CORRECTIONS
AN INTRODUCTION

Stan Stojkovic, Ph.D.
School of Social Welfare
Criminal Justice Program
University of Wisconsin - Milwaukee

Rick Lovell, Ph.D.
School of Social Welfare
Criminal Justice Program
University of Wisconsin - Milwaukee

anderson publishing co.
2035 reading road
cincinnati, ohio 45202
(513) 421-4142

CORRECTIONS
AN INTRODUCTION

ISBN 0-87084-814-3
Library of Congress Catalog Number 91-70609

Kelly Humble *Managing Editor*
Gail Eccleston *Project Editor*

Cover Design by John H. Walker

Preface

The idea for this book began over five years ago at the annual meeting of the Academy of Criminal Justice Sciences. While discussing the topic of corrections with a colleague, the need for a new textbook in the field of corrections was suggested. Further discussions with this colleague and others revealed the need for a text that provides a systemic examination of the corrections field. Encouraged by representatives from Anderson Publishing Co., the project was begun.

This book is the result of a collaborative effort involving many scholars within the discipline of criminal justice. We felt that the incorporation of diverse points of view would enrich the textbook considerably. A great deal of descriptive information is presented in this text, along with much thought-provoking analysis of contemporary issues facing those in corrections. Our intention in writing this text is to provide students, practitioners, and policy-makers with the most relevant and up-to-date information on corrections. To this end, we have incorporated the most recent statistical data available, along with reviews of the most cogent research on the functioning of correctional organizations.

The chapters that follow cover such diverse areas as women in corrections, juvenile corrections, history of corrections, and administration of corrections, to name a few. In addition, controversial topics that are not usually presented in textbooks on corrections are covered. Such topics as sex in prison and prison contraband markets are thoroughly examined.

Moreover, each chapter concludes with a section titled "On the Defensive." In these sections, significant issues are examined. Currently, many of those in control of corrections find themselves, or believe themselves, to be on the defensive. Important factors in the work environment and in the contexts of operation combine to make correctional work difficult. These sections are intended to highlight the nature of the difficulties and controversies facing corrections. The reader should view the "On the Defensive" sections as demonstrative of key issues and ideas expressed within the chapters.

As stated earlier, this book is a collaborative effort. The primary authors are joined by the following scholars: John Conley, State University of New York at Buffalo, who wrote the chapter on the history of corrections; John Klofas, Rochester Institute of Technology, who wrote the chapter on the effects of incarceration; Paul Embert, Michigan State University, who wrote the chapter on correctional law; and David Kalinich, Northern Michigan University and Jeffrey Senese, University of Baltimore, who wrote the chapter on treatment programs for offenders. We think this collaboration has resulted in a high-quality textbook.

We owe a debt of gratitude to many people who participated in the production of this book. First and foremost, we thank John Whitehead, East Tennessee State University, for his thorough reviews of the chapters. In addition to editorial comments, he provided much insight and assistance with ideas for improving each chapter. Second, we extend our appreciation to Mickey and Susan Braswell for their encouragement and aid during the initial writing of the book. Third, we thank Bill Simon for his consideration and patience in bringing this project to completion. Fourth, Gail Eccleston's editing and coordination of production were essential, and we greatly appreciate her efforts. Finally, we recognize MaryAnn Riggs, a close friend and valued colleague.

We hope that *Corrections: An Introduction* provides the reader with insight into the daily workings of correctional organizations. Additionally, we hope that the information presented within these pages provides a greater basis for understanding and asking informed questions about corrections and, especially, challenges the reader to view corrections in a systemic way. We would appreciate any feedback concerning the content of this book, and look forward to hearing from interested readers.

Stan Stojkovic
Rick Lovell

Introduction

Corrections: An Introduction is composed of eighteen chapters. Chapters 1 and 2 examine criminal justice processes and correctional history. The intent of these chapters is to provide an adequate foundation for consideration of corrections as presently practiced. Chapters 3, 4, and 5 present information on various correctional systems, including local, state, and federal arrangements. Chapter 3 highlights the nature of jails. Chapter 4 provides a profile of the contemporary prisoner. Chapter 5 describes state and federal correctional agencies.

The topic of institutional corrections is explored in Chapters 6, 7, 8, 9, 10, and 11. Beginning with Chapter 6, the topic of correctional administration is examined. Chapter 7 focuses on the various treatment programs and activities for prison inmates. Issues concerning prison social structure form the basis of the examination in Chapter 8. Chapter 9 describes the myriad effects of incarceration, along with exploration of problems arising from imprisonment of special category offenders. Causes of, and ways to address, prison violence are discussed in Chapter 10. Chapter 11 describes the nature and extent of sex in prison and prison contraband markets.

The relationship of law to corrections is the focus of Chapter 12. Court cases, rights of institutionalized persons, rights of correctional employees, and liability issues dominate the discussion.

Chapter 13, 14, and 15 focus on community-based corrections. Chapter 13 examines probation and Chapter 14 examines parole. Chapter 15 describes other forms of community-based corrections, including diversion, residential facilities, temporary release programs, and third-level alternatives.

Other significant correctional perspectives are addressed in Chapters 16, 17, and 18. Chapter 16 focuses on the operation of juvenile corrections, while Chapter 17 presents issues related to female corrections. The final chapter of this book—Chapter 18—examines the impending issues facing corrections into the next century, including privatization, professionalization, and policy development.

Table of Contents

Chapter 12

Corrections and the Law　　　　　　　　　　　　　　　　**399**

by Paul S. Embert, *Michigan State University*

Chapter 16
Juvenile Corrections   561

Chapter 17
Female Corrections   595

Photo Credit: Tony O'Brien, Frost Publishing Group, Ltd.

Crime, Criminal Justice Processes, and Corrections

1

After reading this chapter, the student should be able to:

▌ Describe the nature and extent of crime, including an understanding of the Uniform Crime Reports and the National Crime Survey.

▌ Discuss crime control strategies, both liberal and conservative.

▌ Explain the criminal justice process—specifically, system components and dynamics.

▌ Discuss the relationship of corrections to other criminal justice system components.

Introduction

The purpose of this chapter is to provide an overview of the basic workings of the criminal justice system. Included in this description will be the nature and extent of crime in American society according to recent statistics and the various crime control strategies employed by the criminal justice system. In addition, we will examine the various processes of criminal justice agencies, discussing systems' models, components, and dynamics. Finally, the chapter will examine the place of corrections in the larger context of other components of the criminal justice system, i.e., police, prosecution, and courts. We begin our discussion with an examination of the amount of crime in society.

Nature and Extent of Crime

One of the major problems facing those interested in understanding crime is the determination of the actual amount of crime that exists in society. As noted in a number of introductory textbooks on criminal justice, this is not always an easy task. There are, however, two widely accepted measures of crime. The first is known as the Uniform Crime Reports (UCR). These reports are published annually by the FBI and are viewed as the official measures of crime in the United States. The offenses measured through the UCR are divided into two parts. Part I offenses include criminal homicide, forcible rape, robbery, aggravated assault, burglary, larceny-theft, auto theft, and arson. Part I offenses are also known as the *Index Offenses* and are viewed as the more serious offenses measured by the UCR. Part II offenses include a number of minor offenses measured by the UCR. Some examples of these offenses are fraud, embezzlement, and vandalism.

The value of the UCR has been questioned by a number of scholars. Many of the criticisms of the UCR stem from its inability to accurately assess the amount of crime in this country. Criticisms range from its reliability to its measurement procedures. White-collar crime, for example, is not reflected in the UCR. This criticism, along with others, has led academicians to doubt the validity of the UCR. With these *caveats* in mind, the number of known offenses and the crime rate for a 28-year period (1960-1988) are shown in Table 1.1.

Table 1.1
Estimated Number and Rate (per 100,000 inhabitants) of Offenses Known to Police, by Offense, United States, 1960-1988

Population[a]	Total Crime Index[b]	Violent crime[c]	Property crime[c]	Murder and non-negligent man-slaughter	Forcible rape	Robbery	Aggra-vated assault	Burglary	Larceny-theft	Motor vehicle theft
Number of offenses:										
1960 - 179,323,175	3,384,200	288,460	3,095,700	9,110	17,190	107,840	154,320	912,100	1,855,400	328,200
1961 - 182,992,000	3,488,000	289,390	3,198,600	8,740	17,220	106,670	156,760	949,600	1,913,000	336,000
1962 - 185,771,000	3,752,200	301,510	3,450,700	8,530	17,550	110,860	164,570	994,300	2,089,600	366,800
1963 - 188,483,000	3,109,500	316,970	3,792,500	8,640	17,650	116,470	174,210	1,086,400	2,297,800	408,300
1964 - 191,141,000	4,564,600	364,220	4,200,400	9,360	21,420	130,390	203,050	1,213,200	2,514,400	472,800
1965 - 193,526,000	4,739,400	387,390	4,352,000	9,960	23,410	138,690	215,330	1,282,500	2,572,600	496,900
1966 - 195,576,000	5,223,500	430,180	4,793,300	11,040	25,820	157,990	235,330	1,410,100	2,822,000	561,200
1967 - 197,457,000	5,903,400	499,930	5,403,500	12,240	27,620	202,910	257,160	1,632,100	3,111,600	659,800
1968 - 199,399,000	6,720,200	595,010	6,125,200	13,800	31,670	262,840	286,700	1,858,900	3,482,700	783,600
1969 - 201,385,000	7,410,900	661,870	6,749,000	14,760	37,170	298,850	311,090	1,981,900	3,888,600	878,500
1970 - 203,235,298	8,098,000	738,820	7,359,200	16,000	37,990	349,860	334,970	2,205,000	4,225,800	928,400
1971 - 206,212,000	8,588,200	816,500	7,771,700	17,780	42,260	387,700	368,760	2,399,300	4,424,200	948,200
1972 - 208,230,000	8,248,800	834,900	7,413,900	18,670	46,850	376,290	393,090	2,375,500	4,151,200	887,200
1973 - 209,851,000	8,718,100	875,910	7,842,200	19,640	51,400	384,220	420,650	2,565,500	4,347,900	928,800
1974 - 211,392,000	10,253,400	974,720	9,278,700	20,710	55,400	442,400	456,210	3,039,200	5,262,500	977,100
1975 - 213,124,000	11,256,600	1,026,280	10,230,300	20,510	56,090	464,970	484,710	3,252,100	5,977,700	1,000,500
1976 - 214,659,000	11,349,700	1,004,210	10,345,500	18,780	57,080	427,810	500,530	3,108,700	6,270,800	966,000
1977 - 216,332,000	10,984,500	1,029,580	9,955,000	19,120	63,500	412,610	534,350	3,071,500	5,905,700	977,700
1978 - 218,059,000	11,209,000	1,085,550	10,123,400	19,560	67,610	426,930	571,460	3,128,300	5,991,000	1,004,100
1979 - 220,099,000	12,249,500	1,208,030	11,041,500	21,460	76,390	480,700	629,480	3,327,700	6,601,000	1,112,800
1980 - 225,349,264	13,408,300	1,344,520	12,063,700	23,040	82,990	565,840	672,650	3,795,200	7,136,900	1,131,700
1981 - 229,146,000	13,423,800	1,361,820	12,061,900	22,520	82,500	592,910	663,900	3,779,700	7,194,400	1,087,800
1982 - 231,534,000	12,974,400	1,322,390	11,652,000	21,010	78,770	553,130	669,480	3,447,100	7,142,500	1,062,400
1983 - 233,981,000	12,108,600	1,258,090	10,850,500	19,310	78,920	506,570	653,290	3,129,900	6,712,800	1,007,900
1984 - 236,158,000	11,881,800	1,273,280	10,608,500	18,960	84,230	485,010	685,350	2,984,400	6,591,900	1,032,200
1985 - 238,740,000	12,430,000	1,327,440	11,102,600	18,980	87,340	497,870	723,250	3,073,300	6,926,400	1,102,900
1986 - 241,077,000	13,210,800	1,488,140	11,722,700	20,610	90,430	542,780	834,320	3,241,400	7,257,200	1,224,100
1987 - 243,400,000	13,508,700	1,484,000	12,024,700	20,100	91,110	517,700	855,090	3,236,200	7,499,900	1,288,700
1988 - 245,807,000[d]	13,923,100	1,566,220	12,356,900	20,680	92,490	542,970	910,090	3,218,100	7,705,900	1,432,900
Rate per 100,000 inhabitants:[e]										
1960	1,887.2	160.9	1,726.3	5.1	9.6	60.1	86.1	508.6	1,034.7	183.0
1961	1,906.1	158.1	1,747.9	4.8	9.4	58.3	85.7	518.9	1,045.4	183.6
1962	2,019.8	162.3	1,857.5	4.6	9.4	59.7	88.6	535.2	1,124.8	197.4
1963	2,180.3	168.2	2,012.1	4.6	9.4	61.8	92.4	576.4	1,219.1	216.6
1964	2,388.1	190.6	2,197.5	4.9	11.2	68.2	106.2	634.7	1,315.5	247.4
1965	2,449.0	200.2	2,248.8	5.1	12.1	71.7	111.3	662.7	1,329.3	256.8
1966	2,670.8	220.0	2,450.9	5.6	13.2	80.8	120.3	721.0	1,442.9	286.9
1967	2,989.7	253.2	2,736.5	6.2	14.0	102.8	130.2	826.6	1,575.8	334.1
1968	3,370.2	298.4	3,071.8	6.9	15.9	131.8	143.8	932.3	1,746.6	393.0
1969	3,680.0	328.7	3,351.3	7.3	18.5	148.4	154.5	984.1	1,930.9	436.2
1970	3,984.5	363.5	3,621.0	7.9	18.7	172.1	164.8	1,084.9	2,079.3	456.8
1971	4,164.7	396.0	3,768.8	8.6	20.5	188.0	178.8	1,163.5	2,145.5	459.8
1972	3,961.4	401.0	3,560.4	9.0	22.5	180.7	188.8	1,140.8	1,993.6	426.1
1973	4,154.4	417.4	3,737.0	9.4	24.5	183.1	200.5	1,222.5	2,071.9	442.6
1974	4,850.4	461.1	4,389.3	9.8	26.2	209.3	215.8	1,437.7	2,489.5	462.2
1975	5,281.7	481.5	4,800.2	9.6	26.3	218.2	227.4	1,525.9	2,804.8	469.4
1976	5,287.3	467.8	4,819.5	8.8	26.6	199.3	233.2	1,448.2	2,921.3	450.0
1977	5,077.6	475.9	4,601.7	8.8	29.4	190.7	240.0	1,419.8	2,729.9	451.9
1978	5,140.3	497.8	4,642.5	9.0	31.0	195.8	262.1	1,434.6	2,747.4	460.5
1979	5,565.5	548.9	5,016.6	9.7	34.7	218.4	286.0	1,511.9	2,999.1	505.6
1980	5,950.0	596.6	5,353.3	10.2	36.8	251.1	298.5	1,684.1	3,167.0	502.2
1981	5,858.2	594.3	5,263.9	9.8	36.0	258.7	289.7	1,649.5	3,139.7	474.7
1982	5,603.6	571.1	5,032.5	9.1	34.0	238.9	289.2	1,488.8	3,084.8	458.8
1983	5,175.0	537.7	4,637.4	8.3	33.7	216.5	279.2	1,337.7	2,868.9	430.8
1984	5,031.3	539.2	4,492.1	7.9	35.7	205.4	290.2	1,263.7	2,791.3	437.1
1985	5,206.5	556.0	4,650.5	7.9	36.6	208.5	302.9	1,287.3	2,901.2	462.0
1986	5,479.9	617.3	4,862.6	8.6	37.5	225.1	346.1	1,344.6	3,010.3	507.8
1987	5,550.0	609.7	4,940.3	8.3	37.4	212.7	351.3	1,329.6	3,081.3	529.4
1988[d]	5,664.2	637.2	5,027.1	8.4	37.6	220.9	370.2	1,309.2	3,134.9	582.9

Note: These data were compiled by the Federal Bureau of Investigation through the Uniform Crime Reporting Program. On a monthly basis, law enforcement agencies (police, sheriffs, and State police) report the number of offenses that become known to them in the following crime categories: murder and nonnegligent manslaughter, manslaughter by negligence, forcible rape, robbery, assault, burglary, larceny-theft, motor vehicle theft, and arson. A count of these crimes, which are known as Part I offenses, is taken from records of all complaints of crime received by law enforcement agencies from victims or other sources and/or from officers who discovered the offenses. Whenever complaints of crime are determined through investigation to be unfounded or false, they are eliminated from an agency's count (Source, 1988, p. 2).

The Uniform Crime Reporting Program uses seven crime categories to establish a "crime index" in order to measure the trend and distribution of crime in the United States. Crime index offenses include murder and nonnegligent manslaughter, forcible rape, robbery, aggravated assault, burglary, larceny-theft, and motor vehicle theft; the "Total Crime Index" is a simple sum of the index offenses. Arson was designated as a Part I Index offense in October 1978; data collection was begun in 1979. However, due to the incompleteness of arson reporting by police in 1979-87, arson data are not displayed nor are they included in the Total Crime Index of the offenses known to the police.

The figures in this table are subject to updating by the Uniform Crime Reporting Program.

The number of agencies reporting and populations represented may vary from year to year.

This table presents estimates for the United States or particular areas based on agencies reporting.

[a] Populations are U.S. Bureau of the Census provisional estimates as of July 1, except for the Apr. 1, 1980 preliminary census counts, and are subject to change.
[b] Because of rounding, the offenses may not add to totals.
[c] Violent crimes are offenses of murder, forcible rape, robbery, and aggravated assault. Property crimes are offenses of burglary, larceny-theft, and motor vehicle theft. Data are not included for the property crime of arson.
[d] Data for 1988 were not available for Florida and Kentucky; therefore, it was necessary that their crime counts be estimated by the Source.
[e] All rates were calculated on the offenses before rounding.

Source: U.S. Department of Justice, Federal Bureau of Investigation, *Crime in the United States, 1975*, p. 49, Table 2; *1985*, p. 41; *1988*, p. 47 (Washington, DC: USGPO). Table adapted by SOURCEBOOK staff.

Source: U.S. Department of Justice, Federal Bureau of Investigation, *Crime in the United States, 1975*, p.49, Table 2; *1985*, p. 41; *1988*; p. 47 (Washington, DC: U.S. Government Printing Office). Table adapted by *Sourcebook* staff.

It should be noted that the crime index and the crime rate are not the same thing. The crime index refers to the number of known offenses reported to the police. The crime rate refers to the number of known offenses per 100,000 inhabitants. As evidenced in Table 1.1, a number of interesting observations can be made. First, the total crime index has increased over the 28-year period and reflects a fourfold increase. This is also borne out by an examination of the crime rate. Both the violent crime rate and the property crime rate have increased dramatically over the designated period. A cursory examination of this data would suggest dramatic increases in crime over the period under investigation. This leads to our second observation about crime in the United States.

While there is some evidence to support a rapid increase in crime in the United States, one needs to examine the index categories more thoroughly to appreciate the subtle differences among them. An examination of the murder and non-negligent manslaughter category, for example, suggests that while there has been a steady increase in this crime over the designated period, there has been much fluctuation in the rate. Starting with a rate of 5.1 in 1960 and rising steadily to a high of 10.2 in 1980 and decreasing to a rate of 8.4 for 1988 suggests that some crime categories do fluctuate over time. Finally, with respect to current rates of crime, the data suggest that there has been a steady increase for all categories over the designated period.

While the UCR are valuable as a measure of crime in the United States, there is still much concern as to their validity in reporting the "true" level of crime. Because of some of the problems with respect to UCR data, researchers began to develop other methods of assessing the amount of crime in the United States. Another method that was developed in 1973 and sponsored by the U.S. Bureau of Census was the *National Crime Survey* (NCS).

Based on surveys with roughly 50,000 households encompassing 101,000 people over the age of 12, the surveys indicated the following levels of victimization for the year ending 1988. The NCS reported more than 35 million victimizations. About 6 million persons are victims of violent crime each year, according to the survey. In addition, 16 million households were touched by crime in 1988. More importantly, the percentage change in rates of both violent crime (-21.8) and household crime (-28.1) has decreased for the period 1974-1988 (Department of Justice, 1990).

Concerning trends, the NCS indicates a significant decrease in crime over the period 1975 to 1988 (Bureau of Justice Statistics, 1989). The percentage of households touched by selected crimes is portrayed in Figure 1.1.

The number of households victimized in the crime categories of personal theft, household larceny, and burglary during 1988 fell to their lowest numbers since 1975. The crime of personal theft was about 32% below its 1975 peak, with burglary being 30% below its peak in 1975 and any NCS crime down 23% since 1975. With respect to violent crime, the surveys indicate the numbers remained basically unchanged, but they were 12% below their 1981 peak.

Figure 1.1
Households Touched by Selected Crimes of Violence and
Theft, 1975-1988

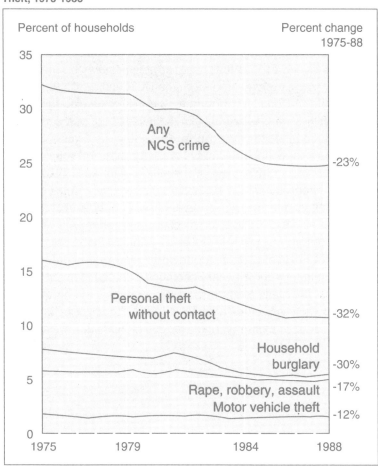

Source: Bureau of Justice Statistics (1989). "Households Touched By Crime, 1988," Washington, DC: U.S. Department of Justice.

Additionally, the data provided by the Bureau of Justice Statistics (1985) suggest that violent crime victims are more likely to be men than women, younger people than elderly, blacks than whites or members of other racial groups, Hispanics than non-Hispanics, and people with low incomes (less than $7,500 per year). Furthermore, the likelihood of being murdered is much higher for blacks than whites; black males have 1 chance in 21 to be murdered while whites have 1 chance in 131. Concerning violent crime in general, besides homicide, the data suggest that males in the age category 16 to 24 have the highest victimization rates regardless of whether one is white or black. Overall, 1 in 12 are victims of a violent crime according to the survey.

Determining the level of crime in the United States is quite problematic given the nature of the phenomenon. All we can reasonably do is to *estimate* that level the best we can. While we can never know the total amount of crime, we can make estimates from both the UCR and the NCS. Each source reveals something different about crime. The UCR reveals the activities of police, while NCS examines crime from the perspective of the victim. While the UCR trends indicate an increase in crime in recent years, NCS reveals that victimization rates have decreased over the past 14 years. Since each source measures crime differently, we should expect such disparate results. What becomes important are the strategies employed to combat crime.

Many strategies of crime reduction are based on the perceived amount of crime present in society. In addition, because these proposals are founded in perceptions of crime, not the true levels of crime, it becomes necessary for defenders of these proposals to be political in their orientation. As a result, the fear of crime among the citizenry becomes a crucial element for those defending various positions with respect to strategies on crime reduction. Whether or not their strategies actually address the issue of crime is problematic at best. It is an examination of these strategies that we address in the following section.

Crime Control Strategies— Liberal and Conservative

According to Walker (1989), we can identify two basic types of crime control strategies in American society. These two strategies are viewed as being political in nature and can be examined on a crime control continuum. Figure 1.2 indicates the major tenets of each of these two approaches to understanding crime. One strategy is referred to as the *liberal* proposal while the other is the *conservative* proposal. Each of these positions espouses views on crime control that are not only political in nature, but in addition, suggests that certain values and beliefs are more important and relevant to crime control than others. It is important to note that each position holds specific beliefs about the nature of crime and what appropriate strategies should be implemented for effective crime control.

Figure 1.2
Two Models of Crime Control Theology

LIBERAL CRIME CONTROL THEOLOGY	CONSERVATIVE CRIME CONTROL THEOLOGY
Posits an idealized world found in bad influences.	Posits an idealized world found in individual responsibility.
Rehabilitation is the key to curing crime.	
	Proper punishment required to change behaviors of criminals.
A belief that people can be reshaped.	
	A belief in the family as a solution to the crime problem.
Social reform is needed to deal with crime, e.g., eliminate discrimination and poverty.	
	Tougher penalties and removing "technicalities" from the criminal justice system.

Source: Developed by Stan Stojkovic.

While this is similar to Packer's (1968) *due process* and *crime control* models of understanding crime control proposals, the approach put forth by Walker is more helpful because it enables one to understand crime control as a political response by criminal justice officials. In this way, one can understand criminal justice operations as reflecting the interests of those who can garner political support for their proposals. An understanding of the political nature of criminal justice operations is relevant here. This approach by Walker is more conducive, therefore, to a deeper understanding of criminal justice agencies as being responsive not only to crime but also to those people who shape the policies designed to deal with crime, i.e., politicians and criminal justice officials. We begin our discussion with an examination of conservative strategies to deal with crime and conclude with an analysis of liberal positions on crime control.

Walker (1989:6) suggests that any analysis of crime control strategies in the United States requires some propositions or ground rules to guide the investigation. Fundamentally, he suggests that much of what liberals and conservatives peddle as crime control strategies is "nonsense." Moreover, he argues that many of the proposals for crime reduction in American society rest on principles of "theology" and not on empirical fact. He further suggests that these strategies perpetuate a crime control theory where a "triumph of faith over facts" is prevalent.

Beginning with conservative views on crime, Walker states that conservatives see crime as an expression of individuals who cannot control their impulses. Because of this lack of self-control, individuals commit crime to meet their daily needs and wants. In effect, self-discipline is crucial to this explanation of crime: criminals do not have the proper motivation and initiative to operate by society's rules, and as a result, the criminal law and the criminal justice system must work toward the protection of society. Thus, individual responsibility is critical within the conservative view on crime. Concerning criminal justice procedure, conservatives believe strongly in fair representation for criminals to guarantee equity in the operations of the criminal justice system, yet they do not believe these procedures should be so cumbersome for criminal justice agencies as to free guilty criminals because of "technicalities." Finally, criminal justice reactions to crime are in tune with an "idealized image of the patriarchal family." In short, crime control rests on the principles of discipline and punishment for wrongdoing on the part of criminals. A fundamental assumption of this strategy of crime control is that punishment will deter the criminal in the future.

Walker argues that the idealized world of the conservative does not exist. In fact, strategies of crime control predicated on increased punishment have not proven to be helpful toward a reduction of crime in society. While these conservative proposals are highly problematic and questionable with respect to effective crime reduction in America, many conservatives still have defended these positions, suggesting that what is required is more certainty of punishment and fewer procedural protections for those individuals being processed by our criminal justice system. This position, however, is not sufficiently supported by empirical evidence. As stated earlier, many of the principles of the conservative position rest on faith and not fact. Its belief in stern discipline and swift punishment guide crime control policies in America regardless of their empirical validity. For our purposes, it is not the empirical validity of the conservative viewpoint that interests us, but the implications that this position presents for the operation of the criminal justice system, specifically, the corrections component.

While conservatives view the world as representative of a large family, the liberal perspective is one of a "large classroom." Within this perspective, the fundamental belief is that criminals are largely determined by the social influences within society. In contrast with the conservative position, in which individual responsibility and blameworthiness are crucial, this opposing viewpoint emphasizes that criminals are influenced greatly by their environment. This perspective on crime control rests on the belief that criminals can be reshaped and turned into more productive citizens. In addition, this position recommends that the criminal justice system be more intricately involved in the change process of the criminal.

With respect to corrections, we can see how this position has been implemented through our prison structures and even supported by many contemporary scholars (Cullen and Gilbert, 1982). Based largely on propositions of faith, the liberal view is still searching for the correct rehabilitation program to change criminals. While scathing criticisms have mounted for years surrounding the effectiveness of rehabilitation programs, defenders of the faith have rallied to continue their support of the concept (Andrews, Zinger, Hoge, Bonta, Gendreau, and Cullen, 1990). As with the conservative position on crime control, the liberal position is equally at fault for perpetuating policies that are founded more on faith than on scientific evidence.

If both conservative and liberal proponents are equally guilty of peddling nonsense about crime control strategies, what does the future hold for producing effective crime control strategies? While we are suggesting here that the policies of crime control are inherently political, whether they be conservative or liberal, we are further suggesting that some policies of crime control representing both political positions do make sense. The challenge for effective crime reduction lies in our ability to select those strategies that are founded in some empirical support and grounded in some realistic expectations of the criminal justice system. At present, such is not the case. It may be wiser for the criminal justice system to do less rather than more. Maybe by being more humble we will be able to develop and implement more effective crime control strategies. In this vein, less is really more.

Moreover, as suggested by Walker, the system of criminal justice is only one part of a larger social system. To view criminal justice as being independent of other institutions in society is naive at best and misleading at worst. One cannot view the operations of any component of criminal justice in a vacuum. This is of extreme importance to corrections, because it is situated at the tail end of the criminal justice system and receives the outputs of the other components. It is an examination of these other components that the next section of this chapter will address. It is the interaction of the components of the criminal justice system that we define as *criminal justice processes*.

Figure 1.3
"If You Want a Successful Drug War, Take It to the Children"

If You Want a Successful Drug War, Take It to the Children

Tough talk and long jail terms have little effect on adult behavior

**By Michael Gottfredson
and Travis Hirschi**

President Bush's long-awaited national strategy to combat the drug problem puts great faith in the potential of conventional law-enforcement strategies and governmental intervention. The Democrats' response differs chiefly in degree, not in kind, with the high ground seeming to belong to those who would spend more.

But the hard-line programs proposed by the president–more prisons, more prosecutors, more hardware for the border patrol, more law enforcement officials, more drug testers–taken together will have little impact on the crime rate or the drug problem.

The $8 billion earmarked by President Bush for the new war on drugs would go atop the $44 billion already spent each year at all levels of government for police and prisons–along with tens of billions more for customs agents, judges, probation and parole officers.

Since the early 1970s and the backlash against Great Society programs, everyone seems to agree that the key to fighting crime and drug abuse is to be found in the criminal justice system–in the workings of the police, courts and prisons–and not in economic or social conditions. This consensus has powered the immense growth in law-enforcement organizations, anti-crime programs (e.g., drug testing, "career criminal" units, mandatory sentencing) and the number of people in jails and prisons.

According to the federal Bureau of Justice Statistics, expenditures for criminal justice in the last few years have increased four times as rapidly as for eduction, and twice as rapidly as for health and hospitals. Since 1980, the number of adults behind bars has doubled. As of January, 627,000 adults were incarcerated in federal and state prisons. The latest figures show that one adult in 55 is under some form of correctional supervision.

But all the effort and money have not bought relief from crime. According to FBI figures, the crime rate peaked around 1980, declined for a few years and then increased during the past four years. (The mild downturn of the early 1980s resulted from the aging of baby boomers. The peak age of incarceration comes a few years after the peak age of crime.

This fact, coupled with tougher sentencing policies, accounts for the increase in the numbers incarcerated.)

No one can substantiate the slightest reduction in drug use or the rate of crime as a consequence of increases in expenditures in the 1980s, and there is no reason to think these failed government programs will now work simply because even more money is thrown their way. In fact, there are good reasons to believe otherwise. The latest scientific research on crime and drug use does not accord with the law-enforcement image of criminals and drug dealers as sophisticated, cunning, persistent and highly organized. Nor does it support the view that strengthening the crime-control apparatus is our only hope.

In fact, the research paints quite a different picture. Studies of the most common criminal events show that they are generally acts of force, fraud or mood enhancement in the pursuit of immediate self-interest. The typical burglary or robbery takes little effort, little time and little skill.

The typical burglar takes advantage of opportunities of the

Figure 1.3—continued

moment; he lives in the neighborhood and victimizes easy targets–such as houses with unlocked doors–carrying away whatever seems of value. The typical car thief finds a car with the keys in the ignition and drives until the gas tank is empty. The typical drug user is satisfied with whatever drug is available at a suitable price. Consequently, most lavish police operations involving costly high-tech hardware are irrelevant to reducing the number of typical crimes. Solid research studies show that most ordinary crimes can be prevented by the presence of even the most minor obstacles: locks on doors, keys taken out of ignitions, reduced late-night hours for convenience stores and the like.

Nor do the crime data indicate that putting more cops on the street will decrease the frequency of offenses. In fact, a growing body of research documents the negligible impact of police patrols in lowering the crime rate.

Moreover, it is becoming clear that criminals and drug abusers are also less complex and less driven than current policies suggest. Indeed, two facts about offenders are directly at odds with the assumptions found in law-enforcement policies. Unless these misconceptions are corrected, there is little hope for efficient and realistic crime policy.

The first fact is this: Offenders are extraordinarily versatile in their choice of criminal and deviant acts. That is, the same people who use drugs also steal cars, commit burglaries, assault and rob others and drive recklessly. Indeed, they are so versatile that knowing their prior offenses does not permit us to predict what crimes they will commit in the future. Despite decades of study, criminologists have failed to discover meaningful numbers of criminal specialists– people who commit particular crimes to the exclusion of others.

For example, when researchers at the University of Pennsylvania followed to age 30 nearly 10,000 boys born in 1945, they discovered virtually no pattern or specialization in each individual's offenses recorded in police files.

The versatility of offenders goes beyond conventional crime categories to include alcohol abuse, spouse and child abuse, accidents, truancy from school and work, and sexual promiscuity. Research repeatedly shows that these behaviors are consistently found together in the same people.

What explains this amazingly dependable correlation among such diverse acts? We believe it is a common element: All of them produce immediate pleasure without regard to potential long-term consequences. This general tendency to engage in such acts we call "low self-control."

Indeed, recent research into offender motivation casts doubt on the standard explanations of drug use and criminal behavior, and on the supposed connection between them. It suggests instead that when adolescents use drugs they are merely seeking an immediate good feeling–and that no deeper social, psychological or economic motives are involved.

This directly contradicts two basic assumptions of contemporary law enforcement: that fear of lengthy prison terms deters offenders from their acts and that a war on drugs can be separated from a war on crime in general.

The second problematic fact about criminal behavior is that all forms of drug use and crime decline sharply as offenders grow older. This phenomenon has proven astonishingly stable through time. Early in this century, the British criminologist Charles Goring reported that age statistics of conviction "obey natural laws of frequency."

Current research reaffirms Goring's findings: The age-distribution curve of crime in the United States today is virtually identical to the one produced by English convicts over three-

Figure 1.3—continued

quarters of a century ago. That is, the propensity to commit crime increases very rapidly throughout adolescence, peaks in the late teens, then declines quickly and steadily through adulthood.

The implications for current drug and crime policy are profound. The decline in crime and drug use with age is so steep that it overwhelms most crime-control strategies that focus on the offender, such as incarceration and rehabilitation. After all, if the vast majority of offenders are teenagers, and if they rapidly quit using drugs and committing crimes of their own accord, what is the point of incarcerating them well into adulthood, or, for that matter, treating them after the problem is over? The present fascination with ever-longer sentences and abolition of parole implies enormous expenditures for almost no payoff in terms of crime reduction.

The age effect is so strong and so obvious to correctional officials that it tends to undermine the resolve to hold prisoners "for the rest of their natural lives." After 30 years in prison, what danger does the 50-year-old "career robber" pose to society? The rate of robbery in that age group is one-fiftieth the rate for 17-year-olds. More to the point of the proposed drug

sentencing policies (and arguments about large financial benefit from imprisonment), what can be the advantage of adding 10 years to sentences that already exceed the active life of the typical offender? Why lock up drug offenders well beyond the age of active substance abuse? Taxpayers may be fooled into thinking they are safer with longer sentences, but when these sentences keep offenders behind bars into middle age (at an average cost, per year, of $25,000 per offender), they should keep their hands more firmly on their wallets.

Any potentially successful plan to combat crime must acknowledge that individual differences in the tendency to commit crimes and use drugs remain reasonably stable over the life course. People who do these things when they are very young tend to do them as adolescents, and to have higher rates than others as adults. People who abstain as adolescents, on the other hand, tend to abstain throughout life.

The president's drug plan conspicuously ignores the notion of prevention. Yet the stability of differences from early childhood suggests that any worthwhile crime or drug policy must focus on the early years of life; that wars on crime and drugs, if they are to be successful, must target children.

Research clearly demonstrates that children who are taught early to respect the property of others, to delay gratifications of the moment if they conflict with long-term goals and to understand the negative consequences of drug and alcohol abuse are unlikely to abuse drugs or commit criminal acts, no matter what the criminal justice system looks like. The same research shows that children not taught these things are likely to run into trouble with the law.

Parents, not police, are the key to the drug crisis. Today, drug and crime policies focus on the wrong institution of social control (the government), treat an inappropriate age category (adults), falsely assume specialization of offenders, falsely assume a causal connection between drug use and criminal acts, and misperceive the motives of offenders. As long as this continues, no amount of taxpayer's money will win the war on crime. ■

Michael Gottfredson and Travis Hirschi are criminologists at the University of Arizona and the authors of "A General Theory of Crime," to be published this winter.

Source: Michael Gottfredson and Travis Hirschi (1989). "If You Want a Successful Drug War, Take It to the Children." Appearing in *The Washington Post National Weekly Edition*, September 18-24.

Criminal Justice Processes

We define criminal justice processes as being composed of three essential elements. The three are: *the systems model, system components, and system dynamics.* The first is a heuristic device designed to aid in the comprehension of criminal justice operations, while the second and third elements are descriptive aspects of the criminal justice system. We will begin by examining the systems model. According to Holton and Jones (1982), a system consists of several parts working together to accomplish some objectives which are held in common among the parts. From this definition, they argue that all systems have seven identifiable components. First, all systems have *components* which operate together toward the accomplishment of goals. The human body, for example, has many parts which operate toward the goal of survival of the body. In this way, the body is easily defined as a human system which functions with the objective of sustaining itself.

Second, all systems operate as an *identifiable whole.* What this means is that systems can be distinguished from one another by their boundaries. Every system has characteristics which distinguishes it from other systems. An example of this would be a political system where identifiable outputs are produced and a boundary is clearly defined.

Third, the components of the system are *interdependent*, whereby each activity of one component in the system will affect the operations of other components in the system. Going back to our human body example, we can say that the functioning of the heart will affect the functioning of the lungs and other vital organs in the human system. If the heart were to stop, then the system would no longer exist. In this example, the heart is a critical component for the human system to exist and it ultimately affects the operations of other components within the same system.

Fourth, every system operates in an *environment*; this environment serves to shape the outputs of the system. The environment can be defined as anything outside of the system's boundary. We can see, for example, that the economic system of the United States is clearly within the environment of the political system and has a significant impact on the American political system.

Fifth, every system has *inputs* which shape the direction of processes in that system. Accordingly, we can identify inputs as taking the form of either *demands* or *supports*. Demands are expressed in many communities as expectations of societal institutions. Criminal justice, for example, is expected to provide protection of citizens and their property. It is these expectations that shape the direction upon which agencies of social control develop and implement policy. Supports are the items that buttress the system in terms of its direction. For example, police receive supports from citizens through their tax dollars. Without these supports, the system of criminal justice as we know it would not exist. These supports are the foundation of the criminal justice system and are required if objectives are going to be attained.

Sixth, every system processes its demands and produces identifiable *outputs*. Outputs are the official measures of what was produced by the system. With respect to criminal justice, we can measure its outputs through arrests, prosecutions, convictions, and numbers of prisoners. The outputs vary from component to component within a system. The outputs enable us to assess what was produced by a component. In addition, an evaluation of a component can only be achieved if one can identify measurable outputs and tie them to the goals of the system.

Finally, all systems receive *feedback* from their environment. This feedback can take the form of new input into the system. Thus, the feedback serves as not only new inputs into the system, but in addition, forces the system to change and adapt to its turbulent and erratic environment. In this way, criminal justice operations can be viewed as a moving picture that is constantly adapting its form to the altering inputs, outputs, and feedback from the environment. This is diagrammed in Figure 1.4. The diagram presented represents all the elements of the system's model and applies it to the system of criminal justice. What requires further attention is an examination of the components of the criminal justice system and how they interact in a dynamic fashion to produce outputs. Our concern at the end of this chapter is to see how this dynamic process affects those people who come under the arm of the corrections component of the criminal justice system.

System Components and Dynamics

One can apply the previously discussed systems model to an understanding of criminal justice. While there is disagreement as to the applicability of the model to the criminal justice system, there still remain some positive aspects of the model that are very relevant to comprehension of the criminal justice system. One such relevant aspect is to view the system of criminal justice as being composed of components. The components of criminal justice are: *police, prosecution, courts,* and *corrections.*

Figure 1.4
System Dynamics

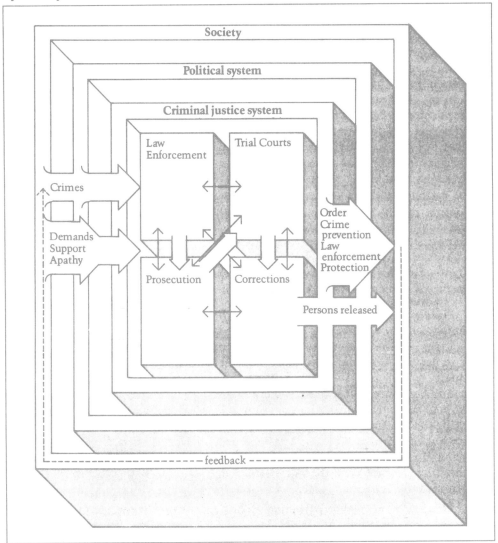

Source: N. Gary Holten and Melvin E. Jones (1982). *The System of Criminal Justice*, Second Edition, p. 16. Boston, MA: Little, Brown and Company.

While the focus of this textbook is corrections, it is necessary to briefly examine the workings of the other components to understand why and how people are funneled into the corrections system. Chapter 4 will discuss the selection process of correctional populations. At present, our purposes are to provide an overview of the police, prosecution, and court components of the criminal justice system and to suggest a systemic understanding of the criminal justice process.

The *police component* of the criminal justice system is probably the most visible and well known. Glamorized by the entertainment profession, the reality of police work is more often boring and tedious rather than exciting and adventurous. It is within this component of the criminal justice system that investigations are conducted, arrests are made, and booking of suspects is completed. Because of their visibility, the police are typically expected to accomplish tasks that are often impossible to achieve. Police behaviors shape the direction of other components of the criminal justice system. Specifically, our concern is with the types and numbers of individuals arrested by the police and how those decisions shape the subsequent actions of prosecutors and judges and ultimately those who end up under correctional supervision. We will discuss this later in the chapter.

After arrests have been made and booking procedures have been initiated, we then move into the second component of the criminal justice system. This component is the *prosecution* of suspected criminals. The process of prosecution is often considered part of an *adjudicatory process* whereby a number of procedures must be initiated. Beginning with the *initial appearance*, suspects are brought before a magistrate and told the charges being processed against them, advised of their constitutional rights, and provided the opportunity to post bail if deemed proper by the judge. This latter procedure is employed to guarantee appearance at the subsequent criminal trial. Typically, the suspect who cannot make bail or who is deemed dangerous to the community will be detained pending the formal trial. These individuals are known as *pretrial detainees*. Much debate has been generated over the years about the relative fairness of detaining defendants and the procedures employed to determine who gets bail and who sits in the local jail awaiting trial. Research has shown how those on bail fare better at their trials than those who are detained awaiting trial (Rankin, 1964; Koza and Doob, 1975).

After the determination of bail is made, a very important procedure occurs which directly determines the outcome of the case for a suspect. This procedure is known as the *preliminary hearing*. During the preliminary hearing, a determination is made as to whether the suspect should be held over for formal charges and brought to trial. At the preliminary hearing the state attempts to show that probable cause exists to bind the suspect over for criminal trial. If the individual is bound over for criminal trial, this is usually done through the issuance of an *indictment* by a grand jury or the presentation of an *information* by a prosecutor. These documents are formal charging mechanisms used by prosecutors. Finally, after the indictment or information has been processed, the defendant appears before a magistrate and is allowed to plead to the charge(s) listed on the indictment or information. Additionally, suspects are notified of their rights and a determination is made as to whether or not they are competent to stand trial. If the defendant cannot afford counsel, one may be appointed by the court. It is at this stage that many suspects plead guilty to the charges listed on the indictment or information. Research evidence has suggested that upwards of 90% of all defendants will plead guilty at this stage of the criminal justice process.

The final element of the criminal justice system is the court component. It is at this stage that the criminal defendant is given his day before the "bar of justice." Estimates vary from courtroom to courtroom, yet the numbers of individuals pleading guilty prior to the actual trial is great, and more importantly, very few defendants receive criminal trials. Fewer than 5% of all felony arrests result in a criminal trial. In fact, the research evidence suggests that guilty pleas outnumber trials by about 20 to 1 (Boland, Conly, Mahanna, Warner and Sones, 1990). Sentencing of the offender takes place subsequent to the trial. Finally, the defendant is allowed to appeal his sentence after the trial. Typically, appeals are over procedural issues surrounding the trial. Very few appeals are actually reversed or even remanded for a new trial.

This brings us to the conclusion of our overview of the criminal justice system. In the final section of this chapter, we will be discussing more specific attributes associated with the police, prosecution, and court components of the criminal justice system and how they affect the corrections system. *We will be arguing that the interactions of these other components of the criminal justice system have a significant impact on the subsequent operations of correctional systems.* How this occurs will be the purpose of this remaining section.

Corrections and the Criminal Justice System

At arrest, the defendant is under the authority of the criminal justice system, and it is the police component of that system that begins the criminal justice process. For our purpose here, we want to know the types of behavior exhibited by police that influence the subsequent actions of other components of the criminal justice system. In short, we need to briefly examine police operational strategies that make some individuals more likely candidates for police intervention than others. There has been a voluminous amount of literature on the police-citizen interaction and the types of individuals who are arrested by the police. Our point is not to review this literature, nor is there space to complete such a task. Instead, we propose to review some key research on the issue and suggest its relevance to understanding the process of selection of offenders for correctional supervision.

According to Manning and Van Maanen (1978), one can examine the arrest strategies of police officers within three fundamental styles. In their words, there are three "generic types" of policing. Table 1.2 depicts these operational styles. The first style is the *preventive* strategy of policing in which the police attempt to discourage the commission of crimes through public awareness and increased visibility. In addition, the police attempt to educate the public through "target hardening" programs and crime prevention methods. The second police strategy attempts to discover crimes while they are being committed and is based on police investigative techniques. It is referred to as the *proactive* style of policing; it relies heavily on the expertise of the police department in crime reduction. Finally, there is the *reactive* strategy of policing, which relies on the police waiting until a crime has been committed and then responding to a call for assistance by the public. Many have argued that this is the most common form of police style used in America.

A combination of these styles of policing is what is evidenced in police departments. Through the proper implementation of these styles of policing, it is hoped that crime can be reduced. We do know, however, that the reduction of crime is not the only reason that police arrest individuals. In fact, as suggested by Reiss (1971), crime reduction is not the primary goal for police in many interactions with the community. Rather, the officer may or may not arrest an individual depending upon other circumstances associated with the event. For example, Manning and Van Maanen suggest the situation and context of the police interaction with the citizen is critical to a decision to arrest.

3 "generic types" of policing are
1) preventive,
2) proactive,
3) reactive

Table 1.2
Types of Police Operational Strategies

	Preventive	Proactive	Reactive
Time	Prior to crime commission	Prior to, or simultaneously with, crime commission	After crime comes to the attention of the police
Aim	Crime is to be prevented, forestalled, or deterred	Crime must be "created" and made court relevant; a case must be presented	Crime must be founded — facts established and a perpetrator brought to task if possible
Place of Agent	Police-citizen obligations similar (cooperative)	Agents ecologically removed from crime commission; Agents rely on informants or own information; Crime often a private transaction involving officer as complainant; Selection of targets (groups, persons, locales) is discretionary	Agents stand in variable relation to commission of crime; Agents rely almost exclusively on citizens' information and complaints
Measure of Effect	Measured by the reduction, absence, or shift in the pattern or level of crime (defined as crimes known)	Measured by arrests and charges, seizures, or warrants served	Arrests and clearance rates
Internal Measures	Not developed	Clearance rates cannot be used because the base number of cases is unknown	Clearance rates can measure extent of effect on founded crime

Source: Peter Manning and John Van Maanen (eds.) (1978). *Policing: A View From the Streets*, p. 144. Santa Monica, CA: Goodyear Publishing Co.

Following this line of reasoning, they examine elements that are crucial to the outcome of a police-citizen interaction. They suggest that the citizen's demeanor, the time and place of the interaction, the officers' perceptions of personal safety, the extent of deference to police authority given by the citizen, and the expectations of the officers about the outcome of the matter will all weigh heavily on whether or not an arrest will be made. Furthermore, the work of Gottfredson and Gottfredson (1980) suggests that the decision to arrest is fairly straightforward when the event is serious and when the victim and perpetrator are strangers. In fact, they argue that the *discretion not to arrest is not often a luxury the police have in these situations.* As a result, it is important to see how decisions by police, based on this multitude of factors, shape the direction of the criminal justice system and determine the eventual offenders who will be placed under correctional supervision.

We can summarize this description of police behavior and its impact on who becomes part of the correctional system in the following fashion: police generally arrest individuals who have committed serious crime upon strangers and the decision to arrest is strongly influenced by characteristics associated with the criminal event. This is not to discount the fact that many arrests by police are for less serious offenses (see Walker, 1990:31-34 for a discussion of this topic). The point is, however, that many individuals arrested by the police are those who deserve some attention by the criminal justice system. As suggested by Walker (1989:26-30), serious crime is dealt with seriously by those who operate the criminal justice system. It all begins with the police and continues with the prosecutorial stage of the criminal justice process.

Our knowledge of the decision to prosecute has been greatly enhanced by a number of recent studies completed by Boland, Conly, Mahanna, and Sones (1990:3-10). They have conducted the most exhaustive examination of the prosecution process to date, and this evidence allows us to make some statements about who ultimately becomes part of the corrections system. We first explore the outcomes of felony arrests made by police and the outcomes of felony arrests that result in some type of indictment. Figure 1.5 diagrams the outcome of 100 felony arrests brought by the police for prosecution for the year ending 1987. According to the data, for every 100 adults arrested for a felony crime, 43 will not be convicted. In addition, of those who are not convicted, 5 will be referred to diversion or diverted, 18 will have their cases rejected for prosecution at screening before court charges are filed, 20 will have their cases dismissed in court, and 1 will be acquitted at trial. A large number of cases are either diverted out of the system or dismissed. More importantly, we can also see that very few people actually go to criminal trial. As indicated in Figure 1.5, of those who are carried forward, a majority plead guilty prior to the trial. Roughly 60% of those who are adjudicated guilty, either through a plea of guilty or through a criminal trial, will actually be subject to some type of incarceration.

Figure 1.5
Typical Outcome of 100 Felony Arrests Brought by the Police For Prosecution

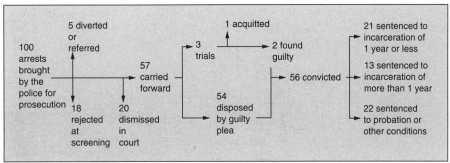

Source: Bureau of Justice Statistics (1990). "The Prosecution of Felony Arrests, 1987." Washington, DC: U.S. Department of Justice.

Figure 1.6
Typical Outcome of 100 Felony Arrests that Result in Indictment

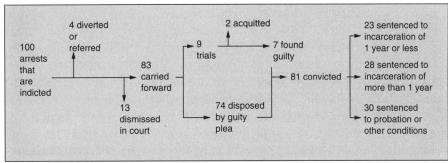

Source: Bureau of Justice Statistics (1990). "The Prosecution of Felony Arrests, 1987." Washington, DC: U.S. Department of Justice.

Figure 1.6 sheds greater light on this phenomenon by examining the outcomes of 100 felony arrests that are carried forward after indictment. These data indicate that close to three-quarters of the defendants plead guilty and less then 10% actually go to trial. Interestingly, of those who go to trial, a majority—over two-thirds—are found guilty. Finally, of those who are convicted, close to two-thirds are sentenced to some type of incarceration while one-third are sentenced to probation. These data suggest that a large number of individuals are not prosecuted, yet of those who are prosecuted and found guilty, a majority receive some type of incarceration. The interesting question arises concerning the great number of dismissals and rejections by prosecutors after arrest has been made by the police. This is portrayed in Table 1.3.

Table 1.3
Reasons Why Felony Arrests are Declined for Prosecution

Jurisdiction	Number of declined cases*	Percent of declinations due to:							
		Insufficient evidence	Witness problems	Due process problems	Interest of justice	Plea on another case	Referral to diversion	Referral for other prosecution	Other
Golden	41	59%	27%	2%	5%	2%	2%	2%	0%
Greeley	235	52	7	0	38	0	1	2	0
Manhattan	995	61	23	5	4	0	-	3	4
New Orleans	4,114	38	30	12	8	0	7	4	-
Salt Lake City	973	58	12	1	8	1	2	19	-
San Diego	4,940	54	15	6	9	1	0	9	7
Washington, D.C.	1,535	30	24	-	13	0	-	3	29

Note: Declined cases include diversions and cases referred for other prosecution. These cases are excluded from counts of rejected cases in other text tables.
- Insufficient data to calculate.
*Excludes cases for which reasons are unknown.

Source: B. Boland and R. Sones (1986). "The Prosecution of Felony Arrests, 1981," p. 17. Washington, DC: U.S. Department of Justice.

The most common reasons among prosecutors for declining prosecution are insufficient evidence and witness problems. Moreover, one of the smallest percentage categories for declining prosecution is the "due process problems" category. This suggests that procedural problems with arrest are not as great an obstacle for prosecutors as commonly perceived by the public, but that concerns over the nature of both the evidence and the witnesses involved weigh heavily among prosecutors in deciding whether or not to continue with the criminal justice process. As we can see, a select few people are actually sent through the court system and then on to corrections. What becomes relevant is an examination of the "Courtroom Work Group" and how it influences the criminal court process in the selection of those defendants who become part of our correctional systems.

The explanation of the Courtroom Work Group is based heavily on the work of Walker (1989:43-54). Accordingly, he describes what he believes to be the basic tenets of this model in his book *Sense and Nonsense About Crime: A Policy Guide*. In this book, he argues that what is evidenced in the courtrooms of this country is something known as the *going rate*, in which there is an "expression of how much a case is worth" in that jurisdiction. Put simply, he states that every courtroom has an accepted level of punishment, as expressed through the likelihood of incarceration and the length of a prison sentence, and that prosecutors, defense attorneys, and judges work together in making sure that this rate is not violated. Much of this is ensured through informal dealings among these workers. As a result, what is created is a "steady state" or criminal justice equilibrium with respect to the operations of the courtroom process. More importantly, according to Walker, this series of interactions produces a situation in which cooperation among the elements of the work group is desired, and the criminal justice process is viewed to be *more administrative than adversarial*. This position is borne out by recent evidence.

Albonetti (1986), for example, examined the prosecutorial decision-making process and concluded that prosecutors seek certainty when screening cases. Specifically, she argued that "uncertainty avoidance" was the goal for many prosecutors, and that they were sensitive to concerns for effective management of victims and witnesses whereby cooperation is enhanced and the career image of the prosecutor is both protected and promoted. Thus, the prosecutor as one element of the courtroom group works toward the maintenance of the going rate largely as a response to protection of image. This same position is equally true for both defense attorneys and judges. If this is the case, a relevant issue is how this going rate is affected or influenced by reform efforts, or more specifically, laws that attempt to alter the rate for equity reasons. Walker (1989:44) states that many criminal justice officials are able "to evade, absorb, or blunt reforms they do not feel are in their interest(s)." In effect, it is an understanding of this going rate which is crucial to the winnowing of defendants during the criminal court process. It is the selection of those defendants who, in the minds of work group members, are the most serious and dangerous who ultimately become part of the corrections system of this country.

As suggested by Walker (1989:44), the going rate within many jurisdictions usually produces the following results. Those people who have committed serious crimes against strangers and have solid evidence against them will be dealt with harshly by the criminal justice system. As stated by Walker (1989:43), "For crimes that count the most, the system (criminal justice) is fairly strong." Finally, when addressing the impact of reform on the court process, Walker believes that in most cases the reforms do not impact in the expected way. What does occur is what he refers to as the "trickle up" effect, where less serious offenses are dealt with more harshly and the serious offenses receive the same attention as was evidenced prior to the reform. In this way, he suggests that many reforms designed to attack serious crime are irrelevant since we already deal with these types of crimes in a serious fashion. More importantly, the unanticipated side effect is to escalate the punishments for those who have committed less serious offenses.

Thus, local systems of criminal justice are relatively autonomous and wield tremendous amounts of power when it comes to the processing of criminal defendants. Additionally, we have seen that through the various interactions among elements in the court work group, specific types of offenders are then sent to correctional systems. As suggested earlier, the percentage of people who end up under the authority of various correctional systems is small, yet as argued by Walker (1989:43), the system is selective in who receives a criminal charge, gets prosecution, and goes to criminal court. However, it would be misleading to suggest that the system of criminal justice in this country is soft on crime. Relying on a reinterpretation provided by Silberman (1978), Walker shows that over two-thirds of those arrested are convicted of either a misdemeanor or felony. Of even greater significance is the fact that of felony complaints, more than 90% are convicted, most through a guilty plea. Moreover, it is equally important to examine the characteristics of those who become part of the correctional system of this country. This will be addressed in Chapter 4.

Summary

The purpose of this chapter was to provide the student with a basic overview of the criminal justice system and to suggest a model for understanding the methods and dynamics of the criminal justice process. From this discussion we concluded that the criminal justice system does the following things. First, our examination of the nature and extent of crime suggested that crime is fairly widespread and that we do not know, in a specific sense, the amount of crime in this country. We concluded that crime is measured through Uniform Crime Reports (UCR) and the National Crime Surveys (NCS). Furthermore, our analysis of these documents indicated that there is much disagreement about the two regarding the extent of crime in this country, yet in some cases, the rates of crime are fairly consistent. These two differing interpretations about the amount of crime may be a function of what they measure. Concerning trends in the crime rate, we have seen it decline over the past three years, with rates of violent crime being fairly constant. In addition, we concluded that the rates of victimization, on the whole, have decreased over a 14-year period.

Second, we examined both liberal and conservative strategies of crime control, suggesting that each is weak by itself in addressing the crime problem in this country. Furthermore, we discussed how the policies of crime reduction are part of a political process and must be understood in this light. Borrowing from the work of Walker, we suggested that many crime control policies are predicated on fiction rather than fact. Concerning the differences between liberal and conservative strategies, we suggested that the former is concerned with social conditions and their relationship to crime along with the belief in rehabilitation, while the latter views crime as a function of individuals who are blameworthy and the purposes of the criminal justice system are to swifty apprehend, prosecute, and punish those guilty of criminal acts against society. Again, our opinion of these strategies was more critical and sober and we suggested that neither of them alone is going to solve the crime problem in this country.

From this discussion, we proceeded with an analysis of the systems model and its applicability to the criminal justice process. We argued that this model enabled us to understand the operations of criminal justice agencies as systems with identifiable components, interdependencies, boundaries, and purposes. In addition, we suggested that this model that applied to the criminal justice system provided us with an opportunity to view the criminal justice process as dynamic and complex. Included in this discussion was a step-by-step representation of the criminal justice process, beginning with arrest and concluding with appeal of sentence. Our position was that the interactions of the components of criminal justice, e.g., police, prosecution, and courts, influence the direction and purpose of correctional agencies.

We expanded on this theme through an analysis of behavior among police, prosecutors, and courtroom personnel. Our review of the relevant literature suggested that the operational strategies of these components contribute greatly to a winnowing of criminal defendants and ultimately those who come under the authority of our correctional systems. Furthermore, we put forth the position that systems of criminal justice and their personnel have much discretionary power to affect the direction of the criminal justice process. As such, we suggested that criminal justice agencies have informal work groups that guide the operations of these systems toward normative positions which they support. Attempts at thwarting or reforming the efforts of these systems have proven to be futile.

In addition, it was noted that serious criminals are treated in a serious manner by those who run the criminal justice system. Finally, we also suggested that any comprehensive understanding of correctional systems requires a fundamental recognition on the part of the student that those who become part of these systems—whether they be institutional corrections, probation, or parole—are a product of a number of interactions among those who operate and control our police departments, prosecutorial offices, and courtrooms. It is this recognition that we sought to achieve in this chapter.

From here, we move into an examination of corrections. The following chapter will investigate the correctional systems of the United States, employing a historical approach. Our purpose will be to examine the development of prison systems in this country and to explore the many different goals associated with corrections today. We will see that the process we call corrections is very complex and often puzzling. The student should begin to realize that an understanding of corrections requires much more than a simple explanation of structures and processes. It must also include an analysis of individuals, their purposes, and interactions. The following chapter will begin this examination. Subsequent chapters will continue this critical process and it is hoped that a greater understanding of corrections is acquired by the student.

Crime Control Theology

The basic problem with most crime control thinking is that faith triumphs over facts. For both liberals and conservatives, certain ideas acquire lives of their own and become, literally, articles of faith. This is the realm of crime control theology.

Ideas about crime and crime control are often based on deeply held beliefs that resemble religious conviction. They cannot be proven or disproven by argumentation over factual evidence. Better to try to prove the existence of God. Over 70% of Americans today support the death penalty because they believe it will deter criminals. This belief persists despite the absence of conclusive evidence to support it. Many liberals continue to endorse rehabilitation in the face of considerable evidence that existing programs do not work.

Conservative Theology

Crime control theologies have compelling power because they imply idealized worlds that reflect the deepest hopes and fears of their adherents. Described in the simplest terms, believers in conservative crime control theology envision a world of discipline and self-control in which people exercise self-restraint and subordinate their personal passions to the common good. It is a world of limits, and the criminal law marks one important set of boundaries. Criminals lack self-control. Their passions get the better of them and they break the rules. They kill because they cannot curb their anger. They steal because they cannot control their desire to possess what they do not have or they cannot defer gratification until they have

earned the right to possess something legitimately. Poverty is no excuse. If they are poor, it is only because they refuse to exercise enough self-discipline to get an education and a job that will lift them out of poverty. James Q. Wilson and Richard J. Herrnstein's conservative theory of criminal behavior holds that crime is essentially a matter of choice: "at any given moment, a person can choose between committing a crime and not committing it."

Individual responsibility reigns in the idealized conservative world. People who break the rules should be punished. Punishment works, for an unpleasant sanction teaches a useful lesson. Criminals learn to obey the rules and others learn by their example that crime does not pay. In criminological jargon these processes are known as specific and general deterrence. There is also an important moral element to punishment. There are rules, and rules are terribly important. To break a rule is to strike at the very foundation of civilized society. Such a transgression deserves an appropriately serious response. We used to call this theory "retribution;" in recent years the term "desert" has become more fashionable, probably because it sounds less biblical. In James Q. Wilson's oft-quoted phrase, "Wicked people exist. Nothing avails except to set them apart from innocent people."

Conservatives are deeply ambivalent, often contradictory about the role of government in the control of crime. Wilson makes a strong argument that government policies cannot affect the basic social conditions that cause criminal behavior. He cites the failure of the liberal social programs of the 1960s.

What he really means is that he doesn't like *liberal* programs: the ones related to job training, income maintenance, family assistance, and so on. Yet he bases his whole approach to crime control on the imposition of tougher penalties that will deter criminals from breaking the law. In short, he is saying that some government policies do influence human behavior while others do not. The real difference between conservatives and liberals is a basic political choice between different government policies. As we shall see shortly, liberals are just as ambivalent on the question of individual responsibility.

Liberal Theology

Liberal crime control theology is not as different from its conservative counterpart as you might expect. It also posits an idealized world and sustains its faith in the face of abundant evidence to the contrary. Liberals and conservatives disagree most sharply on the explanation of criminal behavior. Whereas conservatives attribute it to individual moral failure, liberals see it in terms of social influence. People do wrong because of bad influences in the family, the peer group, or the neighborhood, or because of broader social factors, such as discrimination and lack of economic opportunity. This assumption points in two directions with respect to policy: reshaping individuals and reforming society.

The emphasis of liberal crime control theology on the social environment also underlies its views on the prison. Originally the prison was invented as a controlled environment, one that would cut the inmate off from corrupting influences in the real world. Total isolation was soon abandoned as basic prison policy, but the original assumption remained

unchallenged. Prison reform over the course of 150 years has sought merely to reengineer the prison environment. Environmentalism also points liberal crime control policy in the direction of social reform. If people have adequate opportunities for advancement through legitimate means, they will be less tempted to choose illegitimate activities.

A fundamental article of faith in liberal crime control theology is the belief that people can be reshaped. Much liberal thinking in this area is directed toward a search for an effective rehabilitation program. The history of prison and correctional reform is the story of a continuing search for the Holy Grail of rehabilitation. The prison was launched with great hopes. When it had obviously failed, parole and the indeterminate sentence became the magic keys that would make it work. Successive reforms included individual diagnosis and classification, group counseling, and intensive supervision. Faith continues to survive in the face of repeated failure. Programs are questioned but their underlying assumptions are not.

Liberals are as ambivalent on the question of individual responsibility as conservatives are on the role of government. While liberals emphasize the importance of social conditions in causing crime and reject the conservative obsession with individual responsibility, they do not and cannot completely ignore the role of individual choice. Rehabilitation programs, in fact, are designed to influence individuals to make different (and better) choices. In the realm of the public policy debate, however, they soft-pedal the entire issue of individual responsibility.

Thinking of crime control policy as theology helps us explain the tenacity of various ideas. If liberals have been proposing variations on the theme of correctional treatment for more than 150 years, conservatives have argued the value of swift and certain punishment for just as long. Conservatives have been advocating repeal of the exclusionary rule for more than twenty five years, while for the same length of time liberals have been urging community-based alternatives to prison. These policy recommendations flow from deeply held and unexamined assumptions.

Source: Samuel Walker (1989). *Sense and Nonsense About Crime: A Policy Guide*, Second Edition, pp. 10-17. Pacific Grove, CA: Brooks/Cole Publishing Co.

Key Terms and Concepts

adjudicatory process

conservative crime control theory

crime control model

due process model

going rate

index offenses

indictment

information

initial appearance

liberal crime control theory

National Crime Survey

preliminary hearing

pretrial detainee

preventive policing

proactive policing

reactive policing

system components

system dynamics

systems model

Uniform Crime Reports

References

Andrews, D.A., I. Zinger, R.D. Hoge, J. Bonta, P. Gendreau and F.T. Cullen (1990). "Does Correctional Treatment Work? A Clinically Relevant and Psychologically Informed Meta-Analysis." *Criminology*, 28,4:369-404.

Albonetti, C.A. (1986). "Criminality, Prosecutorial Screening, and Uncertainty: Toward a Theory of Discretionary Decision Making in Felony Case Processings." *Criminology*, 24,4:623-644.

Boland, B. and R. Sones (1986). *The Prosecution of Felony Arrests, 1981.* Washington, DC: Bureau of Justice Statistics.

Boland, B., C.H. Conly, P. Mahanna, L. Warner and R. Sones (1990). *The Prosecution of Felony Arrests, 1987.* Washington, DC: Bureau of Justice Statistics.

Bureau of Justice Statistics (1984). "The Prevalence of Guilty Pleas." Washington, DC.

Bureau of Justice Statistics (1985). "Crime and Justice Facts, 1985." Washington, DC.

Bureau of Justice Statistics (1989). "Households Touched by Crime, 1988." Washington, DC.

Cullen, F.T. and K.E. Gilbert (1982). *Reaffirming Rehabilitation.* Cincinnati, OH: Anderson Publishing Co.

Department of Justice (1990). *Sourcebook of Criminal Justice Statistics—1989.* Washington, DC: U.S. Government Printing Office.

Gottfredson, M.R. and D.M. Gottfredson (1980). *Decision-Making in Criminal Justice: Toward the Rational Exercise of Discretion.* Cambridge, MA: Ballinger Publishing Company.

Holton, N.G. and M.E. Jones (1982). *The System of Criminal Justice, Second Edition.* Boston, MA: Little, Brown and Company.

Koza, P. and A.N. Doob (1975). "The Relationship of Pretrial Custody to the Outcome of a Trial." *Criminal Law Quarterly*, 17:391-400.

Manning, P.K. and J. Van Maanen (1978). *Policing: A View From the Streets.* Santa Monica, CA: Goodyear Publishing Company, Inc.

Packer, H. (1968). "Two Models of the Criminal Process." In H. Packer (ed.) *The Limits of the Criminal Sanction.* Stanford, CA: Stanford University Press.

Rankin, A. (1964). "The Effect of Pre-Trial Detention." *New York University Law Review*, 39:641.

Reiss, A.J. (1971). *The Police and the Public.* New Haven, CT: Yale University Press.

Silberman, C. (1978). *Criminal Violence, Criminal Justice.* New York, NY: Random House Publishing Company.

Walker, S. (1989). *Sense and Nonsense About Crime: A Policy Guide, Second Edition.* Monterey, CA: Brooks/Cole Publishing Company.

Photo Credit: Tony O'Brien, Frost Publishing Group, Ltd.

The Historical Relationship Among Punishment, Incarceration, and Corrections

2

John A. Conley
State University of New York—Buffalo

After reading this chapter, the student should be able to:

- Describe the European model of corrections.

- Explain the historic role of prisons in the punishment process.

- Discuss the influence of the Age of Reason on corrections.

- Provide a description of criminal punishment in Colonial America.

- Trace the incarceration movement in the nineteenth century.

- List the principles of progressive reform.

- Describe the Reformatory Movement and the development of the Big House.

Introduction

The current movement for tighter, more restrictive sentences, the abolition of parole, the massive construction of new prisons, the attack on plea bargaining, and the get-tough attitude toward offenders reflects a general anxiety among the public regarding the effectiveness of current methods of punishment. With ever-increasing crime rates being portrayed by the news media, the public looks for an explanation for the increase in criminal activity and then focuses on the punishment mechanisms in society. For them, if crime is rising, then criminal sentences, prisons, and the agencies of punishment must be failing to do the job. These anxieties and attitudes of the public are not unique to today's concerns over criminal justice. Such reactions to crime and punishment can be found in any period of human history. Not only have societies critically questioned the effectiveness of punishment in the past, but many of the current concerns about punishment are rooted in that past. The purpose of this chapter is to present information about the history of punishment. After briefly discussing the history of punishment from the medieval period in Europe through the American colonial period, the chapter will include a discussion of the development and evolution of prisons and rehabilitation in the United States. You should get a sense of the difficulty of designing an effective system of punishment in any society, the cyclical nature of penal reform, and the variation in attitudes toward and strategies of punishment in the United States.

The European Model in Pre-Modern Times

Prior to the eighteenth century, punishment was a natural part of everyday life and was taken for granted. People were in a constant battle with the environment and suffered heavily and regularly from the effects of wars, plagues, droughts, pestilence, and criminals (Newman, 1978:4-5). So it should be no surprise that they also devised social punishments to help order society. The historical record is replete with examples of a wide variety of punishments available to individuals, groups, the church, and the state. What is most significant for us to understand is that punishment did not develop in a linear way beginning with physical torture in pre-modern societies, moving through imprisonment and fines during the industrial revolution, changing to rehabilitation and treatment during the progressive period (1890-1920), and ending with a search for alternatives to these models in the 1980s. Methods of punishment grew and subsided, changed rapidly and stabilized, and took a variety of forms depending on the social, political, and economic changes occurring in society, and no single method dominated any given historical period.

The Middle Ages, from about the sixth century to the beginning of the sixteenth century, had a very complex mixture of punishments. What may surprise most people, who may believe that physical torture was the norm for this period, is that the most favored types of punishments were economic sanctions. "By the fourth and fifth centuries B.C. . . . an extensive system of fines for a wide variety of offenses" had been developed and continued well into the seventeenth century in England and included confiscation of the offender's property and restitution to the victim (Newman, 1978:114-123; Bellamy, 1971:190-191). Originally imprisonment was used extensively as a means of custody to hold individuals for trial, and by the later Middle Ages it became a popular means of punishment. All these forms of punishment existed simultaneously.

The use of fines continued throughout history. This is not to say that corporal punishment did not exist, because it was common. Mutilation, dismemberment, and branding were common punishments for individuals who committed murder, rape, theft, adultery, or prostitution. The use and persistence of corporal punishment can be explained by its function for small communities. Corporal punishments such as the stocks, pillories, and public whippings served immediate purposes of retribution and deterrence because everyone knew each other in those smaller communities. The physical pain and social embarrassment experienced by an offender were seen by all inhabitants of the community (Newman, 1978:114-123).

There is no record describing a precise philosophy of punishment for the later Middle Ages. The variety of punishments used indicates a practical basis for the punishment that depended greatly on the political interest being served. The preferred punishment of monarchs was either a fine or execution. Monarchs had an interest in deterrence to control and deter threats to their rule as evidenced by the immediacy and overtness of the executions. But punishments also contributed to the king's treasury, as was illustrated by the widespread use of fines for all manners of offenses. Even executions served the king's economic interests, however, because if an offender was executed by proper judicial procedure, all of his possessions transferred to the king. On the other hand, poor victims probably had more interest in retribution and thus relied on physical torture and feuds. The church favored penance, but was not averse to justifying its corporal punishments on the basis of retribution. Intertwined through all these forms of punishment was imprisonment, and by the later Middle Ages prisons and their use became quite common. What is significant is that the popularity of these forms of punishment varied from place to place and from time to time depending on social, political, and economic conditions, and that societies used a mix of these different types of punishments (Bellamy, 1971:180-183).

Prisons as Punishment

It is a distortion of penal history to say that the United States discovered prisons (Rothman, 1971:79-108). Prisons were used in ancient times along with fines, public humiliation, and corporal punishments. Rome, France, Germany, England, and other countries sentenced offenders to prison as punishment from the sixth century well into the fifteenth century. In one form or another prisons existed in England from at least the fifth century and "by the fifteenth century were an important instrument in the maintenance of public order" (Rothman, 1971:162). By the end of the thirteenth century every county and town in England had built jails for the dual purpose of incarcerating offenders awaiting trial and punishing convicted offenders. John Bellamy argues that greater prison space was required by the end of the fourteenth century, and more sentences of imprisonment were issued at this time than in previous centuries. Although the general purpose of the prison was to hold offenders for trial, that purpose changed gradually to one of imprisonment for punishment (Rothman, 1971:164-165).

The reasons for the change from custody to punishment are complex. Imprisonment for suspicion of criminal activity or treason became a rule. Statutes defining certain crimes such as arson, escape from jail, and treason carried no bail provisions or forbade issuance of bail, and thus execution or imprisonment became the standard sentences for these crimes. Crimes began to be seen as a threat to the king's peace in addition to the harm done to individuals by the specific act (such as larceny, assault, etc.). An increasing number of laws emerged with precisely defined prison sentences for offenders (Rothman, 1971:163). Imprisonment was also a common tool of church officials. Church clerks accused of felonies were imprisoned by the Catholic Church. The church used prisons as punishment and used its monasteries as penal institutions. By the fourteenth century the church had developed a penal system and a legal philosophy parallel to the laws and prisons of the state. The parallel legal system was based on religious as well as political issues. The church wanted its subjects punished by God, not by the state, and it wanted political control over its subjects and its expanding empire.

Needless to say, world rulers did not acquiesce to the church's expanding claims to judicial authority over its people and the existence of two separate, but intertwined, systems of punishment flourished through the sixteenth century. By the end of that century the effects of the changing social and economic conditions brought about by the deterioration of the feudal system, the Reformation, and the growth of cities with their expanding middle classes and transient working-class populations created new pressures on social control mechanisms including punishment (Eriksson, 1976:5-6).

In response to a rapidly growing population of vagrants and beggars which seemed not to be affected by corporal punishment, Europe sought other solutions. The first houses of corrections emerged in the sixteenth century beginning in England (Bridewell) followed by the rasphouses (Rasphuis) and spinhouses (Spinhuis) of Amsterdam and quickly spread throughout Europe. The significance of these houses of corrections is that they were operated on the twin dimensions of work and discipline. The Amsterdam model added to and expanded the dimension of punishment by including the idea that prisoners should not just be punished, but also should be taught good work habits, self-discipline, and the benefits of contributing to society. In short, prisoners should be rehabilitated. These two principles would serve as the cornerstones for the treatment of prisoners for centuries to come (Eriksson, 1976:8-17; Spierenburg, 1984).

These houses of corrections were clearly linked to the Calvinistic view that laziness was sinful and consequently these institutions grew rapidly in Protestant areas of Europe. All this penal reform was based on the work ethic of the Reformation and was aimed primarily at vagrants, beggars, and petty offenders. Although referred to as houses of corrections, they had all the characteristics of prisons. Thus it appears that imprisonment was one accepted form of punishment in medieval society and gradually became a primary method of punishment by the end of the seventeenth century. There is no record of mass resistance or opposition to the use of incarceration either in conjunction with fines or restitution, or as a sole means of punishment. The objective of prisons was not rehabilitation, but punishment, where the offender suffered passively society's revenge.

But, as we shall see, the emerging reliance on the prison as a primary symbol of the state's punishing power came under severe criticism as we moved into the eighteenth century. In the context of this period the cliché "yesterday's reforms became today's problems" holds true. The focus of the new penal reform movement, which can be attributed to the intellectual revolution of the eighteenth century known as the Enlightenment, or the Age of Reason, was on the method of punishment.

The Age of Reason: Beccaria and Bentham

The slow emergence of an embryonic science of crime began during a very unreasonable period of European history. The general state of the criminal law and its administration in eighteenth-century Europe was repressive, uncertain, disorganized, arbitrary, and barbaric. The hodgepodge of laws that had accumulated over centuries covered almost every facet of human behavior, included excessive physical punishments for minor offenses, and exhibited widespread duplication. These characteristics and the class-based political conditions allowed criminal justice officials to abuse their authority through corruption, brutality, and unchecked avarice.

Although it may be shocking to us today with the western world's emphasis on individual rights and constrained governmental power, conditions in eighteenth-century Europe allowed the arbitrary execution of punishment and a complete lack of accountability of criminal justice officials. Public officials had the power to deprive persons of their freedom, property, and even their lives without following any principles related to due process of law. Investigators and judges used torture to gain confessions from the accused, and secret trials ended with prison sentences and further torture on the flimsiest evidence. Sentences issued by the courts depended on the power, wealth, and status of the convicted. The severity of the sentence often depended on how much of your wealth you were willing to share with government officials. The death penalty was attached to a wide variety of minor and major offenses including treason, which was defined so broadly that any political utterance fell under its authority. The courts and prison officials made no distinction between accused and convicted, young and old, male and female, murderer and forger. Large cell rooms in prisons housed all these groups together where they intermingled. As you can see, the administration of justice had reached a chaotic level where justice was arbitrary and punishment uncertain (Monachesi, 1973:39).

During this period of chaos in the administration of criminal justice, a revolutionary way of thinking about crime was born. This new wave of intellectual development provided the foundation for what became known as the classical school of criminology. Cesare Beccaria (1738-1794) has been credited with leading the emergence of the classical school of criminology. Born in Milan, Italy of aristocratic parents who had no exceptional political power, Beccaria showed no early signs of his potential to reshape the social perspective on criminal law. Yet encouraged by intellectual friends, Beccaria tackled the current conditions of the criminal law and wrote his now-famous essay, *Dei deliti e delle pene*, which came to be recognized as the foundation of the classical school (and was translated into English under the title *On Crimes and Punishments*).

Beccaria rested his philosophy of punishment on the social contract theory of society espoused by Montesquieu. The contract is based on the willingness of free and independent individuals to unite to form a society by giving up a portion of their individual freedom for the benefit of the security and tranquility of all. The society, the state, then has the right to punish because of the necessity to restrain individuals from infringing on one another's freedoms as defined by the terms (laws) of the social contract. Punishment is necessary to protect the rights and liberties of all the people from usurpation by individuals (Monachesi, 1973:40-43).

Using this philosophical base, Beccaria then addressed the chaotic condition of criminal law in the eighteenth century. The authority for punishment and the types of punishments for crimes should be defined only by the law, according to Beccaria, and the laws should be applied equally to all members of society regardless of their status or power. He argued that the severity of punishment must be related to its usefulness for crime prevention. This latter point is a principle cornerstone of the classical school—*the punishment should fit the crime*. The purpose of punishment is not to torment offenders, but to prevent offenders and the rest of society from committing crimes. Punishment, to be effective, must be prompt and certain and applied equally to all for similar crimes.

Beccaria argued against the death penalty because it was neither legitimate nor necessary; no individual willingly gives to another the right to take his life. Relying on the contract theory, he claimed that the reason to form a society was to protect life, not to take life. The death penalty is also unnecessary, he said, because it has no deterrent effect. The spectacle of an execution is horrible indeed, but it is of short duration and leaves no lasting impression on the witnesses. Only penalties that continue (imprisonment) and are known to be continuous are effective as a deterrent.

Finally, Beccaria argued that the execution of an individual, even if authorized by law, is an act of violence and barbarity that has no place in a civilized society. Beccaria also opposed the use of torture at any step in the process of the administration of justice. He also opposed secret accusations and argued for public trials by one's peers (Monachesi, 1973:45-49).

Beccaria criticized the existing administration of criminal justice and made recommendations for change on the basis of humanitarian grounds sprinkled with concepts related to the relationship of the citizen and the state. His analysis was not based on a scientific approach nor was he interested in developing a scientific model of punishment. Yet his influence throughout Europe and America was significant in setting an intellectual foundation for changing criminal justice administration.

Jeremy Bentham (1748-1832) continued this thrust of reform by developing a systematic categorization of crime and punishment. Bentham's approach to the problem of controlling crime was practical, not theoretical. Although he was an armchair criminologist—formulating his models in the abstract—he devised a focused crime prevention model on the practical problem of eliminating, or at least decreasing, crime. He relied on the ethical principle of utilitarianism, the greatest happiness for the greatest number.

Bentham reduced all human action to one simple definition of motivation: "The pursuit of pleasure and the concomitant avoidance of pain." In this respect, Bentham touches on, but does not develop, an important element of criminological theory—criminal behavior is learned behavior.

Bentham saw the necessity for checks or sanctions to control behavior. Without the possibility of pain (punishment) individuals may learn to seek pleasure from uncontrolled criminal behavior. He saw society's infliction of pain as a means to balance the individual's unbridled pursuit of happiness with the larger interest of society. The legal sanction must be viewed as legitimate, acceptable, by the majority for it to be effective, and he recognized that law was only one form of social control (Geis, 1973:57-59).

Following Beccaria's perspective, Bentham claimed that the function of law was to prevent crime, not to achieve vengeance. He developed a complex mathematical formula in an attempt to state the exact amount of punishment necessary to deter a specific act. Punishment should fit the crime and inflict only that amount of pain greater than the reward of the criminal act. The human element was lost on Bentham because he focused on the situation and its changing characteristics and did not consider the variability across individuals (Geis, 1973:54). Although he has been criticized for treating human behavior from such a rigid and simplistic perspective, Bentham was best in his analysis of the pragmatic uses of various punishments for society.

He argued that the goals of punishment are to prevent recidivism and to deter others from committing criminal offenses. He did not separate these two goals for analysis and he failed to develop a workable model for each, but then, he is in good company because even today criminologists have not succeeded in developing application models that separate the two goals. Nevertheless, Bentham articulated a series of sophisticated criticisms and perspectives that have not been adequately recognized today. He claimed that the less certain the punishment, the more severe it must be in order to have a deterrent effect. (What impact does an inefficient police force or plea bargaining have on punishment today?) If there is an expectation that for any given offense the probability of receiving a punishment is low, then when that punishment is inflicted it must be severe (Geis, 1973:60-62). (Can this explain the long prison sentences awarded in the United States?) Bentham would be very displeased with the excessive time delay between the commission of a criminal offense and trial and the common use of plea bargaining in the United States today. Both conditions violate the requirements of swift adjudication and certain punishment that serve as a foundation for Bentham's model of punishment.

Bentham noted that while punishments should fit the crime in terms of the balance between social threat and the amount of pain necessary to deter, he cautioned against the trap of believing that identical punishments were equal. He allowed that the amount of pain (fine) for one individual (wealthy) would not be the same for another (poor). He warned against a rapid application of punishment without considering its effect. Obviously, we still have not come to grips with these principles in the 1990s.

Against the backdrop of a harsh and cruel administration of justice and an emerging criticism of that cruelty, the American colonies were settled and American criminal law and its forms of punishment emerged.

Criminal Punishment in Colonial America

The colonists obviously borrowed heavily from their English heritage when they settled in America in the seventeenth and eighteenth centuries, so it should not surprise us to find criminal codes that established capital punishment for a wide variety of offenses "as different as murder and arson, horse stealing and children's disrespect for parents" (Rothman, 1971:15). But they added a new dimension, in that they equated sin with crime which made it difficult to separate offenses that violated social order from those that violated God's laws.

Eighteenth-century punishments were harsh, even cruel, and public. The colonists used a variety of punishments singularly or in combination such as fines, corporal punishments, executions, banishment, and psychological torment through shame. The sentence of imprisonment was rare and never used alone. Local jails housed individuals awaiting trial or the execution of their punishment, or debtors who had not paid their debts. Jails were not the primary means of controlling deviants. In the eighteenth century, colonists relied on mechanisms other than penal institutions for punishing deviants.

The most common penalty was a combination of fines and whippings. Those who could afford the fine paid it, and those who couldn't received the sting of the whip. Whipping was a cheap, swift, and useful way to punish the non-propertied class. Another common penalty was to confine offenders in wooden devices (stocks and pillories) that had holes for the head and arms (and in some cases, legs). Offenders sat or stood painfully for hours in the public square which combined physical pain with psychological shame and humiliation. A third common penalty was whipping followed by banishment of strangers (Rothman, 1971:46-49).

The goal of punishment was to deter the offender, not others in society, by reforming the deviant. Punishment by whipping at the local whipping post or by physical abuse while locked in the stocks in the town square served notice to the deviant that if he did not conform to the community's standards, he could expect further, more severe punishment. Clearly the colonists relied on societal retribution as the basis for punishment and viewed the execution of punishment as a right of the society to protect itself and to wage war against individual sin. Deviance was the fault of the offender, not the breakdown of society or the community (Rothman, 1971:18).

One particularly unique penalty involved the banishment of strangers from the community's borders. The goal was to control vagabond strangers, and towns prevented these strangers from entering their communities. They used settlement laws to keep strangers out or to send them on their way. The objective was to insulate the town from deviancy much like a quarantine against disease. Banishment exorcised the external threat of strangers from the close-knit community (Rothman, 1971:50). Clearly, colonists viewed threats to their peace and tranquility as emanating from sources outside the community. This notion still drives much of the law enforcement philosophy (effort) of today such as the federal government's policy that defines the threat of drugs as coming from other countries that supply the drugs. What is also clear is that these smaller, less economically developed communities did not need, nor could they afford, large prisons to punish their deviants.

Capital Offenses

Prisons and imprisonment did not play a significant role even for the punishment of what colonists considered serious crimes. The colonies had a large number of capital crimes. The third-time offender received a sentence of hanging. There was no middle range of sentences between whipping and fines and the gallows. Penal institutions were not common and not commonly used. Jails "held persons waiting for trial or awaiting sentence or unable to discharge contracted debts" (Rothman, 1971:53). Jails were not broadened in their responsibility because of the colonists dependence on the family model of society. A model that relied on state institutions simply did not fit into their view of society. Thus, the Calvinists' view of deviant behavior as sin and their belief in the family precluded them from seeing the jail or prison as an institutional mechanism for individual reform or rehabilitation. For them, reform came from God's benevolence expressed through the family. During the Colonial period, some old and some new mechanisms of punishment were used, and we can see that changes in methods of punishment are directly related to the dynamics of change in the society.

The Commitment to Incarceration in the Nineteenth Century

These views of crime, deviance, and punishment in the eighteenth century did not carry into the nineteenth century. The Enlightenment doctrines of freedom, political independence, and republicanism, bolstered by the colonists' success in applying those doctrines during the Revolution, gave Americans on opportunity to reevaluate the basis of order in a society. Rejecting any ties to the British, they quickly blamed the harshness of the colonial criminal codes for the persistence of deviant behavior and sought solutions other than cruel punishments.

The influence of Cesare Beccaria's treatise, *On Crimes and Punishments*, was clearly evident. John Adams quoted passages from it in "1770 in defense of the British soldiers implicated in the Boston Massacre" (Rothman, 1971:59). Beccaria's argument that severe punishments were ineffective and should be replaced with certain simple and moderate forms became part of the rhetoric for criminal law reform in Pennsylvania, Virginia, New York, and other newly formed states after the Revolution. Death penalties were abolished or limited to a few specific crimes, and corporal punishment was all but eliminated. In its place, the new criminal laws called for incarceration. State after state appropriated funds to build prisons. For Americans, this represented the first break from the punishments of the past (Rothman, 1971:60-61).

The new focus was on reform of criminal law, however, not on prisons. Relying on the perspective made popular by Beccaria's treatise, the reformers located the course of deviancy in the legal system, specifically the cruelty of criminal law. The new goal was to eliminate the cruelty of corporal punishment. Prisons at this point were merely a means to reform the law, not the individual, by providing an alternative form of punishment. Later, in the nineteenth century, a shift in focus occurred that placed the individual at the center of reform which brought prisons into the forefront of penal developments (Rothman, 1971:62).

By the end of the first quarter of the twentieth century, every state in the union had built a penitentiary or had begun construction on one. The focus of reform had shifted from criminal law to the individual's relationship to the society. David Rothman suggests that rapidly changing social and political conditions in communities brought about changes in thinking about order and disorder. The earlier nineteenth-century changes in criminal law, designed around the idea of certain and humane punishment, did not seem to stem the flow of deviancy, nor did the changes seem to contribute to an orderly community or protect society from the threat of criminals (Rothman, 1971:2,79-81).

The penitentiary seemed to be a logical solution to this redefined social problem. Now the root of deviance was not in the individual (the Calvinist view) or in the legal system, specifically the criminal law (the Post-Revolution Enlightenment View), but was located in corruptions within the community and the inadequacy of the family and other social and religious institutions. To protect against temptations, the need was to isolate the offender in a well-structured, orderly environment of a prison. The focus of the reformers shifted from reforming the factors external to the individual (the law) to reforming the individual by concentrating on the internal regimen of the man-made environment of the penitentiary. By placing the convict, who was not inherently criminal but simply was not properly trained to resist community corruptions, in a well-ordered and structured environment, the convict could be retrained and rehabilitated.

Given the emphasis on the internal environment of the penitentiary, it should not surprise us that a debate raged when two different models of internal arrangements for penitentiaries emerged. New York developed the *congregate* system of prison organization between 1816-1823 at its state penitentiary in Auburn. Pennsylvania, in the meantime, had created a different plan, the *separate system*, for its penitentiary in Pittsburgh (1826) and its prison in Philadelphia (1829). The debate is surprising in one respect, however, because it focused primarily on the merits of the two competing systems, not on whether the prisons met their rehabilitative goals. Rothman attributes the intensity of the debate to the importance of the views on the root causes of crime and the expected role of the penitentiary in eradicating the effect of those causes on the individual. Thus, the internal organization of the penitentiary became critical to the solution and to the ideology of the reformers (Rothman, 1971:82-84). Advocates of each system agreed that, in order to rehabilitate the individual, prisons must isolate inmates from society as well as each other and must subject them to a routine of discipline. The dispute centered around the question of how to isolate and discipline. In the Auburn or congregate system prisoners slept alone in individual cells, labored together during the day, marched in a lock-step shuffle, ate their meals in central dining halls, but were forbidden to communicate with each other at all times. This latter requirement earned the system an additional name, the *silent system*. The Pennsylvania, or separate, system isolated each prisoner in a single cell where he worked, ate, slept, and prayed alone.

Each side challenged the other by pointing out the benefits of its model and criticizing the weaknesses of the competing model. Pennsylvania advocates claimed that total separation of the inmates allowed them to repent at their own pace without external interference, which would lead to individual rehabilitation. They charged that the congregate system allowed for contamination among inmates, required excessive and easily broken rules which resulted in harsh punishments and failed to rehabilitate the inmate.

The Auburn advocates defended the principle of separation, but because their system did not maintain absolute separation, they deflected the argument to practical considerations. They claimed that the congregate system allowed flexibility where the Pennsylvania system was rigid. Their main criticism of the separate system was that constant isolation of prisoners was harmful to the convicts and that it bred insanity. The debate raged for over 20 years (Rothman, 1971:86-88).

What can we say about the origin of the penitentiary and the reformers' debate? For one thing, the debate centered only around the New York and Pennsylvania circle of reformers. It was, in essence, a debate that involved a narrow slice of the East coast. Second, only one state, Pennsylvania, modeled its penitentiary on the separate system. All other states, except for the South, which followed a farming-oriented plantation model, copied the Auburn model.

The reason for the popularity of the Auburn model, according to some historians, is that it was less expensive to build and to operate than the Pennsylvania system. Because prisoners worked in shops in the Auburn prison, cells did not need to be large and the congregate work arrangement allowed more goods to be produced with higher income from convict labor. In short, the Auburn model was cheaper and more efficient (Rothman, 1971:88). Other historians have suggested that the two models differed in their view of the work patterns of the future. The Pennsylvania system relied on an individual-based craft model of inmate labor where the Auburn system relied on a mass production factory model using a division of labor. The Pennsylvania system looked backward to an earlier form of production while the Auburn model reflected the new direction of factory-based manufacturing. The expansion and spread of the congregate system westward attests to its attractiveness to the vast majority of state legislatures (Conley, 1980).

The daily operation of the prisons proved problematic for state officials. As soon as prisons were built, they became overcrowded. Maintenance of the silent congregate system required excessive controls which in turn resulted in cruel punishments to secure obedience. Whipping became commonplace, the ball and chain, water tortures, iron gags, and other unusual punishments, if not commonplace, were not rare events. The penitentiary ideology which relied on an orderly environment to achieve rehabilitation, fostered an excessive commitment to enforced obedience. Punitive measures served the reform agenda. Forced labor also was tied to the reform model because idleness was related to criminal activity. Legislators saw convict labor as a means to alleviate the cost of penitentiary operations and were willing to support arrangements to use prison labor. Thus the reformers' "doctrines of separation, obedience, and labor became the trinity around which officials organized the penitentiary" (McKelvey, 1977:21, 55-56, 118-119, 122-124). This commitment to a philosophy of work as discipline (remember the houses of corrections in Europe mentioned earlier) opened the door for a variety of convict labor models tied to the prison environment. Prison industries became major elements of the prison in the late nineteenth and early twentieth centuries in the United States. The prison industries of most states used four open-market systems during this period and one closed-market system after 1940. Under the *lease system* the state relinquished all responsibility for the care of inmates and received a stipulated sum for their labor. This was the most abused system and reform groups effectively forced the states to abandon it by the end of the 1920s. The *contract system* allowed the state to retain control over the prisoners, but sold their labor to private firms or individuals for a specified daily fee per inmate. This system resulted in much graft and corruption and prisoners were still abused by the contractors. The *piece-price method* of production was a variation of the contract system in which the contractor supplied the materials and paid the state a stipulated price for each unit of production. Under the *state account system* the state went completely into the manufacturing business, buying all raw materials, setting up factories, marketing the product, and assuming all financial risks. The *closed-market system* relied on the state-use method, which limited the sale of prison goods to state and local government agencies and non-profit organizations (Rothman, 1971:105).

Regional Variations

One historical fact that should signal caution in accepting the argument that the penitentiary played a critical role as a mechanism for the implementation of state punishment or rehabilitation is that not all regions of the country relied on the massive cell-block model found in the northeastern states. Because of differing social and economic conditions in areas of the country outside the northeast, the nature of punishment and the role of prisons differed from the Auburn and Pennsylvania models.

In the southern states, there was no tradition of relying on the state to provide custody for criminals or to model prisons after the factory. Southern states had economies built on an agrarian, plantation-based infrastructure fueled by the power of slave labor. White criminals were punished with the lash, but black criminals received their punishment on the plantation from their owners. Jails and prisons did not play a large or important role in the southern states. Whatever halting movement toward prison construction in the South in the early nineteenth century was stopped by the devastating effect of the Civil War on the South's economy.

The post-Civil War South had larger concerns of rebuilding their infrastructure such as roads, railroads, and cities destroyed by the war. In addition, there were conditions unique to the South. Unions had no foothold to resist convict labor and blacks freed from the plantations were caught up in the criminal justice net, which placed excessive pressure on custodial facilities. The economically strapped South relied on their own traditions and developed prisons more akin to the old slave system than those massive fortresses in the North. The South combined the old plantation model with the lease system and effectively served the punishment needs of social control and the economic needs of the impoverished southern states (Adamson, 1980).

During the reconstruction period following the Civil War, Mississippi, Georgia, Alabama, Florida, Arkansas, and other southern states established a distinct pattern of penal development that separated them from their northern counterparts. States constructed flimsy, wooden barracks for the temporary housing of convicts until they could be leased to private contractors. Contractors paid the state for the convicts' labor and used them for the construction of the railroads, roads, and (later) highways needed to facilitate the rebuilding of the South's economy.[1] More prisoners meant longer chain gangs

---

[1]   For abuses related to the use of prison labor see Thomas L. Baxley, "Prison Reforms During the Donaghy Administration," *Arkansas History Quarterly*, (1963), 22:76-84; Jane Zimmerman, "The Convict Lease System in Arkansas and the Fight for Abolition," *Arkansas History Quarterly* (1949), 8:171-188; A.C. Hutson, Jr., "The Overthrow of the Convict Lease System in Tennessee," *East Tennessee Historical Society* (1936), 8:82-103; Blake McKelvey, "A Half Century of Southern Penal Exploitation," Social Forces (1934), 13:112-123; Harry Elmer Barnes and Negley K. Teeters, *New Horizons in Criminology* (New York: Prentice-Hall, Inc., 1943, with revisions, 1945), 685-716.

and more construction camps deeper in the mountains, swamps, and mining areas, not more or larger prisons. Finally, the southern states continued the tradition of strong counties and weak state government, which meant that counties had the responsibility for the care of convicts. "County sheriffs showed no lack of initiative in making use of their new labor forces." Everything from cleaning streets to repairing county buildings was done with convict labor, but the primary task for county-controlled convicts was the rebuilding of rural roads (McKelvey, 1977:211).

As in the South and East, social and economic conditions in the West shaped the response to penal needs. The migration of settlers from the East naturally linked the western states to the penal traditions found at Auburn. But the vast distances, mountain chains, and different conditions of settlement on the American frontier served to weaken the natural links to eastern penology. As a result western states and territories in the late nineteenth and early twentieth centuries carved out a penal system different from either the South or the East.

In the mid-nineteenth century the federal territories of Michigan, Oklahoma, Oregon, and other western territories of the frontier had little patience, and little money, for the erection of massive institutions of punishment. Prior to statehood, western territories built log houses as jails to hold offenders until the circuit court convened. The courts used a combination of fines, corporal punishments, and prison sentences, as did their counterparts in the East. Offenders sentenced to prison were transported to federal prisons in the territory, and these prisons were little more than larger log structures (McKelvey, 1977:229-233). These new states struggled with establishing new societies under frontier conditions and, as a result, penal systems were not high on the list of priorities.

Initially the settlers viewed their needs in terms of larger jails. With the increasing cost of maintaining prisoners, the states searched for alternatives short of appropriating massive amounts of capital expenditures to build prisons. At first new states contracted with other, older states or the federal government to house and care for their convicts. This method was inexpensive and easily managed. For example, it cost 50 cents per day per inmate for Oklahoma to send its prisoners to Kansas. County sheriffs transported the prisoners for a fee and both the county and the state saved money on the costs of building and maintaining large prisons (Conley, 1981).

As the western states stabilized their economic base and as they achieved maturity as governments, however, they invested in developing their own penal systems. What is surprising is how quickly these societies built their schools and churches and later their prisons and universities once statehood was achieved. This rapid commitment of the states to build institutions suggests a link between state formation and the establishment of an institutional infrastructure. They borrowed from the Auburn model, but did not duplicate it. For example, western states copied the design of the prisons, but operated them differently. Eastern states relied, at least in rhetoric, on a link between the system of production and convict rehabilitation. Western states had a pragmatic approach and focused more on the economic issues related to prison administration and looked secondarily, if at all, to rehabilitative issues. Prisons were administered by Boards of Charities and Corrections which had the primary responsibility of seeing that prisons were managed efficiently and served the interests of the state. As a result, prison factories in western states tended to supply needed goods and equipment for farmers and ranchers. Convict labor was contracted to private industries, but the work was performed in state prisons (Conley, 1981).

The Progressive Period

By the end of the nineteenth century it became apparent to anyone familiar with penal development that prisons had failed to meet the expectations of prison reformers. Prisons did not maintain a rigid discipline within a controlled environment, discipline was lax, and brutality was the norm (Rothman, 1980:18-20). In fact, investigations from the late nineteenth to the early twentieth century consistently found excessive corporal punishment and widespread corruption in prisons across a number of states. Punishments such as hanging by the thumbs, whippings, beatings, water tortures, solitary confinement in cramped, dark dungeons, and starvation diets of bread and water were commonplace. These punishments and general prison conditions harkened back to the cruelty of the pre-prison days of medieval society.

The question of why these abuses existed and why they went unchecked is of critical importance to our understanding of penal development in America. After all, these institutions were to be the symbols of an orderly society, but they quickly deteriorated into quagmires of brutality and corruption. These institutions and their abusive environments survived because of the functional contributions prisons made to society that had nothing to do with the original intentions of the reformers and because of the powerlessness of the inmates. First, the states administered and controlled the prisons, but the inmates worked for the private interests of the contractors who bought their labor through the lease and contract systems. These contractors made large profits and the states defrayed the costs of prisons by sharing in those profits. Second, the general population, anxious or even paranoid about the hordes of immigrants from abroad and fearful of the poor, saw incarceration as an effective, or at least useful, policy of social control. As long as the poor and the immigrants comprised the vast majority of the inmate population (up to 70% in most prisons), brutal conditions would not generate a massive reform impulse. Americans viewed these groups as the "dangerous classes" and were quite willing to support, or ignore, a policy that banished these deviant strangers, as was done during the colonial period, to the nineteenth-century version of another "community." Finally, penal reformers were trapped by their ideology of rehabilitation. They believed blindly that penitentiaries were the best means to rehabilitate offenders. They feared a return to the brutality of the pre-penitentiary period and could not see the contribution that the nature of the prison itself made to the brutal conditions. As a result of their ideology, they continually focused on the internal regimen of the prison and criticized the corrupt administration, but they never questioned the role they had constructed for the prison as a model of the ideal society, nor did they challenge their belief that crime causation was located in the community. It was at this point in American history that a massive shift in perspective and a rapid rise in optimism about our ability to restructure society occurred.

Historians have labeled the first two decades of the twentieth century as the Age of Reform. Also known as the Progressive Era, this period is characterized by a reform movement that attempted to address a variety of social problems, including the role of prisons. These reformers were college-educated, white, middle-class individuals who were optimistic about the potential of benevolent programs for the lower classes and a wider involvement of government in administering those programs. New programs developed and implemented during this period included the indeterminate sentence, probation, parole, prisoner classification, and individualized treatment based on a case history of the client (Rothman, 1980:3-5). In the field of penology reformers opposed the rigid, uniform, and massive programs, such as those found in prisons at the turn of the century, that treated inmates alike and assumed the single cause of deviancy to be located in the breakdown of the community. Unlike their predecessors in the Jacksonian Period, they rejected the prison as a utopian model for society to emulate. The Progressives proffered a position that viewed the prison as a community. David Rothman called this model a "faithful replication" of society (Rothman, 1980:118). Programs implemented in prisons included *classification*—the separation of prisoners into categories based on a diagnostic analysis of the personal history of the client and the individual's treatment needs which resulted in the minimum, medium, and maximum security distinctions for prisons; *normalization*—the design of programs inside the prison which would place the inmates within a community environment that was controlled but not oppressive; *education*—the implementation of school programs for all grades in order to combat illiteracy which was perceived as a contribution to criminal behavior; *vocational training*—the implementation of labor-intensive work programs that focused on training inmates to function in the job market once released from prison.

The cornerstone of the Progressive's philosophy of criminal justice reform was individualized justice. They viewed their ability to change behavior as unchallengeable—an optimism buttressed by the as yet unchallenged promise of the emerging social sciences. Punishment would be treatment-oriented, which was highly individualistic and based on the scientific models of social work and psychiatry. Treatment programs would be based on a case history of the client, and the social worker, probation officer, and prison staff would serve as benevolent friends. Each justice employee would have wide discretion in deciding upon and administering treatment programs (Schlossman, 1977:55-78).

Criminal justice administrators embraced these progressive reforms because of the benefits to be derived from their implementation. The programs increased the discretion of criminal justice officials. In prisons, classification, normalization, education, and work programs allowed for the maximization of control over inmates and increased the legitimacy of the institutions. Finally, because of the Progressive's belief in the state's ability to change behavior through governmental programs, the state's power and control over clients increased. These innovations widened the net of criminal justice. More people, not less, came under the umbrella of state control with the implementation of probation, parole, and other reforms. These innovations did not replace existing programs, methods or prisons, but added to them as complementary institutions of penal administration (Rothman, 1980:9).

The Progressive programs failed. Normalization did eliminate the lock-step, rules of silence, lock-downs, and striped prison garments, but prisons remained oppressive institutions with little treatment programming. Prisons established some school programs, but they were not well designed and did not have professional teaching staffs. Job training very quickly took a back-seat to the maintenance needs of the institutions or the labor requirements of the contractors. Classification separated inmates into three categories, but the categories served the custody needs of the institutions without the con-comitant treatment programs expected by the reformers. In short, all these programs failed to achieve the objectives sought by the reformers (Rothman, 1980:116,158).

The Progressives failed to recognize that rehabilitative programs cannot occur in total institutions because they are too rigid, too brutal, and not adaptable to the rehabilitation model. Programs were not universally applied or implemented across prisons, not fully implemented in any one prison and had little or no staffing or financial resources committed to them. Where programs were tried, they consistently fell victim to the custody needs of the institution. Work, for example, became a means to minimize idleness in or-der to increase control rather than to serve training objectives. By 1925, prisons resembled factories rather than environments for programmatic reha-bilitation. State prisons suffered from overcrowding with anywhere from one to three thousand inmates behind each prison's walls.

Progressive reformers, social workers, psychiatrists, and criminologists all believed that individual rehabilitation was the key to community safety. One result of this belief was their willingness to study and diagnose behav-ior, but they were unable to prescribe programs for success. As a result the Progressive Period of prison reform is replete with diagnostic analysis and weak on programmatic models. Second, the reformers focused on the indi-vidual and neglected the institutions, particularly prisons. In essence, the re-formers pulled back from daily involvement in prison administration, fo-cused their attention on casework, and left prisons to the wardens and guards to manage (Rothman, 1980:144-145,148-158).

The Reformatory Movement

Even as prisons were built, however, there was a complementary move-ment in penal development that focused heavily on the rehabilitation of the individual convict. Some reformers had witnessed the harsh conditions and brutal effects of prisons on inmates and had become disillusioned with prisons as a means to rehabilitate convicts. The alternative was the reformatory, an institution designed along prison lines, but with the focus turned to internal programs of education and training.

The reformatory was around in the mid-nineteenth century, but did not take on its distinguishing characteristics and did not receive widespread support until the late nineteenth century because of a number of developments that placed pressure on the prison. Private labor organizations attacked the use of inmate labor in prisons and legislatures began to respond with legislation constraining prison industries. This, in turn, began to chip away at the self-sufficiency of prisons. Finally, rising inmate populations also placed severe pressure on prisons because of overcrowding, which created discipline problems.

These conditions created a window of opportunity for the advocates of the reformatory, and policymakers saw the reformatory as a means to relieve public pressure. Although reformers sold the reformatory as an alternative to prisons and we have come to accept that interpretation uncritically, it can hardly be viewed as such. The political conditions described above created a need for a strategy to relieve the pressure on the penal mechanisms. The reformatory, aimed at young adults and designed as an industrial training school, allowed reformers and policymakers to use the "new" institutional model as a symbol of reform and as a practical solution to overcrowding. Because the reformatories were to house young adults, judges had a place to send younger offenders other than the prison. Because the reformatories were designed as industrial training schools to provide job training for inmates, the burden of requiring the institution to be self-sufficient was eliminated. States began building reformatories as another place to send offenders, not as an alternative to prisons (McKelvey, 1977:133-138).

This period of reformatory development has been labeled the period of *pedagogical penology* because of the emphasis on schools and industrial training programs in these reformatories. The reformatory at Elmira, New York, under the leadership of Zebulon Brockway, was the prototype of the reformatory movement. The characteristics of Elmira set the model for reformatories around the nation. Elmira was a humanitarian institution based on treatment through educational and vocational programs and facilitated by the promise of the social sciences. Elmira was the forerunner of the treatment "hospital" for deviants, which criminologists later labeled the "medical model" of corrections. Elmira accepted only first offenders (felony) between 16 and 30 years of age. Sentences were indeterminate with a maximum length that allowed reformatory officials to decide when an inmate was ready to be released. The reformatory's programs emphasized an educational focus that included schools and industrial training. Finally, a system of marks and grade levels was used to reward educational and training improvement. Although these characteristics distinguished reformatories from prisons, the reformatories quickly developed environments identical to prisons, and the educational and reward systems became cornerstones of discipline and control, not rehabilitation (McKelvey, 1977:131-132).

Elmira, through the aggressive leadership of Brockway, served as a model for the nation, but other states merely imitated the shell of Elmira and did not contribute innovations to the model. States continued to mix old and young offenders and repeat offenders with first-time offenders. By the early 1920s the reformatory movement was in full swing, but the environment of the reformatories succumbed to the pressure of the increasing inmate population and the practical needs of custody and discipline. Rehabilitation still was not a realistic expectation for reformatory inmates. Yet Elmira's reformatory model was copied in dozens of states based on its favorable but unchallenged reputation for success in training offenders to reenter society as cooperative, participating members.

Much of that reputation depended to a large extent on Zebulon Brockway's constant and zealous advocacy of his ideas and his model. He was lauded then, and is recognized today, as a pivotal leader of the reformatory movement. Some refer to him as one of the ablest practical reformers of the period. Other scholars have been reevaluating Brockway and the success of Elmira, however, and their conclusions are less adulatory. Scholars have questioned this utopian view of Elmira as either humanitarian or scientific and have placed its leader, Zebulon Brockway, in a different light than the quintessential humanitarian reformer. He was a religious zealot who ignored criticism of his practices, a tyrant who willingly used excessive measures of corporal punishment to maintain discipline, and a reformer who too quickly succumbed to the political pressures of the times.

Elmira's leader, and the leader of the reformatory movement, was an evangelical despot who focused on spiritual rebirth of the inmates, not social rehabilitation for integration into a complex society. His educational and vocational programs were built on an incredible system of pain and brutal punishment. Spiritual regeneration, vocational and educational programs, and the label of reformatory notwithstanding, Elmira and its imitators throughout the nation were first and foremost prisons which had as their practical priority the custody and storage of offenders. Brutal forms of corporal punishment permeated their environments as a means to control, not to rehabilitate (Pisciotta, 1982).

Elmira was a reflection of the social forces of Evangelicalism and temperance of the period. These social movements generated a considerable amount of coercive social policies in an attempt to control and change behavior. Elmira was supposed to implement that posture on criminals and thus did not break with the penitentiary model or become an alternative. The reformatory was an extension of the penitentiary and an expansion of the distributive power of the state to punish. As a result of this recent research we are beginning to achieve a balanced perspective on the role of the reformatory in the development of penology in the United States. We are also getting a clearer picture of the viability of penal reforms and their susceptibility to political pressures (Jenkins, 1984).

The Big House

The term "Big House," made popular by the 1940s prison movies with James Cagney, was used to differentiate the variety of penal institutions such as houses of corrections and reformatories. The Big House of the twentieth century was generally the main prison of a state such as the massive institutions at Columbus, Ohio; Waupan, Wisconsin; Auburn Prison and Sing Sing in New York; "Big Mac" at Macalester, Oklahoma; and Alcatraz in San Francisco Bay. These institutions were built between 1860 and 1930 with additions constructed over time—well into the 1970s—as inmate populations increased. They had massive stone cell blocks and high brick walls with gun turrets for guards. Except for capital punishment, these institutions symbolized the "state's most extreme form of punishment" (Irwin, 1980:5).

These prisons had little, if any, rehabilitative programming, were operated by the combined authority of prison staff and inmate factions, and had pervasive brutality. Finally, it is not very informative to use a label such as Big House to connote such a distinction because in most cases the reformatories and Big Houses during the twentieth century were not distinct either in terms of their programmatic environment or in their function which was primarily punishment and custody in a warehousing atmosphere (Johnson, 1987:47).

Corrections and Prisons:
The Post-World War II Period, 1940-1960

From 1940 well into the decade of the 1960s, penal development once again embraced the rehabilitative philosophy espoused by the reformers of the Progressive period, but with a renewed vigor. After World War II, America rebuilt its economy, became prosperous, more urbanized and educated, and, as a result of the success of America's role in the war, more confident in its ability to solve social problems. The national focus shifted from global concerns to developing solutions to the problems of health, family, and crime. A new breed of post-war professionals emerged in medicine, social work, psychology, and penology, and they began to permeate state penal systems as administrators. What developed from this influx of new leaders was a renewed commitment to rehabilitation, but within a new conceptualization of the prison, the correctional institution. These new institutions were different—in degree, not in kind. They had more educational and therapeutic programs for inmates, less harsh discipline, more privileges and were probably more tolerable. But many of these changes were superficially implemented, whether from administrative ignorance about how to establish rehabilitative programs, or from a lack of resources. In most cases the existing Big Houses and reformatories were relabeled as correctional institutions but did not correct (rehabilitate) and continued to have climates of brutality and warehousing. These institutions became more violent as the overcrowding continued, as prisons became filled with hardened criminals, and as racial and gang conflict over control of the prison environment spiraled (Johnson, 1987:43-45; Irwin, 1980:37-38).

The legacy of corrections is that it left the maximum-security institutions with a level of violence, not unlike that found in previous decades, that was administered by inmates rather than prison administrators and was clearly used for control purposes without any link to rehabilitation or reintegration. Yet some have argued that the administration of punishment through penal institutions today is substantively more humane than in the past. Johnson, in an insightful analysis of the contemporary prison, places today's prison climate in historical context and argues that prisons inflict pain and over time we have "civilized" the administration of pain in our prisons. He claims that punishment was civilized first when we removed corporal punishment from public view and hid it behind prison walls. This decreased the amount of publicity and its concomitant level of mob violence that public executions and corporal punishments generated. We would add that maybe this even began to weaken the legitimacy of violence. Second, we slowly eliminated the acceptability of using physical pain to increase prison production or to control prisoner behavior, even to the point of forbidding the physical pain of an execution. Finally, we have circumscribed or delimited the use of psychological pain to control prisoners. Prison administrators can no longer rely on terror as a means of operating and controlling the prison environment. This use of terror, according to Johnson and others, has been replaced by the use of shame. Shaven heads, inmate numbers rather than names, and other such phenomenon constitute the mechanisms of control. As a society today we are not as bloodthirsty as a century ago, and our prisons reflect that historical shift in attitudes (Johnson, 1987:45-49).

Yet even if most of this analysis is accurate, prisons today are still oppressive, fear-laden, and terroristic climates. Inmates may have more control over their daily lives and may have more access to the outside world, but prisons are violent. The violence now may not be administered by prison officials as in the past, but the violence promulgated by inmates against each other is no less harmful nor is it anything else but a deviant form of punishment for noncompliance to coercive rules even if those rules are part of the inmate culture. (This will be discussed further in Chapter 10.) In short, inmate violence is aimed at controlling inmate behavior. Obviously, this climate is not conducive to rehabilitation. Current interest in supporting a model for compliant and mutual agenda between inmates and prison staff for managing and coping with the prison environment should not be embraced too quickly without a deep reading of the history of punishment and incarceration and the attempts to reform the punishment agenda and the mechanisms of punishment.

These new reformers, however, crystallized a set of assumptions about the causes of criminal behavior and its treatability. They assumed that the causes of individual criminal behavior could be measured precisely and treated in a scientific manner. Based on the three tenets of indeterminate sentencing, classification, and treatment, they set about building new prisons to meet the goals of what became known as the *rehabilitative ideal*. These tenets will be described in detail in later chapters. For our purposes here we need to once again realize that these "reforms" were not totally new, but because of their powerful appeal to reformers, and their acceptance by society in general, they became clear objectives for state prison systems. Once again the prisons were redefined, this time as correctional institutions (Irwin, 1980:39; Allen, 1964).

Prison staff coopted these tenets to serve the custody needs of the prison. Although we can find many correctional institutions, and even Big Houses in the 1950s and 1960s organized along the lines of rehabilitation, the primary function of these new procedures was control of prisoners to achieve an orderly environment. Many prisoners participated in the various programs because of the risk of punishment or the loss of privileges or a delay in parole. As a result, tenuous order was achieved. For those prisoners who refused to participate in the supposedly non-punitive programs, prison administrators created "adjustment centers," segregated units with tighter controls. Essentially these were prisons within prisons and illustrate administrative priority for maintaining order in the institution (Irwin, 1980:60-63).

After a brief slowdown in prison construction during the 1970s, new prisons are being built in the 1990s, states are implementing determinate sentencing which eliminates parole board discretion but increases judicial discretion, and community corrections is losing state support. These developments suggest that the penal systems of the United States are floundering. As John Irwin said, there is "no new powerful correctional philosophy in the making" (1980:216). The 1990s do not appear to have a direction. We may have to wait for a completely new set of research, or a series of cataclysmic events, or maybe a new breed of penal administrators to chart a new course. What is clear, however, is that the cyclical nature of penal reform is intact, and we may be simply in a trough of a cycle.

The 1940s and 1950s saw a resurgence of the movement toward individual treatment. Yet this movement emerged on the heels, some would say as a result, of the failure of the promises of the reformatory objective begun in the 1890s and refined through the 1940s.

Prisons quite literally blew up in the 1950s. More than one dozen state prisons erupted into major riots with a large number of other disturbances in penal institutions throughout the nation. Violence in prisons had escalated, administrators had been powerless or unwilling to manage their prisons, the public was indifferent and rehabilitation had not received sufficient support because of a lack of understanding of rehabilitative goals by all concerned including the inmates (McKelvey, 1977:322-329).

This was not the first time in our history that prison riots occurred across the country. Prisons had erupted in 1912-1915, 1927-1931, 1939-1940, 1950-1953, and in the late 1960s. Although we should be very cautious about making generalized statements about the causes of these riots across such a wide time span, most scholars agree that common threads are evident. Riots did not occur spontaneously. Evidence of rising tensions between inmates and staff and between inmate factions was well documented, and riots usually followed changes in administrative procedures that broke the tenuous and fragile calm of prisons. Yet although riots have been violent, destructive events, they have been relatively rare episodes in our penal history (Irwin, 1980:24-26).

Prison conditions had reached a new low. Overcrowding was rampant and financial support from the states was insufficient. Prison staffs and inmates brutalized each other, living conditions were intolerable, and the situation was getting worse. Legal petitions for redress from inmates fell on deaf ears in the courts. Most courts followed what has been labeled a *"hands-off" doctrine*. They refused to interfere with a state's authority to administer its prison systems.

By the 1970s, however, litigation increased and the courts became increasingly involved in assessing prison conditions through the legal prism of prisoners' rights. By the end of the decade the number of prisoner petitions reached 11,000 annually. There are 46 states that are now (or at one time were) under court order to address prison conditions determined to violate constitutional rights of the inmates. Because some of the violations were so severe and of epidemic proportions, some federal courts have actually taken over the administration of some state prisons (McKelvey, 1977:360-367).

Many states earnestly attempted to address the complex issues surrounding their penal systems, but the most aggressive activity occurred in California. Many rehabilitative concepts were implemented and the penal system was restructured to facilitate those programs. As a result, California earned the distinction of being the leader in the implementation of the rehabilitative model. Punishment had given way to rehabilitation as a policy priority. California exemplified that trend. When the bottom fell out of the rehabilitative movement, California still maintained its commitment and was the primary defender of the rehabilitative ideal (McKelvey, 1977:367-371).

Toward the end of the 1960s a series of scholarly writings challenged the effectiveness of the rehabilitative model by claiming that rehabilitation did not work (Martinson, 1976). Coming at the end of a tumultuous decade that experienced widespread urban rioting, the violence associated with the anti-Vietnam protests and the civil rights movement, and a public perception of rising crime, society looked for new direction for its penal systems. Given the attacks on the rehabilitative ideal with its emphasis on indeterminate sentencing, individual treatment, and wide discretion for criminal justice professionals coupled with a public review of the failure of the system to adequately punish criminals, new models were sought. The determinate sentencing movement gained in popularity because it appeared to limit judicial discretion while at the same time providing equal punishment for similar crimes. The abolishment of parole in many states also attacked the discretion issue, but it also suggested clearly that prison sentences should be served without adjustment. In other quarters, primarily academic, there was a serious attempt to develop a model and an intellectual and pragmatic rationale for the reimposition of corporal punishment as a viable sanction for criminal behavior (see "On the Defensive" at the end of this chapter). Finally, as mentioned earlier, states across the nation responded by building additional prisons to meet what became in the 1980s the overcrowding crisis. Where we are heading in the 1990s is anybody's guess, but what is clear is that society has shifted dramatically away from the rehabilitative model, has moved closer to a punishment model of just deserts as a minimal sanction and has made a commitment to increasing the number of larger and smaller prisons (and thus a larger inmate population) at an extremely heavy financial cost to be paid by the next generation of taxpayers (Irwin, 1980:216-248; Johnson, 1987:161-168).

Summary

The history of punishment, incarceration, and corrections is a fascinating and complex story. We really do not have a complete understanding of the relationship between society's shifting definition of order and the punishment apparatus developed to control those people who challenge those notions of order. We do know that the powerful elements of a society such as kings, vested economic interests, the middle class and reformers all share in the benefits generated by whatever punishment apparatus is used. What we do not know is how and to what extent these elements directly influence the design, development, and implementation of punishment models.

We know, for example, that Beccaria and Bentham wrote and published treatises that criticized the barbaric and dysfunctional punishment mode in place during their lives. But what direct impact did their efforts have on the actual implementation of punishment? Remember that their writings were not distributed by huge international publishing houses or disseminated throughout society by the mass media. At best their ideas circulated through a small cadre of intellectuals. Most prison administrators and certainly all prison guards were illiterate and probably never heard of these great thinkers. The link between reform ideas and practice then is a tenuous one.

We should keep this in mind even today as we discuss the issues of penal reform and practice outlined in this chapter and this textbook. The history of punishment in the United States has been largely a history of the prison. We appear to equate prison with punishment. Much of the history you read in this chapter illustrates the pivotal place prisons play in our punishment apparatus. This history also suggests, however, that our society as a whole does not pay much attention to prisons. It appears that we look to prisons to punish and are surprised when they turn out to be brutal and violent places. Maybe we are too optimistic, in that we look for simple, quick-fix solutions to crime and disorder and are too prone to embrace new reforms too rapidly. Maybe we allow reformers too much discretion in implementing their reforms, such as Brockway's reformatories in the nineteenth century, or the rehabilitative ideals of the twentieth century.

What is clear from this chapter is that the prison is the most important element of our punishment apparatus. All other elements, such as probation, fines, rehabilitation, and sentencing reforms are designed as alternatives to prison. It seems that we refuse to recognize that the prison is a social and political institution, and that we have a responsibility to address the prison on its own terms. We prefer to ignore it and seek alternatives that are discussed in the balance of this book.

A Punishment Manifesto

1. Acute corporal punishment should be introduced to fill the gap between the severe punishment of prison and the non-punishment of probation.

2. For the majority of property crimes, the preferred corporal punishment is that of electric shock because it can be scientifically controlled and calibrated, and is less violent in its application when compared with other corporal punishments such as whipping.

3. For violent crimes in which the victim was terrified and humiliated, and for which a local community does not wish to incarcerate, a violent corporal punishment should be considered, such as whipping. In these cases, humiliation of the offender is seen as justifiably deserved.

4. Every effort should be made to develop a split system of criminal justice: one system for the punishment of *crimes*, and one for the punishment of *criminals*.

5. After an offender has committed a number of repeated offenses, or when the combined injury and damage of his crimes reach a certain amount, he will be treated as a criminal deserving of incarceration.

6. Only criminals should receive prison as a punishment, and only two prison sentences should be allowed: 15 years for the first incarceration, and life if the individual recommits after his release. The 15-year term is the "warning" that the offender is close to the point of no return. There is no more getting off lightly with corporal punishment.

7. The decision to incarcerate will depend on many factors, but should especially depend on how much money the community is prepared to spend on incarcerating repeat offenders.

8. Before pronouncing either a 15-year or a life sentence, the judge should be required to seek a budgetary assessment of the cost of keeping this offender for the respective period. If such money is not approved beforehand by the Division of Budget, the sentence should be disallowed, and corporal punishment substituted.

9. A life sentence means life. If we truly believe that treatment or rehabilitation no longer works, then there is no sense at all, especially from the point of view of incapacitation, in ever letting the "dangerous" criminal out.

10. The measure of the effectiveness of prison as a punishment should not be whether the offender recommits after release. Rather, the notion of prison as retributive considers it entirely possible that a truly terrible offender may not have sufficient time in one life to work through the guilt of his crimes. Furthermore, even if he does work off his guilt, there is no expectation at all, according to the retributive philosophy, that the offender should have learned not to repeat his crime. What he *has* learned is that his crime have a reciprocal cost to him in suffering. Thus, we do not speak of "rehabilitation" of the criminal, but of "redemption."

11. When corporal punishment is used, offenders should receive the same punishment for the same crime, whether it is their first offense or not. The only time an offender's entire record should be taken into account is when we decide to incarcerate. At that point an assessment of the dollar cost of the criminal's offenses may be considered, along with other individual background factors.

12. Because corporal punishment does not discriminate according to the offender's background, no distinction should be made according to age, sex, race or any other social or psychological characteristic when deciding on the amount of deserved corporal punishment. Of course, a medical examination will be required to establish the offender's fitness to receive punishment.

13. The scaling of corporate punishment will be tied (1) the comparative seriousness of offense categories, and (2) the amount of injury and damage of the offense.

14. Corporal punishment may be applied according to intensity, frequency and time, but should never exceed an eight hour period.

15. Corporal punishment should be immediate: applied as soon as possible after the sentence (and preferably upon the finding of guilt).

16. All punishment should be public: corporal punishment should be conducted in the presence of community representatives, including the press, and a description of the offender's crime or crimes should be graphically portrayed to the public at the time of the punishment. Prisons should also be opened to public tours.

17. Corporal punishment should never be used either in combination with prison or in order to "correct" the offender, because in these uses it comes too close to torture, which is barbaric and destructive.

18. Judges must be given more discretion, not less. Corporal punishment, along with a "guidelines" model, is merely a first transitional step towards breaking down sentencing practices which at present are rigid and narrow. By using creative punishments judges will help free the higher courts to break with the purely quantitative notion of crime and punishment, and to begin thinking in terms of *appropriateness*.

19. Fines should be eliminated from the range of punishment alternatives unless they are part of a punishment that tries to reflect a particular offense.

20. When prisons are used as a chronic punishment we must take full responsibility for their harshness and put them to a clear retributive purpose. This means getting rid of the watered down versions of prisons, and making those few prisons that will exist extremely harsh places, reserved only for the terrible few.

21. A prison intensive system will de-emphasize prison as a form of punishment. The advantages of this strategy are obvious: a decrease in the number of people in prison, and a great savings in cost.

But by far the greatest consequence of this de-emphasis in prisons is that fewer persons will come under the direct control of the State (which is what we mean by prisons), and that the major portion of criminal punishment (that is, corporal punishment) will be conducted with the view that it is not criminals *per se* who are being punished at all, but free citizens who have exercised their right to break the law.

In this way the most basic of all freedoms in a society is preserved: the freedom to break the law.

Reprinted with permission of The Free Press, a Division of Macmillan, Inc., from *Just and Painful: A Case for the Corporal Punishment of Criminals*, pp. 139-142, by Graeme R. Newman. Copyright © 1983 by Graeme R. Newman.

Key Terms and Concepts

Age of Reason

Age of Reform

banishment

Big House

Bridewell

Calvinists

capital punishment

classical school of criminology

classification

closed market system

congregate system

contract system

corporal punishment

European model

hands-off doctrine

lease system

medical model

Middle Ages

normalization

penitentiary

piece-price system

post-revolution enlightenment view

progressive period

rasphouses and spinhouses

reformatory model

rehabilitative ideal

silent system

state account system

vocational training

References

Adamson, C. (1980). "Hard Labor and Solitary Confinement: Effects of the Business Cycle and Labor Supply on Prison Discipline in the United States, 1790-1835." *Research in Law, Deviance and Social Control*, 6:19-56.

Allen, F.A. (1964). *The Borderland of Criminal Justice.* Chicago, IL: University of Chicago Press.

Bellamy, J. (1973). *Crime and Public Order in the Later Middle Ages.* London, England: Routledge & Kegan Paul.

Conley, J.A. (1980). "Prisons, Production, and Profit: Reconsidering the Importance of Prison Industries." *Journal of Social History*, 14:257-275.

Conley, J.A. (1981). "Economics and the Social Reality of Prisons." *Journal of Criminal Justice*, 10:27.

Eriksson, T. (1976). *The Reformers: An Historical Survey of Pioneer Experiments in the Treatment of Criminals.* New York: Elsevier Books.

Geis, G. (1973). "Jeremy Bentham, 1748-1832." In H. Mannheim (ed.) *Pioneers in Criminology.* Montclair, NJ: Patterson Smith.

Irwin, J. (1980). *Prisons in Turmoil.* Boston, MA: Little, Brown and Company.

Jenkins, P. (1984). "Temperance and the Origins of the New Penology." *Journal of Criminal Justice*, 12:551-565.

Johnson, R. (1987). *Hard Time: Understanding and Reforming the Prison*. Monterey, CA: Brooks/Cole Publishing Company.

McKelvey, B. (1977). *American Prisons: A History of Good Intentions*. Montclair, NJ: Patterson Smith.

Martinson, R., et al. (1976). *Rehabilitation, Recidivism, and Research*. Hackensack, NJ: National Council on Crime and Delinquency.

Monachesi, E. (1973). "Cesare Beccaria, 1738-1794." In H. Mannheim (ed.) *Pioneers in Criminology, Second Edition*. Montclair, NJ: Patterson Smith.

Newman, G. (1978). *The Punishment Response*. New York, NY :J.B. Lippincott.

Pisciotta, A.W. (1982). "Scientific Reform; The 'New Penology' at Elmira, 1875-1900." *Crime and Delinquency*, 29:613-630.

Rothman, D. (1971). *The Discovery of the Asylum: Social Order and Disorder in the New Republic*. Boston, MA: Little, Brown and Company.

Rothman, D. (1980). *Conscience and Convenience: The Asylum and Its Alternative in Progressive America*. Boston, MA: Little, Brown and Company.

Schlossman, S.L. (1977). *Love and the American Delinquent: The Theory and Practice of "Progessive" Juvenile Justice, 1825-1920*. Chicago, IL: University of Chicago Press.

Spierenburg, P. (1984). *The Emergence of Carceral Institutions: Prisons, Galleys and Lunatic Asylums, 1550-1900*. Rotterdam, The Netherlands: Erasmus University.

Photo Credit: Bill Powers, Frost Publishing Group, Ltd.

Jails and Short-Term Detention

3

After reading this chapter, the student should be able to:

- Discuss the historical foundations of the jail.

- Describe the twentieth-century jail.

- Discuss pretrial detention and the processes of adaptation in jail.

- Outline modern jail management issues, including jail design.

- Provide a description of guarding in jail and the role of correctional law.

- Explain the problems of the mentally ill in jail.

Introduction

As Goldfarb (1975) has noted, "Jails have been little studied, and widely misunderstood." This quotation sums up much of what is known about jails in this country. While we have extensive knowledge and literature on the nature and functions of prison systems, we know very little about the nation's jails. As some have suggested, the jail is considered the forgotten institution in both the criminal justice system and society. It is for this reason that this chapter will examine the history, purposes, and functions commonly associated with the jail. We will begin our investigation by exploring the historical antecedents to the modern jail, focusing on the origin and development of the jail in American society.

This examination will focus on the role of the jail in nineteenth-century America, and conclude with a discussion of the modern jail. In addition, we will explore who ends up in our jails and look at some common jail problems today, such as overcrowding. Our examination of the jail will include a description of the demographic characteristics of individuals who are in jail, along with special problems associated with jail confinement. Our presentation will show how the jail has evolved over time, and the influence that many factors external to the jail have had in changing where the jail is headed as we move into the twenty-first century. The contemporary jail and its design is fundamentally different than when the first jail was built in this country. To understand this difference, we need to begin our examination by exploring the historical roots of the modern jail.

Historical Foundations of the Jail

An examination of the jail in America must begin by identifying what many people believe to be the first jail in this country. The Walnut Street Jail, built in 1790 in Philadelphia, has been attributed the distinction of being the first local institution of confinement in America. While many have noted that other institutions were present prior to the establishment of the Walnut Street Jail, it is still commonly accepted that the modern jail has its roots in the creation of the Walnut Street Jail. This jail, along with other institutions of confinement in society, represented a radical change from the commonly accepted methods of dealing with the social outcast, deviant, poor, or mentally ill. As Rothman (1971) has documented, institutionalization in America did not develop until the beginning of the nineteenth century when the belief in methods outside of the home were viewed as more effective in addressing the common social ills, such as crime, poverty, and mental illness.

This new philosophy led to the creation of a new era of dealing with the criminal, the sick, and the poor and destitute. Essentially, institutionalization was viewed as the panacea to the social ills that were flourishing in early nineteenth-century America. With the growth of the urban city and the concomitant rise in population, the local communities were looking for new approaches to deal with those who were deemed uncontrollable by the traditional methods of social control. Hence, the jail and other confinement institutions, such as prisons later, were viewed as the most appropriate places to deal with society's problems. In this light, institutionalization, of which jails played a integral part, became part of the societal repertoire to combat the evils that were produced through increased urbanization and growth of the city.

Reformers who espoused the development and growth of institutionalization were known as the *Jacksonians*. They represented what Rothman (1980) calls the *Jacksonian Era* in American history, an era firmly entrenched in the belief in institutions of confinement as the solution to the growing crime and deviancy problem in nineteenth-century America. With this belief, these reformers led the way for the development of the jail and other institutions. Fundamentally, their views were shaped by the facts that the cities were not only growing at a rate faster than the local communities were able to handle, but in addition, the attendant problems of the cities could not be addressed by employing the traditional methods of social control. The jail, along with prisons later in the nineteenth century, therefore, embodied a new and radical approach to dealing with social problems.

These institutions were to be places where the criminal, deviant, vagrant, and mentally ill could be housed and their problems dealt with outside of the community, and therefore away from the corrupting influences of society. Ostensibly, the social outcast was out of sight and out of mind in relation to the community. Yet, this process was believed by the Jacksonians to be critical to the solution of the problem, and as such, the growth and acceptance of institutionalization predominated as a progressive way to deal with society's problems, whether it was the mentally ill, the sick and neglected, the poor, or the criminal offender. Thus, the jail became part of a network of institutions that proliferated throughout the early part of the nineteenth century in America. While proposed as a solution, the jail and the prison developed their own problems, most of which were tied to their day-to-day operations. Nevertheless, the early institutions of confinement were a reaction to the cruelty and barbarousness of early methods of social control, such as corporal and capital punishment. *In this way, the jail was viewed as a humane alternative to the draconian methods of dealing with deviants in the past.*

In fact, Goldfarb (1975:10) has suggested that the creation of the early jail, specifically the Walnut Street Jail, was directly related to what early religious reformers—the Quakers—viewed as outrageous and cruel methods of dealing with the poor, the ill, and the criminal. Institutionalization through jails and prisons was viewed as the more humane alternative to the rather cruel and arbitrary practices of the past. As Rothman (1971:15) has stated, however, this justification became part of the repertoire of those who favored institutionalization. By favoring the perpetuation of institutionalization as a proper method of social control, reformers could always argue that their intent was to avoid reverting to practices that were cruel and inhumane. Thus, the history of cruelty and violence against the weakest elements in society—the poor and the criminal—ironically fostered a belief in institutionalization as the only civilized method of social control. The jail, therefore, continued to proliferate throughout nineteenth-century America.

Did, however, the jail really offer a humane alternative to the lash or the hangman's noose? Some social historians have suggested that the cruelty associated with corporal and capital punishments became institutionalized through places of confinement, such as the jail and the prison (Rothman, 1971:19). In other words, while we may have relied less on the physical punishments of the past when dealing with the criminal offender, we created a newer form of brutality as expressed through our jails and prisons. In fact, the jail has historically represented a type of punishment and confinement that is so unique and distinctive that it clearly sets itself apart from other confinement institutions in society, such as the prison. As Goldfarb (1975:10) states, "There was no coherent architectural history or planning of the jail institution; nor has there been much variation in the function and design of the jail to the present time." In short, the jail was viewed as a holding tank, nothing less, nothing more. Jails were built with the sole intent of housing people who could not be handled in any other way in society.

In this regard, the jail was very useful in the growing cities of urban America, where the socially deviant or the poor could be controlled simply by warehousing them in the local jail. Moreover, well into the nineteenth century the jail served the purpose of controlling many gangs of criminals who roamed the western part of America. To control the lawlessness occurring in their towns, communities began building jails. Many of these jails were what Lunden (1959) called nothing but "human squirrel cages." These makeshift jails served the purpose of housing criminals for short periods of time and were consistent with the purposes and designs of the early jails of the nineteenth century—the control of problematic populations of people in the community: the mentally ill, the sick and neglected, and the criminal offender.

By the time the nineteenth century came to an end, most cities and counties had established jails that served the purpose we decribed above, that being the control of problem populations in the community. The Sheriff became the person placed in charge of the jail; this was true early on with the jail and is still true in most counties today. The jail, however, became more critical to communities when crime proliferated and urban centers expanded. While we were still placing the same types of people in our jails, their numbers started to grow considerably. This growth patterned the growth of the communities. The jail became populated by what one writer refers to as "rabble." The rabble class became those people who exhibited behavior that was the most serious and offensive to the local communities. Rabble management, therefore, became the central purpose of the jail in the beginning of the twentieth century and continues today (Irwin, 1986). As Irwin (1986:8) states: "By 1900 Americans had taken England's rabble management invention and modified it to suit their own needs. In particular, in their expanding industrial cities they were ready with large city and county jails to manage the urban rabble, whose numbers and offensiveness were increasing."

The Twentieth-Century Jail

The early jail in America housed primarily those individuals who could not be controlled by more traditional methods of social control. As cities grew and the large populations of people began to aggregate in our urban centers, the problem of crime became more central and visible to the communities. To deal with a growing crime problem, the jail served the purpose of removing those people who were perceived as eyesores to the community. Beginning with the early part of the twentieth century and well into the latter part of that century, "rabble management" became the focus of the jail.

The term "rabble management" is not something exclusive to jails, however. It is clear that the entire criminal justice system, beginning with police, serve to control those people who society finds the most offensive and dangerous. The jail is one institution in society designed to deal with the rabble class. In fact, this idea of rabble control is something that the police have been asked to address in how they deliver services to the community. The problem-oriented style of policing, for example, emphasizes the solving of key problems in the community through cooperation between police and citizens. Many problems are posed by the rabble class; hence, maintaining order in the community and keeping "broken windows" (Wilson and Kelling, 1982) to a minimum is the function of the police. Thus, rabble management is consistent with the broader goals of community order and order maintenance.

What is rabble? Irwin (1986:xiii) defines rabble as those individuals who are "mostly detached and disreputable persons who are arrested more because they are offensive than because they have committed crimes." The rabble class is composed of individuals of whom we all are aware, yet toward whom we are indifferent. They are the public nuisances, the derelicts, the drunks and disorderlies, the vagrants, the mentally ill, and the street persons. Thus, rabble management in the jail involves removing those people from the city streets who offend us, yet who may not be so dangerous when one examines their crimes.

It is the degree of offensiveness that determines how rabble will be handled. In the twentieth century, rabble management means a brief stint in the county jail. As a result, the jail has as its primary function the control of society's rabble, those people who are the most offensive to the prevailing social norms yet who pose very little threat to society. Moreover, since the jail is primarily composed of rabble, the conditions of the jail have not always been the best. It is a sad fact in the criminal justice system that the jail is considered the worst place to be, even though the seriousness of the crimes of many people in the jail is minor.

In fact, a majority of people in our jails are *pretrial detainees*. These are individuals that are awaiting trial and have not been found guilty of a crime, but they somewhat ironically are forced to live in conditions that are much worse than in many state prisons, places where convicted felons are sent! We will see later how modern jail structures have been built to improve the conditions of many jail inmates, even though under the law being a pretrial detainee does not guarantee a jail inmate conditions better than those experienced by convicted felons (see Chapter 12). Later we will examine the characteristics of pretrial detainees in our jails. For now, however, we must more clearly define what the role of the jail is in twentieth-century America.

Irwin (1986:39-41) has argued that the jail in twentieth-century America has evolved into an institution of social control for those people who are not only the most offensive, but in addition, those people who make up the underclass in American society. These are the people in society who have the least power and are the most amenable to jail life. Many have had previous experiences with the criminal justice system and are considered the most "disreputable" in the eyes of the general public. They would include petty hustlers, derelicts, junkies, crazies, and outlaws. Moreover, the jail does house a sizeable number of people who are "mildly offensive" and considered only marginal rabble, such as homosexuals or recent immigrants.

Most important, however, is the fact that the jail is composed of people who have both an element of seriousness and a high degree of offensiveness associated with their crimes. Irwin (1986:40) has suggested that the two taken together make up the jail population, but that offensiveness is the critical variable for most rabble who are arrested and processed into the jail. Surely, the seriousness of the crime is relevant when criminal justice personnel make decisions on whether a person will become involved in the criminal justice system. The point is that many people who are arrested by police are marginal criminals who do not need the intrusion of the criminal justice system into their lives, yet a sizeable number of people in our jails are just those types of people, those who represent a high degree of offensiveness and are the least powerful in society.

Does the jail, therefore, manage the underclass? To some degree there is strong evidence to support this claim. When we examine recent demographic profiles of jail inmates, support for the idea that jails house the most disreputable and disenfranchised members of society becomes rather apparent. Data from the Bureau of Justice Statistics (1990) indicate that a vast majority of jail inmates are male (91%), a little over half are white (51%), with other minority groups making up the difference (black inmates acccount for 47% of all jail admissions, even though they make up only 13% of the U.S. population), and 86% of all jail inmates are non-Hispanic (see Table 3.1). Couple this information with prearrest income data and other relevant socioeconomic indicators, it becomes readily apparent that a sizeable number of jail inmates are from what we would call the underclass.

Table 3.1
Demographic Characteristics of Jail Inmates, 1989

Characteristic	Percent of jail inmates
Total	100%
Sex	
Male	91
Female	9
Race	
White	51
Male	46
Female	5
Black	47
Male	43
Female	4
Other*	2
Male	1
Female	—
Ethnicity	
Hispanic	14
Male	13
Female	1
Non-Hispanic	86
Male	78
Female	8

Note: Data are for June 30 of each year. Sex of all inmates was reported in both years. Race was reported for 91% of the inmates in 1989. Percentages may not add to total because of rounding.
—Less than 0.5%.
*Native Americans, Aleuts, Asians, and Pacific Islanders.

Source: Bureau of Justice Statistics (1990). "Jail Inmates, 1989." Washington, DC: U.S. Department of Justice.

Bureau of Justice Statistics (1988a) data indicate that among jail inmates who were free for one year before their arrest, the median income was $5,486, even though 41% had been working in some type of job. Many of these jobs were low paying, and if the underclass argument is credible, it is, in part, supported by this data. In addition, a vast majority of the jail inmates were not married prior to arrest (79%), 59% had not completed high school, and 47% were unemployed. Clearly, then, it would be reasonable to hold that a great number of jail inmates are disreputable and are those members in society who are the most disenfranchised and alienated from conventional norms and values. Indeed, the data does not paint a rosy picture about the composition of our jails.

Nevertheless, who we confine and what characteristics they bring to the jail may not be as revealing as the conditions under which they must live once in jail. The Bureau of Justice Statistics (1990) reports that the most pressing concern facing jail administrators today is overcrowding. Table 3.2 reveals the extent of the problem. It is clear that when one compares total numbers of inmates over time, the overcrowding of our jails is evident. Table 3.2 also shows that there was almost a 15% increase in the number of inmates housed in our jails from 1988-1989. Additionally, Table 3.3 shows that slightly less than half of the inmates (48%) are pretrial detainees, most of them being male inmates. Most importantly, the data indicate that jail capacity and jail occupancy are nearly equivalent. Table 3.4 highlights the fact that according to the 1978 jail census, 65% of the rated capacity of all jails was occupied, while in 1989 that figure had jumped to 108% of rated capacity.

Table 3.2
Jail Population: One-Day Count and Average Daily Population, by Legal Status and Sex, 1988-1989

	Number of jail inmates		
	National Jail Census 1988	Annual Survey of Jails 1989	Percent change, 1988-1989
One-day count			
All Inmates	343,569	395,553	15%
Adults	341,893	393,303	15
Male	311,594	356,050	15
Female	30,299	37,253	23
Juveniles*	1,676	2,250	34
Average daily population			
All inmates	336,017	386,845	15%
Adults	334,566	384,954	15
Male	306,379	349,180	14
Female	28,187	35,774	27
Juveniles*	1,451	1,891	30

Note: Data for 1-day counts are for June 30 of each year.
*Juveniles are persons defined by State statute as being under a certain age, usually 18, and subject initially to juvenile court authority even if tried as adults in criminal court. Because less than 1% of the jail population were juveniles, caution must be used in interpreting any changes over time.

Source: Bureau of Justice Statistics (1990). "Jail Inmates, 1989." Washington, DC: U.S. Department of Justice.

Table 3.3
Conviction Status of Adult Jail Inmates, by Sex, 1988-1989

	Number of jail inmates	
	National Jail Census 1988	Annual Survey of Jails 1989
Total number of adults with known conviction status	341,893	393,303
Convicted	166,224	189,012
Male	151,810	171,181
Female	14,414	17,831
Unconvicted	175,669	204,291
Male	159,784	184,869
Female	15,885	19,422

Note: Data are for June 30 of each year.

Source: Bureau of Justice Statistics (1990). "Jail Inmates, 1989." Washington, DC: U.S. Department of Justice.

Table 3.4
Jail Capacity and Occupancy, 1988-1989

	National Jail Census			Annual Survey of Jails
	1978	1983	1988	1989
Number of inmates	158,394	223,551	343,569	395,553
Rated capacity of jails	245,094	261,556	339,633	367,769
Percent of rated capacity occupied	65%	85%	101%	108%

Note: Data are for February 15, 1978, and June 30 of 1983, 1988, and 1989.

Source: Bureau of Justice Statistics (1990). "Jail Inmates, 1989." Washington, DC: U.S. Department of Justice.

This problem is accentuated by data on just large jails (jails holding over 100 inmates). These large jails are operating well above their rated capacities. Table 3.5 shows how these large jails in 1989 were at 116% of their rated capacities. As a result, many of these jails are under court order to reduce their populations. In fact, the data indicate (Table 3.6) that a vast majority of the time the court cited crowded conditions as their major concern. The data, therefore, support the idea that jails are not only overcrowded, but in addition, the larger jails are of central concern to the courts. These facilities tend to have a large number of problems associated with them, and therefore, the scrutiny of the courts is much more strict. Table 3.7 lists the 25 largest jails in the country.

Table 3.5
Jurisdictions with Large Jail Populations: Rated Capacity and Percent of Capacity Occupied, 1988-1989

Jurisdictions with large jail populations	Number of jurisdictions		Rated capacity		Number of jail inmates		Percent of capacity occupied	
	1988	1989	1988	1989	1988	1989	1988	1989
Total	508	508	253,226	276,706	281,850	322,314	111%	116%
Jurisdictions with no jail under court order to reduce population	377	374	132,158	138,764	143,242	160,129	108	115
Jurisdictions with at least one jail under court order to reduce population	131	134	121,068	137,942	138,608	162,185	114	118

Note: Data are for June 30 of each year and cover all jurisdictions with an average daily inmate population of 100 or more in the 1988 jail census.

Source: Bureau of Justice Statistics (1990). "Jail Inmates, 1989." Washington, DC: U.S. Department of Justice.

Table 3.6
Jurisdictions with Large Jail Populations: Number of Jurisdictions under Court Order to Reduce Population or to Improve Conditions of Confinement, 1989

		Number of jurisdictions with large jail populations	
	Total	Ordered to limit population	Not ordered to limit population
Total	508	134	374
Jurisdictions under court order citing specific conditions of confinement	118	92	26
Subject of court order:			
Crowded living units	92	84	8
Recreational facilities	51	38	13
Medical facilities or services	41	29	12
Visitation practices or policies	34	25	9
Disciplinary procedures or policies	33	24	9
Food service (quantity or quality)	22	17	5
Administrative segregation procedures or policies	29	22	7
Staffing patterns	41	32	9
Grievance procedures or policies	34	25	9
Education or training programs	17	12	5
Fire hazards	18	15	3
Counseling programs	18	11	7
Other	7	3	4
Totality of conditions	22	17	5

Note: Data are for June 30, 1989, and cover all jurisdictions with an average daily inmate population of 100 or more in the 1988 jail census. Includes only jurisdictions with one or more jails under court order. Some jurisdictions had a jail or jails under court order for more than one reason.

Source: Bureau of Justice Statistics (1990). "Jail Inmates, 1989." Washington, DC: U.S. Department of Justice.

It is not too difficult to realize that it would be a management nightmare to try to control 22,000 inmates as is evidenced in Los Angeles County. It is the large urban jail that poses the most problems for jail managers. The Bureau of Justice Statistics (1990) notes that over 80% of the nation's jail population is housed in the jails of 508 jurisdictions. These consist of 822 jails. However, there are over 3,700 jails in this country. So, what is present is a situation where a small number of jails in the country detain a vast majority of jail inmates. This is why the management of these jails is so problematical. Current research evidence indicates the extent of the problem from the perspective of the jail manager.

Table 3.7
Twenty-Five Largest Jurisdictions: Average Daily Population and 1-Day Count,
June 30, 1989

Jurisdiction	Number of jails in jurisdiction	Average daily population, 1989	One-day count, June 30, 1989
Los Angeles County, Calif.	8	22,426	22,100
New York City, N.Y.	14	16,500	16,597
Harris County, Tex.	2	8,206	8,199
Cook County, Ill.	—	7,000	7,081
Dallas County, Tex.	4	5,800	6,043
Dade County, Fla.	6	4,773	4,726
San Diego County, Calif.	11	4,477	4,987
Shelby County, Tenn.	2	4,452	4,838
Santa Clara County, Calif.	10	4,316	4,162
Orange County, Calif.	3	4,281	4,527
Philadelphia County, Pa.	7	4,277	4,566
Maricopa County, Ariz.	7	3,905	3,896
New Orleans Parish, La.	—	3,700	3,663
Sacramento County, Calif.	3	3,321	2,966
Alameda County, Calif.	4	3,110	3,214
Broward County, Fla.	3	2,979	2,844
Orange County, Fla.	3	2,831	3,305
Baltimore City, Md.	5	2,734	2,783
Tarrant County, Tex.	2	2,420	2,698
San Bernardino County, Calif.	2	2,404	2,395
Kern County, Calif.	3	2,302	2,291
Fulton County, Ga.	4	2,278	2,316
King County, Wash.	2	1,970	2,139
Bexar County, Tex.	1	1,943	2,284
Hillsborough County, Fla.	6	1,939	2,027

—These jurisdictions provided a single report covering all of their jail facilities.

Source: Bureau of Justice Statistics (1990). "Jail Inmates, 1989." Washington, DC: U.S. Department of Justice.

The National Institute of Justice (1988) survey of jail managers shows that jail overcrowding is the most important issue facing them. Over 55% of the jail managers reported that their jails were filled beyond capacity, with 13% between 96% and 100% rated capacity. In addition, over 38% of the jails are under court order with respect to the conditions of confinement. Jail crowding was ranked the most serious problem facing jail managers, followed by staff shortages, and prison crowding which leads to jail crowding. More importantly, the jail managers did provide some ideas as to how jail overcrowding could be dealt with. These included a number of postconviction approaches, such as more liberal work-release programs to pretrial approaches, which included such programs as diversion, citation release, and more flexible release-on-recognizance approaches, and organizational solutions to the problem through more effective internal management programs and greater interagency cooperation between organizations in the criminal justice system.

Whether these approaches will be able to address the problem of overcrowding in jails remains to be seen. We do know that the current attempt to deal with the problem has been through building more jail space. We will discuss this option more thoroughly later in the chapter. For now, we can conclude this section by saying that the jail in twentieth-century America developed out of historical conditions identified with the expansion of urban centers throughout the country. With increased urbanization came the growth of crime and the concomitant rise in jail populations. The purpose, therefore, of the jail must be understood as being related to the urbanization and industrialization of America. With this mind, the jail became the holding tank for those people who could not fit into the mainstream of American society. In the past they were the poor, sick, and often neglected. Today, we refer to them, as Irwin (1986:xiii) suggests, as rabble. Regardless of term, the jail has housed and continues to house many people who not only have committed serious crime, but more importantly, have been identified as the most disillusioned and alienated members of our society.

Pretrial Detention

As shown in Table 3.3, about half of all jail inmates are pretrial detainees. Pretrial detention is a mechanism whereby the court ensures that the defendant remains in the custody of the court until the trial. As our review indicated above, many jail inmates represent the most troubled people in our society. The fact that many jail inmates are poor, may be suffering from some type of mental or emotional disorder, and exhibited a form of behavior that is offensive to most of society really means very little when one examines how these problems are exacerbated by the jail environment. In short, jails do not solve many of the problems people bring with them into jail; if anything, the jail heightens the anxiety of the inmate, and in many cases, may make these problems worse.

Irwin (1986:42-100) has written about the problems that jail inmates experience once they are incarcerated. These problems center around four distinct processes: *disintegration, disorientation, degradation*, and *preparation.* Each one of these processes further removes offenders from the community and firmly entrenches them into the rabble lifestyle. As Irwin (1986:45) states:

> Going to jail and being held there tends to maintain people in a rabble status or convert them to it. To maintain membership in conventional society and thereby avoid rabble status, a person must sustain a conscious commitment to a conventional set of social arrangements. When persons are arrested and jailed, their ties and arrangements with people outside very often disintegrate. In addition, they are profoundly disoriented and subjected to a series of degrading experiences that corrode their general commitment to society. Finally, they are prepared for rabble life by their experiences in jail, which supply them with the identity and culture required to get by as a disreputable.

As such, the jail serves the purpose, in an unintentional way, of introducing people to a lifestyle that is antisocial and unconventional. This may be particularly true of offenders who are pretrial detainees, individuals who may become so alienated with a system and a society that treats them like subhumans when they have not yet been found guilty of a crime.

Disintegration

The distintegration process involves three separate consequences for the jail inmate (Irwin, 1986:47-52). First, the most notable and visible loss of being jailed is the loss of property. Imagine yourself being stripped of all your clothes, your automobile, and all other personal items, and not being sure when you will get them back. On many occasions, the property is either lost or stolen. While the inmate is guaranteed his property upon release, it is not uncommon for clothes and valuables to mysteriously disappear from the sheriff's property room. It is this loss of immediate personal property that begins the disintegration process, and further removes the offender from the outside community.

Second, and a serious deprivation for many jail inmates, is the loss of social ties to the outside world. While inmates are allowed a number of phone calls a day during their period of incarceration, this does not replace the loss of relationships with significant others on the outside. Being cut off from friends and loved ones is expected when being in jail, but the experience is made worse by the limited communication with the outside world. In addition, the disintegration process continues when the jail inmate has no one to communicate with or very little money to purchase basic amenities to survive. Communication tends to center around the jail "grapevine," but it, too, does not meet the needs of the inmate. The disintegration process is heightened when the inmate has very limited opportunities to maintain the key relationships with people in the free community.

Finally, there is a "loss of capacity to take care of business" (Irwin, 1986:51) when one is jailed. This inability to effectively manage one's life behind bars can be devastating for the jailed inmate. For most inmates, the loss of relationships with loved ones and friends is serious enough, but in addition, it is a well-known fact that when a defendant sits in jail as a pretrial detainee, this person does not have the capability to defend himself as well as if he was released on bail prior to the trial. Legal problems behind bars are numerous, and the fact of the matter is that very few jail inmates are able to handle their legal affairs while they are confined. Some inmates, for example, may have holds or detainers from other jurisdictions, and in many situations, they are not able to resolve the pertinent issues involving these holds. As a result, they are further removed from the community and the disintegration process continues for them.

Disorientation

The process of disorientation is continuous for the inmate throughout the entire stay in jail. Beginning with arrest, followed by booking and placement in the jail's "holding tank," disorientation occurs with such power that the inmate is ill-equipped to deal with the experience. This is particularly true among those inmates who are inexperienced with jails and are first-time offenders. During this stage of the jailing process, the inmate becomes more conscious of the fact that he has been arrested and is in jail. In addition, the horrible conditions of the jail leave an impression on the inmate that very few will forget.

Most importantly, the jail inmate becomes "self-disorganized" (Irwin, 1986:63) to the point that feelings of alienation and powerlessness are common. For first-time offenders, the jail experience warps their sense of the outside world, and in some cases may introduce them to a permanent life of rabble. For most, however, the jail experience will wear off upon release, but it is an experience that definitely alters the perceptions of those who go through it. Moreover, for those who go back to the jail in the future, the earlier experience has shaped their subsequent adjustment to the jail and may "propel them further outside" (Irwin, 1986:66) the mainstream of society.

Degradation

Degradation is a word that we all know, yet very few of us have been humiliated by the experience of jail. Many have argued that doing time in jail is one of the most degrading experiences any person would want to go through. The degradation process begins with arrest, and culminates with a judicial determination being made on the individual. Along the way, the defendant has to go through many humiliating experiences, most of which are tied to the routine activities of the jail. This includes strip searches in the presence of other inmates and staff, insults from police and deputy sheriffs who run the jail, and verbal harassment from other prisoners.

The degradation is accepted by the culture of the staff who run the jail, since many are stuck in positions they neither want nor value. For many deputy sheriffs, for example, who work in county jails, the work is viewed as either a punishment for some wrongdoing on road patrol or is an initiation period for rookie deputies. One county official told an author of this book that the jail was reserved for "fuck-ups and rookies." More importantly, the practice of indifference among staff toward inmates in jails is part of an adaptation process by staff. By denying and degrading the inmate the officer is reinforcing some of his own preconceived biases and stereotypes about inmates. It only takes a short period of time in a jail environment before the most well-intentioned individual becomes callous and indifferent to the needs of inmates. By degrading the inmates, the staff provides the necessary grounds for adaptation to the jail environment.

This process of degradation does not end in the jail; it continues well into the courtroom where official and unofficial rules of conduct guide the interaction between the defendant and the presiding judge. The courtroom represents the symbolic form of degradation that defendants experience. It is here that the rabble class learn directly the moral parameters of those who sit in judgment against them. In fact, their demeanor is critical in the courtroom. If the judge feels that their attitude is not consistent with the judge's and the court's moral point of view, it is here that the defendant pays the price. Defendants are coerced into an obsequious position in the courtroom, told what they can say, and when they will say it. Any deviations from the accepted norms of the courtroom can lead to dire consequences for the defendant. If the defendant is recalcitrant or adamant about some issue, this may not bode well for him in the long run. As such, the defendant accepts the degradation process of the courtroom to "cut his losses," and may become less committed to the conventional ways of doings things in society. In Irwin's (1986:84) words, "[r]ejection of conventional values and loss of commitment to society are even more likely to occur when defendants believe that those who punish them in the name of the law are hypocritical and unfair."

Preparation

After the defendant has experienced the disintegration of ties from the outside, has become disoriented because of his experiences in the jail, and has been degraded to a point beyond return, then he is ready for assimilation into the rabble existence. This process is known as preparation. Preparation, according to Irwin (1986:85), involves three steps. To begin, the preparation process includes a hurdle over a psychological barrier that separates the rabble class from other reputable people in society. This barrier is removed after prolonged interaction with other members of the rabble class. Soon the inmate realizes that jail life is not as bad as it first was experienced. In short, the jail inmate has adapted and accepted the rabble mentality. Associated with the removal of this psychological barrier is the fact that the inmate adopts attitudes and behaviors that enable him to survive in the jail, such as wariness and being opportunistic at the right time. The "loss of conventional sensibilities" (Irwin, 1986:85) is a necessary consequence of adopting the rabble mentality.

Second, a process of cultural preparation occurs in most jails, whereby the values and attitudes of the jail become part of the inmate's existence. The parallels to what we know about adaptation to prison are very similar here (see Chapter 8 for further discussion of adaptation to prison). Adopting the rabble mentality means accepting the cultural cues present in the jail. More often than not, this means communicating and accepting the behaviors of those who are the respected members of the jail setting. As such, as Irwin (1986:95-97) describes, the rabble life in jail means discussions about life on the streets, the courts, and what is occurring in the prisons or "joints." Indeed, the preparation process for the rabble existence is powerful and affects all inmates differently. This differential attachment is contingent on past experiences with jails and the rabble class. Prolonged interaction with the rabble class will produce identification and acceptance of their norms, values, and attitudes, and that may be one of the most negative consequences of jail confinement.

Finally, the preparation process enables members of the rabble class to be socially ready once released into the community. This means that the rabble continue to know each other on the streets and interact on a regular basis. The jail provides the network of social relationships which are crucial to existence on the streets upon release. Ostensibly, the preparation process in the jail provides the released offender with the needed connections to continue a life of disreputability once released from jail. In effect, his status as a member of the rabble class is reinforced by doing jail time and making the necessary connections with others who are in the same predicament as he. The release from jail and detention, therefore, is only a physical move for many jail inmates, from the jail to the streets. With the rabble mentality, they are now prepared to continue a life of crime and deviance and are supported in such endeavors by other members of the rabble class who, like themselves, show their allegiance to the rabble lifestyle.

Modern Jail Management Issues

As we can see, the jail of the past was a product of a number of forces. Such is the case today, but in the contemporary jail there are a number of issues which have surfaced that require the attention of jail managers. We begin this section by briefly exploring the conditions in jails, followed by a discussion of the three types of jail design. In addition, we will examine the role of being a jail guard and the attendant problems with such a position. Finally, we will explore the role of correctional law in the operation of jails, and a discussion of the mentally ill inmate in the jail.

Jail Conditions

The conditions of most contemporary jails in this country are quite poor. Despite attempts by many cities to improve conditions in their jails, many jails, on the whole, are terrible places to be. According to the National Institute of Justice (1988:6), jail conditions today are cited as the major area of concern among jail managers. Within this broad topic, six major areas were identified by jail managers about the conditions of their jails that required immediate attention by them. Figure 3.1 shows the percentage of jail managers surveyed, indicating a specific area was a problem for them.

Figure 3.1

Jail facility and equipment needs

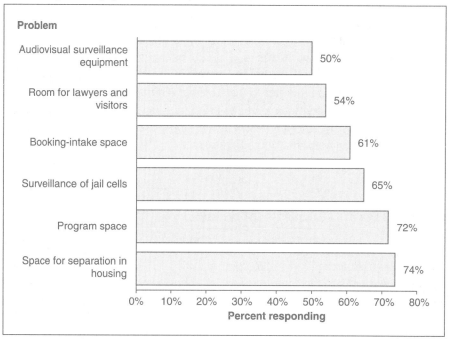

Source: Bureau of Justice Statistics (1988). "Nation's Jail Managers Assess Their Problems," p.6. Washington, DC: U.S. Department of Justice.

As indicated, the major areas are: space for separation in housing (74%), program space (72%), and surveillance of jail cells (65%). It is no secret that many jails do not have the space needed to house the number of inmates they hold. This is consistent with something stated earlier in the chapter—our jails are overcrowded. Couple these problem areas with other conditions in many jails, such as the poor quality of food, unsafe living conditions, and an indifferent correctional officer staff, and it is not too difficult to understand why many people argue that the jail is the worst institution of confinement in this country. As stated by Goldfarb (1975:2), the American jail is the "nation's dumping ground." Until recently, the attitude of many within the criminal justice system and within society was one of indifference.

However, this attitude has changed, and many jail administrators and managers have called for more resources and attention to be given to our ailing and outdated jails. This revolution in thinking has spawned interest in designing jails in a way that makes them more manageable. Jail management and design have become a hot topic for the late 1980s and will continue to draw the attention of many well into the 1990s in this country. Today, we are seeing more and more cities, particularly large urban centers, investing huge sums of money in the construction of new jail facilities. For jail managers and those interested in jail reform, there can be no better time.

Jail Design and Management

The area of jail management and design has captured the attention of many interested in corrections. For example, the National Institute of Corrections (NIC) has invested large sums of money in promoting and training individuals to the modern methods of jail design and management. These more contemporary approaches to jail management and design have received the support of a number of national organizations, including the American Jail Association and the American Correctional Association. Before we examine these contemporary management and design issues, we need to examine other traditional methods of jail design and management.

Nelson (1986) has identified three categories of jail architecture that have been used in this country over the past 200 years. Each differs in how the structure of the jail is built, but in addition, each proposes a different

\

philosophy and management commitment in the operations of the jail. We begin our examination by exploring the *Linear/Intermittent Surveillance* type jail.

This type of jail design is pictured in Figure 3.2. This type of jail design emphasizes the removal of the inmate from the guard. The architectural style is linear or at right angles to the surveillance area of the jail. Under this structural design, the correctional officer or guard has minimal interaction with the inmate. As such, the management philosophy is one of limited interaction between inmates and the officers, hence the name intermittent surveillance. Most important to this approach is the belief about the relationship between correctional officers and prisoners.

Figure 3.2
Linear/Intermittent Surveillance

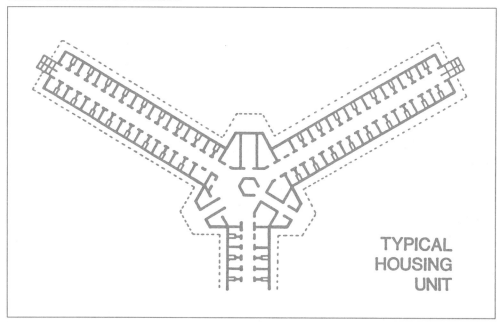

TYPICAL
HOUSING
UNIT

Source: David B. Kalinich and John Klofas (eds.) (1986). *Sneaking Inmates Down the Alley: Problems and Prospects in Jail Management*, p. 169. Courtesy of Charles C Thomas, Publisher, Springfield, Illinois.

This traditional approach to jail design and management sought to isolate the inmate from the correctional officer staff. Historically, remember, the jail was viewed as a holding tank in which minimal interaction between inmate and custodian was expected. However, this is not the case today. In fact, many contemporary writers believe that a number of the problems associated with jails can be traced to this rather antiquated approach to jail design and management. As such, there has been the development of other approaches to jail design, approaches more consistent with a new philosophy about how jail prisoners can be effectively supervised by correctional officer staff.

Figure 3.3
Podular/Remote Surveillance

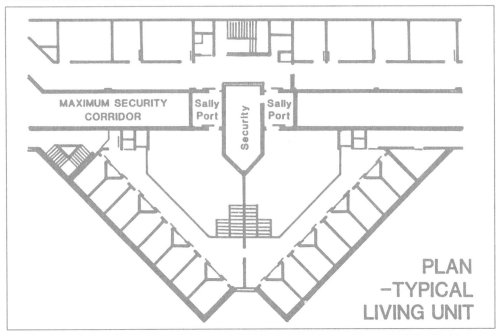

Source: David B. Kalinich and John Klofas (eds.) (1986). *Sneaking Inmates Down the Alley: Problems and Prospects in Jail Management*, p. 170. Courtesy of Charles C Thomas, Publisher, Springfield, Illinois.

The second type of jail design is shown in Figure 3.3. It is known as the Podular/Remote Surveillance type. Under this approach, the correctional officer has limited interaction with the inmate. Prisoners are "observed from a remote, secure observation compartment and the officer has no direct contact with the inmates" (Nelson, 1986:169). This approach to jail design and management has been also referred to as the "Second Generation Jail" concept. It is called this because it is viewed as the next alternative to the more traditional design discussed above. Unlike the linear/intermittent surveillance approach, however, this approach to jail management stresses that some interaction with inmates is needed and inevitable in a jail setting. Nevertheless, its management philosophy is still reactive, like the more traditional approach, in that it holds that inmates will act in a violent and unpredictable manner. Thus, the offficer is separated from the inmate through the podular design. If trouble does occur in the housing unit, the officer is still protected by a fixture and more officers can be summoned if needed in emergencies.

The final type of jail design is shown in Figure 3.4. It is known as the *Podular/Direct Supervision* approach to jail design and management. Under this structural design, the inmate and the officer are placed in the same housing unit with no structural separations present. This design has its origin in the "functional unit" concept developed for usage in federal institutions in the late 1950s and early 1960s. The fundamental premise of this concept was to have single cells for inmates in a self-contained area under the direct supervision of staff. The idea quickly spread to other institutions and was the operating principle behind the construction and operation of Federal Metropolitan Correctional Centers built in the mid-1970s (Zupan, 1991).

Within the podular/direct supervision approach, the housing unit is composed of up to 50 cells, with each inmate occupying one cell. Unlike the other two approaches, this model attempts to be proactive in its management philosophy, relying on the skills and training of the officer to control and supervise the inmate population. To this end, the key to the success of this approach is the proper training of the correctional officer staff.

It is for this reason that many have argued that the podular/direct supervision model is only as good as the staff that is supporting and implementing the fundamental principles associated with it. In short, the correctional officers are at the core of this type of jail design and management. Without the commitment and proper training of officers to this "New Generation" design, the structural characteristics of the approach will not provide the things expected of a contemporary and constitutional jail. While the linear/intermittent and podular/remote types of jail design and management are reactive and involve the correctional officer minimally, the podular/direct model makes the officer the cornerstone of effective jail management and more directly involved in the maintenance of control and security in the jail setting. As some have suggested, this New Generation philosophy to jail management and design allows the correctional officer role to become more rich and rewarding (Klofas, Smith, and Meister, 1986).

Figure 3.4
Podular/Direct Supervision

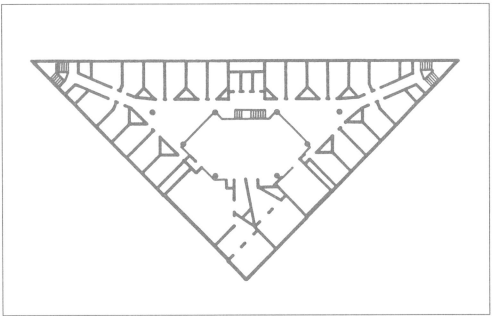

Source: David B. Kalinich and John Klofas (eds.) (1986). *Sneaking Inmates Down the Alley: Problems and Prospects in Jail Management*, p. 171. Courtesy of Charles C Thomas, Publisher, Springfield, Illinois.

Most importantly, as stated by Nelson (1986:174-176), the New Generation design enables jail managers and administrators to overcome the problems they currently experience. Specifically, institutions employing the direct supervision model share eight general principles of operation. They are: safety, control, communications, supervision, manageability, classification, just treatment, and effective personnel. By providing the proper jail design and management approach, the jails of today can become more than the neglected institutions of the past. In fact, current research by the National Institute of Corrections (1987) has shown the benefits of the New Generation concept to jail management.

In their examination of the Manhattan House of Detention, they found that assaults, violence, and the physical destruction of property were all reduced under the New Generation philosophy when compared to the old, traditional-type design and management approach. Moreover, other research has shown how correctional officers are supportive of the podular/direct supervision concept once they are able to experience the visible changes that the new design and philosophy bring to the jail (Lovrich and Zupan, 1987). Couple these findings with the cost savings that are generated by such an approach (Gettinger, 1984), and it is apparent that the podular/direct supervision approach to jail design and management has wide acceptance among those who work and manage American jails.

Guarding in Jail

The role of the correctional officer is the key to effective management of the jail. Yet we know very little about the work of correctional officers in our jails. It has only been recently that researchers have attempted to understand the correctional officer job within prison structures (see Chapter 8). In fact, there has been a research explosion on correctional officers. Much of this literature has examined the effects of the correctional environment on the officer, the problems with correctional officer work, and the attitudes of correctional officers toward their work (see Philliber, 1987, for a review of this literature).

Nevertheless, the amount of information about the correctional officer in jail settings is extremely limited. Much of the research has suggested that the jail is often neglected by those who run it. Throughout the country, the jail is under the control of the sheriff, and in many instances the sheriff views the jail as a low priority. Law enforcement is the central concern of the sheriff, and as a result, the jail does not receive the attention it may require (Guynes, Grieser, and Robinson, 1983). Despite the lack of material on those who work in our jail settings, there has been an attempt by some to examine the phenomenon of jail work and the attitudes of those who work in the jail.

Poole and Pogrebin (1988) have conducted one of the most interesting pieces of research on correctional officers in jail settings. Their research examined the correctional policy orientations and role stress experiences of deputy sheriffs (those who work in jail as correctional officers) during their careers as jail guards. The orientations were attitudes composed of four dimensions—restraint, reform, rehabilitation, and reintegration. This research was designed to see which dimension was predominant among the deputies and their levels of role stress and how that varied over time. Interestingly, they found that deputy sheriffs do vary over time with respect to their correctional policy orientations. In other words, the sheriffs who worked in the jails they studied changed their attitudes toward inmates as time went on. For example, the proportion of deputies who were restraint-oriented was higher toward the end of the jail career, while the proportion of deputies committed to rehabilitation was greater during the beginning of their tour of duty in the jail. In addition, the research indicated that the degree of role stress among deputies varied depending upon career phase.

On the one hand, for those deputies who were restraint- and reform-oriented, higher levels of stress were evidenced during the middle phases of their stay in the jail. On the other hand, those deputies who were rehabilitative- and reintegrative-oriented experienced heightened levels of role stress as their time in the jail increased, with the highest levels of role stress during the late phase of their stay in the jail. This research suggests that those who work in the jail do experience differential levels of role stress depending upon their correctional orientation and the length of time they spend in the jail. Moreover, the authors also suggest that those who work in the jail do not present a unified pattern of attitudes toward jail inmates.

This view is consistent with the research on correctional officers who work in prison settings. That the deputies in the jail exhibit pluralistic orientations toward their work is no strange phenomenon. In fact, this contention supports earlier work by Toch and Klofas (1982) who have argued that subcultural unity in the prison among correctional officers is not present (see Chapter 8 for a further discussion of this issue). This theme is supported by the work of Poole and Pogrebin (1988:206) in the jail environment. Yet it would be premature to comment on the definitive reasons as to why deputies in jails exhibit specific attitudes. At best, our research is tentative and exploratory. More research on the correctional officer in the jail is required before we fully comprehend the role and the many advantages and disadvantages to it.

Despite the paucity of research on correctional officers in the jail, there has been an attempt to modify and enrich the role of the officer in jail settings. Borrowing from the work of Toch and Grant (1982), Klofas, Smith, and Meister (1986:195) have suggested some interesting strategies to enrich the correctional officer role in the jail. These strategies are couched within the belief that correctional officer work in the jail need not be boring, tiresome, and non-productive. Instead, their research suggested that by properly harnessing human resources in the jail, jail managers can have increased training, improved morale, new links to the community, and innovative practices. Fundamentally, the use of human resources in the jail among correctional officer staff revolves around three concepts: participation, information, and productivity.

Participation focuses on the role of the worker in the day-to-day operations of the organization. Correctional officers, for example, could be allowed greater input into the decision-making processes of the organization, and the role of management is to enhance the input of the officer in the workings of the jail. At a minimum, participation requires that managers listen to the ideas, problems, and issues as identified by correctional officers.

Information involves awareness on the part of correctional officer staff about the organization. In this vein, correctional officers are given the critical information generated by research about the organization that they need to complete their daily tasks and functions.

Finally, productivity is a process whereby correctional officer staff are able to see tangible products from their participation in the organization. As such, there have to be written products and plans that address the individual needs of the correctional officer staff and the long-term goals of the organization. These visible products have to be more than "window dressing" or flash; they have to be real to those who work in the jail. In this way, the correctional officers can develop some allegiance to the goals of the organization, since their goals are largely consistent with organizational goals.

Klofas, Smith, and Meister (1986:206-207) argue that by increasing the participation of correctional officers, the jail has the potential of being a productive organization. Most importantly, they argue that because correctional officer work involves great amounts of discretion, it would behoove jail managers to develop participation models, because correctional officers can easily sabotage the best laid plans if they do not agree with them. As a result, participation models among correctional officers enable jail managers to achieve agreement with organizational goals when those goals are defined in the best interests of the correctional officers. In short, participation models allow organizational goals and individual goals of correctional officers to be more congruent.

Guarding in jail, therefore, is a complex task. Thus, new organizational ideas about how to positively interact with the correctional officer staff requires the attention of sheriffs and jail managers. Participation models in jail settings deserve more application in our jails today. Future research will tell us about their advantages and disadvantages. Like much of the research on correctional officers in jail, there is a paucity of research to guide the jail manager. Yet, with the advent of the New Generation jail and other contemporary jail management techniques, we can only improve the current status of many jails throughout the country. With the upgrading of our knowledge about correctional officers in the jail setting, we will be able to provide the training necessary to improve the quality of the correctional officer's role and the functioning of the contemporary jail.

The 1990s begins a new era and interest in the role of correctional officers in jail settings. Much of the information that was generated about correctional officers in prison environments was learned throughout the 1980s. It is now time for research to investigate this same position within jails. We expect this new information will yield some valuable ideas on the correctional officer role in the jail and policy prescriptions for jail managers.

Correctional Law and Jails

No other area has impacted the criminal justice system more than the courts. The law has permeated all criminal justice organizations, and the jail is no exception. Our purpose in this section is to provide a brief overview of the law as it specifically applies to jail settings. A more comprehensive discussion of correctional law is found in Chapter 12. The student desiring a more thorough examination of the evolution of correctional law should refer to that chapter. Our purpose here is to examine the specifics of correctional law as applied to the jail. In addition, we will be examining the phenomenon of jail suicides and how the law mandates that jail administrators take appropriate actions when such events occur. We will be exploring jail suicides as an attempt to lay down some fundamental legal principles that do affect the general operations of the contemporary jail.

According to Embert and Kalinich (1988), the most controversial area in jails today is the problem of suicides. As such, the correctional law dealing with jails and short-term detention facilities has focused on the legal responsibilities of jail administrators to operate safe, secure, and constitutional jails. This includes making sure that the individual does not leave the jail in any worse condition, either physically or psychologically, than when he came into the jail. Embert and Kalinich (1988:4) state "seven deadly sins" associated with suicides and jails under the law.

First, the law recognizes that employers working in the public sector must hire individuals who have been screened for their suitability for the job position. Random or arbitrary placement of individuals into positions of authority over others' lives is not justified under the law and could result in legal action against the jail administrator. In short, jail administrators must show that they did have a satisfactory screening mechanism so that qualified people fill the positions required in the jail.

Second, jail management has the responsibility to discharge or retrain individuals who have been shown to be unsuitable in the performance of their jobs. The correctional officer, for example, who is unable to perform the duties required should either be discharged or retrained in an attempt to bring that person in line with jail policies and procedures. Refusing to discharge or retrain where appropriate brings with it the potential for legal intervention if a problem arises due to the inabilities of the employee.

Third, jail management has the obligation to refrain from assigning unsuitable employees to certain duties. Again, it is encumbent upon the jail administrator, according to the law, to show that the employee is capable and trained to perform various functions required of the position. For example, if the employee has had difficulties in performing the functions of the correctional officer position and is still allowed to continue in that position, the jail administration is liable under the law if inappropriate actions are taken by that employee. Unsuitable employees may include those who are not properly trained and those who have been found to be problematic employees in the position.

Fourth, under the law, jail management has the responsibility to provide overall direction to the jail. Ostensibly, this means that the sheriff and the jail administrator have to produce written policies and procedures about all possible activities that could occur in the jail. These policies and procedures must clearly define the role of the correctional officer, along with steps on how to formally deal with the inmates. The old rituals of doing things informally or without the guidance of any rational policy is no longer acceptable under the law. In addition, claiming that policies and procedures cannot be formalized or that the jail is so idiosyncratic and beyond formal procedures no longer is deemed acceptable by the courts. In effect, the courts have stated that jail administrators must develop rational policies and procedures that are written and enforced within the organization. To do otherwise contradicts with the expectations of the court and can have undesirable effects on the organization should it be shown that jail staff were not given the proper direction to perform their assigned tasks.

Fifth, in addition to the development of policies and procedures for the operation of the jail, jail managers also have the obligation to provide adequate supervision over employees. In the case of the correctional officer, this means that supervision is consistent and evaluations are done regularly. Most importantly, jail administrators must be able to show that the performance of the employee was monitored so that tasks were actually being accomplished. Assuming that the correctional officer, for example, followed the policies with respect to inmate counts in the jail is negligent supervision according to the courts, without some type of documentation that the activity was completed. In this vein, the courts are only asking jail managers to manage and do those things that any reasonable supervisor in any organization would do.

Sixth, jail administrators must ensure that employees who are entrusted with equipment are capable and trained to use such equipment in case it is needed. The principle of entrustment holds that all employees should have the requisite skills to use such equipment in a proper manner. Included in this idea of entrustment is the explicit assumption that the employee is physically and psychologically capable of using the equipment in an acceptable fashion. This, again, means training is critical in the area of entrustment. Examples of situations in which entrustment is important to the correctional officer in the jail are: vehicles used in the transportation of prisoners, weapons used to subdue prisoners, and handcuffs used to restrain inmates.

The final and most critical is the provision of proper training for all aspects of correctional officer work in the jail. This general area is by far the most important when asking questions about liability of jail personnel. The courts have supported professional associations that require a specific number of hours of pre-service and in-service training for all correctional officers who work in jail settings. As stated earlier, one of the most critical areas in jail is suicides, and the proper role that training has in the reduction of such an event occurring the courts have recognized. No longer will the courts accept indifference on the part of jail administrators and correctional officers when it comes to jail suicides. Now it is mandatory that specific training be provided on how to recognize, identify, and monitor suicidal individuals in the jail. Like other behaviors in the jail, suicide can be addressed in a way that not only reduces its frequency, but in addition, relieves the jail of any legal liability.

Our review here of these general legal principles was not intended to be exhaustive. Instead, we sought to present some of the requirements of the law with respect to jail operations. As we can see, the jail is not insulated from the courts, nor should the student be led to believe that the contemporary jail is isolated from the rules and regulations of the external world. Obviously, the courts have had a major influence on the daily operations of jails in this country. It is not probable that their influence will wither away in the coming years, yet it may be limited by future court decisions. Regardless of what the role of the law will be in the future operations of jails, it is apparent that in present times the law is extremely influential in the functioning of the contemporary jail. In Chapter 12 we will continue this discussion of the law and corrections when we delve into the evolution of the law and its impact not only on jails but also state and federal correctional institutions.

Jails and the Mentally Disturbed Inmate

One of the most disturbing factors about the contemporary jail is the number of inmates who suffer from some type of mental illness. According to Steadman, McCarty, and Morrissey (1989), the scope of the problem is so serious that very little is known about the types of services that are available in the nation's jails for those inmates who suffer from mental health problems. Most of the extant research focuses on the prevalence of mental illness among jail inmates. These estimates are quite disparate, but they do indicate that the extent of mental illness problems among inmates in jails is very great. Current research by Teplin (1990) suggests that the rate of severe mental illness has been found to be two to three times the general population even after controlling for demographic variables. Recent research indicates that mental illness among jail inmates ranges from mild depression to advanced forms of psychosis.

Guy, Platt, Zwerling, and Bullock (1985) found that 11% of the inmates they interviewed in the Philadelphia County Prison System (local facilities serving the same functions as jails do in other jurisdictions) required some type of immediate inpatient treatment for mental illness-related problems and that 69% needed some type of treatment, including substance abuse treatment. In addition, Roth (1980) has argued that 3% to 11% of jail inmates suffer from severe forms of mental illness, such as psychosis and that the rate of less severe forms of mental illness, like personality disorders, ranges anywhere from 15-20%. Given the extent of the problem and the limited awareness of the types of services that are available, it is clear that many inmates in the nation's jails are receiving less than adequate treatment for their mental health-related problems.

More importantly, the existing research has suggested that the prevalence of mental health problems in jails only addresses the issue of numbers of inmates suffering from some type of malady, yet it does not reveal the etiology of the problems. Gibbs (1987) has argued that much of what is known about mental illness in jail settings is based on an explanation that is person-centered. This explanation argues that mental health problems are simply brought into the jail by inmates when confined. His research, in contrast, suggests that many mental health problems experienced by inmates can be traced to environmental causes. That is, mental health problems are produced by the jail setting itself, or if a preexisting condition of mental illness is present, the jail setting makes the situation worse. By implication, therefore, this environmental view requires that those who work in the jail modify the setting so that mental health problems do not worsen and that procedures be taken by staff to limit the potential for the development of other mental health problems by inmates.

Lombardo (1985) has suggested that the role of the correctional officer can be enhanced and enlarged so that the delivery of human services to inmates is possible. With respect to those inmates who are experiencing the pains of adjustment to the jail, the officer can serve as a guide to inmates in alleviating the everyday stresses of jail life. This can be accomplished by providing greater training to correctional officers on how to teach inmates to cope with the stresses associated with jail environments. Correctional officers, according to Lombardo (1985:25), can do this by: reading behavioral cues that express inmate distress, assessing the institutional environment for factors that contribute to stress, assessing the environment for resources that might help alleviate stress, and developing strategies for getting troubled inmates and resources together.

This type of strategy not only can help the inmate cope with the environment of the jail, but in addition, it enables the officer to expand and enlarge the correctional role to include other forms of human service delivery in the jail (Toch and Klofas, 1982:27). Moreover, as soon as mental health problems are dealt with by jail staff, it will provide for a more humane and secure environment. Presently, most of the jails throughout the country have limited mental health services available to inmates. Of those that are available, it is not clear if inmate mental health needs are being met. As a result, Steadman, McCarty, and Morrissey (1989:148) state: "There is thus every reason to believe that the quality of mental health care in our nation's jails is as problematic today at it was 15 years ago." Nevertheless, there has been much attention focused on the plight of the mentally ill inmate in our jails, and the direction chosen by many jails has been the development of rational policies to deal with the problem. Only time will tell whether these policies will address the mental health problems of jail inmates.

Summary

The purpose of this chapter was to explore the American jail, from both an historical perspective and a more contemporary view. Our examination indicated that the jail has always been the dumping ground for the most undesirable and disreputable individuals in society. As such, the conditions of many of our jails in both early America and even in more modern times have been poor. In addition, jail demographics indicate that the poor, the uneducated, and the underemployed predominate in our jails. In short, the jail has served as the repository for the most disillusioned and alienated members of society, most of whom have a limited investment in conventional American society.

Moreover, our review of the conditions of many jails indicated that very few do much for those incarcerated. The processes of the jail further push the inmate into what we referred to as the "rabble class," and that the jail's primary purpose in modern society has evolved into rabble management. Today, rabble management has included a number of types of jail designs and philosophies. These philosophies are reflected in the kinds of jails that are used today: the linear/intermittent jail, the podular/remote jail, and the podular/direct jail. Each has its own advantages and disadvanatges, but the podular/direct is the jail of the future supported by many professional associations and jail practitioners.

Besides design issues with jails, we also discussed the role of the correctional officer in the jail. Our review indicated that there is a paucity of research about correctional officers in jail, but that correctional officers in jail settings have a plurality of attitudes, not all focused on any one set of beliefs or philosophies. Moreover, the role of being a correctional officer in jail is very complex and requires further examination by researchers. Most importantly, we examined the possibility of enriching and expanding the correctional officer role by allowing officers greater participation in the formal operations of the jail. Once again, future research will have to guide us as to what role is the most suitable and appropriate for the correctional officer in the jail.

Additionally, we explored the relevance of the law as it relates to the operations of jails. Our purpose was to show where the law has impacted the functioning of contemporary jails, and how it has explicit expectations of jail administrators. Clearly, the law through the courts has laid down specific expectations about how jails should be run so that they conform with the Constitution. Our jails, like our prisons, do not exist in a social vacuum; they, too, must meet the expectations of an evolving society, and it has been the courts that have defined what these expectations are and how the jail should respond to them.

Finally, we examined the problem of the mentally ill inmate. Our discussion focused on the prevalence of mental illness problems among jail inmates and the uncertainty about the types of services that are being provided to mentally ill inmates throughout the nation's jails. We concluded that mental health problems of jail inmates may be occurring with the same frequency as they were in the past, but that efforts were being implemented to deal with those who suffer from mental health problems in jails. It is clear that this problem will not be solved in the immediate future, yet there is hope in the area of training correctional officer staff to be more aware of the problem and to make them more effective in helping inmates to deal with the stresses of everyday life in jail.

Assumptions Underlying
the New Generation Philosophy

The fundamental goal of the architectural design and inmate management style prescribed by the New Generation philosophy is to create an incarcerative environment in which both inmates and staff are safe from violence and predation, and where inmates are treated humanely and in accordance with constitutional prohibitions against punishing pretrial detainees. Both the architecture and inmate management style are informed by a set of theoretical assumptions about the causes of unsafe and inhumane conditions that exist in many traditional jail facilities. In their simplest form, these assumptions maintain that unsafe and inhumane jail conditions are the result of defects in traditional jail architecture and operations which create fear among inmates and staff; which provide opportunities for inmates to engage in predation without fear of detection by staff; which allow inmates to share power and control with jail staff; which isolate inmates from formal and informal mechanisms of social control; which communicate and reinforce the message that inmates are untrustworthy; and, which subject inmates to uncontrollable and unrelievable environmental stress.[1]

Inmate and Staff Fear

A number of deficiencies in the architecture and operations of the jail make detention a dangerous experience for inmates or, at the least, create a perception of peril and insecurity. The most critical include: the linear architectural design that provides ample opportunities for inmates to engage in violent and destructive behavior without detection by staff; intermittent staff surveillance that leaves inmates unsupervised for substantial periods of time; inadequate classification systems that assign predatory prisoners to the same housing units as more vulnerable inmates; heterogeneous inmate populations that bring together ill and healthy, strong and weak, and naive and sophisticated offenders; rapid turnover among prisoners that creates an unstable and unpredictable environment; overcrowding which forces inmates into close proximity with those who have reputations for aggressive and violent behavior; and, understaffing which further reduces staff surveillance of inmate activities.

Although violence is not an everyday occurrence for most prisoners, many live in constant fear that one day they will be confronted by violence from other inmates, knowing that the institution alone cannot prevent or deter it from happening. To a large extent, inmates must depend on their own abilities to protect themselves from victimization. However, the means available to inmates are severely limited. In most cases there are only two options available—fight or flight (Toch, 1977).

In many respects, the nature of the correctional institution makes violence the only effective response to threats or acts of violence. Inmates housed in multiple-occupancy cells or dormitories have few available means to physically escape from victimization—particularly when the victimizer shares a cell or dormitory with the victim. To flee from violence or its threatened use, inmates must request segregation. However, the costs associated with such flight are quite severe. To make such a request, inmates must first admit to themselves that they are too weak to fight off an attack. To enter segregation is to suffer a serious blow to one's self-esteem and to the vision of one's courageousness (Toch, 1977). To flee victimization also requires that the facility have available segregation space and that the staff be willing to cooperate by removing the inmate from the general population. In some cases, staff cooperation may not be readily provided. Staff may respond to the requests of the inmate with ridicule or with the advice that the inmate stand up to other prisoners. Toch (1977:158) cited an interview with an inmate who was advised by staff to counter threats of other inmates with violence.

> And they [staff] told me that you can't run away from it. You have to knock them down, face up to them. The first person that you knock out, you get locked up for three or four days, and then you come out and come back down, and you're going to get a lot more respect . . . I remember one thing that I said to them. I said that these guys were big, and I would have to jump three feet to reach them. And they said that I would have to bring them down to my size. And he told me to kick them in the nuts, and that would bring them down to my size. And he said not to be afraid of lockup . . . And they all agreed with each other . . . they said that there was a recommendation that I would have to start fighting and that that would be the only way to do things . . . One guy started out and said, "Why don't you knock him out on his ass?" And the others said, "Yeah, why don't you?" And then that was the solution, and then they sent me out and said, "Next, please!"

Given the lack of opportunities for flight, as well as the associated costs, fighting back may be the only means of self-protection readily available to inmates. For many, preemptive violence is the only means to survive an impending attack and to prevent future victimization. By demonstrating a willingness to use violence the inmate warns others that an attack will not be without costs.

> Targets of victimization are chosen because they are deemed unmanly, and they are viewed as unmanly because they show fear or resourcelessness. A man loses his target attributes if he provides demonstrations of fearlessness, or if he sports stigmata of manliness. Violence works because it points to a misdiagnosis of the target. Violence also works because aggressors are not as sure of themselves as they pretend. A victim who reacts nonfearfully becomes an uninviting arena for proving one's manliness. He is uninviting because the confrontation can misfire into a demonstration of unmanliness. It is safer to seek other fish in the sea whose reactions are dependably fearful (Toch, 1977:162).

In addition to preemptive violence, inmates who fear victimization by others may make con-

traband weapons, "buy" protection from other inmates, or join gangs. While these alternatives provide some measure of protection, they also add to overall levels of disorder in the facility and reinforce the need for protection. In short, inmates who fear for their safety engage in behaviors that increase the probability of destruction and violence—thereby intensifying perceptions of danger.

Fear is also prevalent among staff. Their fear grows out of their contact with inmates who have reputations for using violence and brutality, and from having to continually deal with a population that appears uncontrolled and uncontrollable. Staff fear is further intensified by the knowledge that the tools necessary to control inmate behavior are lacking. While coercion is the primary and formal means by which the jail organization presumes to maintain order, its use by custodial staff is severely limited by institutional policies, laws and public opinion. Furthermore, force and physical violence are neither effective nor efficient means for controlling inmate behavior (Sykes, 1958; Schrag, 1961; Cloward, 1968). Since the legitimate means available for inmate control are weak and ineffectual, officers find it more expedient and safer to allow inmates to bend or break rules in exchange for at least a modicum of compliance and cooperation (Cloward, 1968; Goffman, 1961; Sykes, 1958). In succumbing to this corruption of their authority, officers demonstrate to themselves, as well as to inmates, the tenuous nature of their control.

Like inmates, officers develop strategies to cope with their fear of inmates and the threat of violence (Jacobs and Retsky, 1975). Some officers become *repressive* and respond to the threat of inmates with their own form of violence. These officers believe that by placing stringent controls on prisoners they can discourage violence. Others try to strike-up *friendships* with inmates in the hope that they will protect them from harassment and violence by others. Still others deal with their fear by *avoiding* contact with prisoners. As with inmates, the coping strategies adopted by officers increase the probability of inmate violence. More importantly, they serve to further reduce what little control officers hold. With the first approach, repression stimulates resentment and promotes expressive bursts of inmate violence against staff. The second approach places staff in the position of performing favors for prisoners. In some cases, these favors include purposely failing to report violence, bringing in contraband weapons, and even allowing inmates access to the segregation units for purposes of victimization (Davidson, 1968). All of these favors hold a potential for additional violent behavior. The third approach, avoiding prisoners, presents inmates with opportunities to engage in violence upon other inmates without staff detection. The less supervision inmates receive from fearful staff members, the less they are deterred from using violence against others. The relationship is cyclical. The more officers avoid prisoners out of fear, the more violent inmates become—and, in so doing, the officers are reinforced in their fear of inmate violence.

---

[1] Five of the six assumptions are inferred from Stephen Gettinger's (1988:14-15) brief description of the psychology of New Generation jails. Credit should therefore be given to Gettinger for providing the initial foundation for these assumptions.

Adopted from: Linda L. Zupan (1991). *Jails: Reform and the New Generation Philosophy*, pp. 73-76. Cincinnati, OH: Anderson Publishing Co.

Key Terms and Concepts

degradation

disintegration

disorientation

Jacksonian Era

linear/intermittent surveillance

podular/direct supervision

podular/remote surveillance

preparation

pretrial detention

rabble management

Walnut Street Jail

References

Bureau of Justice Statistics (1988). "Report to the Nation on Crime and Justice." Washington, DC: U.S. Department of Justice.

Bureau of Justice Statistics (1990). "Jail Inmates, 1989." Washington, DC: U.S. Department of Justice.

Embert, P.S. and D.B. Kalinich (1988). *Behind the Walls: Correctional Institutions and Facilities: A Many-Faceted Phenomena.* Salem, WI: Sheffield Publishing Company.

Gettinger, S. (1984). *New Generation Jails: An Innovative Approach to an Age-Old Problem.* Washington, DC: National Institute of Corrections.

Gibbs, J.J. (1987). "Symptoms of Psychopathology Among Jail Prisoners: The Effects of Exposure to the Jail Environment." *Criminal Justice and Behavior*, 14,3:288-310.

Goldfarb, R. (1975). *Jails: The Ultimate Ghetto of the Criminal Justice System.* Garden City, NY: Anchor Books.

Guy, E., J.J. Platt, J. Zwerling and S. Bullock (1985). "Mental Health Status of Prisoners in an Urban Jail." *Criminal Justice and Behavior*, 12,1:29-53.

Guynes, R., R.C. Grieser and H.E. Robinson (1983). *The Organization and Management of County Jails.* Alexandria, VA: Institute for Economic and Policy Studies.

Irwin, J. (1986). *The Jail: Managing the Underclass in American Society.* Berkeley, CA: University of California Press.

Klofas, J., S. Smith and E. Meister (1986). "Harnessing Human Resources in Local Jails: Toward a New Generation of Planners." In D.B. Kalinich and J. Klofas (eds.) *Sneaking Inmates Down the Alley: Problems and Prospects in Jail Management.* Springfield, IL: Charles C Thomas, Publisher.

Lombardo, L.X. (1985). "Mental Health Work in Prisons and Jails: Inmate Adjustment and Indigenous Correctional Personnel." *Criminal Justice and Behavior*, 12,1:17-28.

Lovrich, N. and L.L. Zupan (1987). "Podular/Direct Supervision Detention Facilities: Challenges for Human Resource Development." Boulder, CO: National Institute of Corrections.

Lunden, W.A. (1959). "The Rotary Jail, or Human Squirrel Cage." *Journal of the Society of Architecture Historians*, 18,4:149-57.

National Institute of Corrections (1987). *New Generation Jails*. Boulder, CO: Library Information Specialists, Inc.

National Institute of Justice (1988). "Nation's Jail Managers Assess Their Problems." Washington, DC: U.S. Department of Justice.

Nelson, W.R. (1986). "Changing Concepts in Jail Design and Management." In D.B. Kalinich and J. Klofas (eds.) *Sneaking Inmates Down the Alley: Problems and Prospects in Jail Management*. Springfield, IL: Charles C Thomas, Publisher.

Philliber, S. (1987). "Thy Brother's Keeper: A Review of the Literature on Correctional Officers." *Justice Quarterly*, 4,1:9-38.

Poole, E.D. and M.R. Pogrebin (1988). "Deputy Sheriffs as Jail Guards: A Study of Correctional Policy Orientations and Career Phases." *Criminal Justice and Behavior*, 15,2:190-209.

Roth, L. (1980). "Correctional Psychiatry." In W. Curran, A. McGarry and C. Retty (eds.) *Modern Legal Medicine, Psychiatry, and Forensic Science*. Philadelphia, PA: F.A. Davis.

Rothman, D. (1971). *The Discovery of the Asylum: Social Order and Disorder in the New Republic*. Boston, MA: Little, Brown and Company.

Rothman, D. (1980). *Conscience and Convenience: The Asylum and its Alternatives in Progressive America*. Boston, MA: Little, Brown and Company.

Steadman, H.J., D.W. McCarty and J.P. Morrissey (1989). *The Mentally Ill in Jail: Planning for Essential Services*. New York, NY: The Guilford Press.

Teplin, L. (1990). "The Prevalence of Severe Mental Disorder Among Male Urban Jail Detainees: Comparison with Epidemiological Catchment Area Program." *American Journal of Public Health*, 80:663-669.

Toch, H. and J. Klofas (1982). "Alienation and Desire for Job Enrichment Among Correction Officers." *Federal Probation*, 46:35-44.

Toch, H. and J.D. Grant (1982). *Reforming Human Services Through Participation.* Beverly Hills, CA: Sage Publishing Company.

Wilson, J.Q. and G.L. Kelling (1982). "Broken Windows: Police and Neighborhood Safety." *Atlantic Monthly*, 249, (March): 29-38.

Zupan, L.L. (1991). *Jails: Reform and the New Generation Philosophy.* Cincinnati, OH: Anderson Publishing Co.

Photo Credit: Tony O'Brien, Frost Publishing Group, Ltd.

Prisoners:
A Profile

4

After reading this chapter, the student should be able to:

∎ Explain the selection of the prison population.

∎ Describe the size of the prison population.

∎ Discuss significant prisoner and prison characteristics.

∎ Provide a description of prison overcrowding.

∎ Describe the profession of guarding in prison.

∎ Differentiate among the needs of prisoners.

Introduction

This chapter will address a number of issues dealing with the selection process of the prison population. To the student this may seem to be very odd language, since it presumes that the agencies of criminal justice actually select specific people for incarceration. While we will suggest that there is some truth to this position, we will further suggest that many of the people who become part of our correctional system have specific characteristics that make them more likely candidates of social control. Therefore, the beginning of this chapter will discuss the process of selection of offenders for imprisonment, with an emphasis on how criminal justice agencies operate as organizations with goals and very directed expectations. From this discussion, we will describe the size of the prison population and selected characteristics of prisoners. Finally, we will conclude with an exploration into the prison overcrowding phenomenon, along with discussions on guarding in prison and prison society. After completing the chapter, the student should have a more thorough understanding of who is in our prisons, what are the key characteristics of prisoners, and an appreciation of some of the problems associated with institutional corrections today.

Selection of the Prison Population

In Chapter 1 we described how the criminal justice process operates, and we further suggested that much of what occurs within the components of the criminal justice system is a function of "work group norms" and the "going rate" established by work process people at the line level of their organizations. We would like to continue that line of reasoning in this chapter by examining how offenders are selected for incarceration. It is our contention that the processes of prosecution, conviction, and sentencing are bureaucratic functions performed by agents on behalf of their organizational interests. In short, agencies of criminal justice will select offenders who meet their bureaucratic criteria for efficient and effective processing. As a result, those who become part of the correctional system have similar characteristics and attributes that are not indicative of greater guilt but are reflective of the demands of the processing agencies of criminal justice, e.g., police, prosecution, and courts.

Moreover, this selection process must be understood within the context of social and economic relations. Economic conditions, for example, have produced a period in history in which there are great numbers of individuals who have limited opportunities. Walker (1989) argues that this situation has fostered the development of an entrenched underclass, many of whom have limited skills. Couple this with a significant loss of manufacturing jobs during the past 40 years, and the product is a society in which crime becomes a legitimate endeavor for many. This is not to suggest that being poor automatically translates into criminality. However, life chances are greatly diminished for these "truly disadvantaged" (Wilson, 1987), and we would be remiss if we did not mention how this context shapes and influences criminal justice operations. We begin this section by analyzing the characteristics of defendants in the selection of the prison population.

In a formal sense, the prosecution of criminal defendants is based on the presumption of innocence and the belief that the "facts of the case" will determine the outcome. While true, it would be rather shortsighted to conclude that other factors in the prosecution process are not of equal value in determining how offenders are adjudicated by prosecutors. The interaction, for example, among the components of the system is critical as to how a case will be adjudicated. How the prosecutor views the facts of the case may be a crucial process as to the likely disposition of the case. Krueger (1981) has shown that prosecutors generally interpret the police version of the facts in a way that ensures a high probability of convictions, and that more often than not, in bargaining situations, appeal to administrative procedures that routinize the disposition in their favor. The prosectorial function, therefore, is constrained by procedures that ensure greater convictability and reduce uncertainty. This position is further elaborated by the work of Albonetti (1986).

In her review of over 4,000 felony cases processed by a superior court in Washington, D.C. in the early 1970s, Albonetti concluded that prosecutorial screening following grand jury indictment was strongly influenced by the desire on the part of the prosecutor to avoid uncertainty about the likelihood of gaining a conviction at the subsequent criminal trial. In addition, this research underscored what previous research had always recognized, that prosecutors are very sensitive to how cases may enhance their careers. Moreover, Albonetti suggests that another possible explanation of prosecutorial decision-making may be related to the resources available to the prosecutor to proceed with a case. This position has been put forth by other researchers and it is possible that a concern over limited resources is a critical variable in the prosecutorial decision-making process. It would be fair to conclude from Albonetti's research that prosecutors seek certainty in their operations and thus select cases that minimize potential uncertainty for them.

Couple this position with what was stated earlier and the developing picture suggests that specific characteristics of offenders make them more likely candidates of criminal trials and possible subsequent incarceration. While we mentioned in Chapter 1 that seriousness of offense is a critical variable when explaining prosecution and courtroom processing, what we are further suggesting here is that the entire courtroom work group is strongly influenced by norms that enhance careers of participants, except the defendant, and more importantly, provide stability and more certainty to the courtroom process.

In an influential piece published by Blumberg (1984), he posits that the adversarial intent of the court system is circumvented, or in his words "coopted" by the organizational demands of everyone in the court social system. As a result, the organizations of prosecution, defense attorney, and judge work together to enhance the efficiency and organizationally defined effectiveness of the court structure. Blumberg states:

> Organizational goals and discipline impose a set of demands and conditions of practice on the respective professions in the court to which they respond by abandoning their ideological and professional commitments to the accused client, in the service of these higher claims of the court organization. All court personnel, including the accused's own lawyer, tend to be coopted to become *agent-mediators* who help the accused redefine his situation and restructure his perceptions concomitant with a plea of guilty (1984:193). [Emphasis added.]

If this is the case, we would expect that many court operations are more *administrative* rather than adversarial, and in fact, this position is borne out by the evidence. Talarico (1979) has shown how prosecutors select cases that not only maximize organizationally defined principles of efficiency, but in addition, support system maintenance and functioning rather than pre-established purposes of the law, e.g., due process and innocence until proven guilty. This has been shown to be true in relationships between probation officials and judges.

Kingsworth and Rizzo (1979) have found that in a majority of cases judges concur with the recommendations offered by probation officials when sentencing defendants. The only point of disagreement between the two came when judges believed primacy of plea bargaining over probation officer recommendations. This, too, may be indicative of other relationships between judges and prosecuting attorneys and their relative importance for both parties. In short, the relationship between the judge and the prosecutor may be more critical to the maintenance of the court organization than the relationship between the judge and the probation officers.

Such is also the case when it comes to sentencing decisions among judges. Research conducted by Frazier and Bock (1982) supports the notion that actors in the court social system interact in a way that supports norms of the organization. Specifically, their research found that in one southern state, sentencing differences were more related to the types of cases judges received rather than the sentencing styles of the judges. Furthermore, the researchers suggested that what may be occurring in many jurisdictions is the creation of "justice subcultures" where sentencing decisions are reflective, to a great degree, of attitudes, values, and norms of the courtroom work group and the shared meanings developed by that work group. More importantly, their position suggests that sentencing outcomes may also be indicative of values reflected in the larger culture, including those outside the criminal justice system, such as political constituencies within the public sector (Walker, 1980).

Thus, the process of selection of defendants for correctional supervision is invariably tied to the organizational constraints and conditions imposed on the criminal justice process by various actors in the system. Most important is the maintenance of the system, with a strong belief in the efficient processing of criminal offenders. From this we can see that those cases that promote greater certainty and chances of conviction will be the most likely ones not only for criminal prosecution but also for confinement in our correctional institutions. If this is a plausible interpretation of the court social system, then we would expect that defendants who end up in prison have certain demographic characteristics that distinguish them from others processed in the criminal justice system. As was stated in Chapter 1, those who become part of the correctional system are different in that they tend to be the more serious criminals and have committed crimes against strangers and have solid evidence against them.

While relevant to know, this information tells us nothing about who these people are and if they represent isolated incidents or are a larger group of people in society who have the same social, political, and economic characteristics. This type of question suggests that the criminal justice system is primarily concerned with certain types of crimes and criminals, and in this way, may be a biased system against particular classes of people. The larger question is, "Why does the criminal justice system focus on specific types of crimes while minimizing or even downplaying other types of criminal events, such as white-collar crime?" Some have suggested that this is due, in large part, to the legislative definitions of crime and the degree to which the criminal justice system is funded. Clearly, the criminal justice system cannot investigate all criminality. We saw in Chapter 1 how most crime goes undetected.

Nevertheless, the issue of bias in the system has raised some interesting questions concerning the fairness of the criminal justice process. For our purposes, we want to know the degree to which some offenders are more likely to become part of the criminal justice system. Are there some similar characteristics of offenders that make them more likely to be the object of the criminal justice system? Can we shed some light on who these "role-ready defendants" are? Borrowing from research gathered by the Vera Institute, the New York Legal Aid Society, the University of Pennsylvania Law School and other sources, Duffee and Fitch (1976) suggest the following characteristics of role-ready defendants.

Typically, the criminal defendant cannot make bail, usually has been arrested before, has no stable family history, is in most situations an urban dweller, more often than not is a member of a minority group, is frequently assigned a lawyer, is probably guilty of some crime, and has committed a crime considered typical rather than sensational. More often than not this type of person will be processed by the criminal justice system and may spend time in a correctional institution. We will see that this is the case when we examine the individual characteristics of prisoners later in this chapter. It is important to note that the connection between police and prosecutors ultimately defines who will become part of the correctional system. In addition, the nexus between police and prosecutors suggests that the system operates in a systemic fashion, something we described in Chapter 1. The student is reminded that the systemic operations of criminal justice are important with respect to the direction and purpose of the system.

Operating in an interdependent way, the system of criminal justice produces the likely candidates of social control. This becomes important when we discuss attempts to deal with these offenders in the institutional environment. In effect, through the selection processes of police, prosecution, and the courts, the component of corrections has its clientele defined. More importantly, how we interact with these offenders is going to be influenced by the characteristics that they bring with them into the institutional setting and the structure of the prison environment itself. More recently in correctional history, the overriding characteristic of prisons that has greatly affected institutional programming is the size of the prison population. It is this topic that we address in the next section.

Size of the Prison Population

Probably no other issue facing corrections today has received more attention than the size of the current prison population. According to the Bureau of Justice Statistics (1991), the prison population has increased 133% since 1980, with actual growth in numbers being 441,422 prisoners. In fact, beginning with the year 1980, we started to see increases in the numbers of people placed in our nation's prisons, reaching a record level of 771,243 people in state and federal prisons as of year-end 1990 (Table 4.1).

Table 4.1
Change in the State and Federal Prison Populations, 1980-1990

Year	Number of inmates	Annual percent change	Total percent change since 1980
1980	329,821		
1981	369,930	12.2%	12.2%
1982	413,806	11.9	25.5
1983	436,855	5.6	32.5
1984	462,002	5.8	40.1
1985	502,507	8.8	52.4
1986	544,972	8.5	65.2
1987	585,084	7.4	77.4
1988	631,669	8.0	91.5
1989	712,557	12.8	116.0
1990	771,243	8.2	133.8

Note: All counts are for December 31 of each year and may reflect revisions of previously reported numbers.

Source: Bureau of Justice Statistics (1991). "Prisoners in 1990," p. 1. Washington, DC: U.S. Department of Justice, May.

Table 4.2
Prisoners Under the Jurisdiction of State or Federal Correctional Authorities,
by Region and Jurisdiction, Yearend 1989 and 1990

Region and jurisdiction	Total			Sentenced to more than 1 year			
	Advance 1990	Final 1989	Percent change, 1989-90	Advance 1990	Final 1989	Percent change, 1989-90	Incarceration rate, 1990*
U.S. total	771,243	712,557	8.2%	739,763	680,955	8.6%	293
Federal	65,526	59,171	10.7	52,208	47,168	10.7	21
State	705,717	653,386	8.0	687,555	633,787	8.5	272
Northeast	123,394	113,965	8.3%	119,062	109,394	8.8%	232
Connecticut	10,500	9,301	12.9	7,771	6,309	23.2	238
Maine	1,523	1,455	4.7	1,480	1,432	3.4	118
Massachusetts	8,273	7,524	10.0	7,899	7,268	8.7	132
New Hampshire	1,342	1,166	15.1	1,342	1,166	15.1	117
New Jersey	21,128	19,439	8.7	21,128	19,439	8.7	271
New York	54,895	51,227	7.2	54,895	51,227	7.2	304
Pennsylvania	22,290	20,469	8.9	22,281	20,458	8.9	183
Rhode Island	2,394	2,479	-3.4	1,585	1,469	7.9	157
Vermont	1,049	905	15.9	681	626	8.8	117
Midwest	145,802	136,338	6.9%	145,493	136,042	6.9%	239
Illinois	27,516	24,712	11.3	27,516	24,712	11.3	234
Indiana	12,732	12,341	3.2	12,615	12,220	3.2	223
Iowa	3,967	3,584	10.7	3,967	3,584	10.7	139
Kansas	5,777	5,616	2.9	5,777	5,616	2.9	227
Michigan	34,267	31,639	8.3	34,267	31,639	8.3	366
Minnesota	3,176	3,103	2.4	3,176	3,103	2.4	72
Missouri	14,919	13,921	7.2	14,919	13,921	7.2	287
Nebraska	2,403	2,393	.4	2,286	2,278	.4	140
North Dakota	483	451	7.1	435	404	7.7	67
Ohio	31,855	30,538	4.3	31,855	30,538	4.3	289
South Dakota	1,345	1,252	7.4	1,345	1,252	7.4	187
Wisconsin	7,362	6,788	8.5	7,335	6,775	8.3	149
South	282,952	262,115	7.9%	274,813	252,614	8.8%	315
Alabama	15,665	13,907	12.6	15,365	13,575	13.2	370
Arkansas	6,766	6,409	5.6	6,718	6,306	6.5	277
Delaware	3,506	3,458	1.4	2,231	2,284	-2.3	321
District of Col.	9,121	10,039	-9.1	6,660	6,735	-1.1	1,125
Florida	44,387	39,999	11.0	44,387	39,966	11.1	336
Georgia	22,345	20,885	7.0	21,605	19,619	10.1	327
Kentucky	9,023	8,289	8.9	9,023	8,289	8.9	241
Louisiana	18,599	17,257	7.8	18,599	17,257	7.8	427
Maryland	17,798	16,514	7.8	16,684	15,378	8.5	347
Mississippi	8,375	7,911	5.9	8,179	7,700	6.2	311
North Carolina	18,412	17,454	5.5	17,713	16,628	6.5	264
Oklahoma	12,322	11,608	6.2	12,322	11,608	6.2	383
South Carolina	17,319	15,720	10.2	16,208	14,808	9.5	451
Tennessee	10,388	10,630	-2.3	10,388	10,630	-2.3	207
Texas	50,042	44,022	13.7	50,042	44,022	13.7	290
Virginia	17,319	16,477	5.1	17,124	16,273	5.2	274
West Virginia	1,565	1,536	1.9	1,565	1,536	1.9	85
West	153,569	140,968	8.9%	148,187	135,737	9.2%	276
Alaska	2,622	2,744	-4.4	1,851	1,908	-3.0	348
Arizona	14,261	13,251	7.6	13,781	12,726	8.3	375
California	97,309	87,297	11.5	94,122	84,338	11.6	311
Colorado	7,018	6,908	1.6	7,018	6,908	1.6	209
Hawaii	2,533	2,464	2.8	1,708	1,752	-2.5	150
Idaho	2,074	1,850	12.1	2,074	1,850	12.1	201
Montana	1,425	1,328	7.3	1,409	1,328	6.1	174
Nevada	5,322	5,112	4.1	5,322	5,112	4.1	444
New Mexico	2,961	2,934	1.0	2,879	2,759	4.3	184
Oregon	6,436	6,744	-4.6	6,436	6,744	-4.6	221
Utah	2,503	2,394	4.6	2,482	2,368	4.8	143
Washington	7,995	6,928	15.4	7,995	6,928	15.4	162
Wyoming	1,110	1,016	9.3	1,110	1,016	9.3	237

Note: The advance count of prisoners is conducted immediately after the calendar year ends. Prisoner counts for 1989 may differ from those reported in previous publications. Counts for 1990 are subject to revision as updated figures become available. Explanatory notes for each jurisdiction are reported in the appendix.
*The number of prisoners with sentences of more than 1 year per 100,000 resident population.

Source: Bureau of Justice Statistics (1991). "Prisoners in 1990," p. 2. Washington, DC: U.S. Department of Justice, May.

When we break down these numbers into meaningful categories, more interesting results appear. For example, the number of sentenced federal prisoners continues to grow at a rate faster than sentenced prisoners in state facilities. Comparing years 1989 with 1990, we find that federal prisoners grew at a rate of 10.7% while state prisoners grew 8.0% (Table 4.2). While both are substantial increases over a one-year period, the growth in the federal system is quite large. These growth rates are also reflected in the total number of people who are incarcerated per 100,000 people in the country. This rate, too, has grown significantly since 1980, when the rate was 139 per 100,000 people compared to 293 per 100,000 people in 1990, an increase of 111% over the period.

In addition, there is considerable variation across regions of the country concerning growth rates in the prison population. Table 4.3 shows the regional totals and the rates of change for the period 1980-1989. It is quite clear that the West had the largest growth rate (202.8%), followed by the Northeast (155.3%), then the Midwest (111.2%), and finally the South (74.8%). Couple this information with the 10 largest state prison populations data, the states with the highest rates of incarceration, and the 10 states with the largest percent increases in prison population between 1988 and 1989 (Table 4.4), it becomes apparent that the nation's prisons are holding more people than ever, and that many of these increases are located in the western region of the country. Finally, there also has been a trend in increasing the number of women in prison. Table 4.5 shows that the female inmate population increased 7.9% between 1989 and 1990.

In sum, the prison population of this country has increased significantly over the past decade, with major increases occurring in the western region of the country. More importantly, we are placing more women in prison, and a larger proportion of our citizenry is becoming part of the prison system of this country. This rate is the highest in the South (see Table 4.2) and the lowest in the northeast part of the country. Moreover, the prison population is also becoming younger and disproportionally represented by minority populations, particularly young, black males.

Table 4.3
Percent Change in Sentenced Prison Population from 1980 to 1989, by Region and State

Region	0-49%		50%-79%		80%-99%		100%-149%		150% or more	
Northeast					Vermont	80.4	Rhode Island	140.1	New Hampshire	257.7
							New York	136.7	New Jersey	249.4
							Massachusetts	130.7	Pennsylvania	162.0
							Connecticut	129.4		
							Maine	113.4		
Midwest	Iowa	44.6	Wisconsin	70.2	Indiana	94.6	Missouri	143.1	Ohio	162.0
			Nebraska	65.5			Illinois	130.4		
			Minnesota	55.1			Kansas	125.4		
							North Dakota	118.4		
							Michigan	109.9		
							South Dakota	109.7		
South	Texas	36.5	Georgia	64.6	S. Carolina	99.4	Dist. of Col.	149.0		
	W. Virginia	22.2	Tennessee	50.4	Maryland	98.9	Oklahoma	138.2		
	N. Carolina	15.5			Florida	97.7	Kentucky	131.0		
					Louisiana	94.1	Arkansas	116.6		
					Virginia	89.6	Delaware	115.0		
							Alabama	113.2		
							Mississippi	103.0		
West			Washington	57.5	Wyoming	92.1	New Mexico	138.6	California	262.5
					Montana	84.6	Idaho	126.4	Alaska	234.2
					Colorado	80.5	Oregon	112.6	Nevada	192.9
									Arizona	191.9
									Hawaii	157.4
									Utah	153.8
Regional totals			South	74.8			Midwest	111.2	West	202.8
									Northeast	155.3
U.S. summary							States	114.0		
							Federal	128.8		
							Total	115.0		

Note: Sentenced prisoners are those with sentences of more than 1 year.

Source: Bureau of Justice Statistics (1990). "Prisoners in 1989," p. 3. Washington, DC: U.S. Department of Justice, May.

Table 4.4
The Prison Situation Among the States, Yearend 1990

10 States with the largest 1990 prison populations	Number of inmates	10 States with the highest incarceration rates, 1990*	Prisoners per 100,000 residents	10 States with the largest percent increases in prison population			
				1989-90	Percent increase	1985-90*	Percent increase
California	97,309	South Carolina	451	Vermont	15.9%	Colorado	107.3%
New York	54,895	Nevada	444	Washington	15.4	New Hampshire	96.5
Texas	50,042	Louisiana	427	New Hampshire	15.1	California	94.0
Florida	44,387	Oklahoma	383	Texas	13.7	Michigan	93.0
Michigan	34,267	Arizona	375	Connecticut	12.9	New Jersey	86.4
Ohio	31,855	Alabama	370	Alabama	12.6	Rhode Island	83.3
Illinois	27,516	Michigan	366	Idaho	12.1	Connecticut	70.8
Georgia	22,345	Alaska	348	California	11.5	Arizona	67.2
Pennsylvania	22,290	Maryland	347	Illinois	11.3	New York	59.1
New Jersey	21,128	Florida	336	Iowa	10.7	Pennsylvania	56.7

Note: The District of Columbia as a wholly urban jurisdiction is excluded.
*Prisoners with sentences of more than 1 year.

Source: Bureau of Justice Statistics (1991). "Prisoners in 1990," p. 4. Washington, DC: U.S. Department of Justice, May.

Table 4.5
Prisoners Under the Jurisdiction of State or Federal Correctional Authorities, by Sex, Yearend 1989 and 1990

	Men	Women
Total		
Advance 1990	727,398	43,845
Final 1989	671,911	40,646
Percent change, 1989-90	8.3%	7.9%
Sentenced to more than 1 year		
Advance 1990	699,443	40,320
Final 1989	643,685	37,270
Percent change, 1989-90	8.7%	8.2%
Incarceration rate, 1990*	566	31

*The number of prisoners with sentences of more than 1 year per 100,000 residents of each sex on December 31, 1990.

Source: Bureau of Justice Statistics (1991). "Prisoners in 1990," p. 4. Washington, DC: U.S. Department of Justice, May.

Prisoners: A Young and Black Majority?

While the nation's prison population has grown considerably over the past decade, some would say that fact alone is overshadowed by a more troublesome fact—that the prisons of this country are becoming blacker and overrepresented by other minority group members. Christianson (1981) raises the issue of how the contemporary prison is disproportionately represented by black males. In fact, his analysis of incarceration trends by race indicated a rather bleak outlook for young, black males in this country. Specifically, he found "strong racial disproportion" in every region of the country, and he further suggests that some legal mechanisms will have to be invoked to deal with the seriousness and extent of the problem.

More contemporary research indicates an even more dismal outlook for the future of prisons in this country. Current evidence indicates that the trend of incarcerating more blacks and other minority group members will become more pronounced as we head into the twenty-first century. More correctly, while the actual numbers of blacks and other minority group members will remain smaller when compared to whites, their rates of incarceration will increase, thereby reflecting a larger percentage of non-majority people becoming part of our prison systems.

California, for example, presently incarcerates 847 blacks per 100,000 people. This is an astronomical figure when we compare it to the numbers for Hispanics (297) and whites (95). As suggested by Irwin and Austin (1987), our current trends of incarceration of blacks and other minorities will lead us into a further separation between those who have (most of whom are white) and those who have not (most of whom are black). As they state, "And we will further divide our society into white affluent classes and a poor non-white underclass, many of them convicts and ex-convicts. In effect, we are putting our own apartheid into place" (Irwin and Austin, 1987:20).

Couple this information with projections by some that the black birthrate will continue to be quite high when compared to the white birthrate (Blumstein, 1988), it becomes apparent that the prisons of tomorrow will become even blacker and overrepresented by other minority group members. This degree of overrepresentation of minority groups will have serious ramifications on the policies of correctional administrators in the not-too-distant future. We offer some ideas and thoughts on this issue and others in Chapter 18. For now, however, suffice it to say that the current and future trends of incarceration in this country do and will reflect the imprisonment of many people who are not of the dominant culture or socioeconomic statuses.

Other Prisoner Characteristics

While there is overrepresentation by blacks and other minority groups in our prisons, there are other factors about prisoners that distinguish them from people in general society. These other factors are presented in Table 4.6. The table indicates that a vast majority of prisoners are male (95.6%), about one-half are white (49.7%), almost three-quarters are under the age of 34 (72.4%), over one-half have never been married (53.7%), slightly under two-thirds have less than 12 years of education (61.6%), over one-half are in prison for violent offenses (54.6%), while a little under one-third are in prison for property offenses (31.0%), and small percentages are in prison for drug offenses (8.6%) and public order offenses (5.2%).

Table 4.6
Sociodemographic and Offense Characteristics of State Prison Inmates

Characteristics	Percentage of Prison Inmates	Current Offense	Percentage of Prison Inmates
Sex		Violent offenses	54.6
Male	95.6	Murder*	11.2
Female	4.4	Negligent manslaughter	3.2
Race		Kidnapping	1.7
White	49.7	Rape	4.2
Black	46.9	Other sexual assault	4.5
Other	3.4	Robbery	20.9
Ethnicity		Assault	8.0
Hispanic	12.6	Other violent	.8
Non-Hispanic	87.4	Property offenses	31.0
Age		Burglary	16.5
Less than 18	.5	Larceny/theft	6.0
18-24	26.7	Motor vehicle theft	1.4
25-34	45.7	Arson	.8
35-44	19.4	Fraud	3.8
45-54	5.2	Stolen property	2.0
55-64	1.8	Other property	.5
65 or older	.6	Drug offenses	8.6
Marital status		Possession	2.9
Married	20.3	Trafficking	5.4
Widowed	1.9	Other drug	.3
Divorced	18.1	Public-order offenses	5.2
Separated	6.0	Weapons offense	1.4
Never married	53.7	Other public-order	3.7
Education		Other offenses	.7
Less than 12 years	61.6		
12 years or more	38.4		
*Includes non-negligent homicide.			

Source: Bureau of Justice Statistics (1988). "Profile of State Prison Inmates, 1986," p. 3. *Special Report.* Washington, DC: U.S. Department of Justice.

In addition, many offenders within the property crime category are not first-time offenders. Many have had some type of experience with the correctional system, whether it be community-based, e.g., probation- or institution-based, prisons, and juvenile institutions. Moreover, while burglary makes up over one-half of all property crimes, it must also be understood as a potential violent crime. This is a crime in which the victim's privacy is invaded and the possibility of violence is high if the victim encounters the offender during the commission of the crime. As such, not all property crimes can be viewed as harmless events. The fact remains that for many offenders who are incarcerated, there is a long history of criminality and involvement in the criminal justice system.

Institutional Characteristics

While we may know the characteristics of individuals in our prisons today, it is equally important to examine some institutional characteristics of the contemporary prison to get a greater appreciation of what prisons are all about. Three characteristics emerge when one is describing prisons today. They are prison overcrowding, guarding in prison, and prison society. We will begin by examining the prison overcrowding issue.

Prison Overcrowding

As stated earlier in this chapter, the number of prisoners in both state and federal correctional institutions is at an all-time high. Many states are under some form of legal mandate to reduce overcrowding in their prisons. The numbers of prisoners have forced correctional administrators to think of new ways to deal with the overcrowding problem. One possible solution is to keep prisoners in local jails.

Table 4.7 shows the number of state prisoners held in local jails because of prison crowding, by state, year-end 1989 and 1990 (Bureau of Justice Statistics, 1991). The table indicates that more than 18,000 prisoners were held in local jails due to overcrowding in the state systems. Three states—Louisiana, New Jersey, and Virginia—accounted for over half of the state-sentenced prisoners in local jails. Five states—Arkansas, Louisiana, New Jersey, Tennessee, and Virginia—held more than 10% of their sentenced state prisoners in local jails.

Table 4.7
State Prisoners Held in Local Jails Because of Prison Crowding, by State,
Yearend 1989 and 1990

States housing prisoners in local jails	Prisoners held in local jails			
	Number		As a percent of all prisoners	
	1989	1990	1989	1990
U.S. total	19,074	18,380	2.7%	2.4%
Alabama	1,018	879	7.3	5.6
Arizona[a]	117	52	.9	.4
Arkansas	596	777	9.3	11.5
Colorado[a]	410	653	5.9	9.3
District of Columbia[b]	821	826	8.2	9.1
Idaho	130	152	7.0	7.3
Indiana[a]	525	757	4.3	5.9
Kentucky	1,411	693	17.0	7.7
Louisiana	4,138	4,493	24.0	24.2
Maine	22	10	1.5	.7
Massachusetts[a]	377	430	5.0	5.2
Mississippi	1,159	775	14.7	9.3
New Jersey	3,024	2,741	15.6	13.0
Oklahoma	0	210	0	1.7
Oregon	127	61	1.9	.9
South Carolina	405	443	2.6	2.6
Tennessee[c]	2,733	1,869	25.7	18.0
Utah	91	0	3.8	0
Vermont[c]	34	34	3.8	3.2
Virginia	1,863	2,325	11.3	13.4
West Virginia[a]	0	102	0	6.5
Wisconsin	73	98	1.1	1.3

[a]For States not including jail backups in their jurisdiction counts, the percentage of jurisdiction population was calculated using the total number of State inmates in jail and prison.
[b]Includes inmates housed in other States as a result of prison crowding.
[c]Inmates sentenced to State prison but held in local lockups.

Source: Bureau of Justice Statistics (1991). "Prisoners in 1990," p. 5. Washington, DC: U.S. Department of Justice, May.

Table 4.8
Reported Federal and State Prison Capacities, Yearend 1990

Region and jurisdiction	Rated capacity	Operational capacity	Design capacity	Population[a] as a percent of Highest capacity	Lowest capacity
Federal[b]	...	...	43,312	151%	151%
Northeast					
Connecticut	9,159	10,075	...	104%	115%
Maine	1,193	1,193	1,193	127	127
Massachusetts	...	...	4,864	170	170
New Hampshire	1,268	1,492	1,112	90	121
New Jersey	...	...	13,383	137	137
New York	55,820	56,833	45,946	97	119
Pennsylvania	...	...	14,338	156	156
Rhode Island	2,396	2,444	2,314	98	103
Vermont	647	647	647	157	157
Midwest					
Illinois	22,691	22,691	18,987	121%	145%
Indiana	10,861	...	...	117	117
Iowa	3,035	3,035	3,035	131	131
Kansas	...	5,405	...	107	107
Michigan	26,266	...	...	130	130
Minnesota	3,198	3,198	3,198	99	99
Missouri	14,822	14,893	...	100	101
Nebraska	...	...	1,666	144	144
North Dakota	...	576	576	84	84
Ohio	...	...	20,598	155	155
South Dakota	1,189	1,130	1,189	113	119
Wisconsin	5,241	5,241	5,241	139	139
South					
Alabama	13,782	13,782	13,782	107%	107%
Arkansas	...	6,535	...	92	92
Delaware	2,915	3,138	2,015	112	174
District of Columbia	8,253	9,121	7,764	100	117
Florida	50,645	45,237	34,826	88	128
Georgia	...	22,424	...	100	100
Kentucky	8,051	7,866	...	103	106
Louisiana	14,697	14,697	14,697	96	96
Maryland	...	17,907	12,246	99	145
Mississippi	8,136	8,594	8,091	88	94
North Carolina	15,942	19,324	...	95	115
Oklahoma	...	8,088	...	150	150
South Carolina	15,438	15,438	11,958	109	141
Tennessee	...	8,803	...	97	97
Texas[c]	49,325	46,859	49,325	94	100
Virginia	13,537	13,537	13,537	111	111
West Virginia	1,700	1,565	1,850	85	100
West					
Alaska	2,808	...	...	93%	93%
Arizona	...	13,884	...	103	103
California	...	...	52,698	185	185
Colorado	...	6,120	4,605	115	152
Hawaii	...	2,141	1,577	118	161
Idaho	...	1,845	1,586	104	121
Montana	1,079	1,407	1,079	101	132
Nevada	5,406	5,406	4,394	98	121
New Mexico	3,225	3,596	3,225	82	92
Oregon	...	6,170	...	103	103
Utah	...	2,911	3,032	83	86
Washington	5,411	6,446	6,446	124	148
Wyoming	793	795	614	140	181

... Data not available.
[a]Excludes inmates who had been sentenced to State prison but were held in local jails because of crowding and who were included in the total prisoner count.
[b]Excludes prisoners housed in contract or other non-Federal facilities.
[c]Excludes 2,743 inmates who resided in boot camps, private prisons, or psychiatric facilities and 726 male inmates in halfway houses.

Source: Bureau of Justice Statistics (1991). "Prisoners in 1990," p. 6. Washington, DC: U.S. Department of Justice, May.

Table 4.9
State Prison Admissions, Relative to Selected Serious Offenses and the Adult
Population, by State, 1980 and 1989

Region and State	Admissions per 1,000 selected serious offenses		Admissions per 100,000 adults	
	1980	1989	1980	1989
U.S. total	25	62	80	172
Northeast	15	52	48	117
Connecticut	37	106	105	242
Maine	28	65	54	81
Massachusetts	8	28	26	62
New Hampshire	14	44	30	53
New Jersey	14	54	49	113
New York	13	52	56	158
Pennsylvania	17	45	33	64
Rhode Island	12	36	35	75
Vermont	32	71	77	110
Midwest	28	62	71	128
Illinois*	32	48	78	124
Indiana	37	64	88	119
Iowa	28	60	50	89
Kansas	26	56	69	121
Michigan	20	54	67	141
Minnesota	12	35	25	57
Missouri	24	65	74	153
Nebraska	35	61	56	85
North Dakota	47	100	36	58
Ohio	45	96	97	193
South Dakota	61	161	71	135
Wisconsin	26	54	46	70
South	38	73	116	220
Alabama	49	69	138	165
Arkansas	50	64	104	342
Delaware	30	88	88	172
District of Columbia	36	69	213	366
Florida	24	98	109	432
Georgia	49	74	156	251
Kentucky	47	70	86	112
Louisiana	31	50	100	157
Maryland	30	70	107	183
Mississippi	43	81	97	167
North Carolina	61	97	158	266
Oklahoma	38	98	111	274
South Carolina	47	63	153	190
Tennessee	33	34	89	79
Texas	38	48	129	180
Virginia	36	111	75	157
West Virginia	30	56	38	58
West	17	51	66	150
Alaska	42	136	115	262
Arizona	24	65	97	204
California	15	50	66	162
Colorado	16	48	55	111
Hawaii	9	14	28	32
Idaho	34	77	78	124
Montana	34	52	55	57
Nevada	26	111	136	302
New Mexico	17	39	53	136
Oregon	27	54	83	139
Utah	15	38	39	69
Washington	14	37	46	100
Wyoming	38	83	71	104

Note: Prison admissions refer to the number of prisoners received from courts with sentences of more than 1 year. Selected offenses are murder, nonnegligent manslaughter, forcible rape, robbery, aggravated assault, and burglary. Adults are defined as the resident population age 18 or older.
*The FBI estimated the number of reported crimes in 1989.

Source: Bureau of Justice Statistics (1991). "Prisoners in 1990," p. 8. Washington, DC: U.S. Department of Justice, May.

Couple this data with capacity data, and we can see that the prison over-crowding problem in this country is significant. Table 4.8 shows a profile of prison crowding, year-end 1990, for all 50 states and the federal system. As indicated in this table, very few states had any reserve capacity. Typically, institutions require added capacity for special prisoner populations, such as those inmates housed in protective custody and disciplinary cases. Table 4.8 shows how only nine states were operating below 95% their capacity. Around 42 jurisdictions and the federal prison system reported operating well over 100% of their lowest capacity, with 34 of these jurisdictions exceeding their highest capacity. Overall, both the state and federal prison systems have overcrowding problems that have stretched existing resources.

Additionally, recent data from the Bureau of Justice Statistics (1990) suggests that the probability of being incarcerated for specific serious crimes has increased dramatically over the period 1980-1988. Table 4.9 reveals that in 1980, 25 commitments occurred per 1,000 reported crimes. By 1988, that ratio had increased to 51 commitments per 1,000 crimes, suggesting that the prison population growth may be due, in part, to an increased certainty of punishment.

Table 4.10
Adult Arrests for Drug Violations, 1980-1988

| Year | Number of adult arrests for drug violations | | |
	Total	Sale or manufacture	Possession
1980	471,165	102,714	368,451
1981	468,056	93,143	374, 913
1982	584,850	119,309	465,541
1983	583,474	128,948	454,526
1984	623,719	137,218	486,501
1985	718,597	170,307	548,290
1986	742,687	186,414	556,273
1987	849,521	219,176	630,345
1988	1,050,576	287,858	762,718
Percent change, 1980-88	123.0%	180.3%	107.0%

Source: Bureau of Justice Statistics (1990). "Prisoners in 1989," p. 9. Washington, DC: U.S. Department of Justice, May.

Moreover, prison populations reflect a large and growing number of offenders who are being sent to prison for the sale or manufacture and possession of illegal drugs. The numbers are staggering. As indicated in Table 4.10, there has been a 123% increase in the number of offenders going to prison for these offenses. Consistent with the nation's attempt to solve the drug problem through the criminal justice system, these data suggest that many people are in prison for drug offenses.

As is evidenced through a review of these tables, the overcrowding problem in this country is quite serious. Overall, we can conclude that overcrowding is a central problem for correctional administrators. It is for this reason, in part, that prison construction has increased dramatically throughout the country. For now, it is important for the student to realize the extent to which overcrowding has affected prisons today. Moreover, it does not seem probable that this problem will be resolved in the 1990s.

Guarding in Prison

Another characteristic associated with the contemporary prison that has received much attention is the phenomenon of guarding. There has been a research explosion on where correctional officers come from, their educational levels, and their general attitudes toward prisoners and corrections as a whole. Interesting information has been developed about how correctional officers adapt to the demands and expectations of their work and the effects of the prison experience on them both as a group and individually. We can begin by examining the concepts of alienation, cynicism, and stress within the correctional officer role. More importantly, we can explore how control is kept in prison by correctional officers, and finally, suggest some new ideas for reformulating the role of the correctional officer so that he or she is a more productive member of the correctional community.

Past research has documented how correctional officers are white, from rural areas, and have very little education (Clemmer, 1940). In addition, current research on correctional officers indicates that many are politically conservative (Athens, 1975) and, as was also found by Crouch and Marquart (1980), only seek positions as correctional officers when no other jobs are available. Couple these facts with the facts that many prisoners are of a minority class, often have low levels of education, and come from predominantly urban areas, and it is plain to see how conflict can arise very easily in the prison context between correctional officers and inmates. Knowing this to be the case, many have called for increased hiring of minority group members to ease the tension (McEleney, 1985).

Whether this solution will be useful in reducing the tension between correctional officers and inmates is problematic at best. Cullen et al. (1985) have reported how black correctional officers were more likely to be dissatisfied with their jobs than their white counterparts. More recent research by Jurik and Winn (1987) supports this position. These researchers found that black correctional officers were more likely to quit their positions because of their conflicts with predominantly white supervisors. Further, Cullen et al. (1989) found support among black correctional officers for custody and greater support for rehabilitation. Additionally, Whitehead and Lindquist (1989) found that the presence of more black officers does not automatically translate into a greater number of officers with more positive attitudes toward prisoners. As such, it is not clear what positive effect would be produced if more minorities were recruited for correctional officer positions. We do know that the job of correctional officer does produce increased alienation, stress, and cynicism among officers. Of the three, stress has probably received the most attention by researchers.

Again, Cullen et al. (1985:520-524) have systematically identified characteristics associated with stress in the correctional officer role. Most notably, they found perceived danger and role problems to be the most significant in creating stressful conditions among correctional workers, yet they, in addition, further suggest that being in a maximum security prison, being female, the amount of experience as a correctional officer, and the lack of support from supervisors, peers, and family to be critical factors to the level of stress felt by correctional workers. This is also borne out by other research conducted by Cheek and Miller (1983), where they found that correctional officers tended to have a greater-than-average number of stress-related illnesses and higher rates of divorce.

Further, Zimmer (1986) has argued that the pressures and stresses of correctional officer work are enhanced for the female officer. Her research pointed out that females who worked as correctional officers experienced strong opposition from the prison community, most notably male counterparts and prisoners. Specifically, they experienced opposition and harassment from male co-workers, discriminatory assignments from male supervisors, and sexual misconduct from male inmates. Unlike male officers, female correctional officers have to develop unique strategies to cope with their work environments, which places undue stress on them.

Moreover, contemporary research has suggested that correctional officers experience very high levels of alienation and negative attitudes toward not only other correctional officers but also administrators and prisoners (Poole and Regoli, 1981). When examining this phenomenon across prisons, Toch and Klofas (1982) found equally high levels of alienation in their sample, and they further suggest that this may be a result of the fact that the sample is urban. Like alienation and stress, the level of cynicism tends to be high among correctional officers. Regoli, Poole, and Shrink (1979) have suggested that the high level of cynicism among correctional officers may be directly related to the move toward professionalization within corrections today. Interestingly, they suggest that since many correctional officers cannot achieve the educational level (i.e., college educated) normally associated with the professional status, they feel a sense of strain between what they are able to achieve and what is desirable in order to be considered a professional. This anomie often produces cynical attitudes among correctional officers.

While correctional officers are often viewed in a negative light by many and experience an inordinate number of problems associated with the job, it would be fair to say that they are an extraordinary group with much creativity when it comes to performing their jobs. The student may ask what their job actually entails, and it is often said that the correctional officer is father, mother, babysitter, counselor, priest, and police officer to the prisoner. This suggests that the role of a correctional officer is multifaceted and often contradictory messages are sent to the officer about exactly what the job requires. Much of the research literature has documented how correctional officers make arrangements with prisoners in order to accomplish the tasks required of them.

Sykes (1958) was the first to suggest that much of correctional officer work relies on the assistance of the inmate. In effect, "symbiotic relationships," according to Sykes, enable both inmates and officers to gain those entities that they both require for a smooth-running institution. For example, the officer may bargain with key inmates for control of a cellblock and in return grant special favors to those inmates (this will be discussed more thoroughly in Chapters 8 and 10). Even recent research by Marquart (1986) and Marquart and Roebuck (1986) suggests that much control in prison is gained by correctional officers through the recruitment of snitches, or inmates who will tell officers about the dealings of other inmates in the institutional environment. This relationship suggests that correctional officers could not accomplish their objectives without the alliance of inmates. Stojkovic (1986) has also documented how this procedure is employed by correctional administrators to control their institutions.

What becomes quite evident is that, like prisoners, correctional officers adapt to their environments and adjust their behaviors accordingly. We will see how this adaptive behavior is represented by correctional officers in Chapter 11 when we explore sexual relations behind bars and prison contraband systems. For now, however, we can say that the role of a correctional officer is often very demanding and requires compromise and adaptation on the part of the officer if he or she is going to survive. It may be the inability of many correctional officers to adapt correctly to the prison environment that contributes to the very high turnover rates among them (May, 1976). While turnover, alienation, cynicism, and stress are very high among correctional officers, there has been a recognition by many researchers that correctional officers are still supportive of prisoners, albeit in small numbers, yet current evidence does suggest that correctional officers attitudes' toward inmates are much more varied than was traditionally the case.

Research by Cullen et al. (1987) supports the position that correctional officers hold still punitive ideals, but in addition, support rehabilitative programming for prisoners. The researchers state, "[a]lthough they see maintaining order as a core feature of their role and harbor some negative attitudes toward inmates, they also appear to define themselves more as 'correctional' officers than as 'guards' and believe in the potential of prison treatment programs to reform inmates" (1987:14).

Stojkovic and Feyerherm (1988) have also found that the attitudes of correctional officers toward inmates may be related to their background and structural characteristics. These researchers found that those correctional officers who were accepting of the rehabilitative philosophy were more likely to gain these attitudes from the organizational setting. In effect, the acceptance of this philosophical attitude may be more a result of the prison organization than some belief they brought in with them when they were hired to be a correctional officer. As a result, there is support for the position that the beliefs and attitudes of correctional workers may be a product of how the organization is structured. This line of reasoning has been supported by research which suggests that more favorable attitudes toward inmates are found in minimum security institutions. Yet this by no means is certain for all correctional officers (see Smith and Hepburn, 1979 and Jurik, 1985).

What is relevant to this discussion is that the attitudes of correctional officers toward inmates are not as similiar as many have suggested and that the punitive attitudes of officers are only reflective of a broad and varied set of beliefs about prisoners. This provides much hope to the correctional officer role, since it becomes quite clear that both correctional officers and the public expect more out of the prison than for it to be a repository for unwanted members of society. The question becomes, "What can be done to the correctional officer role to make it a more productive, enriching, and positive experience for correctional officers and the prisoners they supervise?" A current trend has been to make the correctional officer role much more of a "helping profession" that provides support to the inmate while simultaneously enlarging and enriching the experiences of the correctional officer. This position has been suggested by Klofas (1984) and further developed by Johnson (1987).

Accordingly, Johnson (1987:137-159) supports the idea that correctional officer work should be rooted in the delivery of human services. More importantly, this position suggests that correctional officers are like anyone else in that they seek to do the best job possible given the constraints of their jobs. Additionally, the correctional officer, according to Johnson, is interested in providing human service skills to prisoners, and according to recent research is the most effective in controlling the inmate population. Citing the work of Hepburn (1984), Johnson argues quite persuasively that institutional authority is greatest among those correctional officers who have a less punitive and less custodial orientation, who maintain a lower degree of social distance between themselves and the prisoners, and who express a higher level of job satisfaction. At the heart of this approach, according to Johnson, are personal relationships between correctional officers and inmates. Johnson states, "Correctional authority, in other words, rests in those officers who develop personal relationships rather than with those who play aloof custodial roles" (1984:139). These helping networks and personal-relationship-building ideas can be undertaken by correctional officers in three ways.

First, Johnson suggests that the correctional officer who provides needed goods and services to prisoners on a regular basis is promoting more long-term stability to the institutional environment. Fundamentally, the position here is that officers who provide this approach receive greater respect and support from the prisoner population. It should be noted that what is important here is the fact that the correctional officer becomes viewed by many inmates as *legitimate*; it is this type of legitimate power that is often divorced from the traditional correctional officer-inmate relationship (Stojkovic, 1984). In short, the officer attempts to provide an environment where prisoners legitimize the correctional officer function. This process of legitimation is often associated with the human service approach of correctional officer work.

A second human service activity that can be employed by correctional officers is to serve as an advocate or referral agent for the prisoner. Johnson suggests that this activity may be difficult for many correctional officers because they are required, in most institutions through formal policy, not to get involved with prisoners at any level. Yet much can be said about the normalizing effect of advocacy among correctional officers for prisoners when they have little or no support from the institution's administration, family and relatives, and the general public. This type of support is viewed positively by many prisoners and requires a minimal amount of effort on the part of the correctional officer; the potential return, however, is very great in terms of gaining greater authority and respect among the inmate population. As stated by Johnson, "By observing that some guards go out of their way to ensure that legitimate needs are met, inmates find that they are not alone and powerless. They have allies among the correctional officers who support them and give them a degree of control over their prison lives" (1984:144-45).

Finally, correctional officers can provide inmates with help in the adjustment to prison life. As suggested by Johnson, inmates experience feelings of loneliness, depression, and powerlessness in their present situations. Anyone who has visited a correctional facility can describe the feelings of depression and rejection among many of the prisoners. Correctional officers, nevertheless, have an excellent opportunity to provide inmates the necessary supports that enable them to overcome these often crippling and debilitating feelings. In fact, the premise here is that the correctional officer can easily contribute to a more stable and peaceful prison environment by providing prisoners with the support needed to survive in the prison setting.

Whether this is protection from aggressive prisoners or counseling about specific problems the inmate is experiencing, through the human service approach much can be done for the prisoner with respect to adjustment problems and the prison environment can be much less tense and safer for correctional officers and prisoners alike. Described by Johnson as "helping networks," the prison environment that espouses the human service orientation relies on multiple members of the prison community to work together in the solution of prison adjustment problems among inmates. In this way, correctional officers, counselors, psychologists, and social workers provide a group approach to the treatment of the prisoner.

More importantly, this approach suggests to the prisoner that there is genuine concern for his welfare. We, in addition, add that there is an equal concern for the correctional staff, because it is believed that the human service approach enables the prison to be run more effectively and in the best interests of both staff and prisoners. As stated by Johnson, "human service activities make the officer's job richer, more rewarding, and ultimately less stressful" (1987:154). It is to this end that all correctional work should strive. Without this type of perspective, prisons can only become what they have been in the past: destructive and unproductive institutions where both keeper and kept suffer and experience each other's miseries.

We believe the human service orientation deserves the attention of correctional policymakers, administrators, and the general public. Through experimentation we can see if such an approach is valuable to correctional work. At present, we think it does have potential and certainly requires more critical evaluation before definitive statements can be generalized to correctional facilities. It is a start, however, that correctional administrators will have to explore, because past practices have not proven to be helpful or productive to either the prisoner or his keeper.

Prison Society

Like the correctional officer, the prisoner often experiences many stressful events which shape and alter his perception of the prison world. This final section of the chapter will provide some ideas and positions to the student on how the prisoner copes and adjusts to the prison setting. Chapter 8 will describe these processes and the nature of prisoner social systems more thoroughly, yet our purpose here is to give the student a more comprehensive understanding of the needs of incarcerated men. Moreover, we will attempt to provide some of the rather creative mechanisms of adaptation that men behind bars employ to survive the incarceration process. It is hoped that the student is able to come away from this section of the chapter with a greater appreciation of the effects of incarceration on men and how they attempt to live and function as human beings when removed from the mainstream of society.

Borrowing from Johnson (1987:100-117) and the work of Toch (1977), we can construct an understanding of the various "ecological dimensions" associated with the needs of prisoners. Accordingly, Toch has identified what he believes to be seven major dimensions of prisoner needs and preferences. They are:

(1) ACTIVITY—This is where the prisoner requires some type of stimulation and endeavor which gives a sense of meaning and purpose to his life. Often in prison situations, the prisoner has no activity with which to occupy his time, and the lack of activity produces much stress and discomfort in the prisoner's life. As we will see in Chapter 7, very few prisoners in this country have any work available to them. By limiting an avenue of physical and mental expression to the prisoner, he is not able to meet a fundamental need of all human beings, to be active and involved in the creation of one's own life and immediate surroundings. As an example, the student should attempt to visualize the agony of forced idleness. We are not referring to a vacation, but a situation where there is virtually nothing to do. It is a daily experience for many inmates in this country.

(2) PRIVACY—Among prisoners this is a very important concern because the prison often grants very few moments of privacy. In addition, because many prisons are overcrowded, it becomes very difficult for the prisoner to be alone and at peace with himself. This is particularly disturbing because prisoners are not inherently guaranteed any right to privacy in prison, according to the courts (see Chapter 12), yet it is something that all human beings require for a healthy existence.

(3) SAFETY—Typically, in the prison setting this refers to one's physical safety and the ability to be free of assault from other prisoners. In Chapter 10 we will discuss prison violence more thoroughly; however, we do not want to give the student an incorrect impression. While prisoners often do not feel safe, most are able to satisfy this need through the adaptation of differing lifestyles that are nonviolent and removed from much of the convict world. As stated by Johnson (1987:100),...."[T]he prison accommodates a wide range of nonviolent lifestyles that are sought, and usually found, by the masses of prisoners who studiously avoid the world of the convicts and who, for the most part, survive prison on their own terms."

(4) EMOTIONAL FEEDBACK—This is the need among prisoners, like everyone else, to be loved and cared for by others. In short, it is also the desire to have intimacy in one's life. Again, as with the other needs, this need is often unfulfilled, and more importantly, very few prison programs provide opportunities to the inmate to satisfy this basic need. Typically, this is expressed in the prison through loneliness and a sense of emptiness among inmates. At best, we can say that this could be addressed by the prison organization through greater programming in the areas of prison visitation and furloughs.

(5) SUPPORT—While emotional feedback focuses on the intimate side of human relationships, the need of support seeks assistance and help in the self-improvement process. This is where institutional programming is so critical in prison, yet it is also where very few dollars of the institutional budget are actually spent. This type of programming is usually organized around educational, vocational, and training programs in the prison setting. It is the belief in this type of programming that provides the prisoner with a sense of hope, once released into the free community.

(6) STRUCTURE—The need for structure centers around the issues of certainty and predictability. Like people in the free community, the prisoner seeks a sense of routine to his life. There has to be a plan to the prison organization and what is expected of the inmate as reflected through institutional policy. Most important is the desire for stability in the prison environment. It is on this concern that prisoners and correctional officers, on the whole, tend to agree with each other.

(7) FREEDOM—This concern may seem nonsensical to the student, yet it is something that all prisoners seek in one form or another. As stated by Johnson (1987:102), freedom in the prison context typically represents a perverse game of control between keeper and kept. Much of the concern over freedom among inmates is actually a concern over being treated "like a man" and given some respect. Encroachment on this respect is viewed by the prisoner as an *illegitimate* use of power by the correctional officer. Freedom, therefore, is critical to the prisoner who feels his manhood is being questioned by those who control the institutional setting. As a result, conflict may arise in this situation. Freedom requires that the prisoner have some control over his life when he is quite aware that most control is already exercised by the prison structure.

With these seven dimensions, there is also a great deal of variability among prisoners and prisons. In other words, not all prisoners are going to rate each one of these dimensions as high as the others. Safety, for example, may be a critical dimension for the prisoner who has previously been assaulted, whereas freedom would be more important to the recent arrival to the prison. Moreover, different prisons provide greater opportunities to satisfy some of these dimensions than others. The Federal Bureau of Prisons has one of the most extensive prison industry programs. The support dimension can be met very nicely by many prisoners in the federal system. The critical question becomes, "How do inmates attempt to satisfy these dimensions without resorting to violence?"

Johnson (1987:103-105) employs the concept of a niche described by other writers to suggest adaptability by prisoners to prison life (Seymour, 1977; Toch, 1977). Under this concept, the prisoner affiliates with those people, resources, assignments, and relationships that can satisfy the preferences and dimensions that are the most critical to him. It should be noted that the niche is *not always a gang*. It is a collection of items that makes the prison experience *survivable*, not luxurious. In short, people doing time in prison seek people, events, job assignments, and relationships that afford them the opportunity to satisfy their basic needs and preferences. It is for this reason that many offenders "hang with" members they knew when they were on the streets; this sense of commonality of experience provides the opportunity to share ideas, thoughts, and methods on how to cope with institutionalization.

A student can reflect on his or her experience of when he or she began college to see how this process of niche development works. Most students tend to socialize and interact with other students with whom they have something in common and who can provide them with those essentials required to finish courses and complete college. One of the reasons fraternities and sororities are so important for many college students is that they provide a necessary niche for those students who have particular concerns and needs that these organizations can meet, and ultimately provide them with the opportunity to *survive* the college experience. The prison social system is no diffferent. Like the college environment, the prison environment has not only multiple and varying niches, but in addition, niche creation and perpetuation varies from prison to prison as it does from college to college. Again, like colleges, prisons are different and have to be understood in that light in order for one to understand the complexity of niches and their profound impact on the adjustment process of prisoners.

Prison Life and Beyond

Much of what we know about the prison experience has suggested that institutionalization affects people differently. We will see in subsequent chapters the various adaptation and coping strategies of prisoners. More importantly, the student will see a picture of institutionalization that may not fit his or her preconceived idea of what prison life actually entails. The fundamental questions for the student should be:

"What does the prison experience produce for the prisoner?"

"What are the long-term effects of being incarcerated?"

"Does society benefit by having prisons?"

"If so, what is/are the benefit(s)?"

"How might the prisoner benefit?"

"If there is no benefit, why do we have prisons?"

These are some of the questions that should be asked by the student while reading the following chapters. It is hoped that through reading and probing the following chapters the student will be able to comprehend corrections beyond the prison experience and see how it is tied to other processes in society. Moreover, it should become apparent after reviewing subsequent chapters that the process of corrections cannot be viewed as a separate entity. As stated in Chapter 1, a systemic understanding of corrections suggests that not only is corrections influenced by society, but society is directed, in part, by corrections. In short, what we do in corrections may reflect who we are as a nation. As stated by Dostoyevski, a society can be gauged by how well it treats its prisoners. Whether we are a good society or a bad one is irrelevant for our purposes here. What we seek is a greater understanding of corrections, and it is to this end that the following chapters are directed.

Summary

The purpose of this chapter was to provide the student with an overview of who becomes part of the prison population in this country. From our discussion, we can conclude that there is a selection process in the criminal justice system. In addition, when we examine the patterns of incarceration in this country, it is evident that more people are being incarcerated today than in the past. The trend seems to indicate an increase in the number of people incarcerated in this country, with higher rates of incarceration existing in southern states.

Concerning individual characteristics of prisoners, we find that the prisoner population of this country is disproportionately composed of young black males who have had prior incarceration experiences, with records of both alcohol and substance abuse problems. Moreover, we suggested that many prisons in this country are overcrowded. While prison overcrowding is a problem facing many correctional systems in this country, we also suggested that a key issue in institutional corrections today is guarding in prison.

Our review of the relevant literature indicated that being a correctional officer in today's prison is a very complex task, with the position causing many problems and dilemmas for the correctional worker. More importantly, however, we showed that the correctional officer role is one in which much help can be given to the inmate while simultaneously enriching the job for the correctional officer. Our examination of the correctional officer job suggested that officers hold a wide variety of beliefs and employed a multitude of strategies to successfully complete their jobs. Finally, we concluded this chapter with an overview of prison society and further discussed the needs that prisoners as a group have while incarcerated. The research literature suggested that many cope with incarceration through the development of niches. The chapter concluded with the idea that to fully comprehend correctional systems one must view them in a systemic fashion and to focus on how they affect society and are affected by society. Chapter 5 will continue this line of reasoning by examining the structures and functions associated with federal and state correctional systems.

The Bonus of Bias

We now consider the additional ideological bonus that is derived from the criminal justice system's bias against the poor. This bonus is a product of the association of crime and poverty in the popular mind. This association, the merging of the "criminal classes" and the "lower classes" into the "dangerous classes," was not invented in America. The word *villain* is derived from the Latin *villanus*, which means a farm servant. The term *villein* was used in feudal England to refer to a serf who farmed the land of a great lord and who was literally owned by that lord. In this respect, our present criminal justice system is heir to a long tradition.

The value of this association was already seen when we explored the "average citizen's" concept of the Typical Criminal and the Typical Crime. It is quite obvious that throughout the great mass of middle America, far more fear and hostility are directed toward the predatory acts of the poor than the rich. Compare the fate of politicians in recent history who call for tax reform, income redistribution, prosecution of corporate crime, and any sort of regulation of business that would make it better serve American social goals with that of politicians who erect their platform on a call for "law and order," more police, less limits on police power, and stiffer prison sentences for criminals—and consider this in light of what we have already seen about the real dangers posed by corporate crime and "business as usual."

It seems clear that Americans have been systematically deceived as to what are the greatest dangers to their lives, limbs, and possessions. The very persistence with which the system functions to apprehend and punish poor crooks and ignore or slap on the wrist equally or more dangerous individuals is testimony to the sticking power of this deception. That Americans continue to tolerate the gentle treatment meted out to white-collar criminals, corporate price fixers, industrial polluters, and political-influence peddlers while voting in droves to lock up more poor people faster and longer indicates the degree to which they harbor illusions as to who most threatens them. It is perhaps also part of the explanation for the continued dismal failure of class-based politics in America. American workers rarely seem able to forget their differences and unite to defend their shared interests against the rich whose wealth they produce. Ethnic divisions serve this divisive function well, but undoubtedly the vivid portrayal of the poor—and, of course, the blacks—as hovering birds of prey waiting for the opportunity to snatch away the workers' meager gains serves also to deflect opposition away from the upper classes. A politician who promises to keep working-class communities free of blacks and their prisons full of them can get their votes even if the major portion of his or her policies amount to continuation of the favored treatment of the rich at their expense. The sensationalistic use, in the 1988 presidential election, of photos of Willie Horton (a convicted black criminal who committed a brutal rape while out of prison on a furlough) suggests that such tactics are still effective politics.

The most important "bonus" derived from the identification of crime and poverty is that it paints the picture that the threat to decent middle Americans comes from those below them on the economic ladder, not those above. For this to happen the system must not only identify crime and poverty, but *it must also fail to reduce crime so that it remains a real threat*. By doing this, it deflects the fear and discontent of middle Americans, and their possible opposition, away from the wealthy.

There are other bonuses as well. For instance, if the criminal justice system functions to send out a message that bestows legitimacy on present property relations, the dramatic impact is greatly enhanced if the violator of the present arrangements is without property. In other words, the crimes of the well-to-do "redistribute" property among the haves. In that sense, they do not pose a symbolic challenge to the larger system in which some have much and many have little or nothing. If the criminal threat can be portrayed as coming from the poor, then the punishment of the poor criminal becomes a morality play in which the sanctity and legitimacy of the system in which some have plenty and others have little or nothing is dramatically affirmed. It matters little who the poor criminals really victimize. What counts is that middle Americans come to fear that those poor criminals are out to steal what they own.

There is yet another bonus for the powerful in America, produced by the identification of crime and poverty. It might be thought that the identification of crime and poverty would produce sympathy for the criminals. My suspicion is that it produces or at least reinforces the reverse: *hostility toward the poor*.

Indeed, there is little evidence that Americans are very sympathetic to poor criminals. Very few Americans believe poverty to be a cause of crime (6 percent of those questioned in a 1981 survey, although 21 percent thought unemployment was a cause). Other surveys find that most Americans believe that the police should be tougher than they are now in dealing with crime (83 percent of those questioned in a 1972 survey); that courts do not deal harshly enough with criminals (79 percent of those questioned in 1987); that a majority of Americans would like to see the death penalty for convicted murderers (70 percent of those questioned in 1987); and that most would be more likely to vote for a candidate who advocated tougher sentences for lawbreakers (83 percent of those questioned in a 1972 survey). Indeed, the experience of Watergate seems to suggest that sympathy for criminals begins to flower only when we approach the higher reaches of the ladder of wealth and power. For some poor ghetto youth who robs a liquor store, five years in the slammer is our idea of tempering justice with mercy. When a handful of public officials [tries] to walk off with the U.S. Constitution, a few months in a minimum security prison will suffice. If the public official is high enough, say, president of the United States, resignation from office and public disgrace tempered with a $60,0000-a-year pension is punishment enough.

My view is that, because the criminal justice system, in fact and fiction, deals with *individual legal and moral guilt*, the association of crime with poverty does not mitigate the image of individual moral responsibility for crime, the image that crime is the result of an individual's poor character. My suspicion is that it does the reverse: It generates the association of poverty and individual moral failing and thus *the belief that poverty itself is a sign of poor or weak character*. The clearest evidence that Americans hold this belief is to be found in the fact that attempts to aid the poor are regarded as acts of charity, rather than as acts of justice. Our welfare system has all the demeaning attributes of an institution designed to give handouts to the undeserving and none of the dignity of an institution designed to make good on our responsibilities to our fellow human beings. If we acknowledged the degree to which our economic and social institutions themselves breed poverty, we would have to recognize our own responsibilities toward the poor. If we can convince ourselves that the poor are poor because of their own shortcomings, particularly moral shortcomings like incontinence and indolence, then we need acknowledge no such responsibility to the poor. Indeed, we can go further and pat ourselves on the back for our generosity in handing out the little that we do, and of course, we can make our recipients go through all the indignities that mark them as the undeserving objects of our benevolence. By and large, this has been the way in which Americans have dealt with their poor. It is a way that enables us to avoid asking the question of why the richest nation in the world continues to produce massive poverty. It is my view that this conception of the poor is subtly conveyed by the way our criminal justice system functions.

Obviously, no ideological message could be more supportive of the present social and economic order than this. It suggests that poverty is a sign of individual failing, not a symptom of social or economic injustice. It tells us loud and clear that massive poverty in the midst of abundance is not a sign pointing toward the need for fundamental changes in our social and economic institutions. It suggests that the poor are poor because they deserve to be poor or at least because they lack the strength of character to overcome poverty. When the poor are seen to be poor in character, then economic poverty coincides with moral poverty and the economic order coincides with the moral order. As if a divine hand guided its workings, capitalism leads to everyone getting what they morally deserve!

If this association takes root, then when the poor individual is found guilty of a crime, the criminal justice system acquits the society of its responsibility not only for crime *but for poverty as well*.

With this, the ideological message of criminal justice is complete. The poor rather than the rich are seen as the enemies of the majority of decent middle Americans. Our social and economic institutions are held to be responsible for neither crime nor poverty and thus are in need of no fundamental questioning or reform. The poor are poor because they are poor of character. The economic order and the moral order are one. To the extent that this message sinks in, the wealthy can rest easily—even if they cannot sleep the sleep of the just.

Thus, we can understand why the criminal justice system creates the image of crime as the work of the poor and fails to reduce it so that the threat of crime remains real and credible. The result is ideological alchemy of the highest order. The poor are seen as the real threat to decent society. The ultimate sanctions of criminal justice dramatically sanctify the present social and economic order, and *the poverty of criminals makes poverty itself an individual moral crime!*

Such are the ideological fruits of a losing war against crime whose distorted image is reflected in the criminal justice carnival mirror and widely broadcast to reach the minds and imaginations of America.

Source: J. Reiman (1990). *The Rich Get Richer and the Poor Get Prison*, Third Edition, pp. 129-133. New York, NY: Macmillan Publishing Company.

Key Terms and Concepts

ecological dimensions
helping networks
helping profession
justice subcultures
niche

prison overcrowding
role-ready defendants
symbiotic relationships
work group norms

References

Albonetti, C.A. (1986). "Criminality, Prosecutorial Screening, and Uncertainty: Toward a Theory of Discretionary Decision Making in Felony Case Processings." *Criminology*, 24,4:623-644.

Athens, L. (1975). "Differences in the Liberal-Conservative Political Attitudes of Prison Guards and Felons." *International Journal of Group Tensions*, 5,3, September:143-155.

Blumberg, A. (1984). "The Practice of Law as a Confidence Game: Organization Cooptation of a Profession." In G. Cole (ed.) *Criminal Justice: Law and Politics, Fourth Edition.* Monterey, CA: Brooks/Cole Publishing Company.

Blumstein, A. (1988). Presentation at the 1988 ICPSR Quantitative Program in Criminology, Ann Arbor, MI.

Bureau of Justice Statistics (1990). "Prisoners in 1989." Washington, DC: U.S. Department of Justice.

Bureau of Justice Statistics (1991). "Prisoners in 1990." Washington, DC: U.S. Department of Justice.

Cheek, F.E. and M.D. Miller (1983). "The Experience of Stress for Correctional Officers: A Double-Bind Theory of Correctional Stress." *Journal of Criminal Justice*, 11,2:105-112.

Christianson, S. (1981). "Our Black Prisons." *Crime and Delinquency*, 27,3:364-375.

Clemmer, D. (1940). *The Prison Community.* New York, NY: Holt, Rinehart and Company.

Crouch, B.M. and J.W. Marquart (1980). "On Becoming a Prison Guard." In B.M. Crouch (ed.) *The Keepers: Prison Guards and Contemporary Corrections.* Springfield, IL: Charles C Thomas, Publisher.

Cullen, F.T., B.G. Link, N.T. Wolfe and J. Frank (1985). "The Social Dimensions of Correctional Officer Stress." *Justice Quarterly*, 2,4, December: 505-533.

Cullen, F.T., F.E. Lutze, B.G. Link and N.T. Wolfe (1987). "The Correctional Orientation of Prison Guards: Do Officers Support Rehabilitation?" Paper presented at the Academy of Criminal Justice Sciences Meeting, St. Louis, MO, March.

Cullen, F.T., F.E. Lutze, B.G. Link and N.T. Wolfe (1989). "The Correctional Orientation of Prison Guards: Do Officers Support Rehabilitation?" *Federal Probation*, 53, March: 33-42.

Duffee, D. and R. Fitch (1976). *Introduction to Corrections: A Policy and Systems Approach*. Santa Monica, CA: Goodyear Publishing Company.

Frazier, C.E. and E.W. Bock (1982). "Effects of Court Officials on Sentence Severity." *Criminology*, 20,2:257-272.

Hepburn, J.R. (1984). "The Erosion of Authority and the Perceived Legitimacy of Inmate Social Protest: A Study of Prison Guards." *Journal of Criminal Justice*, 12:579-590.

Irwin, J. and J. Austin (1987). "The Black Prison Population." New York, NY: Edna McConnell Clark Foundation.

Johnson, R. (1987). *Hard Time: Understanding and Reforming the Prison*. Monterey, CA: Brooks/Cole Publishing Company.

Jurik, N.C. (1985). "Individual and Organizational Determinants of Correctional Officer Attitudes Toward Inmates." *Criminology*, 23,3:523-540.

Jurik, N.C. and R. Winn (1987). "Describing Correctional-Security Dropouts and Rejects: An Individual or Organizational Profile?" *Criminal Justice and Behavior: An International Journal*, 14,1:5-25.

Kingsworth, R. and L. Rizzo (1979). "Decision Making in the Criminal Courts: Continuities and Discontinuities." *Criminology*, 17,1:3-14.

Klofas, J.M. (1984). "Reconsidering Prison Personnel: New Views of the Correctional Officer Subculture." *International Journal of Offender Therapy and Comparative Criminology*, 28:169-175.

Krueger, A.E. (1981). *The Organization of Information in Criminal Legal Settings: A Case Study of Prosecutorial Decision-Making in Los Angeles*. Ann Arbor, MI: University Microfilms International.

Marquart, J.W. (1986). "Prison Guards and the Use of Physical Coercion as a Mechanism of Prisoner Control." *Criminology*, 24,2:347-366.

Marquart, J.W. and J.B. Roebuck (1986). "Prison Guards and Snitches: Social Control in a Maximum-Security Institution." In K.C. Haas and G.P. Alpert (eds.) *The Dilemmas of Punishment*. Prospect Heights, IL: Waveland Press, Inc.

May, E. (1976). "A Day on the Job—In Prison." *Corrections Magazine*, December.

McEleney, B.L. (1985). *Correctional Reform in New York*. New York, NY: University Press of America.

Poole, E.D. and R.M. Regoli (1981). "Alienation in Prison: An Examination of the Work Relations of Prison Guards." *Criminology*, 19,2:251-270.

Regoli. R.M., E.D. Poole and J.L. Shrink (1979). "Occupational Socialization and Career Development: A Look at Cynicism Among Correctional Institution Workers." *Human Organization*, 38,2:183-187.

Seymour, J. (1977). "Niches in Prison." In H. Toch (ed.) *Living in Prison: The Ecology of Survival*. New York, NY: The Free Press.

Smith, C.F.W. and J.R. Hepburn (1979). "Alienation in Prison Organizations." *Criminology*, 17,2:251-262.

Stojkovic, S. (1984). "Social Bases of Power and Control Mechanisms Among Prisoners in a Prison Organization." *Justice Quarterly*, 1,4:511-528.

Stojkovic, S. (1986). "Social Bases of Power and Control Mechanisms Among Administrators in a Prison Organization." *Journal of Criminal Justice*, 14,2:157-166.

Stojkovic, S. and W. Feyerherm (1988). "What Prison Guards Believe: A Study of the Philosophical Attitudes of Correctional Officers." Unpublished manuscript.

Sykes, G. (1958). *The Society of Captives*. Princeton, NJ: Princeton University Press.

Talarico, S.M. (1979). "Judicial Decisions and Sanction Patterns in Criminal Justice." *Journal of Criminal Law and Criminology*, 70,1:117-124.

Toch, H. (1977). *Living in Prison: The Ecology of Survival*. New York, NY: The Free Press.

Toch, H. and J. Klofas (1982). "Alienation and Desire for Job Enrichment Among Correction Officers." *Federal Probation*, 46, March:35-44.

Walker, S. (1980). *Popular Justice: A History of American Criminal Justice*. New York, NY: Oxford University Press.

Walker, S. (1989). *Sense and Nonsense About Crime: A Policy Guide. Second Edition*. Monterey, CA: Brooks/Cole Publishing Company.

Whitehead, J.T and C.A. Lindquist (1989). "Determinants of Correctional Officers' Professional Orientation." *Justice Quarterly*, 6,1: 69-88.

Wilson, W.J. (1987). *The Truly Disadvantaged: The Inner City, The Underclass, and Public Policy*. Chicago, IL: The University of Chicago Press.

Zimmer, L.E. (1986). *Women Guarding Men*. Chicago, IL: The University of Chicago Press.

Photo Credit: Tony O'Brien, Frost Publishing Group, Ltd.

Correctional Systems

5

After reading this chapter, the student should be able to:

▋ Discuss the organization of corrections at the federal level.

▋ Describe correctional organization among the states.

▋ Explain strategies of incarceration among the states.

▋ Provide an explanation of sentencing options.

Introduction

Corrections efforts are organized at various levels of political autonomy in the United States. In other words, there are corrections organizations at federal, state, and local government levels. At each level there are organizations that have been established as resultants of the authority and capacities of governing bodies to create, fund, and operate these organizations.

This chapter is primarily concerned with description of the very large corrections organizations exisiting and operating at the federal and state levels of government. Please keep in mind that the various corrections functions are parcelled out among the various governmental levels, that no one organization has the authority or scope of operation for carrying out or for administering all the corrections functions at the federal level and that corrections efforts are not entirely centralized under one organization (Department or Division of Corrections) in any of the 50 states.

Corrections at the Federal Level

At the federal level of government, corrections functions are divided primarily among the Federal Bureau of Prisons (a component of the U.S. Department of Justice), the U.S. Probation Service (organized within the U.S. Administrative Office of Courts, with agents being attached to U.S. District Courts, also providing parole supervision services), and the U.S. Parole Commission (a semiautonomous body). Certain functions are assigned to others. For example, the Federal Bureau of Prisons can only accommodate about one-third of federal pretrial detainees. The U.S. Marshal's Service has responsibility for pretrial detainees and for contracting space in local jail facilities for these accused persons. Given these arrangements, one can readily recognize that corrections functions at this level of government are not strictly centralized, with one agency responsible for policy development, allocation of resources, and centralized management. Nonetheless, the degree of coordination may be deemed significant.

The Federal Bureau of Prisons was created in 1930 to provide for the administration and operation of federal correctional facilities. At year-end 1989, there were 59,171 offenders (including 4,435 females, 7.5% of the total) under the authority of the Bureau of Prisons (an increase of 9,243 from year-end 1988) (BJS:1990). The Bureau operates more than 50 facilities. Table 5.1 shows the distribution of these facilities by region and by type.

Table 5.1
Federal Facilities—U.S. Bureau of Prisons

PENITENTIARIES			
Facility	**Rated Capacity**	**Average Daily Population 3/90**	**Number of Employees**
USP Atlanta, GA opened 1902 (MAX)	797 (includes camp) (MIN)	1,313 (males) (camp 4600)	474
USP Leavenworth, KS opened 1895 (MAX)	988 (includes camp) (MIN)	1,516 (males) (camp 416)	537
USP Lewisburg, PA opened 1932 (MAX)	1,444 (includes camp) (MIN)	1,407 (males) (camp 237)	500
USP Lompoc, CA opened 1959 (MAX)	1,134	1,571 (males)	422
USP Terre Haute, IN opened 1940 (MAX)	919 (includes camp (MIN)	1,629 (males) (camp 386)	435
FEDERAL CORRECTIONAL INSTITUTIONS			
FCI Ashland, KY opened 1940 (MED)	516	1,106 (males)	345
FCI Bastrop, TX opened 1979 (MED)	472	802 (males)	263
FCI Big Spring, TX opened 1979 (MIN)	821	797 (males)	175
FCI Butner, NC opened 1976 (MED)	427	763 (males)	334
FCI Danbury, CT opened 1940 (MED)	615 (includes camp) (MIN)	1,017 (camp 171)	311
FCI El Reno, OK opened 1933 (MED)	852 (includes camp) (MIN)	1,606 (males)	437
FCI Littleton, CO opened 1940	455	923 (youthful males, 18-26)	205
FCI Fairton, NJ opened 1990 (MED)	550	44 (males)	272
FCI Ft. Worth, TX opened 1971 (MIN)	657	927 (males)	332
FCI Jesup, GA opened 1990 (MED)	743 (includes camp) (MIN)	125 (males)	288
FCI Latuna, NM opened 1932 (MED)	657 (includes camp) (MIN)	976 (males) (camp 289)	295
FCI Lexington, KY opened 1974 (MIN)	1,291	1,862 (males/females)	480
FCI Guard Road Lompoc, CA opened 1970 as camp	464	630 (males)	188
FCI Loretto, PA opened 1984 (MED)	274	528 (males)	224
FCI Marianna, FL opened 1988 (MAX CLOSE)	710 (includes camp) (MIN)	269 (males/females)	332
FCI Bradford, PA opened 1989 (MED)	798 (includes camp) (MIN)	967 (males) (camp 201)	266
FCI Memphis, TN opened 1977 (MED)	528 (includes Memphis Detention Center)	1,067 (males)	273
FCI Milan, MI opened 1933 (MED)	732 (includes Milan Detention Center)	1,439 (males)	259

Table 5.1—continued

FEDERAL CORRECTIONAL INSTITUTIONS (cont'd.)			
Facility	Rated Capacity	Average Daily Population 3/90	Number of Employees
FCI Morgantown, WV opened 1968 (YCA)	358	580 (youthful offenders, 18-26)	170
FCI Otisville, NY opened 1980 (MED)	438	867 (males)	310
FCI Oxford, WI opened 1973 (MED)	664 (includes camp) (MIN)	877 (males) (camp 107)	338
FCI Petersburg, VA opened 1930 (YCA)	701 (includes camp) (MIN)	854 (youthful offenders, 18-26)	366
FCI Phoenix, AZ opened 1985 (MED) *satellite camp opened 1988	654 (includes camp) (MIN) 136	983 (males) 199 (males)	334
FCI Dublin, CA opened 1974 (MED)	440 (includes detention center)	712 (males/females)	285
FCI Ray Brook, NY opened 1980 (MED)	510	1,018 (males)	262
FCI Safford, AZ opened 1958 (MED)	221	395 (males)	171
FCI Sandstone, MN opened 1939 (MED)	510	834 (males)	224
FCI Seagoville, TX opened 1940 (MED)	438	753 (males)	222
FCI Sheridan, OR opened 1989 (MED)	760 (includes camp) (MIN)	869 (males) (camp 101)	321
FCI Tallahassee, FL opened 1938 (MED)	577	1,056 (males)	300
FCI Terminal Island, CA opened 1955 (MED)	462	1,144 (males)	320
FCI Texarkana, TX opened 1940 (MED)	646 (includes Texarkana Prison Camp) (MIN)	963 (males) (camp 270)	274
FCI Three Rivers, TX opened late-1990 (MED)	721 (includes camp) (MIN)	N/A (males)	254
FCI Tucson, AZ opened 1982 (MED)	306	651 (males/females)	104
METROPOLITAN CORRECTIONAL CENTERS			
Chicago MCC opened 1975 (MAX, MED, MIN)	363	638 (males/females)	206
Los Angeles MCC opened 1988 (MAX CLOSE, MED, MIN)	544	900 (males/females)	252
Miami MCC opened 1976 (MAX, MED, MIN)	424	1,159 (males)	240
New York MCC opened 1975 (MAX, MED, MIN)	473	841 (males/females)	260
San Diego MCC opened 1975 (MAX, MED, MIN)	546	822 (males/females)	220

Table 5.1—continued

MEDICAL CENTERS			
Facility	**Rated Capacity**	**Average Daily Population 3/90**	**Number of Employees**
Federal Medical Center Rochester, MN opened 1985 (MED)	513	678 (males/females)	400
Medical Center for Federal Prisoners Springfield, MO opened 1933	1,027	961	687
PRISON CAMPS			
FPC Alderson, WV opened 1927 (MIN)	590	824 (females)	228
FPC Boran, CA opened 1979 (MIN)	316	509 (males)	135
FPC Duluth, MN opened 1983 (MIN)	699	700 (males)	142
FPC Eglin AFB Eglin, FL opened 1962 (MIN)	480	874 (males)	134
FPC El Paso, TX opened 1989 (MIN)	93	188 (males)	63

Source: Compiled from the *Directory of Juvenile and Adult Correctional Departments, Institutions, Agencies and Paroling Authorities* (1991), pp. 465-490. Laurel, MD: American Correctional Association. Copyright 1991 by the American Correctional Association. Used with permission.

The Bureau is currently building facilities and gearing for more expansion. As noted above, the federal prisoner population increased by 18.5% from year-end 1988 to year-end 1989. The change in federal sentencing policy to determinate sentencing and abolition of parole, together with intensified federal law enforcement efforts, especially in the area of drug smuggling and related offense areas, promise a dramatic rise in the federal prisoner population within the next few years. The actual effects of these changes are difficult to predict. One large variable to consider is the rate at which new federal facilities may be constructed (as part of his war on drugs package, President Bush suggested the need to channel as much as $1 billion into federal prison construction). The Bureau of Justice Statistics placed the total rated capacity of the Bureau's facilities at year-end 1989 at 32,494, meaning that the Bureau's facilities as a whole were operating at 163% of rated capacity. Obviously, space is an important factor, but one could conservatively predict that the federal prisoner population will reach 100,000 by year-end 1994, if present trends continue.

Community supervision for federal offenders, probation, and parole, is provided by the agents of the U.S. Probation Service. As noted above, these agents carry out their responsibilities under the auspices of the U.S. District Courts. This makes federal probation organizationally a bit complicated. With federal probation officers attached to the district courts and the chief probation officer working closely with the presiding judge of the district, federal probation is not actually as centralized as the federal prison system. At the beginning of 1988 approximately 60,000 persons (45,000+ males and 14,000+ females) were in a federal probation status, and approximately 18,500 persons (17,400+ males and 1,100+ females) were in a federal parole status. At that time, approximately 38% of federal offenders under correctional authority were incarcerated and approximately 62% were under community supervision. As the changes at the federal level produce effects, one may wish to monitor this ratio as one way to examine the place of incarceration as a federal government strategy. Probation and parole supervision are discussed in Chapters 13 and 14.

Parole release decisions at the federal level have been and still are a function of the U.S. Parole Commission. Parole is discussed in Chapter 14. With the implementation of determinate sentencing guidelines in 1988, parole at the federal level has been abolished. Those sentenced under the new guidelines are under a mandatory release mechanism (see Chapter 14). Those who entered federal facilities prior to implementation of the guidelines still fall within the scope of authority of the Parole Commission. The Commission will continue to function until that category of persons has been cycled.

Arrangements in the States

The most common pattern of arrangements for corrections in the states is a combination of local government, state government, and federal government efforts taking place simultaneously. One could say that such an arrangement is a decentralized pattern. Such arrangements allow for local control and local influence of certain corrections efforts (i.e., jails, local probation, juvenile services) while other efforts involving those sentenced to state authority or those sentenced under federal authority are separately administered and carried out.

Decentralized arrangements are sometimes criticized on the basis of duplication of services, the potential for competition for resources available within a given locale, the lack of central accountability for efforts, and for the potential situation of disparity of correctional practice across and within jurisdictions. The strongest arguments for such arrangements focus on the potential for aligning correctional practices (ostensibly those that are locally controlled) with the perceived needs and expectations of the general population within a given locale—community-oriented practice.

In some states (Delaware, South Dakota, Tennessee, Virginia, and West Virginia) corrections functions are more highly unified from the state level. In other words, with the exception of jails and related programs, corrections functions (such as adult probation and parole services, as well as juvenile probation and aftercare services) are provided through the central authority of the State Department of Corrections. Here the typical pattern is to divide the state into regions or service areas with offenders assigned to field service offices all administratively identified with and organized under the central authority. Arguments in favor of such an arrangement emphasize central accountability (instead of several agencies performing similar tasks, with control spread among several governing bodies, control and administration are unified in one agency), greater efficiency in allocation of resources (one large budget rather than many smaller ones, with the possibility present to allocate resources across jurisdictions, making it more likely that resources are allocated according to identified needs), the possibility of closer monitoring of practices to provide greater consistency (consistent criteria and authority to evaluate across jurisdictions), and benefits of economy of scale (flexibility in use of personnel and resources, consolidation of functions and positions). Criticisms of such arrangements typically focus on big bureaucracy (driving locus of control away from the operational setting), the loss of local control of programs and practices, notions that such arrangements do not necessarily guarantee efficiency in allocation of resources (i.e. some areas could finance local programs more generously than might occur where one bigger budget is spread through many regions) and so on.

These variations in arrangements reflect differences in interface primarily between state and local governments. There are other permutations of arrangements, particularly within the state-level of government, dividing authority among agencies at that level, which are discussed below in examination of the State Department of Corrections.

Departments and Divisions of Corrections

In each of the states, there is a large, complex organization, a Department of Corrections or a Division of Corrections. These are part of the executive branch of government. These agencies vary in size, level of funding, structure, staffing, and so on. Beyond this these agencies vary in terms of the correctional functions included within the authority and responsibility of the agency. Table 5.2 shows that all of these agencies have authority and responsibility for adult corrections (meaning those whose sentences place them under the authority of the agency; many offenders will have sentences imposed which place them in correctional efforts carried out by local government agencies) and some have authority and responsibility for certain juvenile efforts, in particular, operation of juvenile institutions.

Table 5.2 also shows that 48 states have a separate executive agency, a Department of Corrections, and two states maintain a Division of Corrections, where the mainline agency is organized as a component of a larger executive agency, a Department of Human Services. (Chapter 6 presents a conceptual image of a Department of Corrections and discusses concerns relevant to such agencies operating as correctional systems at the state level of government.) Obviously, for whatever reasons, the various states have arrived at different arrangements for the distribution of corrections functions at the state level. In a rational sense, any arrangement that facilitates effective and efficient accomplishment of correctional aims could be deemed appropriate. However, just as there is controversy over correctional aims, there is controversy over the appropriate arrangements for organizing correctional efforts within the states.

The arrangements present in the states have been arrived at over time, with some degree of rationality, through political interaction and accommodation, with particular interests being important factors in shaping decisions. In most states these arrangements have been in place for so long that questions concerning their appropriateness would give way quickly to the inertia of big government. Those who do question present arrangements tend to focus on issues such as duplication of structure, duplication of efforts, ambiguity in operationalizing goals and objectives because of fragmentation of efforts, and so on. Some employ the rational logic of centralization, asking whether effectiveness and efficiency would not be better approached by having a superagency that coordinates state-level and local-level corrections efforts, centrally allocating resources, setting policies to dovetail efforts in unified directions, monitoring and evaluating with authority to develop and implement rational changes.

Table 5.2
Positions of Corrections Departments in State Governments (as of June 30, 1990)

State	Adult Departments	Juvenile Departments	Comment and Date of Change
AL	Dept of Corrections	Dept of Youth Services	Bd abolished by court 1979
AK	Dept of Corrections	DHSS-Div of Family & Youth Svcs	DOC separated from DHSS 1981, made independent 3/84
AZ	Dept of Corrections	Dept of Juv Corrections	Ad & Juv from independent bd 1969; Juv separated 7/90
AR	B-Dept of Correction	B-DHS-Div of Children and Family Svcs	DOC created 1968
CA	YACA-Dept of Corrections; Dept of Youth Authority		Changed from Dept Health & Welfare 1980
CO	Dept of Corrections	DI-Div of Youth Svcs	DOC formed 8/77 from Dept Institutions; reorg 12/87
CT	Dept of Correction	Dept Children & Youth Svcs	
DE	Dept of Correction	DSCYF-Div of Youth Rehab Svcs	Ad & Juv changed from DHS 1975; Juv changed from DOC 1984
FL	Dept of Corrections	DHRS-Children, Youth & Fam Prog Office	Ad changed from DHS to DOR 1975, to DOC 1978; DYS formed 1981
GA	B-Dept of Corrections	DHR-Div of Youth Svcs	Ad dept created 1972; name changed to DOC 1985
HI	DPS-Dept of Corrections		DOC est 7/87; moved under DPS 7/90
ID	B-Dept of Correction	DHW-Div of Family & Svcs	DFS est 1/90
IL	Dept of Corrections		Separated from DPS 1970
IN	Dept of Correction		Separated from DHS 1953
IA	B-Dept of Corrections	DHS-Bur of Ad, Children & Fam Svcs	Created DHS 1968; DOC created 1984
KS	Dept of Corrections	DSRS-Youth Services	Ad changed from DHS 1977
KY	Corrections Cabinet	CHHS/DSS-Div Children's Residential Svcs	Changed from DJ 1981, changed to Corr Cabinet 1982
LA	DPSC-Corrections Svcs		Reorg 1984, 1985 (formerly DOC-Ad, HHR-Juv)
ME	Dept of Corrections		Changed from Mental Health & Corr 1981
MD	DPSCS-Div of Correction	Dept of Juvenile Svcs	Juv to independent agency 1987, dept created 1989
MA	HS-Dept of Correction	HS-Dept Youth Svcs	
MI	Dept of Corrections	DSS/OCYS/BJJS-Residential Care Div	DOC created 1953
MN	Dept of Corrections		
MS	Dept of Corrections	DHS-Office of Youth Svcs	Ad changed to dept status 1978; juv formerly div in DOYS
MO	Dept of Corrections	DSS-Div Youth Services	Ad changed from DHS 1983
MT	DI-Corrections Division	Dept Family Services	Corr Div created under DI 1975; Juv trans to DFS 7/87
NE	Dept Correctional Services		
NV	B-Dept of Prisons	DHR-Youth Services Div	Ad changed from Nevada State Prisons 1982
NH	Dept of Corrections	DHHS/CYS/BC-Bur of Residential Svcs	Ad DOC est 1983; Juv trans from Bur of Secure Care 1985
NJ	Dept of Corrections		DOC created from Dept Institutions & Agencies 1976
NM	C-Corrections Dept	YA-Juv Facilities & Programs Div	Ad changed from DPS 1980; Juv changed to separate dept 1989
NY	C-Dept Correctional Svcs	ED-Div for Youth	
NC	Dept of Correction	DHR-Div of Youth Svcs	
ND	DCR-Div of Adult Svcs; Div of Juvenile Svcs		Ad & Juv formerly Dir of Institutions
OH	Dept Rehab & Corr	Dept Youth Svcs	Created from Mental Health & Corr 1971; DYS formerly Ohio Yth Cmsn
OK	B-Dept of Corrections	DHS-Div Children & Youth Svcs	DOC est 1967
OR	Dept of Corrections	DHR-Children's Svcs Div	Est DHS 1971 (Ad), created DOC 1987
PA	Dept of Corrections	DPW/OCYF-Bur of State Child & Youth Prog	Ad changed from Dept of Justice 1980; DOC created 1984
RI	Dept of Corrections	DCTF-Div of Juv Corr Svcs	Juv separated 1980
SC	B-Dept of Corrections	B-Dept Youth Svcs	DYS merged with Placement & Aftercare 1981
SD	B-Dept of Corrections		Separated from DSS 1977; DOC created 1989
TN	Dept of Correction	Dept of Youth Development	DYD separated 1989
TX	B-TDCJ-Institutional Div	B-Texas Youth Commission	Reorganized 1989/90 to TDCJ
UT	Dept of Corrections	DHS-Div of Youth Corrections	Ad reorganized 1983 from DSS; juv from DSS to DHS 1990
VT	AHS-Dept of Corrections	AHS-Dept of Social & Rehab Svcs	
VA	B-Dept of Corrections	Dept of Youth & Fam Svcs	DYFS created 1990
WA	Dept of Corrections	DSHS-Div of Juv Rehab	DOC separated from DSHS 1981
WV	Div of Corrections		Changed from Dept of Public Institutions 1976; to Div of Corr 1990
WI	Dept of Corrections	DHHS-Div Youth Svcs	DOC separated from DHSS 1990
WY	B-Bd of Charities & Reform		

Notes: B = Exec, Admin or Advisory Board; C = Commission; DHSS, DSS etc. = umbrella agencies (see states listings)

Source: American Correctional Association (1989). In the *Directory of Juvenile and Adult Correctional Departments, Institutions, Agencies and Paroling Authorities Directory, 1991.* Laurel, MD: ACA Research Department. Courtesy American Correctional Association.

Table 5.3
Prisoners Under the Jurisdiction of State or Federal Correctional Authorities, by Region and Jurisdiction, Yearend 1989 and 1990

Region and jurisdiction	Total			Sentenced to more than 1 year			
	Advance 1990	Final 1989	Percent change, 1989-90	Advance 1990	Final 1989	Percent change, 1989-90	Incarcer-ation rate, 1990ᵃ
U.S. total	771,243	712,557	8.2%	739,763	680,955	8.6%	293
Federal	65,526	59,171	10.7	52,208	47,168	10.7	21
State	705,717	653,386	8.0	687,555	633,787	8.5	272
Northeast	123,394	113,965	8.3%	119,062	109,394	8.8%	232
Connecticut	10,500	9,301	12.9	7,771	6,309	23.2	238
Maine	1,523	1,455	4.7	1,480	1,432	3.4	118
Massachusetts	8,273	7,524	10.0	7,899	7,268	8.7	132
New Hampshire	1,342	1,166	15.1	1,342	1,166	15.1	117
New Jersey	21,128	19,439	8.7	21,128	19,439	8.7	271
New York	54,895	51,227	7.2	54,895	51,227	7.2	304
Pennsylvania	22,290	20,469	8.9	22,281	20,458	8.9	183
Rhode Island	2,394	2,479	-3.4	1,585	1,469	7.9	157
Vermont	1,049	905	15.9	681	626	8.8	117
Midwest	145,802	136,338	6.9%	145,493	136,042	6.9%	239
Illinois	27,516	24,712	11.3	27,516	24,712	11.3	234
Indiana	12,732	12,341	3.2	12,615	12,220	3.2	223
Iowa	3,967	3,584	10.7	3,967	3,584	10.7	139
Kansas	5,777	5,616	2.9	5,777	5,616	2.9	227
Michigan	34,267	31,639	8.3	34,267	31,639	8.3	366
Minnesota	3,176	3,103	2.4	3,176	3,103	2.4	72
Missouri	14,919	13,921	7.2	14,919	13,921	7.2	287
Nebraska	2,403	2,393	.4	2,286	2,278	.4	140
North Dakota	483	451	7.1	435	404	7.7	67
Ohio	31,855	30,538	4.3	31,855	30,538	4.3	289
South Dakota	1,345	1,252	7.4	1,345	1,252	7.4	187
Wisconsin	7,362	6,788	8.5	7,335	6,775	8.3	149
South	282,952	262,115	7.9%	274,813	252,614	8.8%	315
Alabama	15,665	13,907	12.6	15,365	13,575	13.2	370
Arkansas	6,766	6,409	5.6	6,718	6,306	6.5	277
Delaware	3,506	3,458	1.4	2,231	2,284	-2.3	321
District of Col.	9,121	10,039	-9.1	6,660	6,735	-1.1	1,125
Florida	44,387	39,999	11.0	44,387	39,966	11.1	336
Georgia	22,345	20,885	7.0	21,605	19,619	10.1	327
Kentucky	9,023	8,289	8.9	9,023	8,289	8.9	241
Louisiana	18,599	17,257	7.8	18,599	17,257	7.8	427
Maryland	17,798	16,514	7.8	16,684	15,378	8.5	347
Mississippi	8,375	7,911	5.9	8,179	7,700	6.2	311
North Carolina	18,412	17,454	5.5	17,713	16,628	6.5	264
Oklahoma	12,322	11,608	6.2	12,322	11,608	6.2	383
South Carolina	17,319	15,720	10.2	16,208	14,808	9.5	451
Tennessee	10,388	10,630	-2.3	10,388	10,630	-2.3	207
Texas	50,042	44,022	13.7	50,042	44,022	13.7	290
Virginia	17,319	16,477	5.1	17,124	16,273	5.2	274
West Virginia	1,565	1,536	1.9	1,565	1,536	1.9	85
West	153,569	140,968	8.9%	148,187	135,737	9.2%	276
Alaska	2,622	2,744	-4.4	1,851	1,908	-3.0	348
Arizona	14,261	13,251	7.6	13,781	12,726	8.3	375
California	97,309	87,297	11.5	94,122	84,388	11.6	311
Colorado	7,018	6,908	1.6	7,018	6,908	1.6	209
Hawaii	2,533	2,464	2.8	1,708	1,752	-2.5	150
Idaho	2,074	1,850	12.1	2,074	1,850	12.1	201
Montana	1,425	1,328	7.3	1,409	1,328	6.1	174
Nevada	5,322	5,112	4.1	5,322	5,112	4.1	444
New Mexico	2,961	2,934	1.0	2,879	2,759	4.3	184
Oregon	6,436	6,744	-4.6	6,436	6,744	-4.6	221
Utah	2,503	2,394	4.6	2,482	2,368	4.8	143
Washington	7,995	6,928	15.4	7,995	6,928	15.4	162
Wyoming	1,110	1,016	9.3	1,110	1,016	9.3	237

Note: The advance count of prisoners is conducted immediately after the calendar year ends. Prisoner counts for 1989 may differ from those reported in previous publications. Counts for 1990 are subject to revision as updated figures become available. Explanatory notes for each jurisdiction are reported in the appendix.
ᵃThe number of prisoners with sentences of more than 1 year per 100,000 resident population.

Source: Bureau of Justice Statistics (1991). "Prisoners in 1990," p. 2. Washington, DC: U.S. Department of Justice, May.

Making changes to centralize may make logical sense, but such changes require realignments that encounter political resistance. This resistance may come from other governmental agencies, from interest groups concerned with the effects or potential effects of changes, from other interested parties, and from within the agencies and organizations to be most directly affected. Realignments may mean eliminating positions, changing networks of influence and control, changing the ways of doing business to which many have become accustomed, introducing scrutiny that may be threatening to some or many, and so on. Making changes to bring local agencies and organizations within a centralized structure means changing the nature of the relationship between local and state governments, reducing local autonomy, changing the locus of control and authority, changing funding patterns and perhaps staffing patterns, among other possibilities.

Fragmentation, lack of coordination, lack of centralized leadership, and related issues are frequently raised and directed at the states. While resistance may be overcome, and some form of centralization could occur (some states have created monitoring agencies which formulate standards and have some authority to determine and induce compliance), such changes are difficult to achieve. Among the difficulties to be surmounted by those who would advocate extensive centralization in states is the problem of showing not how the given world of corrections would be different, rather how the given world of corrections would be improved in terms of ultimate outcomes.

At present, one should return to the understanding that correctional functions are divided, both at the state level in many states and between state-level government and local governments to a greater or lesser extent in all states. One should also remember that correctional services of various sorts are provided in every state by private profit-making or non-profit organizations for both state-level and local-level efforts.

Let us turn to a more direct examination of state-level correctional functions. The remaining sections of this chapter cover some basic aspects of the corrections enterprise such as prison populations, budgets, numbers of probationers and parolees, and other descriptive details.

As noted above, incarceration of adults is a major function for all the Departments of Corrections. Table 5.3 shows prisoners under the jurisdiction of state or federal authorities, by region and state, year-end 1989 and advance 1990. Twenty-five states show increases of 8% or more during the one-year period. Rhode Island (23.2%), Washington (15.4%), New Hampshire (15.1%), and Texas (13.7%) show the greatest percentage increases during this period (please note that, except for Texas, relatively smaller numbers result in larger percentage increases as compared to states such as California, New York, and Florida where the already very large numbers of prisoners mean proportionately larger numbers are required for such increases). Oregon (-4.6%), Arizona (-3.0%), Hawaii (-2.5%), Delaware (-2.3%), and Tennessee (-2.3%) showed small decreases in prisoner population. Obviously, some state Departments of Corrections are dealing with very large numbers of prisoners, and some, as might be expected based on general population with far fewer, even with very small numbers of prisoners.

The overall growth of the prison population in recent years is startling, and most of the states' Departments of Corrections are straining their resources to cope with the situation. Table 5.4 shows the percent change in prison population from 1980 to 1989, by state and region, and Table 5.5 shows the overall (entire United States) change in number of inmates, annual percent change, and total percent change during the time period 1985-86 through 1989-90.

On December 31, 1990, the Bureau of Justice Statistics noted that the number of sentenced prisoners per 100,000 residents (in the United States as a whole) was 293, setting a new record (1991:1). Table 5.6 shows the 10 states with the largest prison populations and the highest incarceration rates (all 10 over the national rate) on that date.

It is apparent that the incarceration function for Departments of Corrections in most states is barely under control. Overcrowding is a major problem. Incarceration in most states is assuming a greater proportion of the corrections budget, and corrections budgets are assuming greater proportions of overall state budgets. Table 5.7 shows correctional departments' operating and capital expenditure budgets as of June 30, 1990. The increase in prisoner population from 1988 to 1989 (reported above) alone "translates into a nationwide need for nearly 1,600 new bedspaces *per week*" (BJS, 1990:1) [Emphasis added]. Considering these increases, it is reasonable to assume a continuing need for more and more resources to be devoted to corrections budgets, particularly for carrying out the incarceration function.

Table 5.4
Percent Change in Sentenced Prison Population from 1980 to 1989, by Region and State

Region	Percent Increase									
	0-49%		50%-79%		80%-99%		100%-149%		150% or more	
Northeast					Vermont	80.4	Rhode Island	140.1	New Hampshire	257.7
							New York	136.7	New Jersey	249.4
							Massachusetts	130.7	Pennsylvania	162.0
							Connecticut	129.4		
							Maine	113.4		
Midwest	Iowa	44.6	Wisconsin	70.2	Indiana	94.6	Missouri	143.1	Ohio	162.0
			Nebraska	65.5			Illinois	130.4		
			Minnesota	55.1			Kansas	125.4		
							North Dakota	118.4		
							Michigan	109.9		
							South Dakota	109.7		
South	Texas	36.5	Georgia	64.6	S. Carolina	99.4	Dist. of Col.	149.0		
	W. Virginia	22.2	Tennessee	50.4	Maryland	98.9	Oklahoma	138.2		
	N. Carolina	15.5			Florida	97.7	Kentucky	131.0		
					Louisiana	94.1	Arkansas	116.6		
					Virginia	89.6	Delaware	115.0		
							Alabama	113.2		
							Mississippi	103.0		
West			Washington	57.5	Wyoming	92.1	New Mexico	138.6	California	262.5
					Montana	84.6	Idaho	126.4	Alaska	234.2
					Colorado	80.5	Oregon	112.6	Nevada	192.9
									Arizona	191.9
									Hawaii	157.4
									Utah	153.8
Regional totals			South	74.8			Midwest	111.2	West	202.8
									Northeast	155.3
U.S. summary							States	114.0		
							Federal	128.8		
							Total	115.0		

Note: Sentenced prisoners are those with sentences of more than 1 year.

Source: Bureau of Justice Statistics (1990). "Prisoners in 1989," p. 3. Washington, DC: U.S. Department of Justice, May.

Table 5.5
Annual Change in the Number of Sentenced Prisoners Under the Jurisdiction of State or Federal Correctional Authorities, by Region and Jurisdiction, Yearend 1985 through 1990

Region and jurisdiction	Annual change					Annual percent change				
	85-86	86-87	87-88	88-89	89-90	1986	1987	1988	1989	1990
U.S. total	41,516	38,728	44,678	75,465	58,808	8.6%	7.4%	8.0%	12.5%	8.6%
Federal	3,836	2,992	2,584	5,061	5,040	11.7	8.2	6.5	12.0	10.7
State	37,680	35,736	42,094	70,404	53,768	8.4	7.4	8.1	12.5	8.5
Northeast	6,346	8,441	7,243	14,884	9,668	8.8%	10.7%	8.3%	15.7%	8.8%
Connecticut	283	311	86	1,586	1,462	7.0	7.2	1.9	33.6	23.2
Maine	15	(4)	(18)	212	48	1.2	-.3	-1.5	17.4	3.4
Massachusetts	236	576	483	813	631	4.6	10.7	8.1	12.6	8.7
New Hampshire	99	85	152	147	176	14.5	10.9	17.5	14.4	15.1
New Jersey*	685	3,949	967	2,503	1,689	6.0	32.9	6.1	14.8	8.7
New York	3,942	2,393	3,700	6,685	3,668	11.4	6.2	9.1	15.0	7.2
Pennsylvania	1,046	1,081	1,637	2,575	1,823	7.4	7.1	10.1	14.4	8.9
Rhode Island	44	(16)	188	290	116	4.6	-1.6	19.0	24.6	7.9
Vermont	(4)	66	48	73	55	-.9	15.0	9.5	13.2	8.8
Midwest	7,481	8,141	9,507	15,795	9,451	7.9%	7.9%	8.6%	13.1%	6.9%
Illinois	822	394	1,231	3,631	2,804	4.4	2.0	6.2	17.2	11.3
Indiana	196	671	637	949	395	2.0	6.7	6.0	8.4	3.2
Iowa	90	74	183	550	383	3.3	2.7	6.4	18.1	10.7
Kansas	613	436	154	(319)	161	13.0	8.2	2.7	-5.4	2.9
Michigan	2,987	3,137	3,733	4,027	2,628	16.8	15.1	15.6	14.6	8.3
Minnesota	119	84	253	304	73	5.1	3.4	9.9	10.9	2.4
Missouri	513	1,048	819	1,745	998	5.2	10.2	7.2	14.3	7.2
Nebraska	221	9	145	170	8	12.8	.5	7.4	8.1	.4
North Dakota	(14)	19	34	(10)	31	-3.7	5.3	8.9	-2.4	7.7
Ohio	1,599	1,777	2,222	4,076	1,317	7.7	7.9	9.2	15.4	4.3
South Dakota	13	83	(117)	236	93	1.3	7.9	-10.3	23.2	7.4
Wisconsin	322	409	213	436	560	6.0	7.2	3.5	6.9	8.3
South	11,683	8,823	13,143	23,669	22,199	6.0%	4.3%	6.1%	10.3%	8.8%
Alabama	755	1,098	(245)	1,218	1,790	7.0	9.5	-1.9	9.9	13.2
Arkansas	90	740	520	345	412	2.0	15.7	9.6	5.8	6.5
Delaware	197	203	42	83	(53)	11.2	10.4	1.9	3.8	-2.3
District of Columbia	183	827	700	421	(75)	4.0	17.3	12.5	6.7	-1.1
Florida	3,746	132	2,321	5,285	4,421	13.2	.4	7.2	15.2	11.1
Georgia	487	1,874	294	1,601	1,986	3.2	11.8	1.7	8.9	10.1
Kentucky	307	1,149	717	1,135	734	6.2	21.7	11.1	15.9	8.9
Louisiana	410	1,075	867	1,015	1,342	3.0	7.5	5.6	6.2	7.8
Maryland	256	353	660	1,806	1,306	2.1	2.8	5.1	13.3	8.5
Mississippi	353	158	532	449	479	5.7	2.4	7.9	6.2	6.2
North Carolina	366	(255)	133	377	1,085	2.3	-1.6	.8	2.3	6.5
Oklahoma	1,378	(69)	809	1,160	714	16.5	-.7	8.4	11.1	6.2
South Carolina	1,114	840	1,040	1,906	1,400	11.2	7.6	8.8	14.8	9.5
Tennessee	464	48	2,136	855	(242)	6.5	.6	28.0	8.7	-2.3
Texas	1,002	287	1,616	3,585	6,020	2.7	.7	4.2	8.9	13.7
Virginia	828	386	997	2,345	851	7.1	3.1	7.7	16.8	5.2
West Virginia	(253)	(23)	4	83	29	-14.7	-1.6	.3	5.7	1.9
West	12,170	10,331	12,201	16,056	12,450	14.3%	10.6%	11.4%	13.4%	9.2%
Alaska	136	101	95	46	(57)	8.9	6.1	5.4	2.5	-3.0
Arizona	765	1,520	1,020	1,148	1,055	9.2	16.8	9.7	9.9	8.3
California	9,399	7,087	8,968	10,558	9,784	19.4	12.3	13.8	14.3	11.6
Colorado	418	1,004	957	1,143	110	12.3	26.4	19.9	19.8	1.6
Hawaii	93	11	(22)	242	(44)	6.5	.7	-1.4	16.0	-2.5
Idaho	104	(13)	149	266	224	7.7	-.9	10.4	16.8	12.1
Montana	(18)	96	64	57	81	-1.6	8.6	5.3	4.5	6.1
Nevada	780	(117)	447	231	210	20.7	-2.6	10.1	4.7	4.1
New Mexico	194	280	137	36	120	9.2	12.1	5.3	1.3	4.3
Oregon	394	687	534	753	(308)	9.0	14.4	9.8	12.6	-4.6
Utah	122	92	107	424	114	7.5	5.3	5.8	21.8	4.8
Washington	(316)	(472)	(315)	1,112	1,067	-4.6	-7.1	-5.1	19.1	15.4
Wyoming	99	55	60	40	94	13.0	6.4	6.6	4.1	9.3

Note: Sentenced prisoners are those with sentences of more than 1 year.

( ) Indicates a decline in the number of sentenced prisoners.

*In 1987 New Jersey began to include in its jurisdiction count the number of State-sentenced prisoners held in local jails because of prison crowding.

Source: Bureau of Justice Statistics (1991). "Prisoners in 1990," p. 4. Washington, DC: U.S. Department of Justice, May.

Table 5.6
The Prison Situation Among the States, Yearend 1990

10 States with the largest 1990 prison populations	Number of inmates	10 States with the highest incarceration rates, 1990*	Prisoners per 100,000 residents	10 States with the largest percent increases in prison population			
				1989-90	Percent increase	1985-90*	Percent increase
California	97,309	South Carolina	451	Vermont	15.9%	Colorado	107.3%
New York	54,895	Nevada	444	Washington	15.4	New Hampshire	96.5
Texas	50,042	Louisiana	427	New Hampshire	15.1	California	94.0
Florida	44,387	Oklahoma	383	Texas	13.7	Michigan	93.0
Michigan	34,267	Arizona	375	Connecticut	12.9	New Jersey	86.4
Ohio	31,855	Alabama	370	Alabama	12.6	Rhode Island	83.3
Illinois	27,516	Michigan	366	Idaho	12.1	Connecticut	70.8
Georgia	22,345	Alaska	348	California	11.5	Arizona	67.2
Pennsylvania	22,290	Maryland	347	Illinois	11.3	New York	59.1
New Jersey	21,128	Florida	336	Iowa	10.7	Pennsylvania	56.7

Note: The District of Columbia as a wholly urban jurisdiction is excluded.
*Prisoners with sentences of more than 1 year.

Source: Bureau of Justice Statistics (1991). "Prisoners in 1990," p. 4. Washington, DC: U.S. Department of Justice, May.

The search for relief from spiraling costs has led at least one state, Minnesota, to attempt a different strategy. In that state (1989 prisoner population low at 3,103) the recent strategy has been to place emphasis on development of more community corrections alternatives and on keeping the prison population as small as possible. The state has subsidized local intiatives by directly funding local governments when a convicted offender who otherwise would be assigned to the State Department of Corrections is placed in a community alternative program. In other words, local government receives a portion of the amount of money this offender would have cost if incarcerated under authority of the Department of Corrections, as an inducement to design and implement alternative programs. The long-term effects of this strategy are not yet known. Short-term effects appear to be as intended, at least from the perspective of state-level authority—holding down the prison population and holding down costs associated with incarceration.

Table 5.7
Operating and Capital Expenditures Budgets (as of June 30, 1990)

Fiscal information for adult and juvenile state departments of corrections; biennial budgets have been halved and are noted "B".

ADULT CORRECTIONS

State	Operating Budget	Capital Expenditures Budget	Appropriated Funds	Bond Money	Other Funds	Funds from Previous Year(s)
AL	165,376,526	0				
AK	96,796,000	1,100,000	1,100,000			
AZ	250,117,700	9,156,300	8,640,900		380,000[1]	388,668
AR	54,474,006	23,967,480	2,571,540	21,395,940		
CA	2,288,819,000	2,130,519,532	19,438,000			1,274,336,000
CO	151,987,798	152,000,000	107,000,000			45,000,000
CT	231,468,548	222,200,000		242,200,000		195,932,600*
DE	65,867,209	1,199,328	550,674	648,654	373,800	880,601*
FL	724,033,969	132,148,354	132,148,354			
GA	471,785,537	244,718,360	117,772,360	117,420,000	9,526,000[2]	
HI	68,050,586[B]	86,420,000	86,420,000			
ID	34,613,400	6,321,900				
IL	562,939,500	167,320,500	1,786,000	21,970,000		143,564,500
IN	303,970,216	92,100,000	92,100,000			
IA	109,700,970	0				
KS	126,586,321	35,279,452	1,647,430	29,995,719		3,636,303
KY	86,966,000	24,627,500[B]		19,695,150	4,932,350[3]	
LA	280,476,083	2,260,000		2,260,000		
ME	55,496,447	26,392,610		24,092,610		2,300,000
MD	303,099,785	69,135,000				
MA	224,190,023	0				
MI	803,392,600	4,460,000				
MN	142,475,947	13,121,000	13,121,000			
MS	84,803,636	1,400,000				
MO	204,542,695	2,436,778	2,312,760	124,018		
MT	25,007,837	1,230,600	1,230,600			
NE	57,105,010	3,754,693	2,630,360		1,124,333[5]	
NV	72,646,487	30,737,861[B]	19,689,861	11,048,000		
NH	31,050,616[B]	0				
NJ	558,119,000	88,652,993		82,764,871		5,888,122
NM	101,174,200	0				
NY	1,176,500,000	227,900,000		227,900,000		990,700,000*
NC	398,665,793	1,955,600	1,955,600			9,025,574*
ND	16,719,213	1,908,232	168,733	1,430,670	300,000[6]	8,828
OH	509,077,124	96,673,417		96,673,417		
OK	171,981,898	19,927,917	19,218,936		708,981[5]	
OR	78,766,051[B]	31,491,190[B]	4,057,914		58,924,464	
PA	334,895,000	12,000,000	12,000,000			
RI	82,783,005	119,000,000			119,000,000[9]	
SC	200,203,690	98,154,656		98,154,656		
SD	22,925,761	17,300,000	17,300,000			
TN	267,737,591	17,000,000	2,500,000	14,500,000		
TX	659,073,946	139,241,245	139,241,245	138,761,245		
UT	64,065,600	30,829,564	30,829,564			
VT	26,245,710	2,782,800		2,782,800		
VA	386,156,142[B]	44,974,940[B]	3,342,440	41,632,500		
WA	231,550,787	185,735,733		185,735,733		
WV	26,829,104	0				
WI	210,720,223	36,960,478		36,960,478		
WY	14,343,500[B]	1,071,777[B]	782,500		75,105[10]	214,172
Total	**13,634,868,010**	**4,544,297,986**	**810,727,207**	**1,334,216,728**	**195,345,033**	**2,671,875,368**
FBP	1,371,882,000	374,358,000	374,358,000			
DC	237,501,000	46,364,000		36,364,000	10,000,000[11]	
NYC	766,105,428	244,539,000	145,640,000		46,694,000	52,205,000
PHL	76,120,000	3,875,000		3,875,000		
GU	8,894,432	1,200,000				1,200,000
CSC	806,998,000	110,000,000				
AB	112,140,107	85,610,000				
BC[12]	147,278,754	38,800,000				
MB	45,588,746	23,025,000				
NB	23,382,400	200,000				
NF	15,882,000	484,000				
NS[12]	27,156,900	624,700				
ON	521,046,257	40,300,000				
PEI	9,353,700	0				
PQ	132,736,000	1,460,000				
SK	37,839,500	1,210,000				
YU[12]	2,527,800	80,000				

Other means of funding: AZ(A) St lands earnings $150,000-300,000; CA(A) Lease purchase $692,700,000; CO(A) Lottery $26,000,000; MN(A) Housing of federal inmates $2,173,000; MO(J) Transfer of funds $1,250,000; NM(A) Use of state lands $6,252,800; OK(A) Lease purchase $471,015; OR(A) Certif of participation $25,305,000; RI(A) State master lease; SC(J) Lease purchase $0 currently; SD(A) Correc facility sale/leaseback $2,000,000; UT(J) Oil revenues, school lunch program, support collections, interest on st lands; WA(A) Lease purchase $0 currently

Table 5.7—continued

JUVENILE CORRECTIONS

State	Operating Budget	Capital Expenditures Budget	Appropriated Funds	Bond Money	Other Funds	Funds from Previous Year(s)
AL	25,140,621	300,000	300,000			
AK	16,837,100	3,400,000	3,400,000			
AZ	34,237,600	244,000	244,000			
AR	8,561,967[B]	188,000[B]	168,000		20,000	
CA	294,971,000	10,086,000		10,086,000		
CO	31,497,823	0				
CT	11,315,536	4,840,000		4,840,000		
DE	12,863,400	3,668,000				
FL	141,861,710	8,526,258	8,526,258			
GA	76,020,170	0				
HI	†					
ID	10,780,200	6,000,000	6,000,000			
IL	†					
IN	†					
IA	8,609,622	0				
KS	15,086,719	632,248	632,248			
KY	22,672,000	3,260,800	2,485,800			775,000
LA	†					
ME	†					
MD	98,741,630	1,068,000	1,340,000			7,482,944+
MA	56,669,667	5,700,000				5,700,000
MI	60,946,600	1,147,000	1,147,000			
MN	†					
MS	9,538,290	1,705,000		1,705,000		
MO	16,977,640	410,896	211,816	199,080	1,250,000[4,+]	1,490,799+
MT	5,683,496	0				
NE	†					
NV	6,167,535	83,235	50,000		33,235	
NH	7,426,769	441,440[B]		441,440		
NJ	†					
NM	28,136,400	434,300				
NY	132,459,300	91,867,000	1,867,000	90,000,000		
NC	46,000,000	366,000	366,000			
ND	†					
OH	107,042,299[B]	26,572,135[6]	221,324	26,757,855	7,805,000[7]	622,946
OK	17,127,271	862,924	862,924			
OR	41,113,815[B]	960,000	960,000			
PA	44,319,000	0				
RI	14,572,245	15,175,000	2,305,000	870,000	12,000,000	
SC	36,934,325	2,042,680	85,920			1,956,760
SD	†					
TN	53,425,700	19,212,000	245,000	18,967,000		
TX	63,895,662	21,952,715	2,108,627	19,844,088		
UT	10,578,314	749,000	749,000			
VT	35,880,244	21,782	21,782			
VA	103,151,219	810,690	481,000		329,690[9]	
WA	47,744,265	6,105,945	2,212,000			3,893,945
WV	†					
WI	†					
WY	3,868,670	1,606,676	439,067	1,161,000		445,676
Total	1,758,855,824	249,274,714	37,429,766	174,871,463	21,437,925	22,368,070
FBP						
DC	39,936,000	1,596,000		1,596,000		
NYC	70,485,000					
PHL						
GU						
CSC						
AB						
BC[12]						
MB						
NB						
NF	10,053,500	9,462,000				
NS[12]						
ON						
PEI						
PQ						
SK	14,141,160	3,000,000				
YU[12]						

Notes:
† Combined adult and juvenile departments
✦ Not included in Capital Expenditures Budget
B Biennial (budget amounts divided to cover 2 years)
1. Endowment
2. Interest
3. Bond funds & invstmt income from bond proceeds
4. Transfer of FY '87 funds
5. Revolving fund
6. Loan anticipation note
7. Bond debt
8. Pub Bldg Auth, st master lease, st asset protection fund
9. Lottery
10. Land income fund
11. Federal
12. Data as of 6/30/89

Bond issues pending/date to be determined: AR(A) $14,000,000; CA(A) $450,000,000/11-90; CA(J) $450,000,000/11-90; CT(J) $48,102,590/1991; HI(A) $35,000,000/4-91; IL(A) Undetermined/3-91; KY(A) $39,390,300/3-90; ME(A) $20,250,000/11-90; NC(A) $75,000,000/7-90 and 200,000,000/11-90; NC(J) $9,000,000/11-90

Source: American Correctional Association (1991). In *Juvenile and Adult Correctional Departments, Institutions, Agencies and Paroling Authorities Directory, 1991.* Laurel, MD: ACA Research Department. Courtesy American Correctional Association.

One should begin to think about strategies within states. It is clear that incarceration is a major dimension of the overall strategy in all states. It is also clear that some states incarcerate a greater percentage of offenders sentenced to state authority than do others. As state governments become more heavily bogged down in resource crunches, it may become much more necessary to bring strategies into high relief and press for greater understanding and more intense dialogue on strategies and options. As discussed in Chapter 15, such considerations have begun, with 21 states already involved in attempts to provide "third-level" alternatives, such as house arrest and use of electronic monitoring.

Along with the dramatic increases in incarceration, with overcrowding, and with increasing strain on resources, has come increasing scrutiny from federal courts. The staff of the National Prison Project, ACLU, monitors the status of litigation and court orders concerning the nation's prison systems. As of January, 1990, "[f]orty-one states (plus D.C., Puerto Rico, and the Virgin Islands) [were] under court order or consent decree to limit population and/or improve conditions in either the entire state system or major facilities. (Thirty-three states [were] under court order or consent decree for overcrowding and conditions while eight states [were] under court order or consent decree for conditions only)" (1990:7). The extent of the incarceration problem should be apparent. Some states (for example, Texas at present) have had federal masters appointed by U.S. judges to oversee and insure compliance with court orders. These problems are discussed further in Chapter 9. For now it is important to understand that those who lead Departments of Corrections and others who have responsibilities connected to Departments of Corrections face significant problems. "Only five states have never been involved in some type of litigation challenging overcrowding and/or conditions in their prisons" (ACLU, 1990:7).

Community Supervision and State Authority

"More than eighty percent of those released from prison receive supervision in the community" (BJS, 1989:2). Chapter 14 discusses release mechanisms and points out the changing nature of release strategies among the states—the growing use of supervised mandatory release (30.6% of all prison releases in 1988) and the diminishing use of discretionary release through action of a parole authority (40.3% of all prison releases during 1988) (BJS, 1989).

Table 5.8
Adults on Parole, 1989

Regions and jurisdictions	Parole population, 1/1/89	1989 Entries	1989 Exits	Parole population, 12/31/89	Percent change in parole population during 1989	Number on parole on 12/31/89 per 100,000 adult residents
U.S. total	407,596	305,596	256,395	456,797	12.1%	248
Federal	20,451	10,910	9,949	21,412	4.7	12
State	387,145	294,686	246,446	435,385	12.5	236
Northeast	104,680	56,807	50,940	110,547	5.6%	286
Connecticut	371	101	150	322	-13.2	13
Massachusetts	4,333	5,124	4,769	4,688	8.2	102
New Hampshire	461	259	243	477	3.5	58
New Jersey	18,463	11,202	9,603	20,062	8.7	340
New York	33,962	18,841	16,118	36,685	8.0	270
Pennsylvania	46,466	20,802	19,566	47,702	2.7	519
Rhode Island	442	345	396	391	-11.5	51
Vermont	182	133	95	220	20.9	52
Midwest	51,062	40,437	35,578	55,921	9.5%	125
Illinois	14,369	12,096	11,915	14,550	1.3	168
Indiana	3,411	1,305	1,260	3,456	1.3	84
Iowa	1,945	1,392	1,437	1,900	-2.3	89
Kansas	3,497	3,137	1,841	4,793	37.1	259
Michigan	7,677	7,549	5,336	9,890	28.8	145
Minnesota	1,639	1,912	1,852	1,699	3.7	53
Missouri	7,207	4,228	3,797	7,638	6.0	198
Nebraska	447	679	636	490	9.6	41
North Dakota	134	198	193	139	3.7	29
Ohio	5,991	4,851	4,378	6,464	7.9	80
South Dakota	617	435	542	510	-17.3	98
Wisconsin	4,128	2,655	2,391	4,392	6.4	122
South	156,696	98,397	71,122	183,971	17.4%	292
Alabama	4,701	2,516	1,461	5,756	22.4	191
Arkansas	3,840	2,061	2,401	3,500	-8.9	199
Delaware	1,093	424	504	1,013	-7.3	201
District of Columbia	3,949	2,995	2,029	4,915	24.5	1,057
Florida	2,562	918	1,162	2,318	-9.5	24
Georgia	11,308	15,386	9,257	17,437	54.2	376
Kentucky	3,443	1,759	2,069	3,133	-9.0	114
Louisiana	7,387	5,493	3,703	9,177	24.2	295
Maryland	9,225	5,862	5,225	9,862	6.9	279
Mississippi	3,177	1,641	1,469	3,349	5.4	181
North Carolina	6,191	8,242	6,874	7,559	22.1	153
Oklahoma	1,455	1,195	657	1,993	37.0	84
South Carolina	3,626	1,039	1,035	3,630	.1	142
Tennessee	9,529	4,876	3,705	10,700	12.3	290
Texas	77,827	36,287	22,820	91,294	17.3	758
Virginia	6,576	7,184	6,368	7,392	12.4	160
West Virginia	807	519	383	943	16.9	68
West	74,707	99,045	88,806	84,946	13.7%	224
Alaska	489	555	511	533	9.0	147
Arizona	1,669	3,622	3,243	2,048	22.7	80
California	49,364	84,111	75,967	57,508	16.5	269
Colorado	1,743	1,571	1,515	1,799	3.2	73
Hawaii	1,108	625	446	1,287	16.2	156
Idaho	247	227	236	238	-3.6	34
Montana	671	370	289	752	12.1	128
Nevada	2,100	1,375	1,058	2,417	15.1	290
New Mexico	1,230	1,038	1,117	1,151	-6.4	107
Oregon	3,790	3,864	1,860	5,794	52.9	273
Utah	1,218	848	789	1,277	4.8	119
Washington	10,745	643	1,556	9,832	-8.5	277
Wyoming	333	196	219	310	-6.9	91

Note: Twelve States estimated numbers in one or more categories. Maine eliminated parole in 1976. See the de- tailed parole notes for further information.

Source: Bureau of Justice Statistics (1990). "Probation and Parole 1988," p. 3. Washington, DC: U.S. Department of Justice, November.

Table 5.9
Probation/Parole/Aftercare Service Providers (as of June 30, 1990)

	NUMBER BOARD MEMBERS [*]	ADULT PAROLING AUTHORITIES	ADULT PAROLE SERVICES
AL	3	Bd of Pardons & Paroles	Bd of Pardons & Paroles
AK	5 (PT)	Bd of Parole	Dept of Corrections
AZ	7	Bd of Pardons & Paroles	DOC/Cmty Svcs Div
AR	7 (PT)[1]	Bd of Parole & Cmty Rehab	DOC/Div of Pardons & Paroles
CA	9	Bd of Prison Terms[**]	DOC/Parole & Cmty Svcs Div
CO	7	Bd of Parole	DOC/Div of Cmty Svcs
CT	11 (PT)[2]	Bd of Parole	DOC/Div of Parole[**]
DE	5 (PT)[2]	Bd of Parole	DOC/Div of Cmty Corr
DC	4	Bd of Parole	Bd of Parole
FL	7	Prob & Parole Cmsn	DOC/Prob & Parole Svcs
GA	5	Bd of Pardons & Parole	Bd of Pardons & Parole
HI	3 (PT)[2]	Paroling Authority	Paroling Authority/Field Svcs
ID	5 (PT)	Cmsn for Pardons & Parole	DOC/Div Field & Cmty Svcs
IL	13	Prisoner Review Bd	DOC/Cmty Svcs Div[**]
IN	5	Parole Bd	DOC/Parole Svcs Section
IA	5 (PT)[2]	Bd of Parole	DOC/Div Cmty Corr Svcs
KS	5	Parole Bd	DOC/Parole Svcs[**]
KY	7	Parole Bd	CC/Dept Cmty Svcs & Facilities
LA	5	Bd of Parole	DPSC/Div of Prob & Parole
ME	5 (PT)	Parole Bd [3]	DOC/Div of Prob & Parole
MD	7	Parole Commission	DPSCS/Div of Parole & Prob
MA	7	Parole Bd	Parole Bd
MI	7	Parole Bd	DOC/Bur of Field Svcs
MN	4 (PT)[4]	DOC/Office Adult Release[**]	DOC/Prob Par Supv Rel/ Co Cts or CCA
MS	5 (PT)	Parole Bd	DOC/Cmty Svcs Div
MO	5	Bd of Prob & Parole	DOC/Bd of Prob & Parole
MT	3 (PT)	Bd of Pardons	DI/CD/Cmty Corr Bureau
NE	5	Bd of Parole[**]	DCS/Adult Parole Admin[**]
NV	5	Bd of Parole Cmsnrs	Dept of Parole & Prob
NH	5 (PT)	Bd of Parole	DOC/Div of Field Svcs[**]
NJ	9	Parole Bd[**]	Bureau of Parole[**]
NM	4	Adult Parole Bd	CD/Prob & Parole Div
NY	19	Bd of Parole	Div of Parole
NC	5	Parole Commission	DOC/Div Adult Prob & Parole
ND	3 (PT)	Parole Bd	DCR/Div of Parole & Prob
OH	9 [5]	DRC/Div of Parole & Cmty Svcs & Parole Bd	DRC/Div of Parole & Cmty Svcs
OK	5 (PT)	Pardon & Parole Bd	DOC/Div of Prob & Parole
OR	5	Bd of Parole & Post Prison Supv	DOC/Cmty Svcs Br/Co Cts
PA	5	Bd of Prob & Parole[**] & Co Cts [6]	Bd of Prob & Parole[**] & Co Cts
RI	6 (PT)	Parole Bd	DOC/Div of Field Svcs
SC	7 (PT)	Bd Prob, Parole & Pardon Svcs	Dept Prob, Parole & Pardon Svcs[**]
SD	3 (PT)	Bd of Pardons & Paroles	BP/Paroles/Par Svcs
TN	7	Bd of Paroles	BP/Parole Field Svcs
TX	18	Bd of Pardons & Paroles	TDCJ/PPD/Parole Supv
UT	5	Bd of Pardons	DOC/Field Operations Div
VT	5 (PT)	Bd of Parole	AHS/Dept of Corrections
VA	5	Parole Bd	DOC/Div of Adult Cmty Corr
WA	5	Indeterminate Sent Review Bd	DOC/Div Cmty Svcs
WV	3	Bd of Prob & Parole [8]	Div of Corrections
WI	4	Parole Commission	DOC/Div Prob & Parole
WY	5 (PT)	Bd of Parole	Dept of Prob & Parole
US	9	Parole Commission[**]	Admin Ofc of US Courts

Notes:
[*] All members serve full-time unless coded "PT."
[**] Accredited by Commission on Accreditation for Corrections.
1. AR – 3 full-time, 4 part-time.
2. Chairman serves full-time; members part-time.
3. ME – Parole Board hears pre-1976 cases of parole. Flat sentences with no parole under criminal code effective 5/1/76.
4. MN – Executive Officer & two Deputy Executive Officers (CCA Cmty Corr Act.)
5. OH – Plus 11 hearing officers.

Table 5.9—continued

	ADULT PROBATION SERVICES	JUVENILE PAROLE/AFTERCARE SERVICES	JUVENILE PROBATION SERVICES
AL	Bd of Pardons & Paroles	Co Courts	Dept Youth Svcs ($ only) & Co Cts
AK	Dept of Corrections	No parole/aftercare	DHSS/Div Family & Youth Svcs
AZ	State Courts	DJC/Parole Admin	State Courts
AR	Adult Prob Commission	DCFS/Courts	DCFS/Courts
CA	Co Courts	DYA/Parole Svcs Branch	Co Courts
CO	Judicial Districts	DOI/Div of Youth Svcs	Judicial Districts
CT	Office of Adult Prob	Dept Children & Youth Svcs	Superior Court/Family Div
DE	DOC/Div of Cmty Corr	DSCYF/Div Youth Rehab**	DSCYF/Div Youth Rehab**
DC	DC Superior Ct/Social Svcs Div	DHS/Youth Svcs Admin	DC Superior Ct/Social Svcs Div
FL	DOC/Prob & Parole Svcs	DHRS/Children, Youth & Fam Svcs	DHRS/Children Youth & Fam Svcs
GA	DOC/Prob Div	DHR Div of Youth Svcs & Co Courts	DHR/Div Youth Svcs & Co Courts
HI	State Judiciary/Prob Ofc	DPS/Youth Corr Facility/Cmty Svcs Sect	State Judiciary/Family Courts
ID	DOC/Div Field & Cmty Svcs	Dept Health & Welfare	Dept Health & Welfare and Co Cts
IL	Judicial Circuits	DOC/Juv Field Svcs**	Judicial Circuits
IN	Judicial/County Courts	DOC/Parole Svcs Section	Judicial/County Courts
IA	DOC/Div Cmty Corr Svcs	DHS/Bur Adult, Children & Family Svcs	Judicial Districts
KS	Judicial Districts	DSRS/Youth Svcs	Judicial Districts
KY	CC/Dept Cmty Svcs & Facilities	CHR/Div of Family Svcs	CHR/Div of Family Svcs
LA	DPSC/Div of Prob & Parole	DPSC/Div of Youth Svcs	DPSC/Div of Youth Svcs
ME	DOC/Div of Prob & Parole	DOC/Div of Prob & Parole	DOC/Div of Prob & Parole
MD	DPSCS/Div of Parole & Prob	Dept of Juv Svcs	Dept of Juv Svcs
MA	Office of Cmsnr of Prob/Courts	DYS/Bur of Cmty Svcs	Office of Cmsnr of Prob/Courts
MI	DOC/Bur Field Svcs & Dist Cts	DSS/Ofc Children & Yth Svcs/Co Cts	DSS/Ofc Children & Yth Svcs/Co Cts
MN	DOC/Prob Par Supv Rel/ Co Cts or CCA	DOC/Prob Par Supv Rel/ Co Cts or CCA	DOC/Prob Par Supv Rel/ Co Cts or CCA
MS	DOC/Cmty Svcs Div	DHS/OYS/Cmty Svcs Div	DHS/OYS/Cmty Svcs Div
MO	DOC/Bd of Prob & Parole	DSS/Div Youth Svcs & Jud Circuits	Judicial Circuits
MT	DI/CD/Cmty Corr Bureau	Dept Family Svcs	Judicial Districts
NE	Neb Prob Admin	DCS/Juv Parole Admin**	Neb Prob Admin
NV	Dept of Parole & Prob	DHR/YSD/Youth Parole Bureau	Districts Courts
NH	DOC/Div Field Svcs** & Dist Cts	DHHS/DCYS/Bur of Children	DHHS/DCYS/Bur of Children
NJ	The Judiciary/Prob Div	Bureau of Parole**	The Judiciary/Prob Div
NM	CD/Prob &Parole Div	YA/Cmty Svcs Div/JPB	YA/Cmty Svcs Div
NY	Div Prob & CorrAlt/Co Courts	Div for Youth/Div of Parole	Div Prob & Corr Alt/Co Courts
NC	DOC/Div Adult Prob & Parole	Admin Office of Courts/Juv Svcs Div	Admin Office of Courts/Juv Svcs Div
ND	DCR/Div of Parole & Prob	DCR/Div of Juv Svcs	DCR/Div of Juv Svcs/Supr Cts
OH	DRC/Div of Parole & Cmty Svcs & Co Courts	Dept of Youth Svcs	Co Courts
OK	DOC/Div of Prob & Parole	DHS/Div of Children & Yth Svcs	DHS/Div of Child & Yth Svcs, Co (3)
OR	DOC/Cmty Svcs Br/Co Cts	DHR/CSD/Ofc Juv Corr Svcs	Co Courts
PA	Bd of Prob & Parole** & Co Cts	Co Courts (Prob & Aftercare)	Co Courts (Prob & Aftercare)
RI	DOC/Div of Field Svcs	DCTF/Div of Juv Corr Svcs	DCTF/Div of Juv Corr Svcs
SC	Dept Prob, Parole & Pardon Svcs**	Dept Youth Svcs/Cmty Div	Dept Youth Svcs/Cmty Div
SD	Unified Judicial Sys/Ct Svcs Dept	Unified Judicial Sys/Ct Svcs Dept	Unified Judicial Sys/Ct Svcs Dept
TN	DOC/Div of Prob**	DYD/Prob Div**	DYD/Prob Div**
TX	Cmty Justice Assis Div/Dist Cts	TYC/Cmty Svcs Div/Ofc Par Supv	Co Courts
UT	DOC/Field Operations Div	DHS/Div of Youth Corr	Juv Courts
VT	AHS/Dept of Corrections	AHS/DSRS[7]	DSRS/Div of Social Svcs
VA	DOC/Div of Adult Cmty Corr	Dept Youth & Fam Svcs	Dept Youth & Fam Svcs
WA	DOC/Div Cmty Svcs & Co Cts	DSHS/Div of Juv Rehab	Co Courts
WV	DOC & Judicial Circuits	DOC (Compact) and DHHR	DOC (Compact), DHHR & Jud Circuits
WI	DOC/Div Prob & Par	DHHS/Div Yth Svcs/Co Soc Svcs Depts	Co Social Svcs Depts
WY	Dept of Prob & Parole	Dept of Prob & Parole	Dept of Prob & Parole
US	Admin Ofc of US Courts/Div of Prob		

6. PA – The Board of Probation and Parole administers adult services when sentence is over 2 yrs; county courts when sentence is 2 yrs or less.

7. VT – No functional juvenile parole system. Children in custody go into placement and eventually return to community under supervision of caseworker.

8. WV – Under state statute, parole is considered probation.

The following states have one or more independent county, municipal or city departments: CO,GA,IN,KS,KY,LA,MO,NE,NY,OK,TN,WY.

All Boards are independent except MD, MI, MN, OH, TX, WI.

Source: American Correctional Association (1991). In *Juvenile and Adult Correctional Departments, Institutions, Agencies and Paroling Authorities Directory, 1991.* Laurel, MD: ACA Research Department. Courtesy American Correctional Association.

Table 5.10
Adults on Probation, 1989

Regions and jurisdictions	Probation population, 1/1/89	1989 Entries	1989 Exits	Probation population, 12/31/89	Percent change in probation population during 1989	Number on probation on 12/31/89 per 100,000 adult residents
U.S. total	2,386,427	1,567,156	1,433,104	2,520,479	5.6%	1,369
Federal	61,029	19,858	21,741	59,146	-3.1	32
State	2,325,398	1,547,298	1,411,363	2,461,333	5.8	1,337
Northeast	438,691	215,467	210,364	443,794	1.2%	1,147
Connecticut	46,086	27,839	31,083	42,842	-7.0	1,728
Maine	6,059	4,792	4,000	6,851	13.1	747
Massachusetts	92,353	47,026	50,850	88,529	-4.1	1,935
New Hampshire	2,948	2,552	2,509	2,991	1.5	361
New Jersey	57,903	31,891	23,041	66,753	15.3	1,131
New York	125,256	41,953	38,502	128,707	2.8	946
Pennsylvania	92,296	47,761	50,566	89,491	-3.0	973
Rhode Island	9,824	8,467	6,060	12,231	24.5	1,595
Vermont	5,966	3,186	3,753	5,399	-9.5	1,270
Midwest	510,253	395,440	362,928	542,765	6.4%	1,217
Illinois	90,736	58,023	54,815	93,944	3.5	1,083
Indiana	60,184	57,362	55,685	61,861	2.8	1,497
Iowa	13,099	12,180	11,557	13,722	4.8	644
Kansas	19,580	12,507	9,562	22,525	15.0	1,215
Michigan	115,132	92,400	86,096	121,436	5.5	1,778
Minnesota	56,901	48,079	46,332	58,648	3.1	1,819
Missouri	42,728	27,322	24,799	45,251	5.9	1,174
Nebraska	11,411	15,369	14,153	12,627	10.7	1,064
North Dakota	1,504	558	410	1,652	9.8	343
Ohio	70,088	53,111	44,976	78,223	11.6	967
South Dakota	2,585	4,277	4,146	2,716	5.1	523
Wisconsin	26,305	14,252	10,397	30,160	14.7	835
South	929,936	658,418	601,846	986,508	6.1%	1,565
Alabama	25,301	12,405	11,231	26,475	4.6	880
Arkansas	15,931	5,875	4,234	17,572	10.3	1,001
Delaware	9,576	3,959	3,834	9,701	1.3	1,925
District of Columbia	11,296	8,942	9,887	10,351	-8.4	2,226
Florida	165,475	241,462	214,442	192,495	16.3	1,964
Georgia	121,559	69,142	65,260	125,441	3.2	2,704
Kentucky	7,398	4,142	3,478	8,062	9.0	292
Louisiana	31,218	12,828	11,751	32,295	3.5	1,039
Maryland	78,619	50,145	44,308	84,456	7.4	2,390
Mississippi	6,854	3,142	2,663	7,333	7.0	396
North Carolina	67,164	37,972	32,811	72,325	7.7	1,467
Oklahoma	23,341	11,605	10,706	24,240	3.9	1,022
South Carolina	26,260	15,543	12,151	29,652	12.9	1,159
Tennessee	28,282	24,821	22,197	30,906	9.3	839
Texas	288,906	143,515	141,265	291,156	.8	2,419
Virginia	17,945	10,470	9,330	19,085	6.4	414
West Virginia	4,811	2,450	2,298	4,963	3.2	356
West	446,518	277,973	236,225	488,266	9.4%	1,290
Alaska	2,994	1,755	1,414	3,335	11.4	921
Arizona	25,446	11,490	9,286	27,650	8.7	1,074
California	265,580	163,575	144,137	285,018	7.3	1,335
Colorado	23,230	21,877	18,729	26,378	13.6	1,075
Hawaii	10,704	5,892	5,219	11,377	6.3	1,379
Idaho	3,587	1,976	1,538	4,025	12.2	567
Montana	3,275	1,528	1,344	3,459	5.6	588
Nevada	7,032	3,411	3,119	7,324	4.2	879
New Mexico	5,312	4,508	4,160	5,660	6.6	527
Oregon	27,320	12,018	7,460	31,878	16.7	1,502
Utah	5,595	3,615	3,686	5,524	-1.3	513
Washington	64,257	44,730	34,733	74,254	15.6	2,095
Wyoming	2,186	1,598	1,400	2,384	9.1	703

Note: Nine States estimated numbers in one or more categories. See detailed probation notes for further information.

Source: Bureau of Justice Statistics (1990). "Probation and Parole 1989," p. 2. Washington, DC: U.S. Department of Justice, November.

Table 5.8 shows the number of adults under parole supervision under authority of the states and the federal government during 1988. Table 5.9 shows the providers of probation, parole, and aftercare services by the state and federal governments. Regarding paroling authorities, please keep in mind that, as pointed out and discussed in Chapter 14, a number of states have moved to mandatory release from discretionary release. These states still maintain a discretionary release authority, because there are still inmates who were sentenced prior to changes in the law.

Again refer to Table 5.9. In most states, the Department of Corrections has a component element or division that provides probation services for those sentenced to state authority. As one will note, however, in some states provision of such probation services is a responsibility of other agencies than Departments of Corrections. Table 5.10 shows adults on probation during 1988 by state and the U.S. government. Please keep in mind, as pointed out in Chapter 13, that probation is actually a collection of strategies and is not a singular sort of undertaking—combinations of conditions, differing caseload assignment schemes, and varying levels of supervision make probation vary from jurisdiction to jurisdiction, even within jurisdictions.

Summary

The information provided in this brief descriptive look at the mainline federal and state systems must lead one to consider the enormity of the set of correctional undertakings in the United States. There is no way to speak of corrections in the United States in terms of simple problems. What we have are complex issues and meta-problems (problems that have unspecified numbers of seemingly or actually incalculable variables). The problems of corrections extend far beyond the organizations that are established to deal with corrections and far beyond the capacities of all those concerned with corrections to resolve simply. Each of the chapters in this book should lead to a greater realization of the difficult issues to be faced and hopefully to the realization that these are not problems to be seen solely as problems of the correctional systems.

Expanding Sentencing Options:
A Governor's Perspective

by Pierre S. du Pont IV

Pierre S. du Pont IV was born on January 22, 1935, in Wilmington, Delaware. He is a graduate of Princeton University (1956, B.S.E.) and Harvard University (1963, J.D.), and served as a lieutenant in the U.S. Navy from 1957 to 1960. Now completing his second term as Governor of Delaware, Pierre S. du Pont IV has been a businessman, State representative, and Congressman.

When I became governor in 1977, Delaware was committing about 3 percent of its State budget to corrections. Like all new officeholders, I had a list of things I wanted to improve during my administration. And corrections seemed to me to be one thing that certainly needed improvement. I wanted to cut its demands on tax revenues, which I felt were more urgently needed in other areas. We were, I concluded, pouring too much money into our prisons and jails.

I like to think I accomplished much during my term as governor. But like most officeholders getting ready to step aside, I have to admit that I did not do everything I wished.

This year corrections will account for more than 7 percent of the total State budget, which means that there is still more pressure on the other vital services the State must provide. Indeed, in real dollar terms, our State's corrections budget has grown over 300 percent in just 7 years. This makes it by far the most inflated budget in State government since I took office.

I believe there are answers to the corrections dilemma, and I plan to explore some of them in this article. The proposals that are under active consideration in Delaware are no mere "quick fixes" or exercises in political legerdemain.

Instead, what I propose will require a major overhaul of the corrections system and the establishment of a more flexible and effective sentencing structure. This will require public understanding and acceptance at a time when the criminal justice system is under considerable pressure for not being rigid enough in dealing with criminals.

Balanced against these considerations are the problems of doing nothing at all. The costs in terms of money, of public dismay at growing criminality, and of the waste of human effort are too appalling to permit this to be a viable option.

The failure of the status quo can be shown in what I once considered to be a bright part of the criminal justice system in Delaware. In the 1970s Delaware had built one of the most up-to-date prison facilities in the Nation. It was designed to handle the State's needs until 1990. At least, I was assured as the new governor, there would be no need to worry about building more prisons for some time.

The prison that was to last until the end of this decade was filled to capacity before this decade began. We have since had to construct two major additions to the facility, and a third is in progress today. We have built a multi-purpose correctional facility in Wilmington, and a minimum security institution is now in the planning stages. We are being told to begin thinking about building still more space.

Part of the reason for this alarming growth in spending and in prison population is that only two States incarcerate more people, per capita, than Delaware. We have 274 prison inmates for every 100,000 people. And we are putting them in prison for longer terms under our relatively inflexible criminal justice system. Seven years ago, for each inmate serving a term of 10 years or more, there was roughly one serving a term of less than a year. Today there are four longtermers for every prisoner serving less than a year. And the price to the State for housing, feeding, and guarding these inmates has risen dramatically. It now costs $17,000 per year for us to incarcerate one prisoner.

Despite its great cost, and the promise of more

increases to come, the present system might be largely acceptable if it were working properly. But it isn't. We traditionally rely on incarceration as the primary method of punishing criminals, but—as numerous studies have demonstrated—there is no evidence that higher incarceration rates have any impact on the crime rate. For one thing, prison overcrowding limits whatever chances exist for success in rehabilitative programs.

Despite the evidence that change is imperative, we seem unable to break out of our present pattern of dealing with criminals. It is as if our corrections system is a prisoner, too.

In my judgment, a fundamental reshaping of our approach to corrections is not only in order, it is feasible and imperative. As a start, we must begin to view punishment in terms of certainty rather than severity. The criminal justice system is seriously undermined when men and women are sentenced to probation when they should go to jail, or are released from probation when they ought to remain behind bars. The answer that overcrowding forces these compromises is not acceptable when other answers are available. We must provide sentencing options between the extremes of probation and prison.

Clearly, nothing less than major reform can accomplish these goals. In Delaware, we are beginning to consider an alternative program developed by the Delaware Sentencing Reform Commission. That alternative program stresses accountability—accountability of the offender to the victim and the State, and accountability of the corrections system to the public and other criminal justice agencies. The accountability concept could create an ordered yet flexible system of sentencing and corrections. This system

Restrictions	Level I	Level II	Level III	Level IV
Mobility in the community[1]	100 percent (unrestricted)	100 percent (unrestricted)	90 percent (restricted 0-10 hours/week)	80 percent (restricted 10-30 hours/week)
Amount of supervision	None	Monthly written report	1-2 face-to-face/month; 1-2 weekly phone contact	3-6 face-to-face/month; weekly phone contact
Privileges withheld or special conditions[2]	100 percent (same as prior conviction)	100 percent (same as prior conviction)	1-2 privileges withheld	1-4 privileges withheld
Financial obligations[3]	Fine, court costs may be applied (0- to 2-day fine)	Fine, court costs; restitution; probation (supervisory fee may be applied; 1- to 3-day fine)	Same (increase probation fee by $5-10/month; 2- to 4-day fine)	Same (increase probation fee by $5-10/month; 3- to 5-day fine)
Examples (Note: many other scenarios could be constructed meeting the requirements at each level)	$50 fine, court costs; 6 months' unsupervised probation	$50 fine, court costs; restitution; 6 months' supervised probation; $10 monthly fee; written report	Fine, court costs; restitution; 1 year probation; weekend community service; no drinking	Weekend community service or mandatory treatment 5 hrs/day; $30/month probation fee; no drinking; no out-of-state trips

would be based on the belief that an offender should be sentenced to the least restrictive (and least costly) sanction available, consistent with public safety. That is a standard, by the way, endorsed by the American Bar Association some years ago.

A system built on accountability would structure the movement of offenders into and out of the corrections system, making it fairer and more cost-efficient. It would provide incentives for offenders to work at rehabilitation, since this would permit them to move into less restrictive (and less expensive) forms of control. At the same time accountability would strengthen the safeguards against violent offenders, who could be held in prison as long as necessary, or at least as long as their sentences ran.

Today the sentencing judge in Delaware and many other States is often faced with rigid choices.

The offender before him or her is either sent to prison or put on probation. And as we know, conventional probation is not an adequate answer for every offender whose crime was not serious enough to merit a jail sentence. The options between the two extremes are rarely in place.

And if an offender fails to comply with the conditions of a less restrictive sanction, such as probation, what then? Assuming the probation officer even notifies the court of the violation, the judge's options are limited to sending the violator to prison, or continuing him or her on probation. There is no real flexibility, no real choice of options that will carefully address the needs of society and the individuals involved. Neither is there certainty of punishment in such a system.

Level V	Level VI	Level VII	Level VIII	Level IX	Level X
60 percent (restricted 30-40 hrs/week)	30 percent (restricted 50-100 hrs/week)	20 percent (restricted 100-140 hrs/week)	10 percent (90 percent of time incarcerated)	Incarcerated	Incarcerated
2-6 face-to-face/week; daily phone contact; weekly written reports	Daily phone contact; daily face-to-face; weekly written reports	Daily onsite supervision 8-16 hrs/day	Daily onsite supervision 24 hrs/day	Daily onsite supervision 24 hrs/day	Daily onsite supervision 24 hrs/day
1-7 privileges withheld	1-10 privileges withheld	1-12 privileges withheld	5-15 privileges withheld	15-19 privileges withheld	20 or more privileges withheld
Same (pay partial cost of food/lodging/supervision fee; 4- to 7-day fine	Same as Level V (8- to 10-day fine)	Same as Level V (11- to 12-day fine)	Fine, court costs; restitution payable upon release to Level VII or lower (12- to 15-day fine)	Same as Level VIII	Same as Level VIII
Mandatory rehabilitation skills program 8 hrs/day; restitution; $40/month probation fee; no drinking; curfew	Work release; pay portion of food/lodging; restitution; no kitchen privileges outside mealtimes; no drinking; no sex; weekends home	Residential treatment program; pay portion of program costs; limited privileges	Minimum-security prison	Medium-security prison	Maximum-security prison

There is no one answer to our problems in the criminal justice system. But I believe sentencing reform is the sort of radical surgery that the system must have and have soon. How would this work?

It is not [an] overstatement to say that the proposals of the Delaware Sentencing Reform Commission would completely overhaul our sentencing and corrections laws. They would establish a range of sanctions available to a judge over 10 "levels of accountability." The table displays these 10 levels.

Level I is unsupervised probation; Level X is maximum-security imprisonment. Moving from probation, there is a full range of alternatives, each more restrictive than the last, until the judge—and the criminal—reach a sentence of maximum-security incarceration.

Within each level there are degrees of control and accountability. These involve the offender's freedom of action within the community, the amount of supervision he or she is subject to, and what privileges are to be withheld or what other special conditions are to be attached to the sentence. In addition, the system provides for a range of possible financial sanctions to be imposed, including victims' compensation. Through such flexible controls, we would be able to control the offender's choice of job, choice of residence, ability to drive, ability to drink, ability to travel, and even ability to make telephone calls.

And to all of this we would add the probation fee concept. Successfully used in Georgia and Florida, the $10- to $50-per-month fee is charged to probationers to offset the cost of their supervision. Like the sanctions, the fee could be increased depending on the level of supervision required.

What is so attractive about this idea of accountability is that is applies not only to sentencing offenders, but also to controlling them following sentencing. And the same level of flexibility available to judges would be available to corrections officials responsible for probation.

Let's look at two hypothetical cases to see how the flexible sentencing and control system might work in practice.

First, let's take a drug offender with a minimal prior record but unstable employment record. He might be sentenced in Level II to supervised probation for 2 years, with restrictions on his place of residence, his association with certain individuals, and/or his right to visit high-drug/crime locations. And we might charge him a $10-per-month fee to offset some of the costs of keeping him straight.

If he observes these conditions for the first year of his probation, he could move down the sanctions scale into Level I. This level involves unsupervised probation and levies no fees, but holds out the possibility of certain restrictions on mobility and personal associations to minimize the chance of the offender slipping back into the drug scene and its associated crime. If our hypothetical drug offender violates the terms of his probation, he could be moved to Level III, with heightened supervision, a curfew, and an increased monthly fee. Thus, the offender has a clear incentive to comply with his sentence. And, equally important, the sentencing judge has available options other than prison when probation is violated. Having and using these options will increase the certainty of appropriate punishment.

The second example is near the other end of the offense spectrum. This time our hypothetical offender is a twice-convicted armed robber. He was sentenced to 20 years, with the sentence to begin at Level X, or a maximum-security prison. After serving 2 years, and adhering to all the rules, the man might be moved to Level IX, a medium-security facility, where he might be able to take advantage of expanded rehabilitative programs.

Two years later, with continued good behavior, the offender again could move down the scale, this time to a minimum-security facility with still greater opportunities for rehabilitation. By the same token, if the prisoner's action at Level IX was disruptive and uncooperative, he could be returned to Level X.

Later, at a parole hearing, some appropriate program at Level VI might be selected instead of releasing the offender to a fuller freedom in the streets or leaving him in prison.

When the Sentencing Reform Commission applied the concept of accountability levels to the present offender population in Delaware, it found that only 21 percent of that population fell within Levels IX and X. But that medium- and maximum-security population accounted for 87 percent of the total corrections budget in Delaware. The Commission also found that roughly 70 percent of the corrections population fell between Levels I and III. Less than 10 percent filled the middle ground, and most of these were in some sort of alcohol or drug abuse program. Analysis showed that many in prison could be safely released if the programs were available to restrict their activities properly and closely supervise their rehabilitation. That analysis also showed that many in probation were undersupervised. Many of these men and women clearly needed to be moved into a middle level where they would be subject to stronger, more restrictive programs.

Let me sum up by shifting the focus from corrections mechanics to corrections philosophy. In this regard, I think it reasonable to consider two important goals of sentencing reform. The first is to reverse the long-established trend of growing prison populations and skyrocketing corrections budgets. The second is to redirect the system so that it guides offenders toward a useful life within the law.

Don't expect miracles from the reform proposals I am suggesting. Even with a sophisticated accountability system, we may not be able to reverse quickly the growth of corrections populations and spending. But we reasonably can expect to slow growth in spending and, ultimately, to stabilize costs. A hallmark of the accountability concept is cost avoidance—that is, developing and using less costly alternatives in our corrections programs. And, optimally, the effect of the accountability concept, as the offender moves through the system, will be to help reduce recidivism.

There will be expenses, of course. We must have new programs for those who need to be placed in something less than prison but in more than lightly supervised probation. But again, we can expect cost avoidance. The cost of new programs will be far less than the cost of constructing new prisons, a prospect which currently looms before Delaware and many other States. In fact, we in Delaware expect to rely on the private sector to run many of these programs.

Frankly, I do not see money as the major issue. Nor do I see great reluctance to change within the system itself, although there is strong and healthy debate on the direction that change should take. I believe the major obstacle to sentencing reform is the attitude of the public, an attitude which naturally and properly is reflected in the votes of its elected representatives. I do not consider this a daunting challenge. I believe the winds of change are already blowing in Delaware. Ours was the first state to ratify the U.S. Constitution, and we may again lead the Nation, this time in pragmatic and thorough sentencing reform.

---

[1] Restrictions on freedom structure an offender's time, controlling his or her schedule, whereabouts, and activities for a designated period. To the extent that monitoring is not standard or consistent or to the extent that no sanctions accrue for failure on the part of the offender, the time is *not* structured. It could consist of residential, part-time residential, community service, or other specific methods for meeting the designated hours. The judge could order that the hours be met daily (e.g., 2 hours/day) or in one period (e.g., weekend in jail).

[2] Privileges/conditions; choice of job, choice of residence, mobility within setting, driving, drinking (possible use of Antabuse), out-of-State trips, phone calls, curfew, mail, urinalysis, associates, areas off limits.

[3] As a more equitable guide to appropriate fines, the amount would be measured in units of equivalent daily income, such as 1 day's salary = "1-day fine."

Source: Pierre S. du Pont IV (1985). "Expanding Sentencing Options: A Governor's Perspective," pp. 1-4. Washington, DC: National Institute of Justice, January.

Key Terms and Concepts

centralization

community corrections alternatives

community supervision

coordination

department of corrections

division of corrections

Federal Bureau of Prisons

fragmentation

incarceration

unification

U.S. Parole Commission

U.S. Probation Service

References

American Civil Liberties Union (1990). "Status Report: The Courts and the Prisons." National Prison Project. Washington, DC: American Civil Liberties Union.

American Correctional Association (1989). *Vital Statistics in Corrections.* Laurel, MD: American Correctional Association.

Bureau of Justice Statistics (1990). "Prisoners in 1989." Washington, DC: U.S. Department of Justice.

Bureau of Justice Statistics (1990). "Probation and Parole 1989." Washington, DC: U.S. Department of Justice.

Photo Credit: Tony O'Brien, Frost Publishing Group, Ltd.

Correctional Administration

6

After reading this chapter, the student should be able to:

- Describe the environment for correctional administration at a societal level, a system level, and a service-delivery level.

- Relate the internal environments of correctional organizations to problems of correctional administration.

- Depict the internal and external environments of a maximum-security prison.

- Discuss the administration of a maximum-security prison.

- Provide an explanation as to why many correctional administrators find themselves on the defensive.

Introduction

As Herbert Simon has said, "Administration is most often discussed as the art of getting things done" (1976:1). Actually, the study of administration includes a number of broad realms of consideration and investigation that contribute to a detailed understanding of the organizational structures, processes, and behaviors related to administration. Among these one can include at least concerns with organizational theory and structure, organizational and administrative behavior, leadership or management in complex organizations, decision-making, planning and program evaluation in complex organizations, organizational and interpersonal communication, human resource management (including labor relations), fiscal management, organizational change and development, and concern with various aspects of the context of operation (especially networks of relationships, power, and politics inside any particular organization and networks of relationships, power, and politics connecting a particular organization to others in its operating context).

Obviously, this chapter is not intended to provide a comprehensive discussion of administration in corrections. Rather, we focus on selected aspects of correctional administration—ones we think can assist in developing a fundamental perspective for asking questions about why things happen the way they do in corrections. With this aim in mind, it is important to realize that there is a great deal of diversity among corrections organizations, yet there is a large amount of common ground concerning the administration of these organizations.

Levels of Analysis

We often speak of U.S. corrections as though we are talking about a single entity. We at times refer to the correctional "system" as though the amalgam of agencies and organizations we identify with corrections are component parts of a rather closely coordinated and tightly interrelated structure. The images we draw from such a characterization are at once simplistic and largely inaccurate.

Corrections in the United States encompasses a complex set of endeavors and organizations. As has been discussed earlier, our corrections efforts are not centralized at the national level—we do not have one large organizational pyramid with a designated center for coordination, control, allocation of resources, and so on. Regarding administration, a look at our American "system" results in having to fit together a sometimes-confusing series of "maps" and "overlays" to these "maps." In other words, in seeking to attain a basic understanding of the organization (some might say "the disorganization") of corrections in the United States and the resulting implications for administration, we must confront a complicated set of organizational arrangements.

One way to begin to address the issues concerning administration is to look at American corrections from different levels of analysis, focusing on relevant implications at each level. Our primary interest in doing this is to gain a clearer idea about the context(s) within which correctional organizations are administered and some of the relevant implications for administration.

Societal Level

The United States of America is a diverse society. It is composed of individuals and groups who have beliefs and hold opinions that may differ widely and are often competing. It is composed of individuals and groups who are not equal in terms of wealth, power, or influence. In an organizational sense we must think about our society in a broad manner, as providing the "major option-setting context" (Perrow, 1986:263) within which the amalgam of corrections organizations and correctional administrators must operate.

Although, as we have said, there is no organizational pyramid extending from the national level to the local level in corrections, it is important to gain perspective concerning the types of forces and factors that help shape policies and actions in corrections at this broad level. At this societal level of analysis, we must attend to such considerations as political, economic, and cultural conditions. Politically, correctional administration is shaped by the distribution of power. Our governmental and social arrangements and the ways people operate and their beliefs regarding these arrangements are crucial facets of the overall context for correctional administration.

We have a representative government that is structured to allow varying measures of autonomy at the federal, state, and local levels. Our governmental agencies are supposed to function in a manner that represents the general interest. One of the things to realize and understand is that the "general interest" is not singular or monolithic. Different persons and different groups hold differing conceptions of what best serves the common good, and what directions are appropriate for corrections. In our society, power is distributed among many sets of persons at the various levels of government. There are many avenues for the development and application of influence and power at each of these levels. Persons and groups with differing interests and unequal influence utilize the various avenues to seek to have their interests expressed in the policies that guide or shape directions for corrections. The policies that do emerge are "political resultants" (see Allison, 1973) that reflect the application of power and influence exerted at the different levels of government.

The policies that do result are developed gradually. Past decisions, policies, actions, and beliefs have great force and form the base upon which current policies are argued, expressed, and implemented. Just as there is no single adequate theory concerning the causes of crime, there is no singular adequate approach to corrections. Those with different beliefs about causes and effects and different beliefs about appropriate approaches to corrections may participate in a complicated set of processes for providing directions for the correctional endeavors in this nation. Those who amass sufficient influence tend to have their preferences expressed in policy and tend to have their preferences put into action. Just as there is no encompassing organizational pyramid for corrections, there is no single set of policies or directions that must be followed.

Correctional administrators face a societal context characterized by controversy, competing interests, and differentially powerful persons and groups. Different persons and groups seek to "use" corrections organizations to further their beliefs, their visions, their interests, and because of our complex governmental arrangements there is the possibility for, and the actuality of, many pulls and tugs and many directions. Correctional administrators must respond to those who directly control their situations and to those who have access to and influence with those who directly control their situations. We must also not lose sight of the knowledge that most people in our society know very little about corrections, and if they respond to correctional issues at all, they usually respond in very general ways to very general notions about the operation of government or to selected information that is made available by those with specific interests in government or corrections.

Economically, the most visible concerns have to do with the general state of the economy and potential economic impact on corrections and its administration. Obviously, times of national economic "recession" are times when fewer resources are available to do the work of government in general, or at least this impression is given, depending on the "strength" of the economic downturn. Conversely, times of rapid economic expansion may result in increased resource levels. It is far easier, many say, to administer an agency or organization whose budget is "fat." We must think a bit deeper about corrections and the general economy, though. Several insights may be worth consideration.

First, although many people seem to think differently, our society is not possessed of limitless resources. This means that, at a societal level, we must address the issues involved in the distribution and allocation of resources. Again, because the corrections endeavors undertaken in the United States are organized at various levels of government, and because corrections organizations receive their resources from, and administrators are accountable to, a variety of governing bodies at the various levels, the availability, application, and evaluation of use of resources is subject to being influenced by myriad interests and concerns. In general, those in control of corrections agencies must compete with all other agencies for shares of the available resources. This is done in the many and varied political environments of our governmental structure. Correctional administrators often see their organizations as receiving too little, or less than adequate resources.

Second, this is a society in which wealth and personal resources are unevenly distributed. Increasingly, concerns are being expressed about the possibility of a growing "underclass" in the United States (W.J. Wilson, 1978). It is not our purpose here to enter a debate over the associations or possible associations between lower socioeconomic status and crime causation. However, we must note that there are rather large implications for correctional administration when, looking at aggregate profiles of those funneled into the correctional process, we see that the majority of the "business" for corrections involves correcting persons from the lower socioeconomic levels of society. Those in control of corrections agencies must be concerned with designing strategies, programs, policies and actions for "correcting" people, while being unable to do much about the environments from which offenders emerge and to which they most often must return. Corrections can be, and often is, a frustrating business when one considers meta-level issues and notions of achieving impact or effectiveness where the expected outcomes are dependent to a large extent on social, economic, and political forces which those in corrections cannot harness.

Culturally, we must understand the importance of the attitudes, orientations, and beliefs that predominate concerning just what corrections is supposed to accomplish. Correctional administrators are often forced to engage in a balancing act. They are faced with being placed on the horns of one or another dilemma stemming from debates and political maneuvering concerning what options to pursue. They are faced with reinforcing the image of the government as acting to "solve" large problems where viable "solutions" are not available, where policy development and implementation most often must be derived from compromise negotiated among those who have competing beliefs and interests and varying degrees of power to influence the decisionmakers in government. There are cyclical calls to "reform" corrections—to pursue different options. The force of tradition, custom, habit, and past practices is, however, very strong. It is often very difficult to gain widespread acceptance for pursuit of different options. The overriding political agenda regarding corrections is often a "don't hurt me" agenda, meaning "make as few waves as possible," while showing to the greatest extent possible that something constructive is being done, appeasing as much as possible the significant competing interests, keeping an "acceptable" image.

Obviously, we have only scratched the surface of the possible importance of viewing corrections and administration from a societal level of analysis. At this level the issues and the potential implications for correctional administration are enormous. We hope to convey here the need to think about the larger context, the one in which all our organizations must function, and also to convey a realization that comes to most upper-level correctional administrators—that the larger context for correctional administration is highly political and is shaped by forces over which they have little direct control, where "problems" most often must be addressed as the resolution of varying values and preferences concerning options that are not necessarily supportable as "solutions," but must be seen as acceptable directions for channeling efforts and resources.

The DOC Level

We have chosen to call a second level of analysis the DOC (Department or Division of Corrections) level. This is an arbitrary decision. Our primary concern at this level is with the contexts for administration of corrections organizations such as Departments or Divisions of Corrections, normally structured as major elements of state government, and the large organizations established to carry out corrections efforts for the federal government (e.g., the U.S. Bureau of Prisons). As we have seen in Chapter 5, few of these "systems" could be called centralized; that is, correctional functions in the various states and in the federal government are not all organized under one administrative identity, one large agency. Nonetheless, these large, complex organizations are primary elements in the delivery of corrections services in the United States, and visualizing concerns related to administration at this level is important.

Chapter 5 discusses variations in structure among the state departments/divisions of corrections and the federal structure. Please keep these variations in mind. For the following discussion envision a fairly typical state agency, such as that depicted in Figure 6.1. Our comments will be general in nature.

Figure 6.1 shows DOC, a large, complex governmental organization structured to provide a wide array of correctional services under the authority of a state government. Our mythical state also has correctional services (such as probation in its largest cities, community correctional centers, jails, and some other community-based services) organized under the authority and control of local government. The focus of our attention is the big state agency.

In organizational terms, DOC has an *internal environment* (the composite of formal and informal aspects seen as being within the organization). We will discuss more about the internal environment of corrections organizations in the sections on Common Concerns and Institutional Management. It is important at this time to note that DOC is highly *differentiated*, that the organization has a number of major subdivisions and that many of the organization's members work in specialized subunits. In effect, the set of issues, problems, and tasks to be addressed and carried out by DOC is subdivided, and DOC's structure reflects this parceling out of the overall set. The implications of this subdivision are important. First, those managing and working within each of the major subcomponents and specialized subunits tend to concentrate on their own portions of the organization and to selectively prioritize their roles, their shares of the overall set of problems, and their organizational interests as the most important ones.

Figure 6.1
Department of Corrections (DOC) — Internal/External Environment

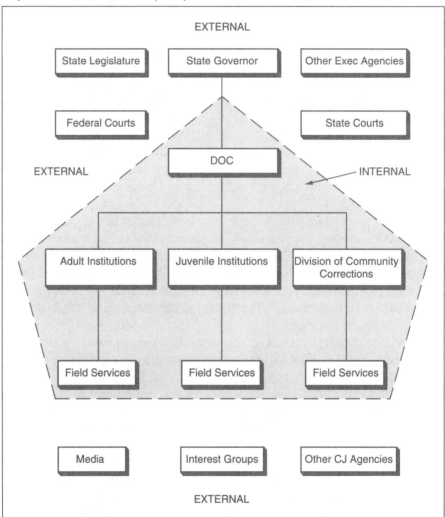

EXTERNAL

State Legislature State Governor Other Exec Agencies

Federal Courts State Courts

EXTERNAL DOC INTERNAL

Adult Institutions Juvenile Institutions Division of Community Corrections

Field Services Field Services Field Services

Media Interest Groups Other CJ Agencies

EXTERNAL

Source: Developed by Rick Lovell.

Top-level management must develop policies and carry out administrative activities which insure that the entire organization functions as a well-integrated entity. Many difficulties may stem from the differentiated structure. We will not attempt to go into all the possibilities. However, consider as an example that DOC has a limited budget (although it may be a large one). Top-level management must allocate resources for the entire organization. At budgeting time, it is not uncommon for those administering the major subcomponents and specialized subunits to compete with one another for what they view to be their appropriate or necessary shares of the budget pie. Organizational tension results from budget maneuvering and attempts to support requests. Top-level management is in the end accountable for the distribution of resources within the organization, and decisions must be made concerning internal priorities. Seldom will these decisions entirely satisfy all those concerned. Similar difficulties emerge in addressing most aspects of the attempt to adequately coordinate and control the operation of DOC.

Second, the subelements of DOC are physically located in different areas of the state. The operations of these subelements do not take place in a vacuum, nor are they confined by any actual boundaries from influences immediate to their locations. This makes control and coordination of the organization a very complicated undertaking. Again, we will go deeper into the associated problems in the section on Common Concerns. For now, consider a basic situation and extend your thinking to other aspects of operation and other parts of the organization. For example, think of one of the probation field offices operating in one of the cities. This office and its probation personnel must establish working relationships with the law enforcement agencies in its immediate area, with the courts in its immediate area, with the local district attorneys' offices, and so on. These relationships may include both formal and informal working agreements, and successful operation requires cooperation among all those involved.

Top-level management may provide general policies to guide the operation of the field office, but the particulars of operation must be dealt with by managers at the lower levels of the organization. In addition, the situations confronted by the various field offices across the state will vary. Even this cursory illustration should lead one to begin to understand that *delegation of authority* and the existence of discretion at all levels of management are important aspects of the internal environment, that coordination and control of such a large agency is difficult, and that, considering the many aspects of operation of DOC (budgeting, personnel decisions, specific task accomplishment, and so on) overall administration is neither simple nor easy.

Beyond this, DOC's administrators confront an *external environment*. As we stated above, DOC's various activities do not take place in a vacuum. Ideally, top-level management is seen as a buffer between DOC and important forces in the external environment. As noted above, however, persons in the various subelements of DOC interact with important forces in the external environment across the state. Our focus in this section is on the major, significant aspects of the external environment confronted by top-level management.

Most top-level correctional administrators recognize their operating contexts as political. As important and time-consuming as their activities are in confronting and resolving internal issues and problems of the organization, its day-to-day functioning and the accomplishment of tasks, the primary focus for most of these top-level managers is actually placed on interactions with significant persons in the external environment. At the system level (Department or Division level) there is a rather large array of significant relationships with other organizations, groups, and individuals important to the operation of DOC. The slate of "significant others" may vary somewhat from state to state, and may vary according to the issues or problems involving the DOC. Our concern here is to emphasize the need for visualizing and thinking about such relationships and the importance of conceptualizing the external environment and implications for administration. We do not think it is necessary to attempt an exhaustive listing of potentially important "significant others," but we offer the following as examples.

To begin with, DOC is an agency within the *executive branch of state government*. Its top administrator is appointed by the *governor*; therefore, the governor has a large amount of influence concerning the direction of overall policy for DOC. Do not lose sight of the notion that governors are elected and respond to influential constituents; also have many demanding responsibilities to occupy their attentions. DOC under one governor could have a top administrator who has a strong corrections background and may be inclined to "do something constructive" with offenders; under another governor the top administrator may have a corporate or "big government" background and may be primarily inclined to operate an "efficient agency." It may be somewhat uncharitable to say so, but many governors develop a "don't hurt me" agenda regarding the operation of DOC—meaning, as we have previously indicated, that the message conveyed to the top administrator is to keep a low profile for DOC, satisfy as many interests as possible, keep things stable and rather efficient, and do as much as possible to avoid allowing problems to surface that may make "waves" for the coalition or party in power.

The *state legislature* is very important to the operation of DOC. DOC's budget is dependent upon the action of the legislature, and top-level administrators must attempt to maintain relationships that put them in a good position to lobby for budget. Also, the legislature passes laws that directly affect DOC'S operations. Again, top-level administrators must maintain relationships that put them in a strong position to lobby for or against legislation important to them and the organization. The legislature has committees, subcommittees, and certain individual members (those who are very interested in corrections for whatever reason) important to DOC. DOC's top-level administrators are particularly concerned about relations with finance committees, judiciary committees, corrections committees (these especially), and individual legislators who take keen interest in corrections as either allies or antagonists.

Both *state* and *federal courts* are significant to those in control of DOC. Regarding the courts, many correctional administrators view themselves as generally on the defensive, responding to litigation and possible litigation that may arise from various sources. Consider our mythical DOC to be currently operating under a *consent decree* (a settlement of a lawsuit in which administration agrees to take certain actions without admitting fault or guilt for the situation that gave rise to the lawsuit) (Oran, 1982:96) issued by a federal district court, stemming from a class action lawsuit filed by inmates. (This is not farfetched. Only five state DOCs have never had a federal court order issued either against the entire system or against one or more of the major institutions.) In such a situation, DOC's administrators, under a plan agreed to in court, are required to take action in a number of areas of operation to alleviate conditions the federal judge has found unacceptable. The court will monitor progress. DOC's top administrators will respond directly to ongoing inquiries made by the federal judge. In addition, other litigation is continually pending. A great deal of top management's energy is focused on creating and maintaining a management posture and sets of policies and operating procedures to provide a strong array of defensible positions to litigation.

The *media* must be recognized. Throughout our mythical state, the various elements of the media are powerful. The media helps set the tone for opinion regarding DOC, often pursues issues resulting in criticism of DOC and its administration, and sometimes pursues issues resulting in favorable publicity. DOC's top administrators are concerned with *image management* and, therefore, with policies and procedures regarding interactions with media personnel and information release. Control is difficult because the organization is large, and its subelements and personnel are spread throughout the state, offering many points of potential access and interaction. The "boundaries" of this organization may be said to be permeable.

The *general public* may be said to be an important portion of the external environment. After all, tax dollars support the organization, and the "public" may quite rightfully be termed the "clients" (or purchasers) of the services provided by DOC. However, as we noted earlier, the "public" is composed of individuals and groups, holding—perhaps advocating—diverse interests and opinions, and these individuals and groups have differing degrees of access to important decisionmakers as well as differing degrees of influence or power. We are better served to think of a variety of *interest groups* existing within the external environment. "An interest group is a 'shared attitude group that makes certain claims upon other groups in society;' ... such a group becomes political 'if and when it makes a claim through or upon any of the institutions of government'" (Dye,1987:26-27).

"External formal and informal interest groups seek to use the organization and its power to affect public policy and values, to appropriate the organization's surplus, to support other organizations or groups, to sell it goods and services, to control its impact on the environment (e.g., [prison] location, wage rates,..., civil rights practices, and so on)" (Perrow, 1986:261). Inmate rights groups, various reform groups (e.g., neo-retributionist reformers), professional groups with vested interests (such as the American Correctional Association), unions (e.g., correctional officer unions—please keep in mind that some groups may be organized "outside" the DOC and have members who also work "inside," and keep in mind that there are internal interest groups that we will discuss more in following sections), community-interest groups (e.g., citizen groups, perhaps local government groups seeking location of a prison in a particular community), and private-sector interest groups (seeking greater reliance on private sector involvement in corrections endeavors through vendor contracts, private sector financing arrangements, even institutional facility management contracts) are examples of potentially important external interest groups.

Top-level managers in DOC must interact with those seeking to make claims on the organization, seeking to influence its operation. Often, these external "significant others" are quite powerful and have a broad base of political support. Many external groups are relatively underpowered; that is, they act in "good conscience" perhaps, but have not amassed the power or support to swing a great deal of weight. The difficulty for top management lies in determining how and to whom to respond. Occasionally, top management wishes to use external interest groups to assist in furthering its own aims. In this case, the issues for management center on developing and maintaining alliances that are considered to be critical for the support of the organization and management's perceptions of DOC's interests. The permutations of DOC/interest group interaction are numerous. Please keep in mind that "the [top administrators] are the chief focal point for external groups, but the boundaries of [the organization] are very permeable, allowing access at any level, sometimes linking an internal group with an external one" (Perrow, 1986:261)

Beyond all this, DOC's external environment includes a number of other organizations important to its operations. For example, *other criminal justice organizations* are important in the rather obvious sense of providing a larger process of which DOC is a part. Policies that are being made (for example, sentencing changes) are important to DOC and its leadership. DOC's administrators must maintain an awareness of potential shifts and may need to provide input regarding policies of other organizations. In addition, *other government agencies*, such as a Department of Administration, or Management and Budget, are very important. DOC's administrators must comply with policies and procedures enacted by outside agencies when resulting actions impact DOC. Again, DOC's top managers may need to have input concerning the development of policies and procedures that affect them; they also may need to establish and maintain good working relationships with the administrators of other agencies to assist in facilitating the smooth operation of DOC as a part of the larger network of government organizations.

As we noted above, it is not our intent to provide an exhaustive listing of potentially important forces or "significant others." Rather, we wish to emphasize the importance of considering administration at the "DOC level;" gaining a measure of sensitivity regarding the complex context for managing and an idea of the role and some of the possibly important concerns for top-level administrators. In asking questions about why things happen the way they do in corrections, such attention is crucial.

Service-Delivery Level

At this level we are interested in visualizing and discussing single organizations directly involved with operational activities in corrections. Our focus is placed on such organizations as correctional institutions, probation field offices, and other organizations established to provide various correctional programs. These organizations may be component parts of DOCs or perhaps the Federal Bureau of Prisons, or one may be considering any of the many organizations established and controlled through local governments (i.e., serving limited areas and limited populations). Earlier we used the term "system" to refer to the DOCs. In the terminology of organizational theory, *system* can refer to a large, multifaceted organization such as a DOC, to a smaller, single organization and its component parts, or to any of the component parts analyzed unto themselves. In other words, a correctional institution may be viewed as an organizational system with an internal and external environment, just as we viewed the DOC as a system.

Please keep in mind that at this level of analysis we are concerned with a very large array of single organizations that may be structured in widely different ways depending on the purposes to be achieved by the organizations. Moreover, these exist in a wide array of operational contexts, but remember to focus on internal environments and external environments and potentially important relationships in thinking about the administration of such organizations. The following sections on common concerns and the focus on institutional management contain comments to be applied at this level of analysis.

Common Concerns

Whether one is considering a DOC, a prison, a probation field office, or any particular program delivery organization, corrections organizations should be understood as complex, bureaucratic organizations. Corrections organizations are not unique in this sense; that is, government organizations in general, and most private sector organizations, may be characterized in the same way.

Bureaucracy is not a dirty word. This term refers to an ubiquitous organizational form. Most of our existing organizations are to a large degree bureaucratic. That is, one may find structure and activities based on the following:

(a) division of labor,

(b) a multilevel formal structure with a hierarchy of positions or offices,

(c) dependence on formal rules and procedures to ensure uniformity and to regulate the behavior of job holders,

(d) an impersonal nature [e.g., sanctions are to be applied uniformly and impersonally to avoid involvement with individual personalities and personal preferences of members],

(e) employment decisions based on merit [i.e., the selection and promotion decisions are to be based on technical qualifications, competence, and performance],

(f) career tracks established to allow for advancement and secure commitment of employees, and

(g) supposedly the separation of the organization member's work affairs and his or her personal affairs [to prevent personal interests from interfering with job performance] (Robbins, 1987: 233).

These characteristics illustrate the classical perspective on organization proposed by Max Weber (1947). "They illustrate "Weber's 'ideal' type of rational [goal-oriented] and efficient organization" (Robbins, 1987:233). Consideration of any corrections organization will reveal formal design features reflecting the above characteristics to a large extent. "Keep in mind, however, that Weber's bureaucratic model was a hypothetical rather than a factual description of how most organizations [are] structured [and operated]" (Robbins, 1987:233). When we consider the internal environments of corrections organizations, we find the formal skeletons to be bureaucratic, both in the sense of structure and in the sense of expected behaviors. Nonetheless, the operation and administration of these organizations does not necessarily closely approximate the ideal in all respects.

Bureaucracy, as an organizational design, may be said to have strong and positive qualities. For example, lines of formal authority and accountability, duties, and responsibilities are at least to be specified. *Standardization* is the central theme of bureaucracy, and the various mechanisms associated with standardizing operations assist in coordinating and controlling the activities of large numbers of people. There are other positive qualities.

The bureaucratic form itself is said to give rise to many organizational dysfunctions; for example, rules and regulations becoming more important than the ends they are designed to achieve, employee alienation arising because of the impersonality inherent in the design, impediments to adaptation or change stemming from the effort to standardize and regulate behaviors through the development of routines and repertoires of action, and so on (see Robbins, 1987). There have been and are many criticisms of bureaucracy as an organizational form.

The formal foundation for corrections organizations is bureaucratic. This foundation in part shapes the context within which correctional administrators operate. However, there is more to consider in thinking about the internal environment and administration. Notably, there is an informal dimension to life in complex organizations. Patterns and networks of communication, networks of influence and power, norms and expectations concerning performance and behaviors in work groups, and many other aspects of administration and operation arise as informal facets of organizational life overlaying and intertwined with the formal design. The informal may supplement, complement, compete with the formal. Correctional administrators must attempt to live with, understand, confront, utilize, and perhaps attempt to change the formal and informal dimensions of their organizations.

Managing

Throughout this chapter we use the terms *management* and *administration* and the terms *manager* and *administrator* interchangeably. "Some writers use the terms administrator and administration to depict managers in the public sector or to describe the jobs of those in the organization who determine major objectives and policies" (Robbins, 1984:9). We agree with Robbins that "there are no significant differences between the terms management and administration" (1984:10). As he states, "The field of management is applicable to business, government, and other not-for-profit organizations" and "the management problems that these varied organizations confront are similar, and the duties of their managers are equally similar" (1984:10). Likewise, the functions and roles of managers in corrections organizations are similar, as is the bulk of the problems they face.

The generic functions of management include planning, organizing, leading, and controlling (Robbins, 1984:6). We have noted that corrections organizations are bureaucratic and that structurally these organizations are hierarchical. In other words, management positions exist at various levels of these organizations. If we refer to the DOC example, we again see a top-level management for the entire organization, another level of management at the major subdivision level, yet another level of management at the single subunit level (for example, there is a warden or superintendent and deputy wardens or deputy superintendents for each prison, a chief probation officer and perhaps a deputy chief probation officer for each probation field office and so on) and within each subunit organization there are levels of management (from the subunit's top managers such as wardens and deputy wardens through supervisors, for example, shift supervisors or living unit managers). Obviously, some organizations have more levels of hierarchy, more levels of management than others.

It is important to think about what managers at different levels do, in a broad sense. "All managers make decisions. They perform planning, organizing, leading and controlling functions" (Robbins, 1984:11). But, as one considers moving from the lower, *operational* levels of an organization (where service-delivery tasks are carried out by line workers) to the upper, *policy-oriented* levels, the nature of the problems confronted, the focus for managers, and the nature and scope of the management functions performed change in degree. Supervisors are most likely to be concerned with technical problems associated with carrying out specific sets of tasks on a day-to-day basis. Their management activities are most likely to primarily involve leading or controlling through direct supervision of line employees. Upper-level managers are most likely to be concerned with problems or issues that often are not well-defined, that involve a large number of interested persons, and that primarily involve resolving questions of value or preference in selecting and organizing options to pursue. We have attempted to give some sense of this in the preceding discussion of the role of top-level DOC administrators. As one's focus moves from middle-level management to top-level management, one would expect to see managers devoting more time to planning and resolution of issues related to broad options, also to organizing to pursue broad options, and less time and involvement in leading and directly controlling the activities of subordinates. The supervisor's role is undeniably important. Often, people speak of first-line supervisors as the backbone of an organization. However, our focus in this chapter is placed more on the upper levels of management.

"Managers affect organizational outcomes [results, successes and failures] by the decisions they make" (Robbins, 1984:13). In order to gain perspective on decision-making in corrections, one should again think about context. We have already given the indication that the external context for decision-making is political. The internal environment and context is also political. As we have briefly noted, those in various subdivisions normally have their own subdivision's interests prioritized as the most essential. Moreover, different individuals and groups throughout the organization may have their own individual or group interests prioritized as most essential, and these interests may not all coincide with management's perceptions of the "organization's best interests." Beyond this, the development of informal networks of influence, communication, and power within the organization overlap formal groupings.

> Internal formal groups, such as departments or work groups, seek to use the organization for such ends as promotion of ideological positions or public policies, protection of groups and expansion of group power, control of working conditions—including degree of effort, safety, interpersonal interactions, and job security—and satisfaction of personal goals. Internal informal groups do the same, but the membership cuts across that of formal groups and tends to offset the centrifugal effects of multiple group strivings by binding groups together, sometimes in unexpected ways. (Perrow, 1986:261)

The section on institutional management will provide examples of the notions concerning groups. For now, it is important to understand that much goes on in complex, bureaucratic organizations, and that "group usage" of the organization may facilitate the decision-making process or it may interfere with it (see Perrow, 1986:260-262).

In their decision-making activities, correctional administrators engage in a process characterized by "bureaucratic politics" (Allison, 1971). Particularly at the middle and upper levels of management, most decisions may be described as *political resultants*, "*resultants* in the sense that what happens is not chosen as a [rational] solution to a problem but rather results from compromise, conflict, and confusion of officials with diverse interests and unequal influence; *political* in the sense that the activity from which decisions and actions emerge is best characterized as bargaining along regularized channels..." (Allison, 1971:162).

Consider the development of a policy, such as the organization's budget, the resultant of a set of decisions concerning the allocation of its financial resources. Inside the organization, in its internal environment, everyone will be affected, and many will take an interest in attempting to influence the budget decision process. Remember the discussion above of internal formal and internal informal groups and "usage." Certain managers, by virtue of their positions, will participate directly in the decision-making process; their positions place them in formal networks or lines of authority, giving them formal responsibility for budget decisions or for input concerning various portions of the overall budget decision. Others may seek to influence those directly involved either through formal avenues for communicating input or through informal lines of communication and influence. *Power* for those involved, formally or informally, is a blend of (1) "bargaining advantages," (2) "skill and will in using bargaining advantages," and (3) "others' perceptions of the bargaining advantages" available to any particular participant in the process (Allison, 1971:168).

> The sources of bargaining advantages include formal authority and responsibility (stemming from positions); actual control over resources necessary to carry out action; expertise and control over information that enables one to define the problem, identify options, and estimate feasibilities; control over information that enables chiefs to determine whether and in what form decisions are being implemented; the ability to affect other decisionmakers' objectives in other [decisions] ...; personal persuasiveness ... (drawn from personal relations, charisma); and access to and persuasiveness with [decisionmakers] who have bargaining advantages drawn from the above (based on interpersonal relations, etc.) (Allison, 1971:169).

What all this means is that those with interests in the budget (as may be the case with many types of decisions or anticipated options and actions) seek to gain support of the most influential decisionmakers. The influential decisionmakers seek to influence one another. There may be many permutations of interests and interested parties in the budget decision. To construct a simple illustration, think of a top-level administrator who wishes to increase the number and quality of programs offered inmates. Imagine the correctional officer force to be unionized and strong, with a primary interest in pay increases, job security (both in the sense of job tenure and in the sense of working in a secure, controlled job situation—physical security), and increasing the number of correctional officer positions. Imagine those with job interests and what are often described as professional interests in various programs (e.g., inmate education programs, various therapeutic programs, etc.) seeking to obtain increases in funding, staffing levels, numbers of programs. Imagine that there is a limited projected increase in monies to allocate for salaries and positions—one item for consideration in the overall budget.

The correctional officer union has bargaining advantages tied to its strength in numbers, its connections inside the organization with decisionmakers who favor its position, and external connections with influential persons that have been gained through political lobbyist activities. The program persons have similar advantages, and although these persons may not have as much a singular voice as the union, they may present support from externally organized professional associations, may have several administrators favoring their positions, and, for purposes of our illustration, may bring to the decision demands from inmates for more programs in a system that is facing court scrutiny.

Again, we are imagining possibilities concerning only one aspect of the budget decision—what to do with the small projected increase for personnel and salaries. Bureaucratic politics within the organization may become quite involved concerning this issue. Add to this maneuvering by significant others outside the organization, and one can imagine perhaps a large measure of intensity among those who must interact directly to reach a resultant decision. The overall budget decision process may involve a number of similarly difficult issues, and ultimately a number of compromises may be necessary, or perhaps those with sufficient bargaining advantages may rather clearly prevail in having their interests expressed in the overall policy.

We cannot provide a full range of illustrations of potential decision issues. The budget illustration is a cursory illustration. Please keep in mind that problems of one sort or another, perhaps involving many interested persons and groups, are emerging continually in corrections organizations, and management often must confront many problems or sets of problems simultaneously. There will be deadlines associated with many of these problems, and where there are deadlines, management's attention will necessarily be forced toward meeting the deadlines, presenting "acceptable" decisions, and designing or providing incentives and controls that result in conformity by those who are involved in carrying out actions to support the decisions.

This may all seem overly complicated. Nonetheless, we have actually only scratched the surface concerning management in corrections. One should remember that the legitimacy of correctional administrators is largely dependent on maintaining fairly stable organizations and on having the organizations achieve, or appear to achieve, something. Do not let the conceptualization of "bureaucratic politics" become a pejorative notion. Use this notion to develop a perspective, for recognizing the extent to which formal and informal interactions involving the internal environment and the external environment are important considerations in asking why things happen the way they do in corrections.

Focus on Institutional Management

Much of the research and thought on correctional administration has emphasized the management of maximum security correctional institutions. In this section, we focus our attention on administration of a maximum security institution as an example of thinking about and analyzing management at the service delivery level in corrections. Please keep in mind that approximately 25% of the confinement facilities in the United States are maximum security institutions. These house approximately 44% of all inmates (Bureau of Justice Statistics, 1987). The average size of the inmate population in these institutions is just under 1,000 (Bureau of Justice Statistics, 1987). Also, keep in mind that there is a good deal of variability among confinement facilities, particularly if one is considering not only maximum security institutions but all institutions, maximum security to minimum security. Nonetheless there is enough commonality regarding administration to allow the extension of the notions to be presented.

We again ask the reader to imagine a typically structured, mythical organization (see Figure 6.2). MAX is located, as are most correctional institutions in the United States, near a small, rural community. The inmate population is approximately 1,000. MAX is a rather large, complex, bureaucratic organization. As shown in Figure 6.2, the structure of the organization is differentiated (i.e., there are major divisions for custody, program services, management operations, each of which is subdivided into a number of sections, and there are several specialized subelements). MAX has a total staff of approximately 400 persons, with administrative positions extending from that of the superintendent through those of the line supervisors. The largest single group among the organization's personnel is composed of the correctional officers (approximately 325 correctional officers staff three shifts in a round-the-clock operation).

Figure 6.2
Maximum Security Prison–Internal/External Environments

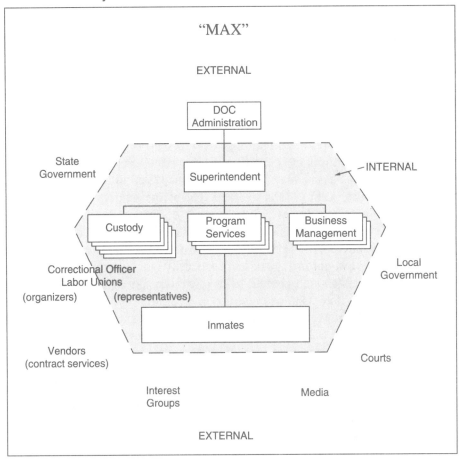

Source: Developed by Rick Lovell.

As a complex organization MAX may be said to have an internal environment and an external environment (remember our previous discussion of DOC and Figure 6.1). Many people seem to have the idea that correctional institutions exist in a vacuum. Such a notion is inaccurate. Managers of correctional institutions must be aware of and confront a rather large array of influences or forces in the external environment and in the internal environment of the institution. In this regard the context for administration of a correctional institution is complex.

External Concerns

To begin with, correctional institutions such as MAX are a part of a larger organization; in the case we are considering, a DOC. The institution must be managed and operated within the parameters and policies established by the top management of DOC. The superintendents of correctional institutions are granted freedom more or less in setting institutional policies, depending on the degree of control their DOC's upper-level management deems necessary. In general, wardens or superintendents have a relatively high degree of autonomy, but keep in mind that these administrators are accountable to administrators such as the director of adult institutions and the chief executive of the DOC.

In addition, MAX is situated near a small, rural community. MAX is a major industry in its area (think of MAX in terms similar to an auto plant existing in such an area). MAX annually provides a multi-million dollar payroll for those who are employed, and the operation of the prison requires the establishment of a number of vendor contracts in the local area (e.g., food service contracts, maintenance contracts, contracts for other services). Local community leaders and groups are interested parties in the operation of MAX. They are quite likely to initiate interactions with the superintendent or other upper-level managers concerning MAX's economic potential in the local area. Also, local leaders and groups may initiate interactions regarding the more visible concerns of community protection or even issues associated with promoting a better understanding of the prison and its operations.

MAX's superintendent must also interact with persons and groups that have interests in the operation of this particular prison because of the inmates who reside there. MAX's superintendent and other upper-level managers may interface with inmate rights' groups, families of inmates (e.g., concerning issues such as visitation policies), and court officials (particularly where litigation specific to the institution is underway). Beyond this, MAX's administrators may interact sporadically with other interested persons, such as researchers seeking entry to the prison to carry out various projects, state legislators who have special interest in MAX's operation, and members of the media. The media are quite important, although for any given institution, media attention and interest may range from sporadic to almost continuous. With such potential topics and issues as escape, deaths in prison, AIDS, prison conditions, the punishment versus rehabilitation issue, and others, MAX's administration must be sensitive to the potential for media interest and to potential staff or inmate and media interaction.

As a final example of significant external interests (we are again attempting to provide directions for thought rather than an exhaustive listing), consider that MAX's correctional officer force is unionized (roughly 50% of the nation's correctional officers are members of unions). The union is actually organized outside the institution and reflects sets of interests developed by a larger constituency than its members working in MAX. MAX's upper-level managers must understand the labor contract and must be prepared to interact with union representatives. Such interactions are particularly important—a large number of members of this externally organized interest group work within the institution (are a part of its internal environment), and these persons (COs) are vital to the functioning of the institution.

We could go on identifying potentially significant others in MAX's external environment. The above, however, should be a sufficient start and a sufficient indication of the types of outside forces that may impact the administration of a correctional institution. The administrators of correctional institutions such as MAX must realize the nature of significant forces in the external environment and must develop an understanding of the degree to which such forces may impact the institution. These administrators cannot hope to harness or control all these forces, but they may seek to shape the environment somewhat through interactions designed to maximize favorable relationships between those connected to the institution and those external parties that have interests in the institution and its operation.

Internal Concerns

MAX has an internal environment that is differentiated and presents complex issues for administration. Figure 6.2 shows the structural complexity. Moreover, managing MAX requires coordinating and controlling diverse work groups (administrative personnel, correctional officers, program services personnel) and the inmate population. Administrators must plan for and manage operations in a variety of areas; for example:

a. Inmate custody and institutional security
    1. discipline
    2. inmate records
    3. grievances
    4. visitation
    5. rights and other privileges

b. Inmate care and welfare
    1. classification and counseling
    2. health and medical care
    3. education and vocational training
    4. recreation
    5. religion
    6. social services
    7. release services

c. Inmate work programs
    1. plant maintenance, perhaps construction
    2. factory management
    3. farm production
    4. inmate wages and account system
    5. hobby management and management of other income-
        producing activities

d. Business and fiscal management
    1. budgets
    2. accounting
    3. procurement
    4. property control
    5. food services

e. General administration
    1. personnel management and labor relations
    2. personnel development
    3. public relations
    4. relations with other government agencies
    5. relations with others in DOC (adapted from McGee, 1981:76-77)

These and other related areas represent matters that are ever present among the concerns of institutional administration.

As indicated above, there are many aims and tasks to be accomplished in operating the institution (these may vary by degree and somewhat by type from institution to institution). We noted earlier that standardization is one of the central features of bureaucratic organization. Rules, regulations, standard operating procedures, and routines for action provide a formal basis for much of what is to be accomplished. These together with the formal system of hierarchy and authority assist in coordinating and controlling efforts at task accomplishment in the institution. MAX is typical of other institutions in that it is highly bureaucratized—in the sense of having several levels of hierarchy and in having myriad policies, rules, regulations, and so on.

The formal arrangements for operation are often complemented, sometimes circumvented, through informal expectations, informal policies, interpretations and use of discretion, and informal routines for action that develop over time. Formal expressions (policies, rules, and so on) do not always cover every possible situation, perhaps do not seem appropriate for given situations (and therefore those involved interpret and use discretion to take action) and at times formal authority (the legitimate power to reward or sanction which is associated with one's position in the hierarchy) gives way to other, informal, forms of power (such as the ability to influence others because one is considered an expert, through force of personality, through the use of certain bargaining advantages, and so on).

From an administrative point of view, managing the institution is to a very large extent a matter of recognizing and utilizing the formal and informal aspects present in the organizational context. This is not simple. The formal and the informal come together in practically everything that is done within the institution. Obviously, it is beyond the scope of this chapter to attempt to address all the possibilities. However, we can gain useful insight by examining the overall question of how control or equilibrium is maintained in the institution.

Think again about authority and power. Authority, as we have defined it, is formally present in the hierarchy of positions in the institution. Most people probably conceive of the institution as being controlled through the formal organizational pyramid of authority—in other words, having broad orders or directives issued by the superintendent, these orders being clarified and further details added as appropriate at the mid-levels of management, then having the ultimate orders for operation presented by first-line supervisors to line personnel who apply them in their areas of operation. This conception does describe the essential notion for operation. It also describes a bureaucratic conception of "total power," in that the expectation is that the power to *reward* or *sanction* will account for task accomplishment and control. Those lower in the organizational pyramid are usually thought of as having a responsibility to obey those who have authority over them.

However, the operation of an institution—the maintenance of control or equilibrium—is not adequately described by the above. The distribution of power in the institution does not simply coincide with the lines of formal authority. Rather, power is distributed in a polycentric manner. At the very least we must recognize that the institution's management and staff are concerned with controlling a large inmate population (management and staff are far outnumbered). This inmate population has no absolute duty to obey those with formal organizational authority (see Sykes, 1958). Moreover, the inmate population is not composed of a single-minded group of persons. The inmate subculture is differentiated, and power and influence within this subculture are distributed in a polycentric manner (refer to Chapter 9). The matter of controlling the inmate population involves a complicated blending of formal authority and informal influence, power that is shared or distributed among those in management, staff, and inmate groupings.

We must also recognize that management is differentiated at least by level and across divisions and that managers in the institution are not necessarily of a single mind concerning the operation of the institution, those tasks that are more important, those activities that should take priority, those approaches that might result in acceptable outcomes. Staff are also differentiated and represent, as we indicated earlier, different interests or at least different perspectives on the operation of the institution and their own roles within the institution. Consider not only differences such as those that may be found between program service personnel and the correctional officer force, but also consider possible differences within these nominal groupings. Think about the different potential roles, aims, perspectives and interests within the correctional officer force. While overall in our mythical MAX, the CO union may present a rather singular perspective in negotiations with management, the correctional officers may themselves present a broad set of concerns with operation of the institution. This may become more apparent when one thinks about the activities, task assignments, and possible aims of cellblock officers, those working in administrative assignments, work detail officers, yard officers, and so on.

It is very important to realize that informal aspects of organization and power may complement, supplement, and circumvent the formal aspects. One must be aware of the large array of concerns in managing and operating an institution. Think of the discussion presented in this chapter and those presented in other chapters in this book. Maintaining equilibrium or stability—control of the institution—is a primary aim for institutional administration. Doing so requires a careful balance among many factors, especially astutely managing a give-and-take relationship among the various work groups staffing the institution and between the inmates and staff.

If one conceives of stability as a primary outcome, then one may think of the various factors that affect power as variables in an equation. Changes in the balance of these factors, these variables, may result in changes in the balance of power and affect stability. Successful institutional administrators understand this and must carefully consider the balance present in any given institution. Success in maintaining stability while accomplishing something constructive requires technical proficiency, conceptual ability, and well-developed social skills among those who manage an institution. Successful administration requires an understanding of the polycentric distribution of power in an institution, as well as the nature and effects of external forces impacting this distribution.

Summary

As a topic, correctional administration covers a broad set of concerns. It is useful to consider correctional administration at different levels of analysis, focusing on relevant implications for administration at each level. One must keep in mind variations in correctional organizations, size, structure, degree of bureaucratic complexity, scope and nature of operations. One may think of a societal level of analysis and identify concerns associated with the "major option-setting context" (Perrow, 1986:263). Here, attention is directed to implications for the development of overall aims and policies.

At a second level, which we have termed the DOC level, attention is directed to the large, complex organizations such as the Departments or Divisions of Corrections and the U.S. Bureau of Prisons. Here, the relationships of these organizations to significant others in an external environment, or operating context, deserve attention. In addition, understanding administration requires appreciation of a complex internal environment that may be characterized by "bureaucratic politics" (Allison, 1971).

At a third level, the "service-delivery level," one focuses on organizations of various sorts involved in directly providing correctional services. These may be parts of large agencies organized as state government agencies, may be locally organized and administered organizations, or may carry out broad or rather limited correctional functions. Here again, attention is directed to the tasks of management in administering complex internal structures and environments while gaining appreciation for the external contexts of operation and administrative requirements.

Correctional administrators face many challenges. As the following "On the Defensive" section indicates, many correctional administrators find themselves in situations in which the pressure to do something positive, combined with intense external scrutiny, may lead to a decidedly defensive posture.

Continuing Administrative Concerns

Regardless of the expressed aims, regardless of the underlying philosophy, those who manage jails, prisons, state DOCs, probation agencies, various programs and other correctional organizations "have the core responsibility to carry out the sentence of the court by whatever means available" (McGee, 1981:2). While addressing this obligation (administrators are called upon to show that something is being done), those in charge must contend with an often unsettling array of surrounding and controlling forces. Many see themselves in situations where they "cannot win," at best they can meet with repeated crises and "keep their heads above water," or at less than best they "lose."

"This is a time when the system as a system is being questioned; its goals and purposes are being debated, and the viability of its methods are being reexamined" (McGee, 1981:3). At the start of the 1980s, McGee outlined some of the major difficulties to be confronted by correctional administrators as they attempt to do something constructive. At the start of the 1990s, his thoughts are yet on target. Consider:

The public is becoming more and more strident in its demands that crime be reduced and that miscreants be locked up or even threatened with execution. The same public wants lower taxes, fewer police, and less money for prisons and jails.

Failure to demonstrate the effectiveness of many of the so-called rehabilitative programs in both community projects and institutions has caused a cloud of cynicism over professional efforts to diagnose and treat convicted law violators.

There is general dissatisfaction with the sentencing laws and a strong movement away from the indeterminate sentence. The mood among political decisionmakers is to turn to harsher punishments as the remedy of last resort, though there is no evidence that this works any better.

The proportion of convicted felons being sent to state prisons instead of the alternatives of local jails, restitution programs, and probation has been increasing in recent years.

More of the tax burden seems to be shifting from local to state governments. Dislocations of programs resulting from this factor alone are not being addressed by responsible public officials.

Due to tax problems and the reluctance of state legislatures to face the financial problem, there are strong indications that federal aid will be sought, especially for the construction of institutions.

The movement toward prisons of smaller size, placed in less-isolated locations, seems to be gaining acceptance, but there has been little implementation of the idea.

Racial and ethnic discrimination and its related problems in prison discipline and order continue, especially in states with large minority populations.

The unionization of public employees is creating special and unfamiliar problems for correctional managers.

The failure to provide constructive occupation for prisoners continues to contribute to prisoner unrest and public dissatisfaction with the prison as a viable social institution.

Reasonable, safe, and politically acceptable alternatives to prisons such as probation supervision, parole, restitution centers, halfway houses, short-term jail sentences, work camps, and variable mutations of these appear to be fighting a rear-guard battle to hold their present positions. There is much rhetoric but no strong forward movement in these programs in the early 1980s.

Overcrowding of jails and prisons is being regarded by both correctional professionals and courts as untenable. These facilities nevertheless are overrun with sheer numbers, making many old outmoded buildings even more untenable.

The costs of both construction and operation of jails, prisons, and correctional institutions have grown to such proportions as to seem unacceptable to many public bodies.

There is a continuing growth of judicial intervention in the administration of jails and prisons. These cases generally attack such issues as overcrowding, "cruel and unusual" living conditions, physical mistreatment, and failure to provide normal access to the courts and the public.

Correctional administrators do find themselves on the defensive. For the past 25 years there has been increasing scrutiny of correctional administration as a "practicing profession." McGee summarizes the primary sort of criticism:

> Most fields of human endeavor produce a few leaders who stand out among their peers for great ideas, great performance, or both.

> This administration of criminal justice has been singularly deficient in this respect....They [administrators] tend to come from miscellaneous backgrounds, often growing up in a limited local bureaucracy producing inward-looking viewpoints and parochial attitudes. Others come in from seemingly related fields.... Most of them do not survive [in their positions] even long enough to learn on the job (McGee, 1981:155).

This sort of criticism has been aimed at correctional administration in general and fired broadside after broadside. Faced with difficult operational contexts, intractable problems, and mounting criticism of a general nature, one may expect reactive postures.

The avenue for optimism for correctional administration has been and is increasing professionalism. This avenue includes not only development and selection of competent professionals but also includes building a coalition of competent practicing professionals and others to lead "corrections" in promising directions, to be "spokepersons for progressive corrections" (Breed, 1986), and to be activists. As yet, such a professionalization has not been achieved. For now, correctional administrators remain largely on the defensive.

Source: Written by Rick Lovell.

Key Terms and Concepts

administration
authority
bureaucracy
bureaucratic politics
consent decree
delegation of authority
"don't hurt me" agenda
executive branch
external environment
formal organization
imager management
informal organization
interest groups
internal environment

judiciary
legislative branch
managerial control
managing
media
organizational system
policy
political resultants
power
service-delivery context
societal context
standardization
system context

References

Allison, G.T. (1971). *Essence of Decision.* Boston: Little, Brown and Company.

Bureau of Justice Statistics (1987). "Prisoners, 1986." Washington, DC: U.S. Department of Justice.

Dye, T.R. (1987). *Understanding Public Policy, Sixth Edition.* Englewood Cliffs, NJ: Prentice-Hall.

McGee, R.A. (1981). *Prisons and Politics.* Lexington, MA: Lexington Books.

Oran, D. (1983). *Oran's Dictionary of the Law.* St. Paul, MN: West Publishing Co.

Perrow, C. (1986). *Complex Organizations: A Critical Essay.* New York, NY: Random House.

Robbins, S.P. (1987). *Organization Theory, Second Edition.* Englewood Cliffs, NJ: Prentice-Hall.

Robbins, S.P. (1984). *Management: Concepts and Practices*. Englewood Cliffs, NJ: Prentice-Hall.

Simon, H. (1976). *Administrative Behavior, Third Edition*. New York, NY: The Free Press.

Wilson, W.J. (1978). *The Declining Significance of Race: Blacks and Changing American Institutions*. Chicago, IL: University of Chicago Press.

Photo Credit: Frost Publishing Group, Ltd.

Activities and Rehabilitation Programs for Offenders

7

Jeffrey D. Senese
University of Baltimore

David B. Kalinich
Northern Michigan University

After reading this chapter, the student should be able to:

▪ List programs and activities provided to prisoners.

▪ Discuss the principles of the rehabilitation process.

▪ Describe the various rehabilitation programs available to prisoners.

▪ Comment on the effectiveness of rehabilitation programs.

▪ Explain the treatment-versus-custody debate.

▪ Discuss the problems associated with managing mentally ill prisoners.

Introduction

Rehabilitation has become a much-maligned term and activity in correctional practice in the late 1980s and early 1990s. Yet there are many in the field of corrections who believe that treatment-oriented programs are an integral part of the day-to-day operations of correctional facilities. However, the creation of a humanitarian correctional environment has not been the result of the treatment orientation. The belief that offenders could be reformed, rehabilitated, or otherwise changed does not appear to have been a widespread result of correctional confinement.

In addition, although researchers claim that true successes in rehabilitation have been virtually nonexistent, it is important that students of corrections understand inmate activities and treatment programs. Although many researchers have demonstrated that rehabilitation may be a conceptual dinosaur, inmate activities and treatment programs are crucial components of most institutional settings that assist in both management and operation of correctional facilities. The general lack of clarity of results in treatment or program activities suggests that further understanding is crucial and that students comprehend that:

> What has developed is a growing awareness that programs and special services are both needed and beneficial components in correctional institutions, but that there does not exist at this time any sure means for changing inmates into law abiding citizens (Snarr and Wolford, 1985).

Therefore, informed students of correctional theory and practice must have a sufficient understanding of the use of treatment programs and activities that are used in order to develop a more complete knowledge base.

It is also important for students to recognize the basic debate about rehabilitation that has taken place. There are several scholars who believe that rehabilitation is untenable. These scholars generally believe that there are no treatment and rehabilitative programs that are effective at changing offenders. On the other hand, there are a group of theorists and policymakers who believe that treatment programs have positive effects on offenders. This latter group suggests that evaluation research has an exclusive focus on recidivism as the criterion of success and does not measure more subtle effects such as institutional adjustment, reductions in institutional tension, and so on. This chapter will describe this debate in some detail, providing the student with a context in which more contemporary treatment programs may be grounded.

This chapter also discusses activities and rehabilitation programs for offenders, supplying students with a general description and providing an awareness of their application in correctional environments. Community-based activities and rehabilitative programs will not be addressed in this chapter, as they are discussed elsewhere in this text. In addition, the focus of this chapter is on active programs that have been developed to provide service to inmates, and that diminish the deleterious effects of incarceration.

It is significant to note at this point that correctional activities and treatment programs are influenced by several factors, both internal and external to the correctional setting. That is, the general context of the institutional setting in the correctional setting is important to the realities of treatment and rehabilitation programs. More specifically, the factors that significantly affect programs offered in a given institution are: (1) the institution's size, (2) the facility's geographic location, (3) the nature of the inmate population, (4) available funding and (5) the personnel resource availability (Embert and Kalinich, 1988). In large institutions it is often difficult to coordinate and administer activities and rehabilitation in sufficient quantities to accommodate more than a small proportion of the population. Additionally, in maximum security facilities inmate movement is restricted. Treatment programs would require intra-institutional movement and would also require more staff, which may in turn result in less cooperation of staff, and consequently programs less accessible to inmates.

This chapter also provides a discussion, and examples, of program activities in correctional institutions. These treatment program activities are those that have been traditionally labeled as rehabilitative in focus. There is also a discussion of inmate activities. Although these activities may not be overtly rehabilitative in focus, they significantly contribute to the day-to-day operation of correctional facilities. The rehabilitative process is also discussed in terms of its objectives, structure, and programs. In addition, the effectiveness of rehabilitation programs is also elaborated on, specifically focusing on the debate between those who report that nothing works and those who believe programs are somewhat effective. This chapter also addresses the conflict, which is typical in many institutions, between treatment and custody. Last, this chapter discusses the special activity and programmatic demand and influence that the mentally ill offender places on correctional settings.

Programs and Activities Defined

This chapter gives the reader a general overview of activities and programs for inmates. However, a major focus of this chapter will be on programs that are created to alter the long-term behavior of offenders. The first step in describing activities and programs for inmates is to clarify the confusion in terms that are used to label things done to offenders while they are under the jurisdiction and authority of the state. The reader is forewarned that certain terminology that typically appears to have something to do with treatment programs for inmates is variously listed as rehabilitation, reform, treatment, treatment programs, inmate programs, inmate activities, and correctional programming—and this list is by no means exhaustive. Practitioners, researchers, and teachers of corrections all apply this array of terms as labels to define one idea; yet these labels are frequently used to represent entirely different processes.

In other words, the notion of treatment for correctional clients is not a clear or concise concept as it covers a variety of activities. In fact, the term "rehabilitation" is fading from the official jargon of correctional vocabularies and is being replaced by the terms "inmate programs" and "inmate services" (Snarr and Wolford, 1985). Additionally, the focus of treatment programs is not as broad as it was at its adoption (during the early 1800s) as a correctional ideology. That is, contemporary programs should provide inmates with basic services, prepare them for their eventual release, and support the custody function (Embert and Kalinich, 1988). From an organizational perspective, almost anything that directly involves the structuring of offender activities, while they are under the jurisdiction of a correctional authority, can be labeled treatment or rehabilitation. Attending weekly Alcoholics Anonymous meetings, church services, performing institutional maintenance duties, and even participating in recreational programs can conveniently be labeled as treatment by correctional administrators. There are both practical and political reasons for this practice. The labeling of routine inmate activities as treatment can enhance the image of a correctional agency. Likewise, textbooks also mix and match, as well as define treatment differently. For example, one textbook includes prison industries, educational programs, treatment programs, work assignments, counseling, social work, and psychological programs in its definition of treatment programs for inmates (Allen and Simonsen, 1988). Another separates rehabilitation programs from that myriad of institutional programs for inmates and includes psychological programs, behavior therapy, social therapy, and vocational rehabilitation in that category (Clear and Cole, 1990). Yet another text asserts that there are six basic areas of institutional programming: education, mental health treatment, medical treatment, religion, recreation, and self-help groups (Snarr and Wolford, 1985). A more rigorous definition of treatment programs for inmates demands that programs have specific goals, are based upon a clear concept or theory, have a specific structure and method, are intense and require time, have a history of success, are run by trained counselors, and are offered to inmates who can benefit from the programs (Gottfredson, 1979).

To add to the confusion, providing dental or medical services to inmates is often called treatment. In addition, mental health services, which technically can be considered a subcomponent of medical services, is clearly a form of treatment. In this chapter, we will attempt to clarify this terminology by arguing there are two universal categories of programs for inmates.

The two major categories of inmate programs are: inmate activities and rehabilitation programs. Although this classification is somewhat simplistic, it does allow one to draw a clear distinction across the myriad of activities and programs. Moreover, it does not restrict the further subclassification of either activities or rehabilitative programs into more discrete categories. While we have consciously eliminated medical programs from our discussion in this chapter, mental health programs, which are a subcomponent of medical services, will be discussed separately. In addition, the reader should be forewarned that the distinction between inmate activities and rehabilitation programs can often be vague.

Inmate Activities

Inmate activities include a variety of programs such as recreation, religious services, and arts and crafts, and are usually available to inmates in prisons (See Figure 7.4 later in this chapter for a list of inmate activities available in many prisons). The purpose of inmate activities is to provide inmates with outlets that help them serve their sentence less painfully and provide them with assistance in solving some of the short-term problems related to their incarceration.

Recreational Activities. Recreational activities, for example, help reduce the enormous burden of boredom and routine that plagues almost all correctional institutions. Correctional institutions have a variety of recreational programs. One traditional recreational program is weight lifting. Inmates who participate in these programs appear to believe in their rehabilitative effects (See Figure 7.1).

Figure 7.1
"Sports Behind the Walls: Weight-Lifting Convicts"

You say it to yourself every time you enter one of these joints. Doors clang or roll or buzz shut behind you, and you think, "If I really had to, if I really really had to, I could do time. Not that I want to, God help me, God help any man who crosses the river into darkness. But if I had to — with the help of sports, maybe — I could do time. I'm sure I could ..."

Who is this man? My name is Gregory Lowe, a.k.a. Beetle. I'm incarcerated at the State Correctional Institution, Graterford, PA. I'm five-foot-six, I weigh 238 lbs. I'm a hungry new lifter. I'm the Ohio Valley Teamsters Prison Postal Meet National Champion in the 242-lb. class. Good competition is hard to find ... I'm calling out to all area lifters in the 242-lb. class. Are you man enough to come in and challenge me? Come on with it.

Beetle — subject and author of that missive, which he sent to lifting clubs and newspapers all over the mid-Atlantic area — stands now with his fellow thieves and murderers amid the tools of their trade, bars and iron. The room is called the Pit, which is exactly what it should be called. The Pit is filled with weights and the sour odor of sweat and the even more acrid odor of penance. It is eight steps down from the main level of the Graterford prison, a dark, aging structure that sits on a rise overlooking the Perkiomen Creek, 31 miles northwest of Philadelphia.

Beetle sits on a bench and proudly holds out the certificate that documents his 825-pound squat, the state powerlifting record he set on Dec. 5, 1987 here in the Pit. He's a champion lifter who is unable to attend outside meets. That, of course, is one of the problems of being a convicted killer. But Beetle, at 32, isn't brash or mouthy like some of the younger lifters around him. He looks at the floor when he says softly, "I thought a lot about it being a pity — being in here. I could've learned it all out there, but I bypassed that." Beetle is black, as is every other lifter in the room. And though the American penal system has a disproportionate number of inmates who are from minorities, Beetle can't blame race for his troubles. He played football at Cheyney (PA) State for two seasons but "got messed up with drinking, mostly," he says, and let the bad guys he hung around with back in Philly "dictate what I did." ...

Beetle stands under the bar and stares into nothingness. Some inmates insult his manhood. They hoot and scream. "He's tightening his belt," Felton (coach) says quietly to the video camera's built-in mike. "He's lifting the straps of his suit ..."

Beetle grabs the bar, lets it sink into his unpadded shoulders and takes two tiny steps backward. His entire body shakes. He drops quickly into a squat, and wraps look as though they are cutting his legs in half. He slowly rises, veins bulging like baby snakes on his temples and forearms, the weight bouncing slightly on his shoulders. It is hard to tell if the screaming inmates are rooting for him to rise or crash to the floor. "Never surrender!" yells Smash (another inmate). "Make a way!"

Beetle quivers and strains and, slowly, every so slowly, stands up straight and puts the bar back on the rack. He has lifted the front end of a small car. His eyes are still not precisely focused. An inmate quickly unwraps his knees. Within seconds the din dies away and the others continue their workouts as though nothing has happened. But for an instant there, Beetle looked as if he were free.

There are many other recreational activities in correctional institutions. Various prisons have running tracks, basketball courts, baseball diamonds, volleyball courts, and tennis courts. Some prisons even have organized intramural sports teams. Moreover, many of these teams play outside teams.

In addition, there are a several non-athletically oriented recreational activities in prisons. There are libraries in many facilities, and occasionally local volunteer groups supply reading materials to inmates. The law library is also perceived as recreational by some inmates. Other activities that are widely utilized to pass the time are card-playing and dominos.

Art. There are also a number of creative or artistically oriented activities. These activities range from crafts to poetry (See Figure 7.2). Hobby craft and art programs, for example, are a creative outlet for inmate energies and a constructive way for inmates to spend their time. Taft contends that despite some spotty acceptance of art programs, most wardens have a very poor view of them and that they are a very low priority, but then again, the general public does not support art activity either (Taft, 1979). However, there are a number of inmates who aspire to artistically oriented activities.

Figure 7.2
Prison Poetry

The World Prison Poetry Center of the Connecticut Correctional Center produces a selection of poetry from prison inmates. In order to be accepted for publication, one must be a prison or jail inmate of any state. Entries are judged by a three-member panel of critics and poets from the New Haven-Hartford region of Connecticut, and the prison poets selected for publication receive an award of twenty dollars and ten free copies. One example of this poetry is titled "My Friend in Jail," by Thomas E. Atwood and it is as follows:

> I have a friend who takes nothing from me
> And it's my friend when I want it to be
> It can make me laugh, cry or be mad
> My friend gets me through the good and the bad
> When they lock me up in my cold cement cell
> It's just me alone in this miniature hell
> So I turn to my friend with a flick of my wrist
> It's moods are selected from a weekly list
> You're probably wondering who this friend can be
> The Electronical
>   workings
>   of a
>   portable T.V.

Source: World Prison Poetry Center (1983). New Haven, CT.

Religion. Various religious services are performed both by inmate lay ministers as well as ordained clergy. Clergy are often called chaplains in correctional institutions. The basic role of the chaplain is to provide spiritual therapy for the inmates. The function of spiritual therapy is to enable a person to internalize the concept of oneself as a whole and spiritual person, a premise based on the ancient philosophical definition of human nature as comprised of body and soul, or body, mind and spirit (Thompson, 1989). Religious services are the among the most commonly offered activities in corrections today.

Prisoner Self-Help. There are a number of self-help type activities in prison environments. These programs are focused on making the time pass as well as making the time easier. There are four general types of inmate self-help activity: adjustment-oriented groups, groups for addicted persons, ethnic self-help groups, and self-awareness groups.

Adjustment-Oriented Self-Help. The adjustment-oriented groups can be illustrated through the example of the "Seventh Step" group founded by Bill Sands.

> Such classes should be conducted by ex-convicts rather than correctional authorities. For two good reasons. One, because such a man knows what must be done, knows what it feels like to be out in the world, branded with a felony record: and two, because the men inside prisons refuse, for the most part, to take moral lessons from the so-called do-gooders (Alcoholics Anonymous, 1976).

The basic orientation here is to enhance the outlook of the inmate, thereby increasing self-esteem and perhaps facilitating a more realistic perception of the reintegration into society upon release. The early Seventh Step groups have developed into a number of other groups which include the Prison Jaycees, Man-to-Man, Lifers Group, People-to-People, Human Dignity, Old Timers' Group, Beyond the Wall, and the Fortune Society (Allen and Simonsen, 1986; Snarr and Wolford, 1985).

Self-Help for Addicted Persons. There are also a range of activities in the realm of self-help that are available to addicted inmates. The most typical forms of groups for addicted persons are Alcoholic Anonymous (AA) programs. The twelve steps outlined in this program summarize the basic guiding principles of AA. In the AA *Big Book* these steps are cited as the "best answers that our experience has yet given to those ever-urgent questions, "How can AA best function?" and "How can AA best stay whole and so survive?" (Alcoholics Anonymous, 1976). In Alcoholics Anonymous there are five prescriptions for sobriety. These are: (1) understanding alcoholism as a disease, (2) recovery begins only after one "hits bottom," (3) one must realize there is a "higher power," (4) self-scrutiny and confession of problem, and (5) carrying the message of AA to other alcoholics. As in rehabilitation programs in the free society, the prison AA groups embrace the values of society and attempt to instill them in participating inmates (Irwin, 1980). There have been a number of similar groups that have resulted from the development of Alcoholics Anonymous. These include Narcotics Anonymous, Cocaine Anonymous, Gamblers Anonymous, Over Eaters Anonymous, Check Writers Anonymous, and Smokers Anonymous (Irwin, 1980).

Narcotics Anonymous has been a somewhat popular inmate self-help group. There are many programs across the country in jails and prisons. The basic principles of the AA program also are present in Narcotics Anonymous (See Figure 7.3). In much of the literature that is distributed by World Service Office (Narcotics Anonymous' publication agency), there is a strong message that alcohol is included in their list of drugs. The focus is on addict solidarity to address and fight individual addictions (World Service Office, 1986).

Ethnic Self-Help Groups. There are also several inmate groups that have organized along ethnic lines for the purpose of building self-respect. These groups attempt to assist inmates coping with their incarceration through the formation of an ethnic solidarity. This approach is used by prisoner groups such as Black Awareness for Community Development, Chicanos Organizados Pintos Aztlan, Afro-American Coalition, Affirmative Action Latin Group, Irish Heritage Group, and the Native American Brothers.

Self-Awareness Groups. There are also self-awareness groups in prisons. These groups attempt to raise the consciousness of the members in an effort to assist inmates in coping with the stress of confinement. Several of these groups have existed in prisons—for example, the Church of the New Song, Ring of the Keys, Inward Bound, Wake Up, Discovery, New Life, Human Potential Seminars, and "est" (Hamm, 1987; Irwin, 1980).

Obviously, inmate participation in one or any of these activities may have a positive long-term effect upon his or her behavior. However, the goal of the activities is to provide inmates with structured programs to occupy their time in an orderly manner, and to ease the pressures of incarceration.

Figure 7.3
What is the Narcotics Anonymous Program and How Does It Work?

The following was reported in a pamphlet published by Narcotics Anonymous. It is an excerpt from their "little White Book," which is similar to the book published by Alcoholics Anonymous. Although these pamphlets are produced to encourage membership, they allow one to gain an accurate perspective of the orientation and practice of the group.

What is NA? Narcotics Anonymous (NA) is a nonprofit Fellowship or society of men and women for whom drugs had become a major problem. We are recovering addicts who meet regularly to help each other stay clean. This is a program of complete abstinence from all drugs. There is only one requirement for membership, the desire to stop using. We suggest that you keep an open mind and give yourself a break. Our program is a set of principles written so simply that we can follow them in our daily lives. The most important thing about them is that they work.

There are no strings attached to NA. We are not affiliated with any other organizations, we have no initiation fees or dues, no pledges to sign, no promises to make to anyone. We are not connected with any political, religious or law enforcement groups, and are under no surveillance at any time. Anyone may join us, regardless of age, race, sexual identity, creed, religion or lack of religion.

We are not interested in what or how much you used or who your connections were, what you have done in the past, how much or how little you have, but only in what you want to do about your problem and how we can help. The newcomer is the most important person at any meeting, because we can only keep what we have by giving it away. We have learned from our group that those who keep coming to our meetings regularly stay clean.

How it works. If you want what we have to offer, and are willing to make the effort to get it, then you are ready to take certain steps. These are the principles that made our recovery possible.

1. We admitted that we were powerless over our addiction, that our lives had become unmanageable.
2. We came to believe that a Power greater than ourselves could restore us to sanity.
3. We made a decision to turn our will and our lives over to the care of God as we understood Him.
4. We made a searching and fearless moral inventory of ourselves.
5. We admitted to God, to ourselves, and to another human being the exact nature of our wrongs.
6. We were entirely ready to have God remove all these defects of character.
7. We humbly asked Him to remove our shortcomings.
8. We made a list of all persons we had harmed, and became willing to make amends to them all.
9. We made direct amends to such people wherever possible, except when doing so would injure them or others.
10. We continued to take personal inventory and when we were wrong promptly admitted it.
11. We sought through prayer and meditation to improve our conscious contact with God as we understood Him, praying only for knowledge of His will for us and the power to carry that out.
12. Having had a spiritual awakening as a result of these steps, we tried to carry this message to addicts, and to practice these principles in all our affairs.

This sounds like a big order, and we can't do it all at once. We didn't become addicted in one day, so remember — easy does it.

Source: Narcotics Anonymous (1986). "Who, What, How, and Why." Reprinted from the *little White Book*. Van Nuys, CA: World Service Office, Inc.

Figure 7.4
List of Activities for Inmates

Art Programs	Jaycees
Native American Groups	Religious Activities
Black Ethnic Groups	Lifer Groups
Paralegal Organizations	Veterans Groups
Hispanic Ethnic Groups	Music Programs
Hobbies	Service Clubs
Public Works	Gospel Clubs

Source: Michigan Department of Corrections (1986). *Annual Report.*

Inmate activities play an important role in prison management and provide direct benefits for inmates. The major concern of prison administrators is to assure a safe and orderly environment. Planned activities structure the inmates' time and behavior, and enhances the ability of correctional staff to control the environment. In addition, activities cut down on idle time and boredom that can be a source of many interpersonal problems among inmates and between staff and inmates. Inmates are also given acceptable channels to utilize their energy and creativity as opposed to developing schemes to beat the system. Spending time at enjoyable activities also cuts down on the stress and frustration that accompanies the monotony of living in prison.

The Rehabilitation Process

Rehabilitation can be defined as a programmed effort to alter attitudes and behaviors of inmates which is focused on the elimination of their future criminal behaviors. Rehabilitation programs are based upon the assumption that a defect within the individual inmate is what causes his or her criminal behavior. "Programmed effort" simply means providing inmates with programs whose goals are to correct the defect suffered by inmates. Correcting defects in inmates by providing them with social or cognitive skills that will, theoretically, reduce his or her tendency toward, or need to return to, criminal activity is, therefore, the goal of the rehabilitation process.

Objectives of treatment programs. To qualify as a treatment program under our definition, the primary objective of a program must be to alter the post-release behavior of the offenders under the jurisdiction of the correctional agency. For instance, the program goal would be to end the criminal behavior of the offender by bringing about changes in the offender client. The change is intended to eliminate the inmate's motivation to engage in criminal behavior upon release from the jurisdiction of the correctional system. To achieve this objective, the treatment program would have as its goals: to understand the causal factors within the client that may have caused him or her to become involved in criminal behavior and provide the client with assistance that would eliminate those causal factors. The basic assumptions underlying treatment programs are that: (1) the offender believes being a non-offender is preferable to being a criminal, (2) the causal factors lie primarily within the offender, (3) the causal factors can be identified and treated, and (4) through the rehabilitation process, the offender will learn and internalize accepted norms.

Structure. A discernible structure premised upon meeting offenders' needs must exist in corrections. In addition, changing the long-term behavior of the inmate must be a major part of the structure. Therefore, a drug dependency program for inmates that meets routinely and has a format that attempts to deal with the participants' drug dependency would be, by our definition, a treatment program. Similarly, a vocational training program that would provide an offender with the skill to earn a legitimate income would also qualify as a treatment program.

The terms "rehabilitation" and "treatment" (which are interchangeable) cover a variety of programs that attempt to treat and cure offenders' specific problems. Traditional rehabilitation programs fall under five general program categories: (1) psychological or therapeutic programs, (2) social therapy, (3) education, (4) vocational training, and (5) individualized treatment. In the following section each program category is individually discussed. The assumptions and dynamics pertinent to each category of programs will be briefly discussed, and the individual programs within each category will be briefly described.

Rehabilitation Programs

Psychological/Therapeutic Programs. Psychological or therapeutic programs are based upon the assumption that an individual's criminal behavior is symptomatic of a defect in the emotional makeup or psyche of the offender. It is further assumed that the defect can be understood or diagnosed by psychologists, psychotherapists, or other trained professionals. Finally, it is assumed that a program or a treatment plan exists or can be developed to treat the emotional defect discovered in the offender. This process of diagnosing and treating an offender is called the medical model. As we will discuss later in this chapter, the medical model is no longer in vogue. However, the psychological or therapeutic programs that were utilized within the medical model are still prevalent in correctional institutions today. The psychological or therapeutic programs generally fall under four subcategories: (1) individual therapy, (2) group therapy, (3) behavior modification, and (4) social therapy.

Both individual and group therapy focus upon the treatment of the mind of the offender. The process of therapy, if properly applied, helps the client understand his or her emotions, attitudes, and motives that have directed his or her behavior. The essential ingredient in the process is the client's acceptance of responsibility for failures. The most important objective of therapy, therefore, is to help the client look critically at his or her own behaviors and their consequences, which, in turn, requires that the client eliminate the use of psychological defense mechanisms in understanding his or her life failures or problems. In brief, psychological defense mechanisms are techniques through which individuals can place the blame for their inappropriate behaviors upon others or upon their circumstances. Students, for example, may claim that an exam was unfair, rather than accept responsibility for the fact that they were partying at the local pub the night before the exam and thus were unprepared. Some inmates may, for example, refuse to understand that they are habitually incarcerated because they seek instant gratification and simply follow their impulses. Rather than admit that they have a problem and are basically immature, they may blame society, their loved ones, or their friends for their problems. In theory, the therapeutic process helps the client to see beyond their psychological defense mechanisms, or excuses for their behaviors, so that they may understand the basic causes of their life problems.

Individual Therapy. In the first type, called individual therapy, a trained and skilled therapist enters a therapeutic relationship with the client. Through their interactions, the therapist helps the client examine himself or herself critically by encouraging and helping the client to set aside his or her psychological defense mechanisms. The process entails frequent, structured discussions between the therapist and the client during which the therapist assists the client in examining himself or herself through discussion and self-disclosure.

Group Therapy. Group therapy, unlike individual therapy in which a therapist and client work together, requires a group of clients who have similar problems. The group is guided by a skilled group therapist who facilitates discussion among the group members. The advantage and purpose of group therapy is that the group members challenge each other when any member resorts to the use of defense mechanisms or excuse-making. It is difficult, if not impossible, for example, to con a con. Thus, inmate group members resorting to fabrication, excuse-making, and refusal to accept responsibility for their actions are likely to be challenged by their fellow group members. Group members also provide support and advice for each other in dealing with difficult, emotion-based problems. Another advantage that group therapy has over individual therapy is that several inmates rather than a single inmate can benefit from the efforts of the therapist during each session. Figure 7.5 provides a list of programs that are considered to be therapeutic programs in a prison system.

Figure 7.5
Therapeutic Programs Available in an Adult Prison System

Psychotherapy—Group	Other Therapy
Family Therapy	Individual Counseling
Psychotherapy—Individual	Substance Abuse Counseling
Group Counseling	

Source: Michigan Department of Corrections (1986). *Annual Report.*

Behavior Modification. The third subcategory, behavior modification, represents a conceptual break from traditional therapeutic counseling. Traditional therapeutic counseling helps the client to understand and reverse the inner defects that have caused him or her to behave irrationally and fail at dealing with life's problems. Behavior therapy, in contrast, assumes that all behaviors of individuals are learned through a system of rewards and punishments to which an individual has been exposed during his or her life. If behaviors are to be changed, a relearning process must take place that will provide a set of rewards and punishments that will eventually evoke appropriate behaviors by the client. In other words, criminal behavior is not symptomatic of anything defective in the inmates' emotional makeup or psyche. The criminal behavior, not the offender's personality or personal defects, is the subject of the change. Criminal behavior is learned and can be unlearned by the same principle. Therefore, behavior modification programs and techniques are utilized instead of traditional therapy that seeks to discover and eliminate the client's defects through the interactions between therapist and client. Behavior modification programs resort to a structuring of rewards and punishments to be received by the client that will facilitate the relearning of behaviors.

In its simplest form, providing "good time" credits for inmates is a form of behavior modification. The mark system, developed by Alexander Maconochie in the 1840s at Norfolk Island, Australia is a behavior modification program to control the behavior of prison convicts during their incarceration. In effect, Maconochie used the mark system as an inmate management tool. The so-called "token economy" has been popular among juvenile detention and correctional centers. The token economy pays inmates tokens for following rules and procedures and takes tokens away from them for noncompliance. In a tightly run program, inmate behavior is closely monitored to impose the reward/punishment system—or the behavior modification system—upon inmates at every possible moment of their incarceration. The goal of the application of the token economy system has been to control inmate behaviors as well as have some long-term impact upon their post-release behaviors.

In the extreme form of behavior modification, programs such as aversion therapy may create physical pain upon the client for improper behavior. For example, alcoholics are often given the drug *Antabuse*. If alcohol is consumed while anabuse is in the client's system, the client will become violently ill. In theory, the client will automatically link the violent illness with the consumption of alcohol. Hence, a conditioned response to the use of alcohol will be created. Correctional clients can be subjected to extremely punitive acts, such as segregation without privileges, to control and modify their behavior. Although such actions, aimed at correcting inmates behavior, are not technically considered behavior modification, they are consistent with that type of treatment. Correctional authorities are not at liberty to force inmates to submit to aversion therapy. When behavior modification is utilized with correctional clients, typically it is a softer form, such as the accumulation of good time or the utilization of the token economy system.

Social Therapy. Social therapy includes aspects of both traditional therapy and behavior modification. Social therapy assumes that the offender must exist within a pro-social environment in which he or she is rewarded for honesty and taking responsibility for his or her behavior and is challenged when acting dishonestly or irresponsibly. In addition, through the liberal use of group therapy and educational programs, the offender is given assistance in dealing with his or her emotional problems or defects that interfere with his or her ability to function properly within the treatment milieu. Social therapy is often referred to as therapeutic community, positive peer culture, and milieu therapy.

The therapeutic community was conceived as an alternative to traditional methods of managing psychiatric patients in hospitals. The focus of the program was to give the patient as much responsibility as possible while incarcerated. In effect, the patient, or inmate, actively participates in all aspects of managing the institution, including inmate rules, regulations, and institutional procedures. In addition, all members of the community, inmates as well as staff, are assigned counselor roles and are obliged to confront those who are not acting responsibly or are being dishonest or playing avoidance games. Everyone is expected to play an active role in the formal governance of the institution, as well as continually reinforce the pro-social norms of the milieu. Each unit, consisting of up to 40 inmates, elects officers and holds unit counsel meetings twice a day to discuss and then resolve problems. In many respects, the community meetings and programs dedicated to the promulgation of pro-social norms take on the security and order-maintenance function of the institution. In addition, inmates participate in group therapy throughout the day and attend formal educational programs. By contrast, rehabilitation programs in typical correctional institutions are often secondary activities. Often treatment programs and staff are viewed as hindrances to custody and order-maintenance. In theory, the therapeutic community is always in action and is the basis of the institution rather than being one of the many aspects of the correctional system.

Education Programs. Educational programs conceivably can assist offenders in their post-release efforts to avoid criminal behavior. Historically, penologists assumed that the almost universal illiteracy on the part of inmates was the root of their criminal and antisocial behaviors. As early as 1870, many penologists argued that when all states implemented mandatory public educational systems, the crime rate would decrease significantly. We are aware, of course, that criminal behavior is a complex phenomenon and is often present among well-educated individuals, such as white-collar criminals. However, the educational level for the majority of inmates is at the sixth-grade level, and many inmates are only marginally literate or even totally illiterate. When limited educational levels or a lack of basic skills impede the offenders' attempts to become law-abiding citizens, educational programs can have an important rehabilitative effect on offenders. Figure 7.6 exhibits educational programs typically available in adult correctional institutions.

Figure 7.6
Educational Programs in Corrections

Basic Education (grades 0 through 8)	Special Education
GED Preparation	Community College
GED	College 3 and 4 years
Life Role Competencies	Graduate Education

Source: Michigan Department of Corrections (1986). *Annual Report.*

The basic education and special education courses provide inmates with fundamental education, and focus on basic reading and math. Completion of these courses will improve basic skills of inmates and prepare them to enroll in the general equivalence program (GED). The general equivalence courses will prepare inmates for the GED. Inmates who pass the GED examination become certified with the equivalent of a high school diploma. Having a high school education (or the equivalence) may enhance an inmate's opportunity to obtain employment that requires a high school education in the primary labor market, which will provide higher pay and stable work.

Community college and four-year college programs are sometimes available to inmates who have an advanced educational level. While these programs are limited due to the number of inmates eligible for college-level work and the cost involved for tuition, community colleges and four-year colleges often offer courses and degrees to inmates. A technical education from a community college or a liberal arts education from a four-year college will provide an inmate with a greater range of occupational choices upon his or her release. Earning a degree while incarcerated may also provide released inmates with a positive self-image and may help to de-emphasize the ex-con label often carried by ex-offenders that typically interferes with their reentry into society. Vocational programs attempt to provide inmates with a marketable job skill, something many inmates do not possess. The ability of inmates to obtain employment which is stable and provides a salary with which they can support their families is perhaps the most important ingredient in an offender's long-term rehabilitation.

Figure 7.7
Types of Products and Services Produced by State Prison Industries

acoustic screens	hosiery and gloves
aquaculture	janitorial products
auto repair/refinishing	key punch
bedding manufacturing	machine shop
binders (3-ring)	meat processing
booklet printing	metal products
box factory	micrographics
broom factory	microfilming
brush manufacturing	office supplies
bus reconditioning	optical labs
canning plant	orchards
chemical products	paint manufacturing
chewing and shredded tobacco	park furnishings
cigarette manufacturing	plant nursery
coffee and tea processing	playground equipment
community service crews	pork products
concrete products	poultry and eggs
construction	pressure-treated lumber
cordwood	printing
dairy/beef cattle	purchasing
decals and seals	sales/customer service
dental prosthetics	sewing
desk accessories	shoe factory
die-cut letters	silk screening
drapery	slaughterhouse
dry cleaning	soap plant
dump bed bodies	sod farm
engraving	solar energy
ethanol production	survey and grade stakes
farming	telephone reconditioning
feed lot	textile products
flag making	timber manufacturing
forestry/sawmill	tire recapping
foundry	typewriter repair
freight trucking	upholstery
furniture	vegetable farm
garment factory	warehousing
graphics	welding
hay production	wood product refinishing

Source: U.S. Department of Justice, National Institute of Corrections, American Correctional Association, January, 1986.

Vocational Programs. Vocational training is one of the earliest concepts applied to the rehabilitation of inmates. Vocational training was applied to inmates in the Auburn Penitentiary in the mid-1800s. The terms "rehabilitation" and "corrections" were not part of the vocabulary of penology at that time. However, inmates were forced to work at textile machines for 14 hours a day in order to prepare them for work in factories after their release. The conditions were harsh. Inmates were chained to their machines while they worked and the silent system was imposed upon them. In addition, the prison sold the products of the inmate labor and made substantial profits. However, the forced labor was presented as beneficial to the inmates' ultimate reform. Figure 7.7 lists the types of products produced by prison industries across the United States. Many of the products are produced in vocational programs. These programs range from heavy industry to high-technology programs.

Later in this chapter we will provide the reader with a critical analysis of rehabilitation programs. However, it is important here to warn the reader that the appearance of an extensive list of vocational programs for inmates in Figure 7.7 is deceptive. To begin with, not all adult correctional institutions have a similar array of vocational programs available. Some may have a great variety, while other institutions may have few, if any, vocational training programs. Second, inmates are typically assigned to tasks that must be completed in order for the institution to function. For example, inmates are often assigned to work in the kitchen and cafeteria to help feed the inmate population. This assignment is often labeled as food management training. When inmates work at menial or routine tasks throughout the duration of their confinement, they are not being trained in the complex business of food service management.

One can argue, however, that specific job skills are not as important for inmates as are good work habits and acceptance of the responsibilities of the workplace. Thus, assigning inmates a 40-hour workweek job that requires punctuality, working with others, conforming to job rules, and taking directions from a supervisor or foreman can create an appropriate work ethic for participating inmates. Through participation in prison employment, inmates can be taught good work habits and can be conditioned to adapt to the workplace culture and, therefore, be good employees after their release. On the surface, this argument makes great sense, especially for inmates who have had limited experience in the legitimate job market or who have had a history of losing jobs. However, a workplace created within a correctional setting must be similar in most respects to the workplace as it is in free society. To the extent that the respective work settings differ, the lessons learned and habits acquired will not match and the rehabilitative potential will be limited.

It is difficult, if not impossible, to make any general comments about the content, quality, and requirements imposed upon employees of the prison workplace or prison industries across all correctional institutions or, for that matter, across all industry in free society. There are some obvious differences however, such as pay rates or union membership. More importantly, total environments differ profoundly from surroundings in free society in many respects besides the workplace. In free society, individuals are responsible for mundane chores such as waking up on time, arranging their transportation to and from work, and investing in clothing, tools, or other items needed on the job. Also, those of us in free society can, on the one hand, structure our leisure time with a great deal more flexibility while, on the other hand, we face a great many more of life's responsibilities. Satisfying our needs and wants and meeting our responsibilities are intertwined with the rewards and demands of our employment. The responsibilities in free society and opportunities to satisfy needs and wants are profoundly different in free society than in prison society. For example, we may be motivated to perform our tasks satisfactorily as we consider the needs of our families. We may also be saving for or paying for a vacation or new fishing boat. These material concerns do not exist within the prison environment.

The medical model becomes a valuable concept when individualized treatment is applied to inmates. The medical model assumes that there are particular defects suffered by the offender that can be identified, and for which treatment can be prescribed to cure the defects. In the terminology of the medical model, the offender is diagnosed and a treatment plan is formulated based upon the diagnosis. The diagnosis may find several defects within one particular offender. He or she, for example, may have poor social skills, an inadequate literacy level, and limited job skills. Hence, the treatment plan for this individual may include group therapy, an educational program and vocational training. Further, the diagnosis may find that the offender has limited intelligence, in which case the vocational training may include janitorial services or training for other occupations requiring limited skills.

By comparison, another inmate may be diagnosed as highly intelligent, well-educated, but incapable of interacting with others in a productive manner. Group therapy and general educational courses will be of little value to this individual. Thus, the treatment plan may include individual therapy and vocational training, such as computer programming, that is challenging and requires limited interactions with others. In other words, each individual offender has a different set of defects that can be discovered through diagnosis, upon which a treatment plan can be created to meet his or her individual needs. This process is referred to as individualized treatment.

An example of individualized treatment in action is contract parole. In this process, the inmate and correctional officials, presumably treatment professionals, enter into an agreement or contract when the inmate first enters the system. The inmate agrees to enter into and succeed in a number of programs and the corrections system agrees to parole the inmate after he or she successfully completes the terms of the agreement. The terms of the agreement are established after the inmate is evaluated, or diagnosed, during the initial classification process. Optimally, the inmate has some input into the terms of the contract and therefore participates in the diagnosis of his or her case and the subsequent treatment plan. Each contract, therefore, is individualized treatment because it is tailored to the individual needs of each participating inmate. Contract parole has not been utilized with any regularity for at least two reasons. First, it requires that the parole board delegate parole decision-making to treatment professionals. Hence, a decision to parole is made when an inmate enters the system rather than after the inmate has served his or her minimum. In other words, contract parole is a radical departure from the traditional parole decision-making process, making it unappealing to correctional administrators. Second, the concept of individualized treatment that is at the core of parole contracting assumes that comprehensive programs exist in the correctional institutions of a system and that inmates can readily be placed in programs during their incarceration. Programs typically are limited, and inmates are enrolled to capacity. Contracts will be altered under these circumstances and the process becomes a function of institutional constraints as well as inmate needs.

To this point we have discussed the various programs that are typically used in the process of rehabilitating inmates. Our discussion has included some critical commentary on the effectiveness and limitations of the programs. The following section focuses on evaluations of the effectiveness of our efforts to rehabilitate criminal offenders in corrections.

The Effectiveness of Rehabilitation Programs

An important question that must be addressed is, "Is rehabilitation an effective intervention?" Before we can address this question, we must define "effectiveness" in this context. For members of the general public, the definition of effectiveness, or a system that works, is based to a great extent on their expectations. For example, the onlooker who has a limited understanding of the criminal justice system and correctional institutions, as well as an unsophisticated understanding of criminal offenders, may believe in the ability of institutional correctional environments to rehabilitate. Through some process of change, the form, substance, and character of the offender is transformed into a productive member of society. Moreover, individuals with this perspective will not settle for less than a system in which all bad people can be dumped into the correctional system and changed into good people with an appropriate orientation toward work, family, and society. Anything less may be considered ineffective by those who expect this mechanical efficiency from the correctional system.

In addition, people who possess this outlook would also expect almost everyone who is subjected to the process to leave the correctional system with appropriate pro-social attitudes. In reality, the correctional function cannot meet such a high standard of effectiveness. We know that prisons are not mechanical systems; and, after being released, many inmates will again commit crimes. Occasionally, released offenders will commit heinous or violent crimes that receive a great deal of media attention. One widely publicized heinous crime can make the entire correctional system look bad. It is clear then that the measure of effective rehabilitation or change must be based upon realistic considerations. As a practical matter, effectiveness can best be defined as changing the likelihood or probability that an offender will commit a criminal offense after having been involved in a rehabilitation program.

Researchers who evaluate the effectiveness of rehabilitation programs, therefore, must establish some acceptable benchmark from which to measure. The benchmark, or criterion, may be a short-term program goal, such as obtaining employment, changing one's self-image, or improving one's social skills. Thus, one could argue that success in achieving the program goals could lead to a longer-term success of a reduced crime rate for inmates involved in the rehabilitation programs. In other words, the recidivism rates of the program participants may be an ultimate measure of effectiveness.

The success rate or recidivism rate of those inmates involved in a rehabilitation program needs to be compared or matched against the success rate or recidivism rate that would have been expected without the benefit of the program. This comparison can be accomplished through appropriate research design and sampling procedures which select a control group or baseline to use for comparison. We will not enter into a discussion of research methods in correctional program evaluation, given that it is clearly beyond our brief description here. We will, however, discuss the essence of the conclusions of past research that has been conducted on the effectiveness of rehabilitation programs over the years.

In the mid- to late-1960s there appeared to be a major change in the reliance on the theory of rehabilitation as a theme in corrections. Much credit for this shift can be attributed to the work of scholars who made broad criticisms of the rehabilitative model as being ineffective. The change in correctional theory was initiated by a number of authors who purported that correctional rehabilitation had failed (Bailey, 1966; Martinson, 1974; Conrad, 1975; Lipton, Martinson, and Wilks, 1975). The work of Martinson solidified the argument against the effectiveness of the rehabilitation or treatment orientation, and created a highly charged debate between those who claimed he was accurate and those who found his interpretations untenable.

Martinson stated "with few and isolated exceptions, the rehabilitative efforts which have been reported so far have had no appreciable effect on recidivism" (Martinson, 1974). This general conclusion did not prevent his more specific criticism of individual programs as having "no appreciable effect on recidivism." Additionally, he also examined a number of specific rehabilitative efforts, and maintains that programs are inadequate and there is a lack of evaluation research to show significant program effects.

In his criticism, Martinson, provides a wide review of educational programs in corrections. Although there is evidence that some of these programs are ineffective, one could argue that Martinson is too pessimistic in his interpretations. It is somewhat inappropriate to generalize about the rehabilitative usefulness of educational programs on the basis of a potential lack of ability of researchers to accurately measure program effects rather than the positive effects on recidivism rates. In fact, Bailey suggested that even though there is impressive evidence of progressive improvement in the caliber of the scientific investigations conducted, the empirical tests have not facilitated progress in the actual demonstration of the validity of correctional treatment (Bailey, 1966). It is apparent that Martinson had not provided convincing evidence that providing no educational programming is either just as good as the programs, or that it is appropriate to discontinue these programs. This may be due to the stringent criteria for success. Martinson believed that for programs to be successful they should demonstrate rather specific and direct program effects and their causes. He concludes by arguing for a straightforward approach to presentation of correctional research.

It is also important to note that Martinson consistently refers to exceptions to the "nothing works" theory, and suggests that programs actually did have some positive effects. Martinson often credits special qualifications of certain individuals with the success of rehabilitative programs. For example, he states that the success of programs "may well have been the therapists' special personal gifts rather than the fact of treatment itself which produced the favorable result" (Martinson, 1974). This contention is surprisingly contrary to the logic of sound research design in that it quickly dispels any positive treatment as intrinsic to those individuals who provide the service regardless of the program under which they function. Moreover, if treatment programs do not affect rehabilitation or prevent recidivism, except in isolated instances, perhaps we are equally inept at evaluating these programs. It is apparent that the "nothing works" perspective sets up correctional programs as straw men that by definition cannot be effective.

The "nothing works" perspective has had a great effect on the study and practice of criminal justice—it appears to have "shaken the community of criminal justice to its roots, and for several months we have been witnessing the phenomenon of 'Martinson-shock'" (Martinson, Palmer, and Adams, 1976). It is also clear that the effects of the school of "nothing works" was still a strong policy influence in the late 1980s.

One of the most vocal opponents to Martinson was Palmer. Palmer's (1975) work was directed specifically at the efforts of Martinson, and received a pointed response from him (Martinson). It is apparent that Martinson did little to pacify the criticism, but engaged in an even broader critique of the literature that addressed correctional treatment programs. For example, in one article Martinson went so far as to claim that, "If the truth be known, correctional research is about nine-tenths pageantry, rumination, and rubbish and about one-tenth useful knowledge" (Martinson, 1976).

The criticisms of the "nothing works" perspective have been on a similar rhetorical tack in which it has been likened to "strangers trying to communicate in different languages by raising their voices" (Gendreau and Ross, 1983). The contentions of this opposing group of authors can be concisely stated as follows: there appears to be a growing recognition that the "almost nothing works credo is invalid" (Gendreau and Ross, 1983). Additionally, this latter group claims that there appear to be a number of programs that do work. They also purport that the notion "offenders could be rehabilitated successfully became a historical oddity, fit only for study by criminal justice paleontologists" (Gendreau and Ross, 1987).

Recently, there have been claims that there is a greater need for consideration of the effectiveness of correctional programs. Some of the recent literature suggests that a more empirically sound approach should be adopted in evaluating the programs and treatments used in corrections. In particular, Burkhart suggests that:

> We face a social dilemma caused by the desire to obtain maximum offender control through imprisonment and a reluctance to support the high public costs associated with prison construction and maintenance of a large inmate population (Burkhart, 1986:75).

That is, the decrease in public budgets to the point at which every expenditure must be justified at a very discrete level, has contributed to a reexamination of the potential of correctional treatments. In addition, society expects, and deserves, to know the probability of an offender recommitting an offense while in the community. The direction that is suggested is one that encourages more vigorous and well-controlled experiments that allow both the public and the criminal justice system to make an adequate assessment of the effectiveness of correctional programs.

Although this recommended approach is quite logical, it is also clear that quantitative solutions are hardly a panacea for improving the quality of evaluation research. However, quantitative solutions are much more amenable to replication and use than other more esoteric techniques. Gendreau and Ross conclude "if we persist in the negative view of correctional treatment, we are encouraging the correctional system to escape its own responsibility. By labeling offenders as untreatable, we make it apparent to one and all that we cannot be held accountable for his improvement or his deterioration" (Gendreau and Ross, 1983). The basic problem for those antagonistic to the "nothing works" perspective does not appear to be the general problems with lack of demonstrated effectiveness of programs, but that through the abandonment of the programmatic approach there is less potential for further experimentation with current or future efforts at change.

The legacy of the debate on the effectiveness of rehabilitation programs, however, left us with a pessimistic view toward rehabilitation for offenders. Although rehabilitative programs still exist in institutions today, the current missions of corrections are primarily the punishment and incapacitation of criminal offenders. In addition, we still grapple for answers. We ask, for example: "Are the programs we offer inmates quality programs that are really good enough to have an effect?" "Do we have a real commitment to the rehabilitation of offenders?" and "Is the total prison environment itself fit for the rehabilitation of inmates?" In other words, when we use a long-term outcome like recidivism to evaluate rehabilitation programs, are we measuring the effects of the specific individual rehabilitation programs or is recidivism a measure of the impact of the total system on its inmates?

When evaluating the effectiveness of our past attempts to rehabilitate criminal offenders, we must also consider the commitment of the correctional system to inmate rehabilitation, as well as the quality of individual rehabilitation programs. Approximately 10% of budgets for prisons and correctional institutions are allocated for inmate programs. Irrespective of good intentions or claims about efforts to offer inmates rehabilitation programs, a limited portion of the total expenditures for institutions is expended on such efforts. The majority of funds go to custody and administrative personnel who are concerned primarily with order maintenance in the institutional environment. Under these financial constraints, only a limited number of inmates can be provided with quality programs.

In our overview concerning the effectiveness of treatment programs, we have been somewhat pessimistic. However, correctional institutions continue to provide activities and programs for the inmate population. In the following section, we will briefly discuss the merits and problems of including inmate activities and treatment programs in correctional institutions. This discussion is typically referred to as the *treatment-custody conflict.*

Treatment Versus Custody

Treatment versus custody describes the conflict that exists between the goals, process, and personnel of the treatment/activities fuctions and custody functions of a correctional institution. The goal of treatment is to help the offender cure his or her defects, while the goal of custody is to keep the inmate population in order and to accustom the inmate to the regime of the institution. These differing goals require different processes. Treatment requires that each inmate be viewed as an individual whose needs and wants must be recognized and attended. In addition, rules must be relaxed in favor of an inmate's progress in his or her treatment program. Custody, on the other hand, requires that all inmates be subjected to one set of rules. Relaxing the rules for inmates in treatment may cause other inmates to demand freedom from regimentation.

Theoretically, psychological programs take place without intrusion on custody staff. During those periods, therefore, the custody staff has no control over the participating inmates. In addition, information shared by inmates during therapy sessions, which may relate to institutional activity, is ordinarily not available to custody staff. In other words, information about illicit activities within the institution that may be revealed during therapy sessions will not be available to custody staff. Custody staff also views closed sessions as opportunities for inmates to trade contraband and set up future illicit activities and deals.

It is not uncommon for the roles of correctional staff and treatment staff to conflict. If treatment staff have greater influence over administrators than correctional officers, treatment staff may attempt to impose their will upon correctional officers through the administrative system. Inmates, who are usually sensitive to conflict and power differentials, will often exploit their relationship with the treatment staff by complaining to treatment staff about correctional officers, hoping that their complaints will reach the prison administrators. When this process of indirect influence is effective for inmates, or is perceived by correctional officers as being effective, correctional officers will have a high degree of distrust of treatment staff and may go out of their way to interfere with the work of the treatment staff. Likewise, if inmates believe that the authority and power of correctional officers is minimized by treatment staff, they may be more difficult to manage.

Problems are created for custody and security by many of the vocational training programs. It is common, for example, for inmates to produce contraband items, such as weapons, in machine shops, etc. Also, inmates who work in food service programs can steal food supplies from the kitchen and cafeteria and resell them as contraband to other inmates. An alcoholic beverage known as spud juice can be prepared by inmates from leftover potato scraps (Kalinich, 1980). Inmates may produce contraband for profit or they may be intimidated into obtaining those goods for fellow inmates, which in turn creates an immediate potential for conflict and violence between inmates (see Chapter 11).

From an administrative perspective, however, custody and security usually are the dominant concerns, receive the most attention and, as we have seen, will get the largest portion of the resources. Therefore, the negative impact that treatment programs and personnel might have on custody and security may not be substantial. In fact, security and order can be strengthened by having an active array of rehabilitation programs and inmate activities. Work assignments, recreation, general inmate activities, and rehabilitation programs all serve to structure time and provide orderly activities for inmates during the day. In addition, many of the programs and activities can provide acceptable psychological outlets for many of the frustrations suffered by inmates during their incarceration.

Mentally Ill Inmates

The main thrust of this chapter has been to discuss traditional programs and activities for traditional inmates. However, the number of mentally ill inmates in prison—and in jails—has increased considerably. Managing mentally ill inmates and providing them with appropriate care and programs is currently a major problem for correctional institutions. In this section, we will discuss managing and treating the nontraditional mentally ill inmates.

Historically, offenders who were mentally ill by legal definitions were incarcerated in state mental institutions; or, as they were frequently labeled, institutions for the criminally insane. Mental institutions also housed individuals who were committed by the probate court. Often, probated individuals were considered dangerous or criminal and candidates for arrest, prosecution, and judicial sentencing. Processing such individuals through the criminal justice system was avoided by probating them directly to the mental institutions. During the late 1960s, mental health professionals reasoned that mental institutions were expensive, did nothing to cure patient inmates, and routinely abused the legal rights of those who were institutionalized. It was also reasoned that mentally ill individuals could only be cured in the natural environment of their respective communities. Hence, laws that defined mental illness and laws that controlled admissions to mental hospitals changed drastically.

Mental illness, as presently defined by law is a "substantial disorder of thought or mood (in an individual) which significantly impairs judgment, behavior, capacity to recognize reality, or ability to cope with ordinary demands of life" (Kalinich, Embert and Senese, 1991:79). Before one can be committed to a mental hospital, however, he or she must first be diagnosed as mentally ill—as defined—and, second, as a result of the mental illness, can reasonably be expected to cause serious physical harm to himself or herself or others or "is unable to attend to his or her basic physical needs such as food, clothing or shelter that must be attended to avoid serious physical harm in the near future" (1991:95). Hence, individuals who are mentally ill and caught up in the web of the criminal justice system will stay in the criminal justice system rather than being transferred to a mental hospital unless they fit the second criteria. Historically, offenders who were merely mentally ill would likely find their way into mental institutions whether they were dangerous or not.

As a result of the abrupt change in the law and philosophy of mental health practitioners, the public mental health systems across the country changed from institutional-based programs to community mental health programs. Mental health clients are to be treated in the community as opposed to traditional mental institutions. As a result, mental hospitals across the country have virtually been emptied within the last two decades. The final effect is that criminal offenders who would traditionally have been incarcerated in mental institutions because of their mental illness are now being incarcerated in prisons.

Prison and jail administrators are, therefore, faced with managing and treating nontraditional inmates. While traditional activities and programs can be utilized by mentally ill inmates, programs aimed specifically at the mentally ill prison population will have to be implemented. A major approach to the treatment of mentally ill individuals is chemotherapy—the use of drugs such as thorazine, to stabilize mental patients. The administration of chemotherapy is restricted to psychiatrists or medical doctors and cannot be employed by prison counselors or social workers. Therefore, a medical staff will have to be added to the complement of correctional institution personnel to provide psychiatric treatment for mentally ill inmates. Social therapy was developed as a treatment modality for mental patients. Given that social therapy is utilized in traditional correctional institutions, it would appear to be a simple procedure to apply social therapy to mentally ill inmates. However, it may not be effective to integrate traditional and nontraditional inmates in the same program. Prison administrators will have to make policy decisions on whether to segregate mentally ill inmates from traditional inmates or allow the two groups to share the same facilities.

In addition, correctional officers and treatment staff will need training to obtain the expertise needed to interact with mentally ill inmates. A major focus of the staff and treatment programs for mentally ill inmates will be to keep them stable and functioning within the prison environment. Mentally ill inmates will not be able to benefit from the rehabilitation programs available in correctional institutions unless those programs are supported with psychiatric programs unique to the mentally ill population.

Initially in this section we provided the reader with a general definition of mental illness. It is important to point out in closing this section that mental illness is not always a clear-cut concept. There are degrees of mental illness, and mental illness is not a static concept. Some inmates may be severely and chronically mentally ill, while others may lapse into mild stages of mental illness and still others may acquire temporary or permanent symptoms of mental illness as a result of the pressures of incarceration (Gibbs, 1986). The problem with providing mental health treatment for inmates or segregating mentally ill inmates from nonmentally ill inmates becomes as confusing and dynamic as the concept of mental illness itself.

Summary

In this chapter we have discussed the range of program activities in correctional institutions. The focus has been on treatment or program activities that have been traditionally labeled as rehabilitative in orientation. We have also examined the range of inmate activities that are typically available in correctional institution environments. Although these activities do not have an exclusive rehabilitative goal, they significantly contribute to the day-to-day operation of most correctional facilities. The rehabilitative process was also discussed and examined in reference to its objectives, structure, and programs. Another area that we examined was the assessment of the effectiveness of rehabilitation programs. We have specifically provided an illustration of the debate between those who report that nothing works and those who believe programs are effective. Additionally, this chapter also addresses the conflict between treatment and custody that is typical in many institutions. Finally, this chapter discussed the special activity and programmatic demand and influence that the mentally ill offender places on correctional settings.

The existence of some form of rehabilitative activities and programs has been constant ever since correctional institutions were relied on as correctional dispositions. Although the magnitude of these programs has clearly been quite different, the general focus on inmate change has persisted. The somewhat recent debate that questioned the effectiveness of rehabilitative programs has changed the orientation of corrections toward a more control-oriented setting. However, many of the programs have persisted and new rehabilitative programs have been added. It is clear that neither operational correctional agencies nor state legislatures have given up on the idea that offenders may be rehabilitated. Although the belief that change is possible exists, the focus on these programs is secondary to security concerns. In addition, there is a broader focus on post-conviction correctional intervention.

The Value of Rehabilitation

There can be little dispute that the rehabilitative ideal has been conveniently employed as a mask for inequities in the administration of criminal penalties and for brutality behind the walls of our penal institutions. Yet as our analysis of the realities of the current swing toward determinate sentencing has revealed, the existence of inhumanity and injustice in the arena of crime control does not depend on the vitality of rehabilitation. Indeed, a punitive "just deserts" philosophy would serve the purposes of repressive forces equally well, if not with greater facility. It would thus seem prudent to exercise caution before concluding that the failure of the criminal justice system to sanction effectively and benevolently is intimately linked to the rehabilitative ideal and that the ills of the system will vanish as the influence of rehabilitation diminishes. As Francis Allen has recently observed, "the contributions of the rehabilitative ideal to these failures has been peripheral."

This line of reasoning is liberating in the sense that it prompts us to consider that the state's machinery of justice might well have been *more* and not less repressive had history not encouraged the evolution of the rehabilitative ideal. This suggests in turn that preoccupation with the misuses and limitations of treatment programs has perhaps blinded many current-day liberals to the important benefits that have been or can be derived from popular belief in the notion that offenders should be saved and not simply punished. In this respect, the persistence of a strong rehabilitative ideology can be seen to function as a valuable resource for those seeking to move toward the liberal goal of introducing greater benevolence into the criminal justice system. Alternatively, we can begin to question whether the reform movement sponsored by the left will not be undermined should liberal faith in rehabilitation reach a complete demise.

Rehabilitation is the only justification of criminal sanctioning that obligates the state to care for an offender's needs or welfare. Admittedly, rehabilitation promises a payoff to society in the form of offenders transformed into law-abiding, productive citizens who no longer desire to victimize the public. Yet treatment ideology also conveys the strong message that this utilitarian outcome can only be achieved if society is willing to punish its captives humanely and to compensate offenders for the social disadvantages that have constrained them to undertake a life in crime. In contrast, the three competing justifications of criminal sanctioning—deterrence, incapacitation, and retribution (or just deserts)—contain not even the pretense that the state has an obligation to do good for its charges. The only responsibility of the state is to inflict the pains that accompany deprivation of liberty or of material resources (e.g., fines); whatever utility such practices engender flows only to society and not to its captives. Thus, deterrence aims to protect the social order by making offenders suffer sufficiently to dissuade them as well as onlookers entertaining similar criminal notions from venturing outside the law on future occasions. Incapacitation also seeks to preserve the social order but through a surer means; by caging criminals— "locking 'em up and throwing away the keys"— inmates will no longer be at liberty to prey on law-abiding members of society. The philosophy of retribution, on the other hand, manifests a disinterest in questions of crime control, instead justifying punishment on the grounds that it presumably provides society and crime victims with the psychic satisfaction that justice has been accomplished by harming offenders in doses commensurate with the harms their transgressions have caused. The following comments by Nicholas Kittrie are instructive here:

> At the very least, the therapeutic programs help set a humanizing climate of new social expectations and aims. . . .Under the traditional criminal

formula, society is the wronged party. It owes nothing to the guilty party, and his rehabilitation remains an incidental accomplishment of the penal sanction. Under the *parens patriae* formula [rehabilitative ideal], the concept of personal guilt is bypassed, if not totally discarded, and much more weight is given the offender's shortcomings and needs. Society accordingly cannot shrug off its responsibility for treatment, since it is inherent in the very exercise of this social sanction.

These considerations lead us to ask whether it is strategically wise for liberals wishing to mitigate existing inhumanities in the criminal justice system to forsake the only prevailing correctional ideology that is expressly benevolent toward offenders. It is difficult to imagine that reform efforts will be more humanizing if liberals willingly accept the premise that the state has no responsibility to do good, only to inflict pain. Notably, Gaylin and Rothman, proponents of the justice model, recognized the dangers of such a choice when they remarked that "in giving up the rehabilitative model, we abandon not just our innocence but perhaps more. The concept of deserts is intellectual and moralistic; in its devotion to principle, it turns back on such compromising considerations as generosity and charity, compassion and love." They may have shown even greater hesitation in rejecting rehabilitation and affirming just deserts had they had an opportunity to dwell on the more recent insights of radical thinkers Herman and Julia Schwendinger:

> Nevertheless, whatever the expressed qualifications, the justice model now also justifies objectively retrogressive outcomes because of its insistence that social policies give priority to punishment rather than rehabilitation. Punishment, as we have seen, is classically associated with deprivation of living standards. Rehabilitation, on the other hand, has served as the master symbol in bourgeois ideology that legitimated innumerable reformist struggles against this deprivation. By discrediting rehabilitation as a basic principle of penal practice, the justice modelers have undermined their own support for better standards of living in penal institutions.

Now it might be objected by liberal critics of rehabilitation that favoring desert as the rationale for criminal sanctioning does not mean adopting an uncaring orientation toward the welfare of offenders. The reform agenda of the justice model not only suggests that punishment be fitted to the crime and not the criminal, but also that those sent to prison be accorded an array of rights that will humanize their existence. The rehabilitative ideal, it is countered, justifies the benevolent treatment of the incarcerated but only as a means to achieving another end—the transformation of the criminal into the conforming. In contrast, the justice perspective argues for humanity as an end in and of itself, something that should not in any way be made to seem conditional on accomplishing the difficult task of changing the deep-seated criminogenic inclinations of offenders. As such, liberals should not rely on state enforced rehabilitation to somehow lessen the rigors of imprisonment, but instead should campaign to win legal rights for convicts that directly bind the state to provide its captives with decent living conditions. Contending that "a free people can make justice live—even in the stark environment of the American prison," John Conrad has thus called for reforms that will grant inmates the essentials of "citizenship," including the "right to personal safety, to care, to personal dignity, to work, to self-improvement, to vote, and to a future."

It is not with ease that those of us on the political left can stop short of completely and publicly embracing the concept that "humanity for humanity's sake" is sufficient reason for combatting the brutalizing effects of prison life. This value-stance is, after all, fundamental to the logic that informs liberal policies on criminal justice issues. In this light, it should be clear that we applaud attempts to earn inmates the human rights enumerated by Conrad among others, and urge their continuance. However, we must stand firm against efforts to promote the position that the justice model with its emphasis on rights should replace the rehabilitative ideal with its emphasis on caring as the major avenue of liberal reform.

Already, we have illustrated in past chapters that support for the principles of just deserts and determinacy has only exacerbated the plight of offenders both before and after their incarceration. But there are additional dangers to undertaking a reform program that abandons rehabilitation and seeks exclusively to broaden prisoner rights. Most importantly, the realities of the day furnish little optimism that such a campaign would enjoy success. In February of 1981, Chief Justice Warren Burger voiced his opinion to the American Bar Association that "too much concern for the rights of criminal defendants may be nourishing America's growing crime rate." In June of the same year, the United States Supreme Court voted a resounding 8-1 that it is not unconstitutional to house two inmates in a cell that measures $10\frac{1}{2}$ by $6\frac{1}{2}$ feet. "The Constitution does not mandate comfortable prisons," wrote Justice Lewis A. Powell. Indeed, "discomfort" is justly deserved: "To the extent that such conditions are restrictive and even harsh, they are part of the penalty that criminal offenders pay for their offenses against society." In this context, it is not surprising that one social commentator has observed that the prisoners' rights movement is in "disarray," a fact that is evident in the disturbing "ease with which the courts now rebuff efforts of prison reformers to win more humane living conditions for a growing prison population." Even justice model advocate David Fogel is aware that "the courts continue to draw narrow issues around prisoner complaints until large stacks are amassed. The Supreme Court then levels them one at a time. Not much," he concludes, "may be expected in the way of enduring correctional change through the drama of litigation when the central actors are reluctant judges and resistant prison administrators.

Further, the promise of the rights perspective is based on the shaky assumption that more benevolence will occur if the relationship of the state to its deviants is fully adversarial and purged of its paternalistic dimensions. Instead of the government being entrusted to reform its charges through care, now offenders will have the comfort of being equipped with a new weapon—"rights"—that will serve them well in their battle against the state for a humane and justly administered correctional system. Yet this imagery contains only surface appeal. As David Rothman has warned, "an adversarial model, setting interest off against interest, does seem to run the clear risk of creating a kind of ultimate shoot-out in which, by definition, the powerless lose and the powerful win. How absurd to push for confrontation when all the advantages are on the other side." In this regard, Illinois inmates under determinate sentencing have won the "right" to challenge the revocation of their good time before the Prisoner Review Board. But the achievement of justice here is more illusory than real: the Board rarely reverses—in fewer than five cases in one hundred—the Department of Corrections' revocation decisions. "A reversal rate that low for a judge," Paul Bigman has observed, "might merit national recognition for extraordinary capability. In the prisons, however, the judge and jury are the co-workers of the accuser."

Moreover, the rights perspective is a two-edged sword. While rights ideally bind the state to abide by standards insuring a certain level of due process protection and acceptable penal living conditions, rights also establish the limits of the good that the state can be expected or obligated to provide. A rehabilitative ideology, in contrast, constantly pricks the conscience of the state with its assertion that the useful and moral goal of offender reformation can only be effected in a truly humane environment. Should treatment ideology be stripped away by liberal activists and the ascendancy of the rights model secured, it would create a situation in which criminal justice officials would remain largely immune from criticism as long as they "gave inmates their rights"—however few they may be at the time. With the movement for prisoner rights now suffering significant defeats in the courts, this concludes a troubling prospect.

Even more perversely, the very extension of new rights can also be utilized to legitimate the profound neglect of the welfare of those under state control. The tragic handling of mental patients in recent years is instructive in this regard. As it became apparent that many in our asylums were being either unlawfully abused or deprived of their liberty, the "mentally ill" won the right to be released to or remain in the community if it could be proven that they were of no danger to themselves or others. With the population in mental hospitals declining precipitously over the past two decades from 420,000 to fewer than 145,000, many can now feel confident that we are well beyond the days of the "Cuckoo's Nest." Yet, what has been the actual result of this "right" to avoid state enforced therapy? It brought forth not a new era in the humane treatment of the troubled but a new era of state neglect. Instead of brutalizing people within institutional structures, the state now permits the [mentally] disturbed to be brutalized on the streets of our cities. While it previously cost between $25,000 and $30,000 annually to hospitalize each patient, the state currently allots ex-patients (through Supplemental Security Income) merely $3,000 on which to survive. Homeless, many of the mentally ill end up in one of the many decrepit boarding houses—"large psychiatric ghettos"—that have sprung up to exploit their vulnerability. Their lives are "hellish at best. They live totally alone, and people don't even know their names or come by and ask them how they feel. They are looked upon as a paycheck and nothing more." In this context, we would do well to keep in mind Charles Marske and Steven Vargo's broader observation regarding the effects of the due process or rights movement in various sectors of our society in recent years: "Unfortunately, the darker side of legalization is its implication in depersonalization. . . . A curious irony emerges: the very groups that called for expanded legalism to establish and protect their individual rights now suffer its consequences."

Source: Francis T. Cullen and Karen E. Gilbert (1982). *Reaffirming Rehabilitation*, pp. 246-253. Cincinnati, OH: Anderson Publishing Co.

Key Terms and Concepts

behavior modification

community mental health

group therapy

individual therapy

individualized treatment

inmate activities

inmate programs

inmate services

medical model

"nothing works"

recreational activities

rehabilitation process

processsocial therapy

therapeutic community

treatment-custody conflict

References

Alcoholics Anonymous (1976). *Alcoholics Anonymous, Third Edition.* New York, NY: Alcoholic Anonymous World Services, Inc.

Allen, H.E. and C.E. Simonsen (1986). *Corrections in America: An Introduction, Fourth Edition.* New York, NY: Macmillan Publishing Company.

Allen, H.E. and C.E. Simonsen (1988). *Corrections in America: An Introduction. Fifth Edition.* New York, NY: Macmillan Publishing Company.

Bailey, W.C. (1966). "Correctional Outcomes: An Evaluation of 100 Reports." *Journal of Criminal Law, Criminology, and Police Science*, Volume 57, Number 2:15-60.

Burkhart, W. R.(1986). "Intensive Probation Supervision: An Agenda for Research and Evaluation." *Federal Probation*, Volume 50, Number 2:75-77.

Clear, T.R. and G.F. Cole (1990). *American Corrections, Second Edition.* Pacific Grove, CA: Brooks/Cole Publishing Company.

Conrad, J.P. (1975). "We Should Never Have Promised a Hospital." *Federal Probation*, Volume 1, Number 1:3-9.

Embert, P.S. and D.B. Kalinich (1988). *Behind the Walls: Correctional Institutions and Facilities: A Many-Faceted Phenomena.* Salem, WI: Sheffield Publishing Company.

Gendreau, P. and R.R. Ross (1983). "Effective Correctional Treatment: A Bibliotherapy for Cynics." *Crime and Delinquency*, Volume 25, Number 4: 469-489.

Gendreau, P. and R.R. Ross (1987). "Revivification of Rehabilitation: Evidence from the 1980s." *Justice Quarterly*, Volume 4, Number 3:348-408.

Gibbs, J. (1986). "When Donkeys Fly: A Zen Perspective on Dealing with the Problem of the Mentally Disturbed Jail Inmate." In D.B. Kalinich and J. Klofas (eds.) *Sneaking Inmates Down the Alley.* Springfield, IL: Charles C Thomas.

Gottfredson, M.R. (1979). "Parole Board Decision Making." *Journal of Criminal Law and Criminology*, Volume 70, Number 1:77-78.

Hamm, M.S. (1987). "The Human Potential Seminar: A Strategy For Teaching Socially Adaptive Behavior in a Correctional Classroom." *The Journal of Correctional Education*, Volume 38, Number 1:4-7.

Irwin, J. (1980). *Prisons in Turmoil*. Boston: Little, Brown and Company.

Kalinich, D.B. (1980). *The Inmate Economy*. Lexington, MA: Lexington Books.

Kalinich, D.B., P.S. Embert and J.D. Senese (1991). "Mental Health Services for Jail Inmates: Imprecise Standards, Traditional Philosophies, and the Need for Change." In J.A. Thompson and G.L. Mays (eds.) *American Jails: Public Policy Issues*. Chicago, IL: Nelson-Hall Publishers.

Lipton, D., R. Martinson and J. Wilks (1975). *The Effectiveness of Correctional Treatment*. New York, NY: Praeger.

Martinson, R. (1974). "What Works? Questions and Answers About Prison Reform." *The Public Interest*, Volume 35, Spring:22-54.

Martinson, R., T. Palmer and S. Adams (1976). *Rehabilitation, Recidivism, and Research*. National Council of Crime and Delinquency.

Narcotics Anonymous (1986). "Narcotics Anonymous: Who, What, How, and Why." Reprinted from the *little White Book*. Van Nuys, CA: World Service Office, Inc.

Palmer, T. (1975). "Martinson Revisited." *Journal of Research in Crime and Delinquency*, Volume 12, Number 2:133-152.

Snarr, R.W. and B.I. Wolford (1985). *Introduction to Corrections*. Dubuque, IA: Wm. C. Brown Publishers.

Taft, P.B. (1978). "Whatever Happened to That Old-Time Prison Chaplain?" *Corrections Magazine*, Volume 4, Spring:54-61.

Telander, R. (1988). "Sports Behind the Walls." *Sports Illustrated*, Volume 69, Number 17:82-95.

Thompson, E.A. (1989). "Chaplains Help Inmates Find Freedom Behind Bars." *Corrections Today*, February: 52, 82-86.

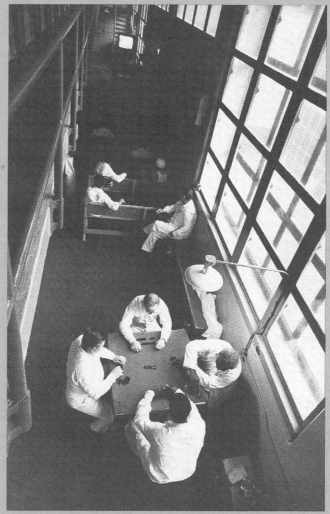

Photo Credit: Bill Powers, Frost Publishing Group, Ltd.

Prison
Social Structure

After reading this chapter, the student should be able to:

▌ Describe early conceptions of the prison social system.

▌ Discuss the theories of prison social organization.

▌ List the fundamental ideas about the contemporary prison social structure.

▌ Comment on the role of the correctional officer.

▌ Explain the differences between the human service model and the control model of prison governance.

Introduction

"This is our home....What you got to remember is that we live here. This prison is nothing but a mini-society that we run. The guards are only here for a job. We are here twenty-four hours a day." This quote, taken from the movie *Other Prisoners*, highlights the importance of the prisoner social structure and its influence on the everyday workings of the prison. From the correctional officer to the "new fish" inmate, there is an understanding of the social world of the prison and how it affects everyone who comes into contact with it. The purpose of this chapter is to discuss the various conceptions about the origination of prison social structures. Our intent is to discuss how the social structure of the prison is influenced by many factors, both internal and external to the prison.

Moreover, our goal in this chapter is to examine the models that have developed to explain the character and formation of inmate societies behind bars. Our discussion will not suggest that any one particular model of explaining the prison social structure is more powerful than another; that decision will be left up to the student after examining the research evidence presented. Rather, we will be highlighting what we believe to be the most important aspects of each specific model on the development of prison social structures. Most importantly, we will show how each model contributes something different to the discussion of prison social structures, and that it is their individual contribution which makes each of them important to both the student of the prison and the person who works and administers such an institution.

We will begin our examination of prison social structure by exploring early conceptions of the prison world. When we say early, we are really talking about ideas that were generated in the 1940s and further developed in the 1950s. Some of these early works definitely shaped the direction of research on prisoner social systems for many years. From there, we will move on to the explanation that has had a significant contribution to the research literature, that being the *functional model* of inmate social systems. This model was heavily influenced by the discipline of sociology and remains today a major explanation for examining social structures behind prison walls. Third, we will explore another model of inmate social systems created, in part, by an ex-offender. This model, known as the *importation model*, will argue that influences external to the prison are the most critical when trying to understand and explain social structures behind bars.

Unlike the functional model, which stresses the role of the environment of the prison and its effects on prisoner behavior, the importation model has received wide acceptance by many contemporary researchers who argue that the prison today is a microcosm of society. To understand the prison requires an examination of the processes of wider society, and how prisoners come to prison with certain attitudes, values, and beliefs emanating from the city streets. These dispositions are critical to an understanding of the prison social world. Once again, this model, like the functional model, will have to be assessed by the student once the evidence is presented. There is no one model that is any more correct than another; they should be considered as competing theoretical models. And as such, their relative contributions have to be weighed by an examination of the research evidence. We hope to provide this evidence to the student. It is then up to the student to weigh the evidence and consider in his/her own mind which model is more compelling and powerful when exploring prisoner social structures.

Moreover, the chapter will examine some contemporary ideas on the creation of the prison social structure. Some of the current research suggests that the modern prison cannot be singularly explained by allegiance to either the functional or importation perspectives. Today, the prison is much more complex and requires other types of models to examine and comprehend the workings of the prisoner social world. We will examine these contemporary ideas and comment on their relevancy to our discussion of prison social structures. Additionally, we will explore the research literature on correctional officers. There has been a research explosion on correctional officers, and the chapter will raise some of the key issues and concerns that face correctional officers today. Finally, we will conclude the chapter by exploring some contemporary ideas about prison management and its relation to prisoner social systems. These ideas are at the forefront of thought about how the social systems of prisoners should be controlled by prison officials.

Early Conceptions of the Prison Social System

Our understanding of prison social structures was quite limited until the middle part of the twentieth century. It was clear that people who ran institutions of confinement were aware of many of the key elements of what we would call a social system today, such as roles, differentiation, organization, and complexity. Nevertheless, the investigation of the prison as having its own social structure did not begin until 1940 when Donald Clemmer published his classic piece *The Prison Community*. In this piece, Clemmer argued that prisoners formed social arrangements inside the institution similar to those found on the outside. More importantly, Clemmer argued that inmates experienced a process whereby traditional values, beliefs, and attitudes were stripped from them. In the place of these traditional values, beliefs, and attitudes, the prison cultural values based on manipulation, deceit, and a criminal lifestyle were emphasized and adopted by prisoners.

This process was coined by Clemmer as the *prisonization* ordeal. In effect, Clemmer's analysis suggested that prisoners experienced a change in their behaviors once incarcerated. This change is focused on the adoption of specific behavioral patterns that are consistent with the culture of the prison. More importantly, Clemmer argued that the prisoner becomes further removed from the conventional and accepted ways of doing things the longer he stays under the influence of the prison society. Known as the prisonization hypothesis, this view argues that prisoners not only internalize non-conventional attitudes in prison, but in addition, these antisocial attitudes become more firmly entrenched the longer the person is removed from society. In effect, the longer the incarceration experience is, the more difficult it becomes to reach and reform the prisoner. As such, we would expect the longer the time spent in prison, the more prisonized the inmate would become and the more difficult to alter behavior toward more acceptable behaviors in society. In short, long prison time is destructive according to the prisonization process espoused by Clemmer.

Clemmer has argued that time served is one of the key factors which affects the degree to which the assimilation to the prison community occurs. In his words, the "[G]reatest degree of prisonization...may be enumerated by a sentence of many years, thus a long subjection to the universal factors of prisonization." Therefore, time is a critical factor in determining the degree to which the prisoner assimilates to the inmate culture or becomes prisonized. To test this hypothesis, many early researchers examined the influence of time served on the behaviors of prisoners. In fact, much of the early research on the prisonization process was designed to examine the relationship between time served and the adoption of the prison culture. This research began our inquiry into the validity of the prisonization process.

Wheeler (1961), for example, sought to test the degree to which the prisoner becomes prisonized over time and how that affects his allegiance and conformity to staff expectations. Moreover, Wheeler was interested in how prisoners conformed to the expectations of staff relative to their involvement in the prisoner social system. Did the inmate who had many contacts with the inmate social system exhibit more of a prisonized experience than the inmate who had fewer contacts with the prisoner social system? In addition, how did the allegiance to an inmate social system vary by the degree of time served in the institution? Were there differences between inmates who had served shorter sentences when compared to those who served longer sentences when it came to their allegiance to staff expectations? Wheeler's analysis largely supported the prisonization hypothesis put forth by Clemmer.

Wheeler found that the degree to which an inmate became prisonized was directly related to his involvement in the informal social system. More importantly, the inmate experiences a sense of role conflict as he becomes more assimilated and accepting of the inmate social system. Wheeler (1961:704) states:

> The dominant normative order among inmates (at least in terms of power and visibility if not numbers) is strongly opposed to that of the staff. The inmate who values friendship among his peers and also desires to conform to the staff's norms faces a vivid and real role conflict. The conflict is not apparent or perhaps is not felt so intensely during the earliest stages of confinement, but with increasing length of time in the prison the strain becomes acute; inmates move to resolve the strain either by giving up or being excluded from primary ties, or by a shift in attitudes.

Even more interesting is the fact that, according to Wheeler, the degree of assimilation to the inmate culture is contingent upon the "career phase" in which the inmate finds himself. Wheeler suggests that prisonization is highly influenced by the amount of time the inmate has spent in the institution. For example, Wheeler found that inmates who were in the early part of their career phase (less than six months served) were very accepting and conforming to the expectations of staff, whereas those inmates who were in the middle phase (those who have served more than six months and have more than six months to serve on their sentences) of their incarceration experience were the least accepting of staff expectations. Moreover, prisoners who were in the late phase of their sentences (those who have less than six months to serve on their sentences) were also more accepting of staff expectations and norms. Are these findings contradictory to the prisonization hypothesis?

To a degree, we can say that the prisonization hypothesis was not supported by Wheeler's research. While Wheeler did find that the degree of involvement in the prisoner social system does affect the degree to which the prisoner is prisonized, he, in addition, found that there is a "differential attachment" to the prison culture, depending upon the time served by the inmate. This differential attachment he describes as taking on a "U-shaped" pattern, whereby greater allegiance to conventional attitudes and staff norms are experienced in the early and late phases of confinement and less acceptance of such norms in the middle phase of incarceration. Thus, the more removed the prisoner is from the community, the less accepting he is of staff expectations, and as a result, the more pronounced the prisonization ordeal. Wheeler, therefore, goes on to suggest that specific methods of dealing with prisoners need to be emphasized depending upon the phase of incarceration. Most importantly, Wheeler's research suggests that inmates are prisonized and deprisonized, and that a direct, linear progression into negative behavior patterns among inmates is not always a result of length of time served. Instead, the adaptive patterns of inmates are complex and require other types of research that investigate how prisoners cope with their environments.

Garabedian (1963) continued the research on the prisonization process by examining the "social roles" and processes of socialization in the prison community. Like Wheeler, Garabedian sought to examine the complexities associated with the prisonization ordeal, but more importantly, he sought to examine how the prisonization process was affected by the adaptive, social roles assumed by inmates. His research sought to typify role types exhibited by inmates. His findings supported many of the findings generated by Wheeler. In short, he, too, found that there is this differential adaptation to prison by inmates, with the most prisonized individuals exhibiting behavioral patterns in opposition to staff norms at the middle phases of their institutional careers.

More importantly, he found specific role types among prisoners. There existed five role types according to Garabedian. They were: *Square John*, *Right Guy*, *Politician*, *Outlaw*, and *Ding*. These role types represented the adaptive responses of prisoners to the problems endemic to the prison setting. On the one hand, the Square John was the inmate most in tune with the conventional attitudes and values of the staff and society. This type of prisoner seeks to do his time with as few problems as possible and in accordance with the expectations of the staff. On the other hand, the Right Guy is the type of prisoner most opposed to the expectations of the staff and is the most respected by the inmate society; he is viewed as the prisoner who is most in tune with the expectations and demands of the inmate society. Both role types, according to Garabedian, subordinate their individual interests to the collective interests of the group. It is the group that counts, not the individual.

Politicians are the keenest type of the inmates, and usually have committed crimes which involved manipulation and deceit. They tend to have contacts with both inmates and staff. Outlaws are the most feared type of inmates. These inmates have resorted to violence or will use violence to get what they want from others. They tend to be isolated from other inmates and staff because of their penchant for violent confrontations. Finally, the Dings are the type of inmates who have no other social characterization that clearly defines their behaviors. In many cases, according to Garabedian, they are the inmates who have committed nonviolent sex offenses. They tend to fade into the background of the inmate culture and are isolated from both inmate and staff contacts. In the prison social system these role types respond differentially to the prisonization ordeal.

Garabedian, like Clemmer and Wheeler, found that inmates do respond differentially to the effects of the prison environment. In short, they are prisonized differently. But in addition, he found that the degree of prisonization is influenced by the social roles exhibited by inmates in the prisoner culture. Specifically, he found that when one examines career phase, the point of heaviest impact varies with different role types. For Dings, the early phase is the most important; for Right Guys and Square Johns, the middle phase; and for Outlaws, the late phase. This differential form of adaptation among prisoners by role type suggests not only the complexity of the inmate social systems in prison settings, but also reinforces a position that similar types of treatment programs may not be the most effective in changing the behaviors of men who hold different roles in the prisoner social system. Garabedian states: "...[S]pecific programs might be geared toward the treatment of certain role types. It is likely that some programs will be more effective for Square Johns and Right Guys, for example, while others will be more effective for Politicians and Outlaws."

Clearly, therefore, the early research on prisons and the prisonization process suggests that adaptations of prisoners to their environments is not only complex, but in addition, the social structures of prisons produce behaviors and role types that vary over time. Accordingly, it would be reasonable to assume that prison social systems do vary by both time and location. For example, is the prisoner social system of a medium-security institution the same as that found in a maximum-security penitentiary and do they remain constant over time? The early research evidence suggests that prisoner social structures represent complex adaptations by prisoners to their individual situations. As such, prison social structures may be viewed as unique responses by prisoners to cope with their environments. Or, they may be the function of attitudes, beliefs, and values brought into the institution by prisoners when incarcerated. These two views seek to answer the most fundamental question about the development of prisoner social structures, that being, "How and why do they originate in the prison environment?" To answer this question, we must explore the two major models of inmate social system development. They are known as the *functional* and *importation models* of inmate socialization. We begin with the functional model.

Theories on Prison Social Organization— The Functional Model

Up until the late 1950s, explanations on the organization of prisoner social systems revolved around the concept of prisonization as described by Clemmer. In 1958 sociologist Gresham Sykes provided the most comprehensive and enlightening accounts of prison life and adaptation to prison life by incarcerated men when he published *The Society of Captives*. Today, this small work is considered a classic in the prison literature. In addition, this work represents the development of a major conceptual model in the understanding of prisoner social systems. This model was called the *functional-adaptive* approach.

This way of viewing the social structure of prison accentuates the fact that prisoners interact and adapt to the prison setting through the development of rules and regulations that enable them to cope with the unique demands of the prison situation. As a result, behavioral patterns in prison are directly *functional* to the environment of the prison. All behaviors among prisoners are viewed as responses to the regimen imposed by the institutional setting. Sykes' contribution to the prison literature was in an identification and classification of such behaviors. He wanted to know how and why prisoners respond the way they do in prison.

To answer these questions, he went to the maximum-security prison in New Jersey and observed the patterns of adaptation exhibited by prisoners.

Fundamentally, Sykes found three interesting adaptive processes at work. First, he argued that prisoners experience *pains of imprisonment* by virtue of being placed in the institution. These pains are unique to the prison environment, and the prisoner social system revolves around trying to cope with them individually and collectively. Second, Sykes found that prisoners create clearly identifiable *argot roles* in prison. Like the pains of imprisonment, these argot roles are functional responses to the deprivations experienced in the prison. Finally, Sykes argues that there is a relationship between prison stability and the social organization of the inmate body. To think of control in the prison requires an examination of the role of the inmate social system in providing stability to the prison. The stability of the prison is inexorably tied to the social organization of prisoners and how they adapt to the day-to-day contingencies of prison life.

Pains of Imprisonment

"The inmates are agreed that life in the maximum-security prison is depriving or frustrating in the extreme," states Sykes. His observations support the notion that prison life imposes various pains on prisoners. The inmate social system represents an attempt to cope and deal with the pains. What are the pains of imprisonment? Sykes argues that prisoners experience five pains of imprisonment. These five represent the kinds of deprivations inmates experience by virtue of being in prison.

First, there is the deprivation of liberty. Probably the most visible and deeply felt pain, this deprivation is the most obvious in the prison, in that the inmate can never leave. The deprivation of liberty is central to the purpose of prison. The inmate is in the state of "involuntary seclusion of the outlaw" (Sykes, 1958:65). Not only is he restricted from making decisions about his ability to move at will, but more importantly, he is rejected by the community through placement in prison. He no longer can be any different. Somehow the inmate must cope with the label of being a prisoner and face the rejection in a way that psychologically deals with the label. Oftentimes this means the rejection of society that has placed him in prison.

Second, the prisoner is deprived of many goods and services when placed in prison. He no longer can have many of the amenities that he enjoyed when he was free. The prison restricts such comforts. More importantly, the prisoner carries with him the stigma of being less of a social being in society's eyes. In a world where material possessions are critical to the definition of oneself, a rather poor disposition is created and perpetuated by the prison when the prisoner cannot even have the basic items that define him as a social being. In short, as Sykes (1958:70) suggests, "[H]e must carry the additional burden of social definitions which equate his material deprivation with personal inadequacy."

Third, the inmate is deprived of normal heterosexual contact in the prison setting. He cannot deal with his sexual needs in ways that are approved by society. As with material possessions, a denial of heterosexual expression is often interpreted in a way which demeans the prisoner's identity as a normal male in society. Being denied normal heterosexual contact calls into question the prisoner's maleness. Since sexual expressions are related to the ability of the male to be a man, it is impossible for the prisoner to express his manhood because of the physical limitations imposed by the prison. As such, many of the homosexual behaviors exhibited by prisoners reflect *functional* adaptations on the part of inmates when other, more socially approved means of expressing oneself sexually are denied, namely normal contact with persons of the opposite sex.

Fourth, there is the denial of autonomy in prison. Autonomy refers to the ability to make daily decisions about one's life. All of these decisions are made for the prisoner, and as a result, the prisoner is dependent upon the wishes of the correctional officer. This situation of dependency reduces many prisoners to the state of childhood. Rudimentary decisions about their lives cannot even be made by them. In this sense, the regimen of the custodians is very demeaning and repulsive to inmates; it violates prisoners' self-image as people who can make their own decisions. By being denied the opportunities to make decisions, the prisoners are forced to live lives of dependency.

Finally, there is the deprivation of security. In this sense, the prisoner does not feel safe in an environment where dangerous people have been placed. As one inmate said to Sykes (1958:77), "The worst thing about prison is you have to live with other prisoners." It is the feeling among many prisoners that the institution is not safe and secure, and that they could be victimized by other inmates at any time. Moreover, the inmate has to face daily the pressure of other inmates who seek to challenge him for favors or property. The pressure places strain on the inmate's self-image when other prisoners test him to see if he has the nerve to face them. This anxiety produces many intense pressures for the inmate. How he reacts will affect his image in the eyes of all inmates in the public arena of the prison.

Taken together, these pains of imprisonment are focal points whereby social interactions among inmates are centered. As Sykes (1958:82-83) suggests, the inmate can either function as an individual where there is a "war of all against all" or he can bind himself into a position of cooperation with other inmates to alleviate the pains of imprisonment. The prison social structure, therefore, represents a compromise between individuals seeking to cope with the pains of imprisonment and a collective body of inmates who negotiate informal rules on how they are to address the pains of imprisonment. It is a mixture of these two positions that defines the nature and extent of social systems in prison. Social systems in prison, therefore, serve the purpose of mitigating the pains of imprisonment. Additionally, the prisoner social world functions as a mechanism to adapt to the "rigors of confinement." These rigors "can at least be mitigated by the patterns of social interaction established among the inmates themselves" (Sykes, 1958:82).

Argot Roles

Argot roles in prison represent the beliefs and attitudes of prisoners expressed in rather distinctive fashion. These argot roles are tied to the prisoner social world by their inherent meanings generated by the prison environment. The language of the prison, therefore, is critical to understanding the social world of prisoners. It is these argot roles that give meaning and an interpretive framework upon which the social world of the prisoner can be understood. According to Sykes, there are a multitude of argot roles found in the prison. The more common of these roles are listed below.

First, there are the *rats* and *center men*. These roles represent behaviors on the part of inmates that are in conflict with the expectations of the inmate body. The rat, for example, is an inmate who "squeals" on other inmates and their dealings. The center man, also, is one who supports the activities of the custodians in their interactions with prisoners. Neither role is valued by a majority of prisoners in the inmate social system. As Sykes (1958:90) states, "And if the rat is hated for his deception and his hypocrisy, the center man is despised for his slavish submission."

Second, there are *gorillas* and *merchants* or *pedlars* in the inmate social system. The former takes what he wants from other inmates through force or threat of force, while the latter exploits inmates by selling them things they need. Additionally, the gorilla and the merchant or pedlar only shows concern for himself and has very little regard for the well-being of the group. In this way, both are indifferent to the concerns of inmates in general and are viewed in a negative light by many inmates.

Third, there are the argot roles of *wolves*, *punks*, and *fags*. These, according to Sykes, are the homosexuals in the prison. On the one hand, wolves represent those inmates who are viewed as the masculine partner in a sexual liaison, whereas punks and fags are the submissive inmates. It is said in prison that punks are made while fags are born. This distinction delineates further the argot roles in prison. Punks are people who have been either coerced into sexual relations with other prisoners or choose such a role to acquire goods and services in the prison. Fags, however, are prisoners who simply prefer the homosexual activity as a lifestyle in prison. Regardless of the sexual role played, the distinctions among prisoners involve clear meanings for the inmate social system. Both the punk and the fag argot roles, for example, clearly mean something in the social world of prisoners. Both are not representations of men; the punk, because he does not have the "toughness" to be a man; and the fag, because he has outward displays of femininity by accepting his homosexual orientation.

Finally, there are *ball busters* and *real men*. The former denotes the inmate role type which is in constant defiance with the custodians. He is the inmate who never gives the guards a break. Initially, one may think of the ball buster as one who is respected by a majority of prisoners, but in reality, he is looked down upon because of his disregard for the negotiations and compromises which make up the social order of the prison. It is these subtleties which keep the stability of the prison intact for custodians, but in addition, allow inmates the ability to make their worlds more liveable under austere conditions. As such, the ball buster is not as revered as one might expect in the inmate social system.

While the ball buster is viewed somewhat negatively by many prisoners, the real men are the most admired in the social world of prisoners. Unlike the ball buster who seeks to upset the order of the prison, the real man does his time without confronting his captors nor does he acknowledge them. In the words of Sykes (1958:102), "[I]t is the man who can stop himself from striking back at the custodians that wins the admiration and thus their image of the hero functions wittingly or unwittingly to maintain the status quo."

Additionally, the argot roles of *tough* and *hipster* do exist in the inmate social system. The tough represents the inmate who, like the ball buster, will not allow himself to be run by the custodial staff, but more importantly, will definitely resort to violence and aggressive behavior if crossed by anyone, including the inmate and the guard. The hipster, however, is the prisoner who talks a good game but is not able to back up his words with actions. In essence, the hipster typifies the inmate who lives a lie and hides behind a façade.

The inmate social system, then, represents a structural makeup of clearly defined roles that enable prisoners to deal with the pains of imprisonment. Inmate roles, in addition, change over time, and prisoners may change their roles depending upon how successful they are in dealing with the pains of imprisonment. Therefore, we would expect inmate social systems to vary from institution to institution and across time. The inmate social system with its attendant roles described by Sykes in 1958 in all likelihood does not exist today. Yet the structural characteristics inherent within prisons have remained rather constant, and given that situation, we would expect that argot roles are still part of prisons today although the language to describe them has changed.

Finally, Sykes does suggest that as the inmate social system becomes more solidified, the greater is the likelihood that the pains of imprisonment are less severe for the entire inmate body. As the inmate has a meaningful system of social interactions with other inmates, he is able to mitigate many of the pains of imprisonment. Thus, prison social structures have utility to most prisoners because they enable them to lessen the severity of the incarcerative experience. And, the prison social structure, according to this functional perspective, is created as a reaction to the harsh realities of the prison structure. By implication, therefore, one can alter the functioning of the inmate social system by modifying the structural conditions of the prison. It is the tenuous balance and relationship between the workings of the inmate social system and the formal rules and regulations of both administrative officials and custodians that define prison stability.

Prison Social Organization and Prison Stability

The functional perspective highlights the importance of the relationship between the formal structure of the prison and the informal workings of the prisoner social system. Prison stability, therefore, cannot be divorced from the workings of the inmate social system. The social world of inmates is a critical component to the smooth operation of the prison. To deny this reality is to fail to accept the kinds of power that prisoners do have in a correctional setting. As Sykes (1958:50) suggests, prison stability is maintained through a series of accommodations when the formal system of rules and regulations cannot provide the control required by custodial staff. He states:

> Unable to count on a sense of duty to motivate their captives to obey and unable to depend on the direct and immediate use of violence to insure a step-by-step submission to the rules, the custodians must fall back on a system of rewards and punishments.

As a result of this give-and-take relationship between the correctional officer and the inmate, the correctional officer provides a modicum of control which is critical to the mission of the institution. In this way, the system of informal rewards and punishments serves the central purpose of the prison, that being stability. Moreover, the guard has many built-in weaknesses in the structure of the prison that make total compliance nearly impossible to achieve. To begin with, throughout the course of a working day, the guard develops a close, trusting relationship with the prisoners. While he may not trust prisoners totally, he learns to respect the inmates as *men* who happen to be in prison, as opposed to *criminals* in prison. Day-to-day interactions with prisoners soften the guard's perception of the inmate, and this makes it more difficult for the guard to demand and expect total compliance from inmates.

Second, the guard role has a foundation in reciprocity. The guard cannot complete all the functions required of him. As a result, many inmates complete functions that are assigned to guards. The reciprocity, in turn, forces the guard to turn his back on rule violations or to be less demanding with inmates when it comes to the enforcement of policies and procedures. The officer exercises his discretionary authority in a way that legitimizes the reciprocal relationship between himself and the prisoner. In this way, the guard's authority is eroded, yet the daily tasks of the job are completed.

Finally, the guard is evaluated on how well he maintains control in his cellblock. By providing rewards and benefits to prisoners, the guard provides more certainty to the environment and greater control over the inmate population. However, guards have limited rewards to give prisoners. If the guard is evaluated on how well he keeps control in the cellblock, then working within the inmate social system through a *sub-rosa* structure of give and take becomes a critical component to the prison's formal structure. More importantly, as stated by Sykes (1958:57), "Now power, like a woman's virtue, once lost is hard to regain." The guard is placed in the middle of an inmate social system that thrives on the reciprocity between the correctional officer and the inmate, and as such, the coercive power presumably inherent within the role of a correctional officer is diminished by the structural qualities of the prison.

The social organization of prisoners is invariably tied to the stability of the prison. Keeping inmates in line requires a recognition on the part of the administrative staff and the custodial officers that it is the balance between the demands of the inmate body and the formal policies which define order in the setting of the prison. Sykes (1958:61) summarizes this position by saying:

> The lack of sense of duty among those who are held captive, the obvious fallacies of coercion, the pathetic collection of rewards and punishments to induce compliance, the strong pressures toward the corruption of the guard in the form of friendship, reciprocity, and the transfer of duties into the hands of trusted inmates—all are structural defects in the prison's system of power rather than individual inadequacies.

The functional model, therefore, holds that many of the behaviors exhibited by both prisoners and correctional officers are directly related to the structural makeup of the prison. If you were concerned with changing the behaviors of guards and inmates, then, you would have to focus on the organization of the prison setting, since it is this structure which determines the behaviors of those who work and reside in it. Definite policy suggestions could include reorganization and restructuring of prison environments to produce other types of behaviors.

The research literature on the adequacy of the functional model has been plentiful. Beginning with Sykes in the 1950s and well into the 1960s, the functional model has been tested to examine a number of phenomena in prisons, including the sexual behaviors and drug habits of prisoners (Akers,

Hayner, and Gruninger, 1974), the informal system of contraband distribution in prison (Williams and Fish, 1974; Gleason, 1978; and Kalinich, 1986), and the adjustment to the pains of imprisonment (Street, Vinter, and Perrow, 1969; Tittle, 1969; Thomas, 1977). All of this research, in part, supports some of the tenets associated with the functional model described above. The research suggests that the functional model is useful in explaining how inmate social systems develop and the purposes they serve in the prison environment.

Theories on Prison Social Organization—The Importation Response

While the functional theory of inmate social organization examines the role of the prison environment in the production of an inmate social system, the importation model suggests that experiences and attitudes of prisoners prior to incarceration are critical to understanding the adaptation processes among inmates. This view holds that pre-prison experiences on the outside world are pivotal in understanding the social system of the prison. This view was originally put forth by ex-offender John Irwin and sociologist Donald Cressey. In a seminal piece published in 1962, Irwin and Cressey presented the basic principles associated with the importation model.

Fundamentally, their position is that not only are the mechanisms of adaptation to prison learned prior to incarceration, but in addition, they argue these modes of adaptation can be tied directly to specific role types. Moreover, they do not deny the pains of imprisonment, nor the prisonization ordeal, as described by the functional model. Instead, they argue that how prisoners adjust to these processes are a function of adaptive patterns learned on the city streets, not functionally related to the prison structure. The prison social system, then, is composed of clearly identifiable roles and referent subcultures. They are: *thief subculture, convict subculture,* and *legitimate subculture.*

Thief Subculture

The thief subculture is composed of individuals who hold specific values. According to Irwin and Cressey, these values are common among

thieves across the nation. The thief subculture values the notion that criminals should neither trust nor cooperate with police, should not betray other thieves, should be reliable and cool-headed, and be "solid" in the eyes of other inmates. Irwin and Cressey describe how the thief subculture thrives on the idea that the individual has requisite skills to be a good thief, but more importantly, is able to hold up and defend the honor of being a thief. In-group loyalties to the thief subculture are more important to other prisoners than skill at being a thief. Finally, the thief subculture supports and lends advice to those group members who are unfamiliar with the workings of the prison and the inmate social system. In effect, the subculture works toward the resolution of conflicts among group members in prison, and the subculture provides the direction to members on "how to do time" behind bars.

Convict Subculture

Unlike the thief subculture, the convict subculture is uniquely tied to the workings of the prison. These are individuals who have had extensive experiences with jails and prisons and have felt their deprivations on many occasions. The central tenet of the convict subculture is utilitarianism and the manipulation of the prison system for personal advantage and gain. Members of the convict subculture work toward the acquisition of wealth when incarcerated and positions of power in the inmate social system. Most importantly, the convict subculture is composed of individuals who have a long record of confinement in institutions, beginning with juvenile institutions. They are able to make transitions from institution to institution because of their extensive experiences with prison systems. Finally, Irwin and Cressey argue that the emphasis on manipulation and ultilitarian values is not a product of the prison environment. Instead, these values reflect an ethic acquired on the city streets and are consistent with beliefs held by many "hard core" members of the lower class, and most prisoners come from this class.

Legitimate Subculture

Unlike the thief and convict subcultures, the legitimate subculture in prison views institutional rules and regulations as part of doing time. They are the inmates who seek status in the prison by following all the approved mechanisms of the prison's administration, such as involvement in the institutional newspaper or the inmate council. They have minimal involvement in the inmate social system and typically do their time with as little trouble as possible. In addition, they make up a large portion of many prisons. Irwin and Cressey estimate that close to 40% of the inmate population can be placed in the legitimate subculture of the prison. In short, members of this subculture are the least problematic for prison officials.

Evidence supporting the importation model is also plentiful (Wellford, 1967; Schwartz, 1971; Thomas, 1975). Additionally, many have attempted to incorporate the importation perspective along with the functional approach into an integrative model of the prisonization process. Proponents of both the importation and functional models have recognized the utility of employing tenets from each approach to explaining the dynamics of the inmate social system. Like the functional model, the importation perspective has provided some deep insight into the functioning of the prisoner social system, yet it, too, has its limitations in explaining much of the activity of the prisoner social system.

For example, it is not clear that all prisoners can be classified into one of three prison subcultures. The prison social structure is more complex and dynamic than was originally stated by Irwin and Cressey. This led Irwin (1980) to comment on the changing social structure of the prison. No longer was the prison primarily composed of three predominant subcultures. Instead, the prisoner social system was viewed as being composed of groups or gangs of prisoners, each with their own identity and purpose. As a result, more contemporary explanations of the inmate social system emphasized the role of gang and racial affiliations when examining the inmate social system. This more contemporary view was more a support of the importation hypothesis than a critique of it. While the original importation model suggested the prevalence of three subcultures in the inmate social system, the more contemporary view expanded on the importation model by suggesting that the inmate social system was much more factionalized and fragmented, defined by gang membership and ethnic or racial identification. As such, a comprehensive analysis of the prisoner social world required a more broadly defined examination of the prison.

Contemporary Conceptions
of Prisoner Social Structure

In an influential book titled *Stateville: The Penitentiary in Mass Society*, James Jacobs (1977) argues that the prison no longer could be understood as being an entity outside of the realm of other processes in society. The prison in contemporary times moved from being at the periphery of society into a more visible position. No longer could the prison be viewed as an institution that was beyond the purview of the public. More importantly, the prison became not only more visible but also more accountable when practices of prison officials could be examined by the public. Jacobs' argument suggests that the prison now, for the first time, became open to public scrutiny. Much of what occurred in the past in the prison was hidden from the public. Yet, for the first time, prison officials had to justify their actions to the public, and more specifically to the watchful eyes of the judiciary.

From his analysis, Jacobs argues that the Stateville penitentiary, like others throughout the country, went through a series of stages that redefined its purpose and the changing structure of the inmate social system. In fact, it is the changing prisoner social world that impacted the environments of the prison and the administrative reactions to them that highlights the modern prison. Thus, Jacobs' analysis of the prison reflects not only the changing nature of the inmate social system and administrative responses to it in one prison, but provides a richer description of how the prison social structure has changed in the modern prison generally. Therefore, his analysis shows how the prison has become more firmly entrenched in the workings and representations of general society. You cannot think of one without the other. No longer is the prisoner social structure explained relative to singular models, such as provided by both the functional and importation models. Instead, analysis of the prisoner social system must include the role of broader social events that define such a structure.

From Jacobs' examination, there were a number of events and processes that defined the character and direction of the Stateville penitentiary over a 50-year period. Two central themes emerged from his analysis: the development of an authoritarian regime at the prison from 1925-1970 and the search for a new equilibrium in the post-1970 years.

The Authoritarian Regime (1925-1970)

Early on, Stateville penitentiary was dominated by the will and charisma of one man: Warden Joseph E. Ragen. Ragen represented a response to an uncontrolled situation prior to his appointment as Warden at Stateville. Influenced by political partisanship of external influences, the prison prior to Ragen could not be run effectively. Ragen stepped into the prison with his own personal philosophy on penal operations as the cornerstone of his administration. He made it clear that he ran the prison. In fact, both inmates and staff were aware of the power of Ragen in gaining the compliance of both groups. His 30-year tenure as Warden can be summarized using Jacobs' (1977:29) words:

> Joe Ragen's thirty year "rule" of Stateville was based upon the patriarchal authority he achieved. In the vocabulary of both employees and inmates, "he ran it." The "old boss" devoted his life to perfecting the world's most orderly prison regime. He exercised personal control over every detail, no matter how insignificant. He tolerated challenges neither by inmates nor by employees nor by outside interest groups. He cultivated an image which made him invincible to his subordinates as well as to prisoners.

The emergence of Ragen onto the scene at Stateville changed the internal machinations of the inmate social system. Fear and intimidation were commonplace, along with strategies to control the inmate population through the cultivation of prison "rats," men who leaked information to guards about the activities of other inmates. Ragen was notorious in instilling fear into the inmate body through the expressions of his power. In addition, he was able to keep the institution out of the public's eye by keeping a quiet, orderly, and peaceful institution. Little was known about the beatings of inmates when they criticized the institution to visitors or through their letters. Ragen was able to control his institution, as suggested by Jacobs, because he prevented external people from coming into the prison and kept a low profile. He literally was out of sight, out of mind.

With the change in the internal composition of the prison, moving from a majority of white prisoners to a majority of black prisoners, in the late 1950s and early 1960s, the inmate social system, with its own rules and regulations, began to change. Couple this with the fact that the national mood toward prisons was changing and the advent of the civil rights movement started to impact on the day-to-day operations of the prison, it was clear that

Ragen's tactics were being called into question by both those internal to the prison, most notably black muslim prisoners, and those external to the prison. In short, the personal dominace enjoyed by Ragen for almost 30 years was now crumbling due to pressures internal and external to the prison. It is in the early 1960s with the retirement of Ragen and changes in the views and expectations of the external world that the prison also experienced great change.

Challenges to institutional authority in the period between 1961-1970 began immediately after Ragen left Stateville and fell into the hands of his successors. His immediate successor could not keep intact the traditional system of doing things in the prison. It is not even clear that Ragen could have maintained the level of control that he enjoyed earlier in the prison's history. The prison now was succumbing to the pressures of the external world. Societal expectations were changing and the ground upon which the authoritarian system was predicated was rapidly shifting. The most critical factor in the erosion of the traditional system was the influence of the legal system, specifically the federal courts.

In 1962, inmate Thomas Cooper filed a claim against the institution claiming he was being punished for his religious beliefs. The institution could provide no justification as to why it denied access to religious materials to black Muslims yet allowed Bibles to be given to Christian prisoners. In a victory for prisoners, the court ruled that there was no legal reason to deny Muslims access to some materials relevant to the practice of their faith. Beginning with this decision and followed by other actions in the prison by the administration, the power of the traditional authoritarian regime became called into question. Not only were black prisoners getting the courts to hear their cases and decide them on their behalf, but more importantly, the prisoner social system started to transform from the white con structure to being predominated by separate social systems of black inmates and white inmates. In short, the social structure of the prison became fragmented along racial lines, something which was critical to later developments in the inmate social system.

As stated by Jacobs (1977:70):

Thus, between 1961 and 1970, Stateville experienced a period of limited change. The loss of a warden who could command absolute authority, the loss of local autonomy, heightened race consciousness among blacks and the penetration of legal norms exposed severe strains in the authoritarian system.

Most importantly, Stateville prison was experiencing changes in the social structure of society. With rising expectations of blacks in society and the growth of the civil rights movement, the prison, like other institutions in society, had to respond to these changes. In most cases throughout the country, the response of prison officials was repression and suppression of inmate leaders and those who challenged the authority of institutional policies and procedures. This approach only created tension in the prison environments, particularly among those prisoners who viewed prisons as representations of a repressive society. As a result, the prisoner social systems throughout the country became fragmented and racial divisions were common. It was the search for equilibrium among prison officials in the 1970s that predominated the institutional agendas of administrators, including at the Stateville penitentiary.

The Search for a New Equilibrium (1970-1975)

The search for equilibrium in the Stateville penitentiary began with a transformation of the organizational structure of the prison. Jacobs (1977:73-74) argues that the change in the prison was fueled by three sources. First, the state of Illinois created a separate Department of Corrections whose charge was to oversee the operations of all institutions. This move enabled the activities of all Illinois prisons to be monitored and controlled through the front office. By centralizing the power of the department, the Illinois Department of Corrections could eliminate the local autonomy of prison officials. In this way, the prison was no longer controlled solely by the warden and his administrative staff. Now, the prison was accountable to a higher authority.

Second, associated with this centralization of authority was the development of a cadre of professional people who were highly educated and considered an elite corp of administrative officials. In short, the central office became a bureaucracy with all the attendant rules and regulations. This bureaucratization fostered a new approach to the operations of prisons. Unlike the past where wardens had local control and ran things the way they saw fit, the new philosophy in Illinois and really the rest of the country was the increased belief in professionalization of administrative personnel through education and training. Now, as Jacobs (1977:73) states: Stateville penitentiary transformed "from a patriarchal organization based upon traditional authority to a rational-legal bureaucracy." It was clear in this search for equilibrium that the central office sought to do away with the old way of doing things.

Finally, the prison began to hire more civilian personnel to fill the roles of teachers, counselors, and social workers. These workers clearly had problems with the authoritarian and patriarchal structure traditionally used by wardens in the Illinois prison system. Ostensibly, these newcomers to the prison would not put up with Ragen's philosophy on employee control in the Stateville penitentiary, and as a result, they demanded that changes be made concerning the processes of decision-making and rule-making.

With the centralization of authority, the rise of a group of professional managers, and the introduction of more civilians into the day-to-day operations of the prison came more problems than solutions as to how prisons were to be run. It is the period between 1970 and 1975 that major problems hit the Illinois Department of Corrections. Specifically, these problems were: Intrusion of the legal system, penetration of the gangs, and transition of the guard force. Each of these problems posed serious tests to the newly formed professional managers who headed the Illinois Department of Corrections.

We do not have the space here to discuss each one of these problems thoroughly. The student is encouraged to review Jacobs' work more completely to see how these problems influenced the direction of the Stateville penitentiary. What can be summarized here is that the legal environment demanded that the prison change its fundamental ways of running the prison and kept correctional administrators busy trying to comply with court orders. In addition, with the rise of the professional administration and its belief in the rehabilitative ideal came much intrastaff conflict, which produced fertile ground for the proliferation and penetration of gangs in the prison. As Jacobs (1977:138) states, the gangs could only proliferate in an organizational environment where certainty did not exist and maintenance and control functions could not be met. As such, Jacobs states: "It was only in the context of this organizational crisis that the gangs were able to organize, recruit, and achieve dominance."

Moreover, the guard force in the Stateville penitentiary went through many changes, much of which affected the operation of the prison. According to Jacobs (1977:175), with the introduction of a "reform minded" administration, the growth of public employee unionism, and the racial integration of the staff came many divisions among staff who worked in the prison. It was clear that the prison was being affected by the changes in the external environment, and that many of these changes were not well received by the traditional guard force. Racial integration of the staff, for example, produced much animosity between older white officers and the newly recruited black officers who often sympathized with the plight of prisoners. These conditions fostered an environment in which staff had no control over the inmate social system. Truly, the prisoner social world in the Stateville penitentiary had become uncontrollable and violent and aggressive prisoner gangs ran the prison. The result was a loss of institutional control by staff and a deterioration between guards and key elements of the inmate social system.

Violent acts against guards increased and the prison was racketed with a greater number of assaults and less control by administrative officals. The search for restoration of control in the prison was difficult and really did not actualize until after 1975 when the status of prisoners was more clearly defined and the reforms of the past were integrated into the formal system of control in the prison. Yet, Jacobs (1977:210-211) argues that there are limits to a professional bureaucracy in the prison. Issues such as resources, the ability of the bureaucracy to meet inmates' needs, the potential conflict with external groups, the role of the guard in a professional bureaucracy, the level of professionalization among administrative staff, and the relationships between prison administrators and the political environment all raise serious questions about the efficacy of bureaucratic methods in running institutions of confinement.

Nevertheless, the real effect that we are concerned with is the inmate social system and how it responds to the changes in administrative style among officals. It was clear that the inmate social system was in a period of control under Ragen at Stateville and slowly changed into a violent subculture dominated by gangs after he left. It is questionable as to what and how administrators should respond to the social systems of prisoners. Clearly, there are some limitations with trying to instill a pure bureaucracy in prison, yet the reforms which have been evidenced in American prisons over the past two decades have drastically altered the functioning of inmate social systems. Can prisons be run without the kinds of relationships that Sykes and other functional proponents argue are inherent within the prison structure, or can we instill other management techniques that improve the conditions of prisoners while maintaining the control required in prison?

These focal questions plague correctional administrators today. As Jacobs (1977:211) so succinctly states:

> What if the attempt to synthesize reform and control in the maximum-security prison fails? What if the prison reverts to arbitrary and capricious management in a situation marked by brutality, favoritism, and staff apathy? The danger is that, in that event, the larger effort to reform our bureaucracies and basic institutions will be dealt a mortal blow. The failure to institutionalize prison reform could reinforce more general cynicism about the capacity of our society to reform itself.

The remaining sections will examine opposing viewpoints as to how prisons can be managed so that they can be useful social institutions and produce more law-abiding citizens for the community. Fundamentally, our goal is to see how inmate social systems can be changed toward more positive ends. The next section will offer specific suggestions as to how the prison can become a place where inmates learn to cope and mature. Under this view, the correctional officer has to be considered an integral part of the rehabilitation process of prisoners. As such, we will, in addition, examine the literature on correctional officers. The final section will explore a control model of prison management, one emphasizing greater involvement and accountability of administrators in monitoring prisoner social systems.

"Hard Time": The Modern-Day Experience of Incarceration

Today, the prisoner social world is much more complex and requires a different viewpoint to understand how prisoners cope with the incarceration experience. One work that has received considerable attention in the 1980s is that of Johnson's (1987). In the book *Hard Time* Johnson (1987:39) states, "Prisons are nothing if not painful, yet the implications of this stark fact have never been fully appreciated by reformers."

Put simply, one cannot conceive of the modern penitentiary without examining the fundamental premise that prisons were designed to be painful, and that the experience of incarceration requires that inmates feel pain. This view is somewhat similar to what the functional model described earlier. Yet, the view offered by Johnson is that the "pains of imprisonment" felt by inmates are much more psychological than physical, and in addition, are what constitute the "hard time" that they experience. As such, the critical question for understanding the contemporary prison is, "How do prisoners cope with the hard time they experience?"

We suggested earlier, according to the functional model on the one hand, that the inmate social system's primary purpose dealt with alleviating the pains of imprisonment. Johnson, on the other hand, suggests that how prisoners today deal with the pains of imprisonment are much more diverse and no consistent pattern of adaptation can be discerned. Moreover, he suggests that the fundamental purpose of prison management is to inculcate among prisoners mature and conventional ways of adapting to prison, with the hope that such behavior patterns will be exhibited when released from prison. The fundamental purpose of prison, therefore, should be teaching correct ways of coping with an inherently painful experience. As Johnson (1987:56) states:

> Prisoners must cope maturely with the demands of prison life; if they do not, the prison experience will simply add to their catalog of failure and defeat. Mature coping, in fact, does more than prevent one's prison life from becoming yet another series of personal setbacks. It is at the core of what we mean by correction or rehabilitation, and thus creates the possibility of a more constructive life after release from prison.

Mature coping, more specifically, is essentially composed of three attributes that prisoners must learn. First, there must be a recognition of common problems of adjustment by prisoners. More directly, this attribute requires that the prisoner recognize that there are both acceptable and unacceptable ways of solving one's problems. Facing one's problems demands that the individual react in a way that is acceptable not only within the constraints of the prison, but in addition, expects from the prisoner that such a coping mechanism is acceptable to the general public. Living lives of illusion and fantasy have been the norm for many prisoners, and such mechanisms are not acceptable among mature people who confront and deal with their problems in a reasonable fashion. Such a skill must be recognized and accepted by the prisoner if successful coping and adjustment are to occur.

Second, mature coping requires that the prisoner not resort to violence and deception as coping mechanisms. For many prisoners, these twin concepts have served as the guiding principles in their interactions with others. In the long run, however, such approaches are doomed to failure. In fact, being in prison actually represents the long-term futility of using such mechanisms of coping. The mature individual does not seek to hide behind deception, nor does he resort to violence when he does not get his way. Instead, the mature individual learns the approved ways of interacting with others and accepts the rules by which conflicts are resolved.

Third and finally, the prisoner must learn that mature coping requires that caring for self and others is an important aspect of successful adjustment to prison. In short, the prisoner has to view his experience in the context of a broader community of individuals, all of whom are seeking to adjust and cope with the pressures of everyday existence. In the words of Johnson (1987:60), there has to be a sense of "altruistic egoism," whereby there is an equal concern for not only oneself but also the other individual. In this way, the individual respects the idea of a community and lives within the parameters as defined by that community. Only through cooperative and agreed-upon rules can the community survive. Whether it be the prison community or the social community, the principle still applies, and it is the purpose of the prison to instill within the prisoner the value of showing concern for others.

The sad fact is that these principles tend not to be reinforced in the context of the prison. As such, Johnson makes a distinction between the *public culture* of the prison and the *private culture* of the prison. It is when public cultural norms of the prison are in opposition to mature coping among prisoners that the prison community has failed. Johnson (1987:63) states:

> Mature coping contradicts standard cultural prescriptions about appropriate prisoner deportment. The public culture of the prison has norms that dictate behavior 'on the yard' and in other public areas of the prison such as mess halls, gyms, and the larger program and work sites. This culture emphasizes an almost automatic use of hostility and manipulation in one's relations with fellow inmates and especially with the staff, and makes friendly and caring behavior, again especially with respect to the staff, look servile and silly.

Therefore, the herculean task that faces correctional administrators is how to reconcile the demands of the public culture with the mature coping strategies of dealing with problems appropriately, avoiding deception and violence, and caring for self and others.

This is no easy task, yet Johnson (1987:66,97-118) does suggest that mature coping strategies are possible among prisoners since many inmates have no desire to exclusively and wholeheartedly accept the norms of the prison's public culture. Instead, they have adaptation strategies that minimize interactions within the public culture of the prison and primarily exist within their own "range of ecological options that support life 'off the yard'" (Johnson, 1987:66). These options are also referred to as niches. The niches serve as mechanisms of adaptation to the prison experience and provide the inmate an outlet for successful adaptation to the prison setting outside the public culture of the prison.

In addition, these niches are vast and very diverse. There is no one monolithic niche nor inmate social system that serves to deal with the pains of imprisonment. The public regards the existing view of prisons as places of violence and deceit, with attendant norms that support such values. However, there are a number of private cultures within the prison that could possibly support mature adjustment among prisoners to the pains of imprisonment. The diversity of these private cultures of the prison is what makes them uniquely distinctive, and places where effective maturing can take place. At present, many of the niches in prison are places where *only* stress reduction occurs and these niches are not conducive to learning acceptable ways of coping with prison life. In short, they are havens for reducing the stresses produced and reinforced by the public culture of the prison.

These niches tend to *avoid* the problems associated with prison life. The goal should be to teach inmates appropriate ways of *facing* the problems that lead toward acceptable behaviors and normal adjustment to the prison setting. One way to accomplish such an objective is to include all actors in the process of developing healthy adjustment among prisoners. This includes those who have the primary role of overseeing and controlling prisoners—the correctional officers. If successful adjustment among prisoners is going to be a reality in the prison of the 1990s, then no other role is going to be as pivotal as the correctional officer role. Much has been written about correctional officers and it is this literature the following section will address.

Correctional Officers at Work: Their Public and Private Agendas

While there has been a plethora of research literature on the workings of inmate social systems, there has been very little research on correctional officers and their work worlds. Traditionally, studies on the role of being a correctional officer have been minimal and many focused only on the meager backgrounds of those people who entered correctional officer work. This situation, however, has changed drastically over the past 10 years. In the late 1980s there has been much research investigating the work environments, expectations, and attitudes of correctional officers. It is clear that contemporary researchers have become fascinated in understanding the correctional officer role (see Philliber, 1987 for a thorough review of the literature on correctional officers). No other area has received more attention than the attitudes of correctional officers.

Much of this research has focused on the determinants of correctional officers' attitudes. These determinants have been portrayed as consisting of two types. The first line of research has investigated the individual backgrounds of officers and how they correlate with attitudes toward prisoners. This line of inquiry has focused on such variables as: race, gender, age, age of entry into correctional officer work, and education. As can be expected, much of the research has not provided consistent findings with respect to attitudes among correctional officers. For example, Toch and Klofas' (1982) study of four prisons in New York found a significantly greater likelihood that nonwhite officers would prefer distance from inmates. Other research, however, found that with respect to race, there were no differences between white and nonwhite officers with regard to custody issues, but that black officers were more supportive of rehabilitation when compared to white officers (Cullen et al., 1989).

Concerning age and education, inconsistent findings were again generated by the research. Jurik (1985) and Cullen et al. (1989:37) both found that gender was not a source of attitudes among correctional officers, while Poole and Regoli (1980) found that there was a negative relationship between education and custody. Yet again, the research has not shown consistent findings when examining these individual variables. Crouch and Alpert (1982) and Jurik (1985:530) both found that there was no relationship between education and attitudes toward prisoners. Interestingly enough, the research suggests that regardless of the officer's race, education, or gender there are no consistent attitudes among officers toward inmates. Like prisoners, correctional officers tend to be a disparate group of individuals who hold no solitary attitudes toward prisoners. Similar findings exist when we examine the effect of age, when hired, of correctional officers and attitudes toward inmates. To summarize, the research evidence is not conclusive as to the importance of individual variables and their effect on the attitudes of correctional officers toward prisoners.

Unlike individual determinants of correctional officer attitudes, a second line of inquiry focuses on organizational determinants of correctional officer attitudes. This research tends to focus on the following variables: role conflict, shift worked, job stress, frequency of inmate contact, and perceptions of danger. Similar to the findings of the individual sources of correctional officer attitudes, the organizational determinants of correctional officer attitudes findings show no consistent pattern. While Smith and Hepburn (1979) found greater punitive attitudes among correctional officers in minimum-security units, for example, Jurik found the exact opposite in her research: there was more optimism among correctional officers in minimum-security units. Finally, Cullen et al. (1989:38) found no relationship between working in a maximum-security unit and support for either custody or rehabilitation. Again, these same inconsistencies are also found when one examines other organizational determinants of correctional officers' attitudes, such as job stress, shift worked, and frequency of contact with prisoners.

Our research is at best inconclusive about the attitudes of correctional officers toward prisoners. What we can say is that correctional officers, like prisoners, are not a homogenous group of individuals. Some correctional officers are punitive, while others are more supportive of rehabilitation. The reasons as to why correctional officers are so diverse and disparate in their attitudes toward prisoners is not so apparent. From our review above of both individual and organizational determinants of correctional officer attitudes, it is not clear what the sources of correctional officer attitudes are and how we can influence them. What is clear is that correctional officers do have attitudes that influence their interactions with prisoners and that these attitudes are fairly diverse among them. A key to understanding the attitudes of correctional officers toward inmates may be acquired by examining the private and public cultures of officers. This returns us to the work of Johnson (1987:119-158).

The idea that correctional officers have diverse and oftentimes divergent attitudes toward prisoners may be understood by examining the differing agenda of officers. On the one hand, correctional officers have a *public agenda*, one that reinforces the stereotype that officers are "hacks," "screws," and "thugs." This view of correctional officers has been portrayed by much of the media and represents only a small percentage of officers. Johnson (1987:119) estimates that only 25% of the correctional officer force can be described in this stereotypical fashion. What is important is that there are correctional officers who do hold these views, and this rather pejorative world view has captured the attention of not only the public but also correctional administrators. As one correctional officer stated to Stojkovic (1984): "We are the screws that no one really cares about."

While the public agenda of correctional officers is relevant to our understanding of correctional officers, it is equally important to examine what Johnson (1987:137) refers to as the *private agenda* of correctional officers. This private agenda entails a much different perception of correctional officers, one that recognizes the correctional officer role as being more complex than what is portrayed by the public agenda. Instead, this view of correctional officers emphasizes that there are multiple roles in being a correctional officer. In addition, the private agenda includes a belief in helping prisoners to adjust to the prison setting. This notion of correctional officers as effective change agents is one which is definitely not in accordance with the traditional view.

Specifically, correctional officers as change agents can involve three separate roles: providing goods and services to prisoners, acting as a referral agent or advocate for inmates, and helping inmates with institutional adjustment (Johnson, 1987:142). Clearly, this view of the correctional officer requires a different perspective on the part of both correctional administrators and the general public. No longer can the correctional officer be viewed as the simple custodian; correctional officers under this view represent the front-line of correctional work, which underscores the importance of human service delivery and its utility to the operation of the institution. As Johnson (1987:154) states:

> Why, then, do some officers persist in activities that take time and effort, are neither recognized nor rewarded by others, and must be hidden or played down for fear of trouble with administrators, peers, treatment staff, or recalcitrant inmates? The reason...is simply this: human service activities make the officer's job richer, more rewarding, and ultimately less stressful.

Once again, this view requires a redefinition of the correctional officer role. Supporters of this view claim that interactions with prisoners will change and the prison will operate on earned authority of the keeper rather than the iron fist of coercion. The questions become, "Will the implementation of these ideas really alter the prison social structure and the organization of prisoners?" "Will the alteration be positive or negative?" These questions are addressed in the next and final section of this chapter.

Governing Prisons:
Human Service or Control?

Much of what is known about prison and prisoners has been received from the sociological literature. It is clear from our earlier presentations that sociology has contributed much to our understanding of prison and prisoners. Most notable has been the literature on prison social structure and how inmates adapt to their incarceration experiences. In addition, much of the prison sociology literature has provided either direct or indirect suggestions as to how the prisoner society is to be run or governed. Take, for example, the functional model of inmate socialization discussed earlier.

The functional model states that a prisoner society is a direct response to the pains of imprisonment imposed by prison structure and prison administration. To alleviate these pains, prisoners not only enter into social relations with each other, but more importantly, develop symbiotic relationships with correctional officers and administrators to keep order and control. Moreover, correctional administration requires that an awareness of the inmate social system and its leaders be recognized and that compromise relationships between inmate leaders and prison officials are structurally induced. In effect, the give-take relations between inmate leaders and prison management are inevitable given the way prisons are designed.

What if, however, prison sociology has taken us down the wrong path? What if it has focused too much attention on the inmate society and too little attention on effective correctional administration? Could it be that both functional and importation theories of inmate socialization have accentuated and even inflated the power of inmate societies or inmate subcultures? Maybe governing prisons can be accomplished largely the same way as other governmental bureaucracies or private companies? These questions raise the issue of how prison social structure can be modified so that prison officials govern and run our prisons, not prisoners?

Such questions have been raised by DiIulio (1987) in his provocative book titled *Governing Prisons*. His work represents a break from the traditional explanations of prison social structure and correctional administration. Through a comparative study of three major correctional systems (California, Michigan, and Texas), DiIulio argues that effective correctional administration can be achieved in the contemporary prison. His approach, however, differs from the works of others in that he argues that correctional administration must begin and end with the managers of the institutions. He does not consider the traditional sociological literature on prisons as persuasive or compelling in the management of prisons. His view is one that accentuates control by those who have been delegated to govern the prison: the prison officials. To run and operate prisons with the implications suggested by traditional sociology is unacceptable and will never restore order, amenity, and service to the prison. In short, he views sociological views of the prison as unacceptable when it comes to prison management. DiIulio (1987:3) states:

> I found it difficult to swallow the notion that the "society of captives" was somehow beyond better government. I began to dig more carefully through the literature on prisons, scrutinizing its empirical findings and tugging at its first assumptions. At the same time I began to gather information on higher-custody prisons in several states. Contrary to much of what I had read, the data indicated that these prisons were not all alike but differed significantly in one or more dimensions of their quality of life: some were clean, others filthy; some were orderly, others riotous; some offered many treatment programs, others few. I wanted to know why. More precisely, I wanted to know under what conditions, if any, better prisons were possible and how, if at all, we could foster such conditions.

DiIulio further argues that the foundation for effective correctional management lies in the ability of correctional administration to direct and lead institutions. Governing prisons in his view requires that the governed are subject to the control of the government. In prison, the government is composed of the wardens and correctional staff. Inmate societies should no longer run the prison. While DiIulio does not deny the existence of inmate societies, he does not see their relevance in the operation of the prison social structure. Clearly, prisoners form social systems behind bars, but correctional officials should control such systems to the benefit of all who live in (prisoners) and run (staff) the institution. In this way, prisoner social structure is dictated by the administration of the prison.

By comparing the prison systems of California, Michigan, and Texas, DiIulio believes that effective correctional administration was best exhibited by the Texas Department of Corrections through a *control model*. Under this model of management, control was centralized in the hands of correctional officials, including line-staff personnel. The objectives of such a system were orderly, rule-oriented, clean prisons. Through a system of rules and regulations, correctional staff kept control of the inmate social system and dictated the day-to-day operations of the prisons, not the prisoners.

Unlike the control model, the *responsibility model* of prison management (the Michigan model) emphasized the idea that prisoners should have as much control as possible over their lives while incarcerated, as long as it did not violate the security considerations of the institution. The central tenet of the responsibility model was that the inmate was to learn responsible behavior while incarcerated, typically through examples offered by correctional staff. In addition, the responsibility model de-emphasized the authority of correctional staff and tried to encourage individual growth and expression among prisoners.

In comparison to the control model and the responsibility model, the *consensual model* of correctional management was one that reflected more the principles of prison sociology and allowed greater involvement of prisoners in the operations of institutions. The fundamental premise of the model was that effective correctional administration required the consent of the governed. In this way, prisoners were viewed as an integral part of the management and administration of the prisons, not in a formal sense but in the view that no prison can be run without the cooperation and consent of those who are being governed. Of the three models, the consensual model ascribed more so to the lessons learned from prison sociology, and in the opinion of DiIulio suffers from them. With no coherent correctional principles and practices, the consensual model really cannot be evaluated like the control or responsibility models.

When examining both the control model and the responsibility model, DiIulio suggests allegiance to the ideas and principles as presented in the control model would be the best for prison management. Given this position, where does human service delivery lie in the hierarchy of the prison? Does it play a role at all? If so, what kind of role? What are the implications of the control model for correctional officers? Can the control model foster an environment where "hard time" is minimized and prisoner growth and development enhanced? Finally, what is the role of prison reform under the control model espoused by DiIulio? Answers to these questions are at the forefront of prison administration today.

Some may argue that the control model as operationalized in the Texas prison system represents the worst form of prison management, particularly from the perspective of the prisoner. How can one, for example, suggest that bureaucratic routines alone will address the needs of prisoners? In fact, could it not be equally argued that intensive rules and regulations may be perceived by many prisoners as oppressive and therefore counterproductive to promoting effective long-term change? As Johnson (1987:77) suggests, "Attributing correctional benefits to bald custodial control perhaps has always been more a rationalization than a rational correctional agenda, and it simply reinforce(s) the legitimacy of the authoritarian regime."

While DiIulio (1987:42) has argued that custody is a precursor to treatment, it is not clear how requiring inmates to be clean-shaven and properly dressed will promote long-term change in them. While clean faces and proper prison attire is a laudable goal, there is no reason to believe that prisoners will internalize behavior patterns that are consistent with societal expectations. We may be producing nice-looking prisons and prisoners, and that may be our real goal, yet it is problematic as to whether we are educating prisoners in a way that promotes constructive change on their parts.

Summary

This chapter has attempted to examine a central topic in corrections—prisoner social systems. We have presented a number of viewpoints about the origination of inmate social systems, attempting to highlight those points that enhance our understanding of the phenomenon. To date, the literature has been extensive on the social worlds of prisoners and their workings. Whether one ascribes to either the functional or importation perspectives, or both, depends on one's own assumptions and examination of the empirical evidence. As our review has shown, there is support for both perspectives in the literature.

Much of what is known from the research suggests that both approaches—functional and importation—are supportable, at least in part. It is a truism that prisoners suffer from the pains of imprisonment, yet it is much more uncertain as to how they cope with said pains, either through an indigenous social structure or through learned behavioral patterns imported from the streets once incarcerated, or both. As such, contemporary examinations have explored not only the questions of origination and adaptation to prison, but more importantly, how the prison is part of broader society.

At present, we are trying to discover what the proper role of the prison should be in society and where prisoner social systems figure into this bigger picture. Some would say that the prison needs to be more focused and committed to the delivery of human services, while others argue that developing and assisting prisoners in their personal rehabilitation first and foremost requires that control be restored to the social order of the prison. These viewpoints are not necessarily mutually exclusive; future research is required to assist us in determining what is the most useful role of the prison into the next century. The following chapters will thoroughly explore what the effects of incarceration are, along with examinations of prison violence and sex and contraband in the prisoner social world. It is hoped that the student will have a more comprehensive understanding of all the complex aspects of the prison after reading these chapters.

Prisons Should be Dehumanizing

Acute corporal punishments are more justifiable than prison because they can be limited in their effects more easily to the offender, often only to his actions, leaving the offender's life generally untouched. Prison takes over the whole of the person's life, so that we must justify it only on the basis that the offender either (1) has committed a crime of such proportions that only a punishment that punishes the whole of the offender's life is adequate to fit the crime, or (2) the offender has committed so many crimes that we are justified in punishing him as a criminal rather than for his particular crimes.

In actual fact, both these justifications boil down to the same thing: we are saying that either because of the horror of his single criminal act or because of the terrible extent of his past record, the offender may be viewed as a person imbued with the aura of criminality—in other words that he is an evil person. Thus, it is only through a punishment of similar aura that we can hope to match him or his deeds.

There are red herrings that are thrown across the path of this argument by many social scientists. They claim that researchers have been unable to find any consistent differences between offenders (of any kind of crime) and non-offenders. The reply is:

1. The scientific evidence is inconclusive. Some studies find differences, others do not.

2. Their claims are, frankly, nonsensical, for they ignore the most obvious fact that those offenders they compare us with have in fact committed serious violent crimes, usually a lot of them, and it is this fact that sets them apart from the rest of us. While this point might be more difficult to defend if we were dealing with the whole range of crimes from least to most serious, since probably everyone has committed a little crime or two in the past, it certainly does not apply to the extreme end of the scale which is what we are concerned with in this chapter.

Morality is the Difference

Very few of those reading this would have committed murder, rape or serious assault or burglary. It is this fact that sets us apart from the criminals who deserve prison. We have little difficulty in judging such criminals as bad persons.

In sum, the difference, the essential difference, between those who have committed a lot of crimes, or just one very serious crime, and the rest of us is one of morality. The modern social scientist, because of their amorality have failed to attend to this difference—in fact they try to explain it away.

[I] suggest that only prison terms of 15 years or more should be allowed. While there are good retributive reasons for such a policy, . . . there is another important reason: the goal is to make the gap between us and the truly horrible criminals even greater in practice than before. This is the opposite to the social scientists who keep trying to fudge over the line.

Indeed, going to prison should be like reaching a point of no return, like descending into Hell.

Making Prisons Retributive

To understand the true functions of prison, we must understand that, in contrast to acute corporal punishments, prisons work on a person's mind as well as his body. This fits in with a special kind of retribution which may be called religious retribution, and which takes a basic principle of retribution—that only the guilty should be punished—far more seriously than the old retributivists did.... They were more concerned with rule-breaking than with guilt. In fact it would be more accurate to describe the old retributivists as secular retributivists.

The religious retributivists naturally take the word "guilt" in its moral sense, which is to say that the offender has a guilty mind, and that only by a series of ritually purgative functions can this guilt be assuaged. Therefore, one must not only fit the punishment to the crime, but one must fit the punishment to the criminal's guilty mind, and the first step in the process is that the criminal must be contrite, or at least work towards contrition.

Criminals Must Recognize Guilt

The individual must be contrite: he must recognize the error of his ways. He must come to want to make amends, and the only way to effect such a transformation since the sins of evil people are so deeply entrenched, is through a long process of suffering. The originators of American prisons, the Quakers, almost understood this when they thought that solitary confinement and the Bible would be enough. But our prisons have long ago lost contact with their religious roots.

Graeme R. Newman, *Just and Painful*, 1983.

Thus, in answer to those murderers who hypocritically say that "they can't bring back murder victims, so what else can they do?" we say to them: they should suffer the long journey towards contrition. They should work off their guilt, and for some not even a lifetime will be long enough. Surely this is not too much to ask when one considers the innocent lives that they have ruined?"

Unfortunately, penologists have lost sight of this important function of retribution, so that they have allowed punishments to destroy souls rather than save them.

One often hears prisons described as soul-destroying. The experience has been likened to Dante's Hell, and aptly so, for the famous inscription above the gates of Dante's Hell is often found scratched on prison walls:

ABANDON HOPE ALL YE WHO ENTER HERE. . .

Prison as Religious Retribution

In Purgatory, Dante, and the Christian religion generally, did not abandon hope, and looked toward the possibility of some kind of salvation, or today we would say cure: salvation is a better word though, since it does not side-step the process of contrition that is inherent in the logic of resolving a crime through its punishment. This is the *religious* as against the *secular* version of retribution.

It is the religious version of retribution that we must apply to the criminals we have locked up, because it is only they whom we have seen fit to imbue with the aura of evil. For those receiving acute corporal punishment and other alternatives, we do not make the leap of judgment to say they are truly evil because they have committed a crime or two of middling seriousness. We punish only their acts, we do not judge their persons. We do not want a Draconian system of criminal justice, and so we save our harshest judgments for only the very few.

Making moral judgments about the quality of lives of people is an arrogant undertaking, one that should not be taken too lightly, or too often. But once we have made the judgment, we must have the courage to follow up our convictions.

The religious version of retribution requires basically two things: the crime must be resolved through its punishment, and the punishment must involve long term suffering.

The Judeo-Christian tradition has long recognized the importance of ritual suffering as a way of resolving or assuaging the terrible guilt that must fall upon someone who has committed a crime or crimes of unspeakable horror. Most religions do in fact have some equivalent system for dealing with guilt. The pagan religions of classical Greece and Rome were clear about this. The bloody cycle of retributive vengeance in the plays of Aeschylus (The Orestian Trilogy) could only be stopped by Orestes spending a long period of time suffering in an effort to assuage the guilt of having murdered his mother. The theme is deeply embedded in western thought.

It is the only way that the cycle of vengeance can be stopped. It is the reason why the trappings of justice—the courts, procedures, dress, etc., have a ritual aura about them. . . .

Treatment in Wolf's Clothing?

The process just described begins to sound very much like a form of "treatment" and not punishment, if one translates it into modern day terminology. For example, instead of talking about the deeper or inner layers of sin that must be penetrated and brought out into the open, one would today talk about uncovering the unconscious, analyzing the offender's inner motives and conflicts.

If this is so, we are in trouble, because criminologists will tell us that it has been found time and time again that treatment does not work, that all manner of treatment programs have been tried out with offenders and none have been shown to produce results any better than chance. That is, criminals who were treated by some method or another who were released, were reconvicted of a subsequent crime in just about the same proportions as those who were released but were not treated.

But the difference between punishment as cure and the treatment model of penology is substantial. When one reads the punishments described by Dante for those in Purgatory, there is little doubt that they *are* punishments, designed primarily to teach a lesson in a painful way; to ensure that the offender suffers while he learns, through his punishment, the quality of his crime. The religious—and logical—assumption is that a crime is by definition a hurt (whether to others or to oneself), so it is only through hurt that any understanding of one's crime can be reached. In contrast, treatment does not require that the offender suffer any pain at all.

In sum, the proper punishment for a despicable

"The Old Prison Discipline"

Custodial, punitive, and productive practices, sometimes called the "old prison discipline," have been outlined by Howard B. Gill. According to Gill, prison discipline stood for the following:

Hard Labor—Ranging from "making little ones out of big ones" and carrying cannon shot from one end of the prison yard to the other, to constructive prison industries.

Deprivation—Of everything except the requisites for a spartan existence and religious instruction.

Monotony—Essentially no variation in diet and daily routine.

Uniformity—Rigidly consistent treatment of prisoners.

Mass Movement—Individuality was squashed through mass living in cell blocks, mass eating, mass recreation, even mass bathing.

Degradation—To complete the loss of identity, prisoners were housed in monkey cages, dressed in shabby, nondescript clothing, and denied courteous contact with guards.

Subservience—To rules, rules, rules!

Corporal Punishment—Among the uses of force were the paddle, the whip, the sweat box, and the famous boot.

Noncommunication—Absolute silence or solitary confinement, without relief from letters, visits, or other contacts.

Recreation—At first none; later a daily hour in the yard.

No Responsibility—Prisoners were denied every social, civic, domestic, economic, and even personal responsibility.

Isolation—Often 16 hours a day, thereby increasing prisoners' egocentricity.

No "Fraternization" with the Guards—This rule prevented any attempts to solve problems through staff-inmate contacts.

Howard B. Gill, "A New Prison Discipline: Implementing the Declaration of Principles of 1870," *Federal Probation*, Vol. 34, No. 2, June 1970.

criminal is one that allows for expiation, for a slow learning through a punishment that expresses his crime. It is essential that the basic sin or sins underlying the crime be played out through its opposite so that the individual will learn the evil of his way. For the terrible few, this can only be done through a process of pain and suffering. This is obviously a long and time consuming process, and it is why prison is a most appropriate medium for contrition. . . .

And although, strictly speaking, according to the old retributivists, one should only match the single crime with the single punishment, it is clear from the religious view of retribution that one must match the despicable criminal's *sins* with the punishments, not his *crimes* with the punishments. In other words, one must go beyond the particular offense to the soul of the offender. By this model, one is justified in matching the punishment to the criminal's entire person. Prison is most apt in this regard. It takes over each inmate's total life.

An Indeterminate Sentence?

Lest this be seen as another form of the indeterminate sentence, we should be clear that this cannot be so if we are to be faithful to Dante's Purgatory. There is hope in Purgatory and it is assumed that eventually all will go through to the top of the mount into Paradise. In fact, Dante even spoke of matching particular amounts of time in Purgatory to the amount of time spent as a sinner on Earth. Without this limitation on punishment, it would be a punishment the same as Hell, with no hope. By placing finite limits on the duration of punishment, one recognizes that there is hope. Hope, indeed, is the central force underlying atonement. This is why the initial prison term for any criminal should be finite and of long duration—say 15 years.

Prison as Atonement

All of this is based, of course, upon the assumption that the offender undergoing atonement is convinced that what he has done requires atonement, that he is really guilty of an evil act, and in the most severe cases of having led an evil life. If he is not convinced of this, then he is no different from those relegated by Dante to Hell. For it is the unbelievers, pagans and heathens, and especially those blatantly so, for whom Hell is reserved. In the same way, the offender who does not believe in the evil of his act, or at least in the right of the judge to pronounce him convicted of a crime and deserving of punishment—for this offender there is no hope of redemption. His punishment will be eternal and it is for him that we say, "lock him up and throw away the key.". . .

Obviously, prisoners cannot be subjected to the same terrible tortures in prison as Dante dreamed up for Hell and Purgatory. But it is time that we took prison seriously as a punishment, and realized that these few criminals, these bad people, have been sent there for punishment and that is what they should get. The chronic punishment of prison must be made to have some meaning. That meaning must hinge on the criminal's recognition of his crimes. It must require acts of contrition, including acts that respond in a direct way to the sin of the crime.

For example, on the simplest level, it seems morally required that incarcerated murderers should devote their time to saving lives in whatever way possible, and that they should see it as quite deserving that they should risk their lives for others. Their use for risky medical research might well be justified on this basis.

We might also note in passing that the saving of one life to make up for one murder would not be sufficient. We do not try to match the injury to the victim in such a specific way, for this would be merely the reflection of the crime without any analogical or educative function to punishment. The criminal must devote himself to saving many lives, for it is the guilt of his own actions that must be assuaged, not the actual injury to the victim (though of course, it plays a part). In some cases there may simply not be enough time for the most evil of criminals to make up for the guilt of the sins underlying his crimes.

In Conclusion. . .

If we were to develop a prison-intensive system based on the use of prisons in ways outlined in this chapter, and on strictly limiting prison terms to 15 years or more, it can be seen that prisons would become very harsh places indeed. But at least there would be a clear purpose to their harshness, and we would have to take direct and clear responsibility for what happened in them. This is in contrast to today where we have all kinds of excuses for not taking responsibility for the violence and aimlessness of prison life.

The prison-intensive system also means that the decision to incarcerate individuals is going to be very weighty indeed.

Who is going to make these decisions? Is there not a chance that the numbers will take over for both acute and chronic punishments and we will end up in a worse mess than we are in already?

There are ways that we can make extra sure that this does not happen. But in order to show how this might be done, we must first break down another myth about criminal punishment: that it is unbridled discretion of judges that is the evil cause of our crazily confused and inconsistent punishment system.

Source: Graeme R. Newman (1985). "Prisons Should be Dehumanizing." In D.L. Bender and B. Leone (eds.) *America's Prisons: Opposing Viewpoints*, Fourth Edition. St. Paul, MN: Greenhaven Press.

Key Terms and Concepts

argot models

consensual model

control model

convict subculture

differential attachment

functional model

hard time

importation model

legitimate subculture

niches

pains of imprisonment

prisonization

private agenda

private culture

public agenda

public culture

responsibility model

social roles

thief subculture

References

Akers, R.L., N.S. Hayner and W. Gruninger (1974). "Homosexual and Drug Behavior in Prison: A Test of the Functional and Importation Models of the Inmate System." *Social Problems*, Volume 21, Number 3: 410-422.

Clemmer, D. (1940). *The Prison Community*. New York, NY: Holt, Rinehart and Company.

Crouch, B.M. and G.P. Alpert (1982). "Sex and Occupational Socialization Among Prison Guards: A Longitudinal Study," *Criminal Justice and Behavior*, Volume 9, Number 2: 159-176.

Cullen, F.T., F.E. Lutze, B.G. Link and N.T. Wolfe (1989). "The Correctional Orientation of Prison Guards: Do Officers Support Rehabilitation?" *Federal Probation*, Volume 1, Number 53, March: 33-42.

DiIulio, J. (1987). *Governing Prisons: A Comparative Study of Correctional Management*. New York, NY: The Free Press.

Garabedian, P. (1963). "Social Roles and Processes of Socialization in the Prison Community." *Social Problems*, Volume 11, Number 1: 139-152.

Gleason, S. (1978). "Hustling: The 'Inside' Economy of a Prison." *Federal Probation*, Volume 42, Number 1: 32-40.

Irwin, J. and D. Cressey (1962). "Thieves, Convicts, and The Inmate Culture." *Social Problems*, Volume 10, Number 2: 142-155.

Irwin, J. (1980). *Prisons in Turmoil*. Boston, MA: Little, Brown and Company.

Jacobs, J. (1977). *Stateville: The Penitentiary in Mass Society*. Chicago, IL: University of Chicago Press.

Johnson, R. (1987). *Hard Time: Understanding and Reforming the Prison*. Monterey, CA: Brooks/Cole Publishing Company.

Jurik, N.C. (1985). "Individual and Organizational Determinants of Correctional Officer Attitudes Toward Inmates." *Criminology*, Volume 23, Number 3:523-540.

Kalinich, D. (1986). *Power, Stability, & Contraband: The Inmate Economy*. Prospect Heights, IL: Waveland Press, Inc.

Philliber, S. (1987). "Thy Brother's Keeper: A Review of the Literature on Correctional Officers," *Justice Quarterly*, Volume 4, Number 1: 9-38.

Poole, E.D. and R.M. Regoli (1980). "Role Stress, Custody Orientation, and Disciplinary Actions: A Study of Prison Guards," *Criminology*, Volume 18, Number 2: 215-226.

Schwartz, B. (1971). "Pre-Institutional vs. Situational Influence in a Correctional Community." *Journal of Criminal Law, Criminology, and Police Science*, Volume 62, Number 4: 530-545.

Smith, C.F.W. and J.R. Hepburn (1979). "Alienation in Prison Organizations." *Criminology*, Volume 17, Number 2:251-262.

Stojkovic, S. (1984). "Social Bases of Power and Control Mechanisms Among Prisoners in a Prison Organization." *Justice Quarterly*, Volume 1, Number 4:511-528.

Street, D., R. Vinter, and C. Perrow (1969). *Organization for Treatment*. New York, NY: The Free Press.

Sykes, G. (1958). *The Society of Captives*. Princeton, NJ: Princeton University Press.

Thomas, C.W. (1975). "Prisonization or Resocialization: A Study of External Factors Associated with the Impact of Imprisonment." *Journal of Research in Crime & Delinquency*, Volume 10, Number 1: 13-21.

Thomas, C.W. (1977). "Theoretical Perspectives on Prisonization: A Comparison of the Importation and Deprivation Models." *Journal of Criminal Law and Criminology*, Volume 68, Number 1:135-145.

Tittle, C. (1969). "Inmate Organization: Sex Differentiation and the Influence of Criminal Subcultures." *American Sociological Review*, Volume 34, Number 1: 492-505.

Toch, H. and J. Klofas (1982). "Alienation and Desire for Job Enrichment Among Correction Officers." *Federal Probation*, Volume 46, March:35-44.

Wellford, C. (1967). "Factors Associated with Adoption of the Inmate Code: A Study of Normative Socialization." *Journal of Criminal Law, Criminology, and Police Science*, Volume 58, Number 2: 197-203.

Wheeler, S. (1961). "Socialization in Correctional Communities." *American Sociological Review*, Volume 26, Number 1: 697-712.

Williams, V. and M. Fish (1974). *Convicts, Codes and Contraband*. Cambridge, MA: Ballinger Publishing Company.

Photo Credit: Tony O'Brien, Frost Publishing Group, Ltd.

The Effects
of Incarceration

9

John Klofas
Rochester Institute of Technology—Rochester, NY

After reading this chapter, the student should be able to:

- ▌ Discuss both planned and unplanned effects of incarceration.

- ▌ Describe the possible harmful effects of incarceration.

- ▌ List the effects of special aspects of incarceration.

Introduction

Criminal penalties are presumed to have an impact on offenders. There may be disagreement about appropriate degrees of harshness or the level of punitiveness or about the conditions necessary for treatment to succeed, but criminal sentences remain the means of implementing policies of retribution, deterrence, and rehabilitation. All of these policies are concerned with the impact of the sanction on individual offenders.

While some of the effects of criminal sanctions are planned this is not necessarily true of all of them. Criminal penalties carry with them a variety of unintentional, if not unanticipated, effects. Some of these are captured in real and fictional accounts of imprisonment which emphasize the stress and violence often associated with incarceration. In this chapter we will examine these effects (or side effects) of incarceration and pay particular attention to the research surrounding them. In order to accomplish this we must first examine the process of incarceration and consider the conditions that are part of that experience and their potential impact. We will then review the research on the impact of confinement on physical and psychological health. Finally, we will consider the effects of specific aspects of incarceration.

Planned and Unplanned Effects

As Johnson and Toch (1988:13) have noted:

One of the striking things about prisons is that we make no bones about the fact that we intend them to be uncomfortable. Punishment by its nature involves the infliction of pain and in the case of prisons it is a chronic pain which even the Supreme Court has acknowledged as legitimate. In a key prison overcrowding case the [C]ourt concluded that the Constitution does not guarantee that prisoners are free from all sorts of suffering and, in fact, 'prisons...which house persons convicted of serious crimes, cannot be free from discomfort' (*Rhodes v. Chapman*, 1981).

There are limits to constitutionally permitted levels of discomfort, however. Drawing those limits has been the chief task facing the courts in prisoners' rights and prison condition cases which raise the Eighth Amendment issue of cruel and unusual punishment. The primary test for this has been whether the conditions are "of such character or consequences as to shock general conscience or be intolerable in fundamental fairness" (*Lee v. Tahash,* 1965). Influencing those limits has also been one of the goals of prison reformers since John Howard first described conditions in British prisons in the late 1700s. While some efforts at line-drawing reflect emotions and sentiments regarding the moral worth of the criminal, Johnson and Toch (1988:15) have pointed out that "No aim of prison—including retributive punishment—is served by arbitrary, gratuitious, ill-distributed distress."

But one need not be limited to arbitrary and gratuitous distress to argue that there may be unintended negative consequences of confinement. The classic delineation of such consequences is offered by Gresham Sykes (1958). Inmates, Sykes argues, find prison life to be depriving and frustrating in the extreme. The deprivations of prison life may in part be seen as unplanned although possibly unavoidable concomitants of imprisoning offenders. While the severe physical suffering of earlier punishments has largely disappeared, the remaining deprivations and the psychological assaults they embody may be as painful as the physical maltreatment they replaced. Sykes described five pains of imprisonment.

The *deprivation of liberty* is the most obvious consequence of confinement. The inmate's world is shrunken to the dimensions of the prison walls. He is cut off from family and friends. But more significant than the physical consequences of confinement are the social-psychological consequences. Confinement represents "a deliberate, moral rejection of the criminal by the free society. By committing his offense the criminal has given up his claim to the status of a full-fledged and trusted member of society" (1958:66).

The *deprivation of goods and services* refers to the necessary material restrictions of the convict's world. It is true that the prisoner's basic material needs are met. He does not go hungry or cold, and adequate medical care is provided. But Sykes argues "a standard of living constructed in terms of so many calories per day, so many hours of recreation, so many cubic yards of space per individual, and so on, misses the point when we are discussing the individual's feeling of deprivation, however useful it may be in setting minimum levels of consumption for the maintenance of health" (1958:68). For Sykes, this deprivation is an assault on the self-concept of the prisoner because of the value placed on material possessions in western societies. The clothes, music, cars, and other means by which people define themselves and express their individuality are stripped from the inmate who is forcibly impoverished by the state.

The *deprivation of heterosexual relationships* also denies inmates a key relationship by which they define themselves. The polarity of the sexes carries with it cultural meanings of both maleness and femaleness. Being cut off from such an anchor endangers the self-image, and the inmate may feel fractured and incomplete. That problem may manifest itself in anxiety and fear over latent homosexual tendencies or in an exaggerated attempt to demonstrate masculinity or femininity.

Inmates experience a *deprivation of autonomy* in the sense that they are subjected to the vast body of prison rules and regulations. Even in the most open of prisons, inmate behavior is closely regulated, with time designated for sleeping, eating, and working, and sanctions for deviating from the prescribed schedule. The social-psychological consequences of this regulation are what most interest Sykes. He argues that the inmate is returned to a childlike state of dependency. The normal self-identification as an adult is lost in a world where inmates make few choices and can seldom find explanations for decisions that affect them.

The final frustration is the *deprivation of security*. The forced association with other criminals is a major source of anxiety among inmates. Fellow prisoners may be viewed as dangerous. Inmates may constantly feel vulnerable or likely to be tested. But the threat is not just one of potential victimization. The fear of exploitation raises concerns about one's ability to cope; about the confidence in one's own inner resources which will allow the inmate to adjust and adapt. The threat to self-concept is more wearing than the physical threats from other prisoners.

Sykes summarizes his view simply: "Imprisonment, then, is painful" (1958:78). As he describes them, the pains of imprisonment are the unintended consequences of intentional conditions of confinement. The pains of imprisonment also have other implications. As is discussed in Chapters 10 and 11 of this book, Sykes argues that they give rise to a prison subculture that supports violence and an underground economy.

The Question of Harmful Effects

That prison life is painful, however, says little about whether or not it is harmful. That is, pain, an immediate aversive condition, does not necessarily result in extended damage (Goodstein and Wright, 1989). The distinction has led to a variety of studies that attempt to systematically examine the possible adverse effects of imprisonment. Recently, efforts have been made to draw together these studies and offer conclusions about the impact of prison. In one such effort Nigel Walker (1983) concludes:

> Imprisonment is almost always boring, irksome and humiliating; in some prisons it is also squalid, and some prisoners suffer from grievances or anxieties. Condemnation of prison conditions is so universal that even to ask how serious is the harm they cause sounds heretical. Yet it does seem possible to exaggerate the harm (1983:69-70).

The reviews of research all offer similar reservations. The studies have not found consistent, enduring negative effects of imprisonment, especially when cognitive, personality, and attitudinal variables are examined. One study recently characterized prison as "the deep freeze" when the authors found neither negative nor positive effects of the experience (Zamble and Porporino, 1988). Walker's caveat, however, is also widely recognized. There are great differences across prison conditions and across prisoners and "an individual's response to confinement is determined by a complex interaction of variables that result in deterioration in some prisoners, improvement in others and no change in still others" (Goodstein and Wright, 1989:242). We will further consider those differences in both prisons and prisoners after examining a range of possible negative effects of incarceration.

Incarceration and Physical Health

In the case of *Estelle v. Gamble* (1976), the Supreme Court ruled that inmates have a right to adequate medical care and found that "deliberate indifference to serious medical needs of prisoners constitutes the 'unnecessary and wanton infliction of pain proscribed by the Eighth Amendment.'" Concern over medical care has been a major issue in prison litigation. Incarceration, however, can affect the health of inmates in a variety of ways, including malnutrition, poor physical conditions, exposure to illness, and exposure to violence.

As Walker (1983) reported for British prisons, in today's institutions, the least likely of these effects is malnutrition. The quality and even the temperature of food is governed by professional standards and while many lawsuits have dealt with problems of freshness or adulteration, such problems are likely to be rare today. Furthermore, special diets, for medical or religious reasons, are readily available. This does not imply, however, that there are no problems in this area. A recent report from New York City, for example described conditions for arrestees who were fed only sandwiches of one slice of baloney and one slice of cheese throughout their four-day stay in the city's holding cells.

The physical conditions of American prisons may be more varied than the quality of the cuisine. The most obvious indicator of this is found in the diversity of the facilities themselves. For example, nearly one-third of prisons are over 50 years old and nearly 50 prisons in service today were built over 100 years ago. Prison conditions also differ greatly by security level. About 25% of prisons are classified as maximum security with an additional 39% described as medium security. The remaining 35% are considered minimum security (Jamieson and Flanagan, 1988).

One approach to examining prison conditions is through inmate litigation. A wide variety of prison conditions have been the subjects of inmate lawsuits. The early suits often dealt with specific conditions such as the adequacy of heating or ventilation systems. Later, however, courts began to consider whether conditions in certain institutions could, as a whole, be so shocking as to constitute cruel and unusual punishment. In 1970, the Arkansas prison system was found to violate the Eighth Amendment when the court concluded that: (1) the prison was run by inmate guards, (2) the open dormitories bred physical assaults, (3) the isolation cells were unsanitary, and (4) there was an absence of rehabilitative programming (*Holt v. Sarver*, 1970).

In 1976, in the Alabama prison case of *Pugh v. Locke*, a federal district court found that the "totality of conditions," rather than any singular aspect of the prisons, violated the Eighth Amendment. Later, in the case of *Hutto v. Finney* (1978), the Supreme Court upheld a lower court decision on conditions in Arkansas segregation and proposed three guidelines for use of the totality of conditions approach. Courts should: (1) consider the totality of conditions of confinement, (2) specify each factor contributing to the violation and the necessary remedial action, and (3) spell out specific minimum standards required to remedy the situation.

The longest and most complex of the cases to utilize the totality of conditions standard was the Texas case of *Ruiz v. Estelle* (1972). After 159 days of hearings Judge Justice concluded in a wide-ranging opinion that:

...it is impossible for a written opinion to convey the pernicious conditions and the pain and degradation which ordinary inmates suffer in the TDC units—the gruesome experiences of youthful first offenders forcibly raped; the cruel and justifiable fears of inmates, wondering when they will be called upon to defend the next violent assault; the sheer misery, the discomfort, the wholesale loss of privacy for prisoners housed with one, two or three others in a forty-five foot cell or suffocatingly packed together in a crowded dormitory; the physical suffering and wretched psychological stress which must be endured by those sick or injured who cannot obtain adequate medical care; the sense of abject helplessness felt by inmates arbitrarily sent to solitary confinement or administrative segregation without proper opportunity to defend themselves or to argue their causes; the bitter frustration of inmates prevented from petitioning the courts and other governmental authorities for relief from perceived injustices (cited in Crouch and Marquart, 1989:125-126).

In Judge Justice's view, these conditions violated the Eighth Amendment and he oversaw dramatic reforms of the Texas Department of Corrections. While such legal analyses provide one source of information on prison conditions, they have not often been complemented by scientific evidence regarding the effects of prison conditions. An exception to this is in the area of overcrowding. That subject has been addressed by both the courts and by social science research.

The Supreme Court addressed the question of overcrowding in the case of *Rhodes v. Chapman* (1981). The State of Ohio appealed a lower court ruling in which overcrowded conditions were found to violate the Eighth Amendment. In reversing that decision the Supreme Court ruled that the crowding conditions fell short of the test largely because inmates were confined to their cells for only part of the day.

For social scientists, the crowding question has been whether crowded conditions affect inmate health or behavior. The studies have measured crowding in a variety of ways, including overall population size, density, and the amount of personal space available for inmates. The research has found both physiological and behavioral effects. The physiological effects of crowding have included findings of elevated pulse rate and blood pressure and increased sweating of the palms (D'Atri, 1975; D'Atri et al., 1981). Crowding has also been associated with increased complaints of illness among inmates (McCain, Cox and Paulus, 1976) and coronary problems (Carr, 1981). Among the behavioral effects associated with crowding are assaults and disciplinary infractions. Some scholars argue, however, that the research on crowding cannot be regarded as definitively demonstrating these effects. Differences in measurement of crowding and the failure to examine alternate explanations, such as loss of control by staff or other variables such as inmate age or transiency, leave the studies open to criticism.

Another issue to consider when addressing the potential effects of imprisonment on physical health is exposure to illness. Inmates run a high risk of acquiring a variety of communicable diseases while incarcerated. There are two reasons for this elevated risk. First, prison and jail inmates are often drawn from a population that has a higher incidence of disease and lower level of medical care than the general population. Second, the conditions of close living in institutions may facilitate the spread of illness among inmates. The two problems are illustrated in studies of tuberculosis in institutionalized populations. In one such study of admissions to Arkansas prisons researchers found the rate of positive reaction to the tuberculosis skin test was 6.5 times higher than the Arkansas population. Another study found 46% of inmates in a Maryland prison were infected with mycobacterium tuberculosis following an outbreak of the disease. In one case, an inmate with active tuberculosis was allowed to remain in population for three months prior to final detection and treatment (Hayne et al., 1985).

These studies are consistent with the idea of increased health risks among prisoners. Other research also supports this view. For example, a detailed comparison of prisoners with probationers and the general population found the greatest number of health problems among the prisoners (Jones, 1976). All of the research is not consistent on this issue, however. Bonta and Gendreau (1990) reviewed several studies that failed to find negative effects on health. They also speculate that for some inmates prisons may actually be conducive to good health due to nutritional diets and adequate medical care.

One area in which there has been great concern regarding the health risks of imprisonment has been with Acquired Immune Deficiency Syndrome (AIDS). For several years the incidence and transmission of the disease in prison has been studied under the auspices of the National Institute of Justice (1989). Over the two most recent years of surveys, the incidence of AIDS among prisoners increased by 61%. That increase, however, was slightly lower than the rate of increase in the population of the United States. Still, prisoners demonstrate substantially higher overall rates of AIDS infection than other citizens. In 1988 the incidence of AIDS in the total U.S. population was 13.3 cases per 100,000 persons. In the prisons (although there was great variability across states) the rate was 75 cases per 100,000. In city and county jails the rate was 183 cases per 100,000. Rates for AIDS-related conditions including asymptomatic HIV seropositivity and AIDS-Related Complex (ARC) showed similar elevations among inmates.

The issue of the transmission of AIDS in prisons and jails is complex due to limited knowledge about the length and variability of incubation periods. Knowledge about modes of transmission may lead one to expect high levels of transmission. The highest incidence of AIDS transmission has been linked to intravenous drug use and homosexuality, both of which have been problems among those sent to prison and within prison itself. Despite presumptions about high-risk behavior, research suggests that the virus is not spreading in prisons and jails at as high a rate as may have been expected. Investigations by the Center for Disease Control have found only modest rates of transmission. As of the end of 1988 there were no cases of work-related transmission of the AIDS virus to corrections staff. To help combat the spread of AIDS, corrections systems have developed a variety of policies including mass screening of inmates, AIDS education programs, and counselling and support services. At least two systems—Vermont and New York City—have adopted policies permitting the distribution of condoms to inmates (*Pennsylvania Prison Society Newsletter*, 1988).

Another threat to physical health of inmates comes from violence in the prison. Many prisons are violent places. But the systematic study of institutional violence has presented several problems that may make inferences difficult. The first problem encountered deals with a suitable working definition of violence. Some researchers have focused on victimization and included a range of behavior from subtle pressures for sex to homicide. Others have restricted the range of their focus to such things as unprovoked assaults. Equally problematic have been the issues of research methods. Official reports, observations by staff, and inmate interviews have all been useful in studying prison violence but each has its limitations as well as its virtues. Those limitations have made it difficult to make comparisons in the nature and distribution of violence in prison and on the street.

Perhaps the best indicator of violence in prison is the fact that each year approximately 100 inmates are murdered by other inmates. Homicide data may provide the most reliable information on prison violence. Their use avoids difficulties over definitions of such terms as assault and they are the easiest to compare with data on street crimes. When that comparison is made, the overall homicide rate for prisoners is approximately equal to the overall homicide rate in the U.S. population (15 to 18/100,000). That has been true since the first national study of prison homicide (Sylvester et al., 1977). But the aggregate figures also hide important differences across jurisdictions. In the national prison homicide study many institutions had no inmate murders while some prisons had murder rates as high as 15 times the population rate. In the most recent available figures, California had 20 of the total 91 inmate murders and New York had 10. Thirty-four states and the Federal Bureau of Prisons had none (Jamieson and Flanagan, 1989).

It also seems likely that there are differences across prisons in other forms of violence. Overall, however, prison research does indicate that violence levels in institutions are often quite high, especially when forms of victimization less serious than homicide are considered. The literature on sexual victimization, for example, has been quite consistent in its findings. Several studies across different jurisdictions indicate that about 1% of inmates are sexually assaulted but that nearly one-third of inmates will be approached, often violently, for sex during confinement (see, Lockwood, 1980; Nacci and Kane, 1983). Estimates of other forms of assaultive behavior in prison also indicate high levels of violence. Some researchers have estimated the rate of assault in prison to be 20 times the rate recorded outside of prison.

Incarceration and Psychological Health

Along with threats to physical health, there has been a great deal of concern over the possible threats to psychological or mental health that may accompany imprisonment. At times the psychological impact of imprisonment has been dramatically portrayed. In a popular description of imprisonment, Jessica Mitford (1973) described correctional officers as possessing a sadistic bent, treatment as *A Clockwork Orange* programming and the prison experience as disheartening, degrading, and dangerous. A more recent description of effects is offered by a self-described state-raised convict:

> When I walk [past] a glass window in the corridor and happen to see my reflection, I get angry on impulse. I feel shame and hatred at such times. When I'm forced by circumstances to be in a crowd of prisoners, it's all I can do to refrain from attack. I feel such hostility, such hatred, I can't help this anger. All these years, I have felt it. Paranoid. I can control it. I

never seek a confrontation. I have to intentionally gauge my voice in a conversation to cover up the anger I feel, the chaos and pain just beneath the surface of what we commonly recognize as reality. Paranoia is an illness I contracted in institutions. It is not the reason for my sentences to reform school and prison. It is the effect not the cause (Abbott, 1982:5).

Such portraits and self-portraits offer testimonial evidence of the psychological effects of imprisonment but are not necessarily representative of the prison experience of all inmates. Researchers have also used other methods to examine the psychological consequences of confinement. Bukstel and Kilman (1980), for example, reviewed 90 studies that examined the psychological effects of imprisonment. They limited their review to "experimental studies" that used quantified measures of outcome variables including performance variables (for example, cognitive abilities), personality measures and attitudinal variables. The reviewers conclude that the evidence does not indicate that imprisonment is harmful to all individuals. Instead, a complex interaction of institutional and individual variables seemed to influence individuals' responses to confinement.

As Walker (1983) points out, one of the complicating factors in investigating the psychological effects of ordinary prison life is the prevalence of mental illness in the offender population. Studies have shown higher than expected levels of mental illness among those admitted to correctional institutions. The most dramatic findings have been with jail populations in which rates of severe mental illness have been found at two to three times the rate of the general population even after controlling for demographic variables (Teplin, 1990). Others have pointed out that such inmates, often depressed, anxious, or agitated, or with other acute symptoms, have a much poorer chance of coping with confinement than other relatively healthy inmates (Wiehn, 1988). One way in which these coping difficulties may manifest themselves is in the form of disciplinary infractions. A study of inmates who received mental health services also showed that they were more likely than other inmates to have a history of disciplinary reports for disruptive behavior (Toch, Adams, and Grant, 1989).

Prison may pose particular problems for mentally ill inmates but there has also been interest in more widespread, if less dramatic, effects. One possible effect that has received attention from researchers has been called *prisonization*. The term, as coined by Donald Clemmer (1940:299), refers to the "taking on in greater or less degree, of the folkways, mores, customs and general culture of the penitentiary." The concept, then, postulates a special-

ized form of environmental influence in which inmates cope with imprisonment by developing a normative system that is opposed to the legitimate authority of staff members. As noted in Chapter 8, other theorists have argued
that attitudes imported into the prison from offenders' street lives may be
more important than the prison experience itself.

Important empirical support for the prisonization hypothesis was obtained by Wheeler (1961) who charted inmates' adherence to an inmate code
and opposition to staff over their prison career. Wheeler found a U-shaped
curve in which inmates displayed decreased attachment to conventional
norms in the middle phases of their imprisonment and stronger attachment to
those norms in the beginning and end of their incarceration. Wheeler's U-
shaped curve has been found in other studies of changing prisoner values, although some of the research has failed to replicate the finding. The dis-
crepant findings may be explained by other variables such as individual and
cultural differences (see Bukstel and Kilman, 1980). In general, however,
studies of inmate attitudes over time suggest that antisocial attitudes increase
with the duration of confinement (see Goodstein and Wright, 1989).

Another effect of incarceration which has been investigated has been referred to as "institutional dependency." Fostered by "infantilizing inmates,
altering their self-concepts, undermining their self-esteem and limiting their
autonomy" (Goodstein and Wright, 1989), institutional dependency is seen as
a consequence of limited decision-making and the inability to control most
aspects of one's life in prison. At its most extreme, the condition was sometimes referred to as Ganser Syndrome, first described in 1898 as a "peculiar
hysterical twilight state," which was marked by a deterioration of personal
habits and standards and an inability to make practical plans (Wormith,
1984). While the diagnostic category is seldom used today, most psychiatrists agree that an identifiable clinical syndrome does exist although they
may disagree on the precise symptoms and the frequency of occurrence.
Perhaps the strongest supporting evidence for institutional dependency
comes from psychological studies showing that "individuals with limited
control opportunities can experience such adverse impacts as depression,
anxiety, and increased health risks" (Goodstein and Wright, 1989:233).

The Effects of Special Aspects of Incarceration

Thus far we have examined the effects of incarceration by considering
the research on institutions and inmates in broad and general terms. Incar-

ceration, however, is a complex experience in which individuals and settings differ markedly. In this section we will focus on several specific aspects of incarceration including long-term inmates, solitary confinement, and jails. Each of these areas involves a unique category of inmate in a unique institutional setting.

Solitary Confinement

Solitary confinement or isolation continues to be the ultimate legal control mechanism available to prison staff and is used with some degree of frequency. A study of disciplinary infractions showed that over one-half of a nationally representative sample of inmates had been charged with a disciplinary infraction since entering prison. Nearly one-third of those rule violators, or 15% of all inmates, were placed in solitary confinement or segregation for their violations (Bureau of Justice Statistics, 1989a). Inmates may also find themselves in segregation for reasons other than disciplinary infractions. They may be subjected to "administrative segregation" because they are viewed as too dangerous or disruptive to remain in the general prison population or they may enter protective custody to be shielded from other inmates.

Inmates may also remain in solitary confinement for prolonged periods of time. In an Arkansas conditions case (*Hutto v. Finney*, 1978) the court set a maximum stay in disciplinary segregation at 30 days and other time limits have been set for other jurisdictions. In the past, isolation for infractions went on for much longer. Cases of inmates spending more than 12 years in disciplinary segregation have been reported (Fox, 1983:52). Typical periods in disciplinary segregation today may range from 10 to 30 days. Inmates may remain in administrative segregation or protective custody for much longer or even for indefinite periods. At the Federal Bureau of Prison's Marion Penitentiary, some prisoners have been in administrative segregation, locked in their cells with minimal out-of-cell exercise time, for over four years. The Federal Bureau of Prisons has also used extended small group isolation on female prisoners at Lexington Penitentiary. States have also turned to the use of long-term administrative segregation.

Figure 9.1
"Most Incorrigible Wind up at Marion"

Most incorrigible wind up at Marion

Behavior control is its chief purpose

By MARK LISHERON
of The Journal staff

Marion, Ill.—For the past six years, this federal penitentiary built next to a national wildlife refuge has operated in a quiet, orderly state of emergency.

Behind the coils of razor wire, pressure sensitive fence and thick concrete walls on 936 acres of rolling hills trimmed as neat as a golf course, prison officials maintain a chokehold on security.

Prison officials instituted a lockdown in 1983. They did it for survival, for inmates and staff alike. Since the prison opened in 1963 in southern Illinois as a replacement for Alcatraz, 32 inmates and three staff members have died violently.

Although violence has dropped dramatically since the new security, no one who works here kids himself: Marion is the repository for the most brutal and some of the most notorious convicts in the country.

If Manuel Noriega is convicted on federal drug charges, he almost certainly will be housed in the prison's underground K-Unit, Warden John L. Clark says.

Convicted Colombian drug lord Carlos Lehder already is serving his sentence—life plus 135 years—in one of the unit's cells.

Spies John Walker Jr. and Jonathan Pollard and Libyan gun runner Edwin P. Wilson share the unit with Lehder.

But they are not the real reason for the perpetual state of siege. Matthew Granger and the 45 other inmates of the Control Unit are. Another unit, called the K-Unit, has slightly larger cells and offers inmates a little more freedom.

Granger is serving a life sentence for stabbing to death a prison officer in 1984 in the Federal Correctional Institution at Oxford, Wis. He had been transferred to Oxford because the Florida prison system, where he was serving another life sentence for murder, could not handle him. He was transferred to Marion because of the murder.

More than half of the 375 inmates here are serving time for murder, more than two-thirds of the total for assault, and all but 2% have some history of violence.

Like Granger, more than a third of the population has plotted or tried to escape from Marion or another institution. The Oxford prison murder occurred during an aborted prison escape.

No Rehabilitation

For these inmates, Marion offers no rehabilitation, no counseling, no classes, said Clark, a former Catholic priest.

"There are no great expectations," Clark said from his office facing the main security tower in the front of the prison. "What we are doing here is to get their behavior under control so they can function in another prison setting. We are dealing with inmates whose whole lives are marked by getting things by being violent and aggressive."

Lt. Walter H. Whaley, the unsmiling head of the Control Unit, said the tight security actually made the job easier.

"There aren't any gray areas," Whaley said. "These are predatory individuals who have killed another human being at the drop of a hat and who have not been controlled anyplace they have been."

Hands cuffed behind his back, surrounded by correctional offi-

Figure 9.1—continued

cers, Granger rocked back in a chair in Whaley's office. With a malevolent, toothless grin he described his killings without conscience.

Both his victims were unlucky, mostly because they happened to get in his way. His victim in Florida had the misfortune to look wealthy.

"I just picked the one who looked the richest," Granger said. "I knocked on his door, he opened it and blew his head off. I was hungry. I didn't get no money, though."

Michael Whitehead, 43, who was captured in 1985 near Rockford, Ill., after critically wounding two federal marshals in Superior, is one month away from leaving the Control Unit.

Whitehead said he had disciplined himself to stay out of trouble by reading, writing letters, and chess, which inmates play by yelling their moves from cell to cell.

The days are pretty much the same. In a tour through the prison the cells are kept tidy, the exercise areas spotless, the linoleum floors spit-polished.

Meals are served to inmates in their 50.8-square-foot individual cells, which are equipped with small black and white televisions and radios.

When moved throughout the prison, inmates are handcuffed and sometimes manacled and always with at least one officer holding onto the cuffs, said Jack Crosley, executive assistant to the warden.

Bars Checked

Cell searches are random and weekly, as is "bar tapping," the deafening hammering at the bars of cells with rubber mallets to make certain they have not been sawed, he said.

Strip searches of prisoners are also random and frequent.

Inmates are allowed five visitors a month. Marion is the only prison in the federal system to bar physical contact between inmates and visitors to prevent exchanges of weapons and drugs, Crosley said.

Control Unit inmates are allowed one hour a day to exercise in isolation, in either an indoor or outdoor cage equipped with one chin-up bar.

Inmates in units of lower security are allowed some gymnasium time and religious services. There is no prison yard, no group meetings.

Those inmates who avoid infractions and pass rigorous investigation and interviews can make it to the Unicor cable shop, become orderlies or barbers.

Cable shop workers, who can earn between 22 cents and $1.50 an hour, manufacture missile and tank cables under defense industry contract, factory manager Kevin Murphy said. Profits are funneled back into the shop program, Murphy said.

Successful performance can mean transfer to penitentiaries with lesser security such as Leavenworth in Kansas, Lompoc, Calif., or Lewisburg, Pa.

Clark said the lack of prison violence was the defense of what some critics call Draconian security.

"People have these terrible images of penitentiaries formed by all those prison movies," Clark said. "The warden is a sadist, the staff a bunch of bozos and the inmates are cute, likable thugs.

"It ain't like 'Cool Hand Luke.' No one is beaten here. What we have here is clean, polite, professional and human."

Correctional officers are more careful but not necessarily more tense, officer Billy Williams said.

Williams, 36, who has worked at the penitentiary for six years, said his wife and oldest of his four children initially objected to the change from a job as a deputy sheriff.

But Williams said the career opportunity, in a coal-mining region beset by double-digit unemployment, was too good to resist.

Figure 9.1—continued

"Sometimes your blood pressure goes sky high, but you always got to keep on your toes," Williams said. "It becomes an everyday kind of job after awhile."

With employment of more than 400 people and an economic impact of more than $16 million on the region, most area residents are glad for the penitentiary, said Rob Wick, who covers the prison for the Marion Daily Republican.

With the prison isolated nine miles southwest of Marion by the watery and beautiful Crab Orchard National Wildlife Refuge, people in the area feel secure, Wick said.

William Craig, whose ranch home is a quarter-mile down a winding road from the penitentiary, said in the years before the lockdown violence and escapes seemed frequent. The lockdown has changed that.

Craig, 49, said he never considered moving his wife and seven children away.

"People has to work somewhere. Prisoners got to be put somewhere. It don't bother me none," Craig said, spitting chewing tobacco into the back of his truck. "I got guns in my house. I guess I can take care of myself."

Source: *The Milwaukee Journal,* April 29, 1990.

Conditions in segregation are often quite spartan. Court decisions in this area provide a patchwork of conditions that have either been accepted or declared to violate the Eighth Amendment. While isolation itself is not unconstitutional, some conditions of life in isolation are unconstitutional. For example, even in solitary confinement an inmate must be provided with the means to maintain personal hygiene, including soap, water, a toothbrush, and toilet paper. Courts have ruled, however, that a shower every seven days and one hour of exercise every 11 days is not unconstitutional. The courts have also ruled that a diet of bread and water with a full meal every third day is not unconstitutional and neither is continuous light or darkness in the prisoner's cell (for a review, see Krantz, 1983). In some states prisoners may even be chained to their beds by their wrists and their ankles in response to disciplinary infractions.

A glimpse of conditions in segregation can also be gleaned from graphic inmate accounts, as in this description:

...he [the warden] inherited a typical northern prison's version of Solitary Confinement. After an inmate had been found guilty in the institution court, which was comprised of three or four officials serving as the prose-

cution but no lawyer for the defense, he was stripped, given a pair of over-
alls, and placed in a bare cell for three to seven days... The surface of the
floor was broken only by a round hole... that served as toilet facilities. It
was covered by a piece of cardboard that did little to prevent the odors of
human waste from permeating your abode...

Your breakfast consisted of two pieces of toast and that cup full of milk. If
you saved one of those pieces of toast, you could also have lunch, or even
dinner if your power was that great (Griswald, Misenheimer, Powers, and
Tromanhauser, 1970:48).

Unsanitary and brutal conditions in prisons have no serious defenders.
But there continues to be a question regarding the harmfulness of solitary
confinement. On one side of the argument are those that regard isolation itself as inhumane. On the other side are those that argue that conditions in
solitary may sometimes be inhumane and that inmates are often treated in arbitrary fashion but that the process of using restrictive confinement, including sensory deprivation does not in and of itself cause harm and may produce
some beneficial results.

One report that is used to argue that isolation itself is harmful is Jackson's (1983) study of solitary confinement in Canada. Jackson described the
effects of solitary confinement from evidence presented at trial in a suit initiated by inmates in administrative segregation. The use of segregation was
described as a means of breaking the spirit of recalcitrant inmates and as resulting in anger, violence, and insanity. Jackson described solitary confinement as "the most individually destructive, psychologically crippling and
socially alienating experience that could conceivably exist within the borders
of the country." Other studies have also concluded that isolation itself is associated with psychological problems, including hallucinations and other
forms of pathology (for a review, see Bukstel and Kilman, 1980).

Proponents of solitary confinement cite the use of anecdotal data and
other methodological shortcomings to argue that some of the studies do not
offer fair assessments of solitary confinement (for a review see Bukstel and
Kilman, 1980). They also cite studies that have failed to find detrimental effects, particularly when relatively brief periods of time, such as four to 10
days, are involved. Their position is also supported by experimental studies
in sensory deprivation. Some researchers have gone further still and argued
that use of solitary confinement under appropriate conditions can have a beneficial effect. Suedfeld (1980) has reported that prisoners released after iso-

lation did not display symptoms of maladjustment. Furthermore, Suedfeld reported positive short-term effects of isolation, in that the male inmates were often better adjusted and posed fewer behavioral problems upon being returned to their normal prison activities.

There is, then, disagreement over the harmful effects of solitary confinement. There is no disagreement, however, that some inmates react very negatively to the experience, especially when isolated for prolonged periods. There is also agreement that the negative effects of isolation can be made more likely by poor conditions and the maltreatment of prisoners which may accompany punitive segregation in prison. Adverse responses are likely when inmates feel that decisions about their placement in isolation and about the conditions of isolation are made unfairly or arbitrarily.

Long-Term Prisoners

American prison sentences are among the longest in the world and are getting longer. Twenty-eight states have passed statutes calling for a sentence of life-without-parole for either homicide offenders or habitual offenders or both (Cheatwood, 1988). Almost every state now has some provision for mandatory sentences for violent offenses, drug offenses, habitual offenders, or crimes committed with guns (MacKenzie and Goodstein, 1985). Long sentences have become common under determinate and mandatory sentencing laws. In Connecticut, for example, a defendant convicted of first degree assault or burglary must be sentenced to a five-year minimum and may receive a sentence of up to 20 years. No longer are lengthy sentences reserved exclusively for murderers.

The lengthening of prison sentences is also obvious from prisoner statistics. In Illinois, for example, during the past decade, the average length of time served by first degree murderers has increased by over three years to a high of nearly 16 years. In that state, increases in sentence length have meant that over half of the prison population is serving time for first degree murder or Class X offenses (including armed robbery and aggravated sexual assault), which can yield sentences of 30 to 60 years. These high proportions of long-term prisoners are found among both male and female inmates (Illinois Criminal Justice Information Authority, 1989).

The growing number of long-term prisoners is composed of diverse groups of inmates. As Flanagan (1982:82-83) has pointed out:

> It includes career criminal robbers in whose lives before imprisonment crime was a daily activity and who adapt to incarceration by continuing careers of deceit and violence. In contrast, other long-term prisoners are essentially non-criminal individuals, whose act of violence was unprecedented and is unlikely to be repeated, and whose interests and perspectives within the prison coincide more closely with those of the officers than with those of fellow inmates. Although murderers make up a large percentage of long-term prisoners, the motives, justifications, and behaviors that are incorporated under the "homicide" label are themselves of broad scope.

These inmates may also represent differences along other important lines. For example, there is increasing concern over elderly offenders in prison. While inmates over age 50 may make up only about 5% of prisoners, that percentage represents more than 35,000 inmates, and that number is growing. Among those inmates will be some who arrive in prison as elderly offenders but there is also a significant number of inmates who have grown old while incarcerated (Teller and Howell, 1981). The over 2,500 inmates on death row across the country represent another special class of long-term inmates. Among inmates executed over the past several years the average length of time between imposition of sentence and execution has been approximately seven years (Bureau of Justice Statistics, 1988).

Like questions about the effects of solitary confinement, there has been considerable debate about the effects of long-term incarceration. Interview and observation studies have described a range of debilitating effects. For example, after extensive discussions with long-term inmates while teaching sociology classes in prison, Cohen and Taylor (1972:109) described prisoners who had endured extended confinement:

> It seems...that many of these men already suffer from what R.D. Laing has called "ontological insecurity." The term describes the state in which one doubts the integrity of the self, the reliability of natural processes and the substantiality of others. In some forms this insecurity can take the form of dread of the "possibility of turning or being turned, from a live person into a dead thing, into a stone, into a robot, an automaton, without personal autonomy of action, an *it* without subjectivity."

Robert Johnson (1981:18) has offered an equally dramatic account of the experience of death row inmates:

> Death row emerges...as an environment in which prisoners feel impotent, afraid, and alone—defenseless against their keepers and unable to alter their fate. A few prisoners deteriorate dramatically; all experience, in varying degrees, a living death. This image of death row as a living death symbolizes the human environment of death row and the human consequences of confinement in this oppressive milieu.

Most of the quantitative analyses of long-term imprisonment have failed to find systematic evidence of deterioration. These studies have included assessments of cognitive ability, personality, health and other variables (for a review, see Wormith, 1984; Bonta and Gendreau, 1990). Such contradictory findings have become part of the controversy over the effects of imprisonment in general and long-term confinement specifically. In the extreme, these positions may be presented as diametrically opposed camps, one positing universal negative impacts and the other arguing that even long-term confinement carries no significant deleterious effect.

Advances in the direction of this research can be found in recent studies. Flanagan (1982), for example, has argued that the safest way out of the controversy may be to suggest that while both positions cannot be correct, they both can be wrong. Recent research recognizes differences in the way inmates respond to their environment. In his own research Flanagan (1982) has sought to identify the sources of stress for long-term inmates and to study how the inmates adjust to them. He has described the loss of relationships with those outside of prison, the difficulty of establishing relationships with younger inmates inside prison, and the fear of physical and mental deterioration that long-term inmates face. He has also investigated the techniques for coping and adaptation employed by these inmates.

In another example of research that recognizes differential responses by inmates, MacKenzie and Goodstein (1985) have examined differences in the effects of incarceration across stages of imprisonment and subgroups of long-termers. They found that inmates in their first six months of incarceration, who had fewer prior records and were facing long sentences, had the most difficult adjustment periods. In later phases of incarceration, inmates found ways to lower levels of stress, anxiety, and psychosomatic illnesses. Such studies bridge the gap between the extreme positions and are illustrations of productive efforts to understand the complexities of prison environments and their inhabitants.

Jail Incarceration

Another area of incarceration in which effects have been examined is confinement in local jails. In this area research has considered a wide variety of effects and has been concerned with sources of stress that are very different from the experiences of long-term inmates. With regard to jail inmates, special attention has been paid to the effects of the transition from being on the street to being incarcerated. Gibbs (1982:35) has described the early stages of jail confinement as:

> ...a discordant limbo. A man has just come from the street where he had some measure of control over his life, and he has not yet been immersed in the daily routine of doing time. He is between worlds, and has mastery over neither. In his situation, feelings of anxiety, confusion, and helplessness surface. A man's sense of control may be destroyed. The need for some measure of predictability, certainty, and order may be very difficult to satisfy.

The stress of prison confinement may be linked to isolation and distance from the street, but the stresses of jail confinement are more often linked to the inmate's temporal, physical, and psychological proximity to the street. Gibbs (1982a:99) has described four interrelated aspects of the pains of jail confinement: withstanding entry shock, maintaining outside links, securing stability in a situation of seeming chaos, and finding activities to fill otherwise empty time.

By entry shock, Gibbs refers to the sudden and dramatic change in status that comes from going to jail. "From the perspective of some prisoners it is almost as if they were gamboling down the street one minute and pondering their fate in a jail cell the next" (1982a:100). After entry shock, the jail inmate finds himself struggling to maintain ties to the street in the wake of his unplanned departure. At the same time he faces uncertainty over his fate and unpredictability in his environment: wondering how long he may be in jail, whether he can make bail and questioning the competence of his counsel, the intentions of prosecutors and "the meaning of a hundred other factors related to his legal predicament" (1982a:100). The turmoil and chaos of early confinement is also accompanied by the intense boredom and physical inactivity that is characteristic of program-impoverished holding facilities.

One area in which the results of jail stress can be seen is in the high rate of suicide found among jail inmates. Suicide is the leading cause of death in jail. While rates of suicide have been constructed from studies of individual jails or samples of jails, the most reliable figures have been presented by Winfree (1988), who used national data to calculate rates for comparable groups in and out of jails. He reports a jails suicide rate of 112.1 per 100,000 compared with a general population equivalent rate of 21.7 per 100,000. Several variables have also been associated with suicide in jails. Self-destructive acts most often occur among inmates in detention (Heilig, 1973), and usually occur relatively soon after arrest and booking (Esparza, 1973). The findings regarding the type of offense and the presence of a history of mental health problems are less consistent. Although suicide profiles are not likely to be robust enough to be useful in developing suicide prevention policies (Kennedy and Homant, 1988), important consistencies have been reported in the literature (Hayes, 1983, 1989). A national study offered this description of the "typical" case (Hayes, 1983).

> An inmate committing suicide in jail was most likely to be a 22-year-old, white, single male. He would have been arrested for public intoxication, the only offense leading to his arrest, and would presumably be under the influence of alcohol and/or drugs upon incarceration. Further, the victim would not have a significant history of prior arrests. He would have been taken to an urban county jail and immediately placed in isolation for his own protection and/or surveillance. However, less than three hours after incarceration, the victim would be dead. He would have hanged himself with material from his bed (such as a sheet or pillowcase).

Some of the most systematic research on the impact of jail confinement has dealt with the legal consequences of pretrial detention. Early studies concluded that pretrial detention, as opposed to pretrial release, carries with it a significant prejudicial effect, resulting in an increased likelihood of conviction (see Rankin, 1964). Further research has introduced control for the seriousness of offenses and for length of criminal histories. In a controlled comparison of bailed and jailed defendants, Rankin (1964) concluded that the prejudicial effects were not as strong as once believed. In his research there was little evidence of a difference in the likelihood of conviction but differences remained in other areas. Jailed defendants were more likely than bailed defendants not to be diverted from the criminal justice system and were more likely to receive sentences of incarceration.

There have also been efforts to study the impact of going to jail on other aspects of an inmate's life. John Irwin (1985:42) has described the jail experience as a process of "disintegration which begins with the separation from the street and marks the initiation into a "rabble" existence (see Chapter 3). He describes three categories of unintended consequences of jail confinement. Almost immediately upon arrest and booking, the inmate begins to lose personal property. Automobiles are impounded, street clothes are taken and, in time, apartments are lost to unpaid rent. Inmates also experience a loss of social ties. Visits, correspondence, and telephone calls are restricted and do not provide an adequate substitute for presence on the street. Finally, there is a "loss of capacity to take care of business and inmates, for example, do not have the ability to clear up criminal cases in neighboring jurisdictions. For many inmates these influences have long-term effects. Irwin suggests that jail inmates learn to be wary and opportunistic and they adopt norms that serve them while in jail and chart their adjustment upon release. Spradley (1970:256) described a similar effect of the jailing process:

> After thirty days in jail a tramp owes himself a drink, not simply because he desires to gratify those impulses which have been denied while incarcerated, but because drinking and drunkenness are the prime symbols of acceptance for the man who has come through a ritual experience of alienation.

In another study on the impact of jail, Weisheit and Klofas (1989) used systematic interviews to assess the tangible consequences of going to jail. Even when inmates were confined for brief periods, the consequences could be quite severe. One-third of the inmates interviewed said they lost their apartments or were evicted by family or friends as a result of incarceration. The same portion reported that personal property was stolen or lost. In many of these cases, apartments were burglarized when associates learned that someone had been jailed. Nearly two-thirds of the inmates who had jobs reported that being jailed would affect their work status, and the same portion of inmates said jail strained their relationship with their family.

The research also examined variables that might aggravate or mitigate the costs of going to jail. Weisheit and Klofas found that resources including financial resources, education, and emotional support were unrelated to the tangible effects of jail. Those effects, however, were often aggravated by other problems such as alcohol, drug, and emotional problems. The research also examined the relationship between the tangible costs of going to jail and adjustment during incarceration. The more jail was disruptive of ones' life in the community, the greater were the adjustment problems during confinement.

Summary

Describing the effects of confinement is a difficult task. Descriptions of anything tend to simplify their subject matter and simplifications are often misleading. We must, therefore, be wary of efforts to encapsulate the experience of incarceration in either eloquently phrased reports of observations or in precise quantifications. In the literature on imprisonment we have moved beyond the misleading simplifications of universal harmfulness or universal harmlessness. The issues of interest have expanded to include effects on physical health and social attachments as well as psychological measures. Our appreciation of differences both across individuals and across institutional settings has also expanded.

The research has also led us to look beyond the question of effects and toward concern about adjustment and coping (see Zamble and Porporino, 1988). In one approach to those studies, prisons are viewed as being composed of sub-environments, of different job assignments, housing units, and social networks, all possessing different degrees of stimulation, safety, privacy, and other attributes (see Toch, 1977). Inmates negotiate these sub-environments seeking, if not constructing, niches to meet their own particular needs (see Hagel-Seymour, 1988). Where negotiation is successful, coping efforts mitigate the stresses of confinement. Where inmates break down, are victimized, or turn to violence, the problem often lies in the unique interaction of the individual and the setting (for review, see Wright and Goodstein, 1989). These understandings help to refine our research and direct us toward what Wormith (1984:435) has described as the "truly important questions" regarding confinement: "What are the adverse effects of incarceration?" "Who will suffer them?" "Why will they experience them?" "How can we ameliorate them?"

The Hole:
Solitary Confinement

There is only *one man* in a cell in the hole for it to really be "the hole." There are rows of cells on a tier, but in the hole—the genuine hole—no two prisoners are ever out of their cells at the same time.

There are always voices in the hole. It's a strange thing. I have seen *wars* take place in the hole. I have seen sexual love take place in the hole. I have seen, as a matter of fact, the most impossible things *happen* under these conditions. Let us say a kind of movement that is not really movement exists there. To illustrate: to walk ten miles in an enclosed space of ten feet is not really movement. There not ten miles of space, only time. You do not go ten miles. To write about the hole, in other words, I would have to explore such common places.

. . . I have been dragged to the hole fighting back many times. I was once carried to the hole in Leavenworth by the security force (goon squad). My hands were cuffed behind me. A pig about six feet two inches who weighed about two hundred and fifty pounds was the boss. He was about forty-five, but he was hard as a rock. The pigs had me face down on the concrete floor, punching and kicking me. It was exactly like a pack of dogs on me. The big one, the boss, ordered me to stand up. He motioned to the others to stand back—and I swear to God, you won't believe this, he knocked my clothes off me with a few swipes of his hands.

The cloth tore my skin like knife cuts. I hit the floor, he hit my shoes (high tops) and knocked them off (broke the laces). All through this thing I tried to keep my head by acting passive and smiling. I thought they were so afraid of me it made them animals, which was true, but I couldn't calm them. That was the time they threw me face down in a dungeon cell. They stood on me while one handcuffed me. The pig who knocked my clothes off was the last to leave the cell. I heard them back out of the cell and I rolled over onto my side. I was hurting everywhere. Well, this pig, who had seemed the least emotional of them all, had his cock out and his face was wrinkled up in a grin and he kind of bounced up and down by bending his knees. He was pretending to jerk off. Then he zipped his fly and left the cell kind of chuckling.

. . . You sit in solitary confinement stewing in nothingness, not merely your own nothingness but the nothingness of society, others, the world. The lethargy of months that add up to years in a cell, alone, entwines itself about every "physical" activity of the living body and strangles it slowly to death, the horrible decay of truly living death. You no longer do push-ups or other physical exercises in your small cell; you no longer pace the four steps back and forth across your cell. You no longer masturbate; you can call forth no vision of eroticism in any form, and your genitals, like the limbs of your body, function only to keep your body alive.

Time descends in your cell like the lid of a coffin in which you lie and watch it as it slowly closes over you. When you neither move nor think in your cell, you are awash in pure nothingness.

Solitary confinement in prison can alter the ontological makeup of a stone.

. . . My years in solitary confinement altered me more than I care to admit, even to myself. But I will try to relate the experience, because you're understanding, and what you do not understand is only what you cannot because *you* have not experienced the hole for years. You *listen* and that is all that counts.

It is hard for me to begin. Beginnings are like that for me now.

But something happens down there in the hole, something like an event, but this event can only occur over a span of years. It cannot take place in time and space the way we ordinarily know them.

Not many prisoners have experienced this event. It *never* fails: most prisoners I know who have been in prison off and on all their lives will tell you they have served *five years* in the hole. Everyone is lying, and I do not know why they must say they served *five years* in the hole. Why *five years*? I cannot understand why that particular duration occurs to all of them. They do not say "I served *four years* or *three years*"—nor even six or seven years. It is *always* five years. I *do* know perhaps a half dozen who *have* indeed served five years or six years, but they are so few and so far between.

At any rate, let me return to the point. Let us say you are in a cell ten feet long and seven feet wide. That means seventy feet of *floor* space. But your bunk is just over three feet wide and six and a half feet long. Your iron toilet and sink combination covers a floor space of at least three feet by two feet. All tallied, you have approximately forty-seven square feet of space on the floor. It works out to a pathway seven feet long and about three feet wide—the excess is taken up by odd spaces between your commode and wall, between the foot of the bunk and the wall.

If I were an animal housed in a zoo in quarters of these dimensions, the Humane Society would have the zookeeper arrested for cruelty. It is illegal to house an animal in such confines.

But I am not an animal, so I do not insist on such rights.

My body communicates with the cell. We exchange temperatures and air currents, smells and leavings on the floor and walls. I try to keep it clean, to wash away my evidence, for the first year or two, then let it go at that.

I have experienced everything possible to experience in a cell in a short time—a day or so if I'm active, a week or two if I'm sluggish.

I must fight, from that point on, the routine, the monotony that will bury me alive if I am not careful. I must do that, and do it without losing my mind. So I read, read anything and everything. So I mutter to myself sometimes; sometimes recite poetry.

I have my memories. I have the good ones, the bad ones, the ones that are neither of these. So I have *myself*.

I have my seven-by-three feet pathway, and I pace, at various speeds, depending on my mood. I think. I remember. I think. I remember.

Memory is arrested in the hole. I think about each remembered thing, study it in detail, over and over. I unite it with others, under headings for how I feel about it. Finally it changes and begins to tear itself free from facts and joins my imagination. Someone said *being is memory*.

It travels the terrain of time in a pure way, unfettered by what is, reckless of what was, what will become of it. Memory is not enriched by any further experience. It is *deprived* memory, memory deprived of every movement but the isolated body traveling thousands of miles in the confines of my prison cell.

My body plays with my mind; my mind plays with my body; the further I go into that terrain of time, into my memories, the more they enter my imagination. The imagination—bringing this memory into that, and that into this, every possible permutation and combination—replaces further experience, which would, if not enhance it, at least leave it intact.

I remember well, with such clarity, I am blinded by the memory. It is as if I had forgotten—but it is that I remember so well, too well:

Why am I here? Because I needed the money? Or was it the palmprint on the counter? What was it—a theft? Or was it that girl by the pond in the flowery dress who smiled at me . . .?

Where was I?

Every memory has an element of pain or disappointment. It scolds a little and in its own way. These elements are normally overshadowed by a familiarity we can live with—we happily forget the rest. The rest: there is no rest—but a quality we can live with in comfort, a degree of quietude.

In the hole after a while the painful elements begin to throw out shoots and sprout like brittle weeds in the garden of memory—until finally, after so long, they choke to death everything else in the garden.

You are left with a wild wasteland of scrubby weeds and flinty stone and dusty soil. They call it *psyche-pain.*

It is the same with ideals. Everyone has a few: a touch of idealism, a little passion. As life in the hole, in the pure terrain of time, continues, your passions are aroused less and less with the help of memories and more and more by your ideals. Love, Hate, Equality, Justice, Freedom, War, Peace, Beauty, Truth—they all eventually become Idols, pure and empty abstract gods that demand your fealty, your undying obedience. Little Hitlers come from every precious feeling, every innocent notion you ever entertained, every thought about yourself, your people, the world—all become so many idols, oblivious to each other, that stridently dictate to you in the prison hole.

You cannot fill them up with your days, your years, for they are empty too. But you try—God, how you try.

The wasteland that is your memory now comes under the absolute dictatorship of idols too terrible to envision.

They are the hard, driving winds that torture the tumbleweeds across the prairie desert of memory—the crazy, hard winds that whip up smaller chaotic columns of dust that twist a few feet in the air like little tornadoes. They are the scorching suns that wither the scrubby vegetation and torture the air that shimmers in waves of suffocating heat that rises from the dead, hard stone. They are the cold, merciless nights of the desert that offer surcease only to the fanged serpents: the *punishment* unfolds.

Don't go near yourself.

Then the mirages in the wasteland. You are far from insanity; you are only living through an experience, an event. The mirages are real reflections of how far you have journeyed into that pure terrain of time. They *are* real. They bring the now out-of-place things back into the desert that was once the felicitous garden of your memory. *There a cherished woman passes into exis-*

tence and you approach, draw close to her, and you touch her and she caresses you and then she vanishes in a shimmer to reveal the man masturbating that you have become and are caressing so tenderly. A beautiful flower is seen at a small distance and opens its radiant wings in a promise of spring among the dusty weeds. More suddenly than it appeared, it disappears to reveal a dark splotch on the wall in the fetid, musky cell. A brook bubbles over the dusty pebbles of the wasteland, promising to quench, to quench—and as you turn, it disappears in a flush of the toilet.

Anything you can experience in the hole, you do to yourself, and after an indecent interval, each occasional experience recalls the old, nice quality of a memory which lies fallow beneath the wasteland. A word in a sentence, a tone in a voice or sound; a fleeting essence in a taste or odor; a momentary texture in a tactile sensation, or a combination of motion and form and color caught by the tail of your visual field. These can revive a good thing. Real things: these are the mirages in the desert.

The real world is out of place in the hole, but the hole is nonetheless really there. It is time that no longer moves forward in human experience. You can walk, placing one foot before the other, across eternity in time. All the space you need is six or seven feet. The hole furnishes only that provision: you are living a demonstration of the theory of the infinite within the finite; the dream within the reality.

But the hole is not the stuff of dreams, of fantasies: it is all quite real. In fact, it is so real it haunts you.

Experience occurs seldom and only in extremes: vividly intense or drably monotonous. Surreal paintings have tried to capture—with some success, I might add—the relationships that are very real in life in the prison hole. It is *not* a dream. *To you* it is not a dream. Your words and thoughts can only reflect this condition of your sensations, your feelings; they do not know their plight. Few thoughts in the hole are conscious of their true grounds.

You become silent, contemplative, because you have become inverted. Your sense perception, having taken in everything, including yourself, within the finite confines of the hole, passes through the monotony and now rises up from the *other side*, the infinite, to haunt you with reality. Those outside the hole, at that moment, would call it a dream—but you inside the hole are in reality, not a dream:

What am I? Do I exist? Does the world exist? Will I awaken to find this is all a dream? Is there a God? Am I the devil? What is it like to be dead? What does toilet water taste like? What is it like to put a finger up my butt? What would happen should I shit on the floor? Or piss down my leg? Am I homosexual? What is it like to sleep on this filthy concrete floor?

The mind deprived of experience because of social sensory deprivation in the hole conceives its intellectual faculty to be capable of putting to use a fictional apparatus in the brain. It will believe that somehow it can learn to control this apparatus and use it to move material things, to destroy or change or create physically real things. Shorn of a gracious God, the mind surrenders to nothing, to Nothingness:

If I concentrated, could I melt or bend the bars of my cell? (Yes, Ommmm.) Should I first try to concentrate to move that scrap of dust on the floor? (Yes. Ommmm.) Did it move? (I saw it move just a hair.)

The intelligence recedes, no more a tool of learning—because knowledge is based on experience—but a tool of the outside world it is deprived of knowing. It tries to contact other minds by telepathy; it becomes the Ancestor. *Words* and *Numbers* come to hold mystic significance: they were invented by some arcane magic older than man. The line between the word and the thing vanishes; the intervals of numbers in infinity collapse with infinity.

The mind now crouches in fear and superstition before the idols of the hole, terrified:

I do not want to take any more. There is nothing you can say of interest. I cannot remember ever being happy. No one has ever been kind to me. Everyone betrays me. No one can possibly understand—they are too ignorant. You have not suffered what I have endured. You call me names (homosexual). You do not understand. You mock me (screwball). This world is nothing. An illusion. Death is the release.

But a kind of genius can come out of this deprivation of sensation, of experience. It has been mistaken as naïve intelligence, when in fact it is *empty* intelligence, pure intelligence. *The composition of the mind is altered.* Its previous cultivation is disintegrated and it has greater access to *the brain, the body*: it is Supersanity.

Learning is turned inside out. You have to start from the top and work your way down. You must study mathematical theory before simple arithmetic; theoretical physics before applied physics; anatomy, you might say, before you can walk.

You have to study philosophy in depth before you can understand the simplest categorical differences assumed in language or in any simple commonplace moral or ethical maxim.

Indeed, it is almost a rule that the more simple and commonplace something is, the more difficult to understand it.

You have come the full circle; experienced that single event that happens down there in the prison hole. How long does it take? Years. I would say five years or more.

. . . They finally put a name on what I have suffered in solitary: *sensory deprivation.* The first few times I served a couple of years like that, I saw only three or four drab colors. I felt only concrete and steel. When I was let out, I could not orient myself. The dull prison-blue shirts struck me, dazzled me with a beauty they never had. All colors dazzled me. A piece of wood fascinated me by its feel, its texture. The movements of things, the many prisoners walking about, and their multitude of voices—all going in different directions—bewildered me. I was slow and slack-jawed and confused—but beneath the surface I raged.

I can guess how wasted I have become now by

the fact that I am no longer disoriented by solitary confinement. It has finally wormed its way into my heart: I cannot measure my deprivation any longer.

Let us say I can no longer measure my *feelings*. I can draw the proportions mentally, however.

. . . I explained to you the other day that the cell regulates the moods of the body. The mind does not regulate its own condition. Mental depression, for example, is a state of the mind caused by the body. In a cell in the hole it only *seems* that there is a separation of mind and body—in fact, the body's condition (of deprivations of sensations; experiences, functions, and so on) controls the moods of the mind more than in any other situation I can think of.

Williams James described this relationship when he said we become sad because we shed tears: we do not shed tears because we are sad. That is our original condition as living beings.

A long time ago in the hole, when I first entered prison, I was on the floor lying on my stomach writing a letter, with my elbows propping me up. So I was bent directly over the page I was writing on.

My mood was "normal"—I mean the normal mood of a prisoner in the hole. I remember I noticed, as I was writing, little spots of water appearing on the paper. I touched them with a finger and wondered at the phenomenon—when suddenly I realized tears were falling from my eyes, and immediately I began to weep uncontrollably. It was the first and only time I have wept since I was a child. I do not know *why* now, nor did I know the cause of it then. I must have been weeping over everything, all of it.

. . . A man is taken away from his experience of society, taken away from the experience of a living planet of living things, when he is sent to prison.

A man is taken away from other prisoners, from his experience of other people, when he is locked away in solitary confinement in the hole.

Every step of the way removes him from experience and narrows it down to only the experience of himself.

There is a *thing* called death and we have all seen it. It brings to an end a life, an individual living thing. When life ends, the living thing ceases to experience.

The *concept* of death is simple: it is when a living thing no longer entertains experience.

So when a man is taken farther and farther away from experience, he is being taken to his death.

Source: *In the Belly of the Beast* by Jack Henry Abbott. Copyright © 1981 by Jack Henry Abbott. Reprinted by permission of Random House, Inc.

Key Terms and Concepts

deprivation
disciplinary segregation
institutional dependency
long-term incarceration
long-term inmates
prisonization

rabble existence
sensory deprivation
solitary confinement
totality of conditions
victimization

References

Abbott, Jack (1991). *In the Belly of the Beast.* New York, NY: Vintage Books.

Bonta, J. and P. Gendreau (1990). "Reexamining the Cruel and Unusual Punishment of Prison Life." *Law and Human Behavior*, Volume 14, Number 3:347-372.

Bukstel, L. and P. Kilmann (1980). "Psychological Effects of Imprisonment on Confined Individuals." *Psychological Bulletin*, Volume 88, Number 3:469-493.

Bureau of Justice Statistics (1988). *Capital Punishment 1987.* Washington, DC: U.S. Department of Justice.

Bureau of Justice Statistics (1989). *Prison Rule Violators.* Washington, DC: U.S. Department of Justice.

Carr, T. (1981). *The Effects of Crowding on Recidivism, Cardiovascular Deaths and Infraction Rates in a Large Prison System.* Unpublished Doctoral Dissertation, Georgia State University.

Cheatwood, D. (1988). "Life-Without-Parole Sanction: Its Current Status and a Research Agenda," *Crime and Delinquency*, Volume 34, Number 1:45.

Clemmer, D. (1940). *The Prison Community.* Boston, MA: Christopher.

Cohen, S. and L. Taylor (1972). *Psychological Survival.* New York, NY: Vintage Books.

Crouch, B. and J. Marquart (1989). *An Appeal to Justice.* Austin, TX: University of Texas Press.

D'Atri, D. (1975). "Psychophysiological Responses to Crowding." *Environment and Behavior*, Volume 7, Number 2:237-252.

D'Atri, D., E.F. Fitzgerald, S. Kasl and A. Ostfeld (1981). "Crowding in Prison: The Relationship between Changes in Housing Mode and Blood Pressure." *Psychosomatic Medicine*, Volume 43, Number 1:95-105.

Esparza, R. (1973). "Attempted and Committed Suicide in County Jails." In B. Danto (ed.) *Jail House Blues: Studies of Suicidal Behavior in Jail and Prison.* Orchard Lake, MI: Epic Publications.

Flanagan, T. (1982). "Lifers and Long-termers: Doing Big Time." In R. Johnson and H. Toch (eds.) *The Pains of Imprisonment.* Beverly Hills, CA: Sage Publications.

Fox, V. (1983). *Correctional Institutions.* Englewood Cliffs, NJ: Prentice-Hall.

Gibbs, J.J. (1982). "The First Cut is the Deepest: Psychological Breakdown and Survival in the Detention Setting." In R. Johnson and H. Toch (eds.) *The Pains of Imprisonment.* Beverly Hills, CA: Sage Publications.

Gibbs, J.J. (1982a). "Disruption and Distress: Going from Street to Jail." In N. Parisi (ed.) *Coping with Imprisonment.* Beverly Hills, CA: Sage Publications.

Goldkamp, J.S. (1979). *Two Classes of Accused: A Study of Bail and Detention in American Justice.* Cambridge, MA: Ballinger Publishing.

Goodstein, L. and K. Wright (1989). "Inmate Adjustment to Prison." In L. Goodstein and D. Layton MacKenzie (eds.) *The American Prison: Issues in Research and Policy.* New York, NY: Plenum Publishing Corporation.

Griswald, H.J., M. Misenheimer, A. Powers and E. Tromanhauser (1970). *An Eye for an Eye: Four Inmates on the Crime of American Prisons Today.* New York, NY: Holt, Rinehart and Winston.

Hagel-Seymour (1988). "Environmental Sanctuaries for Susceptible Prisoners." In R. Johnson and H. Toch (eds.) *The Pains of Imprisonment.* Beverly Hills, CA: Sage Publications.

Hayes, L.M. (1983). "And Darkness Closes in...A National Study of Jail Suicides." *Criminal Justice and Behavior*, Volume 10, Number 3:461-84.

Hayes, L.M. (1989). "National Study of Jail Suicides: Seven Years Later." *Psychiatric Quarterly*, Volume 60, Number 1: 7-29.

Hayne, S.T., T. Allmond, W. Lednar and G. Brown (1985). "Tuberculosis Control in a Military Prison." *Journal of Prison and Jail Health*, Volume 5, Number 1:39-45.

Heilig, S. (1973). "Suicide in Jails." In B. Danto (ed.) *Jail House Blues: Studies of Suicidal Behavior in Jail and Prison.* Orchard Lake, MI: Epic Publications.

Illinois Criminal Justice Information Authority (1989). *Trends and Issues 89.* Chicago, IL: Criminal Justice Information Authority.

Irwin, J. (1985). *The Jail: Managing the Underclass in American Society.* Berkeley, CA: University of California Press.

Jackson, M. (1983). *Prisoners of Isolation: Solitary Confinement in Canada.* Toronto, Canada: University of Toronto Press.

Jamieson, K. and T. Flanagan (1988). *Sourcebook of Criminal Justice Statistics—1988*. Washington, DC: U.S. Government Printing Office.

Johnson, R. (1981). *Condemned to Die: Life Under Sentence of Death*. New York, NY: Elsevier Books.

Johnson, R. and H. Toch (1988). "Introduction." In R. Johnson and H. Toch (eds.) *The Pains of Imprisonment*. Beverly Hills, CA: Sage Publications.

Jones, D. (1976). *The Health Risks of Imprisonment*. Lexington, MA: Lexington Books.

Kennedy, D. and R. Homant (1988). "Predicting Custodial Suicides: The Problems with the Use of Profiles." *Justice Quarterly*, Volume 5, Number 3: 442-456.

Krantz, S. (1983). *Corrections and Prisoners Rights*. St. Paul, MN: West Publishing Co.

Lockwood, D. (1980). *Prison Sexual Violence*. New York, NY: Elsevier Books.

MacKenzie, D. Layton and L. Goodstein (1985). Long-Term Incarceration Impacts and Characterisitcs of Long-Term Offenders: An Empirical Analysis." *Criminal Justice and Behavior*, Volume 12, Number 3:395-413.

McCain, G., V. Cox and P.B. Paulus (1976). "The Effect of Prison Crowding in Inmate Behavior." Washington, DC: Law Enforcement Assistance Administration.

Mitford, J. (1973). *Kind and Usual Punishment: The Prison Business*. New York, NY: Vintage Books.

Nacci, P. and T. Kane (1983). "The Incidence of Sex and Sexual Aggression in Federal Prisons." *Federal Probation*, Volume 47, Number 1:31-36.

National Institute of Justice (1989). *1988 Update: AIDS in Correctional Facilities*. Washington, DC: U.S. Department of Justice.

Pennsylvania Prison Society (1988). *News Letter*. Philadelphia, PA: Pennsylvania Prison Society.

Rankin, A. (1964). "The Effects of Pretrial Detention." *New York University Law Review*, Volume 39, Number 4:641.

Spradley, J. (1970). *You Owe Yourself a Drink*. Boston, MA: Little, Brown and Company.

Suedfeld, P. (1980). *Restricted Environmental Stimulation: Research and Clinical Applications*. New York, NY: John Wiley and Sons.

Sykes, G. (1958). *Society of Captives*. Princeton, NJ: Princeton University Press.

Sylvester, S., J. Reed and D. Nelson (1977). *Prison Homicide*. New York, NY: Spectrum.

Teller, F. and R. Howell (1981). "The Older Prisoner: Criminal and Psychological Characteristics." *Criminology*, Volume 18, Number 4:549-555.

Teplin, L. (1990). "The Prevalence of Severe Mental Disorder Among Male Urban Jail Detainees: Comparison with Epidemiological Catchment Area Program." *American Journal of Public Health*, Volume 80, Number 4: 663-669.

Toch, H., K. Adams and D. Grant (1989). *Coping: Maladaptation in Prisons.* New Brunswick, NJ: Transaction Books.

Toch, H. (1977). *Living in Prison: The Ecology of Survival.* New York, NY: The Free Press.

Walker, N. (1983). "Side-Effects of Incarceration." *British Journal of Criminology*, Volume 23, Number 1: 61-71.

Weisheit, R. and J. Klofas (1989). "The Impact of Jail: Collateral Costs and Affective Response." *Journal of Offender Counselling, Services and Rehabilitation*, Volume 14, Number 1:51-66.

Wiehn, P. (1988). "Mentally Ill Offenders: Prison's First Casualties." In R. Johnson and H. Toch (eds.) *The Pains of Imprisonment.* Beverly Hills, CA: Sage Publications.

Wheeler, S. (1961). "Socialization in Correctional Communities." *American Sociological Review*, Volume 26, Number 4:697-712.

Winfree, L.T. (1988). "Rethinking American Jail Death Rates: A Comparison of National Mortality and Jail Mortality, 1978, 1983." *Policy Studies Review*, Volume 7, Number 4:641-659.

Wright, K. and L. Goodstein (1989). "Correctional Environments." In L. Goodstein and D. Layton MacKenzie (eds.) *The American Prison: Issues in Research and Policy.* New York, NY: Plenum Publishing Corporation.

Wormith, S.J. (1984). "The Controversy over the Effects of Long-Term Incarceration." *Canadian Journal of Criminology*, Volume 26, Number 3: 423-435.

Zamble, E. and F. Porporino (1988). *Coping, Behavior and Adaptation in Prison Inmates.* New York, NY: Springer-Verlag.

Table of Cases

Estelle v. Gamble, 429 U.S. 97 (1976)

Holt v. Sarver, 306 F. Supp. 362 (1970), 442 F.2d 304 (8th Cir. 1971)

Hutto v. Finney, 98 S. Ct. 2565 (1978)

Lee v. Tahash, 352 F.2d 970 (8th Cir. 1965)

Pugh v. Locke, 406 F. Supp. 318 (1976)

Rhodes v. Chapman, 101 S. Ct. 2404 (1981)

Ruiz v. Estelle, F.2d 115 (1980)

Photo Credit: Tony O'Brien, Frost Publishing Group, Ltd.

Prison
Violence

10

After reading this chapter, the student should be able to:

■ Discuss the history of prison violence in America.

■ List the causes of prison violence.

■ Describe methods to reduce prison violence.

■ Comment on prison violence and the future of imprisonment.

Introduction

"Since the first recorded American prison riot, which occurred in 1774 inside a primitive institution built over an abandoned mine shaft at Simsbury, Connecticut, the fear of recurring riots has plagued American correctional systems" (Dillingham and Montgomery, 1985). This statement sums up the view of many concerning prison riots and the attendant violence. Riots represent the worst form of prison violence. The purposes of this chapter are to explore the concept of prison violence and to highlight strategies to reduce it.

When people think of prison violence, more often than not the view of a prison riot comes to the forefront. Yet prison riots are relatively rare events. More common to prison violence is the day-to-day confrontations among inmates and between correctional officers and prisoners. The latter type of violence represents the most difficult task for correctional administrators to address. While not attempting to downplay the importance of prison riots, this chapter will address how violence in prison is much more than the destructive episodes found in major disturbances. Instead, the intent of this chapter is to highlight how violence in prison settings is ingrained into the *structure* of prisons themselves. We will begin the chapter by examining violence in prison through historical lenses. This is where the riot as the ultimate expression of prison violence will be explored.

In addition, we will explore the causes of prison violence, along with methods to reduce it. Finally, we will offer some ideas on the future of imprisonment and prison violence. Unlike the next chapter, which will explore prison sex and violence, this chapter will examine violence more generally by exploring its causes and its more noted forms, such as expressed through person-to-person violence (e.g., stabbings and beatings) and collective violence (e.g., prison riots). It is hoped that by the end of the chapter the student will have a broad understanding of the complexities associated with prison violence.

Prison Violence: A Historical Examination

American prisons have been no places for those with gentle hearts. Much of what is understood about prison violence has been informed by a history of riots or disturbances. Yet, as mentioned earlier, prison riots are only one form of prison violence. Dillingham and Montgomery (1985:20) estimate that to date there have been about 300 riots which have occurred in correctional systems in the United States since 1900. Their definition of a riot included the participation of 15 or more prisoners resulting in property damage and personal injury. Clearly, however, prison violence, as expressed through fights, beatings, and stabbings, between and among prisoners is much more pervasive and common in the contemporary prison.

Bowker (1985) has argued that prison violence can be understood by examining "violence goals." Violence goals can be placed into two types: *instrumental prison violence* and *expressive prison violence.* On the one hand, instrumental prison violence is designed to provide the aggressor with some specific forms of power and status. This type of prison violence attempts to improve the self-image of the aggressor. In addition, the aggressor develops a sense of dominance over the victim. As such, the aggressor gains something through the expression of violence. Bowker (1985:12) argues that sexual assault is largely valued by aggressive prisoners because it defines the dominance an individual has over a weaker prisoner. In much of what is known about prison violence, this type of violence goal is the most prevalent.

Expressive prison violence, on the other hand, is a "nonrational" response to tension produced in the prison environment. Prison riots can be viewed, in part, as expressive violence gone awry among a number of prisoners. This type of prison violence is the most difficult to predict, and as such, correctional staff are often left with very few indicators of such violence, except for increasing tensions among inmates.

In addition, expressive violence and instrumental violence may blend together in the prison setting. A riot, for example, in which hostages are taken could be due to the rational calculations of a small group of aggressive prisoners (instrumental violence), yet could involve the mistreatment of hostages due to the frustrations of prisoners over poor conditions (expressive violence). Each violence goal has its place in explaining prison violence. Whether prison violence goals are expressive or instrumental, the critical result is what is important. One of these results is prison riots.

An examination of the history of prison riots reveals the most vivid description of prison violence, with both instrumental and expressive goals. We, therefore, begin our discussion of prison violence by exploring some major prison riots and explanations of them. The student may want to visualize riots as the expression of many factors in the prison environment. Riots may be the result of the day-to-day violence we find in the correctional setting, or explained by the nature and type of inmates we confine in them. Regardless of causes, prison violence, as expressed by riots, represents the worst part of our correctional history. Only by knowing our history can we become more informed about reducing the possibility of prison riots in the future.

The Attica Experience

Useem and Kimball (1989) argue that to understand the context within which the Attica riot of 1971 took place, one must examine the historical conditions and periods preceeding the riot. According to these authors, two periods of American history developed subsequent to World War II that influenced and shaped the political and social landscape in which the Attica riot occurred. The first period, known as the "Confidence and Rehabilitationism" period (1950-1965), reflected the belief in the institutions of society, including the prison. The prison was to provide the kinds of resources and programs whereby the prisoner could effectively rehabilitate himself.

Prisons were expected to change the offender into a productive citizen, one who could be an active participant in a democratic society. Prison riots of the period represented failure of the prison to meet these demands. More resources needed to be placed into the hands of correctional administrators to effectively promote change in the offender. Additionally, prison riots were viewed to be the workings of unstable men and "deranged thugs" who sought to subvert prison stability. More importantly, prison demographics were changing. With institutions becoming blacker and these prisoners representing the most estranged members of society, many became identified with the Black Muslim movement, a movement that was to make an assault on prison conditions and administrations.

Within this context, the seeds for the second period of American history were developed. This second period, according to Useem and Kimball (1989:11), was known as the "Conflict and Decline of Rehabilitationism (1966-1975)" period. The Attica riot reflected the loss of faith in the traditional institutions of society, and clearly reflected the failure of the prison to produce the results it claimed. In addition, the Attica riot represented deeply entrenched doubts about how social institutions were going to meet the needs of the people. No other social institution was more critically castigated than the prison. The Attica disturbance brought to the forefront of the American consciousness questions about what the purposes of imprisonment should be.

According to Useem and Kimball (1989:16), with the rise of entitlements in society, a backlash against disorder among those who had the most to lose if civil chaos continued, and the decline in confidence in social institutions, a "volatile political environment" was created, whereby the central purposes of the prison were questioned. As such, this period of American history saw more prison riots than ever before. They state:

> In 1967 there were 5 prison riots; 15 in 1968; 27 and 37 in 1970 and 1971, respectively; and in 1972 there 48, more than in any year in American history. To some, the escalation of conflict in prisons was one more element in the rising tide of disorder that was threatening to overwhelm the forces of stability and order. To others, it seemed that American society was on the brink of some sort of major transformation. The Attica riot was an unmistakable symbol of these possibilities (1989:18).

More than any other event in American history, the Attica riot represented much more than the deprivations and frustrations of a number of prisoners; it represented the overall disillusionment of many in society, most of whom who were disadvantaged members of society. These societal frustrations, as expressed by prisoners, all boiled over on September 9, 1971 when a group of inmates seized "A Tunnel" in Attica prison. This seizure, along with concomitant events, was to produce the most deadly and devastating riot to date in American history. It focused the prison into the mainstream consciousness and brought into question the purposes of prisons in a free society.

By the time the riot at Attica was quelled on September 13, 1971, 39 victims lay dead, 10 of whom were hostages. Not to mention the millions of dollars of damage caused by the riot, the riot raised serious and perplexing questions of why such an event occurred and what could be done to prevent such a thing from occurring in the future. Observers of the riot, researchers, and even the official McKay Commission report cited a number of causes of the riot.

First and foremost was the intensive deprivation experienced by the prisoners. It was without question that the Attica prison was a terrible place to live. Even the McKay Commission report devoted a considerable number of pages to the deprivations imposed upon inmates. Yet Attica prison was not different from many prisons in the country. Useem and Kimball (1989:23) report that the significant factors associated with the Attica riot were becoming commonplace in many prisons throughout the country. Most noteworthy was the fact that the standards upon which corrections were to be judged were changing. Many of these new standards were in the form of legal mandates.

In addition, the composition of the inmate population was shifting in prisons across the country. Attica was no exception. With the influx of a greater number of Puerto Rican, Chicano, and black prisoners, the traditionaly white-controlled prisoner society was changing. Furthermore, many of these inmates were more politically conscious and powerless in mainstream society. With changes in the inmate population and the "political consciousness" of these inmates rising, expectations about how the prison was to be run were in a state of flux.

Couple these changes in the inmate population with the fact that the Attica prison had no formal rule system, at least not one that was consistently followed by correctional officers, and the scene was set for a major disturbance. Useem and Kimball (1989:24) state:

> There was one set of rules which applied throughout the New York system, another which was formulated at Attica, and an unknowable number of rules or enforcement standards made up [by] individual corrections officers. Rulebooks were not being printed at this time, so not even the corrections officers had access to them or knew them with confidence.

These forces, along with the reform efforts of the period, saw a radical change in the operation of Attica prison. Three forces, according to Useem and Kimball (1989:25), produced the seeds for change in the operation of Attica prison. First, there were the forces of liberal reform that sought to institute legal reform in the operation of the prison. The U.S. courts were demanding that changes occur in how the prison was run, in particular that constitutional standards be met by prison officials. Next, the "old-line prison officials" constituted a second force. They sought to maintain the status quo in the prison and widen their span of control. With the insurgence of the courts mandating changes in the operation of the prison, this group was most vociferously opposed to any changes, at least changes they perceived weakened their position vis-à-vis the prisoners. Finally, the inmates themselves represented a force in the reform movement of the prison.

The intensive deprivations, the changes in the inmate population, both demographically and politically, the requirement of more constitutional standards in the prison by the courts, the lack of any formal rule system in the prison, along with the pressures placed on the system by inmates, the courts, and the corrections officers all led to the Attica riot. Beginning with some "preliminary skirmishes" on September 8 and the morning of September 9, 1971, the institution was primed for an explosion (Useem and Kimball, 1989:27).

Within a matter of hours of the beginning of the riot, inmates seized "D Yard" of the prison. For the next four days the prison was controlled by prisoners, with the power of the state awaiting orders to retake the prison. With over 1,100 armed men outside of the prison, New York State Commissioner of Corrections Russell Oswald was in a precarious position. On the one hand, he had a prison overtaken by prisoners and an angry mob of corrections officers and state troopers awaiting orders to take the prison back. Many of these officers had "the desire to kill or physically punish inmates" according to Useem and Kimball (1989:37).

On the other hand, New York Governor Nelson Rockefeller was the final decisionmaker in the matter. For Rockefeller, the solution to the problem had to take into consideration the political message being sent by the state. He was adamantly opposed to any negotiations with prisoners holding hostages, and Oswald was not sure that if an assault on the prison was ordered, he would be able to control the assault forces, many of whom were openly opposed to the authority of Oswald himself. Beginning with direct negotiation with the prisoners followed by negotiation through observers, Oswald attempted to end the disturbance on peaceful grounds. All was for naught.

Seeing that the negotiations were to fail, Oswald issued a series of ultimatums to the prisoners. Thinking that the state would never assault the prison, the inmates rejected the ultimatums and refused to relinquish hostages or give back the prison. With no other options available, Oswald ordered the retaking of the prison by armed forces. After the killing of 39 people, 10 of whom were hostages, the bloodiest riot in American history to date was over. Reasons for the armed assault are unclear even today. Yet some have speculated that an armed assault was the only way the state was to maintain its integrity in the face of revolutionary behavior on the part of prisoners.

Useem and Kimball (1989:51) suggest that the retaking of Attica prison was essentially politically motivated by both Oswald and Rockefeller. At stake was the legitimacy of the state and a "decisive reassertion of the state's sovereignty and power." Knowing that the hostages could be killed at any time by the inmates, and that it was next to impossible to save all the hostages in the event of an armed assault, Oswald and Rockefeller sought "the fewest possible casualties" (Useem and Kimball, 1989:51). The prison was retaken and Attica prison continued to exist and operate. The question becomes, "Did the conditions of prisoners improve as a result of the riot, or did the 28 points demanded by the inmates receive any serious consideration on the part of the state?"

Clearly, the conditions of the prison did improve and Attica prison became Attica correctional facility. But, as to the general plight of prisoners in relation to their conditions and the degree of prison violence, the answer is uncertain. It is clear that the Attica riot had both forms of violence goals discussed earlier—the violence that ensued from the Attica riot had both instrumental and expressive goals. The prisoners demanded certain conditions be improved (instrumental violence) and heaped upon both themselves and the hostages many violent acts (expressive violence).

Given the fact that the goals sought by inmates through the use of violence were largely unmet by the Attica riot, the central question becomes, "Why don't prisoners riot more often?" To answer this question, we must turn to a more contemporary riot, one that was to become the bloodiest riot in American history. By examining this riot, we may uncover an answer to our questions about the prevalence of riots and their relationship to prison violence.

The Santa Fe Tragedy

Unlike the disturbance at Attica prison, the riot which took place at the Penitentiary of New Mexico (PNM) was not composed of radical groups seeking to make a political statement. Instead, much of what occurred at this riot was a representation of the worst form of prison violence. Prisoners, many of whom who were labeled as "snitches," were murdered in the most brutal and vicious manners. One inmate was decapitated, while another had a piece of iron run through his skull. The brutality of the riot was unprecedented in the history of American prisons.

In addition to the prisoner-prisoner abuse, 12 correctional officers were taken hostage and many were beaten by inmates and some were even raped, a claim later to be denied by the inmates. While some officers were dealt with harshly by the prisoners, some were treated well; many of the officers who were treated the most brutally were felt to have deserved their fate, at least in the eyes of the inmates (Useem and Kimball, 1989:108). With the correctional officers as hostages, the inmates attempted to negotiate for specific demands concerning conditions at the prison.

These negotiations directly addressed the grievances and deprivations heaped upon the prisoners over a number of years. Like the Attica prison, many of the grievances of the inmates at PNM dealt with the issue of overcrowding. Couple this overcrowding with some massive organizational changes and shifts in the operation of the entire Department of Corrections in New Mexico, and the seeds for a serious disturbance were planted. Notwithstanding these issues, however, the central problem of the administration of PNM was the "snitch system" that had run rampant for many years prior to the riot.

In fact, much of the brutality heaped upon some inmates during the riot could be directly related to the snitch system that was in place at PNM. Some of the most brutal attacks were on perceived prisoner snitches. In addition to the snitch system, there were many inmates during the course of the disturbance who had broken into the institution's pharmacy and stolen narcotics and other mood-altering drugs. Moreover, the riot had begun when inmates in one dormitory were having a "hootch" (homemade beer) party. On the spur of the moment, they decided to attempt a takeover during the night (Useem and Kimball, 1989:101).

With the background of poor living conditions, a disorganized prison and Department of Corrections, and alcohol as an incentive, the prisoners took the prison over on February 1, 1980 and the riot continued for the next 36 hours until the prison was retaken by state police. All hostages were released, but the carnage that was left behind by such a riot was not to be forgotten for many years. In fact, even today, many refer to the riot at PNM as one of the worst, if not the worst, in the history of American prisons. As one inmate who survived the riot put it, "If you owed an inmate a candy bar, all he had to say was that you were a snitch and you were dead...How do you describe a massacre....There has to be a word for what occurred" (*Frontline*, 1988).

The kinds of violence that occurred at PNM can be viewed as both instrumental and expressive, yet it seems that much of the violence was expressive in nature. Without question, the prisoners did have the goal of dealing very harshly with prisoners who were snitches, yet much of the violence was actually an *expression* of hostility and disdain toward specific kinds of inmates. In addition, once the killing started, it is not clear what the instrumental goals of the prisoners were. Wanton and reckless violence became the norm. It is apparent that when alcohol and narcotics were introduced, the violence got out of hand. When there were no more inmates to kill, the aggressors focused on rather gruesome methods to further mutilate the dead bodies. As one inmate stated to a PBS-TV reporter, "When the rats were dead the guys started doing all sorts of crazy shit to the guys [dead inmates]. They were throwing inmates off the tiers and their bodies were crashing on the ground. Guys then would be waiting at the bottom ready to stab the fuckers even though they were dead." Similar accounts are offered by Useem and Kimball (1989:106) in their description of the brutality and violence.

The tragedies at both Attica and PNM highlight extreme forms of prison violence. Whether the goals of the violence were instrumental or expressive, the riots that ensued were costly with respect to human lives lost and millions of dollars in damage and destruction. Nevertheless, riots are only one form of prison violence. As stated earlier in the chapter, a more complete examination of violence needs to explore how it permeates the prison structure. Riots are generally reflective of failures of many areas in the prison, or what Useem and Kimball (1989:218) refer to as "breakdowns in prisons," such as a loss of administrative control and routine. The riot represents the ultimate form of breakdown in the prison community.

In the next section we will examine more thoroughly the causes of prison violence. Much of our discussion will explore the less extreme forms of violence and offer possible explanations for such violence. Later we will examine methods to reduce prison violence.

The Causes of Prison Violence

Three causes for prison violence have been offered by the research literature. They are: (1) the violent inmate, (2) the social climate of violence, and (3) a possible connection between prison violence and overcrowding. None of these causes should be meant to explain prison violence. Instead, the concept of prison violence should be examined as an interplay among all of these factors. Each provides some explanation as to the causes of prison violence.

The Violent Inmate

Much of the early research on prison violence attributed the event to the degree to which the inmate population was composed of inmates who had histories of violence. In other words, much of prison violence can be explained by the histories of prisoners. In short, many have expressions of violence in their backgrounds.

Lockwood (1980) offers this as a possible explanation of men who are involved in sexual violence in prison. His research on prison sexual violence indicated that a vast majority of inmates were incarcerated for crimes in which force or the threat of force was used (84% of his sexual aggressors). This lends support to the idea that violence could be something that originates on the streets and is imported into the prison setting once the offender is incarcerated. Histories of violence in free society are associated with violence in prison. Moreover, many agressors select targets that are much smaller than themselves and, thus, more susceptible to victimization.

Both Irwin (1970) and Abbott (1991) describe the aggressive prisoner as the person who has been "state-raised." These are individuals who have spent much time within institutional settings and have learned violence as the accepted method of dealing with problems. Moreover, of those people who tend to exhibit violent tendencies in prison, many have come from urban settings where violence is an accepted mechanism of dispute resolution. This "subcultural theory" of violence is offered as an explanation of violence in prison.

Lockwood's research (1980:113) on prison sexual violence supports the notion that much of the behavior may have its genesis in the native community of the aggressive inmate. Couple the reinforcement of violence as a mechanism of solving disputes with some institutional characteristics of the prison, and the existence of prison violence is understandable. While individual factors associated with the offender are correlated to later prison violence, these variables do not explain why certain people become violent and others do not. As such, the notion of the violent prisoner must be understood with some caution. It may be that some characteristics of violence are brought with the offender once incarcerated, but that these factors do not influence equally the prevalence of violence among prisoners with similar backgrounds.

The Social Climate of Violence

While prison violence may be rooted within the individual offender, other interpretations of prison violence highlight the structure of the prison setting. This view explores how prison violence has its origin in the "climate" of the institution. Many contemporary researchers have suggested that the structure and design of the prison are major elements in the creation and perpetuation of prison violence.

Toch (1985) has suggested that much of the violence exhibited in prisons today can be traced to the "contextual" makeup of the prison. This view examines the role of the interactions among all actors in the prison environment, including correctional staff and prisoners. Fundamentally, this view holds that the elements of social climate: (1) influence inmates differentially, (2) not all elements of a prison's structure will be well received by all inmates, and (3) positive and negative reactions to features of climate help motivate inmate behavior (Toch, 1985:39).

Further, Toch (1985:41-42) suggests that prisons may promote violence among prisoners by having specific types of climate features. These features serve as harbingers for violence. In addition, these features both increase and decrease the probability of violence occurring. An understanding of these features allows correctional officials to proactively plan to control violent episodes. Toch provides some interesting examples of how contextual factors promote violence in prison:

By Providing "Pay Offs." In this case, the inmate is given status for exhibiting violent behavior, either through peer group approval of violence or through some type of informal reward system. It is common in prison to hear how well respected are those inmates who have resorted to violence as a mechanism of settling disputes. By reducing this type of reinforcement among prisoners, the context for violence is removed.

By Providing Immunity or Protection. Violence in prison is often unheard of and rarely communicated to staff by prisoners. The code of silence that exists in prisons is very strong, particularly informal rules against conversing with staff about inmate problems. No inmate wants to be perceived as a "rat," and as such, very few inmates reveal the nature and scope of prison violence to staff.

By Providing Opportunities. The prison is a violent place. There are many areas and opportunities available to the aggressive inmate who wants to prey on other prisoners. Through the predictability of staff and other prisoners, violence is much more possible.

By Providing Temptation, Challenges, and Provocations. The prisoner social world is filled with many opportunities to test one's manhood. Prisons intrinsically pose opposing groups against each other. Gangs, for example, are a reality of prison and are often intermixed in such a fashion that the climate breeds intergang rivalries and sometimes violent confrontations. It is for this reason that many correctional administrators actively attempt to separate and remove known rival gangs. With the problem of prison overcrowding, however, sometimes this luxury of transfer and removal is not available.

By Providing Justificatory Premises. Some inmates in the prisoner social system are not viewed as deserving of the respect of the other prisoners. Being viewed as less worthy by other inmates makes them the most vulnerable to prison violence. In this way, the inmate justifies violence on another inmate because he may not be viewed as a "real man" or a respected prisoner. By allowing this attitude to exist, the climate breeds many forms of prisoner violence.

By recognizing these features of prison violence, we are able to offer prescriptions on how it can be controlled. No prison will ever be totally devoid of violence, yet much can be done to reduce the prevalence of such events. Today, many have argued that the prison is much too violent and that very little has been done to address the structural and climatic features of the prison that support violence.

Overcrowding and Prison Violence: A Possible Connection?

To the student, the connection between prison overcrowding and violence may seem somewhat intuitive. Nevertheless, the research on this issue has not been definitive as to what, if any, relationship exists between prison overcrowding and violence. Much of the early research attempted to show how prisons breed many physiological and psychological problems due to overcrowding (Walker, Jr. and Gordon, 1980). Yet very little research has been generated that questions the relationship between prison overcrowding and subsequent violence (see Chapter 9).

Farrington and Nuttall (1985), however, have provided some interesting findings on prison size, overcrowding, prison violence, and recidivism. Examining data from England, these researchers concluded that there is no conclusive evidence to support the charge that prison size influences inmate behavior inside, or upon release from prison. Rather than conclude that the relationship does not exist, the authors caution that their research does not mean there is no relationship between prison size and institutional behavior and post-institutional behavor.

Instead, their argument suggests that belief in the relationship between prison size and both prison behavior and post-release behavior is present without data to support it. There is an absence of evidence that size has no effect. In addition, their research was not able to isolate the many factors that may influence the prevalence of violence in prison settings, such as the makeup of the population and the reporting strategies of correctional staff. Finally, one must be cautious in interpreting the relationship of prison size and prison violence based on data collected in English prisons. Prisons in the United States tend to be larger and also house more serious and violent offenders.

Hence, any discussion of prison size, prison population, and prison violence will have to incorporate many different variables for a more comprehensive understanding. At present, there is not much credible research that can provide us with some direction. What the Farrington and Nuttall research does show is that while size may not be correlated with prison violence, overcrowding is associated with prison violence. Their research showed that the most overcrowded facilities tended to have the highest rates of violence. This position is equally supported by the work of Gaes and McGuire (1985) in their study of 19 federal prisons in the United States. In virtually every violent situation, the level of crowding was the strongest predictor of assaults.

Even this research must be questioned because the population under study was the federal system. It would be reasonable to question the generalizability of these findings to larger and more violent state facilities. Future research is going to have to investigate the relationship between prison overcrowding and prison violence in state institutions to more fully comprehend prison overcrowding and prison violence.

It would seem, therefore, that there is some evidence to support the link between prison overcrowding and prison violence. This does not bode well for corrections, since the estimated growth of the correctional system is to be astronomical into the twenty-first century. More than ever before, sound and practical solutions to prison violence will need to be generated if correctional institutions are to be managed in an effective manner.

Methods to Reduce Prison Violence

Proposing solutions to prison violence is no easy task. Many contemporary researchers have suggested that the only way prison violence is going to be reduced is through the introduction of strong administrative controls. Violence in prison is a management problem; therefore, prison managers must take the lead in combatting the problem of prison violence. Nevertheless, it is not clear how this will be accomplished.

DiIulio (1987), for example, argues for stronger control systems in prison settings for more effective management of inmate behavior, including violent behavior. Useem and Kimball (1989:219) reinforce this position when examining prison riots. Their "breakdown" hypothesis suggests that prison violence—most particularly prison riots—is the product of inadequate and poorly managed prisons. As such, they suggest that prison violence is less likely to occur within institutions in which administrative control is direct and maintained by a well-disciplined security system.

Much of the current literature reinforces the belief that prison violence can be reduced through some rational planning on the part of correctional administrators. The literature disagrees, however, on the most appropriate methods to reduce prison violence. All views do not believe that prison violence can be eradicated. At best, management of prison violence is the goal. But how is this most effectively accomplished? There are three general approaches to controlling prison violence. They are the *institutional response*, the *environmental-change approach*, and the *societal-cultural model*.

Institutional Response

Proponents of the institutional response method to controlling prison violence support a strong central administration and well-run prison bureaucracy. Their view is that much prison violence is the function of weak administrators, lax rule systems, and inconsistent rule enforcement, or poorly articulated rules. In short, poor management is the central cause of prison violence. As stated earlier, no one who supports this institutional view would suggest that prison violence can be totally stopped. Their goal, however, is to suggest that more direct action on the part of correctional managers would reduce the incidence and prevalence of prison violence.

As a supporter of this view, DiIulio (1987:33) suggests that much of the "blame" for prison violence has been placed on positions offered by prison sociologists. In fact, and quite suprisingly, many correctional administrators equally support the sociological explanations of prison violence. Why? It seems easier to blame other causes of the problem rather than examining one's own shortcomings as a manager. DiIulio states:

> The popularity of sociological theories of prison violence among correctional practitioners, however, may be less suprising than it seems. Prison managers can hide behind the 'hidden causes' to deflect blame for rapes, assaults, murders, riots that might otherwise be credited to their own managerial shortcomings.

Moreover, contrary to the claims of prison sociology, the best method to run a prison and to control violent episodes is to have tight formal controls within the hands of prison officials. This institutional response to prison violence seeks a centralization of authority among those who have been delegated to manage the prison—prison officials, not prisoners. As a result, prison violence is best handled by those who have the greatest formal authority within the prison structure.

What does this mean with respect to prison structure? Some may think the institutional view supports a highly militarized system of organization to reduce prison violence. Yet, DiIulio and other writers, such as Useem and Kimball (1989:227), support much more than the regimen offered by a military structure. In their view, sound prison administration requires, in addition to tight formal controls, adequate programming, work, cell space, and other necessities that make the prison liveable and reasonable to both correctional officers and inmates. Most importantly, they present evidence from both the Attica riot and the Santa Fe riot that lapses in physical security were instrumental in the development and escalation of the disturbances.

Some may question whether correctional systems can actually provide all of these necessities given the financial crunch and serious overcrowding problems faced by them. In effect, critics suggest that much of what the institutional response method supports can only be given superficially, and once instituted, the fear is that lacking adequate resources and space, prisons will become nothing more than repressive holding centers for prisoners. Most importantly, they will actually foster greater violence among prisoners because of unsatisfactory conditions. Critics present some strong evidence of how prison populations are swelling with no relief in sight, and they are not certain how the institutional response method will be able to address this issue so as to reduce and manage prison violence. These critics are of the view that the future does not bode well for a reduction in prison violence if the institutional response is adopted.

Environmental-Change Approach

Unlike the institutional response method to reducing prison violence, the environmental-change approach seeks to modify the prison environment in such a way that the likelihood of prison violence is reduced. This approach grew out of the work of Toch (1977), Bowker, (1980), Johnson, (1987) and others who suggested that much of the violence in prison could be effectively managed through the identification of specific structural and climatic features that support and foster violence. By identifying these qualities of the institutional environment, policy prescriptions could be generated to reduce the prevalence of violence in the prison setting.

Toch (1977:16) has identified a number of dimensions in the prison environment that relate to the needs of prisoners. One of those needs refers to personal safety. Safety is critical in a prison where the threat of violence is imminent. Many inmates take defensive postures because of the fear of attack by others. In the words of Toch, responding to this need, along with other needs, requires one to understand the "ecology of survival" in correctional institutions.

What is most notable about this view on survival in prison is that prisoners soon realize that "doing time" alone is extremely frustrating and often stressful on a day-to-day basis. As a result, many inmates enter into "niches." These niches serve the purpose of making prisoner adjustment easier and allow some comfort in a world which is usually very depressing and oftentimes stupefying to the prisoner.

Niche development and association becomes a critical element of the inmate social system. The niche allows the inmate to come to terms with his incarceration in his own way (Johnson, 1987:103). By studying and identifying those characteristics in the prison setting that foster certain types of niches, prison officials should be able to understand more thoroughly the nature of prison violence and how prisoners respond to it. This type of information would be invaluable to correctional managers.

Through studies that have examined niche development and the attendant structural characteristics of the prison, Toch and his students have been able to provide correctional administrators with some valuable information on the nature and frequency of prison violence, along with the adaptations of prisoners to this violence. Accordingly, Toch (1985:43-45) has suggested that the following program implications can be helpful in managing prison violence.

First and foremost, there must be a recognition of violence "hot spots" and "low-violence subenvironments." Respectively, these are actually places in the prison where violence either recurs with regularity, or places where violent acts are rare. Data on the location and frequency of violent acts can be easily generated and useful in identifying these areas in the prison. Second, a formal program must be developed that helps both inmates and staff in high-violence areas to address their own violence problem. Interviews with both inmates and staff can be used to develop concrete programs of action against violent encounters. Third, support systems for victims and potential victims of violence would be useful in reducing violent episodes in the prison. This requires active programming on the part of prison administrators so that violent behavior is replaced by more positive outlets and activities. Fourth, Toch suggests "crisis intervention teams" be deployed while violent acts are still "hot." These teams would have the objective of dealing with violent participants and seeing that no residual animosity remains that may erupt at a later time. Finally, the information on violence needs to be assembled in a fashion that is useful for staff training and "inmate indoctrination." Under this approach the information is used in such a fashion to respond to the climatic features that condone and support violence. The result of such training is to identify how these climate features can be minimized in such a way as to effectively manage violence.

In addition, others like Bowker (1982) recommend that more specific structural "interventions" be instituted within the prison to reduce and manage violence. Accordingly, Bowker recommends 13 interventions that could possibly reduce prison victimization and violence:

1. victimization data systems
2. minor structural and utilization changes
3. the correction ombudsman
4. classification by victimization potential
5. increased security
6. facilitating visiting
7. conjugal visits
8. normalizing prison industries
9. more therapeutic roles for correctional officers
10. increased staffing
11. co-corrections
12. unit management
13. lower incarceration rates

Space does not allow for a full examination of all 13 of these interventions. However, there are a few that are the most notable and deserve our attention here.

First, Bowker (1982:73) suggests that data on who the aggressive and most violent prisoners are would be particularly useful to correctional managers. In short, we need a case management system that allows us to devote resources and manpower in areas of prisons or in prisons in an entire correctional system in which victimization is a serious problem. Second, an adequate classification system whereby inmates are scored for their "victimization potential" is needed in the prison. In this way, data can be used to identify those who would be the most likely victims of aggressive assaults. Third, an increase in the types of economic opportunities needs to be enhanced within the prison. At present, because of the lack of legitimate opportunity available to most prisoners, victimization among them is high. In the next chapter, we will discuss how illegitimate contraband systems are very powerful in prison. Part of this is due to the weak legitimate sector of the prisoner economy. By providing more work for prisoners, one can possibly reduce vicitimization.

Finally, a redefinition and restructuring of the correctional officer role is needed to reduce prison violence. The typical correctional officer is stuck in a custodial role in which his or her possibilities of enhancing the developmental process for inmates is minimal. By providing correctional officers with the incentives and requisite training in "therapeutic service delivery," much of the violence in prison could be reduced. More importantly, this would allow the officer to be more than just a "screw," "hack," or "turnkey." Within this type of role, the correctional officer's job is both enlarged and enriched.

Societal-Cultural Model

The final approach to reducing prison violence is premised on the role of societal structure and culture. It reaches beyond the prison to solve the problem of violence, and as such, many might believe it to be unrealistic in its expectations. Under this approach to solving prison violence, an initial attempt is made to understand violence as the product of societal and cultural values deeply ingrained in the American ethos.

This model of prison violence argues that its roots lie in the native communities of the prisoners. Men who are violent on the outside continue to be violent once incarcerated. This is somewhat consistent with the belief held by the institutional response model of violence discussed earlier, yet it differs as to the most effective ways to curb and control violence. While the institutional response approach stresses administrative controls to reduce prison violence, the societal-cultural model argues for greater awareness of prison violence as a mirror image of societal violence. In effect, prison violence is never going to be reduced unless we work to reduce violence in our communities and examine the cultural values that support it.

Lockwood (1980:149-150), for example, argues that prison sexual violence will never be significantly reduced unless we eliminate "the violent subculture of severe poverty" from which many prisoners come. But, what are the possibilities of such a radical change occurring? This, as a realistic alternative to reducing prison violence, is quite slim. Nevertheless, without some type of effort to explore the connection between societal violence and prison violence, we are left spinning our wheels on what is to be done to address the problem. As Lockwood (1980:150) suggests, prison violence may be something we will have to tolerate, and the best we can do is to try to manage it.

But how do we target prison violence and make it more manageable? Lockwood (1980:150-154) has presented a program in New York that has trained many prisoners in nonviolence. This program, known as Alternatives to Violence (AVP), is designed to instill in the participant that nonviolent methods are the most effective when dealing with others. By teaching conflict resolution techniques, the program is able to instill in prisoners the correct methods of dealing with everyday situations. What are the basic themes of the AVP program?

There are four basic themes to the program. First, the prisoner is taught the importance of communication skills, such as listening, speaking, and observation. Through increased communication skills, it is hoped that the prisoner will be able to appreciate the value of interacting with others in an effective manner. Second, the idea of cooperation and community building is stressed in the AVP program. Here, the prisoner is taught to develop and become part of a trusting and supportive atmosphere. Third, the AVP program helps the prisoner to feel good about himself and others. Only by feeling good about oneself can one possibly feel good about others. Finally, and probably the most important, the prisoner explores the many creative solutions that are possible in a wide variety of situations. Through a series of exercises, the prisoner is taught how to solve problems and interact in such a way that nonviolence is stressed.

Lockwood (1980:153) does admit, however, that we may be asking a bit too much from the AVP program when the prisoner is asked to respond nonviolently in an environment that has many violent values present. Asking prisoners to go through a transformation of values in a culture, both prison and societal, which has reinforced violence, and in many cases has shown that violent methods do work, may be very difficult for most prisoners to accept. As asked earlier, however, "What are the other options?" Put simply, we have very few or none. Only through attitude change on the part of society with respect to the use of violence will we see its level decrease. At that point, we would expect as a corollary a reduction in prison violence.

As we can see, the methods to reduce prison violence are many and varied. Each has its role in reducing the prevalence of prison violence. Only through experience and experimentation will we be able to see which methods prove to be the most effective. It is possible that a combination of the approaches discussed above would serve as a foundation for reducing and managing prison violence. Time will tell. Never before has this information been so badly needed. With the astronomical growth in the prison populations of this country, correctional administrators are going to be hard pressed to develop strategies to manage prison violence. What does the future hold with respect to prison violence and the future of imprisonment? It is this question that the final section of this chapter will address.

Prison Violence and the Future of Imprisonment

Violence has always been part of the prison experience. Today, however, many have attempted to look into the future to see what lies in store for correctional administrators. In the view of many, prison populations and the associated prison violence will in all likelihood get worse before it gets better. Why? There are many possible reasons and explanations, yet it seems that much of what the future holds can be tied to one critical issue facing correctional administrators and policymakers—overcrowding. No other issue has forced correctional administrators into thinking about creative ways in which to deal with prison populations.

With the advent of modern correctional techniques, such as electronic monitoring and home detention programs, part of the swell of correctional populations is becoming more manageable. Yet it would be a mistake to assume that these programs will seriously address the prison overcrowding problem. In fact, some researchers have suggested that these new techniques will not reduce the size of prison populations, but instead, will "widen [the] net of social control" that the state has over its citizenry. Time will tell if this statement is borne out by evidence.

What we do know is that prison populations have grown considerably and are expected to continue to grow well into the 1990s. What is this growth going to be like and what possible effect will it have on prison violence? What is the population of offenders going to be like? Will they be more serious offenders serving longer sentences? At present, we can only speculate on answers to these questions. Even our speculations, however, paint a rather bleak picture.

The Changing Nature of Prison Populations and Violence

The nature of prison violence is such that accurately estimating its frequency is a very difficult task. Prison researchers experience a number of problems in trying to gauge the prevalence of violence in prison. Similar to the problems of measurement associated with crime in the free world, official prison statistics often underestimate the frequency of prison violence. Hewitt, Poole, and Regoli (1984), for example, found in their research in the federal prison system that underreporting of prison infractions was a notable problem.

While the 391 inmates surveyed reported 2,265 infractions in a three-month period, and correctional officers reported 1,879 infractions for the same time period, only *66 reports* were filed with the central administration!

Moreover, the researchers did not find that the degree of reporting had anything to do with the seriousness of the offense. Regardless of offense, the reality is that official measures of prison infractions, as one measure of prison violence, are underreported. We would probably expect this phenomenon to occur given that they are offenses, often difficult to detect, and their reporting is left up to the discretion of the correctional officer.

Nothwithstanding these problems in reporting, however, we are still able to get a handle on the extent of prison violence through close monitoring systems. In many states, systematic information on prison violence is kept with an eye for unusual trends over time. Zausner (1985) reports that in 1984 the New York Department of Corrections experienced 3,812 incidents involving close to 6,000 inmates. Most notable was the fact that the number of serious incidents had increased over the previous year. In addition, Zausner (1985:1) reports that there has been a steady increase in incidents over the 1982-1984 period.

Of particular importance to correctional administrators is the location of the violence and who is getting assaulted. The most common location for an assault was in the cellblock (48%), with the prison yard being second (almost 8%) (Zausner, 1985:8). Concerning the type of assault, Zausner found that inmate assaults on staff were the most common (20%) and inmate-on-inmate assaults were the second most common. Finally, Zausner reports that a vast majority (75%) of these assaults occurred in maximum security prisons in the state system.

While some may argue that these data are idiosyncratic of one state system, one that is very large, the reality is that some key issues are noteworthy about prison violence. First, similar to crime in society, we are not made aware of most prison violence. This means that official measures of prison violence are terribly inaccurate. What makes this so shocking is the fact that there are many prisoners who are assaulted, some very seriously, yet these incidents are not brought to the attention of correctional officials. For prison violence to be curbed and managed, this situation must change. Incentives for reporting and documenting prison violence have to be instituted so that prisoners feel compelled to report the violence. Additionally, correctional staff need to be more sensitive to prison violence and take steps to recognize its occurrence and enforce existing polices against it. Too often, correctional staff are insensitive to the problem, which, in effect, tacitly reinforces its presence.

Second, most prison violence seems to be isolated to specific areas of the prison. Knowing this, correctional managers need to highlight these areas for increased security and surveillance. By instituting more thorough, security-conscious measures in the prison, much prison violence can be managed. Finally, there is an overrepresentation of prison violence in maximum security prisons. The very nature of maximum security institutions, with their understaffing and antiquated structures, opens the door for prison violence to flourish. The nature of the prison structure, therefore, may be as critical as the nature of the prison population when examining prison violence.

It is for this reason that many correctional reformers and professional prison groups have argued that new correctional facilities be built with maximum capacity at 600 inmates. The monolithic prison structures of the past are conducive to violence and are ultimately unmanageable. Couple outdated structures with the massive overcrowding experienced in today's prisons and it is clear that solutions to the prison violence problem will not be generated overnight. What does the future hold with respect to incarceration and prison violence? We can only speculate. In the final two sections of the chapter, we will offer some ideas about the trends of incarceration and prison violence and whether prison violence can ever be effectively managed.

Future Trends of Incarceration and Prison Violence

The future incarceration trends in America indicate an upward movement. Already many jurisdictions throughout the country, along with the federal government, are in a massive prison-building frenzy. Take, for example, the Federal Bureau of Prisons (FBP). It is estimated that the FBP will grow well into the 1990s and require almost 100,000 cells by the end of the century. At present, the FBP holds a little over 50,000 prisoners. With growth of almost 100% expected over the next 10 years, dealing with prison violence is going to be extremely problematic.

Who are these prisoners going to be? For what offenses will they be incarcerated? Recent data from the Bureau of Justice Statistics (1989) indicate that a number (over 40%) of offenders coming into the FBP will be for drug offenses, either as dealers or users. Is there something about this population that is particularly noteworthy in relation to prison violence? The answer is yes. Contemporary research has identified drug usage among offenders as predictive of violence in prison settings.

According to Flanagan (1983), the group of prisoners with the highest rate of disciplinary infractions are young, nonhomicidal prisoners with drug problems. Conversely, the group with the lowest rate of infractions is older, homicidal offenders who have no drug problems. His research, based on a representative sample of prisoners released from a northeastern state between 1973 and 1976, serves as an interesting foundation from which we can begin to understand the correlates of prison violence. Given the fact that both the FBP and the state systems are incarcerating more people on drug offenses, and that many of these offenders have drug problems, the future with respect to prison violence is a bleak one.

If one were to select the worst possible group of offenders to incarcerate in relation to correlates of prison violence, drug offenders top the list. As such, it would be reasonable to expect that these young drug offenders will pose many problems for prison officials. One of the most serious of these problems is prison violence. From these trends and the existing data, it seems that prison violence may be on the upswing well into the 1990s.

Not only do we plan to incarcerate drug offenders, but most importantly, we plan to incarcerate *more* of them. In effect, more people will be going to prison. This statement is borne out by projections made by the American Correctional Association (ACA). The ACA (1990) projects that by the year 1993 the population of prisoners will have grown from its present level of 650,000 prisoners to an all-time high of 771,000 prisoners. In addition, the rate of incarceration will have jumped from roughly 258 people per 100,000 citizens to a little over 300 people per 100,000 citizens. Beginning with a rate of 71 per 100,000 in 1910 to the projected rate of 300 per 100,000 in the year 1993 indicates an alarming increase in the percentage of the population that is incarcerated.

These kinds of figures stagger the mind and show how overcrowding may be part of the American correctional scene for many years to come. In relation to prison violence, it is reasonable to assume, again, that the picture being painted is not a pleasant one. With overcrowded prisons and fiscal constraints being imposed on departments of corrections throughout the country, the hope for reducing prison violence seems quite dim. Yet the overcrowding problem is not insurmountable. While some states are attempting to build themselves out of the problem, others are relying on other alternatives to imprisonment.

Such alternatives as electronic monitoring and home detention have been proposed as ways to deal with the overcrowding problem. Many states have instituted these programs, and it is accurate to say that these programs are now considered part of the correctional repertoire. Whether or not these programs will reduce overcrowding or widen the net of social control over citizens remains uncertain to date. What is known is that overcrowded prisons usually translate into violence of some sort.

We do not want to propose a clear link between overcrowding and prison violence, nor do we want the student to infer causality between overcrowding and prison violence, but we would be remiss if we did not consider how prison violence has a *source* in overcrowding. By this we mean that there is some type of connection between overcrowding and prison violence. The nature of that connection is not clear. After reviewing the evidence presented earlier on overcrowding and prison violence, we think it is prudent to be working toward solutions to the prison violence problem, on the one hand, while examining what the future holds with respect to prison violence on the other hand. Given this position, we know that prison violence is a problem today, yet we also speculate that it may get worse rather than better in the immediate future.

Will Prison Violence Ever End?

Given our inglorious history with respect to prison violence, it would seem naïve to suggest that prison violence will just go away. More reasonably, it seems that the best we can do is to try to manage it; this is a theme we have mentioned a number of times throughout the chapter. By instituting some of the ideas generated by the research into actual policy prescriptions, we feel that prison violence can be reduced and managed. We must, however, not expect any alternatives to reduce our problem overnight. Like every complex problem, much work and experimentation will have to be done before concrete and effective solutions can be proposed.

The immediate future is our present concern. With prison populations skyrocketing, the ever present danger of violence in our nation's prisons is imminent. We hope that it does not take another riot or tragedy like those at Attica and Santa Fe to prompt closer scrutiny of the country's prisons and the level of violence found within them. The current situation is unacceptable. No one, including the public, politicians, corrections officials, and prisoners, wants to have violent prisons. Only through some type of national resolve to control violence, both in society and prisons, will we ever see some type of measurable decrease in its frequency. Not to try to find a resolution is to explicitly condone an activity in which there are too many losers and no winners.

Summary

The purpose of this chapter was to explore prison violence. We found that violence in our prisons has a sordid past. Our examination of prison riots showed that this is the worst form of prison violence. By examining the tragedies at both the Attica prison in New York and the Santa Fe penitentiary in New Mexico, we learned how prison riots represent underlying themes of violence, whether they be instrumental or expressive in nature. In addition, we explored the causes of prison violence.

Our review indicated that prison violence cannot be traced to a singular cause, that each cause examined—the violent inmate, the social climate of violence, and the relationship between prison overcrowding and prison violence—explains part of the bigger picture on prison violence. Moreover, the methods used to reduce prison violence are equally complex. Whether one is an advocate of the institutional response, the environmental-change approach, or the societal-cultural model, prison violence is a difficult issue to confront and manage for correctional administrators.

Finally, we concluded the chapter with the future of prison violence and imprisonment in America. It seems that prison violence will continue to flourish in our nation's prisons as long as we send more people to prison than we can accommodate. The picture of the 1990's prison is disconcerting. With fewer cells available and more people going to prison for longer periods of time, prison violence may increase in the coming years. Our speculation was that prison violence would never be significantly reduced and managed until we develop the fortitude to address the problem, both in society and in the prisons.

Empty Bars:
Violence and the Crisis of Meaning in the Prison

Violence and Meaning in the Prison

A special consequence of meaninglessness may be found in the case of prison violence. A close analysis of many cases of prison violence may be related to the gang phenomenon of loss of purpose we have described.

Gang violence is on the increase in virtually every large prison and may be interpreted as an effort to create a meaningful community in an anomic prison environment. As Toch (1977) points out, one of the most important functions served by therapeutic communities or programs in prison is to provide social cohesion and support for inmates. In the absence of organized efforts at community, ersatz groups such as the prison gang emerge. Faced with other prison gangs in the context of the prison, the result is an almost relentless cycle of violence and vengeance.

Another type of violence results from prison "horseplay," almost always because of efforts by adolescents to combat the hopeless boredom of the prison. A dorm wrestling match may literally be the major diversion of the day for many inmates. The intensity of this type of horseplay—sometimes resulting in injury on hard concrete floors—is related both to the absence of any other channels to vent energy and the absence of immediate privileges (such as a good educational or rehabilitative program) which might be lost through the result of such activity.

Baiting by guards—at times resulting in altercations (at times physical)—might be seen as the result of the meaninglessness of the prison experience. Prison guards, themselves without role or purpose, will at times effectively and intentionally seek to frustrate or irritate a particular inmate—at times simply because there is no other realistic mode of relating and also because the prison guard is almost as bored as the inmate.

Often "tickets" will be delivered in the most humiliating fashion or inmates will be left waiting for many minutes simply because the staff member is bored and wants to see the inmates "react."

In maximum security sections (e.g., administrative segregation), one often sees almost pathetic efforts to define meaning in a context devoid of common social value. In one prison an inmate serving a 99-year sentence for multiple murder would every day throw his excrement at the guards, who, in turn, would mace him or throw it back. When this observer once asked the inmate why he did this, he replied quietly: "Hell, there ain't nothing else in here to do."

Often suicidal behavior has an element of socially intelligible meaning to it in terms of the anomie of the prison of 1983. In one prison, an inmate swallowed two razor blades, explaining to the author and a physician that he "thought it was a way to get out of the prison for awhile."

This type of violence is far from atypical. A cycle exists in many prisons where the warehouse prison creates frustrations which Toch (1977) and Sykes (1956) suggest creates psychological deprivations, fears, and frustrations which make violence more likely. Fearing assault, inmates group in protective dyads, friends' "homes' bands," and gangs. Beginning as defensive groups, these groups often eventually initiate violent attacks against others. A recent Ph.D. thesis by Abdul Mu'Min (1981) suggests that such collective groups are most common among inmates who fail to involve themselves among other task, religious, or educational groups in the prison.

Violence in the prison, of course, becomes an obstacle to the discovery of meaning, as well as a result of the anomic reality of the prison. Abraham Maslow, for example, suggests that when safety is a personal reality for a human being, higher order psychological functioning is impossible. Concerned with safety (rape, beatings, or killings), long-term problem solving, life planning, or program development become improbable or impossible. Thus, violence as it becomes an institutionalized reality of prison life hinders the type of conscious evolution of purpose which would make life in prison livable, if not productive.

Hope and Alternatives

What is the hope for the prison? What new metaphor might emerge to restore some useful social meaning to the prison—its inmates and staff members? The history of corrections is the history of social metaphors of the prison emerging and asserting themselves. (Metaphor is used as a general concept; the specific cases are posed as similes.)

Prison as Monastery

The creation of the American prison in Pennsylvania (The Walnut Street Jail) presented a metaphor of the prison as monastery. As the monk retreated from the world into the private experience of prayer and silence, so, too, the first prison "rehabilitation program" assumed a retreat from the world in an antinomian Quaker search for redemption and the return of grade. In this sense, the first metaphor of the prison was that of penitence set in the context of the monastery.

Prison as Workshop

The congregate work prison (Auburn prison model) assumed a notion of the prison as workshop. As portrayed in Ignatieff's *Just Measure of Pain* (1979), the metaphor of the congregate prison approached the reality of the cottage and workshop industry of the era. The regulation of work and discipline used to enforce work approached in many respects the types of work conditions "free labor" experienced in the mid-nineteenth century nonmechanized workshop—

hence the metaphor of prison as workshop.

Prison as Schoolhouse

During the 1850s clergy began visiting the prison in a systematic manner, with the goal of teaching inmates to read and discuss the Bible. By the end of the century, some form of school was common in most prisons. During the past five years, the prison as school metaphor has been revived with the Alaskan University Within Walls program and the Canadian University of Victoria prison education program. Two distinct versions of the prison as schoolhouse exist. There is the metaphor of prison as liberal arts academy with a full curriculum in philosophy, literature, and often the social sciences. A vocational/technical version of the schoolhouse exists—with the well-known Chino (California) Diving Program as an example. What unifies the metaphor is the notion that the goal of the prison should be to educate the inmate in either liberal arts perspectives or vocational skills.

Prison as Hospital

The dominant metaphor of the prison reform era of the 1950s/1960s was the medical model version of prison as "hospital." As Adolphson, a 1950s reformer reasoned, the inmate should be treated much as one who has a physical disease. If we treat a man with infected adenoids by placing him in a hospital, he reasons, so, too, we should treat a person with a criminal disease by placing him in a hospital for criminals—the treatment prison. Ideas such as differential treatment, case management, prescriptions, etc.—common in this reform era—all in effect derive from the metaphor of prison as hospital with treatment being administered for specific criminal problems and release being determined by the degree of the inmates "cure."

Prison as Commune

Another metaphor exists in the gemeinschaft image of the prison commune. In Maxwell Jones' (1953) therapeutic community and perhaps in

Joseph Hickey's and the author's *Toward a Just Correctional System* (1980), there is the notion that the prison should reflect many of the communal values found in the nineteenth century communes. Inmates are expected to feel a sense of bond with one another and make sacrifices for the group; and there is an attempt to create a community within the prison itself which will have greater harmony, communal spirit, and order than the outside society. This metaphor also may be found exemplified in many drug programs which existed in prisons, at least through the 1970s, such as Synanon and Daytop.

Prison as Polis

Reformers Thomas Mott Osborne (1916) and W.E. George (1904) conceived of the prison as a democratic state. In the Osborne Mutual Welfare League (see *Prison Journal*, Winter 1977), inmates constituted a republic with 56 representatives elected from the inmate population-at-large. In the George Junior republic, a minisociety was created to mirror the major legal institutions of the larger society. Murton (1975) and others have recently attempted to reimplement this civic metaphor of the prison finding, as did Osborne, that such efforts, perhaps hopelessly, conflicted with the bureaucracy of the prison and correctional system.

Prison as Enterprise

It is perhaps the sign of the times (i.e., the Ronald Reagan era) that the newest metaphor of the prison and the one most "in vogue" is that the prison should become a capitalist enterprise. Labeled "free venture" programs, this metaphor assumes that the inmate should learn capitalist values by participating in entrepreneurial business ventures housed in the prison. The key assumptions include the notion that the inmate should "pay his way" in the prison and that participation in such programs (which are "seeded" by outside capital sources) will teach inmates capitalistic entrepreneurial work values.

The Evolution of a New Metaphor for the Prison

The question which should be asked is, of course: what metaphor might guide the prison during the coming decade? It might further be asked: what process needs to be undertaken if an alternative to the warehouse is to be found?

An answer to the first question requires a sense of correctional reform revolutions in the past—and, perhaps, a bit of clairvoyance. As Weber (1948) has suggested, most organizational changes begin with a charismatic vision of an alternative mode of operation. Maconochie, Osborne, and Jones, for example, share in common a passionate commitment to what might be called "correctional" prophecy or the ability to move from "what exists" in prisons to the "what could be." What is needed to revive corrections at this juncture is a new correctional vision—an idea with which to restructure the terrible monstrosity of an undifferentiated warehouse, which we have allowed to dominate our correctional agencies.

As to the content of the next correctional revolution, it will certainly mirror larger political and cultural realities. Much as Alexander/Maconochie reflected the spirit of the European revolution of 1848, the democratic prison reform movement of Osborne (1916) was rooted in American progressivism, and the prison therapy movement was contexted by the analytic "couch culture" of the 1960s, so, too, the next correctional revolution will be grounded in the politics and culture of the larger polity.

In the short term, the pragmatism, austerity, realism, and apoliticism of the day will surely be reflected in any new correctional metaphor which emerges. Viewed from this perspective, the prison metaphor of the year 1990 will probably be politically palatable, inexpensive, and provide clear and immediate benefits to the inmates.

Less important, however, than the specific metaphor which will evolve is the restoration of creative thinking, vision, and imagination in corrections. Critical, I suspect, will be the infusion of new personalities into corrections—the present leadership in the field appears to be both morally and intellectually bankrupt. The specific malaise of corrections—violence, overcrowding, boredom, etc.—is inherently related to the fact that in words of a friend of mine (a clergyman and former member of a state parole board), "there is not an honest principle (or fact or number) in the whole field." Unless a new principle and vision comes into being, the prisons will become worse and the people they house will emerge damaged and embittered from their incarceration. The present mentality of "keep the lid on" will reap a horrendous cost to society both in terms of violence within the prison and from those creatures who will emerge without purpose and goals from confinement. The price of almost any rehabilitation program will appear to be a bargain compared with the costs of controlling the graduates from the 400,000-person human "warehouse" system we have created. A true "cost" model is needed to understand the price of keeping people in human suspension for endless periods of time.

The alternative to this vision of the future is obvious. Only by creating an alternative to drift can the present inertia be reversed. Society must have the courage to admit it has failed and to reinvent the future. From this perspective, the "first client" of corrections must be corrections itself. Much as the criminal who drifts into crime, and the criminal justice system, corrections itself has sleepwalked itself into its present plight. It must reawaken if it is to survive.

Any change given this perspective begins with a serious self-analysis by the corrections profession and also requires what Weber (1948) called a sense of charisma on the part of the correctional reformer. In many ways corrections in its present state is a prime candidate for the emergence of a new charismatic vision to guide it (hopefully, sensibly) over the next decades. My best guess, of course, is that this vision will be a quiet, stoic one, but hopefully a vision which weighs such considerations as the responsible balance of risk to citizens with the cost (both financial and human) incurred by the maintenance of the prison system. Critical in the emergence of this charismatic vision are effective educational and vocational models which will restore a sense of dignity and purpose to both correctional staffs and inmates.

The biggest obstacle to any reemergence of a new metaphor of the prison is corrections' poor self-image. In this sense, corrections' image of itself is much like its image of the prisoner. Much as the corrections professional of 1983 does not believe the inmate can change, so, too, it does not believe it, as an institution, can change. Once the prison believes it can create itself, perhaps it will have the faith that it can reform the inmate.

Source: Peter Scharf (1985). "Empty Bars: Violence and the Crisis of Meaning in the Prison." In Michael C. Braswell, Steven D. Dillingham and Reid H. Montgomery, Jr. (eds.) *Prison Violence in America*. Cincinnati, OH: Anderson Publishing Co.

Key Terms and Concepts

Attica riot	Santa Fe tragedy
contextual factors	social climate of violence
environmental-change approach	societal-cultural model
expressive prison violence	structural interventions
institutional response	violent inmate
instrumental prison violence	

References

Abbott, J. (1991). *In the Belly of the Beast: Letters from Prison.* New York, NY: Vintage Books/Random House.

American Correctional Association (1990). "Prisoners in 1990." Laurel, MD: American Correctional Association.

Bowker, L. (1980). *Prison Victimization.* New York, NY: Elsevier Books.

Bowker, L. (1982). "Victimizers and Victims in American Correctional Institutions." In R. Johnson and H. Toch (eds.) *The Pains of Imprisonment.* Beverly Hills, CA: Sage Publications.

Bowker, L. (1985). "An Essay on Prison Violence." In M. Braswell, S. Dillingham and R. Montgomery, Jr. (eds.) *Prison Violence in America.* Cincinnati, OH: Anderson Publishing Co.

Bureau of Justice Statistics (1989). "Federal Criminal Cases, 1980-1987." Washington, DC: U.S. Department of Justice.

DiIulio, J. (1987). *Governing Prisons: A Comparative Study of Correctional Management.* New York, NY: The Free Press.

Dillingham, S.D. and R. Montgomery, Jr. (1985). "Prison Riots: A Corrections' Nightmare Since 1774." In M. Braswell, S. Dillingham and R. Montgomery, Jr. (eds.) *Prison Violence in America.* Cincinnati, OH: Anderson Publishing Co.

Farrington, D. and C. Nuttall (1985). "Prison Size, Overcrowding, Prison Violence, and Recidivism." In M. Braswell, S. Dillingham and R. Montgomery, Jr. (eds.) *Prison Violence in America.* Cincinnati, OH: Anderson Publishing Co.

Flanagan, T. (1983). "Correlates of Institutional Misconduct Among State Prisoners." *Criminology*, Volume 21, Number 1: 29-39.

Frontline (1988). "Shakedown in Santa Fe." PBS Productions.

Gaes, G. and W. McGuire (1985). "Prison Violence: The Contribution of Crowding and Other Determinants of Prison Assault Rates." *Journal of Research in Crime and Delinquency*, Volume 22, Number 1: 41-65.

Hewitt, J., E. Poole and R. Regoli (1984). "Self-Reported and Observed Rule-Breaking in Prison: A Look at Disciplinary Response." *Justice Quarterly*, Volume 1, Number 3: 435-447.

Irwin, J. (1970). *The Felon.* Englewood Cliffs, NJ: Prentice-Hall.

Johnson, R. (1987). *Hard Time: Understanding and Reforming the Prison.* Monterey, CA: Brooks/Cole Publishing Company.

Lockwood, D. (1980). *Prison Sexual Violence.* New York, NY: Elsevier Books.

Toch, H. (1977). *Living in Prison: The Ecology of Survival.* New York, NY: The Free Press.

Toch, H. (1985). "Social Climate and Prison Violence." In M. Braswell, S. Dillingham and R. Montgomery, Jr. (eds.) *Prison Violence in America.* Cincinnati, OH: Anderson Publishing Co.

Useem, B. and P. Kimball (1989). *States of Siege: U.S. Prison Riots, 1971-1986.* New York, NY: Oxford University Press.

Walker, B., Jr. and T. Gordon (1980). "Health and High Density Confinement in Jails and Prisons." *Federal Probation*, Volume 44, Number 1: 53-58.

Zausner, S. (1985). "Unusual Incident Report 1984 Calendar Year." Albany, NY: New York State Department of Correctional Services.

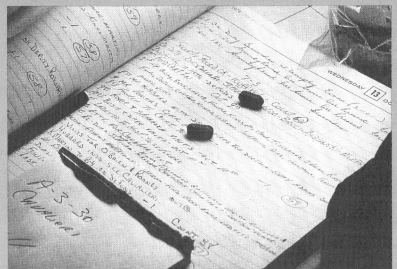

Sex and Contraband in Prison Society

11

After reading this chapter, the student should be able to:

▮ Discuss the nature and extent of prison sex.

▮ Explain the frequency of sexual victimization in prison.

▮ Describe the relationship between prison policy and prison sex.

▮ List types of prison contraband.

▮ Comment on factors that affect contraband flow.

▮ Discuss the value of prison contraband to prison management.

Introduction

While previous chapters have addressed the key elements within the prisoner social system, this chapter will examine two issues that have received considerable attention from researchers interested in the social organization of the prison. These two issues are prison sex and the nature and function of contraband systems in prison settings. The first topic has received much attention through the media and, in addition, much of what people know about prison sex is not predicated on any empirical evidence or research.

Our purpose, therefore, is to review major works done on the issue of sexual relations behind bars. The description will include an analysis of the causes of prison sex, along with a typology of sexual behaviors borrowed from the research literature. In addition, we will examine the frequency of prison sex, including homosexual rape, *yet our intention is to discuss prisoner sexual relations as encompassing much more than homosexual rape.* It is our impression that many people have been led to believe that prison rape is the predominant form of prison sex.

While we will examine prison sexual victimization in this chapter, we will also suggest that this is not a sufficient explanation of prison sexual relations. As a result, we will provide a more exhaustive typological description of the sexual behaviors of men behind bars. Finally, we will attempt to provide some prescriptions for prison policy with respect to prison sex.

Our second topic of this chapter—prison contraband systems—has just recently received the attention of those researchers interested in the social dynamics of the prisoner world. Our purpose here is to describe the types and forms of contraband in prison systems and to examine the factors that facilitate contraband flow in these settings. Moreover, there will be a general discussion of the value of contraband and the role that prison management can play in using the illegal economic systems to their benefit. As with our discussion of prison sex, our intention is to provide a description of how prison contraband systems work in the social world of incarcerated men. Furthermore, since very little is known about these systems and their value to prison administration, our focus will be to help the student to understand contraband functioning in prisons as a necessary component of the prison social system, and as a result, one that must be dealt with appropriately if prisons are to run effectively.

Before we begin our examination of prison sex, we feel it is necessary to justify why we believe these two topics deserve more attention than has been typically given to them by other textbooks on corrections. Our position is based on two reasons.

First, many current textbooks on corrections either fail to address these issues at all or provide nothing more than a perfunctory examination of them. We believe that these two topics have been neglected for too long and that many misconceptions have been created about their role in the workings of prisoner social systems. By providing a separate chapter on these two areas, we are enabling the student to grasp a part of the prisoner world that is substantially different from commonly held perceptions of the prison, as well as one that traditionally has been dominated by myths and misconceptions that have clouded the relevance of these issues to an understanding of the many complexities of the inmate social system.

Second, there has been a greater interest among both practitioners and academic scholars to address these two topics with more vigor and candor over the past 10 years. As a result, there has been a growth in the research literature on these two areas, yet very few textbooks on corrections have incorporated this material into their descriptions of inmate social systems. We felt it was time to provide this material to give the student a more valuable insight into the workings of the prisoner social world. By using this approach, we feel that the student will be more informed about the nature and functioning of the contemporary prison.

Prison Sex

Much of the research literature on prison sex has suggested that sexual behavior behind bars can be explained relative to the two theoretical positions of inmate social system origination discussed in Chapter 8. They are known as the *functional* and *importation* models of inmate socialization. The functional model has its roots in the work of Donald Clemmer (1940) and Gresham Sykes (1958) and emphasizes that sexual behaviors in prison are a function of the deprivations imposed upon prisoners when they are incarcerated. As stated by Sykes (1958:63-84), the denial of normal heterosexual relations in prison engenders homosexual behaviors on the part of prisoners.

In short, homosexual behaviors by inmates are in reaction to the deprivations produced by the prison situation, in which heterosexual avenues of physical expression are not possible.

The importation approach suggests that sexual activities behind bars are largely a reflection of sexual attitudes held on the streets and incorporated into the prison when the offender is incarcerated. The focal point is that prisoners bring into the prison beliefs and attitudes they learned while in the community. Work done by Thomas (1977) suggests that this position is of equal value as the functional approach when explaining the sexual behaviors of prisoners.

More contemporary research supports the position that both theoretical models are useful when explaining the etiology of prison sex. Wooden and Parker (1982), for example, have found that both the functional and importation approaches explain the causes of prison sex. Based on a survey of 200 inmates in a California prison, Wooden and Parker suggest that the deprivation model explains the exploitive and often violent nature of prison sex. In effect, their research has shown that sexual behaviors in prison are reflective of a particular inmate code which stresses dominance of one individual over another, and that coercive sexual behavior on the part of prisoners is rooted in the coercive nature of the prison organization. Exploitation, as a result, is seen in a sexual context and is often expressed through that type of interaction. Additionally, they suggest that the sexual expression of many inmates also includes values and attitudes they bring with them from the city streets and, more importantly, it is distinctive of a particular lower-class ethos. The prison environment only heightens preformed attitudes initially acquired when the offender was not incarcerated. Wooden and Parker (1982:44) state:

> The results of our study demonstrate that both these processes are at work in this prison setting. That is, with regard to sexual behavior in prison there is both forced exploitation (the deprivation model) as well as mutual exploitation (the importation model). Both forms of exploitation involve the use of sex as a means of release....Overriding these patterns in both of these manipulative situations is the convict prison code, shaped by the lower class subculture's emphasis on masculinity and machismo which results in the pattern of extreme dichotomy of sexual scripts.

These sexual scripts provide a typological respresentation of the types of sexual behaviors that can be found in prison. Accordingly, Wooden and

Parker (1982:3) suggest that four sexual scripts existed in the prison community they studied.

The first they referred to as the *kid* or *punk*. This type of sexual script is one in which violence was used to gain sexual satisfaction from the prisoner. In the language of the institution, this type of sexual script is produced when the inmate was "turned out" or forced into a sexual encounter.

Second, according to Wooden and Parker, is the *jocker* or *stud*. This individual has sexual relations with either a known homosexual or a punk. More important, this type of sexual encounter is never viewed as a homosexual act by the jocker. He believes that the sexual act is inherently masculine and "normal" for him, with the recipient being the homosexual. In short, he views sex in prison as an expression of his manhood.

While the jocker or stud does not view himself as a homosexual, the *queen* or *sissy* is without a doubt a homosexual and, in addition, assumes all the effeminate mannerisms of a female and plays the submissive sexual role. It is this type of inmate who is known in the institution as one who is prepared to provide sexual services to inmates, usually for some type of fee or payment. Typically, this type of prisoner can cause many problems in the prison, since there are very few of them and they are sought after by many inmates. It has been documented that the sissy is often the cause of much violence among inmates who compete for his ownership (Stojkovic, 1985).

Finally, the Wooden and Parker typology provides us with a sexual script that is a combination of the aforementioned sexual scripts. This sexual script is known as the *homosexual* or *gay*. These prisoners exhibit diverse sexual scripts while assuming both active and passive roles in their various sexual encounters.

Besides the sexual scripts evidenced in the prison, Wooden and Parker were able to distinguish the types of sexual activity that occurred in the prison. Based on the information provided by 200 respondents, they concluded that all 200 masturbated, with frequency of masturbation varying. Of the sample, 14% reported masturbating once a day; 46% reported masturbating three to five times a week; roughly 30% masturbated one to two times a week; a little over 5% reported masturbating one to three times a month; and only 4% reported masturbating less than once a month.

Concerning prison sex, the researchers found wide disparities *depending upon the stated sexual orientation of the respondents.* Table 11.1 summarizes the sexual behaviors of prisoners by their stated sexual orientation.

Table 11.1
Summary Table

Reported having performed this sexual act	Orientation			Row totals
	Heterosexual	Bisexual	Homosexual	
Prison sex	87 (157) 55.4%	22 100.0%	21 100.0%	130 65.0%
Being orally copulated	69 43.9%	22 100.0%	12 57.1%	103 51.5%
Performing anal penetration	46 29.3%	22 100.0%	9 42.9%	77 38.5%
Performing oral copulation	9 5.7%	13 59.1%	19 90.5%	41 20.5%
Having been anally penetrated	13 8.3%	8 36.4%	20 95.2%	41 20.5%

Source: Wayne S. Wooden and Jay Parker (1982). *Men Behind Bars: Sexual Exploitation in Prison,* pp. 250-251. New York, NY: Plenum Publishing Corporation.

Interestingly, 55% of the professed heterosexuals sampled had some type of prison sex, while 100% of both the stated bisexuals and the stated homosexuals responded that they had some form of prison sex. Of even greater significance were the types of prison sex that occurred. The inmates were asked if they had been orally copulated, performed anal penetration, performed oral copulation, or were anally penetrated. The data show some interesting results when comparing the three types of sexual orientations among the respondents. Of those inmates who stated they were heterosexual in their sexual orientation, well over 43% of the total sample stated they had been orally copulated, over 29% had responded affirmatively to performing anal penetration, with a small percentage (less than 6%) of the total sample performing oral copulation, and roughly 8% of the total sample reporting having been anally penetrated. From this we can say that many of the professed heterosexuals who engaged in sexual encounters were either being orally copulated or performing anal penetration, with very few performing oral copulation or having been anally penetrated. The diversity of sexual services, however, varies when one examines both professed bisexual prisoners and homosexual prisoners.

All 22 bisexual prisoners surveyed by Wooden and Parker admitted to having prison sex; moreover, all were involved in oral copulation and performing anal penetration, with 59% performing oral copulation and over 36% percent having been anally penetrated. From this data, it seems that the bisexual prisoners were performing a variety of sexual acts in the prison setting, with being orally copulated and performing anal penetration the most common and preferred method of sexual interaction. The greatest variety, however, in sexual encounters was exhibited by the professed homosexuals who reported performing all of the sexual acts surveyed by the researchers.

Like the bisexual prisoners, all the homosexuals responded to having prison sex, with performing oral copulation being done by over 90% of the respondents and being anally penetrated reported by over 95% of the homosexual group. Being orally copulated was represented by over 57% of the homosexual group and performing anal penetration was the least common sexual act among the group; a little under 43% of the admitted homosexuals of the sample stated they performed anal penetration. Like the two previous sexual orientations, the homosexual group preferred providing the sexual services as opposed to being serviced themselves. This is borne out by the data in which we see overwhelmingly that performing oral copulation and being anally penetrated are the most common sexual acts practiced by this group. In the words of the researchers, this group would rather "catch" than "pitch."

If we break down the data even further and examine sexual behavior by ethnicity, we find some very interesting results. Table 11.2 portrays the sexual behaviors of professed heterosexual blacks, Caucasians, and Mexican-Americans in the Wooden and Parker research. Interestingly, according to the data, over 80% of the black respondents reported that they engaged in some type of sexual act in prison, while only 38% of white prisoners reported committing a sexual act. For Mexican-American prisoners, over 54% of the prisoners reponded affirmatively as to whether they had some type of prison sex.

With respect to the types of sexual behaviors among the ethnic groups, there are some similarities. Being orally copulated, for example, was the most common sexual behavior expressed by all the ethnic groups, with over 61% of the blacks, 29% of the Caucasians, and 51% of the Mexican-American prisoners stating that they had this sexual service provided to them. Performing anal penetration was the second most common sexual behavior exhibited in the prison. Among black prisoners, over 46% admitted committing this act and a little less than 17% of the Caucasian prisoners admitted performing this same sexual act. The percentage was a bit higher for the Mexi-

can-American prisoners; over 32% of them admitted to performing anal penetration. Performing oral copulation and being anally penetrated were very
low for all three ethnic groups. This makes sense because these prisoners are
those who are professed heterosexuals. Other data provided by Wooden and
Parker suggest that many of the sexual services desired by the heterosexual
population are provided by the bisexual and homosexual prisoners.

Table 11.2
Ethnicity and Patterns of Sexual Behavior of Heterosexuals

Reported having performed this sexual act	Ethnicity			Row totals
	Black (N = 52)	Caucasian (N = 71)	Mexican (N = 31)	
Prison sex*	42 80.8%	27 38.0%	17 54.8%	86 55.8%
Being orally copulated	32 61.5%	21 29.6%	16 51.6%	69 44.8%
Performing anal penetration	24 46.2%	12 16.9%	10 32.3%	46 29.9%
Performing oral copulation	2 3.8%	7 9.9%	0 0%	9 5.7%
Having been anally penetrated	3 5.8%	8 11.3%	1 3.4%	12 7.8%

*Raw chi square = 35.52848 with 10 D.F.; significance = 0.0001.

Source: Wayne S. Wooden and Jay Parker (1982). *Men Behind Bars: Sexual Exploitation in Prison,* p. 251. New York, NY: Plenum Publishing Corporation.

Explanations for why there are different or varying degrees of sexual involvement by the various ethnic groups center largely around the importation
model of inmate socialization. Following this theoretical position, we can offer the following interpretation with respect to the sexual behaviors of men
imprisoned.

First, with respect to black prisoners, a possible explanation is that many
of the sexual attitudes black prisoners bring into prison are reflective of attitudes of black men on the city streets. The researchers suggest that sexual
promiscuity is condoned much more so in the lower-class culture, and as a
result, the sexual scripts evidenced in prison reflect "less possessive attitudes

regarding sexual monogamy and greater acceptance of both selling sex and paying for it (Wooden and Parker, 1982:58).

Second, white inmates are not as involved in prison sex when compared to black inmates; for those who do engage in sexual activity behind bars, an explanation is not as readily available. Wooden and Parker do suggest that many lower-class whites tend to adopt a possessive stance toward the punks or sissies they use to fulfill their sexual desires, yet whether this attitude is brought into the prison or is a function of the environment of the prison is uncertain. It could be that the functional explanation, with its reliance on sexual deprivation as its argument, could be applied to white prisoners, yet that position is speculative at this point in time. More research is required on the sexual behavior of differing ethnic groups in prison before definitive statements can be made.

Finally, Wooden and Parker suggest that the sexual scripts evidenced by Mexican-American prisoners can be explained through the importation model of inmate socialization. Accordingly, it is their belief that the sexual behaviors of Mexican-American prisoners reflect the Catholic influence of the "barrio subculture" from the urban setting. More specifically, this setting promotes the attitude that women can be classified into two distinct groups: prostitutes and "nice girls," with the belief among many Mexican-American men that possession of the woman is central to their role as being a man. Carried over into the prison, this position further suggests that Mexican-American prisoners who are sexually involved with another inmate, in effect, "own" that inmate as property.

Many of the sexual encounters among Mexican-American prisoners are very dominating and controlling. Furthermore, it is prohibitive for a Mexican-American prisoner to "turn out" or assault one of their own ethnic group, because that is the worst possible insult to a prisoner of this ethnic orientation. Again, as with the other two ethnic groups, this interpretation of the causes of prison sex among Mexican-American prisoners requires further investigation before more definitive statements can be made. The problem centers on the paucity of research on this subject matter.

While we have a plethora of research on prison victimization (see Smykla, 1989 for a good review of recent findings on sexual victimization), violence, and rape, there is very little on the *consensual* nature of sexual behaviors in prison. Contemporary research has suggested that prison sex takes many forms, including the development of "quasi-kin relationships" where love letters and attachment among participants are critical elements between them (Propper, 1989). In addition, current research does suggest that the development of homosexual attitudes has its roots in pre-prison experiences, particularly among women prisoners (Leger, 1987). This supports the importation thesis mentioned earlier.

This contemporary research adds substantively to our knowledge about the degrees and types of sexual behaviors exhibited by men and women who are incarcerated. The research informs us of how varied sexual behaviors are in prison and provides us with a more accurate representation of its nature and cause. Nevertheless, all research on prison sex must be cautiously interpreted. The Wooden and Parker study, for example, only surveyed 200 respondents from one state. The sexual behaviors in other prisons throughout the country may vary considerably. The student can understand that given the sensitive nature of the topic, any findings must be understood as having limitations with regard to their generalizability. It is for this reason that researchers have called for more systematic investigations across prisons, comparing men and women's institutions (Propper, 1989:61). Only then will we be able to grasp the degree to which prison sex is prevalent in our nation's prisons.

Prison Sexual Victimization

Sexual victimization in prison has been a topic that many researchers have addressed in the contemporary literature. Much of this research has examined the nature of sexual violence (Bowker, 1982; Parisi, 1982), its form and expression (McGrath, 1982; Nacci and Kane, 1982, 1984; McNamara and Karmen, 1983; Jones and Schmid, 1989; Tewksbury, 1989; and Chonco, 1989), the myths of prison sex (Lockwood, 1985), and methods to reduce the incidence of sexual violence in prison (Lockwood, 1982). One of the most definitive studies done on prison sexual victimization is that of Lockwood's (1980) research conducted over a year's time in the mid-1970s.

In all, he interviewed 107 "targets" of sexual aggression in three prisons in the state of New York. From these interviews, he generated 152 incident descriptions of sexual aggression among the 107 prisoners. Similar to the research on prison sex, this research must be understood as having some limitations. Lockwood's (1980:3) study did not involve the random selection of prisoners to determine the degree of sexual victimization among prisoners. Rather, it focused on targets and relayed their experiences. His research highlighted the fact that sexual victimization is a rare event. This is consistent with research conducted in the federal prison system by Nacci (1982).

According to Nacci (1982:10), only two out of 330 men in his study were compelled to perform an undesired sexual act, while 29% had been propositioned in their institutions. This position suggests that the level of sexual victimization in prison is relatively low, yet Lockwood (1985:89) suggests that the problem of sexual violence in prison actually revolves around the "sexual approaches" exhibited by aggressive prisoners upon other prisoners. It is the measurement of these aggressive behaviors that Lockwood has documented so well in his research. From his research, we can conclude a number of important points about the level of sexual victimization in prison.

Table 11.3 displays the incident characteristics Lockwood found in his study of sexual victimization in three New York state prisons. The table indicates that one-third of the incidents involved either a sexual assault or some other type of violence. The most common form of sexual behavior, however, was of a verbal nature, with propositioning and insulting and threatening language making up over half of the incidents. Again, as stated earlier, actual sexual assault and touching or grabbing are quite rare and make up a small number in the total distribution of incidents.

Table 11.3
Aggressive Behavior in Incidents

Most Severe Behavior in Incident	Number of Incidents in Which Behavior Occurs	Percentage of Total Incidents
Sexual assault	12	8
Other physical violence	39	27
Insulting or threatening language	29	20
Touching or grabbing	11	7
Propositioning only	49	33
Other	8	5
Total	148	100

Source: Daniel Lockwood (1980). *Prison Sexual Violence,* p. 18. New York, NY: Elsevier Books.

Concerning the duration of the incidents, Lockwood indicates that over half of the incidents were single episodes lasting less than two hours; some were only a few minutes long. It must be remembered that very few of the incidents actually involved physical contact between the aggressor and the target victim. As a result, some of the verbal abuse and propositioning, according to Lockwood, lasted up to two days, with the incidents being marked by a number of brief episodes. In fact, Lockwood's data indicates that over one-quarter of the incidents lasted two days or longer in duration, suggesting that the level of sexual victimization must be understood in the context of constant harassment of targets by aggressive and predatory prisoners.

Moreover, the victimization typically occurred within 16 weeks after the target entered the state penal system, and over half of the incidents of sexual aggression took place in the living quarters of the men involved. A small percentage of the incidents also occurred in the institutional schools or prison shops within the direct supervision of staff. This suggests that sexual victimization in prison more often than not occurs in the victim's own surroundings, yet it can occur just about anywhere in the prison setting, adding to an already tense prison situation in which anxiety and distrust are high and fear is commonplace among prisoners. This level of anxiety and fear is especially high among many younger and inexperienced prisoners, because they are the least knowledgeable about the prisoner social world and its norms toward sexual behaviors in general. The typical victim of sexual aggression is the person who is young, white, and of a smaller physical stature in comparison to other prisoners.

This is borne out by the data gathered by Lockwood. His typification of the sexual target included the following: a younger inmate, usually under the age of 21, in half of the cases the victim was white, usually significantly lighter in body weight (on the average, 15 pounds lighter than the aggressor), and with a slender and attractive physical appearance. As described by one aggressor to Lockwood, the physical appearance of the victim is extremely important, and identifiable characteristics are sought after by the aggressively oriented inmate:

> The way he walk. The size of his ass. His facial expressions, his ways and actions. If his face look like a woman, they is going to think he is a woman. The psychological thing about it is that any dude—white or black dude or any Puerto Rican—can come in here looking like a woman. And you say, 'Damn, Man, that man looks like a woman.' He had to be squeeze in a certain institution (1985:32).

If we examine the characteristics of aggressors, we find some interesting differences between them as a group and victims. While the victims and aggressors tend to be younger inmates, the ethnic backgrounds of the aggressors are markedly different when compared to the victims. Lockwood, for example, found that 80% of all aggressors in his sample were black, around 14% were Hispanic, and less than 6% were white.

Of the target victims, 83% were white, 16% were black, and only 2% were Hispanic. This finding suggests that many aggressors, most of whom are black, choose whites, on the whole, as their victims. Why this is the case will be addressed later. Yet, the question becomes, "Are these statistics provided by Lockwood representative of other prison settings?" Research conducted by Wooden and Parker (1982:60) supports Lockwood's findings, along with data gathered in juvenile institutions by other researchers (Bartollas and Sieverdes, 1983). The typical sexual victimization in prison is where the dominant and aggressive prisoner is black and his victim is the young, often frail, white inmate.

Three interpretations have been offered as to why black prisoners victimize white inmates. The first position is that black prisoners sexually victimize white inmates more often because of the perceived repression that the white race has had on the black race since this country has begun. In effect, this position suggests that black prisoners are able to vent their feelings of hostility and anger toward the white race by sexually degrading and victimizing the white inmate while incarcerated. While a plausible interpretation, it is not clear that such an explanation is tenable considering that even black prisoners are victimized by other blacks in the prison setting.

A second interpretation is that the level of *interracial* sexual victimization in prison is actually tied to the level of solidarity among the racial groups. In short, blacks would refuse to sexually victimize other blacks since all are considered part of the same group, sharing similar desires, needs, and expectations. Wooden and Parker (1982:60) make an important distinction, in that black prisoners in the prison they studied would very rarely "turn out" or rape another black inmate, but they would "get down" with an inmate of their own racial orientation if it was agreed upon between both parties. All this aside, there has been no systematic evidence supporting the assertion that sexual victimization of white prisoners by black inmates is motivated from a racial perspective.

A third position suggests that victimization of a sexual nature in prison reflects a larger issue of subcultural violence among many prisoners. Accordingly, Lockwood has suggested that many of the sexual aggressors in prison come from a subculture in which violence is condoned and supported. When one examines the backgrounds of those who are sexually aggressive in prison, the notion of a subcultural link to violence becomes quite apparent. Sexual violence, therefore, becomes inexorably linked to behavioral patterns of violence learned from the city streets and incorporated into the prison setting.

As we suggested earlier in the chapter, the sexual preferences of many inmates may be largely due to the attitudes learned while growing up within a particular cultural setting outside of the prison, and thus lending support to the importation model of prisoner socialization. Couple this subcultural explanation of violence with the individual characteristics of the victims and it is reasonable to see why white prisoners are victimized more often by black inmates.

As suggested by Lockwood, when one is taught that violence is the way to get what you want from someone, and sexual deprivation is high in the prison setting, along with the presence of many young, slight-of-build, white inmates, it is reasonable to assume that sexual victimization is a function of an interplay of all of these factors. The complexity of the sexual victimization issue makes it highly unlikely that probabilistic determinations will be helpful in reducing the level of victimization among many in the target population. Nevertheless, what can be done is to recognize what prison staff and inmates can do together to reduce the *likelihood* of sexual victimization in prison.

Prison Policy and Prison Sex

It should be obvious to the student that sexual relations in prison are commonplace, and that the reasons why these behaviors exist can be tied to both the prison experience and the attitudes inmates bring with them into the institution. As such, theoretical models attempting to explain the etiology of prison sex have been supported by research evidence. In addition, it is equally clear that the problem of sexual victimization in prison is not going to end without some clear and rational policies and procedures to deal with the problem. At present, many writers have suggested a number of alternatives to deal with the prison sexual violence problem, ranging from increasing the number of guards to designing safer institutional environments. This latter approach suggests that prison sexual violence can be reduced by the introduction of more technology to the problem. Even this approach, however, must be considered suspect.

As suggested by Lockwood (1982:141-154), many of the alternatives put forth to reduce prison victimization will not achieve their ends, since the problem may reach outside the prison walls. If it is correct that many of the sexually aggressive people in prison have records of violence or come from what is known as a "subculture of violence," then it is highly suspect whether internal modifications of the prison environment will actually reduce the levels of sexual violence in our prisons. Instead, it would seem more prudent to attempt to teach those who are already violent other methods of coping in the institutional environment. To this end, Lockwood suggests that some programs are effective in accomplishing this goal.

One program described by Lockwood that has shown some potential is the Alternatives to Violence Project (AVP). Since 1975, the program has trained over 400 New York state prisoners on methods to cope with everyday institutional life and to reduce the violent nature of their behavior. Predicated on the principles of communication, cooperation and community building, affirmation, and conflict resolution and problem-solving, this approach has the possibility of reducing sexual victimization in our prisons. Fundamentally, the approach suggests that all types of violence in prison can be reduced if coping mechanisms can be generated by prisoners to deal with their problems.

Contemporary authors have echoed the concerns of their predecessors with respect to effective prison treatment programs. Johnson (1987), for example, has suggested that many of the programs in prisons today fail to alter the violent behaviors of prisoners because they are rooted in a philosophy that attempts to "cure" the prisoner. Such programs have shown to be a dismal failure. Instead, Johnson (1987:171-175) argues quite persuasively that effective change of prisoners' behaviors requires two fundamental principles of operation.

First, that prison programs attempt to teach the inmate how to handle the stress of prison life in a more mature fashion; this means that the structural characteristics of the prison require alteration so that the stress of prison life is more manageable for the prisoner. Second, Johnson mentions that prison programs must provide the prisoner with the ability to handle life's stresses both in prison and when he is released. Both of these principles would seem to be equally applicable to the sexually aggressive prisoners, because many of the violent sexual behaviors in prison represent inadequate coping mechanisms.

In this way, prison programs would serve more of an educative, coping function. Both prison staff and prisoners would be involved in the betterment of the prisoner. In the words of Johnson (1987:174), prison programs would be a "voluntary collaborative training enterprise," in which inmates join with staff to learn how to cope with their institutionalization and the everyday pressures of life. This approach can be applied to the person who sexually victimizes other inmates. We do know that the sexually aggressive prisoner is one who requires help with respect to coping with his life behind bars and the normal pressures that everyone experiences from day-to-day. Ostensibly, the issue which surrounds the prison sexual violence problem in today's prisons is one of making prisons more functional and safe for both the prisoner and the prison staff.

While this will not totally eradicate the sexual violence in our prisons, it may help to reduce the problem so that prisons may be more than places of high stress and potential violence for those who work and reside in them. Of greater significance, however, is that the sexual violence experienced in our prisons must be considered the result, in part, of a violent American culture.

It is impossible to divorce the violent nature of prisons from its roots in the larger American culture. What is required is what Lockwood (1980:153) refers to as the "alteration of our values" on violence in society. In his words, "The problem of prison sexual violence is closely linked to the general problem of sexual aggression in our society: As we progress towards transforming male attitudes towards females, we shall progress toward reducing prison sexual victimization" (1980:154).

While prison sexual violence is a problem within many of our prisons, we would be remiss if we did not reaffirm a point we made earlier in the chapter: prisoner sexual behavior is *not* of a violent nature. As a result, the development of policy in this area must be based on what the empirical evidence has shown about this phenomenon and it must offer the most rational approach to addressing the problem.

Concerning day-to-day sexual encounters among inmates, it is safe to conclude that sexual activity is going to occur and the only reasonable position of correctional staff is that it does not upset the order and stability of the prison. In addition, it is the responsibility of the staff to be continually aware of the possibility of victimization of weaker prisoners by the sexually aggressive inmates. It is, therefore, a rational course of action to attempt to deal with the problems produced by the violent sexual interactions among inmates and to minimize the exploitive nature of these types of encounters. It is here that myths about prison sexual violence need to be clarified and dispelled if policy is going to be effective in dealing with the problem.

Lockwood (1985) has suggested that there are three widely held myths about sexual aggression in prison. The first myth is that sexually aggressive prisoners are more often than not successful in their bids to turn inmate targets into their personal sex slaves. The reality of the situation is quite different, however. According to Lockwood, the most likely occurrence is that an inmate is victimized once. Through either some type of protection by other inmates or the development of a protective lifestyle, the inmate usually is able to protect himself from future assaults.

The second myth mentioned by Lockwood is that the victimized inmate becomes embittered and hostile toward society. Once released, he commits more crime. Lockwood argues that there is no empirical evidence to suggest that this is accurate. While the inmate obviously harbors many ill feelings toward his aggressors and possibly society in general, there is very little to suggest that these feelings are manifested through criminal behaviors once the inmate is released from prison.

Finally, Lockwood states that the crime for which a prisoner is convicted has a very weak relationship with being sexually victimized once incarcerated. Child molesters, for example, have been thought to be more likely candidates of sexual aggression than other types of criminals in the inmate social system. This commonly held myth is not substantiated by any empirical evidence; therefore, its usefulness in predicting the likely victims of sexual aggression in the prison setting is virtually worthless.

While Lockwood has suggested that the only real hope of reducing sexual violence in prison centers around an alteration of values in the general society about violence, others have suggested other novel ideas to deal with the problem. Nacci and Kane (1984:52) have proposed a "target hardening" plan in which inmates are warned about possible mannerisms that attract aggressors in the prison environment. This position suggests that there are attitudes, facial expressions, styles of clothing, and tones of speech that attract the sexually aggressive prisoner to the victim.

While this approach may prove to be workable for some prisoners, it is difficult to believe that its success would be great considering that sexual attractiveness does not seem to be a major factor as to whether an inmate will be assaulted. This approach is definitely worth trying in the prison setting. In addition, Nacci and Kane (1984:51) suggest a more radical approach to dealing with the problem, that being an alteration in institutional policy toward allowing homosexual activity to occur. They argue that many of the sexual relations behind bars are either directly or indirectly condoned by the prison administration. They suggest that prison officials set a different moral tone to control the situation.

While values and attitudes are definitely at the root of the sexual violence problem in our prisons today, it is not clear that a moral uplifting of prisoners on the part of the prison administration is going to significantly address the problem. It is because many of these prisoners have a weak sense of moral development that they are in prison in the first place. While prison officials obviously have the duty to try to instill better moral qualities in prisoners, it is not clear as to how they are going to achieve this objective in the face of more than 200 years of failure. The infusion of morality into our prisons has been a lofty goal, yet we have a very poor understanding of what morality we want to infuse and how we are going to implement it.

Instead of trying to alter the moral character of prisoners, it may be more prudent to propose a plan that encourages them to mature and cope with life. As mentioned in earlier paragraphs, this approach seems to have more promise for many prisoners, and it would behoove institutional administrators to create programming with these goals in mind. We have a long history of what does not work in institutional corrections. This new approach of making prisoners mature and successful coping individuals is more practical and achievable given the structural arrangements of our prisons today. In this way, institutional corrections could potentially do more to decrease sexual violence in prison. In this fashion, doing less is doing more for most prisoners and staff in our institutions.

Hopes of altering inmates' behaviors through various treatment programs have failed miserably and have not made prisons any safer or less violent. A more realistic approach is to teach prisoners how to deal with problems through an interactive model which includes them in the development of an appropriate therapy. By emphasizing a collaborative approach to correctional treatment, there is the potential to significantly reduce the many expressions of violence in our prisons today, including sexual violence.

Prison Contraband Defined
and Forms of Prison Contraband

Prison contraband products and services can be defined as anything that is in the possession or use of the prisoner without the permission of the staff or is defined as illegal by institutional policy. Included in this definition is paper money, illegal drugs, weapons, alcohol, gambling paraphernalia, food, clothing, and other items defined as contraband by the administration of the prison.

The most common forms of contraband are alcohol, marijuana, and homemade knifes, known as "shanks" or "shivs." The prices of such products vary from prison to prison, as does their degree of availability. Current research suggests that the prices of many contraband products are not only varied from prison to prison, but in addition, some prisons are more effective in controlling contraband marketplaces than others (Kalinich, 1986). More importantly, contemporary research on contraband systems in prison suggests that these systems of illegal distribution of goods and services are instrumental to the stability and legitimacy of the prison. Before this position can be explained, it is necessary to examine some of the factors in the institutional setting that facilitate the flow of contraband.

The first question that many students have about illegal goods in the prison environment is how they get into the prison. There are three explanations as to how contraband goods get into prison.

First, and probably the most common explanation, is that visitors smuggle the products into the prison. Many prisons have introduced elaborate methods and procedures to attempt to control contraband flow through increased searches and surveillance of visitors when in the prison. In addition, a number of prisons have listings as large as phone books that prohibit certain people from entering the prison because of their past involvement in contraband smuggling. Cocaine, for example, is a contraband item that is smuggled into the prison by visitors. The most common method by which this is achieved is through a small balloon that is passed from visitor to inmate through a kiss or embrace and then retrieved through the inmate's stool. This, however, does have its limitations. It is common to hear that some inmates have died from swallowing a balloon of cocaine when the balloon ruptured before they could retrieve it.

Second, correctional officers have been known to smuggle contraband goods into the prison. The most common item is some form of narcotic, and the money that can be made by such an activity is often very lucrative. Davidson (1977), for example, has documented how one guard in the San Quentin prison in California made well over $60,000 in one year by smuggling heroin into the prison. While this type of activity occurs occasionally in our prisons today, to suggest that it is that common, or that lucrative, for most correctional officers would be totally erroneous.

Many correctional officers who do enter into this type of arrangement with an inmate or a number of inmates do not make anywhere near this amount of money, yet there are are some who do quite well by involving themselves in the contraband system of prisoners. The most common form of smuggling that occurs among correctional officers is usually small amounts of marijuana. While correctional officers are trained and warned about the dangers and illegalities of contraband smuggling, it is still a widespread activity in many of our prisons today. Besides the economic incentives for getting involved in the contraband system, other structural aspects of the prison make contraband activity on the part of correctional officers almost inevitable. This will be explained more thoroughly later in the chapter.

Finally, contraband items can be brought into a prison setting on the trucks that make major deliveries of food and other goods to the prison. In this situation, certain inmates may get involved with delivery personnel to smuggle goods into the prison for some monetary payment. It is impossible to search all trucks coming into the prison, so it becomes quite easy to bring illegal products into the prison. Occasionally, you hear of situations in which vendors are apprehended and arrested for bringing illegal goods into the prison. This, however, is a very rare event. It is estimated that this method of entry of contraband goods is less common when compared to correctional officer and visitor involvement. Nevertheless, it is a method that is employed by those who are pivotal actors in the contraband market system of the prison.

Factors Facilitating Contraband Flow and their Effects

Kalinich and Stojkovic (1987:4-12) have identified four methods by which contraband flow can be controlled in the prison. The first, and probably the most obvious, is that there can be structural modifications in the prison structure whereby the flow of contraband can be significantly controlled. An increase in the number of security checkpoints or the types of searches done in prison can alter the movement of contraband items in the prison.

Second, there can be a call on the part of the prison administration to "shakedown" prisoners more often to detect contraband items. In most penal institutions, these periodic shakedowns are required. An increase in their frequency or an alteration in the times and places of these searches can produce a change in how contraband goods and services are delivered.

A third method of controlling the contraband flow of the prison is the patrolling and level of interaction between inmates and correctional officers. Much of the contraband activity that occurs in prisons today is predicated on the routinization of correctional officer behavior. Many correctional officers have, in short, predictable patterns of interacting with inmates; these patterns enable prisoners to plan their illegal activities, including distribution of contraband goods and services. In fact, research literature has suggested that knowing this fact is crucial to effective correctional supervision by prison staff. More on this topic later.

Finally, Kalinich and Stojkovic further suggest that the composition of the inmate body is critical to the level of contraband flow in a prison. Many of our correctional institutions today are filled with young, interested inmates who seek either to be buyers or sellers in the contraband system. This desire to get involved in the contraband system of the prison will have a dramatic effect on the flow of commodities in the prison environment. Young drug dealers off the city streets often attempt to continue their trade when incarcerated. Their intrusions into the contraband marketplace of the prison will have profound effects not only on the prices of the illegal goods and services in the prison, but in addition, will have instrumental effects on the long-term stability of the prison.

Marijuana, for example, is a commodity that many prisoners seek when they interact within the contraband system. While most prisoners are not dealers, they are typically buyers of marijuana or other products in the contraband system. In effect, all inmates are either directly or indirectly involved in the sub-rosa system of contraband workings in the prison, whether they be dealers or consumers. To continue our example of marijuana in the prison setting, if an inmate decided to enter into the marijuana business of the prison, he would cause an effect on the supply of the product, the price of the product, and the rules around which marijuana distribution would occur. Most importantly, this sudden increase in the supply of marijuana could lead to instability in the prison setting. Consider the following scenario as a likely result of new entrepreneurs entering the marijuana business of a prison.

To begin with, if the supply of marijuana in the contraband market structure increases as a result of more inmates being able to obtain supplies of it and act as dealers, those inmates with a vested interest in the well-established contraband business will attempt to thwart their new competitors. Their methods can range from undercutting the prices of the new entrants so as to drive them out of business to the use of violence to abruptly remove them from the marketplace. The first method is unlikely in a prison setting because it would require sufficient capital backing to incur losses until the new entrants went broke; this is not possible in prison as such since capital acquisition is often very difficult to achieve for most businessmen in the contraband economy, and as such, the likelihood of them relinquishing valuable capital until the new dealers are removed from the market is slim.

Instead, more often than not, established dealers of contraband will resort either to violence to control their competition or will inform prison officials about the activities of these new entrants. It is the latter alternative that is most commonly employed by entrepreneurs in the sub-rosa economy of the prison. Moreover, by implication, then, prison officials—correctional administrators and correctional officers—become intricately involved in the illegal dealings of prisoners if for no other reason than the stability of the prison setting.

Moreover, this same type of problem can occur if there is a decrease in the quantity and quality of contraband items in the prison market structure. As with an increase in the supply of contraband items in the illegal market of the prison, erratic and uncontrolled fluctuations in the price of contraband items due to the scarcity of goods could possibly cause destabilizing events in the environment of the prison. Thus, the prison administration is placed in a situation in which the integrity of the contraband system has to be maintained through informal linkages with those inmates who are in control of the market structure. In this way, prison contraband systems quite ironically have value to prison administrators through their ability to control large segments of the inmate population through well-known inmate leaders.

The Value of the Prison Contraband System to Prison Stability

Kalinich and Stojkovic (1985) suggest that the real value of a prison contraband system centers around control of an inmate population by a select few prisoners who have an investment in keeping the prison orderly and controllable for both themselves and the prison staff. The creation and perpetuation of a contraband market structure in prison, according to the researchers, creates a situation in which dealers of illegal goods and services exercise a *legitimate* form of power over inmates, and that legitimacy is focused on the contraband market system. In effect, the distribution of contraband products through a marketplace provides the opportunity for key merchants or inmate leaders to develop a normative rule structure that supports the exchange of goods and services, yet in addition, enables stability to reign in the institutional environment. As a result, inmate leaders serve the function of being pro order prisoners and keepers of the organizational status quo which is quite ironically the same interest of the prison administration. Thus, at an informal level, these key inmate leaders form the most important part of the inmate social system, in that they are a crucial part of the informal system of governance which ostensibly controls the prison setting.

Because inmate leaders have an investment in maintaining order in the prison, they are inexorably tied to the prison's formal structure and a key element to the long-term stability and peace of the institution. Any change or alteration in the economic arrangements of the organizational status quo could foster deleterious consequences in the prisoner population. If, for example, the inmate economy became flooded with a greater amount of a specific contraband product and the price for that product began to fall, the incentive for inmate leaders to promote stability and control would become diminished. In effect, the legitimacy, number, and quality of pro order inmate leaders would diminish as a result of a sudden increase in the supply of contraband goods and services, especially with the more popular contraband items such as marijuana. Hence, a crucial sector of the inmate governance system would be weakened and the inmate population would become, in part, relatively ungoverned, creating an atmosphere of instability.

This same situation could arise under conditions of scarcity with respect to contraband goods and services. If contraband products are scarce, the increase in price could cause a concomitant rise in violence and robbery among prisoners in order to gather more money or merchandise to pay for the products provided by the sub-rosa sector. Since many of the products provided in the inmate economy are *price inelastic*, that is, consumption patterns of prisoners would change at a proportionately lower rate than the price change for a particular good or service, inmates will attempt to keep their consumption patterns at about the same level prior to the increase in price of the product. In short, they may resort to violence or theft to get more resources to pay for the product they desire. As with an increase in supply of contraband goods, the effects on the social order of the prison can be very serious and potentially dangerous if an immediate decrease in contraband goods and services occurs. Given a relatively stable prison community, policy changes should be examined in terms of their potential impact on prison stability and order. If policy changes sever the links between the formal and informal power structures that govern the resident population, control of the population could be lost and negative consequences could be suffered by all.

Contraband and Prison Management

The unique focus of our thesis is that contraband systems are not only inherent to the workings of many prison structures, but in addition, critical to the stability of those organizations. As a result, improper manipulations of the contraband system by prison officials can have serious ramifications for prison order. What we will do in this final section is describe some of the unanticipated consequences of the contraband system on prison stability and suggest prescriptions for prison management.

First, within the prison economic sector, stratification occurs and a class structure is noticeable. Within the prisoner social system, the contraband system enables some inmates to gain enormous wealth and resources, usually at the expense of other prisoners. In effect, there becomes a concentration of wealth or capital in the prison setting, and this typically translates into a great deal of power for those prisoners who control the contraband market structure. The power of the contraband dealer lies in his ability to distribute demanded resources to other prisoners (Stojkovic, 1984).

A second unanticipated consequence of the prison contraband system is that for those inmates who thrive on the sub-rosa sector of the prison, it rationalizes and reinforces their existing criminal patterns of behavior. This system of distributing illegal goods and services runs counter to any hope of personal rehabilitation of the offender. Moreover, if the prison contraband system is so influential among inmates, it forces both prison officials and researchers of the contemporary prison to question the efficacy of rehabilitation programs. Surely these programs are of benefit to some prisoners. The proper correctional treatment is not the issue here, however. Instead, if the contraband system is founded on the principles of deceit, manipulation, and extortion, then it is questionable how any treatment approach can alter the power of these illegal activities within the prison structure.

A third, unplanned consequence of the contraband system in prison is the "corruption of authority" (Sykes, 1958:61) that occurs between key inmates involved in the distribution of goods and services and correctional officers. Since correctional officers are evaluated on how well they control their respective areas and the inmate leader's power is rooted in the ability to facilitate contraband flow, there is a necessary link between the two to promote long-term prison stability. Consequently, the prison organization is forced to trade off some corruption for institutional order (Kalinich, 1986:77).

From a management point of view, this link between the informal sector of the prison controlled by inmates and the formal apparatus of the organization as represented by correctional officer staff becomes a critical component of the institution's control and security function, and proper management of the prison requires that administrators be cognizant of the role of this symbiotic relationship in promoting stability to the prison environment. From this analysis, a number of recommendations for prison management can be drawn.

One way to deal with the power of the contraband system is to create more legitimate jobs in the formal sector of the prison. In this way, prisoners would have greater sources of income through legitimate means and possibly reduce the power of the illegal sector of the prison economy. The illegal distribution of food, for example, could be controlled through the provision of increased earning power among inmates in the legitimate sector of the inmate economy. Prisoners, then, could purchase food items through the recognized resident store as opposed to paying often inflated prices through the illegitimate contraband store operation.

Second, it would benefit prison administrators to be aware of any products that could serve as substitutes for existing products in the sub-rosa market of the prison. If a substitute product could be found, then the demand for the contraband item would become *price elastic*, and as such, cutting back on that product would increase price and prison consumers would enter the legal prison market for the substitute product. More importantly, many of the negative effects that come from interfering with the flow of contraband would be curtailed.

Alcohol production in prison, as an example, could be curtailed tremendously if legal forms of alcohol could be brought into the institution and sold legitimately. A warden known to one of the authors had recommended to his bosses in the state correctional system that he thought allowing inmates one shot of whiskey a day would do wonders for the prison, in that it would enable the inmates to get good quality alcohol instead of the often terrible-tasting prison "spud juice" and it would enable the state to make some money from the proceeds of the sales. The idea was routinely dismissed by administrators in the state correctional system as "coddling criminals," and as a result, it was never implemented by the prison, yet this alternative to homemade alcohol in the prison makes a lot of sense considering what we know about how prison contraband systems work. As a viable policy, however, it is unrealistic to expect prisons to sell alcohol to prisoners. The political liabilities far outweigh any potential benefits to prison administration.

A third recommendation to prison administrators regarding prison contraband is that an attempt should be made to eradicate contraband items that pose the greatest risk to prison stability. Weapons, while very rare, have no value to most prisoners. In fact, many prisoners have been known to tell correctional officer staff when dangerous weapons are present in the prison. Through intensive policing of the contraband market by correctional officers for serious weapons, the officers are meeting the objectives of both the inmates and prison officials, i.e., a secure and relatively safe environment. Furthermore, prison administrators would have to be sensitive to the increase in nondangerous contraband activity as a result of intensive policing of dangerous contraband products. This may be a necessary by-product for the long-term stability of the prison facility.

Finally, many of the problems that evolve from the contraband system may be related, in part, to the size of the institution itself. It is a given in prison administration that smaller prisons are more manageable and that custodial staff can control a great deal of contraband activity if there are fewer inmates. Prison staff working in an environment where fewer resources are required to control prisoners would have more opportunities to create conditions that would meet the needs of the prisoners through acceptable means. Thus, the power of the illegal contraband system would decrease, and more importantly, meaningful and flexible programming could be developed that would decrease the incongruity between the goals of the institution and the material needs of the inmate population. This final recommendation may be directed more to correctional policymakers than to institutional administrators, because this recommendation suggests that future construction of prison facilities consider how the size and structure of a prison are critical to the development of an inmate economy as well as other problem areas for prison officials.

Summary

The purpose of this chapter was to examine two rather unconventional topics associated with corrections—sexual relations behind bars and the prison contraband systems. It was suggested, with respect to prison sexual behaviors behind bars, that more often than not prison sex was *consensual* in nature, and that many of the sexual encounters varied among ethnic groups in prison. It was further suggested that the causes of prison sex can be tied to two theoretical positions on the origination of the inmate culture, those being the importation and functional models of inmate socialization. The evidence suggests that while both theoretical positions are supported by empirical evidence, current investigations have found that the importation model is more powerful in explaining the sexual behavior of prisoners.

A review of the literature supported this same position on prison sexual violence. We concluded that much of the sexual victimization in prison can be traced to the subculture of violence that many offenders experience while youths on the city streets. This evidence further suggested that the reduction of prison violence will only be successful in the long run if there is a strategic plan to reduce violence in our general culture. While this may explain why prison sexual violence occurs, it does not provide us with any concrete suggestions as to how to reduce the level of victimization in our prisons. As a result, we suggested some programs that might provide immediate help to the problem, yet our review of them was not positive. It seems that the prison will always be a violent place unless we make a commitment to change its structure and organization. With this in mind, we also suggested that many of our institutional policies on prison sex are based on myths and that these myths need to be dispelled before effective management of sexual behavior behind bars can be achieved.

Finally, we concluded this chapter with a review of the nature, function, and purpose of the inmate contraband system. We suggested that this illegal system of exchange among prisoners was facilitated by many factors in the prison and that there was a relationship between prison contraband systems and the control of the institutional setting. Additionally, we suggested that improper manipulations of the contraband system could have deleterious effects on the prison's stability, and that management could operate effectively with the contraband system to promote greater long-term stability in the prison. We concluded with some suggestions as to how prison officials could deal with illegal systems of exchange in their prisons and make their organizational environments more stable and predictable.

As with prisoner sexual relations, contraband activity in the prison has not been a central topic in many textbooks on corrections. Our purpose in this chapter was to highlight these two phenomena in a way that the student could gain a deeper insight into the workings of the prisoner social system. If this has been accomplished, then we feel that the student has truly gained a greater understanding of corrections. It is to this end that this entire book is written. The subsequent chapter will continue this discussion of life in prison by examining the role the courts have had in shaping both institutional policy and the world of the prisoner. We will see in Chapter 12 the kinds of rights inmates possess as convicted felons. This chapter, too, will suggest that the life of a prisoner is highly restrictive but typically not what the layperson believes it to be. Thus, it will provide us with an even greater understanding of this phenomenon known as corrections.

The Contraband Marketplace:
The Basis of the Informal Social System and Informal Legitimate Governance

The position of this article is that the contraband marketplace is a factor that is instrumental to the development of a legitimate form of inmate governance. Contraband is defined as materials that are unauthorized the formal prison administration. Common examples of contraband are the following: drugs, alcohol, gambling and gambling paraphernalia, real money, and a host of other assorted commodities and services. The demand for contraband is created by the institution's formal goals: the control and punishment of inmates. The supply of contraband products comes about due to the inability of the organization to achieve its primary goal.

The organization cannot totally control its inmate body for a variety of reasons: low officer-to-inmate ratio, lack of normative commitment to the organizational rules by inmates, and the inability to implement an efficient reward/punishment system to gain compliance among inmates. Thus administrators emphasize that which is obtainable: relatively quiet and clean cell blocks that are free of visible violence. This obtainable goal is achieved through a series of relationships developed between the guards and influential leaders. It is at this focal point that the formal system erodes and the inmate social structure begins.

Much activity in the inmate social structure evolves around the maintenance of the contraband marketplace. A vast amount of inmate time is dedicated to the contraband marketplace; inmates are dependent upon the marketplace for material and psychological well-being, and inmates who are influential and are cast in leadership roles are those who contribute to the maintenance of the contraband marketplace (Kalinich, 1980; Stojkovic, 1984).

One of the earliest works on the black market in prison was written about a prisoner of war (POW) camp for American soldiers in Germany during World War II; the work described a flourishing contraband system that included a system of trade between prison camps (Radford, 1945). Since then, a great deal has been written about prisons, particularly in relation to the informal inmate social structure. Although most of the literature does not focus on the contraband marketplace, almost all of it makes reference to contraband flow, with some of the literature describing that phenomenon in detail. McCleery (1960) and Davison (1977) describe active and prosperous contraband market systems that were controlled by powerful inmate leaders. Irwin (1970) depicts the links between inmates' street behaviors and their behaviors in the prison contraband market and the tenuous connection contraband provides among prison gangs. As a result of his research in a Federal Prison, Guenther (1975) concluded that contraband was rather common, and guards attempted to control dangerous contraband (weapons, escape equipment) whereas they, in effect, turned their backs on contraband that was considered a nuisance (drugs, gambling material, homemade alcohol). Shoblad (1972), describing his life as an inmate, discusses with some detail the sophisticated nature of the contraband marketplace and the ease with which inmates provided unauthorized goods and services to the prison population.

Research focusing on the contraband marketplace in a maximum security prison described the existence of a thriving marketplace in which most inmates participated with a great deal of frequency and with an array of goods and services available to them (Kalinich, 1980). The major categories of goods and services available were the following: drugs, alcoholic beverages, gambling, appliances (TV sets, hot plates, radios, and so on), clothing, buying of institutional privileges and reports, weapons, food and snack services, and prostitution. Each of these categories included a number of subcomponents, with complex or simple interactions, and the system was found to be based on a complex monetary operation that included the use of a regular banking system, organized loan sharking in the institution, inmates' prison accounts, inmate script, and real money—"green"—and cigarettes. Similar to Guenther's (1975) research, this study showed that some forms of contraband were considered dangerous by guards—and inmates—such as weapons, whereas much of the contraband was considered a thorn in the side of guards. However, this study found that certain forms of contraband were considered beneficial by custodial staff and were allowed to exist with the tacit but rather open approval of the majority of the staff.

A common and approved contraband service was the "inmate store." Each cell block had one or two inmates who kept a large stock of snacks, pop, instant coffee, and so on, that they purchased at the inmate commissary—the authorized outlet—and resold to inmates in the evenings after the commissary was closed. This form of "convenience store" was found beneficial by the custodial staff as it gave the inmates a method to help structure their free evening time. This was harmless though unauthorized and added to the smooth running of the cell block. Guards' views on drug use by inmates were mixed, even though administrators saw drugs as a definite threat to the security of the institution. Whereas older guards viewed drugs as dangerous, but alcoholic beverages brewed in the institution harmless, younger guards viewed marijuana use as a method of pacifying inmates (Kalinich, 1980).

Other research in a maximum security prison has concluded that narcotics and [their] distribution are equally important in controlling the institutional environment (Stojkovic, 1984). When inmates were asked to describe the influence of drugs within the facility, they stated the importance of the sub-rosa drug market in stabilizing the environment. The consensus among inmates was that the providing of illegal goods and services by pivotal inmates in the inmate social system provided control for correctional officers and comfort to inmates in coping with their incarceration. In effect, the distribution of specific contraband items—differing types of narcotics—was essential for both custodial staff and key inmates in the control of the environment.

What was produced was a situation in which institutional capital was concentrated and power centralized with a few inmates. The short-term effect was that the inmate society was pacified until the next supply of drugs was delivered. In the interim, inmates attempted to cope with imprisonment using illegal means. It was at this juncture that inmate violence, assaults, and robberies surfaced. More important, this is where the value of inmate leaders is pivotal. When institutional violence surfaces, it becomes incumbent upon these leaders to develop compromises among the warring factions to ensure "domestic tranquility." In this way, not only is the institution stabilized through the influence of inmate politicians but the market structure remains intact.

Thus it becomes clear that the contraband marketplace is an important focal point for inmates, around which they focus a great deal of their activities as well as structure their behaviors and interactions with each other and the prison staff, especially custodial staff.

Power of Inmate Leaders, Legitimacy, and Stability

The link between inmates and staff is through the inmate leaders. One of the major roles of inmate leaders is to facilitate the flow of contraband. In doing so, they gain the backing and support of those inmates who value contraband and, thus, can influence them and their behaviors.

The use of formal rewards and punishments to control inmates' behavior is limited. Guards often overlook rule violations by inmates who are not troublemakers and tend to be cooperative overall. As stated earlier, guards depend on influential inmates' cooperation in keeping the cell blocks clean and relatively peaceful. In return for their cooperation, guards will overlook the manipulations of the influential inmates as long as the order of the cell block is facilitated and not disrupted by those manipulations.

There are three elements that are common to inmate leaders. First, they have had extensive knowledge of the informal institutional structure from past experience and are serving long sentences. Second, they have jobs that permit freedom of movement from one area within the institution to another. Third, they have a large number of contacts with fellow inmates who will work for or with them, and some may have criminal contacts outside the institution that can help coordinate the inflow of contraband into the prison black market (Kalinich, 1980). In addition, they are skillful at developing good relationships with inmates and guards. They can usually gain a relationship of trust with inmates and guards, giving both groups the appearance of allegiance to them. In most cases, the inmate leaders have a vested interest in the status quo and the stability of the institution (Cloward, 1960) and, therefore, share the guards' interest in an orderly cell block. They have resources, "business" expertise, are sensitive to the needs of both inmates and prison staff, and can negotiate with the two groups who may otherwise be in constant conflict. In effect, they can contribute to the sense of control and order of the custodial staff, and they can control their constituents—the inmates—through overt and covert means and help keep order in the prison community.

It was found to be a common practice for inmates who were politicians to be selected by prison staff for work assignments, involving some responsibility and trust, such as a clerical position working under a supervisor or counselor. The selection is made on the inmates' potential as a "politician" as staff look for inmates who "know how the prison really works." These inmates, though not expected to be informants, have their finger on the pulse of activities in the institution, and can help legitimize the authority of the staff member they are working for through their influence over other inmates. Staff members enter this employment relationship usually knowing the inmate will use the position for his own benefit. The trade-off of bureaucratic control for stability is considered a rational choice at the operational level (Kalinich, 1980).

The label "politician" suggests that inmate leaders hold legitimate power over their fellow inmates. Their ability to supply contraband goods and services directly and facilitate the behavior of others who are active in the contraband marketplace provides them with the ability to influence and lead their fellow inmates. They nurture and sustain a system that inmates have a normative commitment to in that it concurs with their values, and it provides a material and psychological payoff. Thus a system exists upon which a set of acceptable rules are readily promulgated that reify the system. Inmate leaders are expected to support the rules and system developed at the sub-rosa level and to enforce the rules when necessary and possible. Inmates who inadvertently fall into positions of potential influence with the staff through job assignments or personal interactive skills are expected to become politicians and support the sub-rosa system by facilitating the contraband flow. If they do not take on politician roles and leadership responsibilities as defined by the inmate subculture, other inmates will bring pressures to bear to influence that inmate into accepting at least a partial role as a politician, or will manipulate that person out of the position (Kalinich, 1980). Within this framework of legitimacy, inmate leaders have access to specific forms of power to influence inmate behaviors.

These kinds of power are everchanging within the prison environment. These forms of power vary depending upon the individual and the situation. Past research has suggested that inmate leaders express these disparate forms of power dependant upon how well they influence their peers (Stojkovic, 1984). Accordingly, there are five types of power exercised by politicians: coercive, referent, providing of resources, expert, and legitimate.

Coercive power is defined as the threat of

force or the actual application of punishment to gain conformity among inmates. This type of power has been documented as the primary method inmate leaders employ as a control strategy (Jacobs, 1977; Irwin, 1980). Referent power can be defined as the identification inmates have with a group or gang, and conformity is achieved through a commitment to group norms. This, too, is quite common in our prisons and usually is advanced by various religious groups and "super gangs" in the institution.

Third, providing resources is a particularly important form of power. This kind of power is predicated on the ability of the leader to access goods and services. This type of power is the most relevant to the contraband system. Fourth, expert power is rooted in the knowledge an individual possesses. Typically, leaders who understand the legal system are able to gain much power in the inmate social world and can influence many other prisoners. Finally, legitimate power can be identified; this power base is dependent upon an internalization process, where inmates follow the rules and regulations prescribed by leaders because they perceive them as justified and in the best interest of inmates. We found that those inmate leaders who focused their efforts on facilitating the flow of contraband had access to all of the above-mentioned social bases of power and were the strongest stabilizing force within the informal system. Therefore, conformity is accomplished through a consensus among inmates that adherence to the rules furthers the inmates' needs vis-à-vis the formal administration (Stojkovic, 1984).

Therefore, a loosely defined but strong form of governance develops at the informal level. This promotes stability in that a set of rules is created that inmates can accept; leadership is denied by inmate values, and leaders will develop who contribute to the maintenance of the accepted system. Disturbances in the contraband marketplace will cause similar disturbances in the inmate legitimate governance system. If the contraband system is suppressed through tightening of administrative controls, the basis of legitimate governance is also suppressed. This will, in turn, disrupt the basis for stability in the prison environment.

Key Terms and Concepts

Alternatives to Violence Project (AVP)
bisexual prisoners
consensual sex
contraband
corruption of authority
functional model
heterosexual prisoners
homosexual prisoners
importation model
legitimate power

price inelastic
prison stability
sexual aggressors
sexual approaches
sexual scripts
sexual targets
sexual victimization
subculture of violence
sub-rosa system
target hardening

References

Bartollas, C. and C.M. Sieverdes (1983). "Sexual Victims in a Coeducational Juvenile Correctional Institution." *Prison Journal*, Volume 63, Number 1, Spring/Summer:80-90.

Bowker, L. (1982). "Victimizers and Victims in American Correctional Institutions." In R. Johnson and H. Toch (eds.) *The Pains of Imprisonment*. Beverly Hills, CA: Sage Publications.

Chonco, N. (1989). "Sexual Assaults Among Male Inmates: A Descriptive Study." *The Prison Journal*, Volume LXVIV, Number 1: 72-82.

Clemmer, D. (1940). *The Prison Community*. New York, NY: Holt, Rinehart.

Davidson, T. (1977). *Chicano Prisoners: The Key to San Quentin*. Prospect Heights, IL: Waveland Press, Inc.

Johnson, R. (1987). *Hard Time: Understanding and Reforming the Prison*. Monterey, CA: Brooks/Cole Publishing Company.

Jones, R and T. Schmid (1989). "Inmates' Conceptions of Prison Sexual Assault." *The Prison Journal*, Volume LXVIX, Number 1: 53-61.

Kalinich, D. and S. Stojkovic (1985). "Contraband: The Basis for Legitimate Power in a Prison Social System." *Criminal Justice and Behavior*, Volume 12, Number 4:435-451.

Kalinich, D. (1986). *Power, Stability, & Contraband: The Inmate Economy*. Prospect Heights, IL: Waveland Press, Inc.

Kalinich, D. and S. Stojkovic (1987). "Prison Contraband Systems: Implications for Prison Management." *Journal of Crime & Justice*, Volume X, Number 1:1-22.

Leger, R. (1987). "Lesbianism Among Women Prisoners: Participants and Nonparticipants." *Criminal Justice and Behavior*, Volume 14, Number 4: 448-467.

Lockwood, D. (1980). *Prison Sexual Violence*. New York, NY: Elsevier Books.

Lockwood, D. (1982). "Contribution of Sexual Harassment to Stress and Coping in Confinement." In N. Parisi (ed.) *Coping with Imprisonment*. Beverly Hills, CA: Sage Publications.

Lockwood, D. (1985). "Issues in Prison Sexual Violence." In M. Braswell, S. Dillingham and R. Montgomery, Jr. (eds.) *Prison Violence in America*. Cincinnati, OH: Anderson Publishing Co.

McGrath, G.M. (1982). "Prison Society and Offense Stigma—Some Doubts." *Australian and New Zealand Journal of Criminology*, Volume 15, Number 4:235-244.

McNamara, D.E.J. and A. Karmen (eds.) (1983). *Deviants—Victims or Victimizers?* Beverly Hills, CA: Sage Publications.

Nacci, P.L. (1982). "Sex and Sexual Aggression in Federal Prisons." Unpublished Manuscript. U.S. Federal Prison System: Office of Research.

Nacci, P.L. and T.R. Kane (1982). *Sexual Aggression in Federal Prisons*. Washington, DC: U.S. Department of Justice Federal Prison System.

Nacci, P. L. and T.R. Kane (1984). "Sex and Sexual Aggression in Federal Prisons: Inmate Involvement and Employee Impact." *Federal Probation*, Volume 8, March: 46-53.

Parisi, N. (1982). *Coping with Imprisonment*. Beverly Hills, CA: Sage Publications.

Propper, A. (1989). "Love, Marriage, and Father-Son Relationships Among Male Prisoners." *The Prison Journal*, Volume LXIX, Number 2: 57-63.

Smykla, J. (1989). "Prison Sexuality, Parts I and II." *The Prison Journal*, Volumes LXVIX and LXIX, Numbers 1 and 2.

Stojkovic, S. (1984). "Social Bases of Power and Control Mechanisms Among Prisoners in a Prison Organization." *Justice Quarterly*, Volume 1, Number 4:511-528.

Stojkovic, S. (1985). "Homosexuality in a Prison Community." Paper presented at the annual meeting of the Academy of Criminal Justice Sciences, Las Vegas, Nevada, March.

Sykes, G. (1958). *The Society of Captives*. Princeton, NJ: Princeton University Press.

Tewksbury, R. (1989). "Fear of Sexual Assault in Prison Inmates." *The Prison Journal*, Volume LXVIX, Number 1: 62-71.

Thomas, C.W. (1977). "Theoretical Perspectives on Prisonization: A Comparison of the Importation and Deprivation Models." *Journal of Criminal Law and Criminology*, Volume 68, Number 1:135-145.

Wooden, W.S. and J. Parker (1982). *Men Behind Bars: Sexual Exploitation in Prison.* New York, NY: Plenum Publishing Corporation.

Photo Credit: Frost Publishing Group, Ltd.

Corrections and the Law

12

Paul S. Embert
Michigan State University

After reading this chapter, the student should be able to:

▉ Provide a description of perspectives on corrections and the law.

▉ Discuss the historical background of the law and sources of authority.

▉ Describe the evolution of law in general and correctional law in particular.

▉ List the rights of prisoners, parolees, probationers, and ex-offenders.

▉ Explain other significant issues associated with correctional law.

▉ Describe sanctions for the misuse of correctional authority.

Introduction

This chapter links two imprecise terms—*system* and *process*. Each term refers to the entity we call corrections. It focuses on the impact of law in managing the *correctional enterprise*[1] as well as issues raised in applying specific laws to corrections. That is, it presents various perspectives on how law affects corrections, its clients, and its practitioners.

This chapter also places law into its broader context and describes laws and issues that affect the accused, the convicted, ex-offenders, and correctional employees. It suggests that law is a management issue.

Perspectives on Corrections and the Law

Law is one of the more important variables affecting corrections. This does not mean one need be an attorney to understand corrections, law, or issues related thereto. Nor does this dictate memorization of a variety of legal rules. The rules change, are sometimes contrary or contradictory, and often lack sufficient "crispness" to be useful except as broad guidelines (Kalinich, Embert and Senese, 1990).

Rather, this assertion is prompted by four observations: (1) one's unique position in society may influence his or her perceptions of both corrections and the law, (2) law lies at the essence of what much of corrections is about—management, (3) the relationship between corrections and law is often complex, ambiguous, and beyond providing simple solutions to correctional problems, and (4) law is more than statutes and court decisions—it is a social and political phenomenon (Feinberg and Gross, 1975; Breed, 1986; Embert, 1986).

Some "bad management" contributing to correctional law can be attributed to social and political "forces" outside corrections. Some "bad man-

---

[1]   The term *system* focuses on the interactions of a variety of entities (inside and outside of corrections)—police, courts, prosecutors, etc. *Process* stresses programs and activities involving both accused and convicted—trial, appeal, and treatment programs. *Correctional enterprise* focuses on the many organizations involved in corrections (jails, prisons, probation, parole, etc.). The term *corrections* is also often used as a euphemism, addressing the many ways we deal with offenders; cynically, those things we do with offenders when we don't know what else to do with them.

agement" stems from an individual's particular niche in society. For example, correctional managers may view the law in a different light than line personnel. They may view law related to equal employment opportunity or sexual harassment as more important than, for example, prisoners' rights (Embert and Kalinich, 1988). While labor law is crucial in managing an organization, this body of law is often ignored in discussions focusing on the rights of criminal offenders.

Yet this part of law largely mandates how line officers go about their daily job of managing offenders. Lawsuits, interpretation of the law (and applicable rules) by supervisors, and other factors often result in line officers seeing this part of the law as decidedly tilted toward the rights of probationers, inmates, or parolees. *Correctional clients*,[2] and those who would reform the correctional enterprise and process, debate this viewpoint (Hawkins and Alpert, 1989; Haas and Alpert, 1986; Robbins, 1989; et al.).

Average citizens form contrary views. If an individual is philosophically oriented toward harsh punishment, he or she may see a prison or jail with window air conditioners as an example of "the law coddling criminals." Others might conclude that air conditioners were installed in offices that are used by staff or that house computers.

Some people view inmates' television sets as the law coddling criminals. But correctional officers may view television as a means of keeping inmates occupied—a necessity due to laws and political considerations that often preclude meaningful inmate employment.

In short, one's past experiences with the law, media accounts of court decisions and prison conditions, and other factors combine to give us our unique perceptions of corrections and the law. The task is to recognize that one's perceptions may be incomplete or erroneous. This is essential in understanding and applying the totality of laws to a basic concern of corrections—management.

---

2   The term *correctional client(s)* implies treating, disciplining, rehabilitating, or punishing someone by the correctional system. Although other types of clients receive attention, treatment, and control by various governmental agencies, only correctional clients are dealt with by the correctional enterprise. The reason for this is that correctional clients have "willfully damaged society" (Fox, 1972) and have been labeled "criminals" by the criminal justice system (Embert and Kalinich, 1988).

Correctional Management

Most correctional employees are managers. They may manage large, complex systems (e.g., a state department of corrections). At the opposite extreme they may manage a cellblock or caseload of probationers. Corrections itself is in the business of managing correctional clients. It may have a *goal* of rehabilitating offenders or any other goal commonly ascribed to corrections. But regardless of the goal(s) of a particular correctional system or program, its underlying basis is managing correctional clients.

Correctional and probation officers manage individuals and situations. Their task at any time may be to keep prisoners from climbing over the wall and escaping, breaking up a fight in a dining facility, or initiating a probation revocation action. But when confronted by such situations, they apply principles managers use, including managerial and legal principles and standards.

In effect, management and legal principles and standards merge to underscore much of the technology of corrections: (1) offender assessment and classification, (2) prisoner management programs, (3) treatment programs, (4) inmate disciplinary proceedings, (5) probation or parole revocation hearings, and such custodial technology as the use of force. Accordingly, it is appropriate to view law within the context of overall management.

But management and administration is as much art as science. In fact, Souryal (1980) referred to management as a SCART (Science/Art). In a similar vein, Clear and Cole (1986) noted that a major difficulty in corrections is that the effectiveness of most *correctional technologies* is uncertain. Others argue that the technologies themselves are uncertain (Studt, 1967). In either case, corrections is in the business of applying the science and art of management; using correctional technologies which are part science and part art; and, accomplishing both within a framework of legal rules, often lacking universal applicability.

In this context, Luther Gulick's 1937 proposition of administrative principles, articulated in the acronym POSDCORB (planning, organizing, staffing, directing, controlling, reporting, and budgeting), briefly describes what much of corrections is about. Yet each activity is influenced and constrained by law, however imprecise.

For example, if an inmate is psychologically or physically harmed while confined, a civil suit, writ of habeas corpus, or other legal action is likely. Management issues of negligence in hiring personnel, assigning employees, retaining workers who should have been fired, directing the staff (through sound written policies and procedures), supervising subordinates, training personnel, and entrusting employees (usually with guns or vehicles), may be raised. The physical facility may be challenged as deficient. These eight legal issues, which may be formed into the acronym HARDSTEF, reach to the crux of Gulick's principles.

Staffing (POSDCORB), for example, raises issues of preemployment screening and hiring; proper or improper assignment of people once hired (HARDSTEF); as well as policies, procedures, and training used in directing (POSDCORB) and supervising (HARDSTEF). In effect, the prescriptions of what managers do (or should do) are the substance of many lawsuits. And, when all is said and done, litigation has generated much of the law affecting corrections.

To illustrate, under the federal and state constitutions, all citizens are guaranteed a variety of rights—free speech, freedom of religion, etc. Most do not see a need for such guarantees until someone infringes upon these rights. Then, seemingly inconsequential rights take on fundamental importance. For example, most probably are not too concerned with their constitutional right to avoid incriminating themselves. But when they are arrested and a police interrogation commences, that right becomes very important! The issue becomes recourse.

The answer is often some form of litigation. Our perception of the outcome of litigation may be distorted by media coverage or a summary of a court's opinion. But we will rarely have all the facts, or consider the variables, leading to the lawsuit or court decision. This includes the different laws affecting corrections.

Laws Affecting Corrections

Laws affecting corrections can arbitrarily be categorized into: (1) criminal (or penal) law, (2) civil law, (3) correctional law, and (4) constitutional law. In practice, none of these categories exists in and of itself; each influences and is influenced by the other. Each is restrained by other types of law (Embert, 1986).

Criminal law brings corrections its clientele. It may also remove a client from the enterprise (e.g., when an offender wins an appeal of a criminal conviction). Criminal law provides the input for correctional practitioners, but may leave it with unfinished business if it decides an offender is "guilty in fact, but not guilty under the law."

The concept of "guilty in fact, but not guilty under the law," is symptomatic of the "due process" model of criminal justice, as opposed to the "crime control" model.[3] It results from relations between constitutional and criminal law and exchange relations between the courts and legislatures.

Violations of criminal law are considered wrongdoings against the state, or society as a whole, and are largely a prerogative of the legislative branch of government. Behavior that legislatures label as criminal conduct is, in fact, criminal behavior. But if a legislative body elects to decriminalize acts, they also have that prerogative. For example, legislatures may decide that possession of small amounts of marijuana shall be dealt with as a crime (*felony* or *misdemeanor*), or as a *civil infraction*. This does not imply that legislatures may regulate conduct arbitrarily.

They must show a compelling need to regulate the conduct in question, must not violate the federal or state constitution, and the language of the statute must be very precise (Gardner, 1985). In spite of such restraints, legislatures have considerable power in defining crimes and determining punishments.

Criminal law largely determines how we may deal with an offender (probation, fine, or incarceration), and partially determines where individuals will be confined—county jail, state prison, or federal institution. In these determinations, the judicial process determines specific legal guilt or innocence, and modifies legislative sentencing guidelines to fit a particular individual or circumstance (Embert and Kalinich, 1988).

Some writers have suggested that the courts primarily modify an impossible legislative system (Foote, 1958). While a penal code may prescribe a sentence to a state prison, a local judge may sentence an offender to confinement in a county jail. The court's motivation may be founded in the

---

3   Originally described by Packer (1968). Under the due process model, the law would rather see a guilty person go free than an innocent person convicted. Accordingly, the rights of the accused are protected and the courts play a critical role in the total justice system. As a result, the corrections enterprise is not at liberty to recruit and screen its clientele. This aspect of corrections limits the potential of corrections personnel to have a significant impact on crime in free society. The crime control model would possibly provide the corrections enterprise with a greater proportion of alleged criminal offenders. Given a larger, more representative base of offenders, treatment programs might show higher success rates. Indeed, some people have, cynically, talked about the ability to improve rehabilitation and treatment if corrections had a better caliber of client.

unique circumstances surrounding the offender, the particular crime, or, as a pragmatic decision (based, perhaps on prison overcrowding). In effect, while legislators label certain categories of behavior as crimes, as well as either a felony or misdemeanor, the judicial process (including plea bargaining) modifies the penal code to fit individual cases (Cole, 1989).

This exchange between legislatures and the judicial process has major consequences on corrections. A legislative body may prescribe mandatory prison sentences. Judges may exercise their discretion to impose longer prison sentences than are customary. In either case, prison crowding is imminent. This, in turn, affects parole officers as inmates leave the institution; perhaps due to a parole board using parole to alleviate prison crowding.

Conversely, criminal law is influenced by both constitutional and civil law. For example, police practices and efficiency are constrained by constitutional safeguards in searches and seizures, self-incrimination, and the right to legal counsel. One of the remedies available to individuals who have their constitutional rights violated by the police is litigation under civil law.

Civil law deals with a variety of relationships between individuals (rather than relationships between the state and individuals), and embraces numerous specialities (e.g., contract law, labor law, landlord-tenant law, and tort law. [Statsky, 1986]) Most readers can identify with civil law, particularly contract law. Many enter into contracts with an automobile insurer or a landlord. In return for the payment of premiums, an insurance company agrees to pay for damages in the event of an accident. Similarly, if the tenant pays rent, the landlord allows the tenant to use an apartment. In the latter case, tenants who suffer injuries as the result of inadequate maintenance, or who are assaulted as the result of inadequate security measures, may resort to a tort action to obtain compensation for their injuries.

Tort law (from the Latin word *tortus*, meaning twisted conduct) is a non-criminal, non-contractual suit wherein a *plaintiff* may seek monetary awards (or other actions) as the result of an intentional act or a failure to act (negligence) in carrying out a legal duty (Spain, 1986). Some refer to this duty as "the duty of care," a duty imposed on homeowners and merchants to provide reasonable safety and security for others—household residents (or employees), invited guests (or licensees), and even trespassers.

Tort law often enables citizens to sue the police, and correctional clients to sue probation or correctional officers (and their respective departments), when they have been psychologically or physically harmed (intentionally or through negligence). Such actions may focus on common tort issues (such as negligence in safety measures, which may contribute to a personal injury) or on correctional or constitutional issues.

Correctional law is largely, but not exclusively, a part of constitutional law. That is, it is usually based on a violation of some constitutional prohibition or guarantee (such as the prohibition against cruel and unusual punishment) (Clute, 1980).

Constitutional law is a blend of the written constitution, various laws and rules enacted by legislative bodies and administrative agencies to insure conformance with the constitution, and court opinions. It includes written law, concepts from common law or case law, and a host of social and political influences. Accordingly, it must be placed into perspective with law in general.

Law In General

When we address law in general terms, there are various topics that could be discussed: (1) the philosophy of law (Feinberg and Gross, 1975), (2) the courts' decision-making process (Rohde and Spaeth, 1976), or (3) the processes of constitutional adjudication (Brest, 1975). However, a brief sketch of some historical background and sources of authority in law helps to place law in perspective.

Historical Background

Where the law began, and how it reached the point it is at today, are issues that are neither easily nor authoritatively explained. Native Americans, for example, had laws that were largely unwritten and informal, while ancient China and Egypt had detailed regulations governing their respective societies (Prassel, 1972; 1979).

Among the oldest written laws are those ascribed to the Code of Hammurabi (about 2000 B.C.). In this early Babylonian code, which was based on the concept of *lex talionis*, or revenge, over two dozen offenses called for the death penalty; others called for mutilation, whipping, or forced labor (Allen and Simonsen, 1986). This punitive philosophy pervaded corrections until recently.

Other ancient concepts also became ingrained in the philosophy of corrections and the legal system. Among those having an important effect on corrections was the concept of "civil death." Attributed to ancient Rome, this meant that a criminal suffered complete loss of citizenship, his or her property was confiscated in the name of the state, and the spouse declared a widow (or widower). To society, the offender was legally dead, and lost all legal rights.

Most current laws associated with corrections do not reflect the harshness found in the ancient codes. Although, vestiges of harshness can be found in some of society's philosophy toward corrections and what the law *should* be. Practically, however, correctional law has evolved from its early and harsh beginnings. It is now influenced by legal, social, and philosophical developments since we first adopted English common law.

English common law is "the" principal source of law in the United States. Common law consists of various legal principles that have evolved from analysis of specific court decisions, and has its origins in the Anglo-Saxon period of English history—from approximately 444 A.D. to 1066 A.D. (Bilek, Klotter, and Federal, 1981). Legal principles continue to evolve from an analysis of specific court cases—often referred to as case law. This is not an easy task, and was particularly problematic immediately after the American Revolutionary War.

Following the war there was considerable debate concerning a variety of issues: (1) the roles and privileges of free men (and women), indentured servants, and slaves, (2) the issue of what was to constitute criminal behavior, (3) the extent of legal protection and penalties to be imposed in regulating domestic relationships (husband and wife; parent and child; master and servant, or slave), and (4) the fundamental issue of *sovereignty* (Heffernan, 1985).

Some argued that a multiplicity of rigorous penal laws was repugnant to human nature; others, that criminals were depraved, dangerous, and dependent—terms used to describe both criminals and slaves. Underscoring such debates were issues concerning which laws should be adopted, and the question of who should retain sovereignty—the state or the people (Heffernan, 1985).

Under English common law, anyone who harmed the divine sovereign (King or Queen) forfeited their body. In effect, the death penalty (or other harsh punishment) was appropriate to someone who had harmed the sovereign. Conversely, early English traditions provided that a judge might, "out of mercy," suspend the death penalty and inflict a lesser punishment. Criminals were, in essence, slaves of the sovereign or state (Heffernan, 1985). Accordingly, we see early American court cases ruling that prisoners were "slaves of the state" (*Ruffin v. Commonwealth*, 1871).

Early debates over slavery and women are revealing. Some courts, for example, stated that blacks were properly maintained as a productive lower caste:

> Slavery is with us as an institution founded upon a distinction of races, one of which is subject to the control and domination of the other (*Peter v. Hargrave*, 1848).

Similarly, other courts could rule that whether free or enslaved, blacks could never be protected by the U.S. Constitution (*Dred Scott v. Sanford*, 1856). Comparable thinking dealt with wives, with one writer stating that:

> By marriage, the husband and wife are one person in law: that is, the very being, or legal existence of the woman is suspended during the marriage or at least incorporated and consolidated into that of the husband, under whose wing, protection and cover, she performs everything...under the protection and influence of her husband, her baron or lord...(Blackstone, 1979).

It is evident from these examples that much of the early law and accompanying social theory has been modified—a process that continues today. Modern case law, much of which stems from civil suits, has had a major impact on our criminal justice system.

Among significant recent changes involving corrections were the rise and fall of the *"hands-off" doctrine.* Until the mid-1960s most federal courts uniformly denied relief to prisoners who complained of conditions in prison or jail. Among the reasons given for this policy were notions of civil death and that convicts were little more than slaves of the state. Courts also adhered to the premise that prisons and jails were the responsibility of the executive and legislative branches of government, rather than the judiciary (Haas and Alpert, 1989).

Yet society was changing; with it, the courts began to review their traditional positions regarding convicted offenders, as well as traditional views concerning prisoner litigation (especially under the provisions of 42 U.S.C. § 1983). As the courts began to render decisions affecting corrections, the various legislative bodies were forced into passing new laws. This does not suggest that changes mandated by legislative bodies were due exclusively to the influence of court decisions. The issue of why the law is as it is is far more complex than a simple "courts-causing-legislative reaction" equation.

Indeed, there is considerable controversy over the issue of why the law is the way it is. For example, some writers claim that the law develops as a result of consensus; others, as a result of conflict. The *consensus model* assumes that social and political forces merge to form a law that reflects the values of society as a whole, and transcends the specific interest of particular groups or individuals. The *conflict model* asserts that social and political power is more of an influence of specific groups and elite groups and individuals (Friedmann, 1959; Quinney, 1969).

Regardless of the rationale (consensus or conflict) for the law, or the impact of history on the law, today, law is found in a variety of sources.

Sources of Authority

There is no distinct, separate body of law that can be labeled "correctional law." There are laws that pertain to persons accused of crime, laws that affect persons convicted of crimes, laws that impact upon people following conviction, laws that affect offenders after they have served their sentence, as well as laws that address those who work in corrections. These laws are found in many sources.

Some writers claim that there are four principal sources of law: (1) constitutions, (2) legislative laws or statutes, (3) administrative rules and regulations, and (4) court opinions. While these may be *principal sources of law*, there are at least seven *additional sources* of law affecting corrections: (1) administrative decisions, opinions, or rulings, (2) charters, (3) ordinances, (4) court rules, (5) executive orders, (6) opinions of attorneys general, and (7) international treaties and agreements (Statsky, 1986).

This profusion of governmental entities and individuals contributing to the law partially explains the complexity of legal influences on corrections. Unfortunately, many individuals fail to consider the role each plays in creating the totality of the law and its influence on corrections.

Constitutions are the fundamental laws that create the branches of government and identify the basic rights and obligations of each branch of the federal and state governments. As such, each is the supreme law within its jurisdiction. No other law can legally contradict the provisions of the respective constitution. Charters serve a similar role in local governments.

While *charters* typically have minimal direct impact on corrections, various provisions may restrict the number of police or mandate a local jail—thereby *indirectly* affecting corrections. For example, suicides in police jails and lockups have been targets of numerous civil suits, which have had an impact upon the standards of care required in an attempt to prevent inmate suicides (e.g., *Partridge v. Two Unknown Police Officers*, 1985; *Lyons v. Cunningham*, 1983; *Lightbody v. Town of Hampton*, 1984; *Estate of Cartwright v. City of Concord*, 1985; *Roberts v. City of Troy*, 1985). Similarly, less-than-professional police actions at the local level have resulted in criminal convictions being reversed upon appeal, as well as in civil rights suits (Avery and Rudovsky, 1989).

Public laws or *statutes* must conform with the appropriate constitution. Such laws generally command or prohibit something. While many are precise and complete, others create administrative agencies to explain or carry out the statutes.

In these cases, *administrative rules* or regulations promulgated by the agency (or executive orders issued by the chief executive—the U.S. President or a state governor) take on the effect of law.

In cases involving controversy over a statute, administrative rule, or executive order, *administrative decisions* (or rulings) or opinions of the appropriate attorney general, may be rendered which take on the force of law until overturned by a court opinion.

Court rules, including rules of procedures, govern practices before a particular court and prescribe procedures to be followed in litigation. These may affect criminal or civil cases in a variety of ways that affect corrections. For example, if an individual does not file a civil case in a timely manner, the case (and its particular issue) may not even be considered (Manville, 1989).

When a case is heard and decided, the decision of the trial court may be reversed upon appeal. Even the higher court's opinion (a court's written explanation of how and why it applied the law to reach a decision) may not become *binding* on all lower courts in future similar cases.

Bear in mind, we have a federal court system, and 50 state court systems, each with a hierarchy, as shown in Figure 12.1.

Figure 12.1
Court Hierarchy/Chain of Command

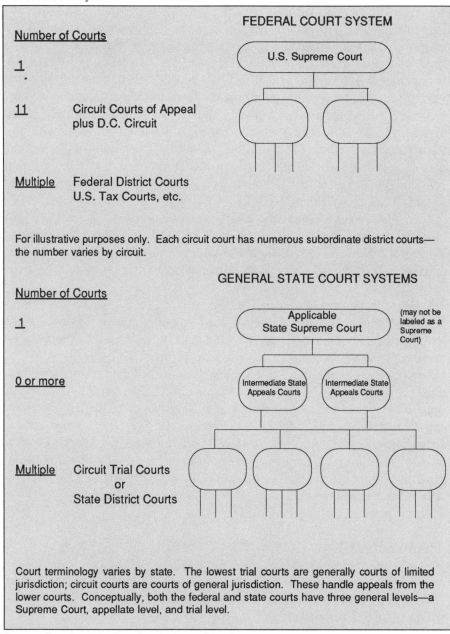

FEDERAL COURT SYSTEM

Number of Courts

1

11 Circuit Courts of Appeal
plus D.C. Circuit

Multiple Federal District Courts
U.S. Tax Courts, etc.

For illustrative purposes only. Each circuit court has numerous subordinate district courts—the number varies by circuit.

GENERAL STATE COURT SYSTEMS

Number of Courts

1

Applicable
State Supreme Court

(may not be labeled as a Supreme Court)

0 or more

Intermediate State Appeals Courts Intermediate State Appeals Courts

Multiple Circuit Trial Courts
or
State District Courts

Court terminology varies by state. The lowest trial courts are generally courts of limited jurisdiction; circuit courts are courts of general jurisdiction. These handle appeals from the lower courts. Conceptually, both the federal and state courts have three general levels—a Supreme Court, appellate level, and trial level.

Source: Developed by Stan Stokjovic and Rick Lovell.

For a decision to be a *binding opinion* on future court decisions, it must be rendered by a court within a prescribed hierarchy or "chain of command." Decisions rendered by courts outside a particular chain of command are merely *persuasive opinions*. Even when an opinion should be binding, a lower court may distinguish a particular case from the general rule. That is, a lower court may accept a general rule of a superior court, but determine that the facts in a particular case are different. An example can be found in cases involving double-bunking of inmates. Two U.S. Supreme Court decisions indicate that double-bunking does not, in and of itself, amount to cruel or unusual punishment (*Bell v. Wolfish*, 1979; *Rhodes v. Chapman*, 1981) Yet this general rule has been circumvented in numerous cases because the "total conditions of confinement" differed from the conditions in both *Bell* and *Rhodes* (Call, 1984; Coles, 1987).

Finally, treaties or international agreements entered into between nations influence corrections. International treaties and agreements can determine whether a host nation or sending nation will try a military offender or civilian employee, and into which nation's justice system an offender will be committed.

Given this array of laws and sources of law, it is inevitable that various laws may conflict. In this case an attorney general's opinion may resolve the issue, or the case may end up in court. In reaching a decision, a hierarchy of laws will generally be followed, as is shown in Figure 12.2.

While the Constitution is the supreme law of the land (as are the respective state constitutions within each state), many court opinions have the same practical effect as the written constitution. For example, the Bill of Rights (the first 10 amendments to the Constitution) does not specifically list any right of privacy. Yet there are a variety of U.S. Supreme Court decisions that impute this right. This right, as well as others, is a fundamental constitutional issue that affects both principal divisions of the law (civil and criminal) and one which has evolved.

Evolution of Law

A brief survey of the historical evolution of law, including correctional law, helps explain why the law is as it is. It also helps us more clearly define the meaning of "the law."

Figure 12.2
A General Hierarchy of Laws

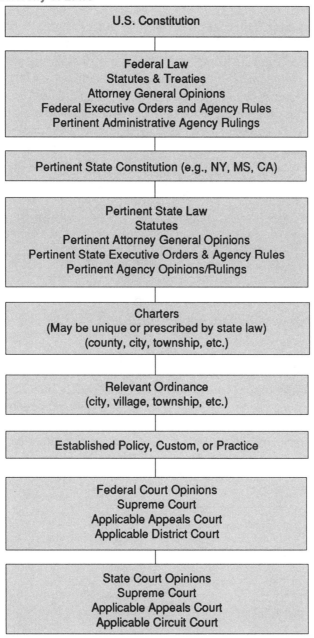

Source: Developed by Stan Stokjovic and Rick Lovell.

Law Defined

We have talked about the law without attempting to define the term. The word almost defies definition; and, as noted by Fisher, O'Brien, and Austern (1987), is the subject of an entire field of study—jurisprudence. Yet these writers define law as a "set of rules or regulations by which a particular group or community regulates the conduct of people within it." While this definition serves our purposes, it should be remembered that the term defies a clear definition because it is often used as a shorthand expression. It may refer to the law in general, or it may refer only to selected aspects of the law (perhaps unique to some particular part of the corrections enterprise). It may also be used as a euphemism, referring to some value-laden concept (e.g., "prisoners' rights").

Used broadly, the term includes criminal and civil law, substantive and procedural law, constitutional law, legislative law, and common (or case) law. Yet this simplistic explanation of law obscures social, political, and other factors bearing on the law.

Law Versus Values and Standards

Constitutions, statutes, administrative agency rules, and court opinions do not materialize in a vacuum. They reflect someone's perceptions of general social values, politics in a broad sense, and the political process, to include the influence of professional associations, political action committees, and other groups.

We can mechanically list constitutions, statutes, or other parts of the law to explain what law is. We can distinguish the law from such variables as American Correctional Association (ACA) Standards,[4] which are NOT a part

---

4   The American Correctional Association (ACA) has published a variety of standards addressing: (1) Adult Parole Authorities, (2) Adult Community Residential Services, (3) Adult Probation and Parole Field Services, (4) Adult Correctional Institutions, (5) Adult Local Detention Facilities, (6) Juvenile Community Residential Facilities, (7) Juvenile Probation and Aftercare Services, (8) Juvenile Detention Facilities, (9) Juvenile Training Schools, (10) Health Care Programs, (11) Food Service Programs, and (12) Small Jail Facilities. These standards are used as management guides for correctional enterprises seeking accreditation, as well as informally by corrections managers, expert witnesses, etc.

of the law. Yet such standards are often used by expert witnesses[5] and attorneys in litigation. They also influence court decisions, as well as correctional agency rules.

For example, one ACA standard prescribes that inmates are to be personally observed by a correctional officer at least every 30 minutes, with suicidal inmates under continual observation (Adult Local Detention Facilities Standard 2-5174, ACA 1981). In litigation, a plaintiff's attorney may often argue that this standard should apply because it is a "state-of-the-art" procedure. Conversely, defense counsel may argue that a state law or state agency rule only requires 60-minute checks on inmates, and more frequent checks of suicidal inmates; and, that this is the law that applies—not the *ideal* standard promoted by the ACA.

When viewed from the foregoing perspective, the law is obviously complex and influenced by its evolutionary nature. This is as true of the law, per se, as it is of the narrower focus of correctional law. Correctional law has evolved as the rights of specific persons and classes of people have evolved.

Rights of Specific Persons and Classes of People

Under English common law all individuals were subordinate to the sovereign. When our new nation was formed, many concepts involving sovereignty and governmental powers were formed and subsequently modified. Even the concept of federally protected constitutional rights has experienced evolution.

The Reconstruction Amendments (13-15) were particularly important in this evolution. They recognized former slaves as being entitled to the protection of the constitution, and extended this protection to violations at both federal and state levels of government. Accompanying these amendments, the Civil Rights Act of 1871—the *Ku Klux Klan Act* (now codified as 42 U.S.C. § 1983, or simply § 1983) created a legal cause of action against any officer or agent of government acting "under color of law" who deprived another of rights guaranteed under the Constitution.

---

5   Expert witnesses may be defined as individuals qualified by training, education, or experience, to render opinions. Some view expert witnesses as consultants. That is, they help attorneys and the trier of fact (judge or jury) understand matters beyond the realm of average citizens. The use of expert witnesses, though widespread, is problematic.

Because it took nearly 100 years (and the Reconstruction amendments of 1865 through 1870) to extend the philosophy of the U.S. Constitution to state government acts, another 100 years of evolution involving constitutional amendment, congressional legislation, changes in social values, standards promulgated by professional groups, and court decisions were necessary to develop a body of law that, today, we refer to as *constitutional law* (Embert, 1986). Constitutional law applies to individuals as well as classes of people. Persons of every race, sex, or religious belief gradually acquired constitutional rights, including the right to sue agents of government (and governmental agencies themselves) for violations of these rights. One of the last classes of people to be brought under the constitutional "umbrella" was accused and convicted criminals.

Rights of the Accused and Convicted

Persons accused of criminal acts are provided with various constitutional safeguards. These include protections against illegal searches and seizures, self-incrimination, the right to be represented by an attorney, the right to a trial by a jury of one's peers, and, upon conviction, protection against cruel and unusual punishment. These rights and safeguards are guaranteed in the Bill of Rights. Yet these safeguards originally protected the citizenry against violations by agents of the federal government only. When the Constitution was adopted in 1787, our concern was oriented toward controlling a newly established central federal government. We thought that we could control state and local governments by means other than our federal Constitution.

Over the next 200 years the basic Constitution and the Bill of Rights were subjected to numerous reviews and interpretations by the courts, reassessments based on the Fourteenth Amendment (adopted following the Civil War of 1860 to 1865). This amendment contains two clauses of major impact. One created the notion of dual citizenship; the other, the concept of "due process." In other words, citizens are citizens of both the United States and a specific state, and no *state* may deprive any citizen of their rights without "due process."

This concept was not implemented overnight. There was much debate over the meaning of the Fourteenth Amendment until about 1970, when, through a gradual process, the major protections of the original Bill of Rights had been incorporated into the amendment. Through this evolution, persons accused of crime were gradually extended various rights not explicitly spelled out in the Constitution.

For example, the Sixth Amendment states that an accused is entitled to the assistance of counsel for his or her defense. The Amendment itself does not address the exact point at which assistance of counsel is to begin or end, or who is to pay for this assistance. Through a series of U.S. Supreme Court decisions, this right now extends from the moment an individual is identified as a *specific* suspect in a crime, through any police interrogations or identification lineups, through preliminary hearings, trial, and appeals. Within some limitations, if an accused cannot afford an attorney, the state must provide one.

Through a comparable evolutionary process, other constitutional provisions have been interpreted and expanded to provide a complex set of both prescriptions and proscriptions for dealing with persons accused of committing a crime. Once the courts focused attention on the rights of persons accused of crime, it was logical, in retrospect, that they would review the meaning of the Bill of Rights and its impact on persons following a criminal conviction.

The courts gradually abandoned the hands-off doctrine and rendered a variety of decisions involving the rights of persons convicted of crime. As in the case of the rights of the accused, a complex set of proscriptions and prescriptions evolved that may be summarized as follows: (1) convicted prisoners do not forfeit all constitutional protections by reason of their conviction, (2) this does not mean these rights are not subject to restrictions and limitations, (3) maintaining institutional security and preserving internal order and discipline are essential goals that may require limitation or retraction of the retained rights of both convicted prisoners and pretrial detainees, and (4) prison administrators should be accorded wide-ranging deference in adopting and executing policies and discipline to maintain institutional security (*Bell v. Wolfish*, 1979).

These basic principles leave many unresolved issues and questions. For example, if prisoners retain some of their constitutional protections—such as the protection against cruel and unusual punishment, what constitutes cruel and unusual punishment? In the 1970s, many court decisions focused upon allegations relating to total prison or jail environments as amounting to cruel and unusual punishment. In these "totality of conditions" lawsuits, many courts entered extensive, detailed decrees, directing governmental and corrections officials to change policies and to renovate their facilities to conform with the mandates of the Constitution.

Other decisions focused on narrower issues, such as the denial of minimal, if not comprehensive, medical care constituting cruel and unusual punishment. In 1976 the U.S. Supreme Court explicitly ruled that inmates incarcerated in correctional facilities had a federal constitutional right to medical treatment, and that "deliberate indifference" to serious medical needs of an inmate violates the Eighth Amendment's proscription against cruel and unusual punishment (*Estelle v. Gamble*, 1976).

Subsequent decisions indicate inmates' rights to medical treatment include a limited right to psychological and psychiatric care, and a right to be protected from themselves. In effect, correctional law has evolved to the point at which it can be said that prisoners have the right to be released from prison or jail in no substantially worse physical or psychological condition than they were at the time they were initially confined (Kalinich, 1986; Kalinich, Embert, and Senese, 1990).

Similarly, probationers and parolees must be dealt with in a manner that affords them at least *minimal* due process considerations—such as by providing them with a notice of pending probation or parole revocation, a hearing, and detailed proceedings following revocation. These considerations are not explicitly spelled out in the Bill of Rights or in the Fourteenth Amendment. They have, however, been made explicit in court decisions. The courts, in turn, have been influenced by social and professional standards.

Impact of Standards on the Law

American society has gradually changed its general philosophy concerning a variety of classes of people. Among the more obvious are societal views towards slavery, ethnic groups, and the sexes. Similarly, society has also changed its view toward dealing with criminals. Whereas death, torture, banishment, and mutilation were once accepted treatments for criminals, today most of society expects criminals to be dealt with *humanely*.

As there is disagreement over equal treatment of protected classes of free citizens, there is also disagreement over what constitutes humane treatment of criminals. A variety of factors have influenced societal views about the "proper" treatment of criminals.

In the former examples, activist groups such as the National Association for the Advancement of Colored People (NAACP) and the National Organization for Women (NOW) have been instrumental in educating the public, the media, legislators, and the courts. Professional associations have played a similar, pivotal role.

These associations include: (1) The American Correctional Association (ACA), (2) The American Jail Association (AJA), (3) The American Bar Association (ABA), (4) The American Medical Association (AMA), and (5) The National Sheriffs' Association (NSA). Each of these associations (and others) has developed and promoted standards of care for inmates, probationers, and parolees.

While the earliest standards were vague and generalized, many have evolved into precise and specific standards. For example, in 1870 the newly formed National Prison Association met in Cincinnati, Ohio, and issued a "Declaration of Principles" stressing the reformation of criminals, rather than the infliction of pain. This association evolved into the American Correctional Association, which published a *Manual of Correctional Standards* in 1946.

Early standards addressed both staff members and prison inmates. For example, one standard focusing on staff members stated that:

> A program of personnel development must be maintained to include the analysis, description and classification of positions, recruitment and selection, in-service training and promotion (ACA 1959).

Today, this broad standard has been expanded into over 25 more precise standards, including:

> Written policy and procedure provide for the selection, retention, and promotion of all personnel on the basis of merit and specified qualifications (Standard 2-4054).

> ...a written grievance procedure for employees which has been approved by the parent agency (Standard 2-4068).

Among standards focusing on inmates are:

> Written policy and procedure ensure the right of inmates to have access to courts (Standard 2-4323).

> A qualified and trained chaplain coordinates and supervises the institution's religious programs (Standard 2-4463).

Such standards, addressing correctional staff, prisoners, probationers, and parolees, mirror philosophies found throughout society. They are, on balance, little more than good management guides that often become the focus of litigation. It is problematic to state that standards promoted by professional groups influenced societal values, or whether such values were ultimately "discovered" and prescribed by the associations (based on prevalent societal and legal standards). It is clear that much of society's philosophy and "state-of-the-art" policies are contained within these standards. They have influenced the entire spectrum of correctional law.

Correctional Law in General

A variety of laws directly affect prisoners, probationers, and parolees. Labor-relations laws and other laws that outwardly affect only staff, also affect correctional clients. Constitutional law, however, is paramount in understanding many of the issues, when applying specific laws to corrections.

Constitutional Law

The rights that apply outside of prisons or jails also apply inside (Clute, 1980). Prisoners, probationers, and parolees have the same constitutional rights as you and me—no more, no less. Constitutional rights are the rights that the government is prohibited from taking away. This does not mean these rights cannot be restricted. Rights can be restricted in free society or in correctional settings.

For example, in free society we have the right to free speech; however, we are not free to recklessly scream "fire" in a crowded theater. Such an utterance would present a "clear and present danger" to others who might be injured in a stampede out of the theater as a result of our prank (*Schenck v. United States*, 1919).

Here we see a balancing of one individual's rights against another's. This balancing exists in prisons and jails, as well as in free society. Prisoners retain basic rights, including the right to reasonable safety and security. They may, for example, retain their right to religious freedom, but this right can be restricted in the interest of safety and security of other inmates and staff members.

This broad approach to restricting rights presents dilemmas. An individual, frequently, will feel entitled to an *absolute* right and resist any attempt to restrict a right. For example, many hunters and shooters have staunchly resisted *any* attempts at gun control.

Corrections officials have often taken similar positions. They have frequently restricted the rights of inmates based on very vague notions about institutional security, or, perhaps, based on some ritual, rather than justifying the restriction based on clearly articulated security or safety concerns. For example, total censorship of all prisoners' mail was a long-standing *ritual*.[6]

By reading all mail and blackening out, or cutting out phrases in a letter, or restricting letters altogether, prison officials kept inmates from being harmed by words, ideas, or things otherwise deemed "unacceptable" (Clute, 1980). In this process an insurmountable workload was prevented only by restricting the volume of mail. This interfered with the freedom of speech guaranteed in the Constitution—including the freedom of speech of inmates' families and friends outside the institution, as well as communications between inmates, their attorneys, and the courts. In balancing the freedom of speech issues, the courts focused on the effects of these rituals on institutional security, and found little correlation.

While prisons and jails have largely abandoned the ritual of censoring "unacceptable" ideas, mail is still screened, read, and restricted in the interest of institutional security. But this form of *inspection*, as opposed to *censorship*, focuses largely on the detection and control of contraband, detecting escape plots, and similar matters. But even these goals make the issues of prisoners' mail and freedom of speech (vis-à-vis institutional security) one of the more complex areas of correctional law. There is an array of issues involving prisoners' mail: (1) religion (2) correspondence with courts and attorneys, (3) inmate publications, (4) mail by and to inmates in isolation, (5) packages, (6) limiting the number of correspondents, (7) mail between inmates, and (8) the issue of negligent (versus intentional) delays in delivering legal mail to inmates (*Procunier v. Martinez*, 1974; *Wolf v. McDonnell*, 1974; *Bell v. Wolfish*, 1979; et al.).

Thus, it is proper to say that inmates, probationers, and parolees have the same constitutional rights as free citizens, and that these rights may be restricted. But the example of prisoners' mail points out the complexities of

---

6   Kalinich (1986) observed that jail managers are trapped between a new set of rules and traditional criminal justice system practices or rituals. The new rules are complex, and developed from standards promulgated by professional organizations and case law. This conflict between old rituals and philosophies and new rules is not unique to jails. It can be seen throughout the criminal justice system.

such generalizations. It also illustrates some of the managerial problems inherent to applying a general rule to specific situations in day-to-day prison operation.

Compounding the situation, the majority of court decisions addressing restrictions on prisoners' mail have come from U.S. District and Circuit Courts, not the U.S. Supreme Court. The Supreme Court has ruled that censorship of prisoners' mail is justified if: (1) an important or substantial government interest is involved, (2) the limitation of First Amendment freedoms is no greater than necessary or essential to the protection of the particular interest involved (*Procunier v. Martinez*, 1974), and (3) that properly identified attorney mail may be opened in the presence of inmates (*Wolff v. McDonnell*, 1974). Such decisions provide broad guidance but do not address many of the *specific* questions dealt with in the daily operation of a prison or jail.

For example, *Wolff v. McDonnell* recognized a legitimate governmental interest in restricting contraband. It saw no harm in restricting inmates to receiving books only from publishers and book-of-the-month clubs. In practice, some systems prohibit inmate purchases from book-of-the-month clubs based on the nature of credit purchasing (Wisconsin Internal Management Procedure No. 4, 11/1/81; *Garner v. Bolden, et al.*, U.S. District Court, Western Michigan, in litigation).

Thus, correctional law presents practitioners with a few broad constitutional principles and an array of specific rulings that may, or may not, apply in *particular* cases. It is left to correctional administrators to sift and sort from a variety of general guidelines and specific court opinions, and fit this array of laws to the management of a particular prison or jail, while dealing with a variety of political, social, physical plant, staffing, and funding differences. Nowhere is the problem more evident than in exercising the general duty of care.

Duty of Care

The concept of acting reasonably to provide safety and security for persons on one's property is well-founded in tort law. Within a correctional context, there is a similar general duty, which may involve constitutional issues or non-constitutional matters.

For example, in *Estelle v. Gamble* (1976), the U.S. Supreme Court stated that deliberate indifference to serious medical needs of prisoners constitutes the unnecessary and wanton infliction of pain proscribed by the Eighth Amendment to the Constitution. Subsequent decisions by federal and state courts have brought dental and mental health care under the rubric of medical care, and extended judicial reasoning to acts of mutilation and other self-destructive behaviors.

The U.S. Supreme Court has even ruled that a private doctor who renders medical services to prison inmates acts "under color of state law;" thus, he or she can be sued for services that fall below constitutional minimum standards (*West v. Atkins*, 1988).

Like the right of free speech, the right to medical care is, at best, a broad guideline and is not a clear, definitive right. For example, some cases have mandated that jails must have a separate psychiatric unit in order to fulfill their duty of providing adequate medical care (*Sykes v. Kreiger*, 1975). However, this rule does not apply to all jails. Similarly, not all cases involving inmate suicides have been ruled to involve constitutional issues.

In cases involving failure to provide medical care, the key to the matter being a constitutional issue is a judicial standard called "deliberate indifference," as opposed to simple negligence, and is an issue for lawyers, judges, and juries to sort out. Briefly, however, if a lawsuit is filed under § 1983, and it is determined that a correctional employee or institution was deliberately indifferent, the duty of care becomes a constitutional issue, and may be considered cruel and unusual punishment (Hurley, 1987).

Apart from the constitutional issue of cruel and unusual punishment, there is the potential issue of medical malpractice. A correctional enterprise may do all the things required, including turning an inmate over to a prison doctor. But that doctor may err, just as a doctor in free society may err.

In such a situation, the doctor (and his or her insurer) may have to fight a medical malpractice suit. While typically a correctional system or institution may not be *directly* involved in malpractice issues, a given case might entail issues of negligence in hiring or assigning a doctor to duties in a prison or jail and might become a civil rights issue, as in *West*.

At a simpler level, the duty of care mandates that prisons and jails be kept in a state of good repair and conform with adequate safety and health standards prevalent in society as a whole. For example, institutions must post warnings of hazardous conditions (such as slippery floors) such as those commonly seen in retail stores. They also must conform with sanitation, fire, and other standards, such as those that generally apply to hotels, restaurants, and other public facilities.

Failing in such matters, a correctional institution or system may be sued by an inmate who is injured. The matter may be handled through a state's claims system or through the inmate grievance system. Should these remedies prove inadequate, an inmate may resort to a lawsuit. In the event of litigation, the issue may be elevated to a constitutional level or may be litigated as a common state tort action.

In effect, prisons and jails must provide reasonable safety and security, as well as health care, for their clients. On balance, it is apparent that correctional institutions face a variety of problems in dealing with their inmates due to the nature of institutionalizing someone against their will.

Prisoners' Rights

The literature and court decisions addressing prisoners' rights are exhaustive. This is because of the array of constitutional and civil rights enjoyed by free people, as well as prisoners.

Constitutional and Civil Rights

Basic constitutional rights typically affecting prisoners are contained in the First, Fourth, Fifth, Sixth, Eighth, and Fourteenth Amendments to the Constitution. Recent U.S. Supreme Court decisions have also focused attention on the Eleventh Amendment. Since many readers may not recall the specific wording in these amendments, it is worthwhile to review each amendment prior to focusing on some specific issues.

> AMENDMENT I: Congress shall make no law respecting an establishment of religion, or prohibiting the free exercise thereof; or abridging the freedom of speech, or of the press; or the right of the people peaceably to assemble, and to petition the Government for a redress of grievances.

The First Amendment addresses five, seemingly straightforward rights: (1) religion, (2) speech, (3) press, (4) assembly, and (5) petition. In practice, each right raises a variety of specific questions and issues unique to prisoners. For example, the rights of prisoners to hold religious services, to conform to religious diets, and the right to wear religious medals and clothing while confined. Most of these issues do not arise in free society.

In discussing the First Amendment, Clute (1980) addressed such additional categories of issues as: (1) differences between personal, legal, and religious mail, (2) publications, (3) grooming and clothing, (4) access to the media, (5) personal visits; and (6) "unions" and other prisoner organizations.

> AMENDMENT IV: The right of the people to be secure in their persons, houses, papers, and effects, against unreasonable searches and seizures, shall not be violated, and no Warrants shall issue, but upon probable cause, supported by Oath or affirmation, and particularly describing the place to be searched, and the persons or things to be seized.

Implied in the Fourth Amendment is the right to privacy. The courts have consistently ruled that in free society, where there is a reasonable expectation of privacy, that right is protected. Conversely, the courts have also consistently indicated that prisoners have little or no reasonable expectation of privacy due to the unique requirements of security within a prison or jail.

Administrators of prisons and jails are responsible for the custody, care, and control of inmates. Given the need for inmate surveillance, inspections, and searches to fulfill these responsibilities, prisoners cannot reasonably expect their persons and belongings to be private. In a similar vein, visitors and employees also lose some of their reasonable expectations of privacy in the interest of institutional security (such as the control of contraband). As a result, employees and visitors may be searched upon entering an institution (see Clute, 1980).

> AMENDMENT V: No person shall be held to answer for a capital, or otherwise infamous crime, unless on a presentment or indictment of a Grand Jury, except in cases arising in the land or naval forces, or in the Militia, when in actual service in time of War or public danger; nor shall any person be subject for the same offence to be twice put in jeopardy of life or limb; nor shall be compelled in any criminal case to be a witness against himself, nor be deprived of life, liberty, or property, without due process of law; nor shall private property be taken for public use, without just compensation.

While many of the rights in the Fifth Amendment have more significance during the accusatory and trial stages, the "self-incrimination" clause has been interpreted to require "*Miranda* warnings," to include inmates accused of new crimes while confined. In addition, decisions affecting individuals "in the land or naval forces, or in the Militia, when in actual service in time of War or public danger..." have generated a separate system of justice for individuals in the military.

The military courts have a unique structure and procedure, claimed (by some) to lie somewhere between the criminal courts and the juvenile courts. The courts, which largely resemble other criminal courts, have, as their authority, the Uniform Code of Military Justice (UCMJ) and include a distinct system of court reviews, including the United States Court of Military Appeals.

In addition, the military has its own distinct corrections systems—run by each branch of the service (Army, Navy, and Air Force). Conversely, each of the military corrections systems is strongly influenced by decisions of both the U.S. Court of Military Appeals and the U.S. Supreme Court.

In the Sixth Amendment we see some seemingly straightforward rights: (1) speedy and public trial by jury, (2) cross-examination of witnesses, and (3) assistance of counsel.

> AMENDMENT VI: In all criminal prosecutions, the accused shall enjoy the right to a speedy and public trial, by an impartial jury of the State and district wherein the crime shall have been committed, which district shall have been previously ascertained by law, and to be informed of the nature and cause of the accusation; to be confronted with the witnesses against him; to have compulsory process of obtaining witnesses in his favor, and to have the Assistance of Counsel for his defence.

The clause in the Sixth Amendment dealing with the assistance of counsel is of particular concern to prisoners, and raises numerous practical issues (including free communications with prisoners' attorneys, the right to "jail house lawyers," and the right to law libraries).

> AMENDMENT VIII: Excessive bail shall not be required, nor excessive fines imposed, nor cruel and unusual punishments inflicted.

The Eighth Amendment is of particular prominence in prisoners' rights cases involving prison conditions, including deficiencies in housing, food, medical care, and sanitation.

> AMENDMENT XIV: Section 1. All persons born or naturalized in the United States, and subject to the jurisdiction thereof, are citizens of the United States and of the State wherein they reside. No State shall make or enforce any law which shall abridge the privileges or immunities of citizens of the United States; nor shall any State deprive any person of life, liberty, or property, with due process of law; nor deny to any person within its jurisdiction the equal protection of the laws.

The Fourteenth Amendment contains important clauses dealing with dual citizenship and due process, as well as the "equal protection" clause. Interpreted in a variety of cases, numerous categories of issues have been developed inherent to these fundamental rights.

For example, Miller and Walter (1987) have categorized some 50 broad issues, including: (1) access to courts, (2) administrative segregation, (3) classification and separation, (4) exercise and recreation, (5) food, (6) grievance procedures, (7) intake and admissions, and (8) visiting.

Constitutional rights of prisoners are abundant and complex. While the same can be said of the rights of free people, the issues are exacerbated by the complexities of providing custody, care, and control of inmates. Conversely, not all inmates' rights involve constitutional or civil rights issues.

Civil rights are guaranteed by the Constitution and supporting federal legislation. Legislation, including the Civil Rights Act, requires prison and jail administrators, as well as the courts, to address three fundamental questions: (1) Is a constitutional right involved? (2) Should the exercise of the right be restricted? and (3) What is a proper reason for restricting the exercise of the right? (Clute, 1980). Depending on the answers to these questions, inmates may file a federal civil rights suit, commonly under § 1983, which provides that:

> Every person who, under color of any statute, ordinance, regulation, custom, or usage, of any State or Territory or the District of Columbia, subjects, or causes to be subjected, any citizen of the United States or other person within the jurisdiction thereof to the deprivation of any rights, priv-

ileges, or immunities secured by the Constitution and laws, shall be liable to the party injured in an action at law, suit in equity, or other proper proceeding for redress...

Research suggests that inmates win monetary awards in only a minuscule number of lawsuits (CONTACT CENTER, Inc., 1985). Many cases are dismissed as lacking a constitutional issue; others, due to various degrees of governmental immunities. (All governments have immunities against being sued, providing for litigation only under certain circumstances.)

Other cases result in some form of declaratory or injunctive relief. That is, the court may render a decision requiring a correctional system to refrain from certain actions in the future, or take actions to fix an unsatisfactory condition. In either case, the inmate receives no direct monetary award.

Where a constitutional or civil right is not involved, inmates may often file suit in state courts based on the general duty of care, or under a general claims law.

Duty of Care: Claims for Losses

Home owners, motorists, private businesses, and governmental entities have a common law duty to provide reasonable safety and security for others. Acts, or failures to act, in violation of common law personal or property rights of another, which do not involve constitutional issues, may result in a victim receiving judicial relief through common law tort actions.

In this regard, there are two principal types of torts: (1) intentional torts, and (2) negligent torts. An intentional tort occurs when an individual purposefully acts in violation of the rights of an individual, and may include assault, battery, or defamation. Most intentional torts (such as assault) also involve criminal infractions. That is, the perpetrator may be tried and convicted in a criminal court, and also sued in a civil court.

Negligent torts typically address failures to act reasonably, and focus on such issues as negligence in hiring an employee, negligence in properly training an employee, or negligence in entrusting an employee with a dangerous instrument (e.g., a car or a gun). In either type of case, a plaintiff may be awarded compensatory damages, and possibly punitive damages.

Nominal damages are awarded when a tort has been committed but the injury is very minor, and may involve an award of as little as a dollar or so.

Compensatory, or actual damages, are designed to financially compensate the victim for a loss. This might include medical expenses and the expenses of "pain and suffering" or the expense of damaged property. Punitive, or exemplary damages, are designed to punish the defendant and are based upon: (1) the conduct of the defendant, (2) the extent of injury, (3) the cost of litigation, and (4) the wealth of the defendant (Spain, 1985).

In summary, when we address the issue of prisoners' rights, it is imperative to recognize that the very term, "prisoners' rights," is a shorthand expression. While some rights can be traced to the Constitution (or the applicable state constitution), others have their foundation in common law. Regardless of the type of right, prisoners enjoy the same rights as you and me. Like our rights, the rights of prisoners can be restricted. With these generalities in mind, we can turn to some fundamental rights of prisoners, and the complex issues associated with these rights.

Fundamental Rights

Prisoners' rights can generally be divided into two categories: *procedural* rights and *substantive* rights. The former refers to due process rights, or the rules guiding and limiting governmental actions against individuals. Substantive rights, on the other hand, deal with the freedom to do something (Hawkins and Alpert, 1989).

Prior to being entitled to either due process or substantive rights, prisoners had to be given *legal status* and *access to the courts*. So long as prisoners were considered "slaves of the state," they could not enjoy any right to due process, let alone any substantive rights.

Bear in mind that prisoners were largely ignored in our Constitution, and were largely at the mercy of state "civil death" statutes. That is, once convicted, offenders generally lacked access to the courts. Even the basic right of *habeas corpus* (Latin for "you have the body," it is a judicial order to someone holding a person to bring that person to court—an effort to be released from confinement due to some constitutional violation) was largely denied prisoners until the early 1940s. In the 1944 case of *Coffin v. Reichard* a federal appeals court ruled that prisoners were entitled to the writ of habeas corpus when deprived of some right to which he or she was lawfully entitled, even in confinement.

Beyond habeas corpus attacks, common law tort actions were, initially, also restrained—most notably by state civil death statutes. Section 1983 suits were, and again are, also problematic, as we shall see. Without belaboring the point, the basic and most fundamental prisoner right is the right to be heard by a court.

Today, inmates have this fundamental right. Hawkins and Alpert (1989) list five basic ways inmates may make legal challenges regarding prison conditions or the practices of correctional officials: (1) a state habeas corpus action, (2) a federal habeas corpus action after state remedies have been exhausted, (3) a state tort suit; (4) a federal civil rights suit (typically under § 1983), and (5) a suit by the federal government against state employees under the Civil Rights of Institutionalized Persons Act of 1980.

While each avenue is problematic, particularly in terms of making *systemic* changes to a corrections system, today it can be said that prisoners enjoy the fundamental right of access to the courts. Albeit, the door may have been somewhat closed, as shall be seen.

The second basic right of significance to prisoners is that of *due process*. The Fifth and Fourteenth Amendments to the Constitution prohibit government from depriving persons of life, liberty, or property, without due process of law. While a criminal trial can clearly deprive persons of fundamental interests, the U.S. Supreme Court has also recognized that other deprivations can take place. While these deprivations may not be as serious as a sentence to prison or jail, the courts have insisted on some form of due process, depending on the seriousness of the deprivation.

As noted, prison officials have wide discretion in administering their facilities. In this regard, every correctional institution has a set of rules governing inmate conduct. Punishments for violations of these rules can range from an oral reprimand to solitary confinement or the loss of good conduct time, and a variety of punishments in between. Due process decisions, such as those described in *Morrissey v. Brewer* (1972) and *Gagnon v. Scarpelli* (1973) led, somewhat logically, to the *Wolff v. McDonnell* decision of 1974 that prison officials cannot impose severe disciplinary penalties without a due process hearing (ACA, 1987).

However, cases subsequent to Wolff have narrowed the extent of prison disciplinary hearings. While the majority opinion required: (1) an advance 24-hour notice of a disciplinary hearing, (2) an impartial hearing body (not the staff member bringing charges), (3) an opportunity to present witnesses and evidence in defense, (4) a statement of the evidence relied upon to reach a decision, and (5) written reasons for the disciplinary action taken, the court did not require inmates to be assisted by an attorney. Similarly, the court left prison officials with the discretionary authority to limit cross-examination of witnesses (based on security reasons).

Thus, while prisoners accused of violating an institutional rule are required to be provided with at least a minimal due process hearing, they are entitled to considerably less than an accused in a criminal trial. In addition, the courts have narrowly interpreted what constitutes a disciplinary action. For example, decisions to transfer inmates from a medium to maximum security facility, transfers from a state to the federal prison system, and even transfers within a prison from the general population to administrative segregation, do not require a formal hearing (Duffee, 1989; Hawkins and Alpert, 1989).

A third fundamental prisoner right—the right to *equal protection of the laws*—has also been narrowly interpreted by the courts. While the equal protection clause of the Fourteenth Amendment prohibits any state from denying any person the equal protection of the laws, prison administrators can rather easily raise a compelling state interest and justify discrimination.

Probably the biggest area focusing on the equal protection argument involves female prisoners. Duffee (1989) noted that most prison experts agree that the rights and programs for women prisoners lag far behind those for men. Nicole Rafter (1989) stated that observers have compared conditions under which men and women are confined and,

> Without exception, they have concluded that women's prisons provide different and generally inferior care. Women have fewer education and vocational programs; less opportunity for work release, recreation and visitation; and fewer medical and legal resources.

Given the fundamental right of access to the courts, minimal due process proceedings, and equal protection of the law, the Eighth Amendment's prohibition against *cruel and unusual punishment* is, arguably, the next most important right of inmates. This amendment has been used to: (1) govern the use of force, (2) govern the use of isolation or segregation cells, (3) govern the availability of medical care, (4) govern the use of some intrusive rehabilitation and treatment techniques, (5) govern the conditions of confinement, and (6) control the length of confinement.

The fundamental rights of inmates are relatively few, but complex. For example, the issue of medical care, including mental health care, is particularly problematic. Even the issue of the "insanity defense" (for avoiding criminal responsibility and punishment for prohibited acts) is problematic. Jurists and social scientists have wrestled with the total issue of mental illness as far back as the landmark *M'Naghten* case in 1843. Although every court has struggled with a variety of rules and issues involving mental illness, the courts failed to recognize a constitutional right to mental health treatment until 1971, when the Court ruled that:

> ...absent treatment, the hospital is transformed into a penitentiary where one could be held indefinitely for no convicted offense...The purpose of involuntary hospitalization is treatment and not mere custodial care or punishment (*Wyatt v. Stickney*, 1971).

Later the U.S. Supreme Court ruled that prisoners in correctional institutions had a right to medical treatment (*Estelle v. Gamble*, 1976). Medical treatment now subsumes some degree of mental health care, and is particularly a problem in county jails (Kalinich, Embert, and Senese, 1990).

On balance, we can conclude that various court cases dealing with prisoners' rights have had a profound effect on the management of prisons and jails, and spawned a variety of rules that constitute the totality of prisoners' rights.

These rights require prisons and jails to be organized and run with definitive written policies, detailed procedures, and well-trained staff members, and address the physical plant, visitation, correspondence, telephone calls, inmate exercise, a law library, religious services, disciplinary proceedings, classification procedures, and even an inmate rule book (Kalinich and Postill, 1981; Miller and Walter, 1989).

Most of the rights of prisoners do little beyond assuring them of reasonably humane treatment. As Hawkins and Alpert (1989) note, the movement and extension of prisoner's rights has forced a bureaucratization of American prisons (fear of lawsuits has forced correctional officials to document their every action). In addition, the movement has generated a need for prison and jail administrators who are trained in law and management.

Conversely, Hawkins and Alpert also noted that any attempt to capture the entire picture of inmate rights is frustrated in a number of ways, including: (1) the inconsistency of U.S. Supreme Court decisions, (2) the failure of lower federal courts to always follow the lead of the Supreme Court, and (3) the fact that many cases do not even reach the Supreme Court.

As an example of the complexity inherent in addressing prisoners' rights, on June 15, 1989, the U.S. Supreme Court ruled that states and state officials are not "persons" as defined by § 1983; hence, they may not be sued under the provisions of § 1983. In this case (*Will v. Michigan Department of State Police*), affirming an earlier Michigan Supreme Court decision, Justice White said that states and their officials enjoy constitutional *immunity* against civil rights suits, and relied on the Eleventh Amendment as the rationale for the decision (*Lansing State Journal*, June 16, 1989).

> AMENDMENT XI: The Judicial power of the United States shall not be construed to extend to any suit in law or equity, commenced or prosecuted against one of the United States by Citizens of another State, or by Citizens or Subjects of any Foreign State.

The implications of this case are uncertain. On the surface it appears that the decision may sharply affect future prisoner § 1983 suits against state departments of corrections. Conversely, attorneys are debating the decision, with some noting that state officials can still be sued for injunctive relief, as well as for damages as individuals (*Michigan Lawyers Weekly*, June 26, 1989).

Additionally, many current rules relating to inmates' rights may be so ingrained in the system that they will survive as a part of state law, or even local custom and practice. If the latter holds, inmates will continue to enjoy minimal humane care and treatment while incarcerated. The frequency of inmate suits and even the process by which inmates gain access to the courts may, however, change. We may see more reliance on writs of habeas corpus or use of the Civil Rights of Institutionalized Persons Act of 1980 when existing rights are willfully and flagrantly violated by the corrections enterprise. Some legal writers have suggested that we may see more § 1983 cases filed in state courts, rather than federal courts (Steinglass, 1988).

In any event, it would appear that inmates have a variety of legal rights that require correctional institutions to be managed with a degree of skill not required in the early days of corrections. The same is true of the rights of probationer and parolees.

Rights of Parolees and Probationers

Although *parole* and *probation* are often used interchangeably, Chapters 13 and 14 distinguish between these forms of community-based corrections. At this point, it is enough to note that parole is a form of release granted by an executive agency to a prisoner who has served part of a sentence in confinement.

As with probation, statutes typically give the paroling authority the right to impose such conditions as it may deem proper. Sometimes statutes dictate that certain conditions be imposed upon parolees. In general, parolees have a right to personal liberty as long as they comply with their conditions of parole. When parolees violate their conditions of parole, revocation of parole (and return to prison) is a possibility.

A similar situation exits in the case of probationers—offenders sentenced by a court to supervision in the community as an alternative to confinement. Probation, as an alternative to confinement, is a creature of statute; accordingly, the appropriate legislature may preclude the courts from granting probation for some types of felony convictions. For those offenders who may be granted probation, the tribunal authorized to grant probation is also typically given the authority to impose and modify the conditions of probation, as well as to revoke probation (Cromwell, et al., 1985).

Eligibility for probation does not convey a right to probation; probation is largely a discretionary function of the sentencing court. However, most states grant a convicted offender a right to be *considered* for probation. Conversely, probation cannot be imposed upon a defendant without his or her *consent* (Cromwell, et al., 1985).

Given these general rules, one might assume that there are few additional rules or rights that might become an issue in cases where convicted offenders willingly submit to a court's discretionary imposition of probation, rather than confinement. However, such is not the case. The U.S. Supreme Court has held, for example, that "due process" mandates both preliminary and final revocation hearings in the case of a probationer (*Gagnon v. Scarpelli*, 1973). Other cases have addressed such issues as searches of probationers by probation officers, vague conditions imposed upon the probationer, and the appropriateness of conditions of probation (*Soroka v. State*, 1979; *Brock v. State*, 1983, etc.). In either parole or probation, the conditions imposed upon an offender are problematic.

Conditions of probation or parole may loosely be defined as: those things an offender must either do, or refrain from doing, to satisfactorily serve a sentence. Ideally, the term and conditions of probation, for example, are tailored to the needs of a specific offender; hence, statutes typically give the courts wide latitude in determining the appropriate conditions imposed upon a convicted offender as a part of probation (Cromwell, et al., 1985).

Given broad discretion in these matters, it is hardly surprising that conditions of probation imposed by trial court judges have been challenged. In retrospect, a majority of such challenges have been based on their impact on third parties, their vagueness, or their unreasonable intrusion on constitutionally protected rights.

For example, banishing a probationer's wife as a condition of probation has been ruled an unreasonable restriction on an innocent person's freedom of travel, and a condition over which the probationer has little or no control (*Parkerson v. State*, 1980). Many can envision a situation in which good judgment would preclude a probationer from having contact with his or her spouse. Conversely, one would also probably challenge the court's authority to restrict a spouse who has not been convicted of any criminal offense.

Similarly, the U.S. Appeals Court has rebuked conditions of probation deemed too broad—such as an individual having to refrain from making any statements advocating disobedience of the law (*United States v. Smith*, 1980). Again, one can see the logic of a condition restricting a person from advocating the disobedience of a specific law, for which the probationer was convicted; however, thoughtful readers might question the court's authority to *totally* restrict a probationer's freedom of expression against *any* law.

In another case, a court order for a probationer to make payments on a $20,000 fine was struck down by a higher court, which ruled that the nonpayment could not be construed as a "failure to rehabilitate" (*United States v. Grant*, 1987). Here, a legal decision applied to the imprecise and imperfect technology of rehabilitation and punishment, impacted on the intended outcome of probation. In this case it is intuitively logical that an offender should pay his or her fine, but it is also conceivable that situations might arise precluding such payment. An unemployed probationer, for example, might not be able to pay a fine. Confining the offender would also do little to enhance payment of the fine.

As a final example, a U.S. Appeals Court ruled that payment of attorney fees and travel expenses was not a proper condition of probation (*United States v. Turner*, 1980). While such a requirement might seem to make sense, in the case of an indigent offender, such a condition conflicts with an accused's right to a court-appointed attorney.

These are but a few examples of issues various courts have addressed in balancing the rights of probationers with the interests of society. Similarly, the courts have attempted to balance conflicting rights and interests in the case of parole, as well as in instances of probation and parole *revocation*, upon an offender's violation of one or more of their conditions of probation or parole.

As in probation revocation, parole revocation requires a minimum due process hearing. In the landmark case of *Morrissey v. Brewer* (1972) the Supreme Court held that the liberty of a parolee includes many of the core values of unqualified liberty, that its termination inflicts a "grievous loss" on the parolee (and others, such as family members), and that its termination calls for some orderly process, however informal.

While the hearing may be informal, certain minimum due process requirements must be met: (1) written notice of the alleged violation of parole, (2) disclosure of evidence against the parolee, (3) the opportunity to be present, heard in person, and to present both witnesses and documentary evidence in defense, (4) the right to cross-examine witnesses against the parolee, (5) a neutral hearing body, and (6) a written statement by the board as to the evidence relied on and the reasons for revoking parole (*Morrissey v. Brewer*, etc.).

Some readers may see these requirements as little more than minimal, and even essential in preventing arbitrary and capricious actions by overly zealous officials. They might, for example, envision being entitled to similar treatment in the event they are threatened with suspension from school. Yet even such relatively simple requirements impose a workload on correctional employees and managers that were not a part of traditional corrections.

While many court cases affecting probationers and parolees focus on the conditions imposed, and the revocation of either status, there are also a variety of court cases addressing the collateral consequences of conviction. These impact on probationers and parolees, as well as those who are confined; hence, are discussed under the section below titled "Rights of Ex-Offenders."

At this point it is important to recognize that mere conviction, and especially a conviction for a crime labeled as a felony, has a major impact on offenders sentenced to probation as an alternative to confinement. While some people may perceive probation as a minor punishment, or "slap on the wrist," when the indirect and collateral consequences of a court conviction are considered, the total punishment imposed upon probationers is hardly considered minor.

Similarly, when a parolee faces revocation of parole, that punishment may be exacerbated by its future impact on such collateral rights. For example, an ex-offender trying to become licensed to practice a profession might have to overcome both the original court conviction and the following parole failure. In effect, probationers, prisoners, and parolees are all affected by collateral punishments which impact on "ex-offenders."

Rights of Ex-Offenders

Among the civil and political rights that may be affected by a court conviction are: (1) all civil rights (civil death), (2) the right to claim good moral character, (3) the right to hold public office, (4) the right to vote, (5) the right to serve on a jury, (6) the right to be a witness, (7) the right to hold a position of trust, (8) the right to full and free enjoyment of property, (9) the right to purchase insurance, (10) the right to certain pension benefits, (11) the right to marry and have children, and (12) employment rights (Cromwell, et al. 1985).

Because of the importance attributed to the direct consequences of a criminal conviction, the collateral consequences of conviction are often overlooked. Nonetheless, the collateral consequences of a criminal conviction are an important aspect in the technologies of corrections. They affect probation and parole services, as well as the value of programs run inside prisons.

The variations among the different states in the application of these collateral sanctions makes generalizations difficult. However, a variety of legal commentators and professional associations have been advocating modification of these traditional barriers for many years.

While convicted felons do not lose their citizenship (*Trop v. Dulles*, 1958; *Kennedy v. Mendoza-Martinez*, 1963) they do lose many civil rights and suffer from many civil disabilities that may adversely affect their ability to reintegrate into society. Legal mandates (whether promulgated in state statutes or agency rules) impact on any hopes for the rehabilitation of offenders or their reintegration into society.

More broadly, ex-offenders face collateral consequences from a court conviction that include social stigma, the loss of some or all civil rights, and administrative and legislative restrictions (Allen & Simonsen, 1986). We will focus on the right to employment to illustrate a variety of ways in which legislative and quasi-legislative forces interact to impact on offender rehabilitation, reintegration, and management.

Barbering, for example, is a needed and respected skill. Prisons need barbers, and must teach the trade to selected inmates. But ex-offenders have traditionally been denied licensure as a barber. Why? Many react to this question with thoughts about murderers being entrusted with razors in a barber's chair. But many felons are not violent offenders; they have been denied licensure as barbers for reasons other than their threat of violence.

These include legislative and administrative agency restrictions on the employment of ex-offenders based on earlier notions of civil death, economic protectionism for various occupations (some dating to the Great Depression), as well as societal views concerning the appropriateness of felons working in various trades and professions.

Social stigma may also make it difficult to obtain employment. That is, a prospective employer may simply refuse to hire an ex-offender. Failure to obtain meaningful employment may be grounds for denial of parole. At a more subtle level, failure to obtain meaningful employment may lead ex-offenders back to a life of crime based on the idea that it is better to earn a decent wage doing something illegal than to join the nation's working poor. In this regard, over one million people work for $4.50 an hour or less (*Lansing State Journal*, July 30, 1990).

The foregoing has implications for the value and appropriateness of prison vocational training and educational programs. Research suggests that prison vocational training programs that do not lead to attractive jobs may be of little value in deterring future criminality (McGee, 1981).

Broadly examined, some 350 occupations or professions have had entry restrictions imposed by federal, state, or local governments. Depending on the state, crime labeled as a felony, a crime involving moral turpitude, and even misdemeanors are sufficient to prevent licensing. Over one-half of the licenses require good moral character, an obstacle in that it is almost universally assumed that persons convicted of crimes lack good character (Cromwell, 1976).

Compounding ex-offender's employment opportunities are restrictions in public employment, based on state constitutions or statutory provisions.

Since most public employment is covered by civil service statutes and regulations, these are often the source prohibiting the hiring of persons found guilty, as well as those arrested, for job disqualification. In some cases an ex-offender may be hired, but only after a lapse of one to five years.

Many ex-offenders may be unable to become bonded. Yet many jobs involving the handling of funds or valuable merchandise require the incumbent to be bonded by a surety company. That company has the authority to approve or deny a bond, and typically will refuse to bond "poor risks."

In effect, when we look at the rights of ex-offenders to employment, there are a variety of legislative and quasi-legislative issues that present barriers to meaningful employment. Also, most corrections professionals recognize that meaningful employment is essential to rehabilitating and reintegrating offenders into society.

There are a variety of other rights affecting ex-offenders and their successful rehabilitation and reintegration into society. Some impact on the offender's self-esteem; others, on the ex-offender's quality of life. The rights to purchase insurance, enjoy pension benefits, to marry, or have or adopt children are some examples. Insurance companies may elect not to issue car insurance to persons convicted of certain crimes; this impacts on job opportunities, as well as the individual's freedom of mobility. In the case of denial of adoption, based on the individual's "lack of fitness" to be a parent, the desire for a family may be so strong as to impact on a marriage. In short, the collateral consequences of a conviction can adversely impact on the most fundamental features of life—employment and family.

Other Legal Issues

We have talked about probationers, inmates, and parolees, focusing on offender rights. This is one way in which corrections and the law interact. There are, however, additional legal issues inherent to corrections: (1) the rights of correctional employees, (2) accreditation, (3) privatization of prisons and jails, and (4) the death penalty.

Rights of Correctional Employees

Like offenders, correctional employees have rights. These include the right to equal employment opportunity, the right to safety and security, and the right to use force in dealing with correctional clients. Each affects, directly or indirectly, the management of a correctional enterprise, and may affect the ability to exercise custody, care, and control over correctional clients.

Equal Employment Opportunity Rights

The most important rights of correctional staff members are, arguably, the right to be hired, assigned, promoted, disciplined, and even fired, without regard to race, sex, creed, age, or national origin. The Fifth Amendment to the Constitution states that "no person shall...be deprived of life, liberty, or property without due process of law." The Fourteenth Amendment imposes similar prohibitions on state and local governments. Additionally, the Civil Rights Act of 1964 (Title VII), as amended by The Equal Employment Opportunity Act of 1972, makes it unlawful for an employer to discriminate in matters involving hiring, firing, wages, or conditions and privileges of employment on the basis of race, color, religion, sex, or national origin.

Correctional staff rights would be meaningless without some means of recourse. A major source of redressing grievances pertaining to employment matters is the Equal Employment Opportunity Commission (EEOC). In practice, most EEOC complaints are deferred to state civil rights agencies empowered to provide relief from discriminatory practices.

The foregoing constitutional amendments and laws; the Equal Pay Act of 1963; The Age Discrimination in Employment Act of 1967, as amended; the Vietnam Era Veterans Readjustment Act of 1972; the General Revenue Sharing Act; and various labor relations acts combine to form what we can loosely refer to as EEO laws and guidelines (Poe and Curry, 1986).

These (and other) guidelines influence correctional staff recruitment, advertising, and selection, as does affirmative action legislation. In this regard, as a result of past job restrictions, many minority and female members of the work force are still disadvantaged in their competition for good jobs. Accordingly, various corrections enterprises have had affirmative actions programs imposed by a court or other governmental entity, as well as through voluntary undertaking.

As a result, today's corrections enterprise has seen an increase in minority and female workers. For example, over 32% of Michigan's 11,043 employees are female; the number of female corrections officers increased from 123 in 1977 to 1,381 at the end of 1987 (Michigan Department of Corrections Annual Report, 1987).

With an increase of female employees in a previously male-dominated profession, issues of *sexual harassment* (as opposed to *sexual discrimination*) have also risen to the forefront of managerial attention. This does not suggest that sexual harassment is unique to corrections or that it is a new phenomenon.

It does, however, serve to point out that according to federal EEOC regulations (March 1980) employers, employment agencies, and labor organizations can now be held responsible if any of its employees sexually harass another employee, and that these responsibilities exist even if policy statements have been issued against sexual harassment. The law also gives victims the right to sue on the basis of sexual harassment (Taylor, 1989).

The result of this issue is that correctional management must now engage in training employees on sexual harassment issues, develop guidelines for dealing with allegations of sexual harassment, and become involved in a variety of other management actions largely alien to past management practices. The application of EEO and affirmative action to corrections has also created new problems, while attempting to solve old problems. In the case of increased numbers of female corrections officers, and the subsequent assignment of both males and females to correctional institutions without regard to the sex of the inmates, prisoners of both sexes have raised objections based on invasions to privacy or on religious grounds.

It might be noted that there are many other unresolved issues involving EEO. For example, the Supreme Court of the State of Washington recently determined that jail correctional officers are significantly different than police officers, and are not entitled to equal compensation. Yet in Michigan, it has been successfully argued that state correctional officers are significantly like state police officers, and this may justify efforts to close the gap in their salaries.

Also, while jails differ from prisons, both must be managed in accordance with similar rules and both involve many complex issues. Yet jail employees are often more attuned to the law enforcement mission of the county sheriff than the corrections mission. Indeed, much staffing in some county jails is by deputy sheriffs. Even where there is a separate type of correctional staff member, they often see their duties as comparable to that of a road officer. For example, they may be more amenable to writing disciplinary reports, rather than counseling or rehabilitating prisoners.

Right to Safety and Security

Frequently overlooked is the issue of staff safety and security. As discussed earlier, all employers have a duty under common tort law of providing reasonable safety and security for their employees. Indeed, this duty, when viewed in the light of equal opportunity and sexual harassment, extends to the right of a generally pleasant work environment.

Use of Force

Generally, society does not allow one person to use force against another; in fact, unlawful use of either verbal or physical force constitutes the crime of assault. (Fisher, O'Brien, and Austern, 1987) Conversely, corrections, by definition, must use coercive force in its relationships with correctional clients. Indeed, the very acts of trying, convicting, and sentencing offenders involve the use of coercive force. Having stated the obvious, we can delve into one of the more complex issues faced by corrections.

First, there is a fundamental philosophical issue facing the entire criminal justice system, not just corrections. This issue is how to best get human beings to conform with the norms, values, and rules of society. The German sociologist, Max Weber, noted three types of compliance: (1) willing compliance (authority), (2) reluctant compliance (power), and (3) forced compliance (might) (L. Radelet, 1986, *citing* d'Entreves, 1967).

Correctional clients, by definition, have not complied with the legal authority. Many, upon arrest and conviction, will only reluctantly comply with their sentence (due to the power of various criminal justice positions). Others must be forced into compliance (through the use of the potential power of the system). This includes, in the case of correctional institutions, compliance with the prison rules.

Institutional correctional officers will typically strive to gain inmates' willing or reluctant compliance with rules. When this fails, the staff must resort to might or force.

When correctional staff members are forced to exceed verbal counseling or coaching, or the force inherent in their authority, the appropriate or inappropriate use of might (force) becomes an issue, often resulting in inmate litigation.

While almost no one questions the need for the occasional use of physical force in correctional institutions, it is equally apparent that correctional staff have used excessive force far too frequently. As a result, the courts have generally ruled that correctional officials have the right or privilege of resorting to the use of physical force against inmates only under the following conditions: (1) in self-defense, (2) in defense of another staff member, visitor, or inmate, (3) to maintain order and enforce institutional rules, (4) to prevent crime, and (5) to prevent escapes.

The issue in all of these cases is the *necessity* at the time of the incident and the *reasonableness* of the degree of force. Force cannot be used minutes or hours after an incident; it must be applied immediately (*ACA Handbook*, 1987). This requirement is fairly straightforward; for example, if two inmates are involved in a fight, finish the fight, and then are subjected to the use of force by correctional officers two hours later, the force would almost certainly be viewed as punishment, rather than the reasonable use of force to end the fight.

The reasonableness of force is another, more complicated matter. As noted by the ACA (1987) courts will look at several factors bearing on the reasonableness of force: (1) need for the application of force in the first place, (2) relationship between need and amount of force, (3) extent of any injury inflicted, and (4) whether the force was applied in a good faith effort to restore discipline or maintain order, or used maliciously and sadistically just to cause harm (*Johnson v. Glick*, 1977).

Distinct from the issue of non-deadly force is that of deadly force. In this case, the courts have generally ruled that deadly force can be used to prevent an act that could result in death or severe bodily injury; but, in effect, only as a last resort, when other means cannot be used; or, if attempted, have failed.

Prisons and jails are confronted with the issue of the use of deadly force to prevent the escape of an inmate. This issue is undecided. (Fisher, O'Brien, and Austern 1987; Hawkins and Alpert, 1989;) It is clouded by the U.S. Supreme Court's decision in *Tennessee v. Garner* (1985), which held that police officers cannot use deadly force to prevent the escape of a fleeing felon unless: (1) necessary to prevent the escape, and (2) the suspect poses a significant threat of death or serious injury to the officer or others.

Garner overturned a long-standing common law principle that police officers could use deadly force to prevent the escape of any fleeing felon. The decision recognized that the early law was based on the facts that: (1) few crimes were labeled as felonies, (2) all felonies carried the threat of the death penalty, and (3) technology made an escape threat more attractive than today; it could readily become a permanent escape. Today, however, numerous crimes are labeled as felonies; few carry the potential for the death penalty; police weapons are considerably more precise; and police communications between communities makes recapture highly likely (thus the temptation to escape is less than in earlier times).

Whether *Garner* applies to corrections has not been decided. Depending on the population of a prison or jail, there may be a mix of felons and misdemeanants; guilty and accused; felons who present a threat to life or limb as well as felons who do not. Given these complex variables unique to prisons and jails, the best that can be said is that when a prisoner attempts an escape the appropriate *state law* applies. Management must develop precise policies and procedures, and implement training programs to preclude wanton and reckless use of deadly force to prevent escapes.

The use of deadly force to quell a prison riot or restore order during a prison or jail disturbance is somewhat less uncertain. The U.S. Supreme Court has addressed this issue, raising the question: "Was the force applied in a good faith effort to restore order, or for the purpose of inflicting harm?" Yet, even in this situation, an inmate may be shot or harmed, and able to raise a legitimate tort suit, if not a § 1983 suit (Fisher, O'Brien, and Austern, 1987).

The issue of the use of force is complex. Correctional officers clearly have the right to use force; they do not, however, have the right to use unbridled force to inflict punishment.

Accreditation as a Legal Issue

In addition to the professional associations, a variety of governmental entities have developed correctional standards—including documents prepared under the auspices of the United Nations (*Standard Minimum Rules for the Treatment of Prisoners*), as well as a variety of governmental entities (the

President's Commission on Law Enforcement and Administration of Justice, and the National Advisory Commission on Criminal Justice Standards and Goals).

Of these standards, American Correctional Association (ACA) standards are unique in that they evolved into an accreditation program. Accreditation of a corrections agency is somewhat comparable to accreditation programs for colleges and hospitals, and somewhat analogous to certification of an individual. That is, an outside authority determines that an agency meets certain "minimal" standards. In effect, accreditation of an agency becomes a "stamp of approval" by a presumedly unbiased organization.

Until 1974 all ACA standards resulted in purely voluntary use, compliance, and self-evaluation, and did not include any outside involvement. In 1974 the Law Enforcement Assistance Administration (LEAA) awarded funds to the ACA to establish the Commission on Accreditation for Corrections. This commission consists of a Board of Commissioners (total of 21) and an executive staff. Its principal responsibility is accreditation, to include participation in standards revision, training of administrators, and research related to standards and accreditation.

Each agency desiring to become accredited will typically commence the accreditation process by voluntarily requesting accreditation. If accepted into a correspondent stage, the agency will receive an orientation and appoint an accreditation manager. This manager will be responsible for developing an internal agency structure about which to marshal agency resources needed to attain accreditation. Ultimately, this manager submits a self-evaluation report describing the agency, its programs, and the extent of compliance with applicable ACA standards. Once accredited (for a three-year period) the agency is expected to continue to comply with the applicable standards, file annual reports, and undergo monitoring visits by impartial auditors.

While such a program has apparent merit, it has not been without its criticism. First of all, accreditation is neither mandatory nor even widespread. Secondly, the standards themselves have been criticized as being political compromises. That is, they were promulgated with a view toward being politically acceptable, rather than as detailed and stringent as they should be. Finally, there is considerable concern over the Commission's audit techniques and process (to include its fee structure); in effect, critics argue that it is in the best interests of the process and individual auditors to approve agency policies, procedures, and programs.

In addition, a former commissioner and Senior Circuit Judge, United States Court of Appeals, resigned from the commission based on a lack of public scrutiny and participation, fundamental flaws in the commission's priorities, and other reasons (Bazelon, 1988). From the standpoint of legal issues, there are those who argue that accreditation is at least an opening argument in defending an agency in the event of litigation. Since plaintiffs' attorneys and expert witnesses use the ACA standards against correctional agencies, it is argued that accreditation helps negate such claims.

According to James George, a professor of law and member of the Commission of Accreditation for Corrections, 57% of accreditation clients perceive accreditation as increasing their ability to defend legal actions. Yet he notes that more frequently the standards are cited as minimum standards (hence, used against agencies). He also notes that institutions considered for accreditation, but denied certification, may be worse off than if they had never sought accreditation. In addition, the Commission itself has concern about the use of its staff and consultants being summoned as expert witnesses in prisoner litigation.

In short, accreditation deals with standards typically perceived as minimal standards. This, in turn, can be used in litigation against a corrections enterprise. It can also be used by politicians as justification for withholding needed funding. Also, it can dupe an uneducated public into thinking their corrections enterprise is more professional and humane than it is in reality.

Privatization of Prisons and Jails

The issue of privatizing prisons and jails has recently generated considerable debate within both the corrections field and the media. For example, the National Institute of Justice has recently produced a head-to-head debate focusing on the value and legitimacy of the free enterprise approach to corrections. Conversely, Collins (1986) has noted that there is little *legitimate discussion* about the pros and cons of privatization; rather, there is debate, which tends to be followed by shouting and name-calling. And, as noted by Robbins (1988), "The privatization of incarceration may be neither constitutional nor wise."

Private involvement in corrections is not a new phenomenon; writers have called attention to the work of the Philadelphia Society for Alleviating the Misery of Public Prisons in 1822 (Duffee, 1989). Similarly, some prison and jail operations have been contracted with the private sector for many years. For example, many prisons and jails contract for medical and food services, and many halfway houses involve a contract with private owners. Because Chapter 18 expands on many facets of privatization, we shall focus on Robbins' view that *total privatization* may not be legal, or not entered into in a legal manner.

The term "privatization" refers to contracting for *total operational* responsibility for a prison or jail; rather than only constructing (or leasing) a physical plant. Similarly, the term does not embrace relatively simple contracts dealing with the provision of institutional services (e.g., food service, vocational or education training, or medical care). This does not suggest that such matters are not problematical. Jails have been built without doors and with other design defects. Contracts have been entered into with doctors and food service companies that have adversely impacted on prisons and jails. Also, contract law and its application is problematic in its own right (witness various news accounts concerning contracting scandals, cost over runs, etc.). In spite of these problems, total privatization, or contracting for total operation of a correctional facility, adds new dimensions to problems inherent in contracting.

From a legal standpoint, Robbins (1988) addresses the following questions (among others):

1. Is it constitutional to contract out for the total operation of an entire prison or jail?

2. Will privatization reduce or eliminate governmental liability?

3. What standards will govern the operation of a private institution?

4. Who will monitor implementation of the standards?

5. Will the public still have access to the institution?

6. What recourse will the public have if it does not approve of the institution's operation?

7. Who will maintain security and control of the institution if the private personnel go on strike?

8. Where will the responsibility lie for quasi-judicial decisions such as classification, discipline, or parole?

There are complex constitutional, statutory, and contractual issues that must be addressed and resolved prior to the complete privatization of a prison or jail. As in many correctional issues, the constitutionality of privatization is a fundamental question. Here, Robbins raises three topics bearing on the greater question: (1) the delegation doctrine, (2) the state-action requirement, and (3) the Thirteenth Amendment.

The issues of delegating a governmental power, versus a governmental function, and the extent of such delegation to private parties raise somewhat different questions at the federal level of government than in state governments. In the case of the federal government, most U.S. Supreme Court cases have upheld such delegations as valid, but in disciplinary measures a governmental agency must have the power to approve or disapprove of the private party's rules. Additionally, a governmental body must retain a power to review disciplinary matters, and make independent decisions regarding a rule violation and the appropriateness of the penalty. Further, Robbins suggests that the cases to date have largely addressed property interests, rather than liberty issues, and that the U.S. Supreme Court could well establish new or different standards in the case of privately operated prisons.

At the state level, Robbins concludes that a state agency will need to retain certain rule-making and adjudicative functions. He speculates, based on principles announced in delegation cases in other contexts, that the courts might uphold the constitutionality of delegations of management functions to private-prison companies. This would include such activities as cell assignment and counting the prisoners. He suggests that disciplinary rules would need to be adopted by a state legislature or an administrative agency with the authority to accept or modify proposed rules.

The Death Penalty

The death penalty has been debated on moral and ethical grounds, data suggesting racial application, its effectiveness as a deterrent to crime, as well as on legal issues. From the standpoint of moral and ethical issues, there are diametrically opposed positions. At one end of the spectrum are those who oppose taking a human life for any reason—to protect country, family, or even self. At the opposite end are those who hold human life no more valuable than the lives of insects. Such extreme values are probably irreconcilable. Indeed, the closer one's value of life lies to either extreme, the less likely it is that there will be consensus on moral or ethical issues.

Figure 12.3
Last Meals, Last Words

LAST MEALS, LAST WORDS

Death penalty experts speculate that modern traditions allowing the condemned a last meal and final statement are ways of comforting both executioner and executee.

Last meals

Hamburger, french fries, Dr Pepper—**James D. Autry**, executed March 1984 in Texas by lethal injection.

Soup, crackers, chili with beans, steamed rice, seasoned pinto beans, corn, seasoned mustard greens, hot spiced beets, iced tea—**Thomas Andy Barefoot**, executed October 1984 in Texas by lethal injection.

T-bone steak, rice, french fries, four slices of toast, strawberry malt—**Earnest Knighton Jr.**, executed October 1984 in Louisiana by electrocution.

Coca-cola, Cheez Doodles—**Margie Velma Barfield**, executed November 1984 in North Carolina by lethal injection.

Unleavened bread—**Stephen Peter Morin**, executed March 1985 in Texas by lethal injection.

Steak, refried beans, tortillas, salad, ice cream, chocolate cake—**Henry Martinez Porter**, executed July 1985 in Texas by lethal injection.

Pink salmon, cole slaw, candied yeams, chilled peaches, grape drink—**Arthur Lee Jones Jr.**, executed March 1986 in Alabama by electrocution.

Lettuce, tomatoes, two cartons of milk—**Chester Lee Wicker**, executed August 1986 in Texas by lethal injection.

Shrimp, crab legs, tossed salad with Thousand Island dressing, apple pie a la mode—**Timothy Wesley McCorquodale**, executed September 1987 in Georgia by electrocution.

Half-gallon of black cherry ice cream—**William Mitchell**, executed September 1987 in Georgia by electrocution.

One pound popcorn shrimp, one pound medium-size shrimp, one pound jumbo shrimp, one loaf garlic bread, french fries, pecan pie, pecan ice cream, iced tea—**Aubrey Adams Jr.**, executed May 1989 in Florida by electrocution.

Last words

"I beg your pardon."—**Marie Antoinette**, queen of France who was apologizing for stepping on her executioner's foot, executed in 1793 by guillotine.

"I'm Jesus Christ."—**Aaron C. Mitchell**, executed April 1967 in California by lethal gas.

"Let's do it."—**Gary Gilmore**, executed January 1977 in Utah by firing squad.

"My final words are, 'I'm innocent' "—**James Dupree Henry**, executed September 1984 in Florida by electrocution.

"I pray my family will rejoice and forgive."—**Doyle Skillern**, executed January 1985 in Texas by lethal injection.

"It's all right."—**Carroll Edward Cole**, executed December 1985 in Nevada by lethal injection.

23rd Psalm—**Michael Marnel Smith**, executed July 1986 in Virginia by electrocution.

"I'd rather be fishing."—**Jimmy Glass**, executed June 1987 in Louisiana by electrocution.

"I hope with all my heart I will be the last sacrificial lamb of a system that is not just, and all these people know it is not just ...."—**Jeffrey Joseph Daugherty**, executed November 1988 in Florida by electrocution.

"Give my love to my family and friends."—**Theodore Robert Bundy**, executed January 1989 in Florida by electrocution.

"I love you."—**Sean P. Flanagan**, executed June 1989 in Nevada by lethal injection. His words were directed at prosecutor Dan Seaton.

"Thank you for letting me die with dignity."—**William Paul Thompson**, executed June 1989 in Nevada by lethal injection.

"We want to die together."—Deposed Romanian dictator **Nicolae Ceausescu** and his wife, **Elena**, executed December 1989 by firing squad.

"One mistake...13 years ago, and that's a long time. Nothing is going to be accomplished. I have peace with myself."—**Dalton Prejean**, executed May 1990 in Louisiana by electrocution.

Source: "Last Meals, Last Words." In *The Washington Times*, June 7, 1990. Reprinted with permission of The Washington Times.

Regarding the death penalty's racial application, the data are more conclusive than emotional, but still subject to debate. For example, most executions have taken place in the Deep South, in the industrialized North, and in California, where minorities represent a large percentage of the population. Some writers point to the disproportionate numbers of minorities executed in these regions as proof that the death penalty is disproportionately applied to minorities. Others suggest that the picture is even worse, based on research noting racial ramifications behind many of the executions of dominant group members (M. Radelet, 1989).

From the vantage point of the deterrent effect of the death penalty, data are far from conclusive. Studies of comparable states, comparisons of crime rates in states abolishing (or implementing) the death penalty, etc., fail to show a consistent correlation between the death sentence and crime rates.

Laying moral, ethical, ethnic, and deterrent issues aside, there are at least three distinct legal issues bearing on the death penalty: (1) the legality of the sentence, per se, (2) the method of carrying out the death sentence, and (3) the conditions on "death row" pending execution.

The legality of the death sentence, per se, has been addressed in light of the Eighth Amendment's proscription against cruel and unusual punishment, especially as compared with "evolving standards of decency that mark the progress of a maturing society" (*Furman v. Georgia*, 1967). The courts have looked at the death penalty in terms of it being a disproportionately severe punishment for a given crime (*Weems v. United States*, 1910), unusual pain (*Louisiana ex rel. Francis v. Resweber*, 1947), and the methods for imposing the death penalty (*Furman v. Georgia*, 1972). While the U.S. Supreme Court has generally upheld the legality of the death sentence, it did impose a brief moratorium on the penalty from 1967 to 1976. But in *Gregg v. Georgia* (1976) the Court determined that the death penalty is not, in and of itself, cruel and unusual punishment, at least in the case of homicide. The court has been less receptive to the death penalty in the case of rape and kidnapping, as well as mandatory death sentences (*Coker v. Georgia*, 1977; *Eberheart v. Georgia*, 1977; *Roberts v. Louisiana*, 1977). Over the years, the U.S. Supreme Court largely avoided the issue of imposing the death penalty on juveniles, but in 1989 ruled that such a punishment was not unconstitutional.

Today, we have the potential for a death sentence in a 37 states and the federal government (*Bureau of Justice Statistics Bulletin*, 1985). Electrocution, lethal gas, lethal injection, hanging, and firing squads have all been used to execute offenders. Hanging has been the most widely used method throughout history but has been replaced by electrocution and lethal injection. Only lethal injection remains a constitutionally questionable method of execution; all other methods of execution have been found to be constitutional (Duffee, 1989).

Turning to the issue of death row conditions, prisoners who have been sentenced to die have complained about being housed under unconstitutional conditions since the mid-1800s. An early case (*In re Medley*, 134 U.S. 160, 1890) involved being placed in solitary confinement pending execution, which was ruled as an additional punishment, and unconstitutional. Following this case, death row conditions received little court attention due to the courts' adherence to the "hands-off" doctrine until the mid-1960s.

Gradually, the concept of the "totality of conditions" evolved and came to apply to death row inmates Thus, today, an inmate's mental and physical well-being must be considered in death row, as well as other areas of prison (*Ramos v. Lamm*, 1980; *Newman v. Alabama*, 1977; *Rhodes v. Chapman*, 1981; also see *Carroll*, 1988).

Sanctions for the Misuse of Authority

Throughout this chapter a variety of sanctions for the misuse of authority were addressed. It was noted that relatively few inmates receive monetary awards as the result of civil suits. Similarly, relatively few appeals of criminal convictions are successful. Despite the overwhelming lack of success, prisoners go to court in record numbers for a variety of reasons. The reader may well ask, "why?" As Manville (1983) advises prisoners, "...when you do obtain victory, the victory is *sweet.*"[7]

The same cannot usually be said from the vantage point of correctional employees or agencies named as defendants in litigation. Accordingly, this section of the chapter addresses some of the more technical issues related to the law and its impact on corrections. It focuses on the sanctions for the abuse of authority or power by correctional staff.

Most abuses associated with corrections can be attributed to the abuse of authority or power. Such abuses may be ascribed to the chief executive of the various state governments, the appropriate legislature, or to specific corrections enterprises and particular individuals.

---

[7]   Manville worked with the National Prison Project, ACLUF, at the time he wrote *Prisoners' Self-Help Litigation Manual*, a publication well known and used by prison inmates.

When we look at the misuse of authority (power or might) by police or correctional personnel, there are three principal sanctions that may be imposed: (1) evidence may be excluded from a criminal proceeding, (2) the offending individual and his or her employing governmental agency may be sued in a civil proceeding, and (3) the individual may be prosecuted under criminal law.

The Exclusionary Rule

We mention evidence being excluded from a criminal proceeding largely to show a complete picture. That is, litigation against the corrections enterprise is only one step in a total process intended to protect the rights of both accused and convicted persons.

Simply stated, the exclusionary rule means that evidence obtained by an unreasonable search and seizure will not be admissible in a court of law. When the rule was first adopted in 1914 (*Weeks v. United States*) it applied only to federal courts and federal agents. In 1961 the U.S. Supreme Court applied the rule to evidence obtained by state or local agents (*Mapp v. Ohio*).

While the exclusionary rule was originally invoked most vigorously, over the past 10 years the U.S. Supreme Court has modified its original stance. As a result, today if the police have acted in "good faith," evidence illegally obtained may in fact be admitted into evidence (Manville, 1988).

Civil Liability

While the exclusionary rule has been somewhat diluted, it is important to recognize that the rule still exists and is a viable sanction against abuses of police authority. From the perspective of corrections, there is no similar rule protecting the rights of convicted offenders. Their recourse is often civil litigation.

We discussed torts and civil rights suits, two of the methods offenders have relied upon to secure a court injunction (a prohibition against actions in the future) or to secure a monetary award. Many suits are settled "out of court;" the attorneys reach an agreement prior to going to trial. Sometimes the accused will enter into a *consent decree* with the court. That is, without admitting any wrongdoing, the government will agree to do certain things as stipulated by the court, to fend off the risk of increased court fees or potentially greater monetary awards to a plaintiff. Readers may well wonder how such decisions can be reached without going to trial. Corrections practitioners may well be puzzled by such settlements. Yet, the legal process, particularly the *discovery process*, has been used by both plaintiff's attorneys and defense counsel to this end.

Discovery involves filing *interrogatories*, which are questions requiring a written response, or the provision of documents. Interrogatories are used in conjunction with *depositions*. Depositions are question-and-answer sessions wherein various individuals provide each attorney with sworn testimony. They are, for all practical purposes, similar to interrogations. Both interrogatories and depositions are used by opposing attorneys in an attempt to find the facts in a given case.

Bear in mind, in civil litigation a good plaintiff's attorney will launch a three-dimensional attack. Typically, this attack will list as many people in the organizational hierarchy (a vertical attack) and as many reasons (HARDSTEF) (a horizontal attack) for the attack as possible. Then, through interrogatories and depositions the attorney will get everyone and every document telling all they can reveal. Finger-pointing will take place as an attorney tries to "divide and conquer." When this overly simplified process is done, both attorneys will have a fair picture of their chances of winning if they go to trial.

Since the burden of proof in civil cases is only a *preponderance of evidence*, neither attorney may want to risk trial. This standard of proof is significantly different than the "guilt beyond reasonable doubt" standard in criminal trials. Convincing a judge or jury of a mere preponderance of evidence (slightly over 50% of the evidence pointing one way) is, at best, risky. Accordingly, each attorney may see merit in settling with a certain decision agreed to out of court, rather than incurring the risks and expenses associated with a trial.

Corrections employees, however, will have to deal with the stress inherent in the discovery process. Often, the work environment will become filled with guilt and hostility. And, once more, management will have to deal with problems generated by the legal process, if not by a court decision.

Criminal Prosecution

It may be recalled that intentional torts are also often criminal acts. A corrections employee can be sued under tort law and prosecuted under criminal law for a single act. He or she may be found guilty in one arena, and innocent in the other, or guilty in both. Certainly employees do not want to be put in such a position.

Accordingly, more managerial attention is now focused on teaching employees the law than was the case previously. For example, in Michigan, all aspiring state correctional officers must take a college course in correctional legal issues prior to being hired. Once hired, they undergo further training in the law.

Summary

Students taking introductory corrections courses often lack academic backgrounds in criminal justice, criminal law, or constitutional law. Similarly, practitioners may know "the rules," but not the reasons behind the rules. This affects their ability to exercise discretion. Because their training is compressed, focusing on "what," not "why," they often understand black or white, but not gray.

Accordingly, this chapter presented some background on law in general, including its evolution. This part of the chapter was intended for readers lacking academic backgrounds related to criminal justice and law. The sections dealing with the rights of offenders and ex-offenders were as much descriptive as prescriptive. That is, they described historical, social, and political influences on correctional law, as well as some prescriptive law.

The section on other legal issues reminds the reader that employees have a variety of rights, as well as the fact that there are a variety of legal issues beyond the rights of offenders.

In broadly examining the many types and sources of law, the chapter conveyed two key messages: (1) law is complex, often ambiguous, and frequently unable to provide simple solutions to correctional problems, and (2) law lies at the heart of what much of corrections is about—management.

This does not mean corrections should not have, as its principal goal, rehabilitation of offenders. Rather, this recognizes a pragmatic fact of life: regardless of the goal(s) of corrections, both offenders and correctional employees must be managed—within a framework of both administrative and legal principles and prescriptions.

Some of the legal prescriptions affect corrections in subtle ways. For example, laws affecting police practices and the rights of the accused affect the work of corrections—correctional clients. Mandatory sentences and other aspects of criminal law affect prison crowding, probation and parole caseloads, and other correctional programs.

Other laws, seemingly only affecting correctional employees, create new problems for corrections. Equal opportunity laws, for example, are designed to eliminate job discrimination, but such laws have contributed to new problems: (1) increased claims of sexual harassment by correctional staff, and (2) religious and privacy issues being raised among inmates.

In focusing on the prescriptive law affecting probationers, prisoners, and parolees, the same rights have evolved as are enjoyed by free citizens. The difference lies in three areas: (1) offender rights can, and are, restricted more so than the rights of free people (due to institutional security and other penal concerns), (2) the courts seem to "find" and protect offender rights more so than in the case of free people, but (3) in reality, the courts typically address offenders' rights for one of two reasons.

First, prisoners lack the choices and mobility of free people. Thus, they need legal safeguards in areas that are not typically a problem for free people. Second, in applying the uncertain technologies of corrections to individual offenders, the rights of free people come into play.

Moreover, much prescriptive law affecting corrections is little more than statements of broad principles. Like Gulick's management principles (POSDCORB), prescriptive law leaves it to corrections professionals to interpret and apply the principles to the realities of their unique situation and environment. Herein lies the problem.

Individual court decisions pinpoint bad managerial decisions. But the courts deal with what legislators, agency administrators, and correctional managers and employees give them. So, we might well ask, "Is it liberal courts or bad management that has underscored the pervasive and invasive movement of law into corrections?"

Litigation Can Be Therapeutic

Richard R. Korn, Ph.D.

Dean, Elmwood College of Criminal Justice
Milpitts, California

Soviet psychiatrists claim to have discovered certain forms of delusion not yet recognized by Western medicine. One of these is "litigation mania," in which a patient continually claims that his confinement is a violation of his civil rights. American psychiatry has generally rejected "litigation mania" as a diagnosis. But, in one case at least, psychiatric and correctional authorities had no problem with it at all. In prisoner Bobby Hardwick they found a patient who fitted the Soviet diagnosis perfectly.

On January 22, 1970, a Georgia psychiatrist found Hardwick, a newly admitted 39-year-old inmate serving a ten-year sentence for armed robbery, to be suffering from paranoid schizophrenia with hallucinations and delusions of persecution. Hardwick spent the next eight years being shuttled back and forth from solitary cells in prison to solitary rooms in mental hospitals. All the while he deluged authorities with complaints about his treatment. Although Hardwick's attacks on the Georgia penal system were purely literary—he presented no behavioral threat—the prison authorities finally lost patience with him, and in 1974 he was transferred from Reidsville prison to a unit for "incorrigibles and security risks" located in H-House of the Georgia Diagnostic and Classification Center (GDCC) at Jackson.

In setting forth his reasons for requesting Hardwick's removal, Reidsville Warden Joseph Hopper unwittingly paraphrased the essential elements of the "litigation mania" diagnosis: "He has written so many writs that it has taken an extra, separate file to hold his legal papers. He has continuously complained about mistreatment. Hardwick has chosen an antisocial path. . . . Therefore it is recommended that he be transferred to GDCC to participate in their behavior modification program in the hope that this will

change his devious trend."

Hardwick's new location, a solitary confinement block, did not modify his litigious behavior. In August 1974 he filed suit in the U.S. District Court of Georgia, claiming several violations of his constitutional rights. Named as defendant in the suit was Dr. Allen Ault, who had participated in the design of the H-House program. Dr. Ault was, at the time the suit was filed, commissioner of the Department of Offender Rehabilitation.

Late in 1975 Judge Wilbur T. Owens, Jr. consolidated Hardwick's suit with 25 other cases which had been filed at Hardwick's instigation. The trial in the case of *Hardwick v. Ault* was set for March 1977, at which point I was called in as an expert witness by the ACLU of Georgia. Given the relative positions and reputations of the two litigants, the outcome hardly seemed in doubt.

But on Jan. 12, 1978, Judge Owens shattered expectations. In a landmark decision, the judge ruled that the totality of conditions in H-House were in violation of the 8th and 14th Amendments. The word of a certified psychotic had prevailed over the diagnosis of his keepers. But something even more remarkable had happened. Throughout the lengthy preparation for the trial, the state's psychiatrists had continued to monitor Hardwick's mental condition. During the same period they also checked frequently on the mental health of his fellow litigants, who were not all mentally ill. After four years in solitary confinement in H-House, the condition of most of the other plaintiff's had deteriorated. But Hardwick, whose diagnosis of schizophrenia had predated his entry to H-House, was clearly getting better in a situation in which normal prisoners were getting worse. Each new report confirmed the trend. By 1978, at the moment of his victory, Hardwick was unmistakably sane. Today he is out of prison and running a successful business in the Southwest.

Under what conditions was Hardwick living during his four-year struggle? In his decision, Judge Owens described life in H-House with numbing specificity: "Inmates are kept in their small individual cells almost all the time. . . . The typical prisoner . . . is out of his cell only slightly over six hours per week. Prisoners . . . are constantly subject to severe security measures. In addition to being constantly under surveillance . . . they are strip searched for any movement out of H-2. During the search two correctional officers keep 'stun guns' trained on the prisoner. The prisoners are fed by the guards who deliver the food in carts while another guard watches with a stun gun. No guard ever goes alone down on the range in front of the prisoners. Almost all of the prison staff's communication with inmates occurs through the porthole in the top of the cell."

The "porthole in the top of the cell" is one of the stranger features of isolation in H-House. It allows prison officials to see and hear without being seen or heard. Prior to his confinement there, Hardwick had already been described as "hearing voices." In H-House, being watched by invisible onlookers and talked to by disembodied voices was part of the program. The porthole was reached by an overhead catwalk. Judge Owens described its use: "The catwalk allows guards to monitor constantly . . . and because [they] follow no set routine the surveillance through the hole in the ceiling . . . is always unexpected. The catwalk is used . . . for nearly all communications with prisoners in H-2. Thus the fate of an H-2 inmate is determined in large part by his conversations with people talking to him through a metal grate. Other than through this grate the H-House inmate has very little contact with other human beings."

But by far the most stressful impact of H-House was the sheer duration of the time spent there. "Punishment in H-House is disproportionate in the sense that it has no proportion with respect to time. . ." wrote Judge Owens. "Because the passage of time is in part a function of space and activity, time truly appears to slow down for the inmate in H-House. This slowing of time is made worse by the indefiniteness of the duration. Without hope or promise as to when the punishment will end, H-House inflicts considerable mental anguish. This anguish was described and testified to by almost everyone who had contact with H-House, including guards, prison counselors, and prison administrators."

Summarizing his assessment of conditions in H-House, Judge Owens concluded: "There can be little doubt that H-House constitutes punishment beyond the original, ordinary incarceration of inmates in the Georgia prison system. . . . Long periods of lock-up in a confined space, limited contact with others, continued and unexpected surveillance and limited exercise eventually take a serious toll on the mental health of the inmates."

Judge Owens' decision was a stinging rebuke to the state's attempt to redefine traditional solitary confinement as a modern form of behavioral treatment. But Hardwick's apparent recovery during the course of his attempts to fight his confinement is an even more fundamental affront to classical psychiatric theory. According to accepted therapeutic doctrine, a paranoid person ought not to be encouraged to believe that his delusions of persecution are valid. Moreover, those who seek to help a paranoid person are supposed to help him realize that his problems are internal rather than environmental, and that his task is to change himself, not his circumstances.

As a former prison psychologist and director of treatment at the New Jersey State Prison at Trenton (1952-1955) I at one time accepted these principles, without question. And I saw it as my professional responsibility to do what I could to dissuade inmates from evading responsibility by merely blaming their environment. One of my duties at the state prison was to monitor the condition of inmates confined to indefinite administrative segregation. As I watched inmate after inmate succumb to the rigors of unrelieved solitary confinement, I described with clinical detachment their struggles to preserve their sanity by fighting back. One of my observations was to be strikingly appropriate to Hardwick 30 years later:

> At the outset the segregated offender typically occupies himself with an ambitious program of protest. Intensive legal activity frequently characterizes this period; the offender busies himself with the search for an effective way to combine the expression of his resentment with a method of obtaining his release. Following the failure of legal appeals, there are attempts to deluge all manner of public officials with a lengthy recital of complaints. As a matter of sound correctional administration, these complaints should be fully and routinely investigated. In addition to providing a precaution against actual injustice, the investigation of unfounded complaints serves a therapeutic purpose. Once again the inmate is provided a demonstration of the failure of his manipulative techniques.

What had not occurred to me, of course, was that indefinite solitary confinement was in itself an injustice, made all the more intolerable by the official belief or pretense that it was for the inmates' own good.

Why, then, did Hardwick not break down under it? One thing was clear not only to me but to others who had observed and interviewed him prior to the trial: Hardwick had recovered his wits even before his legal success. Is it conceivable that it was his struggle, rather than its positive outcome, that was decisive? Or is it possible that Hardwick was never psychotic in the first place?

As an expert witness I was privy to Hardwick's psychiatric reports, which became part of the public record of the trial. I have obtained his permission to reproduce relevant portions of the reports here. Hardwick was first seen by a psychiatrist, Dr. Julius Ehik, in January 1970, shortly after his admission as a new inmate. Dr. Ehik reported: "This inmate . . . will not eat and has not eaten anything for the past three days. He also will not let anybody come close to him and will beg not to be touched. He thinks that he is in the service. He has conversations with a Captain Whitehead who is, according to him, telling him things to do, and keeps him locked up. He stated that he won't eat because he had been told that the food is poison, and that they were trying to get rid of him. . . . From my brief contact with this prisoner, it would appear to me that he is acutely psychotic, that he is paranoid and is hallucinating."

Hardwick's next psychiatric examination took place in September 1974, soon after he had been transferred to H-House. The report, made by another psychiatrist, Dr. J.F. Casey, reflects an unmistakeable concern and sensitivity: "He seems to be hallucinating at the time of the interview. From time to time he would turn his head as if listening to someone, and then when he was asked about this would be very suspicious and insisted that I had heard the same thing that he had heard. . . . He tells at great length of this conspiracy which is not definitely organized other than that it is against him primarily because he is a highly intelligent person and since he is black 'they' whom he would never identify resent his being as intelligent as he is and are taking various steps to suppress him. These steps include his being sent out of the Army and then arrested and having been sent to prison in order to put him away so that he couldn't participate in the takeover of the world which he insists is going to occur in any event. . . . During the interview he tells about hidden microphones in the examining room with us.

"This is a 30-year-old black inmate who is obviously quite hallucinated and delusional and apparently has been for some time. I feel he is suffering from schizophrenia of a paranoid type with relatively little deterioration."

At no point in his assessment does the psychiatrist note the fact that Hardwick is living in a solitary confinement cell where his contact with other human beings is largely limited to communication with their disembodied voices. This omission is consistent with the conventional view that paranoid schizophrenia can best be understood as an internal problem. This same lack of reference to the patient's environment characterizes the psychiatric reports about Hardwick's fellow inmates in H-House. The second point to be stressed is this: While the condition of most of his colleagues was deteriorating, Hardwick's was apparently improving.

Hardwick next saw Dr. Casey two years later, in March 1976. By this time Hardwick was deeply involved in organizing his massive class action suit. He had enlisted the aid of the ACLU of Georgia, and he was in frequent contact with some of the most prestigious attorneys in the state. And he had earned a respect approaching awe by his fellow sufferers. When speaking to him or about him, they rarely used his name. They called him "Lawyer."

In his report of his 1976 interview, Dr. Casey noted an impressive change in Hardwick: "This inmate appears considerably improved from a mental point of view over what he was when last seen. He seems to have fewer ideas of a typical paranoid nature. Some are still with him but not nearly to the extent they were present on the previous exam. . . . Emotionally he is certainly not depressed. He doesn't appear flattened emotionally as when last seen. . . . At the present time he denies any actual hallucinations, which is in some contrast to the previous time when he didn't actually admit it but his nonverbal communication certainly would intimate so. When informed that he though previously he had hidden mikes in the room he was quite doubtful and couldn't remember this and it was obvious that he didn't believe it."

By the time I interviewed Hardwick prior to the trial in 1977, a year after his last examination, there was no evidence whatever of any symptomatology. He was resilient, cheerful, without hostility, and his conversation crackled with wit and good humor. When I first saw him I had not yet read his psychiatric reports. When I saw them I was amazed. My impression of his excellent mental health was shared by all those who worked with him and by those who watched and heard his testimony. One reporter, Marcia Kunstel, wrote: "After watching Bobby Hardwick

testify in a confident, contained manner before a federal judge, it was hard to believe a psychiatrist characterized him as 'delusional, schizophrenic, paranoid and definitely psychotic' only a few years ago."

Conventional psychiatric theory does not have an explanation for Hardwick. According to classical psychiatric doctrine, paranoids remain ill by continuing to blame their environment for their troubles. Their only hope for improvement is to begin to realize that their problems are internal. In a situation well calculated to drive sane people mad, Hardwick had, to all intents and purposes, made himself well. He accomplished this feat in a way that violated every canon of psychiatric treatment. Instead of permitting people to persuade him that his beliefs were delusional, he had succeeded in persuading others that they were valid. This alone should have been enough to confirm and exacerbate his illness. Instead of submitting to his circumstances, he had attacked them. Worse, he had attacked them successfully, which according to accepted doctrine amounts to little more than shifting the burden of his madness onto the world.

Conventional psychiatric theory does have the beginning of an explanation for Hardwick's "symptomatic" improvement. The noted psychiatrist Silvano Arieti has written: "There are persons who, because of unusual circumstances... or because of their ability to organize, succeed in changing and manipulate their environment according to their bizarre wishes, and therefore have no need to develop *overt* paranoid symptoms. These are cases of 'acted out' or 'externalized' psychoses. For instance, people like Nero or Hitler were able to alter the environment in accordance with their wishes, no matter how bizarre these wishes were. As long as they were able to do so on a realistic level, they had no need to become psychotic in a clinical or legal sense.

Dr. Arieti's concept presents some internal difficulties. Is an idea still "bizarre" after many people finally come to believe it? Was Hardwick's wish to change his circumstances irrational? His psychiatrists thought so, but many other rational people, including a federal judge, did not agree. *These* people found H-House rather bizarre. They found it hard to accept a treatment program which somehow managed to fulfill almost every condition of paranoia itself, including conversations with invisible people who appeared and disappeared unexpectedly.

Some years ago the late psychiatrist J.L. Moreno, creator of psychodrama and sociometry, recalled his frustrating work as a young resident in the disturbed wards of the main mental hospital in Vienna. One of Moreno's patients was a former bank clerk who was convinced that he was actually a general being held in captivity as a prisoner of war. Another was an elderly lady who was positive that the ragged doll she constantly clutched to herself was actually her infant.

After spending his day in the wards, fruitlessly trying to convince his patients to give up their delusions, Moreno would gratefully descend into the streets in Vienna. On his way home he would pass young boys playing at being soldiers, and young girls pushing their toy baby carriages and talking with great seriousness about their "children." Moreno then posed for himself a question: Why are the adult fantasists in the hospital wards thought to be insane, while children acting out fantasies in the street are considered normal? And why were the children willing and able to put their fantasies aside when they returned home, while the adults in the wards were not?

Moreno pushed his questioning one step further: Why, he asked, do people, adults and children alike, need to have fantasies in the first place? Why isn't "reality" enough? His answer to his first question provided a clue to the second. People obviously need to relieve themselves with dreams and fantasies when their reality frustrates their inner needs, or violates their inner sense of who they actually are and need to be. Later studies of dream deprivation would confirm Moreno's insight. Waking up experimental subjects when they are about to start dreaming is seriously disturbing. It follows that the ability to indulge in dreams and fantasies, and to believe in them at some level, is essential for coping with stresses of a refractory and frustrating reality. In effect, to be denied the relief and release of dreaming is to be crippled in one's ability to cope on any level.

An indulgent adult world gives children permission to act out their fantasies in play. Children grant each other's fantasies the essential element of credibility by confirming them in vivid and convincing role-playing. A little boy who needs to act out a fantasy of power can mobilize other children to confirm him as a "general" by taking the role of his soldiers. Having satisfied his inner need by expressing it in emotionally authentic action, the boy can relinquish it. He can content himself with playing ordinary soldier to another child's "general," or he can go back to his assigned role of little boy.

Unlike a child, an unhappy adult is not given permission to suspend an accepted but frustrating social identity by acting out his fantasies in the real world. Nor, unless he is a Hitler or a Nero, will he ordinarily find other adults who are willing to confirm his secret self by acting out the counterpart roles of his fantasy with him.

The tragedy of conventional mental hospital treatment is that it intensifies the process that compelled the individual to take on his compensatory fantasy role in the first place. It was to counteract a treatment process that essentially mimicked the disease that Moreno created his system of psychodramatic therapy. Recognizing the metaphorical validity of the patient's fantasies, he also understood that one can relinquish an essential wish only after one has fulfilled it on some psychologically authentic level. So he encouraged his clients to confirm each other's aspirational identities as children do, in dramatic action.

Inmates of prisons and mental hospitals have been drastically "disconfirmed" by their social environments. Like children, their identities are subject to the definitions of others; they are in the clutch of circumstances they cannot control. They have few good choices. To accept their dependency is to accept their neutralization as self-directing human beings. To act out against their circumstances, to try to transform them or to escape from them, is to risk further restriction and neutralization.

All of these conditions are exacerbated in indefinite solitary confinement. There the choices are even more bleak. Inmates can resist by violence. They can retreat into a world of fantasy from which they may not emerge. They can sink into vegetative apathy, or permit themselves to be tranquilized into a state of mindlessness. They can try to escape by self-destruction. The high rates of assault, self-inflicted injury, suicide and psychosis testify to the prevalence of these doomed attempts to transcend the horrors of immobility, isolation and sensory and social deprivation in prolonged solitary confinement.

Litigation offers a striking promise of a better alternative. By persuading outsiders to acknowledge their terrible circumstances, prisoners can obtain confirmation that their difficulties are not merely "internal." By enlisting the aid of these outsiders—attorneys, expert witnesses, judges—they can participate in an attempt to change their circumstances, or to procure their release from them. Whether they are successful or not, the activity of litigation offers an alternative to self-destructive acceptance of a pathological environment, or equally self-destructive violence against it.

There may well be other advantages. Litigation changes the offender's relationship to the law. As a predator, the offender looked at the law and its agents as enemies to be defied or evaded. By definition, the successful criminal is a successful law-breaker. In turning to litigation as his last hope, the offender must enlist the law as his friend. If he is serious, he must take the role of the law, and he must look at himself and his pleadings with a critical eye for their defects. In effect, he must, for perhaps the first time, look at himself as a judge and jury might look at him. The chance exists that he may internalize these attitudes as criteria for his future conduct.

Psychotic or not, Hardwick seems to have succeeded in doing all these things. If he was truly delusional, he was delusional only when he was unable to do anything about his situation in fact. One may not need to feel that he must save the whole world if he can save at least his part of it. The moment Hardwick began to use the law on his behalf, and on behalf of his fellow prisoners, his grander projects were less and less necessary or useful. What was useful now were his powers of observation, his rationality, his ability to persuade. These abilities are preeminently the abilities of a sane human being.

Hardwick was, of course, an exception to the rule. As a result of Judge Owens' court order, H-House was closed and its inmates dispersed in the general prison population. It is now Georgia's death row, and is the subject of a new inmate/ACLU lawsuit charging that confinement there constitutes cruel and unusual punishment.

Source: Richard R. Korn (1981). "Litigation Can Be Therapeutic." *Corrections Magazine*, Vol. 7, No. 5:45-48 (October). Reprinted with permission.

Key Terms and Concepts

access to courts
accreditation
administrative rule
civil liability
conflict model of law
consensus model of law
constitutional law
correctional law
correctional technologies
due process

duty of care
equal protection of the law
governmental immunity
guilt beyond a reasonable doubt
habeas corpus
legal status
lex talionis
preponderance of evidence
procedural law
substantive law

References

Allen, H.E. and C.E. Simonsen (1986). *Corrections in America: An Introduction, Fourth Edition.* New York, NY: Macmillan Publishing Company.

American Correctional Association (ACA) (1983). *Correctional Officer Resource Guide.* Laurel, MD: ACA.

American Correctional Association (ACA) (1987). *Legal Responsibility and Authority of Correctional Officers.* Laurel, MD: ACA.

American Correctional Association (ACA) (1983). *The American Prison: From The Beginning.* Laurel, MD: ACA.

American Correctional Association (ACA) (1990). *Standards for Adult Correctional Institutions, Third Edition.* Laurel, MD: ACA.

American Correctional Association (ACA) (1990). *Standards: 1990 Supplement.* Laurel, MD: ACA.

Archambeault, W.G. and B.J. Archambeault (1982). *Correctional Supervisory Management: Principles of Organization, Policy, and Law.* Englewood Cliffs, NJ: Prentice-Hall, Inc.

Avery, M. and D. Rudovsky (1990). *Police Misconduct: Law and Litigation, Second Edition.* New York, NY: Clark Boardman Company, Ltd.

Bazelon, D.L. (1990). "The Case Against Correctional Accreditation." In I.P. Robbins (ed.) *Prisoners and the Law.* New York, NY: Clark Boardman Company, Ltd.

Bilek, A.J., J.C. Klotter and R.K. Federal (1980). *Legal Aspects of Private Security.* Cincinnati, OH: Anderson Publishing Co.

Blackstone, W. (1979). *Commentaries on the Laws of England,* Chicago, IL: University of Chicago Press.

Blum, J. (1989). Tennessee Association of Criminal Defense Lawyers, in address to National Conference on Sentencing Advocacy, January 26.

Breed, A.F. (1990). "The State of Corrections Today: A Triumph of Pluralistic Ignorance." In I.P. Robbins (ed.) *Prisoners and the Law.* New York, NY: Clark Boardman Company, Ltd.

Brest, P. (1975). *Processes of Constitutional Decisionmaking: Cases and Materials.* Boston, MA: Little, Brown and Company.

Call, J.E. (1985). "Case Law on Overcrowded Conditions of Confinement: An Assessment of Its Impact on Facility Decisionmaking." *Federal Probation* 47 (September 1983): 23-32; also, with editorial adaptations in R.M. Carter, D. Glaser and L.T. Wilkins (eds.) *Correctional Institutions, Third Edition.* New York, NY: Harper & Row, Publishers.

Carter, R.M., D. Glaser and L.T. Wilkins (eds.) (1985). *Correctional Institutions, Third Edition.* New York, NY: Harper & Row, Publishers.

Champion, D.J. (1990). *Corrections in the United States: A Contemporary Perspective.* Englewood Cliffs, NJ: Prentice Hall.

Clear, T.R. and G.F. Cole (1990). *American Corrections, Second Edition.* Pacific Grove, CA: Brooks/Cole Publishing Company.

Clute, P.D. (1980). *The Legal Aspects of Prisons and Jails.* Springfield, IL: Charles C Thomas Publisher.

Cole, G.F. (1989). *The American System of Criminal Justice, Fifth Edition.* Pacific Grove, CA: Brooks/Cole Publishing Company.

Coles, F.S. (1987). "The Impact of *Bell v. Wolfish* Upon Prisoner's Rights," *Journal of Crime and Justice,* Volume X, Number 1.

Collins, William C. (1986). *Collins: Correctional Law 1986.* Olympia, WA: William C. Collins.

Contact Center, Inc. (1985). *Inmate Lawsuits: A Report on Inmate Lawsuits Against State and Federal Correctional Systems Resulting in Monetary Damages and Settlements.* Lincoln, NE: Contact Center.

Cozart, R. (1974). "Civil Rights and the Criminal Offender." In E. Eldefonso (ed.) *Issues in Corrections: A Book of Readings.* Beverly Hills, CA: Glencoe Press.

Cromwell, P.F., Jr. (1976). "Legal Rights of Prisoners." In G.G. Killinger, P.F. Cromwell, Jr. and B.J. Cromwell. *Issues in Corrections and Administration: Selected Readings.* St. Paul, MN: West Publishing Co.

Cromwell, P.F., Jr., G.G. Killinger, H.B. Kerper and C. Walker (1985). *Probation and Parole in the Criminal Justice System, Second Edition.* St. Paul, MN: West Publishing Co.

Duffee, D.E. (1989). *Corrections: Practice and Policy*. New York, NY: Random House.

Eldefonso, E. (1974). *Issues in Corrections: A Book of Readings*. Beverly Hills, CA: Glencoe Press.

Embert, P.S. (1978). *Optimizing the Cost Effectiveness of Military Corrections: An Assessment of Program Evaluations and Related Data*. Washington, DC: Defense Documentation Center.

Embert, P.S. (1986). "Correctional Law and Jails; Evolution and Implications for Jail and Lockup Administrators and Supervisors." In D.B. Kalinich and J. Klofas (eds.) *Sneaking Inmates Down the Alley; Problems and Prospects in Jail Management*. Springfield, IL: Charles C Thomas Publisher.

Embert, P.S. (1991). "Security and the Law." In H.W. Timm and K.E. Christian, *Introduction to Private Security*. Pacific Grove, CA: Brooks/Cole Publishing Company.

Embert, P.S. and D.B. Kalinich (1988). *The Community Mental Health Worker in the Jail Environment*. Lansing, MI: Michigan Department of Mental Health.

Embert, P.S. and D.B. Kalinich (1988). *Behind the Walls: Correctional Institutions and Facilities: A Many Faceted Phenomena*. Salem, WI: Sheffield Publishing Co.

Feinberg, J. and H. Gross (eds.) (1975). *Philosophy of Law*. Belmont, CA: Dickenson Publishing Company, Inc.

Fisher, M., E. O'Brien and D.T. Austern (1987). *Practical Law for Jail and Prison Personnel, Second Edition*. St. Paul, MN: West Publishing Co.

Foote, C. (1958). "A Study of Administration of Jail in New York City." *University of Pennslyvania Law Review* 102 (March):693.

Fox, V. (1972). *Introduction to Corrections*. Englewood Cliffs, NJ: Prentice-Hall, Inc.

Friedmann, W. (1959). *Law in a Changing Society*. Berkeley, CA: University of California Press.

Garner, T.J. (1985). *Criminal Law: Principles and Cases, Third Edition*. St. Paul, MN: West Publishing Co.

Goodstein, L. and D. Layton MacKenzie (1989). *The American Prison: Issues in Research and Policy*. New York, NY: Plenum Publishing Corporation.

Haas, K.C. and G.P. Alpert (eds.) (1986). *The Dilemmas of Punishment: Readings in Contemporary Corrections*. Prospect Heights, IL: Waveland Press, Inc.

Hawkins, R. and G.P. Alpert (1989). *American Prison Systems: Punishment and Justice*. Englewood Cliffs, NJ: Prentice Hall.

Heffernan, E. (1985). "A Note on the Origins of American Prisons." In R.M. Carter, D. Glaser and L.T. Wilkins (eds.) *Correctional Institutions, Third Edition*. New York, NY: Harper & Row, Publishers.

Henningsen, R.J. (1981). *Probation and Parole.* New York, NY: Harcourt Brace Jovanovich, Inc.

Hurley, B.E. (1988). "An Examination of the Legal Duty to Prevent Inmate Suicides and Steps That Can Be Taken to Fulfill That Duty." Unpublished Manuscript, Xavier University.

Johnston, N. (1973). *The Human Cage: A Brief History of Prison Architecture.* New York, NY: Walker and Company, Inc.

Johnson, R. (1987). *Hard Time: Understanding and Reforming the Prison.* Monterey CA: Brooks/Cole Publishing Company.

Kalinich, D.B. and P.S. Embert (1987). *The Fatal Chain of Events: Suicide Prevention in Jails and Lockups, Detention Homes, and Other Secure Facilities, Revised Edition.* East Lansing, MI: KER & Associates, Justice Administration Consultants, Inc.

Kalinich, D.B., P.S. Embert and J.D. Senese (1988). "Integrating Community Mental Health Services Into Local Jails: A Policy Perspective," *Policy Studies Review*, Volume 7, Number 3, Spring.

Kalinich, D.B., P.S. Embert and J.D. Senese (1990). "Mental Health Services for Jail Inmates: Imprecise Standards, Traditional Philosophies, and the Need for Change." In G.L. Mays and J.A. Thompson (eds.) *American Jails: Public Policy Issues.* Chicago, IL: Nelson-Hall Publishers.

Kalinich, D.B. (1986). "New Rules and Old Rituals: Dilemmas of Contemporary Jail Management." In D.B. Kalinich and J. Klofas (eds.) *Sneaking Inmates Down the Alley: Problems and Prospects in Jail Management.* Springfield, IL: Charles C Thomas Publisher.

Kalinich, D.B. and J. Klofas (eds.) (1986). *Sneaking Inmates Down the Alley: Problems and Prospects in Jail Management.* Springfield, IL: Charles C Thomas Publisher.

Kalinich, D.B. and F.J. Postill (1981). *Principles of County Jail Administration and Management.* Springfield, IL: Charles C Thomas Publisher.

Killinger, G.G., P.F. Cromwell, Jr. and B.J. Cromwell (1976). *Issues in Corrections and Administration: Selected Readings.* St. Paul, MN: West Publishing Co.

Klofas, J., S. Stojkovic and D. Kalinich (1990). *Criminal Justice Organizations: Administration and Management.* Pacific Grove, CA: Brooks/Cole Publishing Company.

Krantz, S. (1983). *Corrections and Prisoners' Rights.* St. Paul, MN: West Publishing Co.

Kutak, R.J. (1976). "Grim Fairy Tales for Prison Administrators." In G.G. Killinger, P.F. Cromwell, Jr. and B.J. Cromwell, *Issues in Corrections and Administration: Selected Readings.* St. Paul, MN: West Publishing Co.

Manville, D.E. and J. Boston (eds.) (1983). *Prisoners' Self-Help Litigation Manual, Revised Second Edition.* New York, NY: Oceana Publications, Inc.

Manville, D.E. and G.N. Brezna (eds.) (1988). *Post-Conviction Remedies: A Self-Help Manual*. New York, NY: Oceana Publications, Inc.

McGee, R. (1981). *Prisons and Politics*. Lexington, MA: Lexington Books.

Miller, R.C. and D.J. Walter (1989). *Detention and Corrections Case Law Catalog, Third Edition*. Kents Hill, ME: CRS, Inc.

Morris, N. and M. Tonry (1990). "Between Prison and Probation—Intermediate Punishments in a Rational Sentencing System." *NIJ Reports*, January/February 1990, Number 218.

National Institute of Corrections (1989). *Jail Resource Manual*. Washington, DC: U.S. Department of Justice.

Nelson, W.R. (1986). "Changing Concepts in Jail Design and Management." In D.B. Kalinich and J. Klofas (eds.) *Sneaking Inmates Down the Alley: Problems and Prospects in Jail Management*. Springfield, IL: Charles C Thomas Publisher.

Poe, L.J. and T.H. Curry II. (1986). *Labor Relations for Supervisors and Managers in the Michigan Civil Service System, Third Edition*. East Lansing, MI: School of Labor and Industrial Relations, Michigan State University.

Prassel, F.R. (1972). *The Western Peace Officer*. Norman, OK: University of Oklahoma Press.

Prassel, F.R. (1979). *Criminal Law, Justice, and Society*. Santa Monica, CA: Goodyear Publishing Company, Inc.

Quinney, R. (1969). *Crime and Justice in Society*. Boston: Little, Brown and Company.

Radelet, L.A. (1986). *The Police and the Community, Fourth Edition*. New York, NY: Macmillan Publishing Company.

Radelet, M.L. (ed.) (1989). *Facing the Death Penalty: Essays on a Cruel and Unusual Punishment*. Philadelphia, PA: Temple University Press.

Rafter, N.H. (1989). "Gender and Justice: The Equal Protection Issue." In L. Goodstein and D. Layton MacKenzie (eds.) *The American Prison: Issues in Research and Policy*. New York, NY: Plenum Publishing Corporation.

Reid, S.T. (1981). *The Correctional System: An Introduction*. New York, NY: Holt, Rinehart and Winston.

Rohde, D.W. and H.J. Spaeth (1976). *Supreme Court Decision Making*. San Francisco, CA: W.H. Freeman and Company.

Robbins, I.P. (1990). "The Legal Dimensions of Private Incarceration." In I.P. Robbins (ed.) *Prisoners and the Law*. New York, NY: Clark Boardman Company, Ltd.

Robbins, I.P. (1988). *The Legal Dimensions of Private Incarceration*. Washington, DC: American Bar Association.

Robbins, I.P. (ed.) (1990). *Prisoners and the Law*. New York, NY: Clark Boardman Company, Ltd.

Rudovsky, D. (1973). *The Rights of Prisoners*. New York, NY: Avon Books.

Schwartz, M.D., T.R. Clear and L.F. Travis III (1980). *Corrections: An Issues Approach*. Cincinnati, OH: Anderson Publishing Co.

Sechrest, D.K. and W.C. Collins (1989). *Jail Management and Liability Issues*. Miami, FL: Coral Gables Publishing Co., Inc.

Spain, N.M. (1985). "Civil Law for Security Managers." Pittsburgh, PA: Spain, Workbook.

Statsky, W.P. (1986). *Introduction to Paralegalism: Perspectives, Problems, and Skills, Third Edition*. St. Paul, MN: West Publishing Co.

Steinglass, S.H (1988). *Section 1983 Litigation in State Courts*. New York, NY: Clark Boardman Company, Ltd.

Stojkovic, S., J. Klofas and D. Kalinich (eds.) (1990). *The Administration and Management of Criminal Justice Organizations: A Book of Readings*. Prospect Heights, IL: Waveland Press, Inc.

Studt, E. (1972). *Surveillance and Service in Parole*. Los Angeles, CA: UCLA Institute of Government and Public Affairs.

Taylor, V.H. (1989). "Sexual Harassment in Corrections: A Barrier to Achieving Employment Equity." Unpublished manuscript, Michigan State University.

Timm, H.W. and K.E. Christian (1991). *Introduction to Private Security*. Pacific Grove, CA: Brooks/Cole Publishing Company.

Thomas, J. (1988). *Prisoner Litigation: The Paradox of the Jailhouse Lawyer*. Totowa, NJ: Rowman & Littlefield.

Walters, S. (1988). "Correctional Officers' Perceptions of Powerlessness," *Journal of Crime & Justice* Volume XI, Number 11.

Table of Cases

Baxter v. Palmigiani, 425 U.S. 308 (1976)

Bell v. Wolfish, 441 U.S. 520 (1979)

Bonno v. Saxbe, 620 F.2d 609 (7th Cir. 1980)

Bounds v. Smith, 430 U.S. 817 (1977)

Brock v. State, 299 S.E.2d 71 (Ga. App. 1983)

Bruscino v. Carlson, 854 F.2d 162 (7th Cir. 1988)

Cody v. Hillard, 830 F.2d 912 (8th Cir. 1987)

Coffin v. Reichard, 143 F.2d 443 (6th Cir. 1944)

Coker v. Georgia, 433 U.S. 584 (1977)

Danese v. Asman, 875 F.2d 1239 (6th Cir. 1989)

Dred Scott v. Sanford, 60 U.S. (19 How.) 393 (1856)

Eberheart v. Georgia, 433 U.S. 917 (1977)

Enomoto v. Wright, 434 U.S. 1052 (1978)

Estate of Cartwright v. City of Concord, 618 F. Supp. 722 (N.D. Cal. 1985), *aff'd*, 856 F.2d 1437 (9th Cir. 1988)

Estelle v. Gamble, 429 U.S. 97 (1976)

Fortune Society v. McGinnis, 319 F. Supp. 901 (S.D.N.Y. 1970)

Furman v. Georgia, 408 U.S. 238 (1972)

Gagnon v. Scarpelli, 411 U.S. 778 (1973)

Garner v. Bolden et al., U.S. District Court, Western Michigan, *in litigation*.

Garrett v. United States, 501 F. Supp. 337 (N.D. Ga. 1980)

Gregg v. Georgia, 428 U.S. 153 (1976)

Goldberg v. Kelly, 397 U.S. 254 (1970)

Grummett v. Rushen, 587 F. Supp. 913 (N.D. Cal. 1984)

Hutto v. Finney, 437 U.S. 678 (1978)

Hyland v. Procunier, 311 F. Supp. 749 (N.D. Cal. 1970)

Ind. Dept. of Correction v. Ind. Civ. Rights, 486 N.E.2d 612 (Ind. 1985)

In re White, 97 Cal. App. 3d 141 (1979)

Johnson v. Glick, 481 F.2d 1028 (2d Cir.), *cert. denied*, 414 U.S. 1033 (1937)

Kennedy v. Mendoza-Martinez, 372 U.S. 144 (1963)

Lightbody v. Town of Hampton, 618 F. Supp. 6 (D.N.H. 1984)

Louisiana ex rel. Francis v. Resweber, 329 U.S. 459 (1947)

Lyons v. Cunningham, 583 F. Supp. 1147 (S.D.N.Y. 1983)

Mapp v. Ohio, 367 U.S. 643 (1961)

Monell v. Department of Social Services, 436 U.S. 658 (1978)

Morales v. Schmidt, 494 F.2d 85 (7th Cir. 1974)

Morrissey v. Brewer, 408 U.S. 471 (2d Cir. 1972)

Newman v. Alabama, 559 F.2d 283 (5th Cir. 1977)

Parker v. Williams, 855 F.2d 763 (11th Cir. 1988)

Parkerson v. State, 274, S.E.2d 799 (Ga. App. 1980)

Partridge v. Two Unknown Police Officers, 791 F.2d 1182 (5th Cir. 1986)

Pell v. Procunier, 417 U.S. 817 (1974)

People v. Dominguez, 256 Cal. App. 2d 623 (1967)

Peter v. Hargrave, (Va. 5 Gratt 12-24) (1848)

Plyler v. Evatt, 846 F.2d 208 (4th Cir.), *cert. denied*, 488 U.S. 897 (1988)

Procunier v. Martinez, 416 U.S. 396 (1974)

Ramos v. Lamm, 639 F.2d 559 (10th Cir. (1980)

Richardson v. Ramirez, 418 U.S. 24 (1974)

Rhodes v. Chapman, 452 U.S. 337 (1981)

Roberts v. City of Troy, 773 F.2d 720 (6th Cir. 1985)

Roberts v. Louisiana, 431 U.S. 633 (2d Cir. 1977)

Rose v. Lundy, 455 U.S. 509 (1982)

Ruffin v. Commonwealth, 62 Va. (21 Gratt 790, 796) (1871)

Schenck v. United States, 249 U.S. 47 (1919)

Smith v. Chrans, 629 F. Supp. 606 (C.D. Ill. 1986)

Soroka v. State, 598 P.2d 69 (Alaska 1979)

Sweeny v. United States, 353 F.2d 10 (7th Cir. 1965)

Sykes v. Kreiger, 290 N.E.2d 180 (Ohio 1972)

Trop v. Dulles, 356 U.S. 86 (1958)

United States v. Grant, 807 F.2d 837 (9th Cir. 1987)

United States v. Turner, 628 F.2d 461 (1980)

United States v. Vasta, 649 F. Supp. 974 (S.D.N.Y. 1986)

United States v. Smith, 618 F.2d 280 (5th Cir. 1980)

Weeks v. United States, 232 U.S. 383 (1914)

Weems v. United States, 217 U.S. 349 (1910)

West v. Atkins, 108 S. Ct. 2250 (1988)

Wilkerson v. Skinner, 462 F.2d 670 (2d Cir. 1972)

Will v. Michigan Department of State Police, 109 S. Ct. 2304 (1989)

Wilwording v. Swenson, 404 U.S. 249 (1971)

Wolff v. McDonnell, 418 U.S. 539 (1974)

Wyatt v. Stickney, 344 F. Supp. 373 (M.D. Ala. 1972)

Younger v. Gilmore, 404 U.S. 15 (1971)

Photo Credit: Frost Publishing Group, Ltd.

Probation

13

After reading this chapter, the student should be able to:

- Discuss probation as a set of strategies rather than a singular concept.

- Discuss the growth of probation, particularly the growth of felony probation.

- Describe antecedents to present-day probation practices.

- Contrast advantages and disadvantages associated with probation.

- Discuss the practice of probation supervision.

Introduction

end of '88
over ½ on
(adults) probation

Of the 3.7 million adults under correctional supervision at yearend 1988 in the United States, approximately 64% (about 2.36 million adults) were on probation (BJS, 1989). Probation services are operated at federal, state, and local levels of government and involve the direct efforts of the members of more than 2,000 agencies. Probation services are operated for adults and for juveniles, most often by separate agencies. The focus of this chapter is adult probation.

With increasing numbers of offenders, increasing costs of incarceration, and problems of overcrowding in recent years, the use of probation has expanded. During the four-year period from 1983 through 1987, the adult probation population increased by 42% (see BJS data, 1988), and during 1988 this population increased by yet another 12.5% (BJS, 1989). The trend toward greater use of probation appears likely to continue, and along with the general movement toward greater use has come a trend toward greater use of probation for felony offenders. "The fact is that 'felony probation' is evolving as the sentence of choice for large numbers of convicted felons" (Petersilia, 1985:1). Approximately one-third of the probation population is composed of convicted felons (Petersilia, 1985), and this proportion appears to be continuing to grow. A number of issues accompany the expanding role for probation. These and other issues will be examined in this chapter.

Defining Probation

Probation is a judicial function. In other words, the legal authority to grant probation to an offender in the adult system, and the legal authority to revoke (take away) the grant of probation, rests with the judiciary. As will be discussed shortly, however, other official actors in the criminal justice process have a great deal to do with making these decisions.

Conceptually, the term "probation" refers to "the release to the community of a person convicted of a crime so long as there is compliance with certain conditions of good behavior under the supervision of a probation officer" (Statsky, 1985:604). In practice, probation may closely resemble this definition, or may depart from it to rather significant extent.

Table 13.1
Adults on Probation, 1989

Regions and jurisdictions	Probation population, 1/1/89	1989 Entries	1989 Exits	Probation population, 12/31/89	Percent change in probation population during 1989	Number on probation on 12/31/89 per 100,000 adult residents
U.S. total	2,386,427	1,567,156	1,433,104	2,520,479	5.6%	1,369
Federal	61,029	19,858	21,741	59,146	-3.1	32
State	2,325,398	1,547,298	1,411,363	2,461,333	5.8	1,337
Northeast	438,691	215,467	210,364	443,794	1.2%	1,147
Connecticut	46,086	27,839	31,083	42,842	-7.0	1,728
Maine	6,059	4,792	4,000	6,851	13.1	747
Massachusetts	92,353	47,026	50,850	88,529	-4.1	1,935
New Hampshire	2,948	2,552	2,509	2,991	1.5	361
New Jersey	57,903	31,891	23,041	66,753	15.3	1,131
New York	125,256	41,953	38,502	128,707	2.8	946
Pennsylvania	92,296	47,761	50,566	89,491	-3.0	973
Rhode Island	9,824	8,467	6,060	12,231	24.5	1,595
Vermont	5,966	3,186	3,753	5,399	-9.5	1,270
Midwest	510,253	395,440	362,928	542,765	6.4%	1,217
Illinois	90,736	58,023	54,815	93,944	3.5	1,083
Indiana	60,184	57,362	55,685	61,861	2.8	1,497
Iowa	13,099	12,180	11,557	13,722	4.8	644
Kansas	19,580	12,507	9,562	22,525	15.0	1,215
Michigan	115,132	92,400	86,096	121,436	5.5	1,778
Minnesota	56,901	48,079	46,332	58,648	3.1	1,819
Missouri	42,728	27,322	24,799	45,251	5.9	1,174
Nebraska	11,411	15,369	14,153	12,627	10.7	1,064
North Dakota	1,504	558	410	1,652	9.8	343
Ohio	70,088	53,111	44,976	78,223	11.6	967
South Dakota	2,585	4,277	4,146	2,716	5.1	523
Wisconsin	26,305	14,252	10,397	30,160	14.7	835
South	929,936	658,418	601,846	986,508	6.1%	1,565
Alabama	25,301	12,405	11,231	26,475	4.6	880
Arkansas	15,931	5,875	4,234	17,572	10.3	1,001
Delaware	9,576	3,959	3,834	9,701	1.3	1,925
District of Columbia	11,296	8,942	9,887	10,351	-8.4	2,226
Florida	165,475	241,462	214,442	192,495	16.3	1,964
Georgia	121,559	69,142	65,260	125,441	3.2	2,704
Kentucky	7,398	4,142	3,478	8,062	9.0	292
Louisiana	31,218	12,828	11,751	32,295	3.5	1,039
Maryland	78,619	50,145	44,308	84,456	7.4	2,390
Mississippi	6,854	3,142	2,663	7,333	7.0	396
North Carolina	67,164	37,972	32,811	72,325	7.7	1,467
Oklahoma	23,341	11,605	10,706	24,240	3.9	1,022
South Carolina	26,260	15,543	12,151	29,652	12.9	1,159
Tennessee	28,282	24,821	22,197	30,906	9.3	839
Texas	288,906	143,515	141,265	291,156	.8	2,419
Virginia	17,945	10,470	9,330	19,085	6.4	414
West Virginia	4,811	2,450	2,298	4,963	3.2	356
West	446,518	277,973	236,225	488,266	9.4%	1,290
Alaska	2,994	1,755	1,414	3,335	11.4	921
Arizona	25,446	11,490	9,286	27,650	8.7	1,074
California	265,580	163,575	144,137	285,018	7.3	1,335
Colorado	23,230	21,877	18,729	26,378	13.6	1,075
Hawaii	10,704	5,892	5,219	11,377	6.3	1,379
Idaho	3,587	1,976	1,538	4,025	12.2	567
Montana	3,275	1,528	1,344	3,459	5.6	588
Nevada	7,032	3,411	3,119	7,324	4.2	879
New Mexico	5,312	4,508	4,160	5,660	6.6	527
Oregon	27,320	12,018	7,460	31,878	16.7	1,502
Utah	5,595	3,615	3,686	5,524	-1.3	513
Washington	64,257	44,730	34,733	74,254	15.6	2,095
Wyoming	2,186	1,598	1,400	2,384	9.1	703

Note: Nine States estimated numbers in one or more categories. See detailed probation notes for further information.

Source: Bureau of Justice Statistics (1990). "Probation and Parole 1989," p. 2. Washington, DC: U.S. Department of Justice, November.

As a sentencing option, "probation" is generally used: (1) to suspend the execution of a sentence of incarceration, (2) to suspend the imposition of a sentence, or (3) as a sentence in itself. In suspending the execution of a sentence of incarceration, a judge imposes a period of time for the offender to spend in jail or prison and then suspends all or part of this time, placing the offender on probation. If the offender successfully completes the term on probation, he or she avoids all or part of the incarceration period. If the offender is not successful in completing the term on probation, the imposed period of incarceration remains. At a revocation proceeding (held in court as the official hearing concerning whether or not to continue the offender on probation), a judge may, upon finding that the offender violated probation, order the offender to complete the entire period of incarceration originally imposed, or, by giving the offender credit for the time spent on probation ("street time"), may order the offender to complete what would then remain of the period of incarceration originally imposed. This is the most common use of probation.

In suspending the imposition of a sentence, a judge actually defers the formal sentencing decision, placing the offender on probation for a specified period. Successful completion of the term on probation may either obviate the need to impose a sentence or may be utilized as a positive factor in the eventual sentencing decision. This is the least common use of probation.

As a sentence in itself, a period of probation is the sentence imposed by the judge. This use of probation is widespread but not predominant.

As part of a package of sentencing options, it is also common to find probation combined with other forms of sentencing in a single decision. For example, an offender may be sentenced to a brief or relatively brief period of incarceration to be followed by a period of time on probation ("shock probation" or "split sentence"), or perhaps probation may be imposed in conjunction with a fine, community service, restitution, or other "creative" combination (here probation is usually the overall vehicle for insuring compliance with directions of the court). The judge in most cases has a large degree of discretion in utilizing probation as a sentencing option.

A portion of the above definition of "probation" centers on "conditional release to the community." This means that those offenders placed on probation are obligated to fulfill or abide by a set of *general conditions* (a set of requirements that all probationers in a given jurisdiction must observe), and, often, offenders placed on probation are obligated to abide by or fulfill one or more *specific conditions* (requirements specific to the individual that are imposed by the judge at the time of sentencing). Figure 13.1 shows examples of general and specific conditions.

Figure 13.1
Conditions of Probation

Conditions of probation

Offenders placed on probation must agree to abide by certain rules and regulations prescribed by the sentencing court. This set of rules and regulations is generally referred to as the "conditions of probation." In some states, these conditions are established by the legislature and written into law. In other states, judges have the discretion to impose specific conditions on a case-by-case basis. In still other jurisdictions, the dicretion to impose conditions is left to the probation organization. In most communities probationers must comply with both general and individualized conditions of probation.

The National Advisory Commission on Standards and Goals recommends against applying standard conditions to all offenders. Instead, they suggest a more flexible approach involving three considerations: first, that the conditions be tailored to fit the unique needs of the offender; second, that the conditions imposed be reasonably related to the offender's correctional program; and third, that the conditions imposed not be unduly restrictive or conflict with the offender's constitutional rights.

The American Bar Association supports the advisory commission's recommendations. Additionally, they suggest that the conditions imposed by the court should not be vague and ambiguous, but specific and understandable. The following is a list of the conditions suggested by the American Bar Association:

1. Cooperating with a program of supervision

2. Meeting family responsibilities

3. Maintaining steady employment or engaging or refraining from involvement in a specific employment or reciprocation

4. Pursuing prescribed educational or vocational training

5. Undergoing available medical or psychiatric treatment

6. Maintaining residence in a prescribed area or in a special facility established for or available to persons on probation

7. Refraining from consorting with certain types of people or frequenting certain types of places

8. Making restitution of the fruits of the crime or reparation for loss or damage caused thereby. (It is suggested that repayment schedules be formulated with the probationer's ability to pay in mind.)

Source: Belinda R. McCarthy and Bernard J. McCarthy (1984). *Community-Based Corrections*, p. 114. Pacific Grove, CA: Brooks/Cole Publishing Co.

General conditions of probation may vary from jurisdiction to jurisdiction (obviously, specific conditions are individualized). The nature of general conditions and the degree of discretion available to probation officers in insuring adherence to conditions have been sources of controversy, both in abstract and in practice. These issues will be discussed later in this chapter.

Another element of the definition of probation is supervision. Either directly or indirectly the offender on probation is to be monitored to determine whether he or she is in compliance with the requirements of probation. Supervision is linked to other purposes, namely societal protection and assistance to the probationer. In actuality, supervision may be minimal or may be more intense, and the means of supervising are varied. Much debate surrounds the element of supervision.

Antecedents to Current Notions

The concepts of release to the community, conditions, and supervision (the essence of probation) were in place in the United States by the latter half of the nineteenth century. Probation as it is presently known is the result of the extension of discretionary practices established long ago, and the packaging of these with additional notions during what Walker (1980:17-18) has called "the great institution-building [criminal justice organizations, not simply prisons!] period between 1815 and 1900."

Antecedents of probation include a practice called "benefit of clergy." "The 'benefit of clergy' was an ancient practice inherited from the Middle Ages, when clergymen were exempted from many civil punishments. Gradually, the 'benefit' was extended to laymen who could demonstrate their religiosity by either reading or reciting from memory a passage from the Bible. In [Colonial America] this provided exemption from the death penalty" (Walker, 1980:27).

"Judicial reprieve," another antecedent and a common law practice, "permitted judges to temporarily delay the imposition of sentence and to continue to delay upon evidence of good behavior" (Walker, 1980:88). Additional practices were coming into use in the United States during the early part of the nineteenth century. One should situate these practices within the larger context of neoclassical revisions in the law (formalization of the notions of mitigating and extenuating circumstances; focus on mental disease or defect and issues of criminal responsibility; changing notions about culpability and causation) and moves toward strategies involving the individualization of justice, increasing emphasis on the actor (offender) as a major overlay to the act (offense). The specific features we associate with probation are linked to these more general changes in thinking and to practicalities (limited resources, enormous discretion) in the administration of the growing "criminal justice system."

Examples of additional practices include "an 1836 Massachusetts law [that] authorized security bonds for good behavior as an alternative sentence; the law only ratified practice that extended back many years" (Walker, 1980:88). Also becoming a well-established practice was the "filing of cases." This was tantamount to what today would be called informal prosecutorial discretion. Prosecutors exercised their discretion to suspend prosecution of a case temporarily or, as was often the situation, permanently, if the accused demonstrated appropriately good behavior.

Generally, accounts of the beginnings of probation in the United States point out the influence of John Augustus. Augustus began an avocation as a court volunteer in 1841. Focusing on those with alcohol-related problems and on the indigent, Augustus interceded to pay fines and assist with attempts at recovery and employment. Eventually, the work of Augustus was recognized as contributing to the development of the notion of supervision and the link to court monitoring of those released into the community.

Other notable occurrences mark the development of probation. For example, "Edward Savage, then a captain with the Boston police, conducted 'presentence investigations' following the mass arrest of prostitutes in 1858" (Walker, 1980:88) and, later became the first legitimate probation officer (1878). He is given credit for firmly establishing the presentence investigation (PSI) as a feature of the probation process. The establishment of probation as a recognized element of the criminal justice process was facilitated further by the expressions favoring individualization of correctional practice delivered at the National Congress of Penitentiary Reform and Reformatory Discipline in 1870.

With the foundation for probation emerging and with acceptance of the central notions becoming firmly established, formal institutionalization of this criminal justice element followed. The Massachusetts legislature passed the first probation statute in 1878, followed by a second in 1880, and "in 1891 Massachusetts created a statewide probation system and transferred power of appointment [of probation officers] from municipal officials to the courts" (Walker, 1980:88-89). Rather slowly at first, but by the period 1900-1920, most states had followed suit.

The widening movement and use of probation suffered a mild setback in 1916 when the U.S. Supreme Court ruled that the federal judiciary, which had been granting probation in the absence of specific legislation authorizing this practice, had no basis in the common law to legitimize the practice. This decision resulted in nearly 5,000 pardons being issued to persons assigned to federal probation, and in ensuing Congressional legislation to authorize federal probation.

Widespread adoption of probation was an outgrowth of the Progressive movement. As Rothman indicates (1980) the Progressive ideal of low caseloads, professional (treatment-oriented) officers, and individualized treatment was rhetorically attractive to many and politically convenient for some. The reality of probation has been large caseloads, "non-professionals" (not treatment-oriented), and perfunctory supervision. Practical political requirements to do something with large numbers of offenders and the lack of a singular base of theory, even a singular set of assumptions or directions, have resulted in controversy since the burgeoning of probation in the early part of the twentieth century. One should note that the problems of probation are perennial, and that recent criticisms are not novel.

As noted earlier, the use of probation has grown enormously in the twentieth century. Although particulars of the practice of probation have changed somewhat, the technology, in the sense of basic concepts, has remained essentially the same.

Advantages and Disadvantages of Probation

There is little doubt that probation has become an established item within the rather meager conceptual menu of corrections. Even those who argue most fervently about probation, notably the neo-retributionists, speak primarily about modifying probation practices rather than eliminating the basic notion (there are a few who would argue for elimination, e.g., Thompson, 1983). Political and practical realities, as well as the forces of conceptual acceptance and bureaucratic development, have ensconced this element of correctional practice. To test this notion in a rather crude way, simply try to conceive of the corrections venture in the United States without probation.

In a relatively brief period, the place of probation has become firmly established and the probation industry has burgeoned.

There are a number of advantages to probation as a corrections element. In a practical sense, probation in its varied forms provides the capacity to absorb large numbers of offenders and place them under varying degrees of supervision. Offenders placed on probation do remain in the community. It is argued that these persons do not suffer the physical and psychological deprivations of confinement. Offenders on probation may retain jobs (or look for work), may maintain family and other community ties that may assist them in overcoming their difficulties, may continue to contribute to the support of their families, may continue to meet other financial obligations (incarceration often means that those who depend on the offender must turn to the state for material support, creditors may go unpaid, etc.), may be better able to make restitution to victims, may themselves be able to take advantage of community resources already in place to assist in resolving problems and adjusting to a law-abiding lifestyle, and may suffer less from the stigmatizing effects of conviction.

It is also argued that probation allows a focus on the responsibility and role(s) of the members of the community in correcting offenders. Additionally, it is argued that probation provides a means for dealing with those who have committed less serious offenses, who are one-time or sporadic offenders, who are judged to be relatively stable or more in need of community assistance than incarceration, which generally has severe effects.

From a practical standpoint, probation is more economically attractive than incarceration. The cost of incarcerating offenders is generally recognized to be far greater than the cost of placing offenders on probation. In addition, probation has evolved into a major industry, employing tens of thousands of people in the United States.

There are several disadvantages that may be associated with the use and practice of probation in the United States. Critics of probation usually point out that there is no singular or adequate theoretical base to underlie the practice of probation. "Probation" is not a monolithic correctional approach; rather, the term refers to a collection of strategies that more or less exhibit adherence to the characteristic features discussed above. These features do not in themselves reflect the coherent manifestation of a rigorously derived model. So many approaches to the practice of probation and the use of probation are in evidence in the United States that the meaning and actuality of "probation" is amorphous.

Why is this amorphous character a disadvantage? As the neo-retributionists would point out, it is difficult to determine whether probation is punishment, whether probation (as practiced) legitimately represents
"rehabilitation" or "reintegration" and, so, whether there are clearly ascer-
tainable aims or anticipated outcomes. This is not merely an abstract
dilemma, for when "probation" means many things to many people, those
most directly involved with its realization in use and practice are affected.
Probation most often represents the exercise of a large degree of discretion
by criminal justice officials and "proximate policymakers." For example,
legislatures or other governing bodies provide general parameters for the legitimate use of probation—usually without providing specifics for determining expected outcomes. Prosecutors often utilize probation as a bargaining advantage or tool in plea bargaining, especially when using the tactic of
sentnce recommendation. Judges may impose probation as a permutation of
the sentencing options discussed above and may in general be more concerned with any one or several of the possible advantages discussed above.
Judges may be using probation in the practical sense of doing something with
the marginal case when jail or prison space is limited or filled, where otherwise he or she would normally impose a sentence of incarceration for the
particular offender. Probation agencies, administratively and through the actions of individual probation officers, may in fact focus more on rule watching, rule enforcement, assistance to probationers, or any other focus deemed
appropriate, both agency-wide and for the individual officer and more. Because of this, it may be difficult to ascertain just what the primary aim(s) may
be with any particular individuals or cases and perhaps with probation in
general in any given jurisdiction or among jurisdictions. The disadvantage
lies in having to construct the meaning of "probation" as related to an amorphous set of possible outcomes, possible real-life operationalizations.

It may be argued that the large degree of discretion associated with the
practice of probation and with the imposition of probation is in itself a disadvantage. Some argue that probation is associated with sentencing disparity
(similarly situated offenders receiving dissimilar sentences). Some argue
that probation in many cases unduly depreciates the seriousness of the offense, especially when there is a felony conviction that could result in a
rather severe sentence of incarceration. Generally, these arguments or perceptions are connected to the issue of equity in sentencing, both in imposition of sentence and in the actual sentence served (known as the "effective
sentence"). There are also arguments that when probation is used as a

bargaining advantage in plea negotiation, it distorts due process, where the imposition of probation has more connection to the negotiation than to the process established for making subsequent decisions concerning the offender.

There are also those who argue that probation, especially felony probation, presents a societal protection dilemma. Advocates of incapacitation may focus on the recidivism of probationers to fashion an argument that probationary status does little to deter the convicted offender from committing more crimes, and that retaining the convicted offender in the community merely gives him or her the opportunity to commit additional crimes. For example, in a 40-month follow-up study of felony probationers in California and New York, Petersilia (1985) found that 65% were rearrested, 51% were reconvicted (one-third of these for serious violent crimes), and 18% were sent on to institutions. Those centering attention on societal protection find such statistics important in criticizing the actual effect of probation. On the other hand, such pessimistic statistics may be countered by more optimistic findings (see Vito, 1983, 1984 and see Fichter, Hirschburg, and McGaha, 1987). Depending on one's predisposition, probation outcomes may be seen, more or less, as controversial.

One could identify more advantages and more disadvantages of probation. It is not our purpose here to attempt to resolve questions of the legitimacy of probation as a concept nor is it our purpose to resolve questions concerning the continuation, modification, or termination of particular probation practices. It is our intent to encourage the reader to consider "probation" as a set of strategies pursued differentially in the various jurisdictions at the levels of government where probation is organized. It is our intent to encourage the consideration of different perspectives regarding probation and probation practice and to draw attention to the rhetorical and symbolic arguments that surround probation. Keep in mind the enormity of the probation venture(s) in the United States. It is important to focus on asking more questions about why things happen the way they do, when thinking about probation.

Structure and Operation of Probation

"Probation in the United States is administered by more than 2,000 separate agencies" (Abadinsky, 1987:21). Agencies are organized at federal, state, and local levels of government. As has been noted concerning correctional administration and organization in general (see Chapter 6), these agencies are not parts of a large pyramid that coordinates, controls, or allocates resources, extending from the federal level to the local level. In other words, the agencies providing probation services exist and operate within varying contexts, administratively connected to, and funded by, many different governing bodies. One can expect to find a good deal of commonality, but also different aims, policies, emphases in funding, staffing, and operation resulting from the contexts within which the agencies are administered.

Abadinsky points out that the administration of probation systems can be separated into six categories:

1. *Juvenile*: Separate probation services for juveniles are administered on a county or municipal level or on a statewide basis.

2. *Municipal*: Independent probation units are administered by the lower courts under state laws and guidelines.

3. *County*: Under laws and guidelines established by the state, a county operates its own probation system; this is similar to the municipal system.

4. *State*: One agency administers a central probation system, which provides services throughout the state.

5. *State combined*: Probation and parole services are administered on a statewide basis by one agency.

6. *Federal*: Probation is administered as an arm of the courts. Federal probation officers also supervise parolees. (Abadinsky, 1987:21)

One must also be aware that within states the provision of probation services may reflect variations of the above. Each state has persons who are under supervision of the Federal Probation Service for violations of the United States Criminal Code. There will also be persons who are under supervision of a state-level authority, such as the probation division of a state department of corrections, and, where there are separate county, municipal, and juvenile agencies, there will be persons under the supervision of those authorities. In other words, the total of those on probation within any given state may be composed of persons supervised by different agencies that may pursue different policies, provide different levels of service, have different staffing patterns, and so on. In fact, the realities of probation for these persons may be very different.

Figure 13.2
Notions Concerning Administrative Identity of Probation Agencies

Placement in the Judiciary

1. Probation is more responsive to the courts, to which it provides services, when it is administered by the judiciary.

2. The relationship of probation staff to the courts creates an automatic feedback mechanism concerning the effectiveness of various dispositions.

3. Courts have greater awareness of the resources needed by the probation agency.

4. Judges will have greater confidence in an agency for which they are responsible and thus allow probation staff more discretion than they would allow members of an outside agency.

5. If probation is administered on a statewide basis, it is usually incorporated into a department of corrections. Under such circumstances, probation services might be assigned a lower priority than they would have as part of the court.

Those who oppose the placement of probation in the judiciary note the disadvantages:

1. Judges, trained in law, not administration, are not equipped to administer probation services.

2. Under judicial control, services to persons on probation may receive a lower priority than services to the judge (presentence investigations).

3. Probation staff may be assigned duties unrelated to probation.

4. The courts are adjudicatory and regulative; they are not service-oriented bodies.

Placement in the executive branch has a number of features to recommend it:

1. All other human service agencies are within the executive branch.

2. All other corrections subsystems are located in the executive branch.

3. Executive branch placement permits better coordination of program budgeting and increases the ability to negotiate fully in the resource allocation process.

4. Such placement facilitates a coordinated continuum of services to offenders and better utilization of probation manpower.

Source: Howard Abadinsky (1991). *Probation and Parole: Theory and Practice*, Fourth Edition, p. 29, copyright © 1991. Adapted by permission of Prentice-Hall, Englewood Cliffs, New Jersey.

If one imposes a "national perspective" for viewing probation, the de-centralized character of probation efforts is cast in high relief. It becomes apparent that this decentralized situation exists by level of government and across branches of government, with probation agencies organized within both the executive and the judicial branches. A good deal of attention has been directed to the potential benefits and potential drawbacks of placing probation agencies within either the executive or the judicial branches. Figure 13.2 presents some representative arguments and issues regarding such organizational placement.

Considering the arguments presented in Figure 13.2, one should under-stand that the present organizational arrangements are resultants of incre-mental development. Present varied arrangements then appear to be more the outcomes of political decision-making where differing interests have conditioned the resolution of questions of preference in different political arenas rather than being the outcomes of a coherent and highly rational set of efforts at development. The crux of the arguments regarding organizational alignment appears to more directly involve questions of form (administrative identity and interest, budgetary and policy control, the appearance of and symbolism associated with structure) than to more directly involve questions concerning the anticipated or actual outputs of "probation" (sets of precisely identified objectives). One may wish to ask whether the attention given such arguments may not deflect attention away from more substantive issues con-cerning just what is accomplished or what accomplishments can be expected from the sets of strategies we know as "probation." Going one step further, one may wish to consider whether political realities associated with the orga-nization and operation of probation preclude meaningful consideration of co-herent development from a "national perspective."

Operation: Tasks, Caseloads, and Supervision

Probation field offices are the basic service delivery units for "probation." Whether organized at the federal, state, or local level, there are many tasks to be carried out by those staffing these agencies. As noted above, there is variation across these agencies, in staffing, funding, opera-tional policies, and in the extent and types of services provided. One must keep this variation in mind while considering the practices associated with probation. Our aim in the following discussion is to provide a rough map of the territory commonly covered by those working in probation field offices.

As discussed in Chapter 15, probation is the primary element in community corrections, and the purview of those working in probation has been widened greatly in recent years. Probation officers may be involved in providing services associated with both preconviction and post-conviction phases of the criminal justice process. Depending upon the organization of a given agency, probation officers may be both probation and parole officers, providing services to both probationers and parolees.

Preconviction Services

"The President's Commission on Law Enforcement and Administration of Justice (1972) pointed out that prosecutors often deal with offenders who need treatment or supervision, but for whom criminal sanctions would be excessive" (Abadinsky, 1987:348). Pretrial diversion programs are a reflection of this philosophy. Some probation agencies have become involved in the provision of pretrial diversion services, particularly in the provision of varying degrees of pretrial supervision. Similarly, in recent years, some probation agencies have become involved in the provision of pretrial services in connection with bail projects, especially assisting with screening for those who may be eligible for release from custody and providing varying degrees of pretrial supervision. Some probation agencies, though organized predominantly to deal with adult offenders, carry out additional duties in the area of juvenile intake (see Chapter 16 for discussion of agencies organized to provide juvenile probation services).

Investigation Services

Another set of services provided by probation agencies is the development of presentence and post-sentence investigations. The activities related to the development of these reports obviously may take place either during the pre-conviction phase or the post-conviction phase of the criminal justice process. A PSI is a formal report concerning an offender and the circumstances of the offense. The presentence investigation is developed primarily to assist the court in making an appropriate disposition of the case (Abadinsky, 1987:83). The post-sentence investigation is developed to provide information for further decision-making concerning the offender (the presentence report also may serve the same additional purposes); for example:

- serving as the basis for a plan of probation
- assisting jail or prison personnel in classification and program decisions
- assisting in parole decision-making (see Abadinsky, 1987:83-84)

Figure 13.3
Examples of PSI Inclusions

Typically, a presentence investigation report breaks down into the following categories:

I.   Information concerning the offense. Here the exact nature of the offense to which the individual stands convicted is set forth followed by a narrative account of his and others actions leading up to the commission of the offense. A section is provided wherein the individual reports his version of what happened and this is usually followed by any statements made by codefendants, witnesses and/or victims.

II. Individual's prior record. Here juvenile adjudications as well as adult arrests are listed. Not only is the nature of the arrest, the time, place and disposition given, but also background detail is provided along with verification of the nature of the judicial process which led to disposition.

III. Personal background. A narrative usually verifies defendant's birth date, identifies his parents and siblings and the nature of their relationship. It covers his upbringing, marital situation, educational background, employment, physical, mental, emotional health, military service and the financial situation.

IV. Prosecution comments. The prosecution is given a formal opportunity to enter into the report its beliefs in regard to the offense and what the appropriate disposition should be.

V.   Overall summarization and evaluation. Here a concise review of the foregoing information is drawn together and presented along with the possible sentencing alternatives available to the Court. More and more frequently also appearing here is statistical data indicating the type and length of sentences given to previous similar cases.

VI. Recommendation. Here the probation officer submits to the Court what he believes to be the most appropriate sentence based upon the information in the report. The recommendation should logically follow from all the information compiled as "the probation officer has the responsibility to offer a sound recommendation with supporting rationale which will assist the Court in achieving its sentencing goals."

Source: David M. Crean (1985). "Community Corrections: On the Line." In Lawrence F. Travis, III (ed.) *Probation, Parole, and Community Corrections: A Reader.* Copyright © 1985 by Waveland Press, Inc., Prospect Heights, Illinois. Used with permission from the publisher.

Probation agencies typically have one or more general formats for the development of a PSI. Figure 13.3 shows examples of inclusions. The types and amounts of information, as well as the overall style for presentation, vary across agencies and jurisdictions. Developing a PSI usually requires a probation officer to conduct interviews and to review records and other documents to form the basis of the report. Depending on the offender and the offense, the investigation may be quite extensive and time-consuming. With presentence investigations, judges in many jurisdictions ask that the probation officer deliver a sentencing recommendation along with an overall evaluation of the case. In some jurisdictions, judges prefer not to have a recommendation, but to have the information and an overall evaluation or summary. In either situation, probation officers bear a primary responsibility for the presentation of the information and for the tone of the report. The selection of relevant information and the manner in which information and comments are presented can be influential in the disposition of a case, as well as being influential in the other sorts of decisions for which the PSI may be used.

In a situation in which POs have both probationers and parolees in their caseloads, the probation/parole officers may also develop pre-parole investigations. Pre-parole investigations are similar in nature to PSIs, but these are developed specifically for use in parole decision-making—the decision to grant parole and the later decisions regarding the parolee. McCleary (1978) notes an attitude toward such reports which he characterizes as typical. In his study, he found that parole officers use pre-parole investigations as part of a *typing* process, categorizing offenders generally in terms of *control*, developing reports in a routine (almost perfunctory) manner by focusing on a few key issues. According to McCleary, parole officers (POs) understand that offenders will be released to different environments. Therefore, the PO's main focus is on controllability as related to the offender's potential environment rather than on comprehensiveness in the provision of a total assessment of the individual and circumstances of the offense. Here again, one must consider the large number of agencies, the large numbers of probation/parole personnel, the great amount of diversity among offenders and circumstances, and the increasing requirement of probation/parole personnel to do more with less. Remember that probation may be best envisioned as a set of strategies and that the experience for an individual offender as well as the experiences for probation/parole officers, though similar in some respects, may vary to significant extents.

The provision of investigative services in the development of PSIs and other investigation reports involves a great deal of time and effort for the staff of a probation agency. Criticisms of such investigative services or efforts generally center on the amount of time and energy devoted to these activities in relation to caseload supervision, as well as the quality of information included and the latitude available to probation officers in the presentation of information. Furthermore, the utility of presentence investigations is called into question by some who point out that judges are not bound to base their decisions on the information or recommendations in the PSI. The observation that dispositions seem very often to be in accord with PSIs may counter such criticism; perhaps PSIs are usually well done, perhaps probation officers become well-acquainted with the details of given cases in their jurisdictions and develop PSIs in accord with their perceptions, or both. The actual value of PSIs appears to be difficult to determine. Also, in states where sentencing guidelines are adopted, there may well be need for only a brief PSI or perhaps no PSI, given the nature of the sentencing process under such guidelines.

Supervision

As noted earlier in this chapter, supervision is an essential element defining probation. Varying purposes can be ascribed to probation supervision; for example, community protection, rule enforcement, offender assistance. There is no singular or universally accepted body of theory underlying probation supervision. Various service roles for probation agencies and probation officers have been conceptualized and associated with supervision. Figure 13.4 presents examples of such conceptualizations. Orientations toward service role and toward supervision may vary from agency to agency, from officer to officer, from offender to offender (perhaps dependent on the perceived needs of the offender, perhaps dependent on other factors). Methods of supervision may vary by orientation or other factors.

In practice, probation officers are assigned a caseload for the purposes of supervision. Caseloads may vary, depending on the needs or circumstances of an agency, the needs or circumstances of offenders, the abilities of individual probation officers, and other factors. Caseloads may be *generalized caseloads* (the probation officer supervises a variety of categories of offenders and offense types) or they may be *specialized caseloads* (the probation officer supervises offenders assigned on the basis of certain characteristics of the offender or the offense type).

Figure 13.4
Views of Probation Officer Roles

Treatment Innovations in Probation and Parole

A typology is an attempt to categorize different styles of probation or parole supervision. A typology provides a framework from which to evaluate different supervision styles and to reach tentative conclusions about how probation and parole officers should meet their responsibilities to the offenders they supervise and the communities they protect. There are very few officers who exclusively "fit" into one "type." Most officers perform tasks reflecting each of the types of roles. Also, typologies of roles are seldom "value-free." That is, a particular typology is likely to reflect the biases of the person who developed the typology. The typology discussed below inclues three types of officers: the punitive officer, the welfare officer and the protective officer (Carlson and Parks, 1979).

The *punitive officer* tends to view supervision as a law enforcement function. The punitive officer is likely to emphasize control and surveillance in the supervision process and may attempt to coerce the offender into conforming by threats of punishment. Supervision by punitive officers tends to be highly routinized, with contracts setting strict limits on the probationer's or parolee's associates, hours, travel, employment and other aspects of life. Some probationers and parolees undoubtedly benefit from this type of supervision.

However, the punitive officer may have a tendency to use a punitive style with an entire caseload. As a result, the distinct needs of probationers and parolees may not be served. For example, a youth on probation may also be a school truant because of serious learning disabilities. The truancy could be a contributing factor to more serious legal problems. A punitive probation or parole officer who is concerned with conformity and who has little interest in the individual needs and problems of the offender, will likely miss the unique problems of this probationer. Outward conformity does not resolve the important issues of social development and the problems which contributed to the individual's delinquency or criminality. Compliance is not a measure of change (Street, Vinter and Perrow, 1966).

The major problem with punitive supervision is that it tends to address symptoms rather than problems. At the same time, the task of the probation and parole officer is one of insuring compliance with the conditions of probation or parole. The notion of officer as counselor has tended to confuse the issue because the protection of society has always been paramount, and the counselor role has always been secondary (Marshall and Vito, 1982).

The *welfare officer* can be contrasted to the punitive officer in that the two types are near opposites. Unlike the punitive officer, the welfare officer has as the ultimate goal the improved welfare of the probationer or parolee. This type of officer is committed to the philosophy that the only guarantee of community protection lies in the successful personal adjustment of the client. Ideally, this type of officer is emotionally neutral and works from diagnostic categories and treatment skills which are objective and theoretically based on an assessment of the client's needs and

Figure 13.4—continued

potential.

Various writers have used positive labels to describe the welfare officer and negative labels to describe the punitive officer, reflecting the biases of the author of the typology. However, the welfare officer may place an emphasis on the rehabilitation of the offender, ignoring the importance of protecting the community. Some welfare officers see repeated acts of delinquency or criminality as indicative of problems the probationer or parolee has not resolved. However, the probationer or parolee may have strong commitments to delinquency or, in the case of an adult, to criminality and may be manipulating the officer in order to remain free from any control.

The *protective officer* tends to alternate between protecting the offender and protecting the community. In some instances, the officer may provide direct assistance, and in other instances he may be somewhat punitive. This officer type is sometimes portrayed as vacillating, providing inconsistent supervision for the offender. However, probation and parole include responsibilities to provide programs

and supervision of offenders within a legal framework. This issue cannot be ignored, regardless of the needs of the offender.

While the protective role may seem confusing, with the officer appearing to help at times and to punish at others, this is probably an accurate portrayal of the role, because the role of probation or parole officer involves substantial role conflict (Marshall and Vito, 1982). That is, a wide array of expectations of the officer exists, some of which may appear contradictory. For example, at one extreme, the officer may be expected to provide crisis counseling during moments of acute trauma in the probationer's or the parolee's life. The counseling in this setting may require unlimited patience, empathy skills and considerable professional expertise. At the other extreme, the officer may be expected to deliver an arrest warrant which will result in incarceration or reincarceration of the probationer or parolee. This type of conflict is an inherent part of the role and can create confusion for the probationer and parolee. The officer must have the capacity for performing at both ends of the treatment-punishment continuum, de-

pending on the behavior of the client and the situational context in which the behavior occurs.

The protective role recognized the possibility that probation and parole officer roles cannot simply be typed as surveillance or treatment. Rather, the roles include elements of both surveillance and counseling. The role utilized in a specific situation will be dependent on a number of factors, not the least of which will be the offense and behavior of the offender. For example, if the offender is an active member of a crime syndicate, it is highly improbable that he will be interested in "counseling services" offered by a probation or parole officer.

The reassessment of roles in probation and parole has taken different directions; however, the general theme is that there should be a break with traditional approaches whatever they are. In this process, a new concept has emerged—*resource brokerage*. Resource brokers are less concerned about understanding and changing behavior and more concerned with assessing the concrete needs of the individual offender, making certain the individual receives services

Figure 13.4—continued

from a variety of sources which will directly address those needs. The basic principles of resource brokerage are rather simple.

1. When probationers and parolees are released from supervision it will be expected that they have been prepared to meet community responsibilities.

2. Each individual is accountable for his or her behavior, and responsible behavior is required for freedom.

3. Probationers and parolees generally need the opportunity to learn new workable strategies for handling their life roles while receiving supervision (U.S. Department of Justice, Improved Probation Strategies, 1979).

Under the concept of resource brokerage, the goals of probation and parole can be accomplished through a highly-structured community resource program which provides selective services appropriate to the needs of the offenders. The resource program must include opportunities for ofenders to change themselves *and* those conditions which brought them into the juvenile justice or criminal justice system.

The key to the program is the assumption that most offenders are not pathologically ill, and for this reason, the role of the counselor/therapist is usually inappropriate (Dell'Apa, 1976). A new role emerges for probation and parole officers—that of "advocate-broker." Community resources are seldom organized in the highly-structured system envisioned by the author or resource brokerage. To the contrary, service agencies have their own histories, traditions, biases and myths which may actually impede the delivery of services, especially to persons who have violated the law.

As we attempt to move away from traditional supervision methods in probation and parole to approaches which require different types of assessment methods, we find that those methods have yet to be developed. A major problem limiting the development of new assessment methods and supervision strategies is the absence of scientifically validated procedures which can be used to assess offenders. The validation problem has a number of sources, including lack of agreement on techniques which are appropriate for the assessment and treatment of offender behavior. Before appropriate treatment can be provided through a probation or parole reintegration program, it is imperative that causal factors be accurately defined and classified.

Source: Robert G. Culbertson and Thomas Ellsworth (1985). "Treatment Innovations in Probation and Parole." In Lawrence F. Travis, III (ed.) *Probation, Parole, and Community Corrections: A Reader.* Copyright © 1985 by Waveland Press, Inc., Prospect Heights, Illinois. Used with permission from the publisher.

Supervision of offenders involves direct interaction with, or monitoring of, offenders as well as indirect monitoring of offenders. Probation officers may be required to supervise offenders directly through *personal visits* (interaction with the offender in the probation office, at the probationer's residence, or other places) or through *collateral visits* (interactions with others such as employers, family members, acquaintances of the probationer, who can provide information on the offender's progress). Probation officers may be required to supervise offenders indirectly through the receipt of reports written by the offenders, monitoring jail lists to determine whether anyone in the caseload has been arrested, or through other means suitable to determining the progress of the offender on probation. Supervision also involves the documentation of the offender's progress; perhaps a large amount of paperwork to be regularly completed concerning persons in the probation officer's caseload.

Probationers are often placed into different statuses for the purposes of supervision. This may be done formally, using some type of risk/needs assessment, or may be done informally, as may be the situation when probation officers, due to caseload demands, must decide on whom to focus their efforts. Degrees of supervision may vary from minimum supervision (the probationer may be only loosely supervised in an indirect manner) to intensive (special efforts are made to provide as much direct supervision as possible).

The extent to which supervision may facilitate either community protection or therapeutic assistance to probationers is controversial. Caseloads for most probation officers are large, typically in the range of 80 to 100 probationers, often more, per officer. Given that probation officers may be involved in investigative activities (e.g., developing PSIs), may be involved in preparing documentation on the probationers in their caseloads, may be involved in activities associated with the maintenance of their agencies (staff meetings, and so on), must spend time traveling in the field to meet with probationers and others on a regular basis, must develop documentation and make appearances concerning revocations, and more, critics of probation often argue that little actual supervision can occur.

With the recent explosion in the probation population has come greater attention to special probation programs aimed at focusing supervision efforts on those offenders judged to be high-risk probationers, usually felony offenders. "Intensive probation is currently a hot idea in criminal justice" (Walker, 1989:212). As Walker (1989:212) observes, "This strategy involves a small caseload for each probation officer and more frequent contacts between the office and the offender." Intensive probation involves the concentration of supervision resources on a relatively small proportion of probationers. Such strategies have practical appeal, but, as yet, convincing evidence of the viability of these approaches for connecting supervision to the larger aims of probation has not been produced.

Revocation

When probationers are not succeeding in completing their terms on probation, it may become the task of their probation officers to initiate revocation proceedings. Probationers who commit a crime or crimes while on probation, or probationers who violate the general or specific conditions of their probation, though their acts or omissions would not constitute a new crime (technical violations of probation), may face revocation. Revocation hearings are subject to minimum due process guarantees outlined in the decisions of the U.S. Supreme Court in the cases, *Mempa v. Rhay*, *Morrissey v. Brewer*, and *Gagnon v. Scarpelli* (see Chapter 12 for discussion of these baseline cases). State legislatures may impose stricter requirements for hearings subject to their respective governing authorities.

Usually, revocation involves a process similar to the following. The probation officer initiates the process by making a formal allegation of violation of probation. The allegation is reviewed by a senior probation supervisor, who conducts a preliminary examination or hearing. The probationer may waive a formal preliminary hearing. If sufficient reason is found to request a formal revocation hearing, such a request is sent to the court of appropriate jurisdiction. The revocation hearing is held before a judge, is more or less adversarial in nature (depending upon the extension of due process guarantees beyond those required by the U.S. Supreme Court decisions on revocation hearings), and the result depends upon the decision of the judge regarding the evidence presented. In general, if a judge finds that the probationer has violated probation, several options are available. The judge could decide to issue a verbal or written formal reprimand and continue the offender on probation. The judge could impose new or additional special conditions as requirements and continue the offender on probation. The judge could revoke probation. Obviously, if the judge finds that the probationer did not violate probation, the offender is continued in the previous status.

Figure 13.5
Intensive Supervision

New Dimensions in Probation:
Georgia's Experience with
Intensive Probation Supervision (IPS)

Georgia's Intensive Probation Supervision (IPS) program, implemented in 1982, has stirred nationwide interest among criminal justice professionals because it seems to satisfy two goals that have long appeared mutually contradictory: (1) restraining the growth of prison populations and associated costs by controlling selected offenders in the community and (2) at the same time, satisfying to some extent the demand that criminals be punished for their crimes. The pivotal question is whether or not prison-bound offenders can be shifted into Intensive Probation Supervision without threatening the public safety.

A new research study, partially funded by the National Institute of Justice, suggests that intensive supervision provides greater controls than regular probation and costs far less than incarceration. The study was conducted by the Georgia Department of Corrections, Office of Evaluation and Statistics, and was assisted by an Advisory Board funded by the National Institute of Justice. This *Research in Brief* summarizes the findings.

The Georgia program

The IPS program began in 1982 as a pilot in 13 of Georgia's 45 judicial sentencing circuits. By the end of 1985, it had expanded to 33 circuits and had supervised 2,322 probationers.

While probation programs with varying degrees of supervision have been implemented throughout the country, Georgia's IPS is widely regarded as one of the most stringent in the Nation. Standards include:

- Five face-to-face contacts per week;

- 132 hours of mandatory community service;

- Mandatory curfew;

- Mandatory employment;

- Weekly check of local arrest records;

- Automatic notification of arrest elsewhere via the State Crime Information Network listing;

- Routine and unannounced alcohol and drug testing.

The supervision standards are enforced by a team consisting of a Probation Officer and a Surveillance Officer. The team supervises 25 probationers. In some jurisdictions, a team of one Probation Officer and two Surveillance Officers supervises 40 probationers.

The standards are designed to provide sufficient surveillance to control risk to the community and give a framework to treatment-oriented counseling. The counseling is designed to help the offender direct his energies toward productive activities, to assume responsibilities, and to become a law-abiding citizen.

Most offenders chosen for the IPS pilot program were already sentenced to prison, presented an acceptable risk to the community and had not committed a violent offense. A risk assessment instrument was used to screen offenders. While the majority of those selected fell into the category of non-violent property offenders, a large number of individuals convicted of drug- and alcohol-related offenses also were included as the program developed. Some of these offenses also involved personal violence.

Of the 2,322 people in the program between 1982 and 1985, 370 (or 16 percent) absconded or had their probation revoked. The remaining 1,952 were successfully diverted from prison; many are still under some form of probationary supervision. Some have successfully completed their sentences.

Figure 13.5—continued

From the Director

As the number of offenders behind bars continues to grow—passing the half million mark last year—crime as measured by the National Crime Survey has declined for the fourth straight year. At the same time, there is understandable concern about crowding in our jails and prisons. Reports on the "crisis" in prisons are front page news. But what is less well known is that only one-quarter of offenders under correctional supervision are actually incarcerated. The remainder are in the community on probation or parole.

Overwhelming probation caseloads make it difficult to provide adequate supervision for many of these offenders, who are, in effect, then left unsecured in the communities they victimized. Citizens are placed in jeopardy when offenders, particularly felons, are released without sufficient safeguards. Earlier research by the National Institute of Justice showed that fully two-thirds of a sample of felons on probation in Alameda County, California, were rearrested within 3 years. The majority of charges filed against them were for crimes the public fears the most—robbery, burglary, and theft.

If we do not send convicted criminals to prison, are there alternatives that give probation officers better tools to do their jobs and permit them to exert greater control over convicted felons?

One promising answer to this question is described in this *Research in Brief*. Intensive probation supervision programs are being tried in a number of jurisdictions as a means of providing more control over offenders in the community and keeping them focused on more productive and less threatening behavior. These programs invoke strict curfews and require offenders to maintain employment, receive counseling, provide community service, remain drug and alcohol free, and make restitution to their victims.

This Brief reports on an evaluation of one such program, Georgia's Intensive Probation Supervision (IPS) program, conducted by the State's Department of Corrections and funded in part by the National Institute of Justice.

The results of this study are encouraging. The evaluation suggests that the intensive supervision approach is cost effective and poses less of a risk to public safety than does ordinary probation. Many of the more than 2,300 offenders sentenced to the program

are still on probation. Fifteen percent have successfully completed their sentences. Only 16 percent have been removed from the program and returned to prison for technical violations or new crimes.

Most important, the study suggests that in Georgia, the more stringent supervision reduced the risk to the community. Offenders in IPS committed fewer and less serious crimes than comparison groups of regular probationers and those released from prison.

The Georgia experience, summarized here, offers useful information for policymakers and probation officials searching for ways to make probation a real sanction against offenders. The National Institute will continue to watch with great interest the growing experience with intensive supervision programs to determine what approaches work to control repeat crime by convicted offenders in the community and to ensure a greater measure of protection for the public.

James K. Stewart
Director
National Institute of Justice

Source: Billie S. Erwin and Lawrence A. Bennett (1987). "New Dimensions in Probation: Georgia's Experience with Intensive Probation Supervision (IPS)," pp. 1-2. Washington, DC: National Institute of Justice.

As outlined above, supervision and revocation form the bulk of the post-conviction tasks to be carried out by those working in probation. It should be noted that a number of special programs, such as electronic monitoring and other creative programs, are being associated with probation. These programs are discussed in Chapter 15, Community Corrections.

Summary

"Probation" may be best understood as a collection of strategies. While common characteristics such as release to the community, conditions and supervision may broadly outline the notion of probation, the experience of probation may vary widely for individuals assigned to this correctional status. The use of probation, especially felony probation, is expanding rapidly. As a sentencing option, probation may be a sentence in itself, may be used to suspend the execution of a sentence, or may be used (rarely) to suspend the imposition of a sentence. As a correctional rubric, probation is multidimensional, with many combinations of practices and many variations of practices existing under the general label. As such, probation is a relatively recent development in corrections. A number of historical antecedents underlie twentieth-century practices and concepts and are important in understanding probation as a correctional venture.

Probation allows a very large number of offenders to be placed under correctional authority, at costs substantially lower than costs of incarceration, with the possibility of many arrangements for supervision and control. Recent variations on the practice of probation, notably intensive probation, have been promoted to counter concerns about societal protection and other concerns. As the "On the Defensive" section indicates, probation is politically palatable as an umbrella measure and may be a correctional venture as promising as any.

On the Defensive

"Something which Works"

There is no question that, as an umbrella for a set of many strategies, probation is established as a major item on the U.S. corrections menu. In a practical sense, this umbrella provides for placing large numbers of offenders under some form of correctional authority while promising latitude in attempts to achieve multiple aims (including community protection, doing something constructive with offenders, providing alternatives to incarceration, individualizing justice to some degree, and so on). In a practical sense, probation costs less than incarceration and some other correctional efforts, such as electronic monitoring. In a general sense, many people conceive of probation as an appropriate form of sentence and an appropriate sort of correctional effort for those convicted of offenses viewed as less serious.

If one considers probation in a general sense, one may conclude (as does Walker, 1989) that here is something that works. Probation agencies discharge large numbers of offenders from their sentences of probation as "successes." Usually, success for agency purposes means that these offenders did not suffer reconviction or revocation during the time under supervision. Certainly, this is encouraging.

One must keep in mind, however, the multidimensional nature of probation—the term encompasses efforts undertaken with one-time, sporadic, and chronic offenders, with misdemeanants and with felons, with strategies of minimal supervision to intensive supervision, with lesser resources for many agencies and greater resources for some agencies, with aims of rules-watching for some agencies and "doing something constructive with offenders" (perhaps counseling, perhaps "treatment") for others, and so on. As Walker (1989:210) points out, where probation succeeds, this success may happen "for reasons that are not particularly comforting to the correctional establishment." As he further asserts (1989:212), "[e]ven when probation works, the results may have nothing to do with 'treatment' " (. . .) "that is to say, [most offenders] would do just as well with a suspended sentence (which is simply probation without supervision)."

Critics place correctional personnel on the defensive in asking that they show strong correlations between the actual probation efforts undertaken and the successes reported. Further, critics point to a lack of convincing research evidence to show that focused probation efforts (such as intensive supervision) actually can be counted upon to make a significant difference with offenders. Effectiveness is the issue. Critics appear to place an affirmative obligation upon correctional personnel to show effectiveness, and an inability to clearly show effectiveness (however, this notion may be operationalized and measured) appears to be sufficient for some to severely scrutinize present practices.

Beyond this, the effects of prison overcrowding and increases in numbers of felons convicted are leading to "critical mass" problems for most probation agencies. With approximately half of convicted felons now receiving probation as a primary element of their sentences, correctional administrators and personnel are being called upon to modify strategies and practices to accommodate this burgeoning population. Even with "innovations" such as intensive supervision and house arrest (Chapter 15) the overall situation appears ominous. Numbers of misdemeanants assigned to probation also continue to increase, resources devoted to probation continue to be strained, and no unusual breakthroughs rest on the horizon. Those responsible for providing probation services yet face many of the same questions and problems regarding probation that have been faced for decades. Many of the problems have become more acute. Correctional administrators will be called upon to show that the "something which is being done" responds to these questions and problems, and, so, they are likely to tout modification of present practices and "innovations" as potential "solutions." Controversy will continue.

Source: Written by Rick Lovell.

Key Terms and Concepts

benefit of clergy

collateral visit

community service

filing of cases

fine

general conditions of probation

generalized caseload

intensive probation

judicial reprieve

neoclassical revision

neoretributionists

personal visit

post-sentence investigation

presentence investigation

probation

proximate policymakers

rehabilitation

reintegration

restitution

revocation

sentence

shock probation

specific conditions of probation

specialized caseload

split sentence

street time

References

Abadinsky, H. (1987). *Probation and Parole: Theory and Practice, Fourth Edition.* Englewood Cliffs, NJ: Prentice-Hall.

Fichter, M., P. Hirschburg and J. McGaha (1987). "Increased Felony Porbation: Is it the Answer to Overcrowded Prisons?" Unpublished paper presented at the Academy of Criminal Justice Sciences annual meeting, St. Louis, Missouri (March).

McAnany, P., D. Thompson and D. Fogel (1984). *Probation and Justice: Reconsideration of Mission.* Cambridge, MA: Oelgeschlager, Gunn, and Hain.

McCleary, R. (1978). *Dangerous Men.* Beverly Hills, CA: Sage Publications.

Petersilia, J., S. Turner, J. Kahan and J. Peterson (1985). *Granting Felons Probation: Public Risks and Alternatives.* Santa Monica, CA: RAND Corporation.

Statsky, W. (1985). *Legal Thesaurus/Dictionary.* St. Paul, MN: West Publishing Co.

Vito, G. (1983). "Reducing the Use of Imprisonment." In L. Travis, M. Schwartz and T. Clear (eds.) *Corrections: An Issues Approach, Second Edition.* Cincinnati, OH: Anderson Publishing Co.

Vito, G. (1984). "Developments in Shock Probation: A Review of Research Findings and Policy Implications." *Federal Probation*, Volume 48:22-27.

Walker, S. (1989). *Sense and Nonsense about Crime: A Policy Guide, Second Edition.* Pacific Grove, CA: Brooks/Cole Publishing Co.

Walker, S. (1980). *Popular Justice: A History of American Criminal Justice.* New York, NY: Oxford University Press.

Photo Credit: Tony O'Brien, Frost Publishing Group, Ltd.

Parole

After reading this chapter, the student should be able to:

▮ Define and discuss parole as a set of strategies rather than a singular concept.

▮ Explain the positions of those criticizing parole as a correctional practice.

▮ Differentiate discretionary release and mandatory release from prison.

▮ Describe antecedents to present-day parole practices.

▮ Discuss the use and attendant problems of parole decision-making guidelines.

▮ Comment on the practices of parole supervision.

Introduction

Of the 3.7 million adults under correctional supervision at year-end 1988, approximately 408,000 were on parole (BJS, 1989). In 1988, the parole population was the fastest growing of the four [major] components of corrections and increasing overall by 12.5% (BJS, 1987). Table 14.1 shows the distribution of the parole population among the states and the federal system.

As with probation, the essential features of parole have been in place in the United States since the latter half of the nineteenth century. However, in recent years "parole" has come under heavier attack from critics than has probation. Although a large majority of the states retain parole as a major option in corrections (and, as the above BJS information suggests, are increasing its use), antagonists of parole have been successful in removing this option in several states, as well as from the federal system. This chapter examines common structural and operational features of parole and discusses controversial issues affecting the continuation of parole as a major component of corrections in the United States.

Defining Parole

Parole is "release from confinement after serving part of the sentence; conditional release from prison under the supervision of a parole officer, who has the authority to recommend a return to prison if the conditions of parole...are violated" (Statsky, 1985:559). As is the situation with probation, persons placed on parole serve their terms in the community.

Parole is different from probation in two fundamental ways. First, the concept of parole involves release from confinement under the authority of a state government or the federal government. That is, those persons placed in a parole status are felons who are sentenced to confinement in state or federal institutions and are being granted early release from confinement, while remaining under the supervisory authority of a state government or the federal government. While the reader may be aware of a few instances in some jurisdictions in which misdemeanants are granted early release from confinement in local jails under the rubric of programs called "parole," such programs are not truly parole programs. Nonetheless, such efforts, along with the use of split sentences and shock probation, have created some confusion for those attempting to learn about this area. These "innovations" resemble traditional parole.

Table 14.1
Adults on Parole, 1989

Regions and jurisdictions	Parole population, 1/1/89	1989 Entries	1989 Exits	Parole population, 12/31/89	Percent change in parole population during 1989	Number on parole on 12/31/89 per 100,000 adult residents
U.S. total	407,596	305,596	256,395	456,797	12.1%	248
Federal	20,451	10,910	9,949	21,412	4.7	12
State	387,145	294,686	246,446	435,385	12.5	236
Northeast	104,680	56,807	50,940	110,547	5.6%	286
Connecticut	371	101	150	322	-13.2	13
Massachusetts	4,333	5,124	4,769	4,688	8.2	102
New Hampshire	461	259	243	477	3.5	58
New Jersey	18,463	11,202	9,603	20,062	8.7	340
New York	33,962	18,841	16,118	36,685	8.0	270
Pennsylvania	46,466	20,802	19,566	47,702	2.7	519
Rhode Island	442	345	396	391	-11.5	51
Vermont	182	133	95	220	20.9	52
Midwest	51,062	40,437	35,578	55,921	9.5%	125
Illinois	14,369	12,096	11,915	14,550	1.3	168
Indiana	3,411	1,305	1,260	3,456	1.3	84
Iowa	1,945	1,392	1,437	1,900	-2.3	89
Kansas	3,497	3,137	1,841	4,793	37.1	259
Michigan	7,677	7,549	5,336	9,890	28.8	145
Minnesota	1,639	1,912	1,852	1,699	3.7	53
Missouri	7,207	4,228	3,797	7,638	6.0	198
Nebraska	447	679	636	490	9.6	41
North Dakota	134	198	193	139	3.7	29
Ohio	5,991	4,851	4,378	6,464	7.9	80
South Dakota	617	435	542	510	-17.3	98
Wisconsin	4,128	2,655	2,391	4,392	6.4	122
South	156,696	98,397	71,122	183,971	17.4%	292
Alabama	4,701	2,516	1,461	5,756	22.4	191
Arkansas	3,840	2,061	2,401	3,500	-8.9	199
Delaware	1,093	424	504	1,013	-7.3	201
District of Columbia	3,949	2,995	2,029	4,915	24.5	1,057
Florida	2,562	918	1,162	2,318	-9.5	24
Georgia	11,308	15,386	9,257	17,437	54.2	376
Kentucky	3,443	1,759	2,069	3,133	-9.0	114
Louisiana	7,387	5,493	3,703	9,177	24.2	295
Maryland	9,225	5,862	5,225	9,862	6.9	279
Mississippi	3,177	1,641	1,469	3,349	5.4	181
North Carolina	6,191	8,242	6,874	7,559	22.1	153
Oklahoma	1,455	1,195	657	1,993	37.0	84
South Carolina	3,626	1,039	1,035	3,630	.1	142
Tennessee	9,529	4,876	3,705	10,700	12.3	290
Texas	77,827	36,287	22,820	91,294	17.3	758
Virginia	6,576	7,184	6,368	7,392	12.4	160
West Virginia	807	519	383	943	16.9	68
West	74,707	99,045	88,806	84,946	13.7%	224
Alaska	489	555	511	533	9.0	147
Arizona	1,669	3,622	3,243	2,048	22.7	80
California	49,364	84,111	75,967	57,508	16.5	269
Colorado	1,743	1,571	1,515	1,799	3.2	73
Hawaii	1,108	625	446	1,287	16.2	156
Idaho	247	227	236	238	-3.6	34
Montana	671	370	289	752	12.1	128
Nevada	2,100	1,375	1,058	2,417	15.1	290
New Mexico	1,230	1,038	1,117	1,151	-6.4	107
Oregon	3,790	3,864	1,860	5,794	52.9	273
Utah	1,218	848	789	1,277	4.8	119
Washington	10,745	643	1,556	9,832	-8.5	277
Wyoming	333	196	219	310	-6.9	91

Note: Twelve States estimated numbers in one or more categories. Maine eliminated parole in 1976. See the detailed parole notes for further information.

Source: Bureau of Justice Statistics (1990). "Probation and Parole 1988," p. 3. Washington, DC: U.S. Department of Justice, November.

Second, parole is not a judicial function. The authority to grant and to revoke parole, as well as the authority to establish conditions of parole, is vested in various parole boards and commissions. These organizations are administratively identified with the executive branch of government. Parole authorities make discretionary decisions that affect the nature of sentences imposed upon convicted offenders, but their decision-making occurs during the execution phase of the sentence. Another way of saying this is that parole authorities' decisions affect the effective sentence of the convicted offender.

Figure 14.1
Model Penal Code Guidelines for Parole Conditions

When a prisoner is released on parole, the Board of Parole shall require as a condition of his parole that he refrain from engaging in criminal conduct. The Board of Parole may also require, either at the time of his release on parole or at any time and from time to time while he remains under parole, that he conform to any of the following conditions of parole:

a. Meet his specified family responsibilities;

b. Devote himself to an approved employment or occupation;

c. Remain within the geographic limits fixed in his Certificate of Parole, unless granted written permission to leave such limits;

d. Report, as directed, in person and within thirty-six hours of his release, to his parole officer;

e. Report in person to his parole officer at such regular intervals as may be required;

f. Reside at the place fixed in his Certificate of Parole and notify his parole officer of any change in his address or employment;

g. Have in his possession no firearm or other dangerous weapon unless granted written permission;

h. Submit himself to available medical or psychiatric treatment, if the Board shall so require;

i. Refrain from associating with persons known to him to be engaged in criminal activities or, without permission of his parole officer, with persons known to him to have been convicted of a crime;

j. Satisfy any other conditions specifically related to the cause of his offense and not unduly restrictive of his liberty or incompatible with his freedom of conscience.

Source: American Law Institute (1972). "Model Penal Code: 1962." In *American Law Institute Compendium of Model Correctional Legislation and Standards*, Vol. 3. Washington, DC: U.S. Department of Justice, pp. 58-59.

As defined above, parole involves conditional release to the community. This means that those offenders placed on parole are obligated to abide by or fulfill a set of *general conditions* (a set of requirements that all parolees in a given jurisdiction must observe), and, often, offenders on parole are obligated to abide by or fulfill one or more *specific conditions* (requirements specific to the individual that are imposed by the parole authority at the time of the decision to grant parole). Figure 14.1 shows guidelines for parole conditions.

As was discussed concerning conditions of probation, general conditions of parole may vary from jurisdiction to jurisdiction (obviously, special conditions are individualized). Also, as was discussed concerning conditions of probation, the nature of general conditions and the degree of discretion available to parole officers in insuring adherence to conditions have been sources of controversy. Critics most often have focused on problems of interpretation and application by parole officers.

Another element of the definition of parole is supervision. Either directly or indirectly (usually both in the case of parole) the parolee is to be monitored to determine whether he or she has complied with the requirements of parole. Ideally, parole supervision is to be more intense than supervision for the majority of probationers. Parolees are felons who have been convicted of serious crimes that require severe sanctions, and generally, felons require a higher degree of supervision. Supervision may be thought to serve purposes of societal protection and assistance to the parolee. Regardless, much debate surrounds the element of parole supervision. The issues will be discussed later in this chapter.

Parole as a Release Mechanism

The vast majority of offenders confined in state and federal institutions will be released to various community settings in the United States. Relatively few inmates will live out their lives in prison. Table 14.2 shows state prison releases, by method, during the years 1977-1988 (BJS, 1989). Although figures for release of federal inmates are not included, one may obtain a general idea of the place of parole as a release mechanism.

Table 14.2
State Prison Releases, by Method, 1977-1988

Year	Total releases from prisons	All	Conditional releases				Unconditional releases		
			Discretion-ary parole	Supervised mandatory release	Probation	Other	Expiration of sentence	Commu-tation	Other
1977	115,213	100%	71.9%	5.9%	3.6%	1.0%	16.1%	1.1%	.4%
1978	119,796	100	70.4	5.8	3.3	2.3	17.0	.7	.5
1979	128,954	100	60.2	16.9	3.3	2.4	16.3	.4	.6
1980	136,968	100	57.4	19.5	3.6	3.2	14.9	.5	.8
1981	142,489	100	54.6	21.4	3.7	3.1	13.9	2.4	1.0
1982	157,144	100	51.9	24.4	4.8	3.6	14.4	.3	.6
1983	191,237	100%	48.1%	26.9%	5.2%	2.5%	16.1%	.5%	.6%
1984	191,499	100	46.0	28.7	4.9	2.7	16.3	.5	.9
1985	203,895	100	43.2	30.8	4.5	3.0	16.9	.4	1.2
1986	230,672	100	43.2	31.1	4.5	4.6	14.8	.3	1.4
1987	270,506	100	40.6	31.2	4.4	5.7	16.2	1.0	.9
1988	301,378	100	40.3	30.6	4.1	6.0	16.8	1.0	1.2

Percent of prison releases

Note: The data are from the National Prisoner Statistics reporting program. The total releases from State prison are those for which the method of release was reported. Deaths, unspecified releases, transfers, and escapes were not included. Altogether, 320,805 persons were released or removed from State prisons in 1988.

Source: Bureau of Justice Statistics (1989). "Probation and Parole 1988," p. 4. Washington, DC: U.S. Department of Justice, May.

As the reader will note in Table 14.2, a relatively small percentage of the state prison inmates (16.8 in 1988) serve their entire sentences in confinement ("expiration of sentence," or "flat time"). Smaller percentages are released to probation (4.1 in 1988), through commutation (1.0 in 1988), and through other means (7.2 in 1988, with conditional and unconditional release considered). The two categories of "discretionary parole" and "mandatory release" clearly account for the large majority of releases. As the reader will also note, from 1977 through 1988, the distribution of releases through discretionary release versus mandatory release has changed dramatically.

"Discretionary parole" is the term used to describe releases that result from decisions by parole boards or commissions. "Unlike releases on discretionary parole, mandatory releases from prison do not result from decisions by parole boards or commissions; however, like those leaving prison on discretionary parole, prisoners with a mandatory release enter community supervision for some specified period of time" (BJS, 1987:2). With mandatory release, there is no board action and no parole hearing (these will be discussed later in this chapter). Rather, "[correctional] authorities subtract time off for good behavior in prison from the offender's sentence to determine the time of mandatory release from prison" (BJS, 1987:2). As Table 14.2 indicates, discretionary parole release has diminished appreciably in recent years while mandatory release has increased about fivefold.

The release figures reflect the manifestation of discontent with discretionary parole release. Several states have shifted from discretionary parole to mandatory release, and the federal government is making this transition. One practical effect is the reduction in number (eventually) and reduction in scope of authority of parole boards or commissions, while, as indicated above, community supervision may remain. Issues surrounding this shift are discussed later in this chapter.

Antecedents to Present Notions

A number of antecedents may be identified as milestones or precipitous developments in the emergence and establishment of parole in the United States. During the mid-1800s, conditional release became the basis of a "new penology" which found its most coherent articulation at the Cincinnati congress in 1870 (see Chapter 2; also see Walker, 1980:92-98). However, as Walker observes, "The laws [which followed] creating the indeterminate sentence and parole simply formalized existing practice, clarifying and often relocating responsibility for decision-making" (1980:92).

Walker (1980:92-98) explains that parole, which has a history somewhat similar to that of probation, became established in practice because the conceptual foundations served to assist in achieving a number of purposes. These purposes included providing additional avenues for criminal justice officials to practice discretionary leniency and individualize justice, to present an option that could be understood as both less expensive and more convenient than incarceration, and to present a somewhat palatable strategy for dealing with overcrowding (a perennial problem in corrections).

"Parole" followed other strategies for early discretionary release. Executive pardons, good-time release, and commutations of sentences all were items on the conceptual menu predating parole. As Walker states,

> The pardoning power was exercised liberally during the nineteenth century. Wines and Dwight found that the incidence of pardon increased in proportion to the length of sentence. Between 1828 and 1866, 12.5 percent of all prisoners in Massachusetts received pardons. But the percentage increased from 20.5 percent for inmates with sentences of five to ten years, to 32 percent for those with sentences longer than ten years, and 50 percent for inmates sentenced to life imprisonment. In fact, 'lifemen' in Massachusetts served an average of only seven and three-quarters years in prison (1980:93).

Used so liberally, the power to pardon became a problem, placing governors in the awkward position of frequently having to address requests for pardons. Also, the liberal use of the pardoning power engendered controversy concerning arbitrary application. Parole would promise, at least in principle, to provide a more coherent and more politically acceptable means for discretionary release.

New York passed the first good-time law in 1817 (see Walker, 1980:94). Gradually, other states followed suit. As noted above, good-time laws served multiple purposes. Maintenance of control over inmates was perceived to be one of the most important purposes (Walker, 1980). Parole would promise to fulfill similar purposes.

The establishment of parole was gradual and was at least somewhat uncertain. The foundational rubric for the practice of parole is generally credited to the development of the "mark system" by Alexander Maconochie during the 1840s at the British penal colony on Norfolk Island, near Australia, and to Walter Crofton, who established the Irish system of parole ("ticket of leave") during the 1850s.

Maconochie experimented with what is known today as the indeterminate sentence. Maconochie assigned a number of "marks" or points (to be earned on the basis of work and good behavior) to each sentence. "Under this arrangement the convict could progress through several grades [levels] and in due course earn a ticket of leave [conditional release]" (Walker, 1980:95).

The English Parliament passed an act in 1853 allowing prison inmates to receive early release (on a "ticket of leave") under supervision of the police (Abadinsky, 1987). Subsequently, Walter Crofton assumed leadership of the

Irish prison system and instituted a conditional release system that influenced later developments in the United States. As Abadinsky summarizes, the *Irish system* also involved levels or stages:

1. The first stage involved solitary confinement for nine months. During the first three months the inmate was on reduced rations and was allowed no labor whatsoever. It was reasoned that after three months of forced idleness, even the laziest prisoner would long for something to do. He would then be given full rations, instructed in useful skills, and exposed to religious influences.

2. In the second stage, the convict was placed in a special prison to work with other inmates, during which time he could earn marks to qualify for a transfer to the third stage.

3. Stage three involved transportation to an open institution, where the convict, by evidencing signs of reformation, could earn release on a Ticket of Leave.

4. Ticket of Leave men were conditionally released and, in rural districts, supervised by police; those residing in Dublin, however, were supervised by a civilian employee who had the title of Inspector of Released Prisoners. He worked cooperatively with the police, but it was his responsibility to secure employment for the Ticket of Leave men. He required them to report at stated intervals, visited their homes every two weeks, and verified their employment: in short, he was the forerunner of the modern parole officer. (1987:145)

The Irish system provided supporters of parole in the United States with several of the essential elements currently associated with parole practice. It also provided advocates of the "new penology" with a milestone undertaking which was used to indirectly reinforce their notions concerning individualizing justice and expanding the discretionary power of those in control of the sets of strategies we presently refer to as "corrections." Still, the formal establishment of parole as an institutionalized feature of U.S. penal practice did not occur immediately.

Zebulon Brockway was a prominent official who advocated making conditional release a formal part of American correctional practice (Walker, 1980). At Elmira Reformatory (see Chapter 2), where Brockway was superintendent from 1877 until 1900, a mark system and a set of "innovative" programs (primarily education and industrial programs) were introduced to individualize the penal effort. Early release was initiated as a portion of the set of inducements and practice supporting the discretionary ideals of the indeterminate sentence. Decisions to advance inmates to parole status were made by the institutional board of managers. Parolees would remain under the supervision of reformatory officials for six months, reporting each month to an assigned "guardian" (official) (Abadinsky, 1987). Walker (1980) notes that the Elmira Reformatory was no more successful than other prisons. Walker explains that, "Because there were nearly fifteen hundred inmates, the demands of custody prevailed over the ideal of individualized treatment" (1980:97).

Brockway's system was replicated in several reformatories in other states. By 1900, parole was still a limited element in U.S. corrections practice. However, the Progressive Era (see Chapter 2), especially during the period 1900 through 1915, brought rapid expansion of the practice of parole. Thirty-four states had adopted parole by 1915. However, as Rothman (1971) would observe, parole was rhetorically appealing, but the central notions were not implemented as intended or promised.

Parole fit within the strategies of those who saw themselves as Progressives and those who found convenient partnerships with the Progressives (see Rothman, 1971). Progressives concerned with corrections sought to reform practices in the United States. "In effect, all Progressive programs assumed one outstanding feature: *they required discretionary responses to each case*" (Rothman, 1971:6). Individualizing correctional practice would be the hallmark of the collection of strategies identified with the Progressives. That parole (as well as the other central strategies) was based more on impressionistic logic than "proven" principles did not deter the Progressives. "That these measures [the collection of practices making up parole and other central strategies] would expand the power of the state, enlarging the freedom of action of public officials, did not disturb reformers" (Rothman, 1971:6). And, for those interested in enlarging the discretionary realms of action in corrections, as well as others primarily looking for something that might work and would be politically palatable, the strategies of parole, probation, et al. seemed to fit. Alliances were formed, and the practices were rapidly adopted.

Current Notions

As noted earlier, parole, as a set of strategies, may be said to serve multiple aims. Those supporting parole as a concept may center attention differentially on various aims. Critics of parole may do the same. Parole may be said: (1) "to provide a timely release from prison, enhancing the potential that the sentence served will meet the needs of the inmate and adequately protect society" (Culbertson and Ellsworth, 1985:130), (2) "to lessen the harshness of some long prison sentences" (Culbertson and Ellsworth, 1985:131), (3) "to provide a 'safety-valve' for overpopulated prisons" (Culbertson and Ellsworth, 1985:131), and (4) "to provide prison authorities with a tool which can be used to maintain social control over prison popula- tions" (Culbertson and Ellsworth, 1985:132). Parole may also be said to pro- vide an avenue for programmatic (treatment type) intervention aimed at suc- cessful personal adjustment of the parolee, based upon interactions with a pa- role officer who "works from diagnostic categories and treatment skills which are objective and theoretically based on an assessment of the [parolee's] needs and potentials" (Culbertson and Ellsworth, 1985:135).

It is clear that current notions and practices that fall under the general rubric of "parole" may vary substantially. Consider the possible aims pre- sented above and consider organizing and operating parole systems to pursue one, some, or all of these general aims. The federal system and the states with their systems are not following a singular aim or set of aims. We have already indicated in this chapter a very strong shift in the nature of release from prison, as shown in the patterns of discretionary release (board or com- mission action) compared to patterns of mandatory release across the states during the period 1977 through 1986. As noted earlier, the large shift toward mandatory release reflects the recent "assault" on parole as discretionary re- lease, resulting in changing notions and practices. There have been, and there presently are, notable debates concerning community supervision and conditions of parole, resulting in varying notions and practices in the realm of community supervision.

Parole Decision-Making

Zebulon Brockway's discretionary early release system vested the parole decision-making authority in an institutional board of managers. By the 1920s debates in various states concerning the objectivity of parole decision- making and variability in parole decision-making created impetus for the es- tablishment of decision-making bodies which would be independent of direct institutional management. During this period there was also a general movement toward the centralization of administration of correctional functions (see McElvey, 1977:267-298). This general movement added to the impetus for creation of decision-making bodies organized with administrative identities either independent of the large correctional systems (*independent boards* or *commissions*) or within the large correctional systems, yet as semiautonomous elements (*consolidated boards*). Institutional boards have died away, but since this time period there has been a variety of parole decision-making arrangements generally following the independent and consolidated schemes. In recent years, the movement (in several states and in the federal system) toward mandatory release changes the nature of the decision-making function and promises the eventual elimination of the parole board or commission in some systems.

Criticism and debates concerning discretionary board decision-making and discretionary release in general have been focused in a number of directions. In an abstract sense, neo-retributionists question whether parole is actually punishment or is instead the amelioration of punishment. Neo-retributionists also question whether parole is defensible as a rehabilitative venture (notwithstanding the attachment of the general notion to other aims such as those above).

In an applied sense, many have critically scrutinized the practices of discretionary boards or commissions. Most notably, the degrees of objectivity of such bodies and the mechanics of intendedly rational decision-making have received attention. These issues have been present and have been addressed since the beginning of the twentieth century, especially since the 1920s. The administrative identity (location within the overall government hierarchy) has resulted in varied authoritative relationships, as noted above. The composition of discretionary boards/commissions and the manner in which board/commission members acquire their positions has been questioned in various systems, resulting in differential arrangements among the states and the federal government. In particular, attention has been directed to whether board members should be direct political appointees (as in some states, where selections to fill vacancies are made by the governor, with the determination of qualifications made by the governor) as opposed to the use of more elaborate schemes (as in some states, where general qualifications for board members are predetermined, there is a screening and nominating panel, and there are more established regulations for the appointment process), which is thought to provide greater assurance of appointing those most competent to decide parole matters.

Table 14.3
Guidelines for Decisionmaking

APPENDIX A GUIDELINES FOR DECISIONMAKING Effective 9/1/81 [Guidelines for Decisionmaking, Customary Total Time to be Served before Release (including jail time)]				
OFFENSE CHARACTERISTICS: Severity of Offense Behavior (Examples)	**OFFENDER CHARACTERISTICS:** Parole Prognosis (Salient Factor Score 1981)			
	Very Good (10-8)	Good (7-6)	Fair (5-4)	Poor (3-0)
LOW Alcohol or Cigarette law violations, including tax evasion (amount of tax evaded less than $2,000)[1] Gambling law violations (no managerial or proprietary interest) Illicit drugs, simple possession Marihuana/hashish, possession with intent to distribute/sale [very small scale (e.g., less than 10 lbs. of marihuana/less than 1 lb. of hashish/less than .01 liter of hash oil)] Property offenses (theft, income tax evasion, or simple possession of stolen property) less than $2,000	ADULT RANGE			
	< = 6 months	6-9 months	9-12 months	12-16 months
	(YOUTH RANGE)			
	(< = 6) months	(6-9) months	(9-12) months	(12-16) months
LOW MODERATE Counterfeit currency or other medium of exchange [(passing/possession) less than $2,000] Drugs (other than specifically categorized), possession with intent to distribute/sale [very small scale (e.g., less than 200 doses)] Marihuana/hashish, possession with intent to distribute/sale [small scale (e.g., 10-49 lbs. of marihuana/1-4.9 lbs. of hashish/.01-.04 liters of hash oil)] Cocaine, possession with intent to distribute/sale [very small scale (e.g., less than 1 gram of 100% purity, or equivalent amount)] Gambling law violations—managerial or proprietary interest in small scale operation [e.g., Sports books (estimated daily gross less than $5,000); Horse books (estimated daily gross less than $1,500); Numbers bankers (estimated daily gross less than $750)] Immigration law violations	ADULT RANGE			
	< = 8 months	8-12 months	12-16 months	16-22 months
	(YOUTH RANGE)			
	(< = 8) months	(8-12) months	(12-16) months	(16-20) months

Table 14.3—continued

APPENDIX A (Continued) **GUIDELINES FOR DECISIONMAKING** Effective 9/1/81 [Guidelines for Decisionmaking, Customary Total Time to be Served before Release (including jail time)]				
OFFENSE CHARACTERISTICS: Severity of Offense Behavior (Examples)	**OFFENDER CHARACTERISTICS:** Parole Prognosis (Salient Factor Score 1981)			
	Very Good (10-8)	Good (7-6)	Fair (5-4)	Poor (3-0)
LOW MODERATE (Continued) Property offenses (forgery/fraud/theft from mail/embezzlement/interstate transportation of stolen or forged securities/receiving stolen property with intent to resell) less than $2,000				
MODERATE Automobile theft (3 cars or less involved and total value does not exceed $19,999)[2] Counterfeit currency or other medium of exchange [(passing/possession) $2,000-$19,999] Drugs (other than specifically categorized, possession with intent to distribute/sale [small scale (e.g., 200-999 doses)] Marihuana/hashish, possession with intent to distribute/sale [medium scale (e.g., 50-199 lbs. of marihuana/5-19.9 lbs. of hashish/.05-.19 liters of hash oil)] Cocaine, possession with intent to distribute/sale [small scale (e.g., 1.0-4.9 grams of 100% purity, or equivalent amount)] Opiates, possession with intent to distribute/sale [evidence of opiate addiction and very small scale (e.g., less than 1.0 grams of 100% pure heroin, or equivalent amount)] Firearms Act, possession/purchase/sale (single weapons: not sawed-off shotgun or machine gun) Gambling law violations—managerial or proprietary interest in medium scale operation [e.g., Sports books (estimated daily gross $5,000-$15,000); Horse books (estimated daily $1,500-$4,000); Numbers bankers (estimated daily gross $750-$2,000)] Property offenses (theft/forgery/fraud/embezzlement/interstate transportation of	ADULT RANGE 10-14 months (YOUTH RANGE) (8-12) months	14-18 months (12-16) months	18-24 months (16-20) months	24-32 months (20-26) months

Table 14.3—continued

APPENDIX A (Continued)			
GUIDELINES FOR DECISIONMAKING			
Effective 9/1/81			
[Guidelines for Decisionmaking, Customary Total Time to be Served before Release (including jail time)]			

OFFENSE CHARACTERISTICS: Severity of Offense Behavior (Examples)	**OFFENDER CHARACTERISTICS:** Parole Prognosis (Salient Factor Score 1981)			
	Very Good (10-8)	Good (7-6)	Fair (5-4)	Poor (3-0)
LOW MODERATE (Continued) stolen or forged securities/income tax evasion/receiving stolen property) $2,000-$19,999 Smuggling/transporting of alien(s)				
HIGH Carnal Knowledge[3] Counterfeit currency or other medium of exchange [(passing/possession) $20,000-$100,000] Counterfeiting [manufacturing (amount of counterfeit currency or other medium of exchange involved not exceeding $100,000)] Drugs (other than specifically listed), possession with intent to distribute/sale [medium scale (e.g., 1,000-19,999 doses)] Marihuana/hashish, possession with intent to distribute/sale [large scale (e.g., 200-1,999 lbs. of marihuana/20-199 lbs. of hashish/.20-1.99 liters of hash oil)] Cocaine, possession with intent to distribute/sale [medium scale (e.g., 5-99 grams of 100% purity, or equivalent amount)] Opiates, possession with intent to distribute/sale [small scale (e.g., less than 5 grams of 100% pure heroin, or equivalent amount) except as described in moderate] Firearms Act, possession/purchase/sale (sawed-off shotgun(s), machine gun(s), or multiple weapons) Gambling law violations—managerial or proprietary interest in large scale operation (e.g., Sports books (estimated daily gross more than $15,000); Horse books (estimated daily gross more than $4,000); Numbers bankers (estimated daily gross more than $2,000)]	ADULT RANGE 14-20 months	20-26 months	26-36 months	34-44 months
	(YOUTH RANGE) (12-16) months	(16-20) months	(20-26) months	(26-32) months

Table 14.3—continued

APPENDIX A (Continued)
GUIDELINES FOR DECISIONMAKING
Effective 9/1/81
[Guidelines for Decisionmaking, Customary Total Time to be Served before Release (including jail time)]

OFFENSE CHARACTERISTICS: Severity of Offense Behavior (Examples)	OFFENDER CHARACTERISTICS: Parole Prognosis (Salient Factor Score 1981)			
	Very Good (10-8)	Good (7-6)	Fair (5-4)	Poor (3-0)
HIGH (Continued) Involuntary manslaughter (e.g., negligent homicide) Mann Act (no force—commercial purposes) Property offenses (theft/forgery/fraud/embezzlement/interstate transportation of stolen or forged securities/income tax evasion/receiving stolen property) $20,000-$100,000 Threatening communications (e.g., mail/phone)—not for purposes of extortion and no other overt act				
VERY HIGH Robbery (1 or 2 instances) Breaking and entering—armory with intent to steal weapons Breaking and entering/burglary—residence; or breaking and entering of other premises with hostile confrontation with victim Counterfeit currency or other medium of exchange [(passing/possession/manufacturing)/amount more than $100,000 but not exceeding $500,000] Drugs (other than specifically listed), possession with intent to distribute/sale [large scale (e.g., 20,000 or more doses) except as described in Greatest I] Marihuana/hashish, possession with intent to distribute/sale [very large scale (e.g., 2,000 lbs. or more of marihuana/200 lbs. or more of hashish/2 liters or more of hash oil)] Cocaine, possession with intent to distribute/sale [large scale (e.g., 100 grams or more of 100% purity, or equivalent amount) except as described in Greatest I] Opiates, possession with intent to distribute/sale [medium to a very large	ADULT RANGE 24-36 months (YOUTH RANGE) (20-26) months	 36-48 months (26-32) months	 48-60 months (32-40) months	 60-72 months (40-48) months

Table 14.3—continued

APPENDIX A (Continued) GUIDELINES FOR DECISIONMAKING Effective 9/1/81 [Guidelines for Decisionmaking, Customary Total Time to be Served before Release (including jail time)]				
OFFENSE CHARACTERISTICS: Severity of Offense Behavior (Examples)	OFFENDER CHARACTERISTICS: Parole Prognosis (Salient Factor Score 1981)			
	Very Good (10-8)	Good (7-6)	Fair (5-4)	Poor (3-0)
VERY HIGH (Continued) scale (e.g., 5 grams or more of 100% pure heroin, or equivalent amount) unless the offense is described in Greatest I or Greatest II] Extortion [threat of physical harm (to person or property)] Explosives, possession/transportation Property offenses (theft/forgery/fraud/embezzlement/interstate transportation of stolen or forged securities/income tax evasion/receiving stolen property) more than $100,000 but not exceeding $500,000				
GREATEST I Aggravated felony (e.g., robbery: weapon fired or injury of a type normally requiring medical attention) Arson or explosive detonation [involving potential risk of physical injury to person(s) (e.g., premises occupied or likely to be occupied)—no serious injury occurred] Drugs (other than specifically listed), possession with intent to distribute/sale [managerial or proprietary interest and very large scale (e.g., offense involving more than 200,000 doses)] Cocaine, possession with intent to distribute/sale [managerial or proprietary interest and large scale (e.g., offense involving more than 1 kilogram (1000 grams) of 100% purity, or equivalent amount)] Opiates, possession with intent to distribute/sale [managerial or proprietary interest and large scale (e.g., offense involving more than 50 grams but not more than 1 kilogram (1000 grams) of 100% pure heroin or equivalent amount)] Kidnaping [other than listed in Greatest II;	ADULT RANGE 40-52 months .... (YOUTH RANGE) (30-40) months	52-64 months (40-50) months	64-78 months (50-60) months	78-100 months (60-76) months

Table 14.3—continued

APPENDIX A (Continued) **GUIDELINES FOR DECISIONMAKING** Effective 9/1/81 [Guidelines for Decisionmaking, Customary Total Time to be Served before Release (including jail time)]				
OFFENSE CHARACTERISTICS: Severity of Offense Behavior (Examples)	**OFFENDER CHARACTERISTICS:** Parole Prognosis (Salient Factor Score 1981)			
	Very Good (10-8)	Good (7-6)	Fair (5-4)	Poor (3-0)
GREATEST I (Continued) limited duration; and no harm to victim (e.g., kidnaping the driver of a truck during a hijacking, driving to a secluded location, and releasing victim unharmed)] Robbery (3 or 4 instances) Sex act—force [e.g., forcible rape or Mann Act (force)]				
GREATEST II Murder Voluntary Manslaughter Aggravated felony—serious injury (e.g., robbery: injury involving substantial risk of death or protracted disability, or disfigurement) or extreme cruelty/brutality toward victim Aircraft hijacking Espionage Kidnaping (for ransom or terrorism; as hostage; or harm to victim) Treason Opiates, possession with intent to distribute/sale [managerial or proprietary interest and very large scale (e.g., offense involving more than 1 kilogram (1000 grams) of 100% pure heroin or equivalent amount)]	ADULT RANGE 52+ months .... (YOUTH RANGE) (40+) months Specific upper limits are not provided due to the limited number of cases and the extreme variation possible within category	64+ months (50+) months	78+ months (60+) months	100+ months (76+) months

GENERAL NOTES

A. These guidelines are predicated upon good institutional conduct and program performance.

B. If an offense behavior is not listed above, the proper category may be obtained by comparing the severity of the offense behavior with those of similar offense behaviors listed.

C. If an offense behavior can be classified under more than one category, the most serious applicable category is to be used.

D. If an offense behavior involved multiple separate offenses, the severity level may be increased.

E. In cases where multiple sentences have been imposed (whether consecutive or concurrent, and whether aggregated or not) an offense severity rating shall be established to reflect the overall severity of the underlying criminal behavior. This rating shall apply whether or not any of the component sentences has expired.

Table 14.3—continued

OTHER OFFENSES

(1) Conspiracy shall be rated for guideline purposes according to the underlying offense behavior if such behavior was consummated. If the offense is unconsummated, the conspiracy will be rated one step below the consummated offense. A consummated offense includes one in which the offender is prevented from completion only because of the intervention of law enforcement officials.

(2) Breaking and entering not specifically listed above shall normally be treated as a low moderate severity offense; however, if the monetary loss amounts to $2,000 or more, the applicable property offense category shall be used. Similarly, if the monetary loss involved in a burglary or breaking and entering (that is listed) constitutes a more serious property offense than the burglary or breaking and entering itself, the appropriate property offense category shall be used.

(3) Manufacturing of synthetic drugs for sale shall be rated as not less than very high severity.

(4) Bribery of a public official (offering/accepting/soliciting) or extortion (use of official position) shall be rated as no less than moderate severity for those instances limited in scope (e.g., single instance and amount of bribe/demand less than $20,000 in value); and shall be rated as no less than high severity in any other case. In the case of the bribe/demand with a value in excess of $100,000, the applicable property offense category shall apply. The extent to which the criminal conduct involves a breach of the public trust, therefore causing injury beyond that describable by monetary gain, shall be considered as an aggravating factor.

(5) Obstructing justice (no physical threat)/perjury (in a criminal proceeding) shall be rated in the category of the underlying offense concerned, except that obstructing justice (threat of physical harm) shall be rated as no less than very high severity.

(6) Misprision of felony shall be rated as moderate severity if the underlying offense is high severity or above. If the underlying offense is moderate severity or less, it shall be rated as low severity.

(7) Harboring a fugitive shall be rated as moderate severity if the underlying offense is high severity or above. If the underlying offense is moderate severity or less, it shall be rated as low severity.

REFERENCED NOTES

1. Alcohol or cigarette tax law violations involving $2,000 or more of evaded tax shall be treated as a property offense (tax evasion).

2. Except that automobile theft (not kept more than 72 hours; no substantial damage; and not theft for resale) shall be rated as low severity. Automobile theft involving a value of more than $19,999 shall be treated as a property offense. In addition, automobile theft involving more than 3 cars, regardless of value, shall be treated as no less than high severity.

3. Except that carnal knowledge in which the relationship is clearly voluntary, the victim is not less than 14 years old, and the age difference between offender and victim is less than four years shall be rated as a low severity offense.

DEFINITIONS

a. 'Other media or exchange' include, but are not limited to, postage stamps, money orders, or coupons redeemable for cash or goods.

b. 'Drugs, other than specifically categorized' include, but are not limited to, the following, listed in ascending order of their perceived severity: amphetamines, hallucinogens, barbiturates, methamphetamines, phencyclidine (PCP). This ordering shall be used as a guide to decision placement within the applicable guideline range (i.e., other aspects being equal, amphetamines will normally be rated towards the bottom of the guideline range and PCP will normally be rated towards the top).

Table 14.3—continued

c. 'Equivalent amounts' for the cocaine and opiate categories may be computed as follows: 1 gm. of 100% pure is equivalent to 2 gms. of 50% pure and 10 gms. of 10% pure, etc.

d. The 'opiate' category includes heroin, morphine, opiate derivatives, and synthetic opiate substitutes.

e. Managerial/Proprietary Interest (Large Scale Drug Offenses):

Managerial/proprietary interest in large scale drug cases is defined to include offenders who sell or negotiate to sell such drugs; or who have decision-making authority concerning the distribution/sale, importation, cutting, or manufacture of such drugs; or who finance such operations. Cases to be excluded are peripherally involved offenders without any decision-making authority (e.g., a person hired merely as a courier).

Salient Factor Score (SFS 81)

Register Number _____   Name_____

Item A: PRIOR CONVICTIONS/ADJUDICATIONS (ADULT OR JUVENILE) .... ☐

None..	=	3
One..	=	2
Two or three	=	1
Four or more..............................	=	0

Item B: PRIOR COMMITMENT(S) OF MORE THAN THIRTY DAYS (ADULT OR JUVENILE)........... ☐

None..	=	2
One or two.................................	=	1
Three or more............................	=	0

Item C: AGE AT CURRENT OFFENSE/PRIOR COMMITMENTS... ☐

Age at commencement of the current offense:

26 years of age or more...........	=	2***
20-25 years of age	=	1***
19 years of age or less.............	=	0

***EXCEPTIONS: If five or more prior commitments of more than thirty days (adult or juvenile), place an "x" here _____ and score this item .... = 0

Item D: RECENT COMMITMENT FREE PERIOD (THREE YEARS).. ☐

No prior commitment of more than thirty days (adult or juvenile) or released to the community from last such commitment at least three years prior to the commencement of the current offense ..... = 1
Otherwise................................ = 0

Item E: PROBATION/PAROLE/CONFINEMENT/ESCAPE STATUS VIOLATOR THIS TIME.............. ☐

Neither on probation, parole, confinement, or escape status at the time of the current offense; nor committed as a probation, parole, confinement, or escape status violator this time...................... = 1
Otherwise................................ = 0

Table 14.3—continued

Item F: HEROIN/OPIATE DEPENDENCE.. ☐

No history of heroin/opiate
    dependence ....   =   1
    Otherwise...............................   =   0

TOTAL SCORE .... ☐

NOTE: For purposes of the Salient Factor Score, an instance of criminal behavior resulting in a judicial determination of guilt or an admission of guilt before a judicial body shall be treated as a conviction, even if a conviction is not formally entered.

Sec. 2.21 *REPAROLE CONSIDERATION GUIDELINES.*

    (a) If revocation is based upon administrative violation(s) only [i.e., violations other than new criminal conduct] the following guidelines shall apply.

Positive Supervision History: (Examples)	*Customary Time to be Served Before Rerelease*
a. No serious alcohol/drug abuse and no posses-sion of weapon(s) [and]	
b. At least 8 months from date of release to date of violation behavior [and]	< 6 Months
c. Present violation represents first instance of failure to comply with parole regulations of this term.	

Negative Supervision History: (Examples)	
a. Serious alcohol/drug abuse (e.g., readdiction to opiates) or possession of weapon(s) [or]	6-9 Months
b. Less than 8 months from date of release to date of violation behavior [or]	
c. Repetitious or persistent violations.	

    (b)(1) If a finding is made that the prisoner has engaged in behavior constituting new criminal conduct, the appropriate severity rating for the new criminal behavior shall be calculated. New criminal conduct may be determined either by a new federal, state, or local conviction or by an independent finding by the Commission at revocation hearing. As violations may be for state or local offenses, the appropriate severity level may be determined by analogy with listed federal offense behaviors.

    (2) The guidelines for parole consideration specified at 28 C.F.R. Sec. 2.20 shall then be applied. The original guideline type (e.g., adult, youth) shall determine the applicable guidelines for the parole violator term, except that a violator committed with a new federal sentence of more than one year shall be treated under the guideline type applicable to the new sentence.

    (3) Time served on a new state or federal sentence shall be counted as time in custody for reparole guideline purposes. This does not affect the computation of the expiration date of the violator term as provided by Sections 2.47(b) and 2.52(c) and (d).

    (c) The above are merely guidelines. A decision outside these guidelines (either above or below) may be made when circumstances warrant. For example, violations of an assaultive nature or by a person with a history of repeated parole failure may warrant a decision above the guidelines. Minor offense(s) (e.g., minor traffic offenses, vagrancy, public intoxication) shall normally be treated under administrative violations.

Source: Barbara Stone-Meierhoefer and Peter B. Hoffman (1982). "Presumptive Parole Dates: The Federal Approach," *Federal Probation,* June (1982):45-55.

Many have questioned the procedures utilized by various parole authorities, primarily from the standpoint that most parole boards have not published explicit decision-making criteria, have retained a high degree of discretion and/or flexibility in the decision-making process, have perhaps conducted their activities without a high degree of public visibility. One point to keep in mind is that parole authorities are required to conduct their activities within parameters established by state legislatures or the Congress, in keeping with codes of procedure and other relevant legislation. Legislative bodies have typically provided parole authorities with broad-based autonomy—the idea is and has been discretionary release in these situations.

The central dimension advocated for countering potential difficulties in discretionary decision-making has been to develop and implement parole decision-making guidelines. Adopted by the Federal Parole Commission (keep in mind that this body is going out of business after a transition period already begun) and later in several states, such guidelines are intended to formalize the decision-making process and make decision criteria explicit. Table 14.3 show examples of parole decision-making guidelines, the federal authority's "salient factor score."

Parole decision-making guidelines are based on the development of weighted factors concerning: (1) the offense committed and certain aspects of the circumstances in the fact situation of the offense, and (2) the offender and certain factors considered important in the offender's personal history. Also, other factors may be included, such as institutional record, when such factors are considered important in making a decision to grant or deny parole, as well as the conditions of parole, if granted. Parole decision-making guidelines were initially advocated and introduced in an effort to structure parole board discretion and reduce disparity in parole decision-making. Advocates also pointed out that the development of parole guidelines would require the explicit statement of paroling policy (Gottfredson and Gottfredson, 1988). The initial movement toward the use of guidelines was not intended to eliminate parole authorities. Rather, guidelines were to make the decisions of paroling authorities more objective, more rational. Please keep in mind that where mandatory release has supplanted discretionary release, one may find decision-making guidelines in use, but these are sentencing guidelines, and the focus for their application is assisting the judiciary rather than assisting a paroling authority in a parole decision.

While parole guidelines have been put into use in a number of states and in the federal paroling process, these have not provided a panacea for discretionary release. The primary concern regarding guidelines involves the difficulty of predicting the future behavior of people. The development of parole guidelines is based on ascertaining factors about the offense and the offender that promise to be most "salient" in describing (some say predicting) an offender's likelihood of succeeding (completing the parole sentence successfully, and remaining a law-abiding person thereafter). These factors are established by conducting research involving relatively large numbers of offenders and parolees to determine variables that are most closely associated with potential for success (success can be defined in different ways; for example, completion of sentence on parole without revocation) or perhaps to determine those variables that are most closely associated with some conception of the "social dangerousness" of the offender (for example, attempting to ascertain a person's propensity to commit a violent act).

Hawkins and Alpert discuss difficulties confronting those involved with the development and implementation of decision-making guidelines (1989:120-124). As they state, "No predictions about the future behavior of human beings are going to be completely accurate." The dilemma then becomes a value-relative question concerning how much inaccuracy can be tolerated. Difficulties can arise in several areas.

Hawkins and Alpert focus on the prediction of violent behavior to illustrate potential sources of inaccuracy. As they state (1989:121):

> The assessment of the degree of inaccuracy which should be tolerated in predictions of social dangerousness hinges on the ratio of two types of error. The first error involves persons predicted as good risks, but who later prove to commit one or more violent acts. In prediction jargon, they are termed *false negatives*. The second type of error is *false positive*. These individuals are predicted as dangerous but do not commit a violent act, that is, would not offend if released. They have been termed poor risks, but falsely labeled as regards the target behavior—being violent. There would be two types of accurate predictions, true positive (predicted as violent and turns out to be so) and true negative (predicted as not violent and was so).

Policy problems follow the possibility of the types of error described above. Legislators and other public officials must decide how strongly the decision-making authority must guard against the possibility of such errors actually occurring (this decision reflects the resolution of a question of preference regarding the degree of risk to be tolerated in conjunction with pragmatic concerns such as overcrowding and other broader questions such as budget). *Overprediction* is a term used to describe the situation in which the paroling authority tries to reduce the potential for false negatives obtaining parole and thereby denies parole to an unknown number of false positives, who would not have committed a violent act but who at that time cannot demonstrate that fact. This situation can, in turn, compound the difficulty for further research in a jurisdiction, and this situation is unpalatable to those who would term the unnecessary retention of an inmate an injustice.

Conversely, *underpredicting* (making decisions that allow parole for those who might engage in a violent act according to the prediction scheme) can cause image problems for the paroling authority, presents a higher degree of risk in terms of the possibility of societal protection, and can cause further difficulties for the validation of the decision-making scheme. In some states (see Chapter 15), "third-level alternatives" are being tried (for example, intensive parole supervision schemes, electronic monitoring) to attempt to deal with the issue of granting parole to "marginal cases." Where such projects are underway, they are being presented as avenues for addressing a variety of political, technical, and pragmatic concerns.

Predicting violent behavior is made more problematic because, even though there are large numbers of violent acts in our society, the occurrence of violent behavior relative to other behaviors is rare. When using statistical techniques to attempt to predict, greater accuracy is obtainable when the target behaviors subjected to analysis approach a 50-50 ratio of occurrence-nonoccurrence. From a statistical perspective, the rarer the occurrence, the greater the margin for error. This introduces another qualification to the sorts of analysis underlying guideline development.

Regardless of whether potential for violent behavior is the central target or whether some other constellation of potential behaviors form the central target, guideline development depends on the analysis of aggregated data, that is, looking at a large or rather large group of offenders in a given jurisdiction. Inferences and conclusions are drawn from the data concerning the group, the guidelines are formulated, and the guidelines are then to be applied in decision-making concerning individual offenders. Hawkins and Alpert (1989:123) quote David Stanley (1976:56) to make a point concerning the possibility of inefficiency in applying guidelines to individuals:

> The trouble with prediction is simply that it will not work—that is, it will not work for individuals, only for groups. A parole board may know that of 100 offenders with a certain set of characteristics, [such as] 80 will

probably succeed and 20 will fail on parole. But the board members do not know whether the man who is before them belongs with the 80 or the 20.

This quote may overstate the case somewhat. One would not want to lose sight of the possibility of decision-making taking place with the greatest degree of attention by those presenting evidence and those using guidelines to make the parole decision.

Guidelines may hold the possibility of introducing rigidity into the discretionary release decision. Where guidelines have been implemented, there have generally been provisions that enable parole boards to make decisions outside the guidelines. Usually, decisionmakers are required to state their reasons for doing so. Additionally, guidelines may be modified and updated, giving some flexible character to the scheme that is in place at any given time. Advocates argue for the desirability of some flexibility; critics argue that too much flexibility shortcuts the aim of reducing potential disparity in decision-making. The controversy remains. One should reflect upon the effort to provide structure to discretionary decision-making, remembering that the intent is to introduce some degree of continuity. One should also consider the parole decision-making context; decision-making occurring within the complex reality of political, economic, social, value-oriented concerns.

Community Supervision

As is the situation with probation, "parole" is actually a collection of strategies attached to a few primary images, such as community supervision. Those who are placed under supervision in the community may enter from discretionary release or from mandatory early release. Remember also that parole may be said to serve many purposes; therefore, the community supervision aspect may be seen as supporting varying purposes. Parole may serve some purposes more appropriately ascribed directly to political or bureaucratic interests, in which officials wish to be seen as doing something constructive under conditions of uncertainty concerning what to do.

Parole supervision is a function of the state governments and the federal government. In other words, parole supervision is carried out through organizations established at these levels of government. Although in a few states there are parole supervision specialists, it is not uncommon (as in most states and in the federal structure) to find that those who are to supervise parolees also supervise probationers. In the federal structure, probation and parole officers are part of the bureaucracy of the Administrative Office of the U.S. Courts and at the operational level are organized in conjunction with the U.S. District Courts. In a few states, parole agencies are organized outside the Division or Department of Corrections, directly subordinate to the governor. In most states, the parole supervision element is organized as a major subunit of the Division or Department of Corrections.

As is the situation with probation, parole supervision may serve a multitude of aims rather than a singular purpose. One should keep in mind that underlying notions and practices forming the basis of parole supervision may vary from jurisdiction to jurisdiction; these may also vary among individual agencies and agents, as well as in application to individual parolees.

The discussion in Chapter 13 concerning potential variation in probation supervision may be applied to parole supervision with some additional considerations taken into account. It is important to keep in mind that by virtue of having served time in prison and having at least one felony conviction, parolees are generally thought to require more intense supervision than most probationers (remember, though, that felony probation is increasing). The number of parole cases assigned to parole officers is usually smaller than the number of probation cases assigned to probation officers, but in many jurisdictions officers may have large caseloads composed of both probationers and parolees—the nature and intensity of supervision may depend on a number of factors. Culbertson and Ellsworth (1985:131) point out that "[t]he roles adopted by probation and parole officers as they carry out their responsibilities are determined by a variety of issues, ranging from the personality of the officer to the political-social-legal philosophy of the agency administering supervision."

Walker (1989) charges that parole supervision is inherently superficial, largely bureaucratic, and that "no correctional treatment" is provided. Given burdensome caseloads and the perhaps pragmatic orientations of most agency leaders to emphasize "rule watching" over "counseling," such a change is not surprising. Yet, much is made of the relatively high degree of discretion afforded parole officers in carrying out their responsibilities.

For many, discretion connotes the capacity to individualize justice. How then, can Walker's charge that parole supervision is bureaucratic be supported? In one sense, large caseloads mean little time for interaction with those assigned (we have noted already that caseloads may be "mixed" for some officers, with few parolees but usually many others). Time and task requirements are obvious.

If one considers the research literature on parole practice (e.g., McClearly; 1978, Studt, 1972; Waller, 1974) a more substantive picture emerges. Parole officers tend to act as "street-level bureaucrats" (Lipsky, 1980). What this means is that, while parole officers at times use their discretion to deal differentially with individuals in their caseloads, the actual thrust of their use of discretion is more toward agency "ways of doing business." In other words, laws and formal agency policies set broad parameters for the actions and judgments of parole officers. However, one will probably not find a work group of 10 parole officers acting individually within these parameters basing their differences in discretionary authority. What one is more likely to find is a group of 10 officers most often acting in a similar fashion, occasionally manifesting differences, basing their similarities in discretionary authority.

Informal policies, expectations, and norms are created in each work group. These provide the substance of practice. As with most sorts of work groups (think of any organization in which you have worked) parole officers assimilate these informal expectations (to greater and lesser degrees, to be sure) and these norms/policies are reinforced through discretionary behavior. The result is a tendency to similarity rather than difference in practice.

As McClearly (1978) would observe, this is all part of a socialization process within which the novice parole officer becomes a "professional" and the "professionals" maintain stability, a status quo. The ultimate purpose is to provide a relatively manageable set of work expectations and to address bureaucratic issues of doing something acceptable and maintaining job tenure.

Formal attempts to provide coherence to the supervision function include assessment and classification of those to be supervised in the community. The generally espoused aims of assessment and classification are to provide rational means for estimating the risk of probation/parole violation and the degree of dangerousness of the offender (therefore ascertaining the nature and level of supervision required) and to provide rational means for determining needs of the offender being supervised (therefore projecting nature and extent of services that would assist the offender in resolving his or her real-life difficulties). Although assessment and classification strategies hold the promise of contributing much to the decision-making process in probation and parole agencies, realizing that promise has proven difficult.

A number of concerns emerge as one considers the potential of assessment and classification efforts. Classification efforts are plagued with the same problems of prediction discussed earlier in this chapter regarding development of parole decision-making guidelines. As Culbertson and Ellsworth point out (1985:138-139):

> There is a great deal about human behavior we do not understand, and, therefore, cannot quantify. Our failure to acknowledge the extent to which we *do not understand* often limits the potential to which we can understand.

As they also point out (1985:139):

> Classification is an attempt to place individuals in various categories, based on assumptions and, hopefully, data concerning the offender and his or her behavior. The category in which one is placed requires a supervision plan reflecting the rationale for category placement. The problem is [that] there is little agreement as to what should be accomplished with individuals once they are classified.

Assessment and classification to support the element of community supervision of parolees has not been shown to be *the* definitive direction for making parole supervision rational, objective, and ultimately effective. This strategy for improving decision-making becomes an element set within the overall operating context of the organization(s) providing the community supervision services. As Culbertson and Ellsworth (1985:139) further observe, "[T]here has been a general failure to recognize and address the constraints imposed by agency policy and politics when there is an effort to implement new strategies." Agency staffing levels, budgets, formal and informal policies concerning the actual aims and practice of supervision, and pressures to do something with relatively large numbers of offenders—even in the absence of clear aims—may contribute to separation of the rationale for classification from the actual practice of supervision in a given jurisdiction.

Conversely, the argument may be made that classification does represent one avenue for making a necessary attempt to impart coherence to the supervision process. Efforts at classification and linking classification decisions to implementation may at least force consideration of expected outcomes and the potential for achieving positive outcomes through the process of community supervision. Whether or not classification contributes much to coherence in the supervision process apparently will remain an arguable question, given the potential problems discussed above and given the variation in operating contexts among the many agencies utilizing assessment and classification.

Revocation

When parolees do not succeed in completing their terms on parole, revocation proceedings may be initiated by the parole officer. As is the situation with probation, parolees who commit a new crime, or parolees who violate the general or specific conditions of their parole, though their acts or omissions would not constitute a new crime (technical violations of parole), may face revocation. Similar to the situation with probation revocation, parole revocation proceedings are subject to minimum due process guarantees outlined by the U.S. Supreme Court (see the discussion of the decision in *Morrissey v. Brewer* in Chapter 12).

Unlike probation, the parole revocation decision is made by the paroling authority (board or commission), not by a judge. Usually, parole revocation follows a process similar to the following. The parole officer initiates the process by making a formal allegation of violation of parole. Most often this allegation is accompanied by a request that the parolee be arrested and detained in jail until a determination is made. The allegation is reviewed by senior agency officials, who conduct a preliminary examination. The purpose of this review is "to determine whether there is probable cause or reasonable grounds to believe that the arrested parolee had committed acts which would constitute a violation of parole condition" (*Morrissey v. Brewer*, 1972).

If sufficient reason is found to continue the revocation process, the paroling authority holds a revocation hearing. At this stage the due process guarantees established in *Morrissey v. Brewer* (1972) apply. These include: (a) written notice of the claimed violation, (b) disclosure to the parolee of evidence against him or her, (c) opportunity to be heard in person and to present witnesses and documentary evidence (d) right to confront and cross-examine adverse witness (unless the hearing body specifically finds good cause for not allowing confrontation), (e) provision of a neutral and detached hearing body, and (f) a written statement of the fact finders as to the evidence relied on and the reasons for revoking parole. Parole boards/commissions have been considered sufficiently neutral and detached to conduct revocation hearings, and these bodies have discretionary authority concerning the disposition of the proceedings. If a parolee is found to have violated parole, the parole board/commission may decide to return the offender to prison (often the outcome) or may decide on other options (such as imposing special conditions).

Summary

Parole may best be understood as a collection of strategies. While common characteristics such as release to the community, conditions, and supervision broadly outline the notion of parole, the experience of parole may vary widely for individuals assigned to this correctional status.

Parole as discretionary release involving decisions of a parole board or commission changed dramatically in the decade of the 1980s. Mandatory release, in which release is a matter of law and those released early through good time mechanisms are placed under supervision, increased substantially. Where discretionary parole accounted for 70% of releases from prison in 1977, by 1988 discretionary release accounted for 40.3% of releases, and mandatory release had grown from just below 6% of releases to account for 30.6%. The trend continues.

As an item on the correctional menu, parole in the form most people recognize has been around for a relatively short time. A number of historical antecedents gave rise to recent and present practices, and these are important in understanding parole in the twentieth century. Parole and parole practices have been heavily criticized—particularly discretionary release decisions, attempts to predict through the use of guidelines, conditions, and practices of supervision. As shown in the chapter and in the "On the Defensive" section that follows, the parole debate continues.

Is Parole Defensible?

Parole is the unwanted child of American criminal justice, arousing the fury of both conservatives and liberals. Conservatives argue that it allows prisoners to get out too soon. Softhearted parole boards turn dangerous criminals loose to prey on law-abiding people. Parole boards (along with "good time" provisions) do in fact shorten prison terms to a considerable degree. Only a small percentage of prisoners serve their full terms. Convicted robbers serve an average of about three or four years; the going rate for second-degree murder is about five or six years.

Some liberals have had second thoughts about parole and now defend it on the grounds that the sentence-shortening function is essential. The real problem, in their view, is the indeterminate sentence. Sentencing statutes typically provide the judges with a wide range to choose from (one to fifty years, ten to life, and so forth). As a result, they dish out extremely long sentences. With the exceptions of the Soviet Union and South Africa, our two rivals for penal excess, no other country in the world gives such long sentences as the United States. By shortening sentences, parole boards moderate punishment. In effect, two bad systems tend to balance each other out.

The real question, of course, is how much time is enough. Conservatives assume that longer sentences have a greater deterrent and incapacitative effect. Liberals reply that the available evidence suggests that prisoners who serve short sentences do just as well (or as poorly) as those who serve long terms. Thus we can achieve the same ends at much less cost to society and less suffering to the inmate by giving shorter prison terms.

Liberals indict parole on the due-process grounds. Parole boards routinely make decisions about people's liberty with no rational or scientific basis. Parole release decisions are arbitrary in general and often discriminatory against minorities. The decisions are inextricably linked with the original criminal sentences, which liberals also view as examples of uncontrolled discretion. The idea of determinate sentencing initially attracted a great deal of support among liberals because they thought it would bring the discretion of both judges and parole boards under control. For the most part, their enthusiasm quickly disappeared when it became obvious that in the current political climate, legislators would prescribe very long determinate sentences.

Parole Survives

Despite the broad-based attack, parole continues to survive (except in the federal system, where it was abolished by the 1987 sentencing guidelines). This is not the first time it has weathered a major assault. David Rothman has found that parole was everyone's favorite whipping boy in the 1920s as well. It survived because it serves the practical needs of prison officials, specifically their ability to manage prisoners. The power of a guard to "write up" an inmate for an infraction is a large factor in the length of time that inmate will serve. Parole boards give heavy weight to an inmate's behavioral record, and of course they have only the official records of infractions to go by. Prison officials have always argued that they need these carrots and sticks in order to maintain control over the prison population.

At the same time, parole serves as a safety valve for the prison population. Prisons have always been overcrowded, and parole has permitted some leeway in keeping the problem from getting completely out of hand. One of the interesting new developments in the 1980s is a series of prison overcrowding laws. Michigan and Iowa require the automatic release of prisoners (by the speeding up of parole eligibility dates) whenever their prison populations exceed a certain limit. This innovation simply makes explicit what has long been one of the latent functions of parole.

Whither Parole?

The question remains: What to do about parole? Can it be improved substantially, or should it be abolished altogether? The main argument in its defense has a curiously negative thrust: we need to correct other problems. Parole is necessary to shorten excessively long sentences and to allow us to manage the behavior and size of the inmate population. This is hardly a principled defense of one of the cornerstones of our criminal justice policy.

Source: Samuel Walker (1989). *Sense and Nonsense About Crime*, pp. 223-225. Pacific Grove, CA: Brooks/Cole Publishing Co.

Key Terms and Concepts

classification

commutation

consolidated board

decision-making guidelines

discretionary release

flat time

general conditions of parole

good time

independent board

Irish system

mandatory release

mark system

overprediction

pardon

parole

progressives

revocation

specific conditions of parole

ticket of leave

underprediction

References

Abadinsky, H. (1987). *Probation and Parole: Theory and Practice, Fourth Edition.* Englewood Cliffs, NJ: Prentice-Hall.

Bureau of Justice Statistics (1987). "Probation and Parole 1986." Washington, DC: U.S. Department of Justice.

Bureau of Justice Statistics (1989). "Probation and Parole 1988." Washington, DC: U.S. Department of Justice.

Culberton, R. and T. Ellsworth (1985). "Treatment Innovations in Probation and Parole." In L. Travis (ed.) *Probation, Parole, and Community Corrections.* Prospect Heights, IL: Waveland Press, Inc.

Gottfredson, D. and M. Gottfredson (1988). *Decision Making in Criminal Justice: Toward the Rational Exercise of Discretion, Second Edition.* New York, NY: Plenum Publishing Corporation.

Hawkins, R. and G. Alpert (1980). *American Prison Systems: Punishment and Justice.* Englewood Cliffs, NJ: Prentice-Hall.

McClearly, R. (1978). *Dangerous Men.* Beverly Hills, CA: Sage Publications.

McElvey, B. (1977) *American Prisons: A History of Good Intentions.* Montclair, NJ: Patterson-Smith.

Rothman, D. (1980). *Conscience and Convenience: The Asylum and its Alternatives in Progressive America.* Boston, MA: Little, Brown and Company.

Stanley, D. (1976). *Prisoners Among Us: The Problem of Parole.* Washington, DC: The Brookings Institution.

Statsky, W. (1985). *Legal Thesaurus/Dictionary.* St. Paul, MN: West Publishing Co.

Studt, E. (1972). *Surveillance and Service in Parole*. Los Angeles, CA: UCLA Institute of Government and Public Affairs.

Walker, S. (1980). *Popular Justice: A History of American Criminal Justice*. New York, NY: Oxford University Press.

Waller, I. (1974). *Men Released from Prison*. Toronto: University of Toronto Press.

Photo Credit: Bill Powers, Frost Publishing Group, Ltd.

Community Corrections

15

After reading this chapter, the student should be able to:

▌ Discuss "community corrections" as a general model encompassing many potential strategies.

▌ Explain diversion and pretrial release as correctional practices.

▌ Comment on third-level correctional alternatives—in particular, house arrest and electronic monitoring.

▌ Describe the concepts of restitution and community service.

▌ Define and explain temporary release programs and residential programs as correctional ventures.

Introduction

For many, the dominant concept of U.S. corrections is incarceration of offenders in state and federal prison facilities. Although the number of adult offenders dealt with in this way is enormous (approximately 710,000 offenders in such facilities at year-end 1990) and is growing at an unprecedented rate (more than a 100% increase since 1983), more than 80% of adult offenders are at the same time under other forms of correctional authority, in "community corrections." At year-end 1990 approximately 2.5 million adult offenders were in a probation status, approximately 450,000 were in a parole supervision status (including those exiting prison through discretionary release and through mandatory release with a requirement for supervision), approximately 375,000 were in the nation's jails (including those serving sentences and those awaiting trial, the latter not convicted), and an unspecified yet large number of offenders were in other community-based corrections programs. Clearly, "community corrections programs serve more people and touch more lives in any given year than do prisons" (Travis, 1985:3).

This chapter presents an overview of community corrections efforts. Without question, probation and parole efforts are the major elements of community corrections. These efforts are discussed in separate chapters. It is our position that jails should be considered as an element of community corrections, especially because in 45 states jails are locally administered, locally funded, and their operations are a function of local government. Jails are discussed in Chapter 3. Other elements of community corrections are discussed in this chapter, along with issues of importance in these areas of corrections. Not the least of the difficulties in addressing community corrections is the attempt to discern the definition of community corrections.

Defining Community Corrections

The term "community corrections" is a broad umbrella under which a large array of practices and programs are generally included. As such, almost any correctional practice or program other than those carried out within prison facilities could be deemed a community corrections effort. However, making such a gross distinction is unsatisfactory to some and does little to further an understanding of community corrections as a concept.

Those who attempt to provide substance to a distinctive concept of community corrections often rely upon the notion of *reintegration* in the search for a unifying foundation, a central doctrine. "Reintegration" can be an elusive term. According to McCarthy and McCarthy (1984:6):

> Reintegration is based on the premise that crime and delinquency are as much symptoms of community disorganization as they are evidence of the psychological and behavioral problems of individual offenders. Reintegration has its roots in the social sciences. [Various social factors] ...are all evidence of the community's failure to promote the development of law-abiding behavior.

As a correctional aim, reintegration is most often seen as the individual adjusting to a law-abiding lifestyle, making use of the opportunities available in the community. The individual is encouraged to pursue law-abiding life options. The "community" collaborates, in that conscious attention is directed to providing opportunities, such as employment, and in providing assistance to the individual as he or she learns to make use of legitimate opportunities. The offender is expected to adopt new attitudes and beliefs as the process continues, and the offender is expected to translate these into law-abiding behavior.

Community-based programs founded on the notion of reintegration would be designed to foster change within the offender and to encourage the community change necessary for the programs to succeed. McCarthy and McCarthy present a number of design characteristics which they consider essential for a community-based program to achieve the reintegration objective, including:

1. A location within, and interaction with, a meaningful community.

2. A nonsecure environment.

3. Community-based education, counseling, and support services (these are provided by noncorrectional public and private agencies as well as by correctional staff and are organized into a comprehensive service delivery network).

4. Opportunities [for the offenders] to assume the normal roles of citizen, family member, student, or employee.

5. Opportunities for personal growth.

6. Efforts to change the community by encouraging tolerance for nonconforming behavior that is nevertheless law-abiding and developing opportunities for self-sufficiency and self-realization. (1984:8)

The logic of reintegration to provide fundamental doctrine for a unifying concept of community corrections is appealing. Attempting to encourage and implement the interactions and moments of community corrections program interface such as those alluded to above is important and appealing. Nonetheless, in thinking about community corrections, there are several observations worth consideration.

First, think about the use of the term "community" and a conception of "community." In the United States "communities" are diverse—the larger the area identified as a community and the greater the population encompassed, the more diverse. Obviously, a large Standard Metropolitan Statistical Area (SMSA) includes groups with diverse interests and unequal influence, individuals with varying conceptions of what is important, governing bodies and agencies with agendas that do not necessarily mesh, limited rather than limitless resources, persons with perhaps conflicting notions about what purposes the application of the criminal law is to serve, citizens who may be amenable to accepting responsibility and a role in corrections, citizens who are apathetic regarding corrections, citizens who do not want corrections programs associated with their neighborhoods, among other possibilities.

Second, think about what reintegrating the offender means in a practical sense. What yardstick is to be employed in determining whether reintegration of an individual has been achieved? Law-abiding behavior is the usual focus, which usually means that the offender is not recidivistic (which could mean any of the following: is not rearrested, is not rearrested for certain types of offenses, is not reconvicted, among other possible operationalisms of the term). If such is the focus, then one takes a legalistic approach, assuming that the criminal code and the actual applications of the criminal code are the important bases for determination of community standards of reintegration. This is legitimate and acceptable to many, but does not mean that there is consensus on a standard for determining reintegration of an individual or that there is a consensus as to what standard would represent reintegration in the abstract.

Third, it is clear that the logic employed above would lead one to focus upon the nature and extent of community-correctional program interface and interaction to determine whether a given effort is "community corrections." One would focus on issues such as whether program design and plans for implementation include development of ties to the local community and reliance upon resources available within the local area. For example, whether program personnel are required to develop and rely upon alliances with community members, private organizations, and public organizations to provide networks of employment possibilities, educational opportunities, medical and counseling services, perhaps citizen involvement such as volunteer probation officer, and so on. Obviously, one would focus on questions concerning the degree to which program design and program operation are aimed at fostering community change; for example, direct attempts by program personnel to educate community members about community responsibilities in the overall corrections effort, to inform local leadership and citizens about conditions that should be addressed to assist in the overall corrections effort, and to encourage interactions which facilitate program-community involvements.

If one attempted to judge whether a given program was a community corrections effort or something else, based upon the nature and extent of community corrections program involvement, then correctional efforts that exist in community settings, yet exhibit few or no such involvements would be outside the umbrella. For example, if a probation agency's personnel focused attention on rule enforcement, made little or no use of referral possibilities for persons in their caseloads, did little or nothing to network the agency's resources with available community resources, one might consider the effort to be something other than "community corrections." However, distinguishing community corrections in that way may be more semantic than substantive. There is no easily determined standard for judging the nature or extent of involvement. Most community corrections efforts or programs have some planned involvement and at least tangential use of locally available resources.

Furthermore, determining the degree of reciprocity (willingness to be involved, dedication of resources) by members of any given community would be an important consideration in making a distinction. Again, there is no established measurement for judging. It is also important to keep in mind that there are thousands of correctional agencies and organizations (public and private) in operation throughout the United States. Most operate in jurisdictions that are overburdened with offenders. Some are set within communities having few resources to commit. Some operate where available resources are more plentiful or more accessible. Often correctional efforts overlap within a given community (e.g., federal, state, and local probation efforts commonly coexist in larger SMSAs) and there may be competition as well as cooperation among the efforts. There also may be competition as well as cooperation among most or all social service agencies and organizations within a given community.

Finally, the point to be made here is that examining "community corrections" requires an awareness of much complexity and an understanding of the ambiguity associated with the term, as well as an understanding of the "softness" of the notions utilized to provide conceptual substance. Community corrections and reintegration have rhetorical appeal as well as value in identifying ideals, aims, and directions. It is very important to be attuned to the message of community-based corrections. Correctional administrators and corrections personnel can do little to change the environments from which offenders come and to which offenders must return. To have any hope for corrections efforts to succeed consistently, there must be recognition of a larger collective responsibility.

Community Corrections Programs

As discussed "community corrections" is a broad term. Beyond probation, parole, and jail programs, there is a rather wide array of efforts designated as community corrections efforts. Some of these efforts or programs are carried out in conjunction with probation, parole, or jail efforts, yet deserve individual mention. Some efforts are conducted as separate from the predominant three sets of endeavors. Following is an examination of other important community corrections efforts.

Pre-Conviction Efforts

Although one usually thinks of corrections as dealing with convicted offenders, there are efforts carried out during the pre-adjudicatory stages of the criminal justice process or, as alternatives to prosecution, that many include within the rubric of community corrections. The bulk of such efforts falls within the areas of diversion and pretrial release.

Diversion

Diversion programs offer alternatives to the usual arrest and prosecution processes. As defined by the National Advisory Commission on Criminal Justice Standards and Goals (NAC), diversion efforts are "formally acknowledged and organized efforts to utilize alternatives to initial or continued processing into the justice system. To qualify as diversion, such efforts must be undertaken prior to adjudication and after a legally proscribed action has occurred" (NAC, 1973:73). In other words, the candidate for diversion is a person who could be or has been arrested for an alleged offense and who could be taken to trial as the defendant in a criminal prosecution for the alleged offense.

With diversion, criminal justice officials use discretion to decide not to invoke the usual formal criminal justice process. For example, a law enforcement officer could decide not to arrest a person, instead referring the person to a social service agency, or a prosecutor could allow a defendant to avoid a trial, offering the accused an opportunity to successfully complete a domestic violence couseling program, a substance abuse program, or other requirement in lieu of prosecution.

As a legitimate use of discretion by individual criminal justice officials, diversion has a long history. When officials use discretion individually, and not as part of an organized diversion effort, use of such discretion could be termed *informal diversion*. In recent years there has been increasing interest in formalizing diversion, with formal screening of cases to determine the accused's suitability for diversion, the development of diversion casework positions, and formalized arrangements linking networks of community resources to the formal diversion efforts.

Diversion may take a number of forms. Officials are relatively free to be creative in using available resources to design strategies. For example, instead of arrest, a person accused of battering his or her spouse could be asked to agree to attend a family crisis counseling program. A person accused of an offense involving public drunkenness could be asked to attend an alcohol abuse program. In lieu of prosecution, an accused person could be offered the option of attending treatment programs, educational programs, or participating in any other effort that may be deemed appropriate by the prosecutor.

Diversion often benefits an accused person. The accused person may retain his or her job, whereas confinement could result in the loss of a job. The accused may avoid costs of hiring an attorney and other direct costs associated with prosecution. The accused avoids the stigma of being labeled "convicted" and avoids a record of conviction—perhaps even avoids a record of arrest. The accused may receive necessary treatment at little or no cost, or may receive other forms of direct assistance in resolving problems.

However, diversion does involve controversy. The accused person gives up the due process guarantees that accompany the usual, formal prosecution.

It could be argued that persons who may have an adequate defense may opt for diversion unadvisedly. Some argue that diversion "widens the net" of criminal justice, providing avenues for an unwarranted extension of social control by expanding discretionary options. Others argue that a focus on victims and justice may be obscured in efforts to expand the use of diversion. Nonetheless, diversion is viewed by many as a pragmatic approach to dealing with cases in which the accused may benefit and in which the usual, formal processing would result in misapplication of resources in an already overburdened system.

Pretrial Release

Pretrial release is distinguished from diversion in that the aim is to provide alternatives to secure detention while the defendant awaits trial. The candidate for pretrial release is not avoiding prosecution or further formal processing.

Obviously, a variety of problems may be associated with pretrial detention for a defendant. Family difficulties may be exacerbated, if the detainee was employed he or she could lose his or her job, among other possible problems. Additionally, jail space for pretrial detention (actually, jail space in general) is a scarce resource. For example, during 1989, the nation's jails operated at 108% of rated capacity (Bureau of Justice Statistics, 1990). These sorts of concerns, coupled with concerns about conditions in the nation's jails, have led many to focus on the alternative of pretrial release.

Pretrial release options may be financial or nonfinancial, may involve supervised release or (most often) unsupervised release, may be conditional release or release without conditions other than the requirement for the defendant to appear for trial.

Pretrial release may happen prior to the actual jailing of a defendant or after an accused person has been placed in detention.

Conceptualizing pretrial release efforts as part of community corrections may require expanding the umbrella. Those who do so appear to focus on community protection and on the potential for assisting the accused as part of a larger set of individualized responses.

Financial options involve the defendant posting bail in the form of cash or some other financial pledge to obtain release. Nonfinancial options involve a pledge which is not secured, as in release on recognizance, in which the accused's signature is accepted to obtain release. The preponderance of pretrial releases fit within the scope of these options. Here, there may be little that connects to community corrections, perhaps only the thinnest thread—if the process is part of the punishment.

However, since 1960, formalized pretrial release programs have been developed and implemented in scores of jurisdictions. Generally, these programs incorporate conditions for release and may involve supervised release. The aims of such programs generally involve screening candidates for release to determine both suitability and needs, ascertaining whether the candidate has problems or needs that could be addressed while on pretrial release through use of community resources, conditions, or supervision, and taking appropriate steps to insure the defendant's appearance in court. Some programs include pretrial work release (the defendant being employed, working outside the jail during work hours and returning during non-work hours).

Pretrial release can be controversial. Legal issues concerning the constitutionality of imposing certain conditions (such as limiting involvement with particular groups or individuals) on the not-yet-convicted defendant have surfaced. Also, some argue about the appropriateness of supervision (in the programs that have this feature) of the not-yet-convicted defendant, again looking at constitutional issues as well as "net-widening" effects. Nonetheless, expansion of pretrial release options may be seen as a pragmatic direction for assisting certain individuals and augmenting the scarce resources that are present in the nation's jails.

Post-Conviction Efforts

Post-conviction efforts are much more easily conceptualized as fitting under the corrections umbrella. In addition to probation, parole, and jail efforts, there is a rather well-reconized set of community-based endeavors including restitution and community service programs, temporary release programs (work release, study release, furloughs), various residential programs, and an array of nonresidential programs. Beyond these, there is a growing movement to deal with offenders in the community by establishing what are being called "third-level" alternatives. Third-level alternatives are characterized as "tough," "punitive," and not compromising to public safety (Petersilia, 1988). The core third-level programs are intensive supervision—assignment of risky probationers of parolees to a maximum supervision caseload, involving small numbers of offenders supervised by a team of agents, house arrest (also called home confinement), and electronic monitoring. The following discussion focuses first on the third-level alternatives.

Third-Level Alternatives

The growing number of offenders flooding the criminal justice system, overcrowded prisons and jails, and an increasing interest in public protection as well as punitive rather than "treatment-oriented" sanctions, have led to attempts to conceptualize and establish an intermediate level of criminal sanctions. The options advocated, being pressed into the corrections menu, are somewhere between incarceration and the less restrictive components of community corrections. House arrest and electronic surveillance are providing appealing directions as intermediate sanctions.

The Community Control Program in Florida was the first statewide home confinement program. Figure 15.1 gives the details of the Florida program. Additional conditions may be imposed upon an offender sentenced to house arrest. These could include paying restitution, paying a fee (usually monthly) to defray the costs of supervision, or, among other possibilities, the requirement to submit to electronic surveillance or monitoring. "In at least 20 States, 'electronic bracelets' are being used to detect violations of house arrest" (Petersilia, 1988:1).

Petersilia presents a discussion of advantages and disadvantages of house arrest (1989). As she observes (1989:2), the financial appeal of house arrest is great (saving on average about $10,000 to $15,000 on the yearly cost of incarcerating an offender), there are social benefits (offenders who had jobs can keep them, the stigmatizing effects of incarceration are avoided, psychological and physical disruption of family relationships can be avoided), house arrest is flexible enough to allow response to local and offender needs (it can become a preconviction option in connection with diversion or pretrial release and can be molded to deal appropriately with individual offender needs), and there is ease of implementation and timeliness (pressure to reduce prison and jail overcrowding is here now and the house arrest options may require few new facilities, especially if electronic monitoring is not used).

Figure 15.1
House Arrest

What Is House Arrest and Why Is It So Popular?

As prison crowding worsens, the pressure to divert non-dangerous offenders to community-based alternatives has increased. Since it is generally agreed that the public is in no mood to coddle criminals, such alternatives must be tough and punitive and not compromise public safety. House arrest sentencing is seen by many as meeting these criteria.

House arrest is a sentence imposed by the court in which offenders are legally ordered to remain confined in their own residences. They are usually allowed to leave their residences only for medical reasons and employment. They may also be required to perform community service or to pay victim restitution or probation supervision fees. In at least 20 states, "electronic bracelets" are being used to detect violations of house arrest.

While the goal of "house arrest" is easily understood—to restrict freedom—the mechanisms used to confine an offender to his home vary considerably. Typically, offenders participating in Intensive Probation Supervision programs are required to be in their residences during evening hours and on weekends. House arrest programs of this type now exist in Georgia, New Jersey, and Illinois.

In some instances, curfews are added to the offender's court-ordered parole or probation conditions. While curfews permit individual freedom in the community except for particular hours, more intrusive home incarceration programs restrict the offender's freedom in all but court-approved limited activities. These more intrusive programs now exist in Kentucky, Utah, Michigan, Oregon, and California. Several have been modeled on the house arrest program operated by the State of Florida.

Florida's Community Control Program

Florida's house arrest program, known as "Community Control," was established in 1983 to help alleviate prison crowding in the State. It is the most ambitious program of its type in the country, with about 5,000 offenders "locked up" in their homes on any one day. Leonard Flynn, a panelist on this Crime File segment, oversees the program's operations for the Florida Department of Corrections.

Florida's program targets "incarceration-bound" offenders, including misdemeanants and felons. Each offender is supervised by a community control officer, whose primary function is to ensure that the offender is adhering to court-ordered house arrest restrictions. The community control officer works nights and weekends to monitor compliance. For the more serious offenders, an electronic monitoring system is used. This system operates by having a central computer randomly telephone the offender during designated hours. The offender responds to the telephone call by placing a receiving module (contained in a watch-like wristband) into a modem. The computer verifies the action via a remote printer.

Offenders are permitted to leave their residences only for court-approved employment, rehabilitation, or community service activities. Participants must pay monthly supervision fees of $30 to $50 to offset the costs of supervision, pay restitution to victims, and provide for their own and their family's support.

Figure 15.1—continued

Officials in Florida consider the house arrest program to be a resounding success. Since 70 percent of those 10,000 persons were believed likely to have been sent to prison otherwise, real cost savings have been realized. In Florida, it costs about $3 per day to supervise a house arrest offender, compared with $28 per day for imprisonment.

Florida's success, coupled with the intense pressure that nearly every state is feeling to reduce prison commitments, ensures that interest in house arrest will continue to grow. An additional impetus is provided by manufacturers of electronic monitoring equipment, who promote their products as a means to achieve public safety without incurring exorbitant costs. Consequently, it is important to consider the major advantages and disadvantages of house arrest programs as well as the larger conceptual issues that such sentencing practices raise.

Source: Joan Petersilia (1988). "House Arrest," pp. 2-3. Washington, DC: National Institute of Justice.

According to Petersilia (1989:2-3) disadvantages may include: that house arrest may have net-widening effects (providing another set of options that could result in expansion of the population under correctional authority rather than reduction), and if house arrest does widen the net, costs will obviously increase for corrections rather than decrease; that house arrest may not be satisfactory to some as a punishment (for example, the MADD organization "sees such sentencing as a step backward for efforts to stiffen penalties [for drunk drivers]"); that house arrest focuses primarily on offender surveillance rather than assistance; that house arrest is intrusive and possibly illegal (involving the state's presence in individuals' homes); that house arrest may involve race and class bias (so far those who have been eligible have tended "disproportionately to be white collar offenders, programs involve payment of fees, and the offender must have a home and a telephone, all of which mediate against those living in poverty), and that house arrest does not necessarily insure public safety or protection.

As noted above, house arrest may involve electronic monitoring or may involve other forms of surveillance. As Figure 15.2 indicates, Florida's program uses supervision by a community control officer for each offender, and more serious offenders are monitored electronically. The material technology of electronic monitoring is achieving a degree of fascination among some policymakers, some practitioners, and some members of the public. Figure 15.3 explains how electronic monitoring equipment works.

Figure 15.2
How Electronic Monitoring Equipment Works

How electronic monitoring equipment works

Electronic monitoring equipment receives information about monitored offenders and transmits the information over the telephone lines to a computer at the monitoring agency. There are two basic types: **continuously signaling devices** that constantly monitor the presence of an offender at a particular location, and **programmed contact devices** that contact the offender periodically to verify his or her presence.

Continuously signaling devices

A continuously signaling device has three major parts: a transmitter, a receiver-dialer, and a central computer.

The transmitter, which is attached to the offender, sends out a continuous signal. The receiver-dialer, which is located in the offender's home and is attached to the telephone, detects the signals sent by the transmitter. It reports to the central computer when it stops receiving the signal and again when the signal begins.

A central computer at the monitoring agency accepts reports from the receiver-dialer over the telephone lines, compares them with the offender's curfew schedule, and alerts correctional officials about any unauthorized absences. The computer also stores information about each offender's routine entries and exits so that a report can be prepared.

Programmed contact devices

These devices use a computer programmed to telephone the offender during the monitored hours, either randomly or at specified times. The computer prepares a report on the results of the call.

Most but not all programs attempt to verify that the offender is indeed the person responding to the computer's call. Programmed contact devices can do this in several ways. One is to use voice verification technology. Another is to require the offender to wear a wristwatch device programmed to provide a unique number that appears when a special button on the watch device is pressed into a touchtone telephone in response to the computer's call.

A third system requires a black plastic module to be strapped to the offender's arm. When the computer calls, the module is inserted into a verifier box connected to the telephone. A fourth system uses visual verification at the telephone site.

Note:
Since the survey, several manufacturers have introduced a "hybrid" form of equipment. It functions like the continuously signaling devices, but when the central computer notes that the offender may have left at an unauthorized time, it telephones the offender and verifies that the person responding is the offender. If verification does not occur, notification is made of the violation.

Source: *NIJ Reports*, "Electronic Monitoring of Offenders Increases," Jan./Feb. 1989, p. 4.

Figure 15.3
**Number of Offenders Being Electronically Monitored on February 12, 1989, and
Percent Change From 1988**

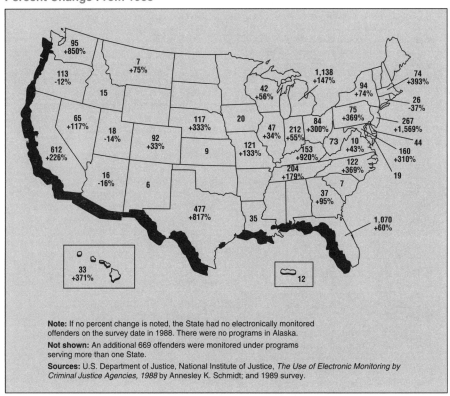

Note: If no percent change is noted, the State had no electronically monitored offenders on the survey date in 1988. There were no programs in Alaska.

Not shown: An additional 669 offenders were monitored under programs serving more than one State.

Sources: U.S. Department of Justice, National Institute of Justice, *The Use of Electronic Monitoring by Criminal Justice Agencies, 1988* by Annesley K. Schmidt; and 1989 survey.

Figure 15.3 — continued

Monitored Offenders by Offense Category, 1987-1989

Offense Category	1987 % of Total Number	1988 % of Total Number	1989 % of Sample
Crimes against the person	5.6	9.7	11.8
Drug offenses	13.5	15.3	22.0
Frauds	3.3	3.8	2.3
Major traffic offenses	33.4	25.6	18.9
Property offenses	18.2	20.1	31.7
Sex offenses	2.8	4.0	1.4[a]
Weapon offenses	1.2	1.3	2.2
Multiple offenses	10.2	6.1	.9[b]
Other offenses	11.8	14.2	8.9

[a] Neither of the jurisdictions best known for the monitoring of sex offenders was included in the 1989 sample—this decline is likely an accident of sampling rather than a significant trend.

[b] The decline in "multiple offenses" is probably an artifact caused by form design. The 1989 form offered respondents an opportunity to precode responses and only limited space for multiple offenses.

Type of Termination by Months on Monitoring, 1989 Sample

Duration of Monitoring	Successful Terminations	Technical Violations	New Offense Violations
1st month	271	94	16
2d month	211	71	7
3d month	170	43	6
4th month	128	26	9
5th month	67	16	3
6th month	46	11	0
7-12 months	66	12	6
13-24 months	14	2	1
Total	973	275	48

Successful Terminations are those in which the offender completed the assigned term or was removed for administrative reasons.

Technical Violations include curfew violations, substance abuse violations, absconding, and other rule violations that caused the offender to be removed from monitoring. The usual but not invariable consequence of technical violations was incarceration.

New Offense Violations were those in which the offender was arrested for an offense during electronic monitoring.

Source: *NIJ Reports*, Nov./Dec. 1990, p. 10.

One should note that electronic monitoring may be used as a "front-door" strategy or as a "back-door" strategy. Offenders, either in sentencing decisions (front door) or in decisions concerning early release from prison (back door) could face electronic monitoring. One should also note that electronic monitoring is a relatively recent development in its application to corrections, but its use is increasing rapidly. The National Institute of Justice reports that the first electronic monitoring program was initiated in Palm Beach, Florida, in December, 1984; that on February 15, 1987 there were 826 persons being monitored electronically in the United States; that on February 14, 1988, 2,277 offenders were being monitored electronically, with Florida and Michigan monitoring 49.5% of those counted on that day (NIJ, 1989). The program in the state of Michigan started as a back-door strategy, to facilitate early release of potentially risky parole candidates.

Reported success with electronic monitoring is providing impetus for more use. One should also understand that "[a]n additional impetus is provided by manufacturers of electronic monitoring equipment, who promote their products as a means to achieve public safety without incurring exorbitant costs" (Petersilia, 1988:2). Cost savings may be the major selling point for electronic monitoring. It is difficult to generalize about cost savings (the cost of incarcerating an individual could range from $15 to $50 or more per day and the cost of monitoring would depend upon whether an agency bought its own equipment or leased the services and equipment, though a ballpark estimate of $7 to $11 per day would seem appropriate), but most projections appear to center on reductions of as much as one-half to two-thirds of the cost of supervision.

It is too soon to tell just what the effects of house arrest and electronic monitoring are. Although reports of success are strong ("[g]enerally less than 25% of participants fail to complete the programs successfully" [Petersilia, 1989:4]), most of the programs have been highly selective. In other words, those persons selected to participate have been very good risks (this is called "loading for success"). Much rigorous research will be necessary to make some rather definitive statement. Nonetheless, interest in and implementation of these types of programs is increasing steadily. One can look for third-level alternatives to remain.

Restitution and Community Service

Restitution (in which the offender makes a financial payment to restore damage done to a victim) and community service (in which the offender does service work as ordered by the court to atone, perhaps symbolically, for the offense) are usually imposed in conjunction with probation (as special conditions). These could be sentences in themselves. These also could be required as conditions of diversion programs.

Restitution and community service have become very widespread sentencing options, and correctional programs based on restitution or community service have made appearances in most jurisdictions. There are so many potential variations in such programs that one should focus on these as collections of strategies rather than as single options.

The primary issues surrounding restitution involve the offender's ability to make payments, the potential nature of the offender-victim relationship during the period of restitution (whether the offender will pay directly to the victim or, as in many jurisdictions, through a probation agency or other intermediary agency), and how to enforce payment. To enforce payment, the court may provide an inducement such as sentencing the offender to a period of incarceration, suspending the sentence and relying on the threat of imminent incarceration. In some jurisdictions, the court may assign the offender to an intermediary agency that assists the offender in finding a job, requires payment to be made on a certain schedule, and can return the offender to court for failure to pay. With community service, primary issues involve determining what type and how much of what type of service will be appropriate to the offense, as well as determination of eligibility and selection of offenders to participate in community service options.

Restitution and community service programs have not been shown to reduce recidivism. However, due to potential economics and the logic employed in the rationales for such efforts, and due to the need to provide sanctions for large numbers of offenders convicted with less serious offenses, these options (strategies) are well ensconced in community corrections.

Temporary Release Programs

Temporary release programs involve incarceration and mechanisms for inmates to spend time in community settings. Work release, study release, and furloughs provide the avenues for temporary release.

Work release refers to programs that allow prison or jail inmates to work in a community setting. The inmates reside in the prison or jail or in a designated facility, go to work in the community setting for a specified period during the day, then return to the place of incarceration. Study release allows inmates to spend time in the community enrolled in academic or vocational education programs. There are many variations on each of these sorts of programs. These may be thought of as strategies for the purposes of general consideration.

Both work release and study release involve attempts to achieve the general aim of preparing incarcerated persons for a better chance at a law-abiding lifestyle upon release from incarceration. Work release may result in economic benefits to the inmate and perhaps to the inmate's family. The working inmate pays taxes, and many programs require that the working inmate pay a fee to cover room and board expenses, thereby defraying costs of incarceration. Study release may assist in personal development, which may, in turn, assist the inmate in finding employment or in other beneficial ways. Both sets of strategies involve crucial issues regarding inmate eligibility and selection. Typically, programs are limited, and attention is usually directed to means for selecting the most deserving inmates—those most likely to successfully complete such programs, those most likely not to cause problems while in such programs, and other similar issues. Both sets of strategies depend upon resources available in a given locale and upon the inclinations and efforts of corrections personnel in developing networks of resources. Work release is particularly dependent upon the inclinations and needs of employers as well as upon the marketable abilities and skills of inmates. Study release programs are particularly dependent upon education and vocational education resources that are available in a given area and upon the baseline preparations of the inmates (i.e., whether inmates have attained levels of educational preparation sufficient to allow them to participate in meaningful ways in certain programs).

Furloughs allow inmates to leave their places of confinement to return to the community for a short period of time, usually for a few days. During the furlough the inmate is not directly supervised. A number of purposes could be served by granting a furlough. The inmate approaching release could search for employment or for a place to live upon release. The inmate could make connections with support groups or with family members or others. Additionally, there may be other reasons for prison administrators to grant furloughs.

One should keep in mind that almost all persons incarcerated in the United States will one day be released to community locale. During the past two decades the use of furloughs has quietly grown into the tens of thousands across the United States. Although recent political campaigns have drawn unfavorable media attention to the use of furloughs, resulting in expressions of concern over the potential for those on furlough to commit crimes or abscond, such difficulties are relatively rare.

Temporary release programs have not been shown to significantly affect recidivism. Nonetheless, because of the logical appeal of such programs and because of the pragmatic aims that such programs attempt to serve, these are a staple on the community corrections menu.

Residential Programs/Halfway Houses

Halfway houses are residential facilities that usually provide more structure and a greater degree of supervision for court-ordered residents than do many other sorts of community corrections endeavors. Placement of offenders in such facilities is most often combined with probation (halfway in) or parole or other early release (halfway out). These types of facilities have rules, usually have curfews, and provide stricter supervision than general probation or general parole. Because of the variety of possible component program elements that may be in place in any given residential program, it is difficult to generalize about these types of facilities. It is quite common for residents to be required to hold a job or look for work, to participate in group counseling along with other residents or to participate in individual counseling, to attend education or vocational education programs or substance abuse programs, among other possibilities.

The preeminent difficulty facing those implementing residential programs is neighborhood acceptance. Most residential programs are relegated to being located in the least desirable sites because of resistance from property owners in more desirable sites. Proposals for locating residential programs in established neighborhoods where property values are in the mid-to-upper ranges most often result in significant resistance and the prospective location is changed to a less desirable site. Residential programs are widespread, however, and can offer much to offenders. However, as with most community corrections endeavors, results concerning effectiveness are mixed.

Summary

"Community corrections" is a term that subtends many approaches, many practices. Probation and parole are clearly the largest and most identifiable elements of community corrections. However, diversion, pretrial release, restitution programs, community service programs, work release, study release, furloughs, and a variety of residential programs fit beneath the community corrections umbrella. Recently, "third-level alternatives," notably house arrest and electronic monitoring programs, have been added and are garnering much attention as attractive corrections endeavors that promise greater degrees of control of offenders in the community.

Reintegration is a prominent concept underlying the notion of community corrections. Both "reintegration" and "community corrections" are elusive terms. One must consider just what "community" means while attempting to decide what the substance of "reintegration" may be. In practice, convicted offenders and, sometimes, those who have not yet been convicted are dealt with in diverse community settings, each of which uses different community corrections programs. As the following "On the Defensive" section indicates, community corrections was once touted as a panacea for corrections. Now, the tenor of discussion and expectation appears to have changed.

[handwritten margin note: 3rd level alternatives = - house arrest - electronic monitoring]

The Panacea Pendulum

The Decline of Community Corrections

The prospects for a comprehensive community corrections movement initially seemed bright. The policy of treating offenders in the community promised to be cost effective, fundamentally humane, and a therapeutic panacea for all but the most sociopathic among us. But, remarkably, the appeal of this policy agenda was not sustained for long. Conservatives, as might be anticipated, criticized such notions as diversion and deinstitutionalization as merely more attempts by liberals to coddle offenders and rob the criminal sanction of its deterrent powers. What was unexpected, however, is that commentators on the political left also launched an attack on the concept of community corrections. Sensitized to the ways in which past reforms had been corrupted, they were quick to scrutinize community-based programs and to illuminate their shortcomings. They uncovered such problems as the lack of an emergent consensus concerning the goals of community corrections (Coates, 1981), and the local community resistance to halfway houses (Krajick, 1980). More worrisome, a number of commentators asserted that the latest panacea had, in the end, done little to facilitate the improvement of offenders and much to serve class and organizational interests (Austin and Krisberg, 1982; Lerman, 1975; Scull, 1977; Van Dusen, 1981; Rothman, 1980). These issues are touched upon below.

Many of the newly established programs suffered from a lack of clear program objectives. One of the reasons for this lack of direction was that the reformers had concentrated all their efforts on deinstitutionalizing offenders, with the assumption that getting people "out of institutions, even if the community is not geared to serve them, is all to the good" (Foster, 1973:33). As Coates (1981:88) remarked:

For too long, we have accepted the notion that a halfway house or a group home is somehow inherently better than the institution it replaces. Little thought has been given to what factors differentiate a group home from an institution.

Community reactions to a program were also crucial in determining how well it could function. As Warner (1977:14) has stated:

Without the support and positive involvement of good neighbors, a group home is not a community based program at all, but simply another asylum isolated from the world which has, in the first place, alienated the child. If the task of a group home is to reintegrate children into the community, this cannot be done without the support of good neighbors.

Frequently, the newly established programs lacked such support. Nearby residents, fearing victimization and declining property values, exerted strong pressure to prevent programs from opening. Often the pressure was political in nature, involving complaints to public officials or the local zoning board. A 1974 study by the American Society of Planning Officials found that:

The reasons cited most often why zoning boards refuse to grant permits to halfway houses were "substantial opposition from nearby landowners" and "community prejudice toward the persons to reside in the facility" (Krajick, 1980:16).

As administrator Robert Bright noted, "community corrections was officially a good idea, but if you made enough noise, you didn't have to have it in your neighborhood" (Quoted in Krajick, 1980:16). Such resistance caused some programs to close, and others to relocate in non-residential urban areas. Such sites, however, were far from ideal. "Sticking a center out between the dog pound and the peat moss factory is no answer," observed administrator Ray Messegee, adding that "It's better to get into a residential area, because that's where inmates are returning to" (Quoted in Krajick, 1980:19).

A more fundamental attack has come from commentators arguing that the community corrections movement is merely a new and subtle means by the repressive state to expand social control over citizens. Andrew Scull set forth early insights into this issue. Scull (1977) maintained that the community corrections movement occurred not because it was more therapeutic to treat people in the community, but because it was cheaper to do so. Scull pointed to the increases in the cost of institutional care, and to the rising crime rates which has increased the number of offenders to be dealt with, as factors which necessitated the rise in community-oriented alternatives. Scull noted that the extensive use of community corrections allowed the system to avoid the expense of constructing costly new facilities. In Scull's (1977:144) words:

> to the extent that the adoption of diversionary policies obviates the need for massive expansion of the physical capacity of the existing institutional system . . . decarceration provides a direct and immediate source of relief to the state's fiscal crisis whose importance is obvious, even while its dimensions are extraordinarily difficult to estimate with any degree of precision.

On a more general level, historian David Rothman (1980) demonstrated how the existing interest groups within the criminal justice system had historically used efforts at reform to further their own ends. While Rothman did not deal with the deinstitutionalization movement directly, he did illustrate how many of the community-oriented reforms advocated by the Progressives (e.g., parole and probation) had persisted, not because they achieved the changes that Progressives had proposed, but because they served the judges, prosecutors, and correctional officials within the system. In short, the ideals or "conscience" of the reforms had been corrupted by the pragmatics or "convenience" at the core of the legal process. Notably, Austin and Krisberg's (1982) recent review of the effectiveness of alternatives to institutionalization in terms of reducing the use of incarceration suggests that the conscience versus convenience dichotomy is still with us today. Their analysis of existing research has led Austin and Krisberg (1982) to argue that the community corrections movement is best characterized as an "unmet promise." "In each instance," they observed of community-based programs, "the non-incarcerative options were transformed, serving criminal justice system values and goals other than reducing imprisonment" (1982:405-406). Despite expressed intentions, reform efforts thus did not result in a lessening in levels of incarceration or in government surveillance over people's lives. Instead, a close inspection of these undertakings reveals that their "conscience" has typically been corrupted and that they have ultimately been used to protect or bolster the organizational interests of the justice apparatus. As Austin and Krisberg (1982:377) have concluded:

> Alternatives to incarceration have been introduced for the espoused purpose of altering the nets of criminal justice. Organizational research, however, suggests that the reform strategies are frequently distorted, shifting their original purposes and producing unintended and undesirable consequences. The evidence indicates that alternatives have created:
>
> 1. Wider Nets, in the sense that reforms have increased the proportion of persons whose behavior is regulated and controlled by the state.
> 2. Stronger Nets, in that reforms have augmented the state's capacity to control citizens through an intensification of its powers of intervention.
> 3. Different Nets, through the transfer of jurisdictional authority from one agency to another, or the creation of new social control systems (cf. Van Dusen, 1981).

Panaceas and Policy

There can be little doubt that liberal and more radical critics of community corrections, such as those discussed above, did a service in counteracting the naive conclusion that this latest reform agenda would somehow be immune to the kinds of difficulties that previous reforms have suffered. Yet, while instructive in this way, the tarnishing of the appeal of community corrections had a less attractive consequence as well: it meant that those on the political left were now bereft of any panacea for the crime problem that it could offer to policymakers and the public. In the matter of a few years, they had reached the conclusion that not only was it foolish to imagine that crime-curing communities could be fashioned within the prison, but also it was equally misconceived to anticipate that prevailing realities would ever allow for humanistic and efficacious reforms outside the penitentiary's walls. It was manifest that "nothing works" (Martinson, 1974), and that well-intentioned criminal justice reforms unwittingly were "dangerous" undertakings (Doleschal, 1982). With hopes of curing criminality dashed, the best that could be done was to try to insure that offenders would be treated justly both before the courts and while incarcerated (Fogel, 1975; von Hirsch, 1976). Beyond this, meddling in criminal justice matters simply risked making things worse. Capturing this sentiment, Doleschal (1982:151) has remarked, "That we should leave the system alone, intervening as little as possible and only when necessary, is an idea whose time has come, and an increasing number of authors are expressing it."

To an extent, this sobering perspective was more honest than past attempts that promised unattainable achievements in the realm of crime control. But again, there is a negative side to all this. Panaceas, for all their simplicities, have one advantage: they energize correctional reform by offering the prospect that things can get better. In the absence of any easily believed panacea, those of the left have been robbed of their enthusiasm for embarking on campaigns to improve the criminal justice system. "Today," LaMar Empey (1979:10) has written, "optimism has turned to pessimism, fervent hopes to despair." In a context such as this, it is not surprising to learn that the best [of] those on the political left have to offer are the admonitions that nothing works and to leave the system alone (Travis and Cullen, 1984).

This does not mean, however, that a new panacea has not emerged to grasp the fascination of criminal justice policymakers. If liberal elements in society are now refraining from claiming that they have the key to solving the crime problem, their conservative counterparts have shown no such reluctance. Indeed, there is no hint of despair on the right, only answers. As Bertram Gross (1982:137) has noted with a measure of hyperbole, they advocate a forceful if "simple remedy: 'Police 'em, Jail 'em, Kill 'em." In real terms, this means that it has become plausible to suggest that juveniles of all sorts can be "scared straight" by letting them witness the horrors that reign within adult prisons (Finckenauer, 1982). For older offenders, there is the assumption that stringent, mandatory prison sentences have the power to enforce conformity. At the very least, lengthy stays behind bars will insure that the dangerous do not roam free in the community (Wilson, 1975; cf. Gordon, 1980). Caging the habitually wicked may create a Hobbesian state of all against all within the society of captives, but the high walls of the prison will insulate the innocent from such people. The widespread appeal of this philosophy of incapacitation is best seen in the constant escalation of the state and federal prison population—doubling in the last decade to the point where it now has surpassed the unprecedented figure of 425,000 (*Justice Assistance News*; 1983).

When these considerations are combined with our knowledge of the past, it becomes inescapably clear that the panacea pendulum is swinging steadily away from the conclusion that the cure for crime lies in either the "community" or "corrections." It would be premature to assert that this is a permanent state of affairs. For one thing, while many citizens believe we should get tough on crime, they nonetheless express the opinion that offenders should still be given an opportunity to be rehabilitated (Cullen et al., 1983). For another, the contradiction inherent in the conservatives' simultaneous call to hold the line on taxation while urging that large expenditures be allocated for the construction and operation of an enormous prison apparatus may place limitations on how far the reliance on imprisonment as a preferred response to crime can proceed. Yet it is too much to expect that underlying attitudes supporting rehabilitation or financial exigencies will, by themselves, halt the current trend in justice policy. The punitive panacea at present has no competition, and all evidence suggests that its influence in the correctional arena is growing. Unless those with more reformist impulses begin to offer policy agendas that at once reveal the inadequacies of "getting tough" and furnish answers to the crime problem, the salience of the conservatives' vision of justice thus promises to remain undiminished in the time immediately ahead (Cullen and Gilbert, 1982; Cullen and Wozniak, 1982).

In this regard, reformers would do well to reconsider whether it was a wise decision to have abandoned community corrections as their panacea when no alternative other than pessimism was at hand. Some might argue that to embrace anything as a cure-all in light of knowledge to the contrary is both disingenuous and dangerous. Perhaps so. But one must also face the reality that policymakers have shown little inclination to stop the justice process so that empirical research can instruct them on how to implement complex solutions to deal with the complex problem of crime. As such, the decision to popularize a crime panacea should transcend the issue of whether a cure-all has in fact been discovered, and consider whether the consequences of the panacea are better or worse than the policy agenda that will take its place. Such pragmatism to the noble may be unappealing, but in the end, it may prove to be the most humanistic avenue of reform to follow.

Source: Mark C. Dean-Myrda and Francis T. Cullen (1985). "The Panacea Pendulum: An Account of Community as a Response to Crime." In Lawrence F. Travis, III (ed.) *Probation, Parole and Community Corrections: A Reader*. Copyright © 1985 by Waveland Press, Inc., Prospect Heights, Illinois. Used with permission from the publisher.

Key Terms and Concepts

community

community control office

community corrections

community service

diversion

electronic monitoring

furlough

halfway house

house arrest

loading for success

net widening

panacea pendulum

pretrial release

recidivism

reintegration

residential program

restitution

study release

third-level alternatives

work release

References

Bureau of Justice Statistics (1990). "Prisoners in 1989." Washington, DC: U.S. Government Printing Office.

McCarthy, B.R. and B.J. McCarthy (1984). *Community-Based Corrections*. Pacific Grove, CA: Brooks/Cole Publishing Co.

National Advisory Commission on Criminal Justice Standards and Goals (1973). *Corrections*. Washington, DC: U.S. Government Printing Office.

National Institute of Justice (1989). "Electronic Monitoring of Offenders Increases." *NIJ Reports*, Jan./Feb. (1989):4.

Petersilia, J. (1988). "House Arrest." *An NIJ Crime File Study Guide*. Washington, DC: U.S. Government Printing Office.

Travis, L.E., III (1985). "Probation, Parole, and Community Corrections in Contemporary America." In L.E. Travis, III (ed.) *Probation, Parole and Community Corrections: A Reader*. Prospect Heights, IL: Waveland Press, Inc.

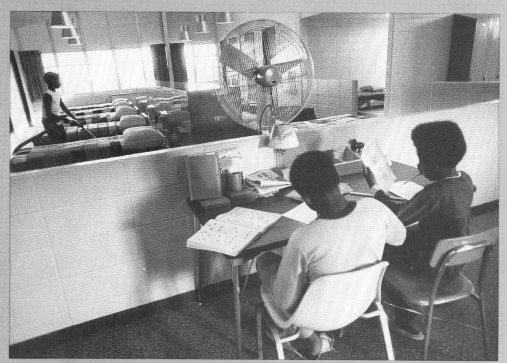

Photo Credit: Bill Powers, Frost Publishing Group, Ltd.

Juvenile Corrections

16

After reading this chapter, the student should be able to:

▮ Discuss the origins of the juvenile justice system.

▮ Describe the role and development of the juvenile court.

▮ Explain the operation of the juvenile justice system.

▮ List landmark legal decisions in juvenile justice and juvenile rights.

▮ Describe types of juvenile institutions.

▮ Comment on the effectiveness of both secure and nonsecure programs for juveniles.

Introduction

No other component of the criminal justice system has undergone such dramatic change over the past 20 years than the juvenile justice system of this country. We have seen drastic changes with respect to legal decisions and juvenile justice operations, increased concern over juvenile rights, the "widening of the net" of social control over juveniles, debate over the issue of juveniles committing more serious crime with increased frequency, and discussion centering on the institutionalization of juveniles. All of these issues are relevant to the investigation of the juvenile justice system of this country, yet our purpose here is not to deal with each and every one of these controversial topics, because each would require separate chapters to adequately accommodate the essential material.

Instead, our purpose is to examine the correctional aspects of juvenile justice. This will include a brief description of the origin of juvenile justice, an overview of the juvenile justice system, identifying focal points of entry and exit from the system, landmark legal decisions dealing with juvenile justice operations and the concomitant rights that juveniles do have, and finally an analysis of the types of institutions found in the juvenile justice system. This will include an exploration of detention centers, training schools, camps and ranches, and foster homes. This final section of the chapter will provide the reader with relevant questions and answers about these institutions and the implications for future juvenile justice policy concerning the institutionalization of young offenders. It is hoped that the student will gain a comprehensive understanding of the juvenile justice system, along with a complete picture of the types of programs and institutions within this component of the criminal justice system. This more complete understanding of the juvenile corrections system will be enhanced through the integration of empirical literature on the various program areas. These research findings are intended to give the student a more critical and contemporary understanding of juvenile corrections. We begin with an examination of the origins of the juvenile justice system.

Origins of the Juvenile Justice System

The beginnings of the juvenile justice system can be traced to early England and the operations of many poorhouses and Houses of Refuge. Accordingly, Finckenauer (1984) suggests that much of what is contemporary juvenile justice has its roots in the concepts of family solidarity, more specifically the role of the father in the perpetuation of the family unit. Interestingly enough, he further describes how institutions of confinement were predicated on the philosophy of rigid discipline and the instillation of proper habits into youths. The student should recognize that much of this same philosophy dominates many of our institutions today. While philosophical approaches to juvenile corrections may be found somewhat similar when comparing the past with the present, the conditions of early institutions were miserable.

As described by Empey (1982), these early systems of child care and control demonstrated one simple fact—children were treated, at best, with indifference, if not with cruelty. While we are aware of the many cruelties heaped upon children today, it was nothing like the events of the past. In fact, much of what we call juvenile justice today grew out of the concern people had over the mistreatment of juvenile offenders. While we will later see a different interpretation of the creation of the juvenile justice system in the United States, we can say that there was, initially, a concern among many that operations of institutions for the care of young people were, for the most part, brutal and indifferent to their needs. This led to the formal development of legal principles and concepts which were to distinguish adults from youths, in legal terms, and to improve the plight of these young people who were institutionalized.

The guiding legal principle, which was created in the case *Ex parte Crouse* (1838), was *parens patriae*. Under this principle, the state assumed the role of the guardian when it was shown that the natural parents could not assume control of the child. In effect, this case created the fundamental legal principle upon which modern systems of juvenile justice were founded. In *Crouse*, the father of a young girl petitioned the Pennsylvania Supreme Court for the release of his daughter, who had been incarcerated under the *parens patriae* doctrine. The father claimed that the institutionalization of his daughter without the benefit of a jury trial was tantamount to denial of her Sixth Amendment right to a jury trial. In response, however, the high court held that the distinction between juveniles and adults is based in the *parens patriae* doctrine, and more importantly, that the location of the child in the House of Refuge was not equivalent to a prison structure, but to a school, and as such, the purpose of the institution was the protection and welfare of the child, not punishment, as was the case in the more confining adult institutions.

This case was the first to unequivocally delineate the power of the state with reference to juvenile system operations and the legality of institutionalizing young offenders for their best interests and society's. Much debate has been generated over the past 150 years concerning the legal rights of juvenile offenders with respect to their handling and care by the juvenile justice system. We will discuss some of those major decisions in subsequent pages. At present, however, what *Ex parte Crouse* did was grant extraordinary discretionary powers to those who run our juvenile justice system. Some of this power has been circumscribed in recent times, yet it is problematic as to whether these court actions over the years have really helped those who come into the American juvenile justice system. This issue will be examined more critically in the next section.

The Role and Development of the Juvenile Court

The invention of the juvenile court, as described by Rothman (1980), can be seen in the degree of concern put forth by the dominant reform group of the times, that being the Progressives. According to Rothman (1980:205-235), the Progressives were particularly interested in the plight of children, or in his words, they were in a "remarkable degree child oriented." Much of the Progressives' concern with children arose when immigrants groups and their progeny started to fill the major urban centers. Seeing the conditions of the city as not being conducive to the change of children, the growth of the juvenile justice system began as a logical response to the overcrowding of the cities. As such, juvenile justice was perceived to be a response to the increased urbanization of many American cities. Recent evidence indicates that the creation of the juvenile court can be traced to the degree of urbanization experienced by the state (Sutton, 1985).

While urbanization and the growth of cities was a major factor leading to the development of the juvenile court in the United States, revisionist historians saw the growth of the juvenile court as a response to the threat these new urban immigrant groups posed to the existing economic and political structure of American society. This line of reasoning has its roots in two specific types of analyses. On the one hand, there is the *critical* or *radical interpretation*. It has its theoretical foundation in the work of critical criminologists who question the role of the state in the creation of social structures, like the juvenile court. On the other hand, there is the view that suggests that the creation of the juvenile court was primarily in response to demands put forth by those for whom the juvenile court would be of benefit, either directly or indirectly. This second view is referred to as the *functional interpretation*. The first position has its origin in the work of Platt (1977).

functional interpretation [handwritten margin note]

Platt (1977:introduction) recognized that the "invention of delinquency" could not be divorced from other social processes occurring during the same period. His emphases lie on the integration of political and social phenomena intersecting into a specific position on juvenile justice affairs. More directly, Platt was concerned with answering the question of why the juvenile justice system developed when it did, and how it related to these other processes—economic, political, and social in nature. Drawing his analysis from the Illinois juvenile justice system, he has argued rather persuasively that the delinquency phenomenon was largely a product of forces concerned with the social control of the poor's progeny, not the benevolence of reformers. He states:

Platt [handwritten margin note]

> The child-saving movement was not a humanistic enterprise on behalf of the working class against the established order. On the contrary, its impetus came primarily from the middle and upper classes who were instrumental in devising new forms of social control to protect their power and prestige. The child-saving movement was not an isolated phenomenon but rather reflected massive changes in the mode of production, from laissez-faire to monopoly capitalism, and in strategies of social control, from inefficient repression to welfare benevolence. This reconstruction of economic and social institutions, which was not achieved without conflict within the ruling class, represented a victory for the more 'enlightened' wing of corporate leaders who advocated strategic alliances with urban reformers that supported liberal reforms (1977:xx).

More recently, Rothman (1980:225-226) has suggested that the Progressive desire to invent the juvenile court went beyond the benevolent ideological considerations of reformers and included the interests of those who would run the system. His examination of the juvenile court suggests that the power of what he refers to as the "functional" advantages of juvenile court to a number of Progressive-minded interest groups. In this way, Rothman argued that the creation of the juvenile court was rooted in specific ideological positions, yet it was the intended by-products of the juvenile justice system among supporters that ultimately lead to its creation and perpetuation. In the words of Rothman, the system of juvenile justice became "convenient" for some interested groups of reformers. He states:

> The rapidity with which the juvenile court won legislative approval reflected not only ideological considerations—the appeal of its rhetoric and its all-encompassing goals—but *functional* ones as well. A diverse group of its supporters, ranging from members of voluntary and philanthropic organizations to administrators of criminal justice, discovered that the enlargement of the powers of the court generally fit well with their own particular needs. Shifting the balance of authority from the private sector to the state furthered their own concerns and agendas. The added reach of the court promised to enlarge their influence and freedom of action. [Emphasis added.]

This interpretation of the invention of the juvenile court differs to a large degree from the critical perspective offered by Platt. Yet the point that can be made by this is that the system we call juvenile court was not created in a vacuum, and to suggest that it operated without the direct and indirect influences of broader social, economic, or political interests would be naïve in its best possible interpretation and incorrect in its worst possible interpretation. Somewhere between the two perspectives is where the true explanation of the development of the juvenile court system lies. As suggested by Finckenauer (1984:116), what we know as the juvenile court system today may be a direct result of both benevolent reformers and repressive capitalists. All this aside, what is relevant is to see where the contemporary juvenile court system had its roots and where it has gone.

The first juvenile court in the United States was founded in Cook County, Illinois in 1899. This court dealt not only with cases of a delinquent nature, but in addition, handled all cases of dependency and neglect. With the proliferation of juvenile courts throughout the land beginning in the twentieth century, the doctrine of *parens patriae* became a predominant concept in these courts. More important, the distinction between treatment and punishment became blurred, and as a result, there was no inherent logic to separate delinquent children from those who were determined to be dependent; all children were to be treated by the guiding hand of the juvenile court. As far as the state was concerned, all children who were in need of some type of supervision, regardless if it was due to their delinquent behavior or due to their lack of parental supervision, were being protected, not punished, by the state. Additionally, the belief in the expertise of the state was critical to the functioning of the juvenile court.

In effect, the juvenile court developed and sustained its existence through the belief in the rising knowledge about crime and delinquency. Positivism had begun to flourish and there was a growing acceptance of the so-called expert in determining the causes of delinquency and its subsequent treatment. An associated consequence of this arrangement was the increased discretion of the juvenile court. As stated by Rothman (1980:211) "Once again, an individual (an expert) approach presuppposed *wide discretion* [emphasis added]; and since the object of treatment was a youth, (progressives were) ready to expand this discretion well past recognized adult standards." Consequently, this discretionary power enabled juvenile court workers to have tremendous control over the youth under their authority. This kind of uncontrolled power provided the foundation for determinations of whether juveniles were institutionalized, yet it had very little effect on what happened to juveniles once they arrived at the institutions.

While institutionalization of juveniles was within the power given to the juvenile court, by far, the most important aspect of the court was probation. Through the use of wide discretionary authority, juvenile probation officers at the turn of the twentieth century had much input into how juveniles were to be treated and processed by the juvenile court. All efforts of the juvenile court became predicated on the belief that the best interests of both the state and the child lie within itself and its procedures. "In sum, to the courts as to the reformers, according to Rothman (1980: 235), the innovation of the juvenile court was all light—no darkness intruded. The potential for abuse or mischief did not have to be explored. Here was an effort to promote the best interest of the child and the state." Ostensibly, however, it became an overriding concern among many that the juvenile court had too much authority and power and that a checking of state power through the juvenile court was warranted.

This concern was not vocalized, however, until some 60 years after the invention of the juvenile court when the President's Commission on Law Enforcement and Administration of Justice in 1967 voiced some strong concerns about the fairness of juvenile justice proceedings. Much of what was occurring was a revolution in thought concerning the etiology of delinquency and appropriate methods of treatment of juvenile offenders. With the growth of new theoretical models, suggesting that the denial of opportunity and the creation of labels for juveniles by the system of criminal justice led to delinquent behavior, a new call was being proposed by the President's Commission that juveniles be diverted from the juvenile justice system, that delinquency treatment should be expanded, and that some offenses should be decriminalized (Empey, 1982:401-422). Moreover, the courts were no longer taking a passive posture with reference to juvenile justice operations, particularly juvenile court procedures. It was in the late 1960s that we began to see major decisions from the courts on the operations of the juvenile justice system.

The Operation of the Juvenile Justice System

As was stated in Chapter 1, much of the crime in this country is committed by young offenders. This statement is borne out by evidence compiled by the Federal Bureau of Investigation (FBI) through the Uniform Crime Reports. In addition, we can identify the types of dispositions given juveniles after they have been arrested by the police. Table 16.1 identifies the percent distribution of juveniles taken into custody, by method of disposition, for the period 1972-1988. The table shows some rather erratic fluctuations in the data, yet some stable referral methods by police over time. The most common method of disposition was the referral to juvenile court, followed by handling by the police department, and finally, an equal distribution of referrals to criminal, adult court, another police agency, or a welfare agency. It becomes apparent that juvenile court is the most likely disposition of juveniles who are arrested by the police.

While the workings of the juvenile court are important for understanding later correctional options with young offenders, it is equally important that an overview of the juvenile justice system be provided. Our purpose here is to give an overview of the juvenile justice system and how that process affects who becomes a part of the juvenile correctional establishment. Figure 16.1 identifies the major components of the juvenile justice system as recognized by the National Advisory Committee on Criminal Justice Standards and Goals. As mentioned earlier and as is shown in the diagram, the police have a number of options after arrest. If juvenile court is the option selected by the police, then the offender is received through a process called *intake screening*. At this stage of the juvenile justice process, a determination is made as to whether the juvenile offender should be held for further action by the juvenile court, whether the case should be dismissed, or whether some informal judgment should be rendered, such as ordering some type of restitution to the victim or to society.

Table 16.1
Percent Distribution of Juveniles Taken into Police Custody

By method of disposition, United States, 1972-88					
	Referred to juvenile court juris-diction	Handled within depart-ment and released	Referred to criminal or adult court	Referred to other police agency	Referred to welfare agency
1972	50.8%	45.0%	1.3%	1.6%	1.3%
1973	49.5	45.2	1.5	2.3	1.4
1974	47.0	44.4	3.7	2.4	2.5
1975	52.7	41.6	2.3	1.9	1.4
1976	53.4	39.0	4.4	1.7	1.6
1977	53.2	38.1	3.9	1.8	3.0
1978	55.9	36.6	3.8	1.8	1.9
1979	57.3	34.6	4.8	1.7	1.6
1980	58.1	33.8	4.8	1.7	1.6
1981	58.0	33.8	5.1	1.6	1.5
1982	58.9	32.5	5.4	1.5	1.6
1983	57.5	32.8	4.8	1.7	3.1
1984	60.0	31.5	5.2	1.3	2.0
1985	61.8	30.7	4.4	1.2	1.9
1986	61.7	29.9	5.5	1.1	1.8
1987	62.0	30.3	5.2	1.0	1.4
1988	63.1	29.1	4.7	1.1	1.9

Note: See Note, table 4.1. Arrest data for 1988 were not available for Florida and Kentucky; therefore, these States were omitted by the Source.

Source: U.S. Department of Justice, Federal Bureau of Investigation, *Crime in the United States, 1972*, p. 116; *1973*, p. 119; *1974*, p. 177; *1975*, p. 177; *1976*, p. 220; *1977*, p. 219; *1978*, p. 228; *1979*, p. 230; *1980*, p. 258; *1981*, p. 233; *1982*, p. 242; *1983*, p. 245; *1984*, p. 238; *1985*, p. 240; *1986*, p. 240; *1987*, p. 225; *1988*, p. 229 (Washington, DC: U.S. Government Printing Office).

It is the intake decision that has received much attention in the criminological literature. Much of this research has suggested that, beyond legal variables, other variables such as race and public demeanor at the hearing are critical to the decision of the intake worker. Bell and Lang (1985), for example, found that prior criminal record and demeanor at the intake hearing were critical in the final disposition of the juvenile offender. Moreover, they also found that the race of the juvenile offender was not a critical factor when compared to these other factors. Specifically, they found no evidence to support the position that black and Hispanic youths were differentially treated when compared to white youths. Interestingly though, they did find that white youths were less likely to receive the most lenient disposition—that being counsel and release—or the most harsh disposition—a detention petition. Other research by Fenwick (1982) suggests that additional variables may also be critical in the intake decision-making process of juvenile court, such as the level of "family disaffiliation" in the offender's life. By this, Fenwick is referring to the lack of integration with family members or designated family representatives.

From this brief analysis it becomes apparent that the intake decision is very important and can include a number of decision criteria as to whether a juvenile will be formally processed by the juvenile court. Current analyses suggest that prior conviction and the degree of legal and nonlegal control in the youth's life are all relevant variables to the juvenile disposition (Staples, 1987). All this aside, what is important to note is that the intake screening process is one in which many variables are taken into consideration by the intake worker, and more important, that this will affect who moves into the next step of the juvenile justice process.

This next step is referred to as the *detention hearing* stage of the juvenile justice process. It is at this stage that a determination is made as to whether or not a youth will be released to his parents or detained. Recent case law has developed concerning the use of detention prior to the adjudicatory process. In _Schall v. Martin_ (1984), the court ruled that juveniles suspected of committing certain types of crime may be preventively detained if it can be shown that the actions of the juvenile offender are so serious as to pose a threat to the safety of the community.

Subsequent to the detention hearing is the *adjudicatory inquiry*. This inquiry is designed to determine the facts of the case and whether further action is required by the juvenile court. This inquiry is typically heard before a magistrate or commissioner, and, in most instances, he or she has three options available: (1) to dismiss the case, (2) to request a formal hearing, or (3) to refer the matter elsewhere in the juvenile justice system, such as a diversionary program.

If the magistrate determines that more formal intervention is necessary, then the case may be referred to the juvenile court through a *petition*. If a petition is granted, the case then would move to what is known as an *adjudi-*

catory hearing. This is not a formal criminal trial, but the purpose of this hearing is to determine the facts of the case and to arrive at the best possible disposition for the juvenile offender. Remember, the foundation of the juvenile court is rooted in the *parens patriae* doctrine discussed earlier in the chapter, and as a result, the concern is what is best for the juvenile and for the state. More importantly, the hearing is less formal than in the adult system and is a *civil* matter, not a criminal one. If the presiding judge determines that no wrongdoing has been committed by the juvenile, the case is dismissed. If, however, a determination was made that a crime has been committed by the juvenile, then a *disposition hearing* is held.

As indicated in Figure 16.1, there are many options available to the juvenile court judge once a determination has been made that a juvenile has committed an offense. These alternatives range from restitution to custodial detention. More often than not, the most probable disposition is probation, but we are seeing an increased use of both restitution programs and institutional confinement. It is the latter that we will be describing in subsequent pages of this chapter. Before we begin that discussion, we need to examine some of the major court decisions that have affected the operations of the juvenile justice system. This review will provide us with a foundation for understanding how and why juveniles are treated differently from adults.

Landmark Legal Decisions in Juvenile Justice and Juvenile Rights

We have already discussed how the juvenile justice system originated with the intent of granting juvenile justice officials enormous amounts of discretionary authority. In addition, it was mentioned that the challenge to this arrangement did not occur until well into the late 1960s, with the intervention of the courts in the operations of the juvenile justice system. With this intervention came a redefinition of what, in a formal and legal sense, could be done to juvenile offenders. It was in the 1960s, as a result, that we saw a proliferation of case law on issues pertaining to juvenile justice. During this period, we saw three specific cases which had a profound effect on the future operations of juvenile justice systems.

Figure 16.1
The Juvenile Justice System

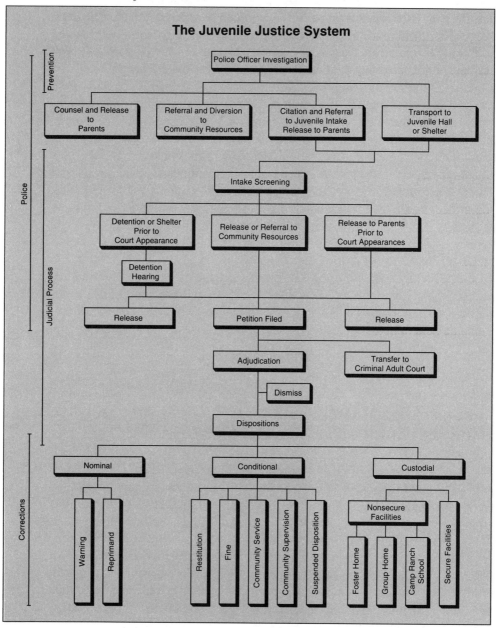

Source: National Advisory Committee on Criminal Justice Standards and Goals (1976). *Report of the Task Force on Juvenile and Delinquency Prevention*, p. 9. Washington, DC: Law Enforcement Assistance Administration.

In *Kent v. United States* (1966), the Supreme Court ruled that juveniles, for the first time, did have some constitutional protections. This ruling seemed antithetical to the purpose of the juvenile justice process, being more civil rather than criminal, and as a result, the decision was not in line with previous actions taken by juvenile courts throughout the country. The specific issue in *Kent* dealt with the waiver of a juvenile to adult court without the benefit of minimal due process protections. The Supreme Court ruled that such an important decision must be made with minimum requirements of due process and fair treatment demanded by the Fourteenth Amendment of the U.S. Constitution. While *Kent* was the first to address some constitutional questions of due process with respect to the processing of juvenile offenders, it was not until the following year that the Supreme Court addressed more thoroughly the constitutional rights of juveniles in the juvenile justice system.

In re Gault (1967) was a case that more thoroughly defined the constitutional protections afforded juvenile offenders. The particulars of the case dealt with an obscene phone call made by the defendant, Gerald Gault, and his subsequent detention in the State Industrial School for a period equal to six years. Gault was 15 at the time of the offense and under state law could be held until he reached the age of 21, a penalty which if committed by an adult would be punishable by no more than a fine of $50. The Supreme Court was concerned not so much with the penalty imposed, as with the procedures used to determine Gault's guilt or innocence. From this decision, the Supreme Court ruled that juveniles who face the possibility of incarceration must be afforded the following constitutional protections: notice of charges, right to counsel, right to confrontation and cross-examination of witnesses, privilege against self-incrimination, right to a transcript of the proceedings, and a right to appellate review. Subsequent to the *Gault* decision, we saw an increased willingness of courts to extend more due process protections to juvenile offenders.

In 1970, the Supreme Court in *In re Winship* held that the standard of proof required for an adjudication of a delinquent is proof "beyond a reasonable doubt," not what traditionally had been a lower standard of a "preponderance of the evidence." Later, we also see the double jeopardy protection extended to juveniles (*Breed v. Jones*, 1975), yet these protections do not include the right to a jury trial for juvenile offenders (*McKiever v. Pennsylvania*, 1971). However, it should be noted that the Supreme Court did not rule that juries could not be granted in juvenile proceedings, only that

[handwritten margin notes:]
Kent v. US. (1966)
— constitutionality – 14th amm.
In re gault (1967) constitutional protections & procedures
In re Winship (1970) beyond a reasonable doubt
Breed v. Jones (1975)
Mc Kiever v. Penn (197)
not required for juveniles

they are not required for these hearings. There are jury trials for juveniles, even though their numbers are relatively low.

Moreover, the courts have become more conservative in recent times with regard to juvenile rights. Current court opinions have held that juveniles may waive their *Miranda* rights (*Fare v. Michael C., 1979*) and that students have minimal protections against searches and seizures in their lockers in school (*New Jersey v. T.L.O., 1985*). Such decisions have led many to believe that there has been a significant retrenchment of juvenile rights. Contemporary scholars disagree as to the extent of this retrenchment and its effect on the fair operation of the juvenile justice system.

Whether or not these due process rights have actually increased the fairness of the juvenile justice system is problematic, with many scholars arguing that the impact of legal decisions on the operations of juvenile justice systems has been minimal at best. Many have suggested that the impact of the due process protections on the operations of juvenile justice systems has been negligible (Platt et al., 1971; Kittrie, 1974; and Nejelski, 1976). Currently, scholars have questioned the actual change in juvenile justice processing when one examines the level of resources available to the system. According to Block (1985), decisions by the Supreme Court were offset when one examined the level of funding granted to state courts to oppose the interests of juvenile offenders. Increasingly, according to Block, state court systems were able to evade the intentions of juvenile court reform through the law by having a larger share of resources to combat the interests of the juvenile. In effect, the status quo was being supported and "many gains made by the juvenile in 1969 were offset by power resources granted to the court." The idea that minimal change has actually occurred in the juvenile justice system is borne out by other research evidence.

Mahoney (1985) has discussed how the right to trial for juveniles does not increase the likelihood of a positive outcome. Instead, she argues that when compared to non-trial cases, juveniles fare no better in jury trials. In addition, she found that the use of a jury in a juvenile proceeding lengthens the trial considerably. She further argues that the "right to a jury trial for juveniles may be less a *right* to an impartial jury of peers as conceived in the Constitution, than a *ritual* with little substantive meaning" (Mahoney, 1985:564). Again, this raises questions as to the actual impact of court decisions on the processing of juveniles. More contemporary research on juvenile court processing has gone so far as to question whether status offenders (less serious offenders) are treated less formally than nonstatus offenders (more serious offenders). The evidence suggests that each is treated with the same degree of formality; status offenders are treated more harshly than their criminal counterparts when examining detention decisions, and the more serious criminal offenders receive more severe final dispositions (Marshall et al., 1983).

On the whole, therefore, it would be fair to conclude that the legal system, through court decisions, has had some impact on the system of juvenile justice in this country, at least to the degree that it has attempted to formalize the processing of juveniles in the system. Whether it has actually changed the operations of the juvenile justice system, or made the process more fair, remains to be questioned and answered by social scientists. Without a doubt, court decisions have had an impact on who becomes part of the juvenile correctional establishment of this country. It is a greater understanding of this part of the juvenile justice system that the final section of this chapter will address.

Types of Juvenile Institutions

Nonsecure Institutions

Foster homes, shelters, group homes, camps & ranches.

According to Finckenauer (1984:151-154), one can view juvenile institutions as being one of two types. First, there are *nonsecure* facilities, which are composed of institutions in which the security level is not as great as more traditional institutions. Included under this definition are the following:

Foster homes. These are home-like environments in which the juvenile lives with a family. Many foster homes are temporary in nature and are used in lieu of some type of shelter or detention facility. More often than not, the foster home is used for neglected and nonserious delinquent youths.

Shelters. Shelter is typically used for the youth who is awaiting some form of court action and is not able to reside in the family home. As mentioned by Finckenauer (1984:151), this type of facility is used for status offenders and runaways. In addition, many shelters have minimal restrictions and are used for those youths who are not security risks. There is no intention to punish the offender or to correct him or her.

Group homes. Like the previous two, a group home is a nonsecure residential facility which emphasizes treatment of the juvenile offender. Moreover, unlike the foster home, the group home does provide a structure whereby the needs of the juvenile can be addressed by the home. It, too, is a nonrestrictive and residential placement that attempts to reintegrate the juvenile offender into society. A good example of a group home is the Middlefields project opened by Dr. Harriet Hollander in North Brunswick, New Jersey in 1980. Its goal was to instill in the juvenile individual learning through a four-step Levels System in which the youth would earn points for showing responsibility and compliance with the rules and regulations of the program. Based on what is referred to as "psycho-education," this approach has its roots in "some psychological disturbance or disorder to be the cause of delinquency, and therefore employ(s) psychological and mental health correctional strategies" (Finckenauer, 1984:176).

Camps and ranches. These types of facilities are employed for those youth who have already been adjudicated by a juvenile court. In many situations, these facilities are substitutes for the more confining and restrictive conditions of reform schools or training schools. Additionally, they are non-secure in nature and are often located in rural areas. The notion behind these programs is to instill in the youth the importance of responsibility and discipline in their lives. Through participation in outdoor activities, it is hoped that the juvenile will gain some type of rehabilitative effect. A strong emphasis is placed on developing proper work habits, self-discipline, and proper interpersonal skills (Finckenauer, 1985:152). The Outward Bound program is a good example of this approach. With an emphasis on self-discipline, this approach attempts to instill a more positive self-image in the juvenile, and in addition, it is hoped that these learned behaviors can be transferred to societal living. It is this transference process that is the most critical when evaluating such a program. As suggested by Finckenauer (1984:82), this type of program may be the most effective for those juveniles who are more "action-oriented adolescents." It definitely is not for every juvenile offender. The research literature is scant at best and future evaluations will have to be completed before any definitive statements can be made about its long-term effectiveness.

Effectiveness of Nonsecure Programs for Juveniles

It is the question of effectiveness of these nonsecure programs which has received much attention in the research literature. While it is difficult to indentify any one program that is more effective than another in curbing delinquency tendencies, we can make some preliminary statements. Finckenauer (1984:210-213) does suggest that a set of conclusions can be drawn from what we know about juvenile treatment programs. His conclusions come from his own personal evaluation of many treatment programs. One type of treatment program he described emphasized *individual factors* associated with delinquency. These factors include learning disabilities and absence of supportive family relationships, irresponsible thinking and acting, and poor impulse control and low frustration tolerance.

Additionally, he examined treatment programs which emphasized *social factors* associated with delinquency. Such programs as Highfields and Higher Horizons are rooted in the belief that much of delinquency is the product of social forces independent of the individual delinquent. Fundamentally, this approach has its origin in much of the sociological literature of the 1950s which emphasized the delinquent subculture and the normative system which supported delinquent acts.

After reviewing these two types of programs, Finckenauer concludes that many of these treatment programs are eclectic in nature. In effect, there are multiple approaches being employed in many programs, and more importantly, it becomes very difficult to identify what parts of a program are actually producing an effect on delinquent behavior. Conceptually, it becomes difficult to plan efficiently and effectively one's treatment resources, not to mention the danger of "shotgunning" treatment approaches. Second, in many of the programs reviewed by Finckenauer, there were no clearly defined treatment criteria for intake purposes. As a result, a side effect of such poorly designed programs is that the wrong people are placed in the wrong programs. The long-term effects for the program and the individual are potentially disastrous. In fact, current research has suggested that this has been one of the most critical problems facing correctional treatment today (Gendreau and Ross, 1980).

Third, according to Finckenauer, is the fact that many treatment programs have poor internal operations. He suggests that a critical problem in juvenile corrections today is that many juveniles do not complete the treatment programs. Because of poor intake and classification procedures, completion rates are low for many treatment programs. In addition, low completion rates can be tied to insufficient program auditing and monitoring. It becomes very difficult to understand specific program effects on delinquents if program monitoring cannot be accomplished. Finally, Finckenauer does suggest that any successful program of juvenile intervention must have a solid staff. Juvenile corrections has suffered for years because of poorly trained and unqualified staff.

A fourth problem discussed by Finckenauer is that many treatment programs have no systematic information on the outcomes of their clients. As a result, administrators of treatment programs have no way of knowing whether or not their programs have any long-term effect on the delinquent. While they may have some information on their clients, the kinds of information which would be critical are often lacking. What program, for example, has worked with what client is crucial information for future planning purposes, yet many administrators do not have any idea of what, if any, effect their program has had on the subsequent behavior of the youth. Therefore, it would seem imperative that constant program evaluation is critical to a successful juvenile treatment program. As stated by Finckenauer (1984:213), "Research and program evaluation are necessities, not luxuries, in juvenile corrections."

Finally, Finckenauer suggests that juvenile aftercare must be an essential to any juvenile treatment program. The juvenile requires support and supervision not only from family and friends, but in addition, needs the guidance provided by agencies in the community. This includes a constant reinforcement of what was learned in the treatment program when back in the community. Juvenile aftercare is the agency that can provide this support.

Secure Institutions detention facilities, training schools, cottage systems.

While much of what has just been reviewed applies to nonsecure institutions for juveniles, there are other types of juvenile institutions which are more secure in their structure. Generally speaking, these types of institutions fall into two categories.

Detention facilities. These types of institutions are designed to keep juveniles either before or after their adjudication in the juvenile justice system. Most commonly referred to as "lockups," these institutions are secure in their structures. Juveniles placed in these institutions are those who have committed more serious crimes and cannot be placed either at home or in a less secure facility. Because of their confining nature, very little treatment is actually conducted in these institutions. Instead, the fundamental purpose is the secure handling of young offenders until some future action is taken by the juvenile court.

Training schools. These are also known as "reform schools" and more recently have been called cottage systems. The fundamental purpose of such an institution is the control of delinquent offenders. Like their counterparts in the adult correctional system, training schools have institutional security as their primary purpose. Additionally, there is a concern with treatment of juvenile offenders, but as stated by many, treatment is very difficult to achieve in such an environment. One reason is the fact that many juveniles stay for such short periods of time that it is difficult to achieve any type of treatment effect. A second reason is the confining nature of such institutions. Finckenauer, for example, (1984:166), suggests that community treatment is the best possible option for young offenders since it is less coercive, more humane, more cost-effective, more replicative, and as effective in reducing recidivism rates among juveniles when compared to institutional treatment.

Data on the numbers and types of offenders incarcerated in juvenile institutions is plentiful. Table 16.2 displays the average daily population and one-day counts for both public and private juvenile custody facilities, 1975-1985. From this table, we can make a number of interesting observations. First, of all 85,514 residents housed in the 3,036 public and private juvenile detention and correctional facilities in the country, well over 97% were juveniles. Moreover, when we compare 1975 with 1985, we see an increase of about 41% in the total number of juvenile facilities. Public facilities held about 60% of the total number of residents on the census date in 1985. Second, the average daily population in juvenile facilities increased 12% between 1975 and 1985.

Concerning the demographic characteristics of the confined juvenile populations between the years 1975-1985, we see in Table 16.3 that males constituted close to 80% of all juveniles in custody. Whites were 65% of the custodial population, while blacks were 33%, and 2% other races. In addition, well over 80% of confined juveniles are in the age group 14-17, with the average age being 15.4 years for public facilities and 14.9 years for private facilities. Finally, a vast majority (67%) were incarcerated for acts which, if committed by an adult, would be considered criminal.

This view of the juvenile offender as committing serious crime has attracted the nation's attention. This is the most notable if we focus on public juvenile facilities. According to the Office of Juvenile Justice and Delinquency Prevention (OJJDP, 1991), over 95% of all offenders in public juvenile facilities for the year 1989 were incarcerated for acts if committed by an adult would be considered a crime. Recent data suggest that these include property offenses, offenses against persons, and drug-related crime. It is clear from this data that juvenile institutionalization has become a primary alternative in dealing with juvenile offenders.

Table 16.2
Average Daily Population and One-Day Count of Residents in Juvenile
Facilities, 1975-1985

	1975	1977	1979	1983	1985	Percent change 1975-85
All facilities						
Number of residents						
One-day count						
All residents	76,576	75,297	74,113	82,272	85,514	12%
Juveniles	74,270	73,166	71,922	80,091	83,402	12
Male	57,078	57,308	57,679	64,424	66,393	16
Female	17,192	15,858	14,243	15,667	17,009	−1
Adults	2,306	2,131	2,191	2,181	2,112	−8
Number of facilities	2,151	2,592	2,576	2,900	3,036	41
Public facilities						
Number of residents						
One-day count						
All residents	49,126	45,920	45,396	50,799	51,402	5%
Juveniles	46,980	44,096	43,234	48,701	49,322	5
Male	37,926	36,921	37,167	42,182	42,549	12
Female	9,054	7,175	6,067	6,519	6,773	−25
Adults	2,146	1,824	2,162	2,098	2,080	−3
Average daily population	48,794	48,302	47,803	50,208	49,480	1
Number of facilities	874	992	1,015	1,023	1,040	19
Private facilities						
Number of residents						
One-day count						
All residents	27,450	29,377	28,717	31,473	34,112	24%
Juveniles	27,290	29,070	28,688	31,390	34,080	25
Male	19,152	20,387	20,512	22,242	23,844	24
Female	8,138	8,683	8,176	9,148	10,236	26
Adults	160	307	29	83	32	−80
Average daily population	26,740	29,611	28,566	31,685	33,121	24
Number of facilities	1,277	1,600	1,561	1,877	1,966	56

Note: One-day count data were collected on June 30, 1975; Dec. 31, 1977 and 1979; and Feb. 1, 1983 and 1985. Average daily population data for 1975 are for the annual period ending June 30, 1975. Data for 1977, 1979, 1983, and 1985 are for the calendar year.

Source: Bureau of Justice Statistics (1989). "Children in Custody, 1975-1985," p. 27. Washington, DC: U.S. Department of Justice.

Similar to the adult system, the juvenile correctional system has been asked to deal with more offenders, many of whom have committed very serious crimes. An interesting fact is that the fastest growing crime category among juveniles is alcohol and drug violations. According to OJJDP (1991:5), this crime category grew a whopping 58% when compared to 1987 figures and presently accounts for 12% of the custody population within public juvenile facilities. It is clear that juvenile institutions are places where more serious offenders are being sent, and the data indicate that this trend will continue into the forseeable future.

Research on Training Schools and Deinstitutionalization

Much of the research on juvenile institutions has emphasized two predominant themes: organizational structure and inmate social systems. We will examine these two topics and then turn to the topic of deinstitutionalization. We begin by reviewing one of the most comprehensive works ever done on juvenile institutions. In a book titled *Organization for Treatment*, Street, Vinter, and Perrow (1966) describe the organizational structures of six juvenile institutions, examining their goals and program objectives. The institutions were placed on a treatment/custody continuum.

In addition, the six institutions varied in their goals and structures. Two institutions emphasized *obedience/conformity*, two put forth the goals of *reeducation/development*, and two had primarily goals of *treatment*. Moreover, the institutions supported structures which enhanced their goals. For example, the institutions that put forth development and reeducation as their goals were places where rules were enforced, yet there was an equal concern for the education of the youth in community schools. Conversely, the two institutions that emphasized obedience and conformity had a strong commitment to custody and rule enforcement, while the treatment-designed institution promoted individual guidance to the juveniles by working with them through their confinement.

As can be expected, the differing types of institutions produced different attitudes among the juveniles. The institutions emphasizing obedience and conformity to goals engendered behaviors among the youths that were the most opposed to staff norms, not trusting of staff members, and held attitudes that were defined as antisocial. Interestingly enough, the researchers found that the level of conformity was not as high as expected, and that ironically, the juveniles exhibited behaviors that were in direct opposition to the stated goals of the institution.

The juveniles in the treatment-based institutions exhibited behavioral patterns that were the exact opposite of the custodial institution: there was greater agreement to staff norms, a more trusting attitude toward the staff members, and a genuine concern toward working out their problems. From these findings, the researchers suggested that the *structure of the institution* greatly affects the behavioral patterns exhibited by the youths being confined, and that more importantly, the way the program was organized was the treatment. In short, the degree of "social distance" between staff and juvenile inmates is largely a function of the organizational structure of the institution.

This position is further supported by more recent evidence gathered about juvenile institutions and the development of an inmate code among juveniles. Yet this more contemporary research also suggests that there is a different response to institutionalization by juvenile offenders depending upon their race. Bartollas, Miller, and Dinitz (1975, 1976) have suggested that black juvenile inmates follow a different normative code to institutionalization than their white counterparts. While an inmate code existed for all inmates, there were noticeable differences between black and white prisoners. Black inmates, for example, held the following set of norms: "exploit whites," "no forcing sex on blacks," "defend your brother," and that the "staff favor(s) whites." With respect to white inmates, the code reinforced the beliefs that "you don't trust anyone" and "everybody for himself." Moreover, the research concluded that the acceptance of the inmate code was more prevalent during the middle stages of institutionalization, when compared to initial and final stages of confinement. This position is consistent with the work done by others in adult institutions (Wheeler, 1961; see Chapter 8).

Even more contemporary research has suggested that the security levels of institutions are critical in determining the behavioral responses of juvenile offenders. Work done by Sieverdes and Bartollas (1986) indicated that there was a differential response among juveniles toward staff and peers contingent upon the security level of the institution. In their work, Sieverdes and Bartollas concluded that the greatest peer cohesion existed among residents in maximum security institutions where inmates had longer confinements and previous training school experiences. These attitudes were also prevalent in minimum security institutions where inmates' attitudes were strongly influenced by behaviors they had adopted while still in the community. Initially, these inmates viewed the staff as being helpers in gaining early release for them, but this attitude waned as time progressed and disagreement with institutional staff began to escalate.

With respect to the medium security institutions, the researchers found that increased conflict among inmates reduced an allegiance to an inmate code and feelings of hostility toward staff. This was explained by examining the populations of these types of institutions, where conflict among inmates was expected to be greater because of the heterogenous character of the institutions. The medium security institutions had serious offenders along with first-time referrals and long-term recidivists. This mixture in an institutional setting is bound to promote greater antagonism among inmates according to the researchers.

As with early research, Sieverdes and Bartollas concluded that the social distance between inmates and staff was greater in maximum security institutions than either medium or minimum security facilities. More important, they suggested that their findings have serious implications for the operations of juvenile institutions, and that future policy decisions must consider the feasibility, humaneness, and justice of juvenile institutionalization. At a minimum, we would suggest that alternative decisions concerning the proper organizational structure for juvenile institutions be generated. Some reasonable suggestions have been made with respect to adult institutions. It would seem appropriate that such ideas be applied to institutional corrections for juveniles as well. One approach that has received attention in adult institutions and is being tried in juvenile institutions is self-government.

Evaluations of self-government programs in juvenile institutions are relatively rare in the research literature, yet there has been some work done in the recent years. McNeil and Hart (1986) reported that self-government in the juvenile institution they examined was related to a reduction in aggressive behaviors among the youths. According to their procedure, self-government was designed with the following principles: the students established their own rules concerning aggressive behavior, the students monitored the violations of the rules and all rule violations were reported to a "chairman," and student-run trials to determine the guilt or innocence of the rule violator and a selection of punishment were created. The researchers suggested that this type of structural arrangement promoted "socially acceptable alternative ways of resolving conflicts" among the youths. This research, however, is by no means definitive, and future research is going to have to address some of the problems and prospects associated with self-government in juvenile institutions. At present, not enough evidence is available to determine the efficacy of this type of program on the behavior of juvenile offenders.

While some have suggested that structural modifications are required for any constructive change to occur in juvenile institutions, others have been more radical in their suggestions. One of the most drastic measures that has been advocated by a number of individuals, yet applied by only a few, is the move toward deinstitutionalization of juvenile populations. Beginning with the *deinstitutionalization* of juvenile offenders in Massachusetts in 1972, there has been strong support for such a position throughout the country. Initially created and implemented by Jerome Miller in Massachusetts, this approach to juvenile corrections held as its fundamental premise that institutions for juvenile care were of little or no value to many juvenile offenders. With this in mind, the deinstitutionalization movement gained strong support in the early 1970s and is still advocated by many who are interested in the plight of institutional youth.

The *Juvenile Justice and Delinquency Prevention (JJDP) Act of 1974*, for example, recommended that the diversion and deinstitutionaliztion of certain types of juvenile offenders, i.e., status offenders, be accomplished before the end of the calendar year 1985. In addition, the Act required that juveniles be separated from adult populations when confined. The Act also stated that for any state to receive federal funds for their delinquency programs it had to meet the requirements set forth by the legislation. While many jurisdictions have complied with the mandates set forth by the JJDP, there are still many juveniles housed in adult institutions and status offenders (see Table 16.3) still placed in juvenile institutions.

Reasons as to why so many status offenders are still being incarcerated center around two fundamental positions. The first position is that when agencies of social control decrease their influence over problem populations in society, e.g., juvenile offenders, other types of social control rise to meet the challenge. Thus, when the deinstitutionalization movement began to decrease the numbers of status offenders being incarcerated in juvenile institutions, other agencies of social control picked up the slack. Privately owned facilities began to flourish at a time when there was a decreased reliance on publicly operated institutions of confinement for juveniles (Sarri, 1981). A second position suggests that privately run facilities serve a useful purpose in controlling the "escalation" of status offenders into hard-core delinquents.

Table 16.3
Demographic Characteristics and Reason for Custody of Juveniles Held in
Public and Private Juvenile Facilities, 1975-1985

	Number of juveniles				
	1975	1977	1979	1983	1985
Public facilities	46,980	44,096	43,234	48,701	49,322
Sex					
Male	37,926	36,921	37,167	42,182	42,549
Female	9,054	7,175	6,067	6,519	6,773
Race					
White	:	27,963	26,053	27,805	29,969
Black	:	14,865	13,752	18,020	18,269
Other[a]	:	1,045	950	1,104	1,084
Not reported	:	223	2,479*	1,772	0
Ethnicity					
Hispanic	:	4,009	4,395	5,727	6,551
Non–Hispanic	:	40,087	38,839	41,202	42,771
Not reported	:	0	0	1,772	0
Age on census date					
9 years and younger			:	42	60
10–13 years	:	:	:	3,104	3,181
14–17 years	:	:	:	39,571	40,640
18–20 years	:	:	:	4,804	5,409
21 years and older	:	:	:	86	32
Not reported	:	:	:	1,094	0
Reason for custody					
Delinquent[b]	34,107	37,846	39,519	45,351	46,086
Status offender[c]	4,494	4,916	2,789	2,390	2,293
Dependent, neglected, or abused	451	706	520	383	431
Emotionally disturbed or mentally retarded[d]	9	115	56	81	81
Other[e]	7,403	84	49	129	132
Voluntarily admitted	516	429	301	367	299
Average age	:	15.3 yrs	15.3 yrs	15.4 yrs	15.4 yrs
Private facilities	27,290	29,070	28,688	31,390	34,080
Sex					
Male	19,152	20,387	20,512	22,242	23,844
Female	8,138	8,683	8,176	9,148	10,236
Race					
White	:	21,917	21,654	22,377	23,999
Black	:	6,005	5,843	7,822	9,204
Other[a]	:	1,148	1,191	916	877
Not reported	:	0	0	275	0
Ethnicity					
Hispanic	:	2,096	1,906	2,117	2,510
Non–Hispanic	:	26,974	26,782	29,273	31,570
Not reported	:	0	0	0	0
Age on census date					
9 years and younger	:	:	:	619	672
10–13 years	:	:	:	5,419	5,862
14–17 years	:	:	:	24,237	26,258
18–20 years	:	:	:	1,086	1,243
21 years and older	:	:	:	29	45
Not reported	:	:	:	0	0
Reason for custody					
Delinquent[b]	9,809	9,484	9,607	10,712	11,657
Status offender[c]	4,316	7,438	6,296	6,652	6,726
Dependent, neglected, or abused	4,844	5,296	5,031	6,625	6,917
Emotionally disturbed or mentally retarded[d]	1,913	1,739	1,383	1,594	1,851
Other[e]	529	26	167	49	76
Voluntarily admitted	5,879	5,087	6,204	5,758	6,853
Average age	:	14.9 yrs	14.9 yrs	14.9 yrs	14.9 yrs

Note: The data were collected on June 30, 1975; Dec. 31, 1977 and 1979; and Feb. 1, 1983 and 1985.
*Includes 1,976 juveniles in 51 Florida facilities for whom race data were not reported.
: Not available.
[a]Other includes American Indians, Alaska Natives, Asians, and Pacific Islanders.
[b]Criminal acts if committed by adults.
[c]Acts not criminal for adults, such as running away, truancy, and incorrigibility.
[d]1975 data represent emotionally disturbed or mentally retarded juveniles awaiting transfer to another jurisdiction.
[e]1975 data include those held pending court disposition or awaiting transfer to another jurisdiction. 1977-85 data include unknown and unspecified acts.

Source: Bureau of Justice Statistics (1989). "Children in Custody, 1975-1985," p. 39. Washington, DC: U.S. Department of Justice.

The premise operating here is that if institutions of confinement did not intervene and institutionalize young status offenders, they would move on to more serious crime. In this way, the institutionalization of youths is for their own good. Rankin and Wells (1985:179) tested this position in their analysis of a national panel of boys based on self-report measures of delinquency. They concluded that "While our results indicate that some escalation from status to delinquent offenses occurred, most boys showed patterns of offense persistence. Respondents were most likely to remain in the same offense category over time, regardless of how they were initially categorized (nonoffenders, status offenders, or delinquents) and of how the offense categories were operationalized." Additionally, while the researchers were more concerned in their research about the jurisdictional control of young offenders by the juvenile court, we can also say that to justify institutionalization of status offenders because of a perceived need to control the escalation into more serious crime by juveniles is not warranted by existing empirical evidence.

Finally, we must comment on the policy direction of many deinstitutionalization plans. Sarri (1981:36) has suggested that the move toward deinstitutionalization in many communities reflects more political and environmental pressure rather than the needs of wayward youths. Again, it seems that organizational, political, and bureaucratic needs of agencies of social control are instrumental to the process of "decarcerating" many of the problem populations in society (Scull, 1981). This idea is equally applicable to matters concerning juvenile offenders. As stated by Rothman (1980:214), "[I]n juvenile justice, as in adult justice, reforms satisfied the most humanitarian of impulses and, at the same time, some very narrow and self-interested considerations."

Summary

The purpose of this chapter was to provide the student with a basic understanding of the juvenile justice system and a specific working knowledge of the types of institutions of confinement for juvenile offenders in this country. In addition, the chapter highlighted the major cases that have had an impact on the operations of the juvenile justice system. From a review of the case law, it would be accurate to conclude that the role of the law has drastically changed over the years with respect to juvenile justice operations.

While early in the development of the juvenile justice system the law had a minimal influence on the workings of the juvenile court, this changed during the 1960s. With many courts questioning the intentions behind the *parens patriae* doctrine, there was an increase in the formalization of the juvenile justice process. This formalization gave more legal rights to the juvenile offender and made the system of juvenile justice more in line with the operations of the adult system. However, we also saw how current court decisions may be limiting the rights of juvenile offenders.

From this discussion, we examined the kinds of juvenile institutions in this country and their distinguishing characteristics. Moreover, we discussed how these institutions differed with respect to their purposes and objectives. The descriptive information provided suggested that there are a large number of juveniles being held in both public and private institutions. Moreover, a position was presented that differing institutions produce differential attitudes among juvenile offenders and that new ideas needed to be generated to deal with this population.

The ideas of self-government in juvenile institutions, and, in particular, the movement toward deinstitutionalization have been a reaction to the perceived failures of traditional programs in juvenile corrections. These rather novel approaches have been suggested as ways of making the juvenile correctional process more productive, humane, and just in its operations. Whether these approaches accomplish their objectives remains to be seen, and the role of researchers is to provide the necessary evaluations of new approaches to juvenile corrections. With this broader base of knowledge we can develop programs that are more practical and equitable to both the juvenile offender and society.

On the Defensive

Juvenile Crime:
The Offenders Are Younger
and the Offenses More Serious

Peter Applebome

Special to The New York Times

FORT WORTH—After the judge read the jury's verdict last week, the defendant looked up for an explanation to his attorney, who told him softly, "We lost."

With that, the 10-year-old boy in the blue and gray athletic jacket buried his head in his hands and began to cry. He had just been found guilty of delinquent conduct in the stabbing and beating of a 101-year-old woman in December.

The woman, a neighbor, had identified the boy as her assailant while testifying from her wheelchair in a two-day trial in juvenile court here. A jury trial, which is not usually held in juvenile cases, was conducted in open court at the request of the boy's attorney.

It was a jarring scene, but similar ones seem to be occurring with increasing frequency, according to juvenile experts around the country. They say younger children are becoming involved more often in serious criminal activity usually associated with older youths or adults.

Wary of Generalizations

Figures in juvenile crime can be elusive because much of the crime involving young children is not handled through conventional judicial channels.

Some officials say that serious crime by preteen-agers remains a minor part of the juvenile crime picture, and for that reason they are wary of generalizations about major changes in the nature of juvenile crime.

But interviews with juvenile justice officials around the country indicate that the age at which youngsters are committing serious crimes is declining steadily, and that cases that seemed like bizarre anomalies a few years ago are now becoming more common.

Crime figures compiled by the Federal Bureau of Investigation, based on reports from 11,249 agencies in 1985, reported that youths 15 years old and younger were responsible for 381 cases of murder and non-negligent manslaughter, 18,021 aggravated assaults, 13,899 robberies and 2,645 rapes. Children 12 and under were responsible for 21 of the killings, 436 of the rapes, 3,545 aggravated assaults and 1,735 robberies, the F.B.I. said.

Increase in Younger Criminals

Officials at the National Center for Juvenile Justice, a private, nonprofit research organization in Pittsburgh, said that from 1978 to 1983 the fastest-growing areas in juvenile crime were the youngest age groups. The rate of referrals to juvenile courts rose 38 percent for 12-year-olds, 37 percent for 13-year-olds, 22 percent for 11-year-olds, and 15 percent for 10-year-olds, the youngest age for which figures were available.

"Without question, all the biggest increases are in the younger ages," said Hunter Hurst, director of the center. "Once you pass 13, all the increases begin to drop."

Explanations range from increasing drug and gang activities in elementary schools, including criminal activity involving a highly potent form of cocaine, crack, to the high level of violence in the society as a whole and to increasing stress on families, particularly in poor urban areas.

Many experts say that as crime becomes more prevalent among younger teen-agers, a trickle-down effect among younger children is inevitable.

"Not only is the age dropping at which kids are

getting involved in crime, but violent crimes are being committed by younger and younger kids," said Daniel P. Dawson, chief of the juvenile division for the Ninth Circuit State Attorney's office in Orlando, Fla.

"Four or five years ago, even two or three years ago, it was very unusual to see a child younger than 12 or 13 in the system, particularly with multiple charges," he said. "Now you see kids aged 7, 8 or 9 come in with a whole string of burglaries."

Officials in the New York City area say the overall rate of juvenile crime has been decreasing for several years, and some lawyers question whether there is any documentable increase in crimes by children.

Child Abuse Up in New York

"Younger kids are more likely to be the victims than the offenders," said Janet Fink, assistant attorney in charge of the juvenile rights division of the Legal Aid Society. "It's partly a result of demographics, but in New York City the juvenile delinquency rate is down in sharp contrast to cases of child abuse and neglect, which have gone off the charts."

But judges and police officials say that while the overall number of youthful offenders may not be rising, there is no question that the severity of the crimes is increasing.

James A. Payne, chief of Family Court for New York City's Law Department, said that in 1985 the court heard 4.2 percent fewer cases than in 1984, but there was a 7.3 percent increase in serious crimes.

"A 10-year-old is now like a 13-year-old used to be," Sgt. Richard J. Paraboschi of the Newark Police Department's Youth Aid Bureau. "And the 16-year-olds are going on 40."

Guns Make a Difference

Sergeant Paraboschi said one of the biggest changes in recent years has been the dramatic increase in the number of children involved in gun incidents. Judges see the same trend.

"When I was first on the bench in 1978, if I had one gun case a year it was a lot," said Justice Richard Huttner of the State Supreme Court in Brooklyn. "Now from what I hear it's not unusual to have one or two in a week."

Justice Huttner, a former head of New York City's Family Court, added: "I don't think we see more young kids than we did, but they used to be kids arrested for stealing Twinkies from a grocery store. Now it's different. An 11- or 12-year-old is not big enough to rob most people, but with a gun it's a different story."

Judge Tom Rickhoff of San Antonio District Court, who hears only juvenile cases, said he was struck by the alarming increase in young children who have already veered toward persistent criminal behavior.

'Exceptionally Dangerous People'

"When you see a 10-year-old in your court you almost want to reach out and pat them and tell them they'll be all right, but these are exceptionally dangerous people," Judge Rickhoff said.

"I see more and more children of parents who are mentally ill or on drugs," he added. "Some of them are kids who've dropped out of school in the fourth or fifth grades. If you drop out in the fourth or fifth grade, you're dead in the United States."

Some recent cases range from a 10-year-old baby sitter in California who strangled a child she was taking care of to a recent incident in Queens in which a 12-year-old faced 27 charges, including first-degree rape, robbery, aggravated assault and grand larceny, in a case that also involved another 12-year-old and an adult.

Of particular worry nationwide is the increasing drug use in elementary schools, especially the use of crack and of such inhalants as paint or glue. Officials say that although the national incidence of drug use is decreasing, its use by children is increasing dramatically.

"Drug use used to be a decision of adolescence," said Mr. Hurst of the juvenile justice center in Pittsburgh. "Now it's a fourth-grade decision."

Mr. Payne of New York's Family Court said drug use was part of the reason for a marked increase in violent activity by younger juveniles in recent years. Drugs accounted for 4.2 percent of all juvenile arrests in 1985 and 6.8 percent last year, he said.

"We've had almost a 50 percent increase in drug crime," Mr. Payne continued. "Crack is the main reason. We are seeing kids as young as 10 or 11. They can make $800 a week. They only stay in school because that's where their constituency is."

In other areas of the country gangs are blamed for a major impact on juvenile crime. Officials in California say the average age of gang members is steadily dropping as older children bring in younger ones.

"We have a great number of gang children," said Ron W. Hayes, deputy director of Prevention and Community Corrections for the California Department of the Youth Authority. "There are about 500 gangs and about 50,000 members. You put drugs and gang behavior together and you get violent behavior."

Implications are Troubling

Officials say the implications of a lowering of juvenile crime ages are extremely troubling.

One problem, officials say is that the juvenile justice system is poorly equipped to deal with young children committing serious crimes. Beyond that, any lowering of the age at which young people begin to commit crimes has ominous implications for the overall crime rate.

"We've considered the prime criminal activity years to be from 16 or 17 to 22 or 23," said Mr. Dawson, the Ninth Circuit State Attorney's official in Orlando. "Now we're seeing increases in crime not because of population shifts in that age group, but because there's more crime involving young kids. If you expand that bell curve in which you see the most crime down to 13 or 14, the total crime rate is going to skyrocket."

One aspect of juvenile crime that is being treated with increasing concern is the racial issue. The nation's crime rate has dropped since the 1970s, primarily because there are fewer youths in the prime criminal ages.

Demographers say that the trends are now becoming more worrisome, and that the bulk of the increase among juveniles will involve those who are members of minority groups.

In 1965, 50 percent of the inmates of youth facilities operated by the California State Youth Authority were white, 19.7 percent were Hispanic and 28 percent were black. In 1986 25.3 percent of the inmates were white, 32 percent were Hispanic and 39 percent were black.

"There has been a rise in the crime rate," said Dr. Alfred Blumstein, dean of the School of Urban and Political Affairs at Carnegie-Mellon University in Pittsburgh. "And it come[s] at a time when there should be a decline."

Changes in Juvenile Laws

"What we may be seeing is a disproportionate number of children who are coming from the underclass, which has had higher fertility rates than the middle class," Dr. Blumstein continued. "We may be seeing the children of the middle class baby boom and the grandchildren of the underclass."

The juvenile justice system has been trying for years to cope with the steady drop in the age of criminal activity, and officials say the nation is slowly changing the way it looks at juvenile offenders. In New York for example, the Juvenile Offender Law of 1978 made it possible for 14- and 15-year-olds charge[d] with serious felonies and 13-year-olds charged with murder to be tried in adult courts.

Roland Henley was one of the jurors in the case of the 10-year-old boy charged with delinquent conduct in the attack on the 101-year-old Fort Worth woman. The boy, whose mother and father have served prison terms, faces sentencing this week that could include placement in state youth facilities until he is 21.

Asked why the jury deliberated for two hours, Mr. Henley replied, "I just wanted to be fair to the man."

A Downward Trend for Juvenile Crime

To the Editor:

An old and popular myth is that today's young people are worse than those of previous generations. It was reinforced by your Feb. 3 article on juvenile crime in the United States, which concludes that offenders are younger and the offenses more serious. You presented interesting statistics, but other pertinent facts support different conclusions.

Most important, arrests of juveniles declined steadily from the mid-1970s until 1984, when the Federal Bureau of Investigation reported the first modest increase in juvenile arrests in more than 10 years. Juvenile arrests for serious crimes in 1985 were 21 percent less than in 1976. This drop was primarily due to the declining number of teen-agers in the U.S. The arrest rate per 100,000 youths makes the 1985 juvenile-crime rate quite similar to that of 1976.

The data show little change in the number of arrests of those younger than 15 (the focus of the alleged crime wave). For example, their 1985 arrest rates for murder, robbery and aggravated assault were similar to rates a decade ago. Arrest rates of children for burglary in 1985 were way down, compared with 1976.

The one area of increase was for the crime of rape. Between 1976 and 1985, arrests of juveniles and adults for rape climbed dramatically. Some of this increase may be attributed to the greater likelihood of victims to report rape and more aggressive law-enforcement efforts.

Court-referral data are highly dependent on juvenile-justice policies. Thus, if there are fewer community programs, more arrested youths will be sent to court. These data are more an indication of public policies attempting to "get tough" with lawbreakers.

Indeed, in the last decade, as juvenile arrests have dropped, the number of incarcerated youths has increased dramatically. The juvenile-justice system has become more restrictive, formal and oriented toward punishment than rehabilitation. Research evidence strongly indicates that expanded incarceration of juveniles does not protect public safety and may actually increase rates of serious youth crime.

Barry Krisberg
President, National Council
on Crime and Delinquency
San Francisco, Feb. 5, 1987

Key Terms and Concepts

adjudicatory hearing

adjudicatory inquiry

camps

deinstitutionalization

detention facilities

detention hearing

discretionary authority

disposition hearing

foster homes

functional interpretation

groups homes

individual factors

intake screening

Juvenile Justice and Delinquency
   Prevention Act of 1974 (JJDP)

Office of Juvenile Justice and
   Delinquency Prevention (OJJDP)

parens patriae

petition

radical interpretation

ranches

shelters

social factors

training schools

References

Bartollas, C., S.J. Miller and S. Dinitz (1975). "The Informal Code in a Juvenile Institution: Guidelines for the Strong." *Journal of Southern Criminal Justice*, Volume 1, Number 1:33-52.

Bartollas, C., S.J. Miller and S. Dinitz (1976). *Juvenile Victimization: The Institutional Paradox*. New York, NY: Halstead Press.

Bell, D., Jr. and K. Lang (1985). "The Intake Dispositions of Juvenile Offenders." *Journal of Research in Crime and Delinquency*, Volume 22, Number 4:309-328.

Block, K.J. (1985). "Balancing Power Through Law: The State v. The Juvenile in Delinquency Proceedings." *Justice Quarterly*, Volume 2, Number 4:535-552.

Empey, L. (1982). *American Delinquency: Its Meaning and Construction, Revised Edition*. Homewood, IL: The Dorsey Press.

Fenwick, C.R. (1982). "Juvenile Court Intake Decision-Making: The Importance of Family Affiliation." *Journal of Criminal Justice*, Volume 10, Number 6:443-454.

Finckenauer, J.O. (1984). *Juvenile Delinquency: The Gap Between Theory and Practice*. Orlando, FL: The Academic Press and Harcourt, Brace & Jovanovich.

Gendreau, P. and R.R. Ross (1980). *Effective Correctional Treatment*. Toronto, Canada: Butterworth Publishers.

Kittrie, N.N. (1974). *The Right to be Different*. Baltimore, MD: Penguin Books.

Mahoney, A.R. (1985). "Jury Trial for Juveniles: Right or Ritual?" *Justice Quarterly*, Volume 2, Number 4:553-566.

Marshall, C.E., I.H. Marshall and C.W. Thomas (1983). "The Implementation of Formal Procedures in Juvenile Court Processing Of Status Offenders." *Journal of Criminal Justice*, Volume 11, Number 3:195-212.

McNeil, J.K. and D.S. Hart (1986). "The Effect of Self-Government on the Aggressive Behavior of Institutionalized Delinquent Adolescents." *Criminal Justice and Behavior*, Volume 13, Number 4:430-445.

Nejelski, P. (1976). "Diversion: Unleashing the Hound of Heaven?" In Rosenheim (ed.) *Pursuing Justice for the Child*. Chicago, IL: University of Chicago Press.

Office of Juvenile Justice and Delinquency Prevention (1991). "Public Juvenile Facilities: Children in Custody 1989." Washington, DC: U.S. Department of Justice.

Platt, A.M., H. Schechter and P. Tiffany (1971). "In Defense of Youth: A Case of the Public Defender in Juvenile Court." In D. Hopson, et al. (eds.) *The Juvenile Offender and the Law*. New York, NY: De Capo Press.

Platt, A.M. (1977). *The Child Savers: The Invention of Delinquency, Second Edition, Enlarged*. Chicago, IL: University of Chicago Press.

Rankin, J.H. and L.E. Wells (1985). "From Status to Delinquent Offenses: Escalation?" *Journal of Criminal Justice*, Volume 13, Number 2:171-180.

Rothman, D.J. (1980). *Conscience and Convenience: The Asylum and Its Alternatives in Progressive America*. Boston, MA: Little, Brown and Company.

Sarri, R.C. (1981). "The Effectiveness Paradox—Institutional vs. Community Placement of Offenders." *Journal of Social Issues*, Volume 37, Number 3:34-50.

Scull, A.T. (1977). *Decarceration: Community Treatment and the Deviant—A Radical View*. Englewood Cliffs, NJ: Prentice-Hall Publishing Company.

Sieverdes, C.M. and C. Bartollas (1986). "Security Level and Adjustment Patterns in Juvenile Institutions." *Journal of Criminal Justice*, Volume 14, Number 2:135-146.

Staples, W.G. (1987). "Law and Social Control in Juvenile Justice Dispositions." *Journal of Research in Crime and Delinquency*, Volume 24, Number 1:7-22.

Street, D., R. Vinter and C. Perrow (1966). *Organization for Treatment*. New York, NY: The Free Press.

Sutton, J.R. (1985). "The Juvenile Court and Social Welfare—Dynamics of Progressive Reform." *Law & Society Review*, Volume 19, Number 1:107-145.

Wheeler, S. (1961). "Socialization in Correctional Communities." *American Sociological Review*, Volume 26, October:697-712.

Table of Cases

Breed v. Jones, 421 U.S. 519 (1975)

Ex parte Crouse, 4 Wharton 9 (Pa. 1838)

Fare v. Michael C., 442 U.S. 707 (1979)

In re Gault, 38 U.S. 1 (1967)

In re Winship, 397 U.S. 358 (1970)

Kent v. United States, 383 U.S. 541 (1966)

McKiever v. Pennsylvania, 403 U.S. 548 (1971)

New Jersey v. T.L.O., 105 S. Ct. 733 (1975)

Schall v. Martin, 35 Cr. L. 3103 (1984)

Photo Credit: Tony O'Brien, Frost Publishing Group, Ltd.

Female
Corrections

17

After reading this chapter, the student should be able to:

- Discuss the history of women's institutions.

- Describe women's institutions.

- List and discuss problems associated with women's institutions.

Introduction

No other offender in the criminal justice system has been so systematically neglected than the female offender. Much of the research literature and descriptions of the criminal justice system center on the role of men. No one doubts that men are at the focus of criminal justice operations. This is no more apparent than in the corrections component of the criminal justice system.

Of the 680,000 people incarcerated in this country, roughly 640,000 are men. Women only account for about 40,000 offenders, or 7% of those offenders incarcerated today (Bureau of Justice Statistics, 1990). Despite these small numbers, women are still part of the corrections component and deserve serious attention among academicians, correctional policymakers, and the public. Pollock-Byrne (1990) has stated that there are three basic characteristics of women's institutions.

First, they are smaller than prisons for men. There are no mega-prisons (over 1,000 inmates) for women in this country. Most are very small, housing anywhere from 200 to 300 prisoners. Second, there are fewer women's prisons than men's prisons. Most states in this country either have only one facility for women or contract with another state or the federal system to house their inmates. Finally, and most importantly, these institutions are markedly different than men's prisons. Whether one examines their history, or the methods with which female prisoners adapt to their incarceration experience, there are noticeable differences.

More than just noting them, however, we must use a different set of assumptions about female offenders and practical implications for how women's institutions are run. It is without question that the understanding and management of these facilities has been dominated by those methods found to be the most conducive to men's institutions. Yet, many of these methods are totally unacceptable toward the effective operation of women's facilities. Again, whether one is talking about prison programming, or health care needs, as examples, the needs of women offenders are much different from their male counterparts.

Therefore, the purpose of this chapter is to address many issues pertaining to the female offender, with a particular emphasis on female correctional institutions. We will be examining issues such as the history of women offenders in American society, the contemporary female prison, including information on the size of the inmate population, social structure of the female prison, and prison programming for women to mention a few, problems with female prisons, and other salient issues that face female offenders.

Our focus is not simply a comparison between men's prisons and women's prisons. Instead, we seek to examine the needs of women in their own light. It is our opinion, as that of other writers (Pollock-Byrne, 1990:153), that past attempts to understand female criminality and female institutions have relied on the measurement of male performance. We seek to view female offenders and female institutions on their own terms.

It is without question that there are some similarities between male and female offenders and their abilities to adapt to the incarceration experience. Nevertheless, too often these similarities have been used as justifications to deny female offenders the practical programs and treatment modalities because they do not "measure up" to the standard created by men. We view this to be counterproductive to aiding the female offender. Our intention here is not to downplay either similarities or differences, but instead, to view female offenders in a light that gives them legitimacy.

Once legitimacy is granted, then more effective questions about policy and programmatic concerns can be addressed. Historically, we have treated the female offender in a way that has demeaned her and not created the climate in which effective change can take place in her life. The history of how the female offender was treated by those in charge of society is one of indifference. While, on the whole, the male offender was to be punished for his transgressions, the female offender was to be saved. How she was to be saved is the history of women's institutions in America.

History of Women's Institutions

The history of women's institutions in this country is rooted in the practices of early England. Many of the later practices to be incorporated into the treatment and confinement of female offenders were directly tied to ideas created by the English. In fact, the overriding ideas of how women were to be treated was not only English in origin, but in addition, was influenced by the belief in fundamental differences between male and female offenders.

As Dobash, Dobash, and Gutteridge (1986) have stated, many of the early conceptions of female offenders rested on the notion that women were morally weak, in relation to male offenders, and in need of more direct methods of supervision and control. On the one hand, the female offender was viewed as less culpable than the male offender; on the other hand, the irony of the situation was that this meant more control and the justification of all sorts of brutality, all in the name of saving her.

As such, many of the early practices imposed on female offenders were very cruel and often took place under the supervision of male jailers. Moreover, prior to their incarceration, women in society were considered the chattels of men, and this meant that if the women were not respectful of their husbands, the men had the option of sending their wives to either a poorhouse or a monastery. Once removed from the home, the woman often had to fend for herself. This translated into abject poverty for many women and a life of crime as a method to survive (Pollock-Byrne, 1990:38).

These methods of survival meant such criminal activities as theft or begging. More often than not this led toward the institutionalization of many women for rather trivial offenses. This pattern has continued into contemporary times. Many institutionalized women today have committed property crimes, sexual crimes (such as prostitution), and drug offenses. So, from the beginning, women were left out of the mainstream of society, but in relation to institutionalization, were also viewed as morally bankrupt and deserving of very severe punishments. What did these punishments translate into in practice?

There are many accounts that have described the plight of women who had fallen from the good grace of society. With everything from public floggings to the placement of an iron cage over the head of the female offender to prevent her from talking, early punishments were harsh. These punishments were intended to make the woman more obedient and subservient to the wishes of her husband (Dobash et al., 1986:23). If these proved to be ineffective in bringing the woman into line, then more severe measures were taken. Institutionalization represented society's worst form of punishment and correction for women.

Early types of prisons or reformatories for women were typically sections of prisons for men, reserved for women. This arrangement did not work well for too long, as the abuse of women by male correctional staff was common, along with the indifference paid to women's needs by a male society. Typically, men and women were housed together, and there was no goal of separation of the sexes. This meant that the women were usually at the mercy of the stronger and more violent male offenders. Even when institutions began requiring the separation of male and female offenders, the women did not fare much better (Pollock-Byrne, 1990:39).

It was truly a system in which women were not only sent to prison or reformatories for less serious offenses when compared to men, but in addition, once incarcerated, these women were usually under the control of men who abused them, and very little was done to improve their situations. When states in the middle part of the eighteenth century started to separate male and female offenders, women were also neglected. They were not viewed as important enough to deserve any modicum of care from their keepers, all of whom were men.

As a result, whether they were separate sections of men's prisons, or institutions for women, they lagged far behind men's institutions with respect to general treatment. This is not to imply that male institutions were nice places to reside—they were not. Nevertheless, places where women were incarcerated were much worse when compared to men's institutions and not much productive activity was done with the women. As Rafter (1985) reports, many of the early institutions of confinement for women, particularly in the South and the West, were places where very little was done, even though the numbers of women coming to those institutions were steadily increasing throughout the middle part of the nineteenth century.

In short, women were neglected, even as more of them became institutionalized. This same general attitude of "benign neglect" exists in many states today. In fact, we will find out later how this neglect has led to legal steps on the part of women to achieve parity and equality with male institutions. For now, we can conclude that the early treatment and confinement of women was controlled by men, that it lacked any substantive programming, and that it exhibited poor conditions in comparison to male institutions. These faults, along with a growing concern among some reformers about how women were treated in institutions run by men, led to the development of the reformatory movement by women for women.

The Reformatory Movement and Female Corrections

In the latter part of the nineteenth century in America, there was a growing concern about the role of the prison in society. Many reformers, including the Progressives, sought a better system of institutionalization for prisoners (Rothman, 1980). While male institutions had become firmly entrenched within the existing correctional repertoire, ideas on how institutions for women were to be run were lacking. Many of the ideas on incarceration were molded to fit the needs of men, with very little concern for women prisoners. Most important, however, was the belief among women reformers that the female institution should be run by women and for women.

This idea was most forcefully expressed by Elizabeth Fry. Being concerned that women's prisons were places where male superintendents could coerce and exploit women, Fry, in England, and other reformers in America fought for the idea that women's institutions should be run by women. She advocated women superintendents (known as warders) for three specific reasons. First, they would prevent sexual abuse by male guards. Second, they would set "moral examples" of true womanhood for the female offenders. Finally, they could provide a sympathetic ear for female inmates (Pollock-Byrne, 1990:41).

With these ideas in mind, reformers in the middle part of the nineteenth century sought to transform the institutional experiences of female offenders. They viewed themselves as individuals who could serve as an advocate for women who had fallen from grace. In addition, they sought the development of specific institutions for women. These institutions were to be places where "feminine values" could be instilled in the offenders. Hence, the reformatory movement for women became a reality and part of the correctional system of many states.

Taking the lead of many private institutions for women created in the 1830s in America, the public institutions for women were not commonplace until the latter part of the nineteenth century. States like Indiana (Women's Prison, 1873), Massachusetts (Reformatory Prison for Women, 1877), and New York (House of Refuge for Women, 1887) were the first to erect publicly run institutions for women. Soon after, other states joined and by the middle part of the 1970s virtually all 50 states had at least one institution for women. Pollock-Byrne (1990:44) argues that four factors led toward the development of women's prisons in America.

First, there was an increase in criminality among women during the period of the Civil War. Offenses such as prostitution and abortion were offenses that could result in incarceration. Second, the women's Civil War social service experience. Third, the simultaneous development of the charities organization movement and of prison reform which emphasized criminality and the realization of the reformatory ideal. Fourth, the initial development of the feminist ideal and the role of women in society.

Couple all these factors together and the reformatory movement for women became an ideal for many prison reformers. What were these reformatories like? Like the hopes of reform in early men's prisons, there were hopes of reform in women's prisons. Yet the reality often overshadowed any true reform efforts. In fact, while many of these institutions were different from the institutions for men where early female offenders were housed, the fact was that they were not much better in their operation or treatment of women.

With the changeover in the staff from very devoted and religious-minded reformers to a cadre of "professional administrators," the reformatories for women exhibited some of the insensitivities and abuses that were so common in men's institutions. Rafter (1985:77) writes of how these professionally run institutions had inadequate resources and lacked programs. Staff abuse, in the form of physical punishments, was prevalent, and the reformatories for women started to experience the problems often thought to be exclusive to men's institutions. More importantly, many of these early reformatories for women were used to morally educate women and to segregate black and white offenders.

Rafter (1985:126) describes two different types of institutions for women, each with differing purposes and offenders. While the reformatory was used for primarily young, white, female offenders, the custodial institution was used to house offenders who were older (between the ages of 30 and 50) and nonwhite (black). Even though black women were disproportionately represented in prison commitments, they were not to be found in large numbers in reformatories for women. Instead, many were housed in the custodial institutions, which, on the whole, were much worse when compared to the reformatories. Black female offenders who were confined to reformatories were usually segregated from the mainstream women's population and housed in cottages (Rafter, 1985:37).

It is without question that the early reformatory movement for women did improve the lot of many female offenders, yet it would be shortsighted to suggest that fulfillment of the needs of women improved dramatically under this movement. Nevertheless, the plight of women caught in the criminal justice system started to be recognized among both reformers and society. No longer was the female offender institutionalized under the sole direction of male penal philosophy. Beginning in the late nineteenth century and well into the twentieth century, we saw the incremental improvement of the female offender's condition in the prison setting.

While the conditions of women offenders improved on the whole during the reformatory movement, what remained was a legacy of presumed differences between male and female offenders. Coupled with the belief that women were different from men, they needed "domestic training," and they were not so much criminal as sexually immoral, the reformatory movement framed a consciousness that was to hold back progress in the treatment of female offenders up until the present day (Pollock-Byrne, 1990:54). Somewhat ironically, while the reformatory movement for women improved the conditions under which women experienced incarceration, it also set up a philosophy that was to enslave them.

It is without question that the student reviewing female correctional history has the advantages of hindsight. Early reformers did not have the benefits of modern technology and health systems and all truly believed that they were aiding the female offender. They made due with what was available. Their philosophy toward female corrections was filled with good intentions; nonetheless, the cumulative results produced many unintentional and harmful effects. What is injurious to the female offender today is this philosophy of the past that still entraps many correctional systems. It is the critical examination of this philosophy that current reformers of women's prisons are addressing. We will discuss how this is being done today later in the chapter. We now turn our attention to the workings of the contemporary women's prison.

Contemporary Women's Institutions

Size of Female Prison Population

According to the Bureau of Justice Statistics (1990:79), the U.S. prison population has reached an all-time high of slightly under 700,000 prisoners. When one compares the rates of growth between male and female offenders, female offenders are outdistancing their male counterparts. In the first six months of 1989, the number of female prisoners grew 13%, compared to an increase of 7% for male prisoners. This trend began in the early 1980s and is continuing. Since 1980 the number of female prisoners has increased 175%, while the number of male prisoners has risen 101%.

While the total number of female prisoners as of 1989 has increased to just below 40,000, compared to roughly 640,000 male prisoners, the rapid increase has caused many to question why the number of female prisoners has grown at such a fast rate. The reasons for such growth underlie our understanding of female crime and the contemporary female prisoner and women's prisons. These reasons reflect our understanding of female criminality and society's response to it. Four reasons can be explored as to the growth of female crime and the rate of imprisonment among women (Pollock-Byrne, 1990:20-32).

First, some have suggested that female crime can be traced to the women's liberation movement. The argument claims that with increased opportunities among women come increased opportunities to commit crime. This line of reasoning suggests that women are becoming more like men, and as a result, one would expect increases in crime among women. The research evidence on the connection between female liberation and criminality is weak at best. While some do suggest a connection between female criminality, especially property crime, and female liberation (Simon, 1975), the more recent evidence shows a very weak, if not nonexistent, connection (Giordana and Cernkovich, 1979; Bowker, 1981; and Weisheit, 1984). In fact, many have suggested that studies explaining female crime due to the women's liberation movement suffer from many stereotypes and methodological weaknesses (Naffine, 1987).

A second explanation for the increase in female crime is one of a statistical interpretation. This view holds that the increase in female crime is not all that great in *real numbers* when compared to men. While the Uniform Crime Reports have shown an increase for women in every major category except murder and nonnegligent manslaughter between 1978 and 1987, the fact remains that the *percentage* increases mask the reality that for most offenses the numbers are quite low. When it is argued that female crime has exploded over the past 10 years, one needs to interpret this statement cautiously.

For example, when exploring the Crime Index total for the period of 1978-1987, we see an increase in arrests of 15.8% for men while arrests for women increased a total of 25.5%. This, on the surface, would suggest a large increase in female crime. Yet, a closer inspection of the real numbers reveals men outnumbering women by more than three to one (1,584,596 arrests for men versus 438,187 arrests for women). Increases in the number of arrests among women is misleading unless one breaks down the aggregate statistics. Increases in the aggregate crime figures for the period hide the fact there are huge increases in some categories, for example, drug usage, while in other categories such as violent crime, the numbers have stayed relatively stable (Pollock-Byrne, 1990:29). Without identifying the differences across crime categories, we are left with a picture of female crime that is inaccurate.

Another explanation of female crime is rooted in both psychology and biology. This explanation suggests that female crime can be tied either to the psychological makeup of the female offender or to biological processes, such as menstruation and menopause. Both of these views have been discarded by many contemporary writers. Much of this research has not been able to isolate the specific conditions under which some women become criminal and others do not. As Pollock-Byrne (1990:20) has suggested, any adequate theory of female criminality is going to have to explain both why women commit crime, but in addition, why they commit it less often when compared to men. Neither a psychological nor a biological approach is capable of addressing this issue. As such, this psychological/biological explanation generally has been discounted by contemporary researchers.

A final explanation suggests the role of both opportunity and socialization as strong factors in female criminality. Under this view, crime among women is caused by the limited opportunities available to them and the differing kinds of socialization experiences found between boys and girls. While boys have more free time and are socialized into activities that support criminal pursuits, young girls are often socialized into being good housewives and traditionally domestic. This form of socialization limits opportunities for crime, regardless of age. Thus, one would expect female crime to be related to those activities in which women are given greater opportunities and are reinforced through a specific socialization process. Crimes such as shoplifting, forgery, and passing bad checks are not only the most common female offenses but are also consistent with the traditional social role of women (Pollock-Byrne, 1990:22).

Regardless of the cause, it is clear that female offenders are becoming more commonplace within American correctional institutions. These women, on the whole, are involved in crime for many reasons. Yet, the current research evidence does point to the fact that for many of them crime is rooted in denied opportunities and faulty socialization. Couple this reality with the fact that society has gotten tougher on crime, both male and female, and it is apparent why overcrowding is a problem in our institutions today. If this current research is correct, then the female offender should have some identifiable qualities. Before examining the characteristics of female prisons, we need to thoroughly explore qualities of the female offender to see how, if at all, they influence the delivery of services to women within correctional institutions.

Characteristics of Female Offenders

Research on female offenders has blossomed over the past 10 years. Much of the early work on female offenders has focused on demographic profiles. Beginning with the work of Glick and Neto (1977), we find that the common characteristics of female offenders are the following: most are poor, disproportionately represented by black women, a vast majority have children, with many having more than one child, and drugs and alcohol are significant problems in their lives. This picture, painted over a decade ago, has not changed much into the 1980s and probably will not change significantly into the 1990s and beyond.

Current research by Crawford (1990) found similar results to the Glick and Neto survey. The results indicate that black women are still disproportionately represented in state prison populations (36%). Overrepresentation of Hispanic women is also a problem (15%). In addition, only one-fifth were married, with over 80% being either divorced or never married. Only 40% had graduated from high school or attained some type of equivalence degree. Additionally, more than 80% had at least one child. So, since the original Glick and Neto survey, the characteristics of female offenders have not changed much. Many of these women exhibit characteristics that make them noncompetitive in society. Thus, it would be expected that many commit economic crimes. This fact is borne out by the data, when one examines crimes among female offenders.

36% African-Am.
15% hispanic.
80% divorced/
    single.
less than 1/2
had HS dip.
more than 80%
had at least 1
child.

Studies vary slightly as to the types of crime women commit that lead to imprisonment. Goetting and Howsen (1983), for example, found that 49% of their sample had committed violent crimes, 39% property crimes, 10% drug-related offenses, and 2% public order offenses. Similar to research on male offenders, the most serious female offenders are incarcerated. Additionally, with public demand for tougher sentences for serious offenders and those involved in drugs, we should expect more women to go to prison for longer periods of time. As stated earlier, drug offenses among female offenders are increasing and this will have an impact on the female prison population. Finally, we should clear up a misconception held among many about the female offender.

over 1/2 violent
    crime.
39% property
10% drug
2% pub. order

While official measures of crime, like the Uniform Crime Reports, suggest that well over 80% of the offenses that women are arrested for are property offenses, a majority of the offenses for which women are imprisoned are of a serious nature. The misconception is that the female prison population is simply composed of property offenders. This is not the case. While we said earlier that many women commit crimes for the reasons of denied opportunities and poor socialization, the crimes that warrant incarceration are very serious, and those who commit the most serious crimes are generally the ones who are imprisoned. As such, one can say that a majority of female offenders are arrested for relatively minor offenses, but those who are incarcerated are the more serious offenders.

Social Structure of Female Prisons

Like their male counterparts, female prisoners develop their own social structure during incarceration. While research on the experiences of male prisoners is plentiful, similar research about the experiences of women who are incarcerated is limited. Nonetheless, there has been some seminal research on the social structure of women's prisons, the socialization of women behind bars, and the application of the prisonization concept to the experiences of incarcerated women.

Most of the research has concluded that women experience and adjust to incarceration much differently than do men. Much of the research, however, is dated, and as a result, our understanding of how women "do time" is limited. In spite of the limited research, there are some things that we can comment on with respect to social structure and female prisons.

First, the inmate code, as described in Chapter 8, is not as prevalent or as powerful in women's prisons when compared to men's prisons. Various reasons have been posited as to why this situation exists, yet the fact remains that women are not as committed to an inmate code as described by the early research on men and prison. While there may be a set of norms that guide the behavior of incarcerated women, the power with which a code is adopted and accepted by female prisoners is limited. One example in which a tenet of the male inmate code is not as readily accepted by women prisoners deals with interactions with correctional staff. The inmate code for men has strong proscriptions against such behavior, while such a tenet is not common within women's institutions (Pollock-Byrne, 1990:131).

Second, the argot roles for women are noticeably different when compared to men's institutions. Sykes' (1958) description of real men, toughs, politicians, merchants, and the like are not as common in women's institutions. Research has suggested, however, that certain roles do exist among female prisoners. Both Giallombardo (1966) and Heffernan (1972) describe role types that both are similar and different to the roles found by Sykes in male prisons. Giallombardo, for example, describes snitchers, jive bitches, rap buddies, and boosters. Heffernan, in addition, describes three role types that are similar to the subcultural types examined in Chapter 8.

Heffernan's descriptions of the "square," "cool," and "the life" are very similar to the subcultural adaptations of "square," "thief," and "con" as described by Irwin and Cressey (1962). Heffernan's research suggests and supports an importation concept of inmate socialization among female prisoners. Additionally, Heffernan's research supports the idea that the three role types among female prisoners react differently to the prison experience. This is consistent with research in male institutions where adaptation to prison and the acceptance of the inmate code is dependent upon role type (Wheeler, 1962).

Heffernan "Square", "Cool", "Life."

Current research by Mahan (1984) also suggests that the inmate code may exist to some degree in women's institutions. Specific tenets of the traditional inmate code may be found among female prisoners. In particular, proscriptions against "ratting" and "taking care of oneself" are of importance to many female prisoners. What does differ is the degree to which violence is used to support these tenets. While violence is fairly common in men's institutions (see Chapter 10), the same is not true in institutions for women. Thus, what is exhibited is some allegiance to specific elements of the inmate code and a reluctance to use force to enforce the code.

Third, the social organization of women's prisons is much different when compared to men's institutions. Pollock-Byrne (1990:135-138) suggests that the social organization of women's institutions differs in three areas. First, while racial gangs and racial violence may be common in men's prisons, such is not the case in women's prisons. Most of the research on race relations in women's prisons is limited, yet it does support the idea that integration, not segregation, is the norm. Second, while inmate leaders in male prisons are often fragmented, usually on racial and gang dimensions, such is not the case with respect to leaders in women's prisons. More often than not these leaders occupy roles found within family structures. As such, leaders are usually those individuals who assume the traditional male role in the family setting of the prison. These women are fulfilling the role as defined by the social organization of "kinship" relationships in prison. Finally, much of the social organization in the women's prison centers around families, pseudofamilies, friendships, and homosexual liasons. The allegiance of women to these families is on the emotional and personal dimensions. As a result, we would expect these kinship relationships to be small and rather closely grouped.

Fourth and finally, the presence of pseudofamilies is extremely important to many women who are incarcerated. The pseudofamily is one in which the traditional roles of the family on the outside are reinforced within the context of the prison. This includes the father role, the mother role, the child role, and parent-sibling relationships. With female prisoners assuming these roles, a pseudofamily is formed. Why do these families exist and how common are they in women's prisons? Remember, the inmate code for men reinforces independence and the belief in going one's own way. Our discussion in Chapter 8 highlighted the concept of "niches" and how male inmates form such groupings to meet their needs. The analog to the niche in the female prison is the pseudofamily. This family, more often than not, serves the purpose of supporting the inmate during her incarceration experience. More importantly, the pseudofamily's role in shaping the prison experience for women varies.

Current research has suggested that the degree to which these pseudofamilies influence women has changed over time. No longer is it appropriate to view the pseudofamily as the only way in which women adapt to the prison environment. Fox (1984) underscores this fact when he states that the presence of the pseudofamily is not as common today as it was in earlier days. Today, there are many more programs available to women, and outside groups can access the prison much more easily. As such, women prisoners are able to maintain some type of relationship with others much more so than in the past. This has decreased the reliance on the pseudofamily as a mechanism of adaptation. As with male institutions and niche development, the degree to which an individual adopts the social organization of the pseudofamily is contingent upon her needs and how the pseudofamily can meet those needs.

Programs and Services in Women's Prisons

Much of the programming available within women's prisons is quite dismal. As we stated earlier, the women's prison often suffered from the stereotypes of female offenders as being either lazy or incapable of taking charge of their lives. Positive role models, as defined by men, often meant that programming in women's prisons inculcated upon women the virtues of domestic work. Since the beginning of women's prisons in this country, the domestication of women has guided programming. Women were to be taught the roles of housekeepers and mothers. Prison programming was not intended to do any more.

Even today much of the programming found in women's prisons accentuates the domestic role for the female offender. We will find later how this role is unsuitable for most female offenders, that it further places female offenders in situations that do not promote fairness or long-term positive change among them. Nevertheless, the domestic-based programming that occurs within women's facilities is the most common. Pollock-Byrne (1990:88-89) has identified five major categories of programming within prisons.

First, there are maintenance programs in women's prisons. Like their male counterparts, women prisoners become involved in clerical programs, food service, and general cleaning jobs. More often than not these programs have more women seeking them than there are jobs available. Many women who enter into these programs have waited a long time before they were actually given the jobs. Because there are too few jobs, most women who seek these positions are turned away. Second, there are educational programs for women. Again, like male prisoners, many female prisoners have some type of educational deficiency. Third, there are vocational programs in women's prisons. Many of these programs are rooted in traditional "female" positions, such as clerical training or cosmetology programs. The fourth type of programming focuses on change or personal rehabilitation of the female offender. Such programs as drug and alcohol therapies and psychological treatment programs fall under this rubric. Finally, the fifth area of programming found in women's prisons deals with medical care. Because of the special needs of women prisoners, many of these types of programs are essential in prison.

Figure 17.1
"Washboard Rehabilitation"

Washboard rehabilitation
House of Correction offers few opportunities over long haul

By PATRICK JASPERSE
of The Journal staff

Michelle Denice Jones' rehabilitation program consists of cleaning bathrooms, watching TV, eating and sleeping.

The 20-year-old inmate, who is serving a 7½-year term at the Community Correctional Center in Milwaukee, complains about the lack of programs in a facility designed for short-term stays.

"If you don't give me an education, if you don't give me something to do, how do you expect me to change? How can I be anything?" she asked.

Jones was sentenced in May for 10 counts of theft. Circuit Judge Dominic S. Amato gave her 10 consecutive terms of nine months in jail. Because the offenses were misdemeanors and because each term was under a year, state law required her to be put in a local facility.

The Community Correctional Center, 1004 N. 10th St., is a branch of the county-run House of Correction, which is designed for short-tem offenders.

State prisons take felony offenders with sentences of one year or longer.

Jones is one of 105 inmates serving sentences longer than a year here. The long-term inmates were given consecutive sentences for several misdemeanor offenses.

Franklin M. Lotter, superintendent of the House of Correction, said longer sentences posed treatment problems and made crowding problems worse. The House of Correction's two Franklin facilities and one downtown location were designed to hold 800 inmates, but a recent count showed they housed about 1,300 inmates.

In addition, House of Correction programs are not designed to serve inmates longer than a year.

"The majority of these cases do not include community access, such as getting out for study, work or chld care," Lotter said. "We try to give them a job assignment and keep them occupied, but it's too long of a time in a local facility."

The facility offers chemical dependency programs, high school equivalency degree classes and a few vocational programs.

By contrast, Taycheedah Correctional Institution, the state prison for women where Jones otherwise would be sent, offers everything from high school equivalency classes to one-year vocational degrees and two-year associate degrees from the University of Wisconsin-Platteville and UW-Parkside.

Jones, who has the longest sentence of any inmate in the House of Correction, already has exhausted most of the facility's programs. Since May 9, she has completed courses in cooking, science and math.

"My books gave me a sense of responsibility and gave me something to do," she said. "I want to change my life. I don't want to go back to stealing."

She said there were no more classes for her to take, and instead she is one of two inmates assigned to clean her

Figure 17.1—continued

dormitory of 80 women.

Wearing a green prison uniform, white T-shirt and tennis shoes, Jones speaks articulately and openly. She talks frequently about the need to learn so that she can make something of her life once she is released.

"I'm not whining. I can do my time, but let me do it in a place where I can do something," she said. "After I clean all day, what is there to do? Watch soap operas, and I don't watch that stuff."

Jones will be eligible for parole in two years, Lotter said. If she does not get parole, her release date will be Aug. 27, 1994, assuming she gets one day of credit for every four days of "good time" she serves.

Lotter said state prisons were better equipped with re-habilitation programs for prisoners such as Jones. He wants a state law enacted that would allow such prisoners to be placed in state institutions. A County Board committee also has recommended such legislation, but no one has taken it up in the Legislature.

Amato, the judge who sentenced Jones, said the answer to the problem was not lighter sentences, but a change in state law that would allow prisoners such as Jones to go to state prisons.

"It's extremely frustrating, because No. 1, there are better rehabilitation facilities at the state institution systems and, No. 2, some of the people who have received long sentences should be at a maximum-security prison.

Amato said one factor in the high number of long sentences for misdemeanor offenders was that felony charges sometimes were reduced to misdemeanors during plea bargaining.

Jones pleaded guilty to 10 theft charges, but an additional 13 were read into the record for consideration in sentencing, said Asst. Dist. Atty. Thomas McAdams. Most of the victims were elderly people, he said. Jones would gain entrance to the victims' homes by pretending she was in trouble, needed to use a telephone or was a police officer, and then would steal wallets or purses while the victims were not looking, McAdams said.

Jones, the oldest of six children, said she was forced to steal because her mother used drugs and did not provide for the family.

Source: *The Milwaukee Journal*, Metro Section, Monday, November 13, 1989.

All of these types of prison programming are sorely needed in womens' prisons. Today, however, it seems that drug and alcohol treatment programs, along with educational programs, are the most essential for female offenders. With the ever-growing number of women entering prisons today who are both drug dependent and illiterate, many states have begun an intensive effort to address these problems. Weisheit (1985) found, for example, in his survey of women's prisons that almost all prisons offer some sort of treatment programs, with alcohol programs, drug programs, and mental health programs being the most common. In addition, the research literature has identified the need for educational programs for female offenders (Chapman, 1980). If one theme is recurring among both male and female offenders, it is that educational needs are great among them. Prison programming will have to address this issue if long-term change of offenders is going to be possible.

Problems with Women's Institutions

A general theme of this chapter has been how women's prisons suffer from many stereotypes. Most important is the fact that women's prisons, more so than men's prisons, also suffer from neglect. By this we mean that not only are women's prisons viewed differently by society and hence treated differently, but more importantly, there are many problems for female offenders that are directly related to institutionalization. These problems are often neglected and reflect society's indifference toward the female offender. There are three problems directly related to women's prisons. They are: female offenders and their children, limited job training and educational opportunities, and legal problems.

Female Institutionalization and Children

It is estimated that over 80% of all women who are incarcerated have children. Many of these women have more than one child. Institutionalization and the separation of children from their mothers is one of the most painful experiences for women who are incarcerated. The problems associated with the loss of children are great for the incarcerated mother. Concern with who will support their children and the loss of custody rights are of paramount concern to incarcerated mothers. Trying to adjust and address these issues from a prison cell is extremely difficult. In many states the mother has very few rights when it comes to her children (we will address this issue more thoroughly later in this chapter).

Recent research by Crawford (1990:6) suggests that many of the children of incarcerated women are taken care of by relatives, and that most of the mothers retain custody of their children. Even so, however, there are still the day-to-day problems that incarcerated mothers experience with respect to their children. The most noteworthy is the effect of the mother's incarceration on the children. Even though the mother has legal custody while she is incarcerated, in most cases the traumatic effects on the nurturing of the children, particularly young children, can be devastating.

While Baunach (1985) found that over 50% of incarcerated mothers in her study reported no problems or were unaware of any problems with their children, close to another 50% did report that their incarceration caused a myriad of problems for the children, including emotional problems, academic problems in school, and aggressive behavior. Other research has also supported the notion that the separation between mother and child produces negative behaviors by the child because of the disruption in the child's life due to the incarceration of the mother (Stanton, 1980). Clearly, the incarceration of the mother produces a stressful situation for both the mother and the child.

To address this issue many states have initiated programs for prisoner mothers and their children. In one program initiated in New York, the Bedford Hills Correctional Facility allows children of incarcerated women to visit and stay with their mothers for short periods of time. The intent of the program is to get children and their mothers together so that the bond between the two is not severed. The children stay with a "host family" in the community for a specified period of time and visit with the mother during the day. All those involved report a very positive interaction for both the children and the mothers (Public Broadcasting System, 1988).

Variants to this type of program for children and their incarcerated mothers have sprung up all over the country. Now it is an accepted fact that many women in prison have children, most of whom are very young, and that prison programming must address this issue. This is not to say that there are not a number of pressing problems that face mothers who are incarcerated. While most states have attempted to address the problems created by mothers who are incarcerated, the fact remains that for most of these female prisoners, being a mother separated from her children is a devastating harshness heaped onto the incarcerative experience. Some suggest that the feeling of separation from one's children is the most painful thing for the female offender. Additionally, the modest accommodations provided by the prison are not enough to satisfactorily deal with the pain felt by most incarcerated mothers.

Limited Job Training and Educational Opportunities

By far one of the most telling criticisms against women's prisons revolves around the lack of quality educational and vocational programming. Critics of women's prisons have voiced their concern over the poor quality of programming in these areas. Litigation has questioned what, exactly, female prisoners are entitled to with respect to programming. Much of the controversy about programming in women's prisons centers on its quality when compared to men's facilities. At present, the legal community has tended to side with advocates for women's prisoners. Much of the concern has been with the notion of equal opportunity for female prisoners, particularly in the areas of vocational training and educational opportunities.

This equal opportunity argument was addressed in the case of *Glover v. Johnson* (1979), in which a Michigan court held that women could not be denied the equal opportunity to quality prison programming. The court's intent in this case was to increase the number and quality of prison programs for women. It was one of the first cases to examine the differences in programming between men's and women's prisons. No longer could prison administrators justify programs for female prisoners solely on stereotypes about women. Traditionally, prison programming for women meant only cosmetology programs and clerical services training. Today, the courts have ruled that programs in women's prisons should be comparable to the programs found in men's prisons, and many states have already instituted such programs.

What does this mean? On the surface, this means more programs for women prisoners that previously have been solely reserved for men prisoners. Now we see in some institutions such diverse programs as welding, carpentry, computer, electrical, and plumbing. While these programs are still not as common in women's institutions as they are in men's institutions, they are slowly moving into institutions for women. On the whole, therefore, the educational and vocational opportunities for female prisoners have improved greatly throughout the 1980s and hopefully will continue to improve into the

1990s. It would be shortsighted, however, to suggest that these programs have come far enough. Like male prisons, the quality of many programs for women is questionable. The real accomplishment in prison programming for women has been the acceptance among prison administrators that female prisoners can be trained and educated in areas similar to male prisoners. In short, stereotypes about women prisoners are being debunked. Programming for female prisoners has come a long way but requires further progression if we are to have a significant impact on the life chances of women once released from prison.

Current research has also suggested that if programs are offered, women will enroll in them. Quite interestingly, much of the enrollment of women in prison programs is in the traditional areas. In fact, some institutions have problems getting women to enroll in the more contemporary programs, such as welding and carpentry. Why such hesitance on the part of women prisoners to enter these nontraditional areas? One interpretation is that many female prisoners may be more traditional in their outlooks on life, and that if enrollments are going to increase in these nontraditional areas, "consciousness raising" is going to have to exist before women become more interested in them (Pollock-Byrne, 1990:92). Regardless of the type of program, it is clear that traditionally programming in women's prisons has suffered. With a greater number of women being incarcerated, and a majority of them lacking any marketable skills, prison programming will become an important issue for administrators of women's prisons into the 1990s.

Legal Problems of Incarcerated Women

Many of the problems women face once incarcerated relate to the two issues discussed above. Women in prison face legal challenges concerning their children and the right to have a greater number of quality programs for their betterment. Historically, however, women have spent very little time and effort defending themselves in the nation's courtrooms. It is a relatively recent phenomenon to see female prisoners contesting the conditions of their confinement. Unlike male prisoners, female prisoners tend to litigate less often, and this may represent an underlying frustration that incarcerated women have with the criminal justice system (Aylward and Thomas, 1984).

In spite of the hesitancy of women to litigate, there has been a growing number of lawsuits that have challenged the conditions under which women are imprisoned. The two areas into which case law has expanded for women prisoners are: suits that challenge the quantity and quality of prisoner programs, and suits that argue for differential treatment of female offenders for medical reasons (Pollock-Byrne, 1990:163).

We discussed earlier the effect of *Glover v. Johnson* (1979), which provided female prisoners with the right to more programming. In addition, other cases have called into question the practices of prison officials with respect to prison programming. In *Barefield v. Leach* (1974), a court held that small numbers and economic hardship could not justify the absence of quality programming for female prisoners. Similar cases have arisen throughout the 1980s and many of them have been settled by a consent decree mandating that both the state and the litigants arrive at a consensus about programs for women prisoners. In many cases these decrees have given women prisoners greater access to higher quality programs.

Similar cases have arisen with respect to medical services and female prisoners. One such case was *Todaro v. Ward* (1977). In this particular case women at the Bedford Hills Correctional Facility in upstate New York claimed that the medical services provided by the institution were in violation of the Eighth Amendment's prohibition against cruel and unusual punishment. The court concurred with the prisoners and held that the provision of medical services was not an issue in the case. Instead, the court stated that the provision of medical services was based on arbitrary procedures that granted too much discretion to correctional officials. This meant that the administration of medical services in the prison was handled so haphazardly that prisoners were being denied adequate medical treatment. The court cited cases of gross abuse and mishandling of female prisoners. They ordered a more coherent system of medical treatment for the prisoners.

Other cases have also arisen with respect to female prisoners and their right to adequate prenatal services and the termination of parental rights. In *Morales v. Turman* (1974), the court addressed the issue of care for women who are pregnant while incarcerated. Nationally, it is estimated that 6% of women who enter prison are pregnant (Crawford, 1990:32). In *Morales*, pregnant women were encouraged to exercise and to ingest unidentified pills so that miscarriages would occur. The court documented the lack of medical care for prisoners and the miscarriage of one prisoner. Today, such abuses are no longer tolerated by the courts; nevertheless, it would be fair to say that very few states have the kinds of services that are needed for the adequate medical treatment of female prisoners, particularly in the areas of pregnancy counseling and gynecological services (Pollock-Byrne, 1990:173).

Finally, an issue that has generated much controversy in women's prisons is child custody and the loss of parental rights. Much of what the court has said on this issue has favored correctional officials. These decisions have granted correctional administrators latitude in deciding what is in the best interests of both the child and the institution. In most states, the prisoner does not have the right to keep a newborn child within an institution. Moreover, even if the prisoner is allowed to keep the newborn child for a short period of time, this does not mean that the imprisoned mother will keep her parental rights.

In *Los Angeles County Department of Adoptions v. Hutchinson* (1977) the court ruled that a woman may have her parental rights terminated involuntarily because of her incarceration. An issue that the court seeks to address in such matters is the capability of the mother to support her children upon release. With little or no programming available to most women offenders, it is not clear how they will be able to support their children upon release. As such, many courts have terminated the parental rights of women. Even if the mother tries to keep the child under the custody of family members while incarcerated, the lack of communication between agencies that handle such matters, the incarcerated mother, and relevant family members is often poor. As a result, the incarcerated mother loses in the battle to keep her children.

As with the other issues raised in this section, the incarcerated mother is usually on the short end of the stick when it comes to her rights. More often than not the female prisoner is stuck in a vicious cycle of failure. Because prison programming is often inadequate in many women's prisons, it is unclear how women will be able to escape a life of crime. Couple this fact with the reality that more women are going to prison and the picture that is being painted is not a pretty one. Moreover, it is not clear how the courts will address the plight of women prisoners in the future. We know that more women are going to prison and that this trend will probably continue into the near future. What is unclear is how the courts and the legal system will address the concerns of incarcerated women. Only time will tell how and when the courts will respond to the issues most pressing to female prisoners.

Other Issues

There are two other issues that are currently associated with female offenders and corrections. The first is the existence of co-correctional institutions. These facilities are designed to recreate the environment of the free
world. By "normalizing" the prison environment, for both men and women
prisoners, the prison is more conducive to the effective change of individuals.
Begun in the early 1970s, these types of institutions are found throughout the
United States. Some have suggested that such institutions offer a glimmer of
hope in changing the attitudes and behaviors of prisoners (Smykla, 1980).
To date, however, very little systematic evidence has been generated to prove
or disprove the efficacy of such institutions in producing long-term change
among prisoners.

Much of what we know about such institutions relates to their composi-
tions and the kinds of services provided. Current evidence reports that very
few states have such an institution, and that if co-correctional programs are
provided, they are provided in the vocational training area. Under an arrangement with male institutions, female prisoners are bused to institutions
where vocational programming is available (Ryan, 1984). Six states do have
co-correctional facilities, and they are a small part of their correctional systems.

In addition, the presence of such facilities in the correctional repertoire
is not significant. It could even be argued that such facilities were created as
part of a "correctional fad" in the 1970s. It is clear that they have had a
minimal impact on the correctional systems of most states. The future of
such institutions is uncertain, particularly in times when prison space is rare
and the advantages of such a facility may be outweighed by practical constraints, such as budgetary concerns. Given that the country is searching for
more bedspace, and the primary purpose of institutions has become societal
protection and retribution, it is unclear what role, if any, co-correctional institutions will play in corrections into the 1990s.

A final issue which has drawn the attention of many has been the growth
in the number of women being sent to prison. We mentioned earlier that the
rate of growth for female prisoners had passed the rate of growth for men for
the 1980s. Will this trend continue into the 1990s and beyond? There is every reason to believe it will. One of the primary reasons has been society's
penchant for incarcerating the drug dealer and user. With many more people
going to prison for drug-related offenses, we will see into the 1990s more

women being placed behind bars. Current statutes, at both the state and federal levels, have escalated penalties for drug offenses. Women, in particular, are the fastest growing group with respect to drug offenses and incarceration. There is no reason to believe that this trend will be interrupted in the near future.

In spite of this growth in the number of female prisoners, their presence in the correctional systems of this country will be small when compared to men. Crime, on the whole, will still be dominated by men. Given this fact, we should see more women going to prison, but proportionally they still will be a relatively small number and percentage of the total population of prisoners. What will be critical for women prisoners is how they will be treated by correctional systems. We have seen in this chapter how, historically, women prisoners were not treated well. One of the challenges facing correctional administrators in the future is to improve the conditions under which so many female offenders exist. We know this may be a tall order, especially because male offenders preoccupy most of the time and efforts of correctional officials; nevertheless, without a firm commitment to the issues that are important to female offenders, what will continue is a form of benign neglect that has been the anathema of female corrections.

Summary

The purpose of this chapter was to examine the key issues and trends that affect female corrections. We began the chapter by exploring the prevalence of women in the nation's correctional institutions. We found that while women make up a small percentage of the total incarcerated population, their numbers are growing. This fact was not always true in American corrections.

By exploring the reformatory movement of the past, we saw how female prisoners were treated by the criminal justice system. Our examination of the reformatory movement suggested that many correctional systems for women were rooted in unfounded assumptions about female criminality, and thus, many of the programs structured to lead women out of crime were ineffective. Beginning with a misguided perception of the female criminal, strategies to reduce crime, more often than not, served the purpose of suppressing women even further. Not only were women offenders viewed with disdain by society, but in addition, such a view was to dominate thinking about female offenders well into the twentieth century.

With a history of benign neglect and indifference toward female offenders, contemporary institutions lacked the adequate programming that could lead women out of crime and toward more productive lives. We found out that not only was the female prison population growing, but more importantly, modern institutions for women exhibited specific social structures and normative systems, some of which were similar to male institutions. In addition, the lack of programming for women was in sharp contrast to that found in men's institutions. Couple this indifference of society toward women's institutions and the lack of adequate programming, it was easy to see how problems were common to the contemporary women's prison.

Three main problems were stated as being common to women's institutions. The most noteworthy was loss of children and the inability of the female offender to maintain parental rights. Additionally, we saw what kinds of programs were available to women prisoners and how women have fought through the courts to increase the quantity and quality of these programs. Finally, we discussed how women have been hesitant to use the courts to defend their rights, but that this situation is changing today. Significant cases have arisen that address the concerns of incarcerated women. Whether or not the courts will expand their review of issues pertinent to women prisoners is uncertain.

Finally, the chapter examined two other issues facing female corrections. These two issues were: co-correctional institutions and whether or not more women will be going to prison in the future. On the former issue, we found that co-corrections is not as relevant an issue today as it was when it was proposed in the early 1970s. Nevertheless, these institutions are part, albeit a small part, of correctional systems throughout the country. With respect to the latter issue, we said that more females will be going to prison in the future, even though their actual numbers and percentages will still be small when compared to those of men. The challenge that lies ahead for correctional administrators will be how the female offender will be treated when dollars are limited and the country is more focused on crime committed by men.

The Female Offender:
What Does the Future Hold?

The American Correctional Association's Task Force on the Female Offender set out to study the policy implications of the rapid growth in the number of women being sent to prison. The Task Force and its subcommittees set the following goals:

- To ascertain the current and future needs of correctional programs to meet the challenges of the increase of female offenders being confined and in need of correctional programs.

- To aid in policy and procedure development for women's programs both in institutions and in the community.

- To examine the issues that will allow legislatures and other policy makers to better understand the needs and services of female offenders.

- To suggest strategies for dealing with the issues of child care and incarceration.

- To examine and suggest methods by which women can have equal access to all types of correctional programs.

This publication is intended to provide a summary of three surveys conducted by the American Correctional Association's Task Force on the Female Offender. The Task Force surveyed adult and juvenile female offenders, local government jail facilities, and state correctional facilities in late 1987. The information provided from the surveys, follow-up interviews with administrators, and previous studies. Also included are recommendations from the Task Force.

The Female Offender Survey Project is designed to assist the Task Force in its policy deliberations by examining (1) the backgrounds, attitudes, and program needs of the nation's estimated 43,000 female inmates and (2) the administrative principles and practices of federal, state, and local government correctional institutions responsible for housing and supervising them.

Critical Social Problems

The critical social problems that emerged during the 1980s and continue into the 1990s that affect the female population also affect local corrections and long-term state facilities. The issues of homelessness, mental health, drugs, AIDS, and unwanted pregnancies confront jails and prisons daily, and as social services remain inadequate, crime results. Although law enforcement and corrections were not intended to solve these social problems, they are the last line of defense to stabilization and treatment of these problems when crime occurs.

Increased Numbers

The number of female offenders in state and local correctional facilities has increased dramatically in the last fifteen years. Although "population explosion" has been the theme for all of corrections and detention in that time frame, the female population has had a greater increase in percentage each year since 1981 than the male population.

Major Issues

The issues that need to be addressed for the female offender are virtually unchanged over time: facilities, programs, and security that meet the needs and requirements of the female offender and proportional share of the resources.

Facility Design

The female offender has often been housed in facilities designed for the male population. This is changing, but slowly. Female offenders are given lower priority for resources since their numbers are small compared to the male population. The population explosion continues to divert attention from the female offender as bed space is obtained for a male population boom that, although not greater proportionally, is greater in numbers.

Detention Facility Locations

According to the survey, and not surprisingly, local detention facilities tend to be urban, located in commercial or industrial areas, and in use less than 20 years. Long-term facilities tend to be located in rural areas and in use for more than 20 years. A greater number of jails and prisons than expected had housing for female offenders as its original purpose (79 percent of jails and 67 percent of prisons). Long-term facilities are being planned in 68 percent of state jurisdictions surveyed and in 43 percent of local jurisdictions. Maximum security facilities were identified as a need by 30 percent of both local and state jurisdictions. Minimum security needs were identified by 42 percent of state and 23 percent of local jurisdictions. Most jurisdictions indicated multiple needs, with greater emphasis (number of beds) on higher security at the local level and emphasis on medium security at the state level.

Population

In 1990, the prison population exceeds 600,000, with females representing more than 32,000 of that population. The jail population exceeds 300,000, with the female population estimated at a higher percentage in this status. Jail space, however, is short-term confinement in which 64 percent of women obtained pretrial release and served from three to four days. The overall length of stay is 40 days for the last year surveyed. Local facilities, with bed space for as many as 20,000 female offenders, are processing and treating at least nine times that number (180,000) during each twelve-month period.

Administration

The administration of female facilities at the state and local levels is most often under the direction of male administrators. In the survey, 82 percent of local facilities and 51 percent of state facilities are directed by males. The survey does not specify whether the indicated administrators have multiple responsibilities or at what level the administrator has specific responsibility for women. Most often in state facilities, the women's facility administrator is solely responsible for operations, advocacy on behalf of the female offender, and meaningful futuristic planning. In local facilities, the operational responsibility for the female offender may be delegated to an even lower level, with the jail administrator having multiple responsibilities. In very few states and local systems are there administrative staff, removed from operations, who plan and advocate for the female offender as a primary function.

Security Issues

According to the survey, the incidence of major disturbances and escape in female facilities is quite low. More than 80 percent of long-term and local facilities have experienced no serious demonstrations in the previous five years. Nearly one-half of the women's prisons and 90 percent of local jails had no escapes in the previous 12 months. The other indicator of management problems is lawsuits filed by or on behalf of women inmates. Women's prisons have an average of 3.5 and women's jails an average of 5.3 lawsuits pending. The area most often in dispute in local facilities is health services. In state facilities, health services is also the most frequent cause of disputes, but is followed closely by facility and program deficiencies.

Classification

Classification is seen as the most effective management tool in corrections, and its misuse is most often blamed when operational problems exist. There is a belief by many practitioners that classification issues are very different for women; a lower percentage of women require close custody and supervision and are less of a threat to each other, staff, or property. Yet, in the survey, only 24 percent of state facilities and 26 percent of jails recognize those differences and use specific systems for women. That number is not surprising for local facilities, since the length of stay is normally quite short; it is, however, very significant for state facilities.

Visitation

Concerning visitation and the problem of female offenders who have custody and responsibility for children, the survey indicates that child visitation for inmates at state facilities is always allowed. The concept of extended visitation is allowed in more than 40 percent of these institutions nationwide. Local facilities tend to be more conservative in this area, but contact visitation is allowed in 38 percent and extended visitation in 15 percent of jails.

Needs and Opportunities

A needs and opportunity survey of inmates is difficult, and only a few questions were asked in this survey. There is an obvious interest in substance abuse and education and training levels. In the jail survey, 68 percent indicated that only 20 percent of their clients at intake had substance needs. In the state facilities, 60 percent indicated that more than 60 percent of their population needed substance abuse treatment. These data indicate that substance abuse problems are not being detected at the local level, or that substance abuse becomes a consideration only at time of sentencing, i.e., a drug offender or a property offender with a serious drug abuse problem is more likely to be sentenced to prison than to be offered community options.

Work assignments for women are available to 45 percent of the population in jails and to 95 percent of the population in prisons. Twenty percent of jails offer some vocational education. As for educational achievement by highest grade attained, the survey shows that 48 percent in jails and 33 percent in state facilities have high school diplomas, while 18 percent in jails and 30 percent in state facilities have less than an eighth-grade education. Recognizing that this information is self-reported, there is also an indication that more frequently, those with education deficiencies are more likely to be sentenced to state facilities.

Profile of the Adult Female Offender

Personal History

The average adult female offender is a minority (57 percent) between the ages of 25 and 29 who had either never been married (37 percent) or who before incarceration was a single parent living alone with one to three children (62 percent). Upon release she plans to live with either her parents or grandparents (27 percent). She plans to maintain custody of her children (72 percent), who are currently being cared for by her mother or grandparent (48 percent).

Home Life

The average female offender comes from a single-parent or broken home, with 50 percent having other family members incarcerated, of which 54 percent are brothers or sisters. The most important people in her life are her children (52 percent) and her mother. She has run away from home at least one to three times (65 percent) because she felt insecure about parental love and acceptance while growing up (56 percent). She is easily influenced by her peers (65 percent) and uses drugs to make her feel better emotionally (39 percent). She had most likely attempted suicide (28 percent) an average of one to two times (70 percent) because she was depressed, felt that no one cared, and that life was too painful to continue (69 percent).

Physical Abuse

The average female offender has likely been a victim of sexual abuse (36 percent) a minimum of three to 11 times or more (55 percent) between the ages of five to 14 (57 percent). She most likely was sexually abused by a male member of the immediate family (49 percent), such as a father or stepfather (23 percent). Reporting the incident resulted in no change or made things worse (49 percent).

Alcohol/Drug History

The average female offender first started using alcohol or drugs between the ages of 13 and 14 (74 percent), has used alcohol at least one to two times a month (74 percent), has used cocaine (49 percent) on a daily basis (22 percent), and has used speed (40 percent) and marijuana (56 percent) on a daily basis (22 percent).

Criminal History

The average female offender has been arrested an average of two to nine times (55 percent), beginning between the ages of 15 to 19 (34 percent). The most common offenses include property crimes (39 percent) and crimes of violence (22 percent). She received a sentence of two to eight years (50 percent), will serve less than one-fourth of her sentence, and committed crimes for the following primary reasons: to pay for drugs, relieve economic pressures, or poor judgment. Thirty-five percent react to their first incarceration with disbelief, 28 percent react with resignation, and 27 percent react with fear. If a program had been available to help or assist her, she would have participated (88 percent). She expresses remorse and regret at being incarcerated (42 percent), and indicates gains in self-awareness and personal growth (36 percent) as a result of incarceration.

Treatment Programs

The average female offender has participated in either a drug and/or alcohol treatment program (68 percent) and feels that the most helpful of these programs are alcohol (94 percent) and drug (86 percent) treatment programs, and Job Corps (66 percent).

Educational Background

The average female offender is a high school dropout with one to two years of education and no GED (26 percent), or one to three years of education and a GED (24 percent). Fifty-nine percent failed to complete their education because they were bored or tired, and 34 percent failed to graduate because of pregnancy. Forty-nine percent attended vocational school, studying business, secretarial skills, medical or dental skills, and cosmetology.

Work History

The average female offender has previous work experience in the fields of sales, services, and clerical work (73 percent). Fifty-four percent held an average of one to three jobs a year prior to incarceraton, with the highest salary earned ranging from $3.36 to $6.50 an hour (48 percent). Sixty percent received welfare assistance, and 65 percent feel qualified to perform either clerical or service-oriented jobs. Forty percent have received on-the-job training, 22 percent attended vocational school on the outside, and 11.5 percent received some vocational training in prison. Eighty-one percent realize that they need more education and experience and want to obtain jobs in the following areas: clerical (22 percent), services (23 percent), and professional (16 percent).

Program Benefits

During incarceration, the average female offender finds the education program the most helpful (21 percent), followed by substance abuse, Alcoholics Anonymous, and chaplaincy/church programs.

Source: American Correctional Association (1990). "The Female Offender: What Does the Future Hold?," pp. 1-3, 6-7. Copyright 1990 by the American Correctional Association. Used with permission.

Key Terms and Concepts

argot roles
benign neglect
co-correctional institutions
kinship relationship

pseudofamily
reformatory movement
subcultural adaptations
warders

References

Aylward, A. and J. Thomas (1984). "Quiescence in Women's Prison Litigation: Some Exploratory Gender Issues." *Justice Quarterly*, Volume 1, Number 2: 253-276.

Baunach, P. (1985). *Mothers in Prison*. New Brunswick, NJ: Transaction Books.

Bowker, L. (1981). "The Institutional Determinants of International Female Crime." *Journal of Comparative and Applied Criminal Justice*, Volume 5, Number 1: 11-28.

Bureau of Justice Statistics (1990). "BJS Data Report, 1989." Washington, DC: U.S. Department of Justice.

Chapman, J. (1980). *Economic Realities and Female Crime*. Lexington, MA: Lexington Books.

Crawford, J. (1990). *The Female Offender: What Does the Future Hold?* The American Correctional Association. Washington, DC: St. Mary's Press.

Dobash, R., R. Dobash and S. Gutteridge (1986). *The Imprisonment of Women*. New York, NY: Basil Blackwell.

Fox, J. (1984). "Women's Prison Policy, Prisoner Activism, and the Impact of the Contemporary Feminist Movement: A Case Study." *The Prison Journal*, Volume 64, Number 1: 15-36.

Giallombardo, R. (1966). *Society of Women: A Study of a Women's Prison*. New York, NY: John Wiley & Sons.

Giordana, P. and S. Cernkovich (1979). "On Complicating the Relationship Between Liberation and Delinquency." *Social Problems*, Volume 26, Number 4: 467-481.

Glick, R. and V. Neto (1977). *National Study of Women's Correctional Programs*. Washington, DC: U.S. Government Printing Office.

Goetting, A. and R. Howsen (1983). "Women in Prison: A Profile." *The Prison Journal*, Volume 63, Number 2: 27-46.

Heffernan, E. (1972). *Making It In Prison: The Square, The Cool and The Life*. New York, NY: John Wiley & Sons.

Irwin, J. and D. Cressey (1962). "Thieves, Convicts, and the Inmate Culture." *Social Problems*, Volume 10: 145-167.

Mahan, S. (1984). "Imposition of Despair: An Ethnography of Women in Prison." *Justice Quarterly*, Volume 1, Number 1: 357-385.

Naffine, N. (1987). *Female Crime: The Construction of Women in Criminology*. Sydney, Australia: Allen & Unwin.

Public Broadcasting System (1988). "Women In Prison." Boston, MA.

Pollock-Byrne, J. (1990). *Women, Prison, & Crime*. Monterey, CA: Brooks/Cole Publishing Company.

Rafter, N. (1985). *Partial Justice: State Prisons and Their Inmates, 1800-1935*. Boston, MA: Northeastern University Press.

Rothman, D. (1980). *Conscience and Convenience: The Asylum and Its Alternatives in Progessive America*. Boston, MA: Little, Brown and Company.

Ryan, T. (1984). *Adult Female Offenders and Institutional Programs: A State of the Art Analysis*. Washington, DC: National Institute of Corrections.

Simon, R. (1975). *Women and Crime*. Lexington, MA: Lexington Books.

Smykla, J. (1980). *Coed Prison*. New York, NY: Human Sciences Press.

Stanton, A. (1980). *When Mothers Go to Jail*. Lexington, MA: Lexington Books.

Sykes, G. (1958). *The Society of Captives*. Princeton, NJ: Princeton University Press.

Weisheit, R. (1984). "Women and Crime: Issues and Perspectives." *Sex Roles*, Volume 11, Number 7/8: 567-580.

Weisheit, R. (1985). "Trends in Programs for Female Offenders: The Use of Private Agencies as Service Providers." *International Journal of Offender Therapy and Comparative Criminology*, Volume 29, Number 1: 35-42.

Table of Cases

Photo Credit: Bill Powers, Frost Publishing Group, Ltd.

Impending
Issues

After reading this chapter, the student should be able to:

■   Discuss the reasons for slow and incremental change in corrections.

■   Explain the administrative tendency to deal with uncertainty by minimizing or avoiding risk.

■   Describe general concerns regarding the future of corrections.

■   Discuss the nature and extent of private involvement in corrections.

■   Comment upon key issues concerning privatization and corrections.

■   Depict various scenarios for the immediate future of corrections.

Immediate Issues

For citizens and residents of the United States, the decade of the 1990s has begun in a disquieting manner—recession on the homefront and warfare in the Persian Gulf. The United States is still plagued with problems of poverty, racism, violence, drug abuse, and other ominous difficulties.

For all of us the complex problems of crime and what to do with offenders continue to increase. The larger societal problems significantly shape the natures and definitions of corrections problems, as well as significantly influencing attempts to address the internal issues of corrections. As pointed out earlier, the problems usually designated as corrections problems have roots in focus/factors/conditions that correctional administrators cannot harness or control. As pointed out throughout this book, problems of racism, violence, conditions, overcrowding, resources, and direction (or lack of it), are among a host of pressing immediate issues demanding attention.

As Figure 18.1 suggests, "corrections" is being heavily burdened with a staggering number of present problems. The search continues for "answers," "solutions," and dramatic change. As Travisono asks, "so what can we look forward to?"

We now turn to a brief consideration of things to come in corrections. *Predicting* the future is a virtual impossibility; corrections is a complex undertaking—there are so many possible events, we are faced with so many uncertainties regarding the present (and, actually, regarding the *past* in corrections) that making precise projections is very difficult. When policymakers and planners engage in *forecasting* (applying themselves and certain methods—some crude, some more sophisticated—to making projections) they are normally dealing with time horizons of from one to five years. Looking forward 10, 20, or more years becomes very difficult for most matters, even if the objective is to achieve a moderate degree of certainty. Nonetheless, it is important to attempt to gain some perspective on possible futures in corrections, and to gain a measure of sensitivity to the issues we may be facing.

Figure 18.1
"Zooming and Booming in the '90s"—Editorial

Editorial

Zooming and Booming in the '90s

It is no secret that the criminal justice system has been running on empty for the past several years. But the question is: How much longer can this tired old system roll on without a major infusion of resources or some reduction in the load it is asked to carry? As we begin the last decade of the 20th century, everyone asks what the future of corrections looks like. Well, let's see where we are as we begin 1991:

- Prison census — 716,172 and zooming
- Jail census — 350,000 and zooming
- Probation — 2,386,427 and zooming
- Parole — 407,596 and zooming
- Rate of Incarceration: per 100 thousand — 285 persons (zooming)
- Number of prisoners on death row — 2,397 (sobering)

According to the Bureau of Justice Statistics, the total number of adults under supervision by correctional authorities is now more than 4 million persons—a staggering increase of 9.2 percent since 1988 and 34.6 percent since 1985. An estimated one of every 46 adults in the United States was under some form of correctional supervision on any given day in 1989. As we all know, statistics will show a great many more were under supervision in 1990. One out of every four black men is under correctional supervision.

Although correctional budgets have increased, they are still behind what is needed—a consequence of inflation and the slowness with which services are added.

Hundreds of adult and juvenile institutions and jails are under court order because of conditions of confinement issues. All suffer from crowding, and there appears to be no relief in sight.

Are these numbers going to continue to zoom in the '90s? I think they are.

Are we going to struggle and still not have all the answers? I think we are.

Are our political leaders going to allow us the resources we need? I think not.

So what can we look forward to?

The final answers to our problems are outside the criminal justice system. Either prevention systems must be developed in our schools or community agencies to target potential offenders, or we must learn to punish less expensively and for shorter periods of time.

Shorter sentences—hah! The October 1990 issue of Corrections Compendium reported that life sentences have increased by 45 percent in the last two years. We have approximately 60,000 men and women serving life—for many of them it's life without parole. As mentioned earlier, 2,397 men and women are now on death row. Are prisons going to become places for lifers with very little to do? Or are we going to begin to look more closely at what we are doing as a society and why we continue to punish so expensively?

Looking at the big picture, we have always said that when 75 percent of the offenders are in community programs and 25 percent are in institutions, we will have a balanced system. The current balance has not changed in more than 25 years—75 percent of the offenders are in community programs and 25 percent are in institutions. So what's wrong?

What's wrong is the volume. The skyrocketing number of intakes is killing the system. We haven't been able to stem this flood of offenders with programs acceptable to the public and politicians.

So my solution for the '90s is that we—the criminal justice system—must tell the whole sordid story, over and over again, to all who will listen. It is up to us to find ways to handle the volume—or to live with it. ◆

Source: Anthony P. Travisono (1991). *On the Line*, A Publication of the American Correctional Association, January, Vol. 14, No. 1, p.1. Reprinted with permission of the American Correctional Association.

Change and Corrections

The organizations and agencies discussed in this text are all part of, or are intimately related to, the complicated governmental undertaking we call corrections. The policies and subsequent actions developed and carried out must be understood as parts of the larger public policy context. As we have discussed (Chapter 6), the networks of relationships and interdependencies involving these thousands of organizations and agencies provide a sometimes confusing set of overlays to our picture of corrections. On the one hand, we must consider the uniqueness present in the operating contexts of particular organizations and agencies. On the other hand, there is a good deal of commonality or similarity among the many contexts. In thinking about the years to come, we must necessarily think about change. Although we must keep uniqueness in mind, and therefore be fairly circumspect, there are some general insights we can draw concerning change and corrections.

Even if it may appear at times that change in corrections is rapid and dramatic, overall, the process of change in corrections is slow and incremental. There are important reasons to expect a continuation of this type of change process. Consider the following:

1. To begin with, the state of knowledge about crime and responses to offenders does not show promise of revolutionary breakthroughs. The technological core of American corrections is composed of some "hard" knowledge, a great amount of impressionistic logic, and a number of varying, sometimes contradictory perspectives. Present practices have been arrived at gradually, most often through a process of trial and error involving attempts to test or implement variations on previous themes. Seldom has the "new" been actually innovative. Moreover, there are conflicting expectations of the correctional process and the outcomes that those concerned with corrections are to achieve. As has been noted earlier, various groups and individuals attempt to have their perspectives, their interests, their visions, expressed in correctional policy. This is neither necessarily healthy nor necessarily unhealthy. It does often lead to confusion, unclear goals, and perhaps unrealistic expectations of those in corrections. In short, there is no singular, well-defined purpose for our correctional venture. The near future promises no abatement to controversy, and this situation tends to promote a conservative approach to change.

2. Our American political structure and processes are geared to and are characterized by gradual, incremental change. The term *policy succession* (in which "new" policies grow from previous policies and substantially reflect attempts to "solve" the same problems—or, as is often the case, the problems created by previous policies) more accurately describes the approach to change than the term *policy innovation* (in which previously unrecognized problems, previously unencountered problems are addressed in a truly unique way, or in which problems are reconceptualized or redefined in such a revolutionary way as to require completely different approaches in attempting to address them). "In reality, 'new' policies are rarely written on a *tabula rasa*, but rather on a well-occupied or even crowded table of existing laws, organizations and clients" (Hogwood and Peters, 1983:1).

In looking at corrections we find myriad efforts at the various levels of government and we find varying degrees of autonomy, complicated sets of relationships regarding authority and responsibility, and interrelationships among organizations that have developed over rather long periods of time. Throughout, we find that politics is the means through which choices concerning direction, mission, and guiding policy are made. If we look closely we find that those in power share basic interests in the preservation of the system, and, although there is variation in attitude and there is often debate, those in power share fundamental agreement on principles underlying the system—e.g., private property, separation of powers, inheritance rights, means for attaining political office, and so on.

There is a tremendous force to habit, custom, and tradition in our political system. Because of: (1) its complicated nature, (2) the convergence in decision-making and policy-making of persons with diverse interests and unequal influence, and (3) the reality that decisions and policies in this context result from the gradual accretion of many previous decisions and actions, the overriding tendency is for changes to develop rather slowly and to be primarily conservative in nature.

3. Our organizations (yes, corrections organizations, other governmental organizations, commercial organizations) are bureaucratic. As we have stated, bureaucracy is not a dirty word; the term refers to a ubiquitous organizational form. Some characterize bureaucratic organizations as "rigid," the antithesis of changeable, and "bureaucrats" as persons who do not desire change. This is misleading. While we cannot here enter a detailed discussion of the processes and concerns

in complex, bureaucratic organizations, we can begin to think more accurately about change and bureaucratic tendencies. To simplify, *uncertainty* (about the present, about the future) is associated with change and with certain tendencies in complex organizations. Those in control of corrections organizations are faced with complicated, potentially turbulent (or unsettled, unsettling) environments.

The administrative tendency is to deal with uncertainty by attempting to minimize or avoid risk. This is done in part by relying on strategies, routines, and repertoires for both decision-making and action that have been shown to be or are thought to be relatively safe in their overall consequences for the organization. It is not the case that adaptations do not occur; nor is it the case that changes are not made. But, changes that are made are very likely to represent small deviations from past practices and policies, marginal adjustments, which hold the probability or the expected promise of being relatively safe. When faced with the need to adapt, the tendency is for administrators and others involved to consider and adopt, if possible, *previous* strategies or actions, alternatives already in existence, which satisfy the requirements of the situation and which tend to minimize anticipated risk. When none of the available strategies or actions are sufficient to meeting these broad criteria, the tendency is to take such alternatives as do exist and modify one or several (depending on the perceived need) only to the extent required to satisfy the need to adapt in a relatively safe manner.

Obviously, we are talking about tendencies. Occasionally, risky ventures are undertaken. However, over time, we suggest that incremental change is the usual pattern. Remember, administrators are dealing with many complicated problems simultaneously, and they are doing so in a context which is often unsettled, while they are faced by sets of constraints to possible actions. One large question is whether existing policies have been designed for ready change. For example, some directions for action involve the development of enormous "sunk costs" (commitments that cannot easily be reversed or given up), as in the construction of prisons. Not only is the construction cost involved, but also jobs are created, contracts established, interests developed, all of which contribute to inertia, diminishing the practical reality or possibility of changing the course of action taken. Designing policies for change would mean anticipating decision stages, assessing ongoing activities, and structuring and operating programs and actions in such a way as to facilitate changes through a design amenable to change.

Altogether, we can expect change in corrections to be slow and incremental. We think one cannot accuse those in corrections of not being responsive; of not making changes. However, we are all better informed if we think about and try to understand why we see few truly dramatic changes—why we can usually expect a process of marginal adaptation. It is not our purpose to crush idealism, nor is it our purpose to explain away the possibility of, or perhaps the need for, dramatic change in corrections. We do think, though, that those who anticipate "reforming" corrections, who zealously approach the implementation of innovative ideas, can: (1) avoid some degree of frustration, and (2) *be more effective* through attempting to develop and continuing to develop a deeper understanding of change in complicated contexts.

General Concerns Regarding the Future

As noted earlier, we must be aware of the uniqueness of the organizations and contexts in corrections—variations among states and the federal system and variations among particular components of the corrections endeavor at all levels. We should, however, attempt to find a way to think about the problems to be faced by policymakers in the future. It is helpful to attain some measure of sensitivity to general sets of concerns. Several are presented below. The attempt is to identify broad realms from which forces necessitating change may arise.

Changing Problems

The first broad area is that of *changing problems*. Our discussion here may seem a bit circular—that is, changing problems obviously appear to require change and change results in new problems. What we wish to do, nonetheless, is suggest that one must focus some attention on the possible direction of change and the resultant need to think ahead about the nature of problems—as opposed to taking a posture of simply reacting to changing problems. For example, overcrowding is a problem that is already present for federal, state, and local corrections operations. Already, there are those who are emphasizing the need to characterize overcrowding as an input problem—meaning that there are simply too many offenders for corrections agencies to handle. If we look back 20 to 30 years we see far less concern with "input." What we are seeing now is a strong need to understand corrections as a "scarce resource"—the need to reorient thinking to the actual limitations of corrections in terms of capacity, resources, ability to meet demands.

This problem is a complex problem which is very likely to remain with us for the foreseeable future. The changing nature of the problem must be associated with not only increases in crime (more offenders) but also with our notions about the practical ends those in corrections are to accomplish. Various demands for greater use of incarceration, for greater use of corrections in general, are being expressed in a very real way through changes in sentencing practices, changes in the criminal law and sanctions, increasing efforts to arrest and process offenders. The central issues no longer can be argued in some nebulous way as problems of "rehabilitation" versus "punishment," in an abstract sense. Faced with the reality of limited, rather than limitless resources, the practical problems become preeminent. It is clear that fundamental choices must be made concerning what to do, how to proceed. The rather general set of issues wrapped in the notion of "correcting" offenders has given way to an even more difficult set of problems regarding the use of scarce resources (scarce in the sense that there are too few resources, even though spending levels are enormous). We can expect no simplistic "large solution," since portions of this problem result from changes in policy in other components of the criminal justice system, as well as from broader political, social, and economic difficulties. Addressing the central issues may require a strong reorientation in thinking about "corrections;" it will at least require much greater thinking about the relationship of "corrections" to the judiciary and to law enforcement and to American society.

The above is an illustration—a real one. The definitions of and nature of many problems change over time. Thinking about the future requires attention to the changing nature of problems. There must be strategic thought in considering the direction of change and in addressing the need for design of new policies, or the redesign of existing policies (Hogwood & Peters, 1983:244).

Changes in the Prevailing Wisdom About "Solutions"

"As well as the nature of the problems changing, the conventional wisdom about how to address the problems also changes" (Hogwood and Peters, 1983:244). The history of American corrections reflects a series of rather strong shifts in emphasis concerning our responses to those who violate the law. For example, think about the cyclical playing-out of the emphasis on "punishment," "rehabilitation," and "reform" in the twentieth century—think of the difference in practice necessitated by adopting one or another view as more prominent.

One point to be aware of is that overall we do not tend to shift completely from one emphasis to another. The often-used dichotomies of "punishment" versus "rehabilitation" or "the act" versus "the actor" can confine our thinking. For nearly 200 years competing perspectives have coexisted in American corrections. In other words, although we designate "eras" in which one or another emphasis appears to have held greater sway, the other perspectives have not vanished. Rather, there is an intermingling and one or another emphasis appears to be more prevalent. This is important to understand in thinking about the future, for it is unlikely that truly radical departures will occur. Instead, direction will not be singularly focused, seemingly contradictory perspectives will coexist, a middle ground of compromise (perhaps appeasement) will exist, and the force of our previous and present perspectives will carry forward with great strength.

Changes in the Resource Base

Concerns in this area are critical in corrections. Insufficient resources place severe constraints on the capacity to adapt, the capacity to innovate. "From the strategic perspective, governments may face at least two types of strains on resources which will influence their ability to pursue certain types of policies" (Hogwood and Peters, 1983:245). One is the result of choices concerning the application of available resources. Those in corrections compete with all other agencies for a share of the government budget pie. Choices regarding allocations to corrections can serve to inhibit or to facilitate meaningful changes. "The second and more severe problem arises when there is a reduction, or at least a slowing of growth, of real resources" (Hogwood and Peters, 1983:245). In this situation the budget pie actually shrinks, or increases are smaller than expected. Agency leaders must find ways to perform with less or with less than expected. Planned changes may be greatly affected or unplanned changes may be required in order to provide necessary services with lower levels of resources available.

Attention to these broad realms of concerns is important in thinking about the direction of and nature of change for corrections. Obviously many factors are important and many more can be specified. Our intent in presenting the concerns discussed above is to encourage further thought about change and corrections.

One particular set of changes, which is already underway and which is illustrative of much of the foregoing discussion, is termed *privatization*. The potential "privatization of corrections" is controversial and the current debate contains many important issues. The next section presents a brief description of the present nature and scope of corrections—private enterprise alliances, plus a brief discussion of key issues.

Privatization

As we have seen earlier (see Chapter 2), private involvement in corrections is not a new notion. Since the early nineteenth century, private enterprise has been allied in various ways with American corrections. The stringent restrictions placed on private involvement and the marketing of prison-made products, as well as other legal restrictions concerning private involvement from the 1930s into the 1970s resulted in declining interest and low levels of emphasis regarding ties with the private sector. However, "crowding and the escalating cost of American prisons and jails are [along with other less visible factors] prompting public officials and the private sector to experiment with new alliances in the field of corrections." (National Institute of Justice, 1985:iii).

"Few proposals in the field of corrections have stimulated as sharply divided opinions as the prospect of enlarging the role of the private sector in corrections..." (National Institute of Justice, 1985:7). Nonetheless, private involvement has recently been gradually expanding, and a consideration of future possibilities must focus particular attention on this area. Following is a brief description of recent private sector involvement and a look at the issues that will figure prominently in the developing controversy.

Nature and Extent of Private Involvement

The reemergence of interest in private sector/corrections alliances has been, in part, fueled by the Law Enforcement Assistance Administration's (LEAA) Free Venture program initiated in the 1970s. Although LEAA is no longer in existence, the effects of Free Venture continue. This program promoted a prison industries model encouraging:

1. a full workday for inmates;

2. wages based on productivity;

3. productivity standards comparable to industry;

4. industrial management to have hiring/firing decision;

5. enterprises to become self-sufficient after a reasonable start-up period;

6. active coordination between prison industries and post-release placement;

7. optional partial reimbursement for room/board/restitution (National Institue of Justice, 1985:12-13).

Eventually, seven states were funded to attempt efforts under Free Venture. Although Free Venture did not specify private sector involvement, two states (Minnesota and Washington) did include the private sector. Further impetus to private sector alliances was provided in 1979 when "the Percy Amendment was passed, thus marking the first major change in federal laws concerning prison industries since 1940" (when the Sumner-Ashurst Act proscribed interstate shipment of prison-made goods) (National Institute of Justice, 1985:13). The Percy Amendment created exemptions to the interstate commerce ban for five states: Arizona, Kansas, Minnesota, Nevada, and Utah. The effect of the exemption has been to widen available markets for these states. Kansas, Minnesota, and Utah developed programs in conjunction with private enterprise.

The federal government has, since 1980, encouraged greater private involvement in corrections. The posture of the Reagan administration was to encourage private sector/government alliances whenever feasible. "More than half the states have now adopted legislation to provide for some form of private sector involvement in their prison work programs, [and] the (federal) Justice Assistance Act of 1984 increased the accessibility to interstate markets necessary for the success of prison industries managed or operated by private business" (National Institute of Justice, 1985:1). The Bush administration has followed with emphasis on private involvement. Private sector involvement in corrections has not yet proceeded beyond a relatively limited degree of involvement, but nonetheless the range of involvement, and the diversity already present may be somewhat surprising and is suggestive of a potentially widening role in future years. Although still limited in each, private sector/corrections alliances include the following general areas:

1. *Prison industries*. (See Figure 18.2 for examples of states involved and types of programs.)

2. *Private sector financing*. Efforts are already underway to make private sector financing available for corrections undertakings, primarily prison and jail construction. Examples of corporations involved include Merrill Lynch Capital Markets, E.F. Hutton, Shearson Lehman/American Express, and Dean Witter, among others. Examples of services provided include *lease contracts*, in which private enterprise finances and constructs a facility—then leases it to the government agency, and *lease-purchase contracts*, a variation in which ownership is eventually transferred. Private sector financing could be more or less expensive than traditional means of financing, depending on the conditions surrounding construction. Such arrangements can allow the government: (a) to move more rapidly, (b) to avoid official assumption of total debt, and (c) to continue to build where bond referenda fail, and construction is considered essential (National Institute of Justice, 1985). Industry advantages include: (a) tax breaks, (b) steady, long-term cash flow, and (c) transfer of some of the owner's risk to the lessee, e.g., insurance against accidental damage or loss, when paid by the lessee (National Institute of Justice, 1985).

Figure 18.2
Examples of Private Sector Participation in Prison Work Programs

---

Prison-Based Private Industries

- In 8 states, the private sector is involved in 13 different types of DOC-operated prison industries:

  — In Minnesota, 45 inmates manufacture disc drives for Control Data Corporation; another 140 inmates will reportedly manufacture light metal products for a private firm.

  — Computer terminals have been installed by Best Western in an Arizona women's facility where 30 inmates make reservations for the hotel chain.

  — In Mississippi, 20 inmates manufacture condensing units for KOOLMIST.

  — In Iowa, Kansas, Nevada, Utah, and Washington, private sector firms also employ inmates for a variety of small enterprises.

Privately Managed Prison Industries

- In Florida, PRIDE (a non-profit corporation) operates 50 percent of all state prison industries and plans to take over the balance by October 1984.

- In Oregon, Senate Bill 780 will create a privately managed prison industry arrangement similar to Florida's.

- In Minnesota, Stillwater Data Processing Systems, Inc. employs 10 inmates as computer programmers in its independently managed company at Stillwater Prison.

- In Michigan, City Ventures Corporation is building a model industries program for the Huron Valley correctional facility.

- A unique privately managed prison industry operates outside the walls of Kansas State Penitentiary. Staffed almost entirely by prison inmates who are bused to and from work, Zephyr Products, Inc. is a sheet metal company developed specifically to reduce prisoner idleness.

Source: J. Mullen, K. Chabotar and D. Carrow (1985). "The Privatization of Corrections," p. 3. Washington, DC: National Institute of Justice.

Figure 18.3
Prison Contracting: The Issues

Legal Issues

1.   What are the legal issues in prison contracting?

2.   What liability protection will a government agency and contract need?

3.   How should the responsibility and authority for security be divided between the contracting agency and private operator?

4.   What provision is there for protecting inmates' rights, including mechanisms for inmates to appeal decisions affecting them?

Policy and program issues before deciding to contract

5.   What specific preanalysis should a State undertake prior to the contract decision (e.g., cost analysis, legal issues analysis)?

6.   What are the reasons for considering or not considering contracting prison operation with private enterprise, particularly with for-profit firms?

7.   How should publicity regarding a change in private operations be handled (e.g., agency, media, public)?

8.   Should contracting be for (a) existing facilities; (b) a new institution replacing an existing facility; or (c) a new institution not replacing an existing facility?

9.   What level of offender should be assigned to the contracted facility? What are the differences in attempting to contract minimum versus medium versus maximum security facilities? Are there different considerations for contracting facilities for specific populations (i.e., service vs. geography, protective custody, mentally ill, women, death row, mothers, and children)?

10.   How many inmates should the contractor be expected to house? What provisions should be made for fluctuations in that number? What control does the contractor actually have over the number of inmates? Should minimums, maximums, or both be established in the contract?

11.   How will inmates be selected? Will the private organization be able to refuse certain inmates (e.g., AIDS victims, psychologically disturbed offenders)?

12.   What authority and responsibility should a private contractor have for effecting the release date of inmates? What will be the relationship of these decisions to the State Board of Parole?

RFP and contract issues

13.   Should contracting be competitive or noncompetitive? Are there enough prospective contractors to provide real competition? What are the relative merits of for-profit and non-profit organizations as prison operators?

14.   What criteria should be used to evaluate private proposals (e.g., percentage values for cost and quality of service)?

15.   On what basis should the contract price be established (e.g., firm fixed price, fixed price per unit, cost plus fee)?

16.   What provisions should be made to reduce service interruption (e.g., problems with transition periods, defaults by contractors, work stoppages, fallback provisions)? Should there be provisions to protect the private contractor (e.g., government obligations)?

17.   What performance standards should requests for proposals and contracts establish?

18.   What should be the duration of the contract and what provisions made for renewal?

19.   What provisions for monitoring performance are needed in the RFP and proposal?

20.   What provisions should be made for present correctional employees (e.g., rehiring rights, job benefits)?

Monitoring and evaluation

21.   How and to what extent should contractor performance be monitored?

22.   How should government evaluate the results of contracting?

23.   What results can be expected from contracting (e.g., cost, service effectiveness and quality, alleviation of crowding, effects on other prisons in system)?

Source: Judith C. Hackett, Harry P. Hatry, Robert B. Levinson, Joan Allen, Keon Chi and Edward D. Feigenbaum (1987). "Contracting for the Operation of Prisons and Jails," p. 3. Washington DC: National Institute of Justice.

3. *Confinement Service Contracts (facility and/or program management).*
   Contracts to manage operations are, as yet, rare in adult institutional corrections. Many persons are calling private sector ventures in this area
   "prisons for profit." In many states, private contractors have provided
   components of community-based undertakings for some time. Also, in
   the area of juvenile corrections, private service contracts have been more
   prevalent. The largest amount of controversy concerns adult institution
   management contracts. Although private service contracts in the area of
   community-based programs seem to have presented less of a problem,
   the entry of the private sector into adult facility management appears to
   cause great concern (see Figure 18.3).

   Already the federal government—through the Immigration and Natural-
   ization Service (INS), U.S. Marshal's Service, and Federal Bureau of
   Prisons—has moved into the area of contracting confinement services—for "warehousing" illegal aliens. The states have been much
   slower to respond, although Kentucky, in 1984, issued a request for proposals for a 200-bed facility.

   A number of private corporations (including Corrections Corporation of
   America, National Corrections Corporation, Buckingham Security Ltd.,
   and Eclectic Communications Incorporated, among others) are already
   organized and actively promoting/lobbying for confinement service
   contracting. Several jail facilities across several states are contract-op-
   erated, and those in the corporations predict expansion of their activities
   (see Figure 18.4).

Key Issues

Certain forms of private sector involvement in corrections undertakings
appear to be almost noncontroversial. For example, as mentioned earlier, the
contracting of community-based services in both adult and juvenile areas
seems to be well enough established that the major issues center on the speci-
fication of particular contracts. Both profit-making corporations and non-
profit organizations provide a fairly extensive array of services nationwide.

Figure 18.4
Trends in Private Operation of Correctional Facilities

Trends in private operation of correctional facilities

Approximately 1,200 adults are held in secure correctional facilities privately operated for State and local governments in the United States. Among the institutions, by jurisdiction:

State of Kentucky, Marion Adjustment Center, 200 males, minimum security, for-profit contractor.

State of Florida, Beckham Hall Community Correctional Center, Miami, 171 males, unsupervised work release, for-profit contractor.

Bay County, Florida, Jail and Annex, 350 men and women, for-profit contractor.

Hamilton County (Chattanooga), Tennessee, Silverdale Detention Center, Workhouse, 340 men and women, for-profit contractor.

Ramsey County (St. Paul), Minnesota, Roseville Detention Center, 42 females, not-for-profit operator.

The Tennessee Department of Corrections issued a request for proposals in 1986 for operation of a medium-security prison, but received no bids it considered responsive. The department is now considering revision and reissue of the RFP.

Many States contract extensively for work release, prerelease, and other nonsecure detention space. For example, California contracts for 1,700 nonsecure beds, Alaska has contracted out a correctional restitution center, and 5 of Illinois' 15 community correctional centers are privately operated.

Private companies or organizations operate juvenile facilities in 12 States; secure juvenile facilities in Pennsylvania, Tennessee, Massachusetts, and Florida were considered in the preparation of this report.

Source: Judith C. Hackett, Harry P. Hatry, Robert B. Levinson, Joan Allen, Keon Chi and Edward D. Feigenbaum (1987). "Contracting for the Operation of Prisons and Jails," p. 2. Washington DC: National Institute of Justice.

Similarly, certain forms of private sector involvement in adult institutional corrections, and in the area of jail programs, apparently are familiar enough to present few issues. For example, it is common to find vendor contracts at all levels—food service, medical and mental health services, and other essential services—in which private suppliers or professionals provide specified products or services.

The areas in which the greatest number and most ardently contended issues are arising are: (1) the expansion of the role of private enterprise in prison industry ventures, and (2) the rather newly emerging facility management and operation ventures. These areas promise to generate the more difficult questions in the coming years—and the resolution of certain of these questions will require the attention of a wide array of public officials, interest groups, and members of the public. The more important issues may be categorized among several general headings:

1. *Conceptual Issues.* The fundamental questions to be addressed are: (a) is any part of the administration of justice an appropriate market for private enterprise, and (b) if so, to what extent should private enterprise be allowed to enter or develop the market?

2. *Strategic Issues.* Beginning as long ago as 1888 (with a strong position taken by the American Federation of Labor (AFL)), organized labor has, to varying degrees, presented opposition to the development of private sector ventures in prison industries. Although organized labor has tolerated what may be seen as minimal-level involvement, the expansion of private sector enterprises in this area may evoke strong responses. The conditions under which organized labor would sanction a large-scale expansion remain to be seen.

   In the area of facility management and operation, we can expect questions and potentially strong opposition from public employee unions and locally organized correctional staff unions. Furthermore, while we can expect some degree of acceptance from those in correctional management, there is a rather large likelihood of opposition. "As a...survey by the National Institute of Corrections has noted, 'loss of turf' may, in fact, be more of an inhibitor to expanding the role of the private sector than the actual loss of employment for state workers" (National Institute of Justice, 1985:74). Here, the issues center on control, loss of power, and the possible realignment of networks of control and influence in the corrections sector.

3. *Administrative Issues.* In addition to the above-mentioned issues of "turf," control, and power, accountability emerges as a potential question. The primary question is "How do we insure that those involved in private sector/prison industry ventures or facility management/operation ventures meet prescribed criteria and contract specifications?" Ancillary issues include at least: (a) "What should be specified?" (i.e., problems and issues must be anticipated and made explicit before granting contracts), (b) "What types of monitoring and inspection procedures can

best preserve and protect accountability?" (c) "What new avenues must be explored for public input?" and (d) "If there eventually is a rather limited number of qualified and interested private sector providers, how does the state approach the situation of canceling a contract when doing so might leave no other alternative than reestablishing a state-managed operation?"

4. *Legal Issues.*   Among the thornier issues raised, especially by the prospect of facility management, is the question of liability.

> Because private facility management contracts are a recent innovation, no body of case law has yet emerged to clarify the respective liabilities of public and private agencies. There is, however, no legal principle to support the premise that public agencies will be able to avoid or diminish their liability merely because services have been delegated to a private vendor. Liability will be limited only to the extent that it might already be constrained by the (rapidly disappearing) defense of sovereign immunity or statutes establishing specific monetary limits on claims against the state....Thus, if the contractor errs, the state has retained its authority and may share the liability (NIJ, 1985:77).

The range of possible liability problems is large, and resolution of these problems will involve lawmakers, the judiciary, executive branch officials, interest groups, offenders, and the general voting constituency. Moreover, legal issues do not end with liability. In many states the legal authority to contract for facility management is not explicitly provided. Similarly, in some states, certain governmental units are required either by legislation or by constitutional provisions to maintain direct responsibility for facility management and operation—the responsibility cannot be delegated. In these and other situations, expansion of the role of private enterprise would require changes in legislation, perhaps constitutional amendments, and a rethinking of the role and structure of the established governmental agencies involved.

5. *Financial Issues.* Financial issues ostensibly center on the dollar benefits or dollar costs resulting from private sector contracting. Most often these issues will be discussed as "benefit-cost" issues, and those considering these issues will think directly of the dollar accounting balance.

However, "costs" and "benefits" also must take into account effects on offenders, effects on the image of corrections and justice, resulting changes in public confidence and support, as well as myriad anticipated and unanticipated outcomes. These effect and outcome issues are difficult to measure, and sometimes are difficult to identify or conceptualize. They are therefore the types of issues that promise to elicit greater controversy and require more fundamental considerations concerning just what the value of extensive privatization is or might be.

Does Privatization Place Corrections On the Defensive?

Private sector alliances are not new to the American prison. Private enterprise is, in fact, no stranger to much of the operation of corrections in the United States. However, the role of private enterprise has long been debated, and there has been a good deal of disagreement over the appropriate balance between government operations and private operations in corrections.

As the foregoing discussion illustrates, there are many facets to the privatization issue. Overall, the 1980s emphasis on private sector involvement has placed those committed to public sector corrections on the defensive. While the most visible issues seem to involve funding alternatives to reduce the stress on increasingly overburdened correctional systems—that is, finding complementary and supplementary arrangements for service delivery—the nature of the 1980s emphasis presents a challenge to an existing order. To gain a measure of perspective regarding this challenge, conceive of corrections as a huge industry, a public industry for the most part, but nonetheless a multibillion-dollar industry that has many constellations of interest surrounding the allocation of resources and aims associated with its decentralized operation.

For the past 50 years or so, there has been little challenge to the legitimacy of those who control the various portions of this industry. The ground rules for the operation of this industry—its ways of doing business, so to speak, have been firmly established and fairly well recognized. Laws and formal structural arrangements, as well as slowly developed networks of influence and control (among the primary agencies—corrections agencies, legitimizing organizations such as governing bodies and other governmental agencies, and constituent organizations and groups—those which exist because of various interests in the industry such as professional organizations, contractors, etc.) have supported the primacy of the public bureaucracies and their ways of doing business.

While overriding concerns are certainly "correcting" offenders or at least "doing something constructive" with offenders, concerns also focus on the authoritative allocation of the enormous resources pumped into this industry and on the myriad groups and interests that "depend" on the day-to-day, year-to-year operations of the various elements of the industry. Most of the visible issues regarding private-sector government alliances in corrections could probably be taken care of through compromises, contracts, changes in legislation, and so on. However, think about the deeper, more fundamental problems privatization presents or is said to present. The greatest degree of resistance and greatest amount of controversy occurs when proposals for private management and operation are advanced. One can begin to think of the sub-rosa issues in terms of struggle for control of the industry. Certainly, it is unlikely that corrections would become completely privatized—there are many obstacles. However, expanding the role of the private sector to one of management and operation of facilities, combined with an increased role in financing and constructing facilities challenges the hegemony of the established corrections structures. Extensive privatization would challenge the established organizational and group relations in and among the various systems, the established networks of organizational and group influence and control, and the established ways of doing business such as personnel practices, contracting for services, the ascription and recognition of status to those working within corrections, and so on.

The correctional bureaucracies must be seen as interest-oriented structures in themselves. Those who administer the bureaucracies and those who otherwise work within these structures have strong interests tied to them. Furthermore, the constellations of groups and individuals whose interests coincide or are symbiotic with those of the bureaucracies have adapted to the established patterns. Think briefly about the challenge to those whose jobs are vested in government civil service, about the increasing degree of unionization in corrections and what has been a long process of compromise in reaching a rather stable position with management, about the positions carved out over time for groups of educational, therapeutic, medical, and other service providers.

Significant privatization would mean large change in many of the current arrangements. Large change means uncertainty for all involved, especially for those who could see loss of position, loss of status, and changes in comfortable routines. There is little definitive evidence to suggest that private enterprise moving into corrections on a grand scale would much improve or much diminish corrections outcomes in the United States. Much would be different in the corrections industry, however. Privatization is a challenge to legitimacy and power in an industry in which the present dominant interests have been relatively unchallenged. Grasp this understanding, think further about it, and one can begin to conceptualize the central issues and gain insight regarding the actual nature of the controversy. Yes, privatization places corrections on the defensive when the suggested role of private enterprise challenges the existing order.

Summary

Most of us expect change to bring progress. Many of us equate change with reform, expecting something better than what was. Moreover, many of us have an image of relatively rapid improvement through a rather amorphous idea of change.

Predicting or forecasting the future becomes more difficult the further ahead one looks. A few sets of concerns, changing problems, changes in prevailing wisdom about "solutions," changes in resource bases, among others, may guide us in trying to be more precise.

As this chapter discussed, corrections is a part of a complex world. As we have stated, we do not aim to crush idealism; neither do we wish to promote cynicism. Hope for the future lies in better understanding the difficulties and dilemmas, sometimes the contradictions, associated with change. As Walker (1989) has indicated, we are engaged in situations in which theories (beliefs and belief systems) hold sway, in which impressionistic logic and sometimes contradictory perspectives dominate dialogue, in which there is little "hard" knowledge to dictate which directions to pursue.

We must plan for change and understand the slow, incremental nature of change in corrections. Please consider the ideas that we have presented concerning change, and accept the challenge to become better informed. As the following "On the Defensive" indicates, there may be reasons to consider differing scenarios for the future in corrections.

The Near Future: Possibilities

The Bleaker Scenario: Continuing Crises

As Jurik and Musheno (1986) have noted, U.S. corrections has entered yet another in an almost continuous series of crises. "Like earlier crises, the instability of corrections today revolves around a reconsideration of system goals with a renewed emphasis on deterrence and incapacitation, and an exploding population of inmates unaccompanied by adequate fiscal support for correctional bureaucracies" (1986:457). The current set of dilemmas is complex. There may be varying conceptualizations and characterizations of the major problems confronting those in control of corrections in the United States, but there can be little doubt that, absent some remarkable change in directions, the near future for corrections looks bleak.

As we have noted, there appears to be little reason to expect a dramatic breakthrough in the technological core of corrections. In fact, the conceptual menu in corrections is quite limited. Although a number of potential remedies are being tried ("They include construction of new prisons, alternatives to incarceration, privatization of corrections and professionalization of [the] bureaucracies" [Jurik and Musheno, 1986:457]), these essentially represent returns to previous themes or variations on previous themes used to confront previous crises.

The current crises (set of dilemmas), as outlined above, appears to be so complex and so problematic that the overall situation may become even more difficult in the near future. As we have discussed earlier, resources for the work of government in general are not limitless. As more resources are directed toward amelioration of current correctional dilemmas, those in charge of other social service programs and agencies are likely to feel the effect through cutbacks in their areas of interest. The consequences may include a reaction in which coalitions form to lobby against greater allocation of resources for corrections. Such a reaction would promise to place the search for "solutions" in corrections into the realm of budget battles rather than some perhaps more constructive realm of trying to coalesce on realistic notions concerning just what those in corrections are to accomplish. In short, the current situation looks bleak for the near future.

The Brighter Scenario: Professionalization

The brighter scenario for corrections in the United States must involve attempts to break the cycles of crisis alluded to above. In general, this will require developing, at all levels, more realistic conceptions of the purposes and possible outcomes to be achieved in corrections. Our correctional programs do have real world effects. These effects may be anticipated ones and/or may be unanticipated ones. The continuation of certain programs may have more to do with the strategies of strong interests served than with some rational connection putting theory into practice. In other words, as we have tried to point out, much of what is done in corrections is an incremental continuation of previous policies and actions—often we do not know whether what was done/what is done has positive results; much of what is continued simply turned out to be relatively acceptable, politically and otherwise.

What is needed for a brighter scenario is meaningful assessment of directions for corrections. This is not simple. In a clear-cut way those concerned with corrections must articulate directions. This requires concerted effort at revealing the nature of the policy-making process for corrections; exposition of the parameters to be expected in correctional outcomes; an attempt at locating the correctional venture and its potential, as well as its limitations, within the larger criminal justice framework and within the larger societal framework of the United States of America. Some very difficult questions must be addressed, including: what are the substantive aims of corrections and the larger criminal justice process?; where can corrections fit within larger societal aims?; how do we effectively utilize corrections as a scarce resource in fulfilling these larger aims?; what aims does corrections currently fulfill?; and more.

As Alan Breed has observed, "[T]here has to be a message, a plan, a policy that is clearly articulated and understood" (1986:8). Perhaps a message is more practically attainable than a big plan, a big policy. Regardless, it is clear that someone, some set of persons must take the lead in expressing this message. The brighter scenario for corrections would involve the active commitment of corrections professionals in developing such a message. Perhaps the first step is the recognition that the arena for policy decision regarding corrections is political. Politics, bargaining, and interaction are the basic mechanisms of policy-making. As Breed (1986:7) has also suggested, there must be a "coalition of strong professional groups, civic organizations and independent groups who can work within the political process without being controlled by it." Such a large effort may be termed utopian. Given the many directions already being pursued, the many levels of autonomy and interaction, the competing interests in our society, such thinking may be termed naive by many. Nonetheless, the alternative is to relegate the future in corrections to a disjointed process of incrementalism; one in which constructive change is serendipitous occurrence, and one in which there is little attempt at understanding corrections as a societal undertaking.

Although it may seem embarrassingly optimistic, we must think that there is a brighter scenario for corrections. There is already, we think, a professional core in corrections which is expanding. There is also a set of interested professionals not directly employed in corrections, but who are concerned about directions for corrections. The brighter scenario for corrections is dependent on the realization of Breed's suggestion. Those concerned about corrections, who have knowledge about corrections and can de-velop knowledge about corrections, must become politically active. The professionalization of corrections means the establishment of a large coalition of persons committed to addressing the broad questions outlined above and to addressing the particular questions that result. Absent this, the cycle of crisis is likely to continue to unfold.

In-Between: Pluralistic Ignorance and Business as Usual

Alan Breed (1986) has utilized the term "pluralistic ignorance" as "the term central to the current correctional dilemma." According to Breed, pluralistic ignorance is "the systematic inaccuracy in the assessment of group opinion by members of the group." He is referring to the "great difference between what one thinks, and what one thinks others think," and Breed observes that this sort of condition "discourages the expression of controversial opinion."

We think that the notion of pluralistic ignorance should be expanded and broadly applied in the consideration of U.S. corrections. Most people in the United States are simply ignorant about corrections. Many do not wish to be informed. Even those persons who work in or are intimately related to the operation of the criminal justice and corrections organizations in the United States are ignorant about corrections. These correctional workers more appropriately fit Breed's conception. They may not truly be uninformed; more likely they are unwilling (1) to become better informed about corrections and about the processes of decision-making affecting corrections and (2) to engage among one another in controversial dialogue which highlights the potential and limitations of corrections and results in advocacy for progressive corrections.

As we have stated in Chapter 6, the political agenda for corrections is often a "don't hurt me" agenda. This means preservation of the status quo. It also means making acceptable changes, when necessary, which give the impression that problems are being solved when, in actuality, little more is being done that posturing and the symbolic appeasement of various interests. Breed is quite critical in stating the following:

> [W]e must recognize that today's correctional leaders are qualified survivors. They are not activists, and they have not been spokespersons for progressive corrections. They are persons attractive to whatever party is in power. Even so, there tenure is short, stability virtually unknown, and long-term major policy changes are rare events. Sadly, this absence of correctional leadership will not change in the immediate future (1986:6).

Those seeking to engender constructive change in criminal justice and in corrections face an overwhelming undertaking. The forces and interests impacting their organizations, their jobs, make it so. It is far easier to focus on one's immediate set of day-to-day problems than to become involved in larger efforts at change. To be fair, those working in the criminal justice system and in corrections are under strong pressure to get something done, face multiple problems and deadlines, and, to be effective in any great sense, must face an unsettled and unsettling environment. This is compounded by the real world situation that criminal justice and corrections as undertakings are largely decentralized; the organizations and persons who work in them are operating in sets of complicated contexts, serving many masters.

One effect of the real world situation for those in corrections may be to encourage a parochial view—to encourage an attitude of accomplishing the day-to-day tasks of an immediate nature and to lose interest in applying energies to the very difficult problem of building the base necessary to move from the status quo. Business-as-usual for corrections has generally meant maintaining stability rather than exposing the limitations inherent in corrections or exposing the nature of the processes of decision-making affecting corrections. "Crisis" appears to have become a convenient rationale for various strategies aimed at reinforcing the status quo in corrections. Unwitting ignorance, especially on the part of those most directly concerned with corrections, and intentional ignorance, accepting the "don't hurt me" approach or the parochial view, have similar outcomes in the long run for corrections. Absent concerted effort, the near future for corrections could quite easily be a replay of past decades—business as usual.

Source: Written by Rick Lovell.

Key Terms and Concepts

accountability

benefit-cost

Buckingham Security Limited

Bush administration

"business as usual"

confinement service contracts

Corrections Corporation of America

Eclectic Communications Incorporated

forecasting

Free Venture program

"hard" knowledge

impressionistic logic

innovation

Justice Assistance Act of 1984

lease contracts

lease purchase contracts

liability

National Corrections Corporation

National Institute of Corrections

Percy Amendment

pluralistic ignorance

policy innovation

policy succession

prevailing wisdom

prison industries

prisons for profit

private sector financing

privatization

professionalization

Reagan administration

resource base

"soft" knowledge

Sumner-Ashurst Act

sunk costs

tabula rasa

turbulent environment

uncertainty

vendor contracts

References

Breed, A. (1986). "The State of Corrections Today: A Triumph of Pluralistic Ignorance." Proceeds of Address to Guests of the Edna McConnell Clark Foundation, New York, February, 1986.

Hogwood, B.W. and B.G. Peters (1983). *Policy Dynamics*. New York, NY: St. Martin's Press.

Jurik, N. and M. Musheno (1986). "The Internal Crisis of Corrections: Professionalization and the Work Environment." *Justice Quarterly*, Volume 3, Number 4, Dec. 86, 457-480.

Mullen, J., K. Chabotar and D. Carrow (1985). "The Privatization of Corrections." Washington, DC: National Institute of Justice.

Smart, B. (1983). "On Discipline and Social Regulation: A Review of Foucault's Genealogical Analysis." In D. Garland and P. Young (eds.) *The Power to Punish*. London, England: Heinemann Educational Books.

Indices

Subject Index

Name Index

Case Index